Exploring Social
Psychology

❖

Exploring Social Psychology

FOURTH EDITION

❖

David G. Myers
Hope College

Boston   Burr Ridge, IL   Dubuque, IA   Madison, WI   New York
San Francisco   St. Louis   Bangkok   Bogotá   Caracas   Kuala Lumpur
Lisbon   London   Madrid   Mexico City   Milan   Montreal   New Delhi
Santiago   Seoul   Singapore   Sydney   Taipei   Toronto

The McGraw-Hill Companies

EXPLORING SOCIAL PSYCHOLOGY

Published by McGraw-Hill, a business unit of The McGraw-Hill Companies, Inc., 1221 Avenue of the Americas, New York, NY, 10020. Copyright © 2007, 2004, 2000, 1994 by The McGraw-Hill Companies, Inc. All rights reserved. No part of this publication may be reproduced or distributed in any form or by any means, or stored in a database or retrieval system, without the prior written consent of The McGraw-Hill Companies, Inc., including, but not limited to, in any network or other electronic storage or transmission, or broadcast for distance learning. Some ancillaries, including electronic and print components, may not be available to customers outside the United States.

This book is printed on acid-free paper.

3 4 5 6 7 8 9 0 DOC/DOC 0 9 8 7

ISBN-13: 978-0-07-353187-8
ISBN-10: 0-07-353187-1

Vice President and Editor-in-Chief: *Emily Barrosse*
Publisher: *Beth Mejia*
Executive Editor: *Michael J. Sugarman*
Developmental Editor: *Katherine C. Russillo*
Marketing Manager: *Melissa S. Caughlin*
Managing Editor: *Jean Dal Porto*
Project Manager: *Catherine R. Iammartino*
Art Director: *Jeanne Schreiber*
Designer: *Srdjan Savanovic*
Cover Designer: *Srdjan Savanovic*
Senior Photo Research Coordinator: *Nora Agbayani*
Media Producer: *Stephanie George*
Production Supervisor: *Jason I. Huls*
Composition: *Techbooks*
Printing: *45# New Era Matte, R. R. Donnelly & Sons*

Credits: The credits section for this book begins on page 461 and is considered an extension of the copyright page.

Library of Congress Control Number:

2006923293

The Internet addresses listed in the text were accurate at the time of publication. The inclusion of a Web site does not indicate an endorsement by the authors or McGraw-Hill, and McGraw-Hill does not guarantee the accuracy of the information presented at these sites.

www.mhhe.com

About the Author

❖

David G. Myers (davidmyers.org) is the John Dirk Werkman Professor of Psychology at Michigan's Hope College, where students have voted him "Outstanding Professor." Myers's love of teaching psychology is manifest in his writings for the lay public. His articles have appeared in three dozen magazines and he has authored or co-authored 15 books, including *The Pursuit of Happiness* (Avon, 1993), *Intuition: Its Powers and Perils* (Yale University Press, 2002), and *What God Has Joined Together: A Christian Case for Gay Marriage* (Harper-SanFrancisco, 2005).

Also an award-winning researcher, Myers received the Gordon Allport Prize from Division 9 of the American Psychological Association for his work on group polarization. His scientific articles have appeared in more than two dozen journals, including *Science, American Scientist, Psychological Science,* and *American Psychologist.*

He has served his discipline as consulting editor to the *Journal of Experimental Social Psychology* and the *Journal of Personality and Social Psychology.* In his spare time he has chaired his city's Human Relations Commission, helped found a community action agency that assists impoverished families, has spoken to hundreds of collegiate and religious groups, and became an advocate for an assistive listening technology that serves fellow people with hearing loss (hearingloop.org). David and Carol Myers are parents of two sons and a daughter.

Contents

❖

Foreword

❖

W hen social psychology works best, it touches the soul of society and the heartbeat of its individuals. Of course, it is an academic discipline with its own history, heroes, theories, methodologies, and jargon. As such, in recent years it has gradually moved to a central position within the field of psychology. In earlier days, it was looked upon as a peripheral curiosity, more akin to cultural anthropology than hard-nosed brass instrument and animal psychology that dominated a psychology proudly branded "Made in the U.S.A.," at least until the 1960s. As cognitive psychology has restored the mind and tongue to behaving organisms, social psychology has put them into a meaningful and lively social context. And as other domains of psychology have come to recognize the importance of the social setting and interpersonal dynamics in understanding the whys of human thought, feeling, and action, they too have added a social dimension to their studies. So we now have social-cognition, social-learning, social-developmental, social-personality, and many other hyphenated alliances that enrich the study of the individual. The individual person, though usually taken alone as the unit of psychology's research focus, is more fascinating when seen as part of the complex social fabric from which human nature is woven.

But what is unique among social psychologists is that their concern for experimental rigor and creativity in the laboratory equals their concerns for real-world relevance and viable interventions that may improve the quality of our lives. Virtually all of the most significant areas of application and extensions of psychology out of academia into the everyday life of ordinary people have come from, and are continuing to be energized by, social psychologists. What are those realms of social-psychologically inspired contributions to the human condition? Let us count but a few: health psychology, psychology and law, organizational behavior, environmental psychology, political psychology, peace psychology, and sports psychology.

When a former president of the American Psychological Association urged his colleagues to "give psychology away" to the public, it was primarily the social psychologists who took his message to heart and went to work in the field of everyday little hassles and big-time troubles. So while some of us are proud to uncover a significant statistical effect in a laboratory test of key hypotheses derived from a theory, others are deriving joy from showing politicians how to negotiate more effectively, companies how to structure energy conservation programs, or the elderly how to take more control and personal responsibility over their lives. We all recall the admonition of our inspirational leader, Kurt Lewin, who told us that there is nothing so practical as a good theory. But we now add to that intellectual call to arms that there is nothing as valuable as theoretically inspired practical applications. Furthermore, there is no reason not to embrace all of it—the abstract theory that unifies our singular observations and points us in new directions, the ingenious experimental test, the convincing demonstration of a social phenomenon, or the perceptive application of what we know to solving social problems facing our society and the world.

Despite this range of interests among social psychologists, most would agree on the basic "lessons" of social psychology that emerge from a variety of sources.

Five principles can be identified. First, the power of the situation influences individual and group behavior more than we recognize in our individualistic, dispositionally oriented, culture. The second principle concerns the subjective construction of social reality, by which we mean that the social situation is a shared construal of a reality that does not exist "out there," but is created in our minds and passed on in gossip, rumors, ritual, folklore, school lessons, and racist tracts, among other sources of social communication. The third lesson is about the irrationality of some human behavior and the concurrent fallibility of human intuition even among the best and brightest of us. Because we have shown that the presence of others, whether in groups of friends or coworkers, or in unstructured settings of strangers, influences the decisions and actions of individuals, our fourth lesson centers on group dynamism. Finally, social psychologists add the principle that it is possible to study complex social situations and generate practical solutions to some emerging problems, as well as apply what we already know to improve personal and societal functioning. But such lessons are not merely the stuff of textbooks, they are the stuffing, or stories of life itself. Let me share a personal tale with you about the first two lessons, which, now that I think of it, also slips over into the rest of them. Growing up in a South Bronx ghetto as a poor, sickly kid, I somehow learned the tactics and strategies of survival, known collectively as "street smarts." At first they were put to use to avoid being beaten up by the big tough guys through righteous utilization of ingratiation tactics and sensitivity to nonphysical sources of power. Then they worked to make me popular with the girls at school, which in turn enhanced my status with the less verbal neighboring big shots. By the time I got to junior high school, I was being chosen as class president, captain of this or that, and was generally looked to for advice and leadership. However, a strange thing happened along the path through adolescence. In 1948 my family moved to North Hollywood, California, for my junior year of high school. The initial wonder at being in this western paradise soon became a living nightmare. I was unable to make a single friend during the entire year, not one date. Nobody would even sit near me in the cafeteria! I was totally confused, bewildered, and of course very lonely. So much so that I became asthmatic. I became so with such intensity that my family used this newfound sickness as the excuse it needed to leave the polluted palms and general disillusionment we all felt to return to the dirty but comprehensible reality of the Bronx. Still more remarkable, within six months I was elected as the most popular boy in the senior class, "Jimmy Monroe" or James Monroe High School! I was talking about this double transformation to my friend in homeroom class 12-H-3, Stanley Milgram, and we acknowledged that it wasn't me that had changed but the situation in which I was being judged by my peers, either as an alien New York Italian stereotype or a charming, reliable friend. We wondered how far someone could be changed by such divergent situations, and what was the stable constant in personality. "Just how much of what we see in others is in the eye of the beholder and the mouth of the judges?" Stanley wrote the senior class squibs for the Year Book and helped me to reclaim my California-lost ego by penning, "Phil's our vice president, tall and thin, with his blue eyes all the girls he'll win." So my Bronx street smarts were still working, at least sometimes, in some situations, for some people. Naturally, thereafter we both were heard to repeat loud and clear whenever asked about our predictions of what someone was like or might do:

"It all depends on the situation."

Stanley went on to study conformity with Solomon Asch, a major contributor to early social psychology. At Yale, where we were on the faculty together for a short while, Milgram then conducted a series of now-classic studies on obedience to authority that have become the most cited experiments in our field because of their definitive demonstration of the power of the situation to corrupt good people into evil deeds. My way was not too divergent, since I studied how anonymity can lower restraints against antisocial acts and how putting normal, healthy young men in a mock prison ended up with their behaving in abnormal, pathological ways.

The irrationality lesson? It was the prejudice toward me created by applying an ill-fitting stereotype of being Mafia-like because of my ethnic identity and urban origins—by otherwise nice, intelligent white kids. The influence of the group prevented individual students from breaking through the constraints imposed by prejudiced thinking and group norms, even when their personal experience diverged from the hostile base rate. As a student at Brooklyn College I studied prejudice between allegedly liberal Whites and Blacks in their self-segregated seating patterns in the school cafeteria and also Black versus Puerto Rican prejudices in my neighborhood. Then when I became president of my White-Christian fraternity, I arranged to have it opened to Jews, Blacks, Puerto Ricans, and whoever made the new grade as a "good brother"—a first step in putting personal principles into social action.

You can see now why I feel that social psychology is not merely about the social life of the individual; for me, it is at the core of our lives. People are always crucial to the plot development of our most important personal stories. The McGraw-Hill Series in Social Psychology has become a celebration of that basic theme. We have gathered some of the best researchers, theorists, teachers, and social change agents to write their stories about some aspect of our exciting field which they know best. They are encouraged to do so not just for their colleagues, as they do often in professional journals and monographs, but rather for intelligent undergraduates. With that youthful audience in mind, we all have tried to tap into their natural curiosity about human nature, to trigger their critical thinking, to touch their concerns for understanding the complexity of social life all about them, and to inspire them toward socially responsible utilization of their knowledge.

No one achieves those lofty goals better than the author of this text, David Myers. David writes with a clarity, precision of style, and graceful eloquence unmatched in all of psychology. He is the author of the best-selling introductory psychology textbook and also the best-selling social psychology text, a rare feat of effective writing and mind-boggling focused energy. What sets him apart from his talented peers is David's clear vision of his audience, to whom he talks as if they were welcomed guests at his dining table. We see him sharing his wealth of knowledge of psychology and of literature, posing just the right questions to pique their interest, or calling up the apt metaphor that clarifies a complex thought, and always integrating it all within a compelling story.

The McGraw-Hill Series in Social Psychology provided David Myers with a new option for his talents, enabling him to go beyond traditional textbook writing with its compressed, encyclopedic presentation of information. Why not tell a series of stories, each built around a distinctive theme of social psychological interest? They would be points-of-view pieces, personal perspectives of this senior researcher, writer, teacher. Taken as a whole, these modules would represent the breadth of the field while also enabling David the freedom to plumb some of its depths more fully than is possible in traditional texts. This new orientation freed David to burst out of the constraints imposed on textbook authors and fashion a novel approach to introducing students to the joys and challenges of social psychology. In a sense, David Myers moved from master writer to master chef by creating wonderfully enticing little dishes, with 31 separate flavors, as in an Indonesian rice table, a rijstafel. Skillfully blended are many expected ingredients—attribution, persuasion, aggression, prejudice, and group dynamics—along with unfamiliar ones—pride, corruption of nice people, dislike of diversity, peacemakers, and psychology of religion, to name but a handful of his dishes.

These 31 "magical modules," as I have come to think of them, form a fabulous feast suitably rich for new students at the table of social psychology, yet quite satisfying for the more jaded tastes of mature faculty colleagues. Whole sets of research are skillfully summarized, critical questions posed for pondering, perceptive conclusions subtly extracted, and meaningful implications for students and society are adroitly drawn.

The success of the first three editions of *Exploring Social Psychology* (1994, 2000, 2004) has inspired David Myers to try his hand at improving the module mix, blending them better within and across categories, while updating some to reflect contemporary research and theorizing. What was excellent earlier now becomes simply superb.

As usual, David Myers is never satisfied with leaving good enough alone. As a perfectionist, he is always working to improve his presentation of the science and practice of social psychology, and it shows again in this new edition. Virtually every chapter has something new and hot off the press, new research data, new examples of social psychology in action, new commentary and analyses, as well as David's provocative insights into connections between ideas about human nature. It is such a delightful blend of basic research wed to practical applications organized around issues that are so relevant to the concerns of our contemporary students.

Before you start your first course, let me note one personal flaw of my own—this was not the first book I read in my undergraduate social psychology course. Had it been, I would have known instantly that there could be no more exciting adventure than to spend one's life as one of Them—social psychologists who make a difference through their research and theories in enhancing the quality of the Human Condition. As Allen Funt's *Candid Camera Classics* reveal that it is possible to learn while laughing, David Myers's *Exploring Social Psychology* reveals that it is possible to be entertained while becoming educated. So sit back, read, and enjoy this master of the trade weaving his wonderful tales for your pleasure, each tasty in its own way.

Philip G. Zimbardo,
Series Consulting Editor

Preface

———— ❖ ————

This is a book I secretly wanted to write. I have long believed that what is wrong with all psychology textbooks (including those which I have written) is their overlong chapters. Few can read a 40-page chapter in a single sitting without their eyes glazing and their mind wandering. So why not organize the discipline into digestible chunks—say forty 15-page chapters rather than fifteen 40-page chapters—that student could read in a sitting, before laying the book down with a sense of completion?

Thus, when McGraw-Hill psychology editor Chris Rogers first suggested that I abbreviate and restructure my 15-chapter 600-page *Social Psychology* into a series of crisply written 10-page modules I said "Eureka!" At last a publisher willing to break convention by packaging the material in a form ideally suited to students' attention spans. By presenting concepts and findings in smaller bites, we also hoped not to overload students' capacities to absorb new information. And, by keeping *Exploring Social Psychology* slim and economical, we sought to enable instructors to supplement it with other reading.

As the playful module titles suggest, I have also broken with convention by introducing social psychology in an essay format. Each is written in the spirit of Thoreau's admonition: "Anything living is easily and naturally expressed in popular language." My aim in the parent *Social Psychology*, and even more so here, is to write in a voice that is both solidly scientific and warmly human, factually rigorous and intellectually provocative. I hope to reveal social psychology as an investigative reporter might, by providing a current summary of important social phenomena, by showing how social psychologists uncover and explain such phenomena, and by reflecting on their human significance.

In selecting material, I have represented social psychology's scope, highlighting its scientific study of how we think about, influence, and relate to one another.

I also emphasize material that casts social psychology in the intellectual tradition of the liberal arts. By the teaching of great literature, philosophy, and science, liberal education seeks to expand our thinking and awareness and to liberate us from the confines of the present. Social psychology can contribute to these goals. Many undergraduate social psychology students are not psychology majors; most will enter other professions. By focusing on humanly significant issues such as belief and illusion, independence and interdependence, love and hate, one can present social psychology in ways that inform and stimulate all students.

This new fourth edition features updated coverage throughout. In addition, the fourth edition features technology components designed to assist both professor and student. Icons throughout the text guide the student to the Online Learning Center (OLC) (www.mhhe.com/myersesp4) to gather more information on each module by viewing excerpts from The Social Connection video modules, participating in interactive exercises and taking module quizzes to test their knowledge. The Social Connection video modules, produced by Frank Vattano at Colorado State University, enrich classic experiments by recreating or providing footage from classic experiments, seasoned with interviews of leading social psychologists.

A comprehensive teaching package also accompanies *Exploring Social Psychology*. The acclaimed Instructor's Resource Manual CD-ROM (IRCD) has been revised to reflect changes in the fourth edition text. The IRCD includes a Test Bank, which has also been revised to include a higher concentration of conceptual questions, and a set of PowerPoint slides to use in the classroom. The instructor's side of the OLC will also include the instructor's manual and Power-Point presentations.

ACKNOWLEDGMENTS

I remain indebted to the community of scholars who have guided and critiqued the evolution of this material through seven editions of *Social Psychology*. These caring colleagues, acknowledged individually therein, have enabled a better book than I, alone, could have created.

I am grateful not only to Chris Rogers, for venturing this book, but also to series editor Philip Zimbardo for his encouragement. As my friendship with Phil has grown, I have come to admire his gifts as one of psychology's premier communicators. Others on the McGraw-Hill team also played vital roles. Psychology editor Mike Sugarman encouraged and commissioned this new edition, and Kate Russillo supported us by gathering reviews from thoughtful colleagues, including:

Michele Breault, Truman State University
Shawn Meghan Burn, California Polytechnic State University
Deborah Davis, University of Nevada
Susann Doyle-Portillo, Gainesville College
Krista Forrest, University of Nebraska at Kearney
Kellina Craig-Henderson, Howard University

Richard Miller, University of Nebraska at Kearney
Peggy Moody, St. Louis Community College
Rosann Ross, University of Northern Colorado
Darrin Sorrells, Oakland City University

Although these generous colleagues bear no responsibility for any lingering errors, I am indebted to each of them for their conscientious and helpful contribution to the teaching of social psychology.

Here at Hope College, Kathryn Brownson helped digest the *Social Psychology,* eighth edition material into these modules and prepare them for production. As in all of my published social psychology books with McGraw-Hill, I again pay tribute to two significant people. Were it not for the invitation of McGraw-Hill's Nelson Black, it surely never would have occurred to me to try my hand at text writing. Poet Jack Ridl, my Hope College colleague and writing coach, helped shape the voice you will hear in these pages.

To all in this supporting cast, I am indebted. Working with all these people has made my work a stimulating, gratifying experience.

David G. Myers
davidmyers.org

The McGraw-Hill Social Psychology Series

This popular series of paperback titles is written by authors about their particular field of expertise and is meant to complement any social psychology course. The series includes:

Berkowitz, Leonard:	Aggression: Its Causes, Consequences, and Control
Brown, Jonathon:	The Self
Burn, Shawn, M.:	The Social Psychology of Gender
Brannigan, Gary G., and Matthew Merrens:	The Social Psychologists: Research Adventures
Ellyson, Steve L., and Amy G. Halberstadt:	Explorations in Social Psychology: Readings and Research
Fiske, Susan T., and Shelley E. Taylor:	Social Cognition, 2/e
Schroeder, David, Louis Penner, John Dovidio, and Jane Piliavan:	The Psychology of Helping and Altruism: Problems and Puzzles
Keough, Kelli A., and Julio Garcia:	Social Psychology of Gender, Race, and Ethnicity: Readings and Projects
Milgram, Stanley:	The Individual in a Social World, 2/e
Myers, David G.:	Social Psychology, 9/e
Pines, Ayala M., and Christina Maslach:	Experiencing Social Psychology: Readings and Projects, 4/e
Plous, Scott:	The Psychology of Judgment and Decision Making
Ross, Lee, and Richard E. Nisbett:	The Person and the Situation: Perspectives of Social Psychology
Rubin, Jeffrey Z., Dean G. Pruitt, and Sung Hee Kim:	Social Conflict: Escalation, Stalemate, and Settlement, 2/e
Triandis, Harry C.:	Culture and Social Behavior
Zimbardo, Philip G., and Michael R. Leippe:	The Psychology of Attitude Change and Social Influence

❖

PART ONE

Introducing Social Psychology

"We cannot live for ourselves alone," remarked the novelist Herman Melville, "for our lives are connected by a thousand invisible threads." Social psychologists study those connections by scientifically exploring how we *think about, influence,* and *relate* to one another.

Video
1.1

In the first two modules I explain how we do that exploring, how we play the social psychology game. As it happens, the ways that social psychologists form and test ideas can be carried into life itself, enabling us to think smarter as we analyze everyday social thinking, social influences, and social relations.

If intuition and common sense were utterly trustworthy, we would be less in need of scientific inquiry and critical thinking. But the truth, as Module 2 relates, is that whether we are reflecting on research results or everyday events, we readily succumb to a powerful hindsight bias, also called the *I-knew-it-all-along phenomenon.*

1

❖

Doing Social Psychology

T here once was a man whose second wife was a vain and selfish woman. This woman had two daughters who were similarly vain and selfish. The man's own daughter, however, was sweet and kind. This sweet, kind daughter, whom we all know as Cinderella, learned early on that she should do as she was told, accept insults, and not upstage her vain stepsisters.

But then, thanks to her fairy godmother, Cinderella was able to escape her situation and go to a grand ball, where she attracted a handsome prince. When the love-struck prince later encountered a homelier Cinderella back in her degrading home, he at first failed to recognize her.

Implausible? The folktale demands that we accept the power of the situation. In one situation, playing one role in the presence of her oppressive stepmother, the meek and unattractive Cinderella was a different person from the charming and beautiful Cinderella whom the prince met. At home, she cowered. At the ball, Cinderella felt more beautiful and walked and talked and smiled as if she were.

The French philosopher-novelist Jean-Paul Sartre (1946) would have had no problem accepting the Cinderella premise. We humans are "first of all beings in a situation," he believed. "We cannot be distinguished from our situations, for they form us and decide our possibilities" (pp. 59–60, paraphrased). Social psychology is a science that studies the influences of our situations, with special attention to how we view and affect one another. "Our lives are connected by a thousand invisible threads," said the novelist Herman Melville. Social psychology aims to illuminate those threads. It does so by asking questions that have intrigued us all:

- How and what do people *think* of one another? How reasonable are the ideas we form of ourselves? of our friends? of strangers? How tight are the links between what we think and what we do?
- How, and how much, do people *influence* one another? How strong are the invisible threads that pull us? Are we creatures of our gender roles? our groups? our cultures? How can we resist social pressure, even sway the majority?
- What shapes the way we *relate to* one another? What leads people sometimes to hurt and sometimes to help? What kindles social conflict? And how might we transform the closed fists of aggression into the open arms of compassion?

A common thread runs through these questions: They all deal with how people view and affect one another. That is what social psychology is all about: attitudes and beliefs, conformity and independence, love and hate. To put it formally, **social psychology** is *the scientific study of how people think about, influence, and relate to one another.*

Tired of looking at the stars, Professor Mueller takes up social psychology.
Source: Reprinted with permission by Jason Love at www.jasonlove.com.

Unlike other scientific disciplines, social psychology has nearly 6 billion amateur practitioners. People-watching is a universal hobby—in parks, on the street, at school. As we observe people, we form ideas about how human beings think about, influence, and relate to one another. Professional social psychologists do the same, only more systematically (by forming theories) and painstakingly (often with experiments that create miniature social dramas that pin down cause and effect). And they do it frequently, in 25,000 studies of 8 million people by one recent count (Richard & others, 2003).

*F*ORMING AND TESTING THEORIES

We social psychologists have a hard time thinking of anything more fascinating than human existence. If, as Socrates counseled, "The unexamined life is not worth living," then simply "knowing thyself" seems a worthy enough goal.

As we wrestle with human nature to pin down its secrets, we organize our ideas and findings into theories. A **theory** is *an integrated set of principles that explain and predict* observed events. Theories are a scientific shorthand.

In everyday conversation, "theory" often means "less than fact"—a middle rung on a confidence ladder from guess to theory to fact. But to a scientist, facts and theories are apples and oranges. Facts are agreed-upon statements about what we observe. Theories are *ideas* that summarize and explain facts. "Science is built up with facts, as a house is with stones," said Jules Henri Poincaré, "but a collection of facts is no more a science than a heap of stones is a house."

Theories not only summarize, they also imply testable predictions, called **hypotheses**. Hypotheses serve several purposes. First, they allow us to *test* a theory by suggesting how we might try to falsify it. In making predictions, a theory puts its money where its mouth is. Second, predictions give *direction* to research. Any scientific field will mature more rapidly if its researchers have a sense of direction. Theoretical predictions suggest new areas for research; they send investigators looking for things they might never have thought of. Third, the predictive feature of good theories can also make them *practical*. A complete theory of aggression, for example, would predict when to expect it and how to control it. As Kurt Lewin, one of modern social psychology's founders, declared, "There is nothing so practical as a good theory."

Consider how this works. Say we observe that people who loot, taunt, or attack often do so in groups or crowds. We might therefore theorize that the presence of other people makes individuals feel anonymous and lowers their inhibitions. Let's play with this idea for a moment.

Perhaps we could test it by constructing a laboratory experiment simulating aspects of execution by electric chair. What if we asked individuals in groups to administer punishing shocks to a hapless victim without knowing which one of the group was actually shocking the victim? Would these individuals administer stronger shocks than individuals acting alone, as our theory predicts?

We might also manipulate anonymity: Would people deliver stronger shocks hiding behind masks? If the results confirm our hypothesis, they might suggest some practical applications. Perhaps police brutality could be reduced by having officers wear large name tags and drive cars identified with large numbers, or by videotaping their arrests—all of which have, in fact, recently become common practice in many cities.

But how do we conclude that one theory is better than another? A good theory (1) effectively summarizes a wide range of observations and (2) makes clear predictions that we can use to (a) confirm or modify the theory, (b) generate new exploration, and (c) suggest practical application. When we discard theories, usually it's not because they have been proved false. Rather, like old cars, they get replaced by newer, better models.

_C_ORRELATIONAL RESEARCH: DETECTING NATURAL ASSOCIATIONS

Most of what you will learn about social-psychological research methods you will absorb as you read later modules. But let us go backstage now and take a brief look at how social psychology is done. This glimpse behind the scenes will be just enough for you to appreciate findings discussed later and to think critically about everyday social events.

Activity
1.1

Social-psychological research varies by location. It can take place in the _laboratory_ (a controlled situation) or in the **field** (everyday situations). And it varies by method—**correlational research** asks whether two or more factors are naturally associated, and **experimental research** manipulates some factor to see its effect on another. If you want to be a critical reader of psychological research reported in newspapers and magazines, it pays to understand the difference between correlational and experimental research.

Using some real examples, let's first consider the advantages of correlational research (often involving important variables in natural settings) and the disadvantage (ambiguous interpretation of cause and effect). Today's psychologists relate personal and social factors to human health. Among the researchers have been Douglas Carroll at Glasgow

Commemorative markers in Glasgow
Cathedral graveyard.

Caledonian University and his colleagues, George Davey Smith and Paul
Bennett (1994). In search of possible links between socioeconomic status
and health, the researchers ventured into Glasgow's old graveyards. As
a measure of health, they noted from grave markers the life spans of 843
individuals. As an indication of status, they measured the height of the
pillars over the graves, reasoning that height reflected cost and therefore
affluence. As Figure 1-1 shows, taller grave markers were related to
longer lives, for both men and women.

   Carroll and his colleagues explain how other researchers, using contemporary data, have confirmed the status-longevity correlation. Scottish
postal-code regions having the least overcrowding and unemployment
also have the greatest longevity. In the United States, income correlates
with longevity (poor and lower-status people are more at risk for pre-
mature death). In contemporary Britain, occupational status correlates
with longevity. One study followed 17,350 British civil service workers
over 10 years. Compared with top-grade administrators, those at the
professional-executive grade were 1.6 times more likely to have died.
Clerical workers were 2.2 times and laborers 2.7 times more likely to
have died (Adler & others, 1993, 1994). Across times and places, the
status-health correlation seems reliable.

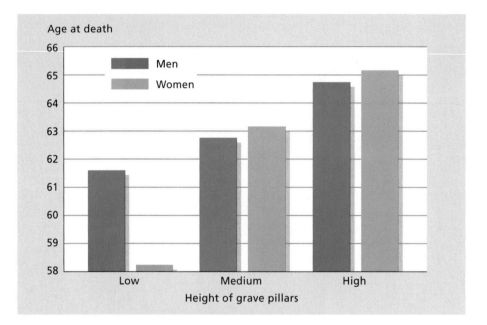

FIGURE 1-1
Correlating status and longevity. Tall grave pillars commemorated people who also tended to live longer.

Correlation Versus Causation

The status-longevity question illustrates the most irresistible thinking error made by both amateur and professional social psychologists: When two factors like status and health go together, it is terribly tempting to conclude that one is causing the other. Status, we might presume, somehow protects a person from health risks. Or might it be the other way around? Maybe health promotes vigor and success. Perhaps people who live longer accumulate more wealth (enabling them to have more expensive grave markers). Correlations indicate a relationship. Correlational research allows us to *predict,* but it cannot tell us whether changing one variable (such as social status) will *cause* changes in another (such as health).

The correlation-causation confusion is behind much muddled thinking in popular psychology. Consider another very real correlation—between self-esteem and academic achievement. Children with high self-esteem tend also to have high academic achievement. (As with any correlation, we can also state this the other way around: High achievers tend to have high self-esteem.) Why do you suppose this is (Figure 1-2)?

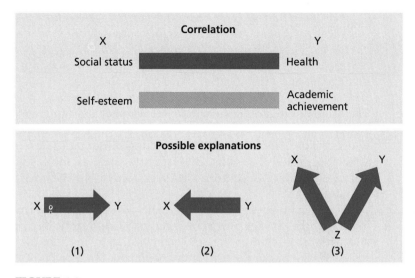

FIGURE 1-2
Correlation and causations. When two variables correlate, any combination of three explanations is possible.

Some people believe a "healthy self-concept" contributes to achievement. Thus, boosting a child's self-image may also boost school achievement. Believing so, 30 U.S. states have enacted more than 170 self-esteem-promoting statutes.

But other people, including psychologists William Damon (1995), Robyn Dawes (1994), Mark Leary (1998), Martin Seligman (1994), and Roy Baumeister and colleagues (2003), doubt that self-esteem is really "the armor that protects kids" from underachievement (or drug abuse and delinquency). Perhaps it's the other way around: Perhaps problems and failures cause low self-esteem. Perhaps self-esteem often reflects the reality of how things are going for us. Perhaps self-esteem grows from hard-won achievements. Do well and you will feel good about yourself; goof off and fail and you will feel like a dolt. A study of 635 Norwegian schoolchildren suggests that a string of gold stars by one's name on the spelling chart and praise from the admiring teacher can boost a child's self-esteem (Skaalvik & Hagtvet, 1990). It is also possible that self-esteem and achievement correlate because both are linked to underlying intelligence and family social status.

That possibility was raised in two studies—one a nationwide sample of 1,600 young American men, another of 715 Minnesota youngsters (Bachman & O'Malley, 1977; Maruyama & others, 1981). When the researchers statistically removed the effect of intelligence and family status, the correlation between self-esteem and achievement evaporated.

Advanced correlational techniques can suggest cause-effect relations, statistically extracting the influence of confounded (extraneous but associated) variables. Thus, the researchers just mentioned saw the correlation between self-esteem *and* achievement evaporated after extracting intelligence and family status. (Among people of similar intelligence and family status, the self-esteem-achievement relationship was minimal.) The Scottish research team wondered whether the status-longevity relationship would survive their removing the effect of cigarette smoking, which is now much less common among those higher in status. It did, which suggested that some other factors, such as increased stress and decreased feelings of control, must also account for the greater mortality of the poor.

So the great strength of correlational research is that it tends to occur in real-world settings where we can examine factors like race, gender, and social status that we cannot manipulate in the laboratory. Its great disadvantage lies in the ambiguity of the results. The point is so important that, even if it fails to impress people the first 25 times they hear it, it is worth making a 26th time: Knowing that two variables change together enables us to predict one when we know the other; but *correlation does not specify cause and effect.*

EXPERIMENTAL RESEARCH: SEARCHING FOR CAUSE AND EFFECT

The near impossibility of discerning cause and effect among naturally correlated events prompts most social psychologists to create laboratory simulations of everyday processes whenever this is feasible and ethical. These simulations are roughly similar to aeronautical wind tunnels. Aeronautical engineers don't begin by observing how flying objects perform in a wide variety of natural environments. The variations in both atmospheric conditions and flying objects are so complex that they would surely find it difficult to organize and use such data to design better aircraft. Instead, they construct a simulated reality that is under their control. Then they can manipulate wind conditions and observe the precise effect of particular wind conditions on particular wing structures.

Control: Manipulating Variables

Like aeronautical engineers, social psychologists experiment by constructing social situations that simulate important features of our daily lives. By varying just one or two factors at a time—called **independent variables**—the experimenter pinpoints how changes in these one or two things affect us. As the wind tunnel helps the aeronautical engineer discover principles of aerodynamics, so the experiment enables the social psychologist to discover principles of social thinking, social influence, and social relations. The ultimate aim of wind tunnel simulations is to understand and predict the flying characteristics of complex aircraft. Social psychologists experiment to understand and predict complex human behaviors. They aim to understand why behavior varies among people, across situations, and over time.

Historically, social psychologists have used the experimental method in about three-fourths of their research studies (Higbee & others, 1982), and in two out of three studies the setting has been a research laboratory (Adair & others, 1985). To illustrate the laboratory experiment, consider an experiment that typifies a possible cause-effect explanation of correlational findings: the correlation between television viewing and children's behavior. Children who watch many violent television programs tend to be more aggressive than those who watch few. This suggests that children might be learning from what they see on the screen. As I hope you now recognize, this is a correlational finding. Figure 1-2 on p. 9 reminds us that there are two other cause-effect interpretations that do not implicate television as the cause of the children's aggression. (What are they?)

Social psychologists have therefore brought television viewing into the laboratory, where they control the amount of violence the children see. By exposing children to violent and nonviolent programs, researchers can observe how the amount of violence affects behavior. Chris Boyatzis and his colleagues (1995) showed some elementary school children, but not others, an episode of the 1990s most popular—and violent—children's television program, "Power Rangers." Immediately after viewing the episode, the viewers committed seven times as many aggressive acts per two-minute intervals as the nonviewers. The observed aggressive acts we call the **dependent variable.** Such experiments indicate that television can be one cause of children's aggressive behavior.

So far we have seen that the logic of experimentation is simple: By creating and controlling a miniature reality, we can vary one factor and then another and discover how these factors, separately or in combination, affect people. Now let's go a little deeper and see how an experiment is done.

Every social-psychological experiment has two essential ingredients. We have just considered one—*control*. We manipulate one or two independent variables while trying to hold everything else constant. The other ingredient is *random assignment*.

Random Assignment: The Great Equalizer

Recall that we were reluctant, on the basis of a correlation, to assume that violence viewing *causes* aggressiveness. A survey researcher might measure and statistically extract other possibly pertinent factors and see

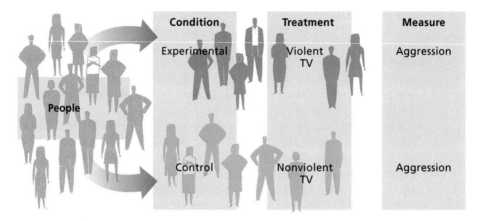

Condition	Treatment	Measure
Experimental	Violent TV	Aggression
Control	Nonviolent TV	Aggression

People

FIGURE 1-3
Random assignment. Experiments randomly assigning people either to a condition that receives the experimental treatment or to a control condition that does not. This gives the researcher confidence that any later difference is somehow caused by the treatment.

if the correlations survive. But one can never control for all the factors that might distinguish viewers of violence from nonviewers. Maybe violence viewers differ in education, culture, intelligence—or in dozens of ways the researcher hasn't considered.

In one fell swoop, **random assignment** eliminates all such extraneous factors. With random assignment, each person has an equal chance of viewing the violence or the nonviolence. Thus, the people in both groups would, in every conceivable way—family status, intelligence, education, initial aggressiveness—average about the same. Highly intelligent people, for example, are equally likely to appear in both groups. Because random assignment creates equivalent groups, any later aggression difference between the two groups must have something to do with the only way they differ—whether or not they viewed violence (Figure 1-3).

The Ethics of Experimentation

Activity
1.2

Our television example illustrates why there are ethical issues with some conceivable experiments. Social psychologists would not, over long time periods, expose one group of children to brutal violence. Rather, they briefly alter people's social experience and note the effects. Sometimes the experimental treatment is a harmless, perhaps even enjoyable, experience to which people give their knowing consent. Other times, researchers find themselves operating in a gray area between the harmless and the risky.

Social psychologists often venture into that ethical gray area when they design experiments that engage intense thoughts and emotions. Experiments need not have what Elliot Aronson, Marilynn Brewer, and Merrill Carlsmith (1985) call **mundane realism.** That is, laboratory behavior (for example, delivering electric shocks as part of an experiment on aggression) need not be literally the same as everyday behavior. For many researchers, that sort of realism is indeed mundane—not important. But the experiment *should* have **experimental realism**—it should absorb and involve the participants. Experimenters do not want their people consciously play-acting or ho-humming it; they want to engage real psychological processes. Forcing people to choose whether to give intense or mild electric shock to someone else can, for example, be a realistic measure of aggression. It functionally simulates real aggression.

Achieving experimental realism sometimes requires deceiving people with a plausible cover story. If the person in the next room actually is not receiving the shocks, the experimenter does not want the participants to know this. That would destroy the experimental realism. Thus, about one-third of social-psychological studies (though a decreasing number) have used deception in their search for truth (Korn & Nicks, 1993; Vitelli, 1988).

Researchers often walk a tightrope in designing experiments that will be involving yet ethical. To believe that you are hurting someone, or to be subjected to strong social pressure to see if it will change your opinion or behavior, may be temporarily uncomfortable. Such experiments raise the age-old question of whether ends justify means. The social psychologists' deceptions are usually brief and mild compared with many misrepresentations in real life, or even on some of television's "Candid Camera" and reality shows. Nevertheless, do the insights gained justify deceiving and sometimes distressing people?

University ethics committees now review social-psychological research to ensure that it will treat people humanely. Ethical principles developed by the American Psychological Association (2002), the Canadian Psychological Association (2000), and the British Psychological Society (2000) urge investigators to do the following:

- Tell potential participants enough about the experiment to enable their **informed consent.**
- Be truthful. Use deception only if essential and justified by a significant purpose and not "about aspects that would affect their willingness to participate."
- Protect people from harm and significant discomfort.
- Treat information about the individual participants confidentially.
- Fully explain the experiment afterward, including any deception. The only exception to this rule is when the feedback would be distressing, say by making people realize they have been stupid or cruel.

The experimenter should be sufficiently informative *and* considerate that people leave feeling at least as good about themselves as when they came in. Better yet, the participants should be repaid by having learned something about the nature of psychological inquiry. When treated respectfully, few participants mind being deceived (Epley & Huff, 1998; Kimmel, 1998). Indeed, say social psychology's defenders, professors provoke far greater anxiety and distress by giving and returning course exams than researchers provoke in their experiments.

GENERALIZING FROM LABORATORY TO LIFE

As the research on children, television, and violence illustrates, social psychology mixes everyday experience and laboratory analysis. Throughout this book we will do the same by drawing our data mostly from the laboratory and our illustrations mostly from life. Social psychology displays a healthy interplay between laboratory research and everyday life. Hunches gained from everyday experience often inspire laboratory research, which deepens our understanding of our experience.

This interplay appears in the children's television experiment. What people saw in everyday life suggested experimental research. Network and government policymakers, those with the power to make changes, are now aware of the results. The consistency of findings on television's effects—in the lab and in the field—is true of research in many other areas, including studies of helping, leadership style, depression, and self-efficacy. The effects one finds in the lab have been mirrored by effects in the field. "The psychology laboratory has generally produced psychological truths rather than trivialities," note Craig Anderson and his colleagues (1999).

We need to be cautious, however, in generalizing from laboratory to life. Although the laboratory uncovers basic dynamics of human existence, it is still a simplified, controlled reality. It tells us what effect to expect of variable *X*, all other things being equal—which in real life they never are. Moreover, as you will see, the participants in many experiments are college students, which are hardly a random sample of all humanity. Would we get similar results with people of different ages, educational levels, and cultures? This is always an open question.

Nevertheless, we can distinguish between the *content* of people's thinking and acting (their attitudes, for example) and the *process* by which they think and act (for example, how attitudes affect actions and vice versa). The content varies more from culture to culture than does the process. People from various cultures may hold different opinions yet form them in similar ways. For example, college students in Puerto Rico report greater loneliness than do collegians on the U.S. mainland.

Yet in both cultures the ingredients of loneliness are much the same—
shyness, uncertain purpose in life, low self-esteem (Jones & others, 1985).
Our behaviors may differ yet be influenced by the same social forces.

CONCEPTS TO REMEMBER

social psychology   The scientific study of how people think about, influence, and relate to one another.

theory   An integrated set of principles that explain and predict observed events.

hypothesis   A testable proposition that describes a relationship that may exist between events.

field research   Research done in natural, real-life settings outside the laboratory.

correlational research   The study of the naturally occurring relationships among variables.

experimental research   Studies that seek clues to cause-effect relationships by manipulating one or more factors (independent variables) while controlling others (holding them constant).

independent variable   The experimental factor that a researcher manipulates.

dependent variable   The variable being measured, so-called because it may *depend* on manipulations of the independent variable.

random assignment   The process of assigning participants to the conditions of an experiment such that all persons have the same chance of being in a given condition. (Note the distinction between random *assignment* in experiments and random *sampling* in surveys. Random assignment helps us infer cause and effect. Random sampling helps us generalize to a population.)

mundane realism   Degree to which an experiment is superficially similar to everyday situations.

experimental realism   Degree to which an experiment absorbs and involves its participants.

informed consent   An ethical principle requiring that research participants be told enough to enable them to choose whether they wish to participate.

2

❖

Did You Know It All Along?

Anything seems commonplace, once explained.

Dr. Watson to Sherlock Holmes

D o social psychology's theories provide new insight into the human condition? Or do they only describe the obvious? Many of the conclusions presented in this book may have already occurred to you, for social psychology is all around you. We constantly observe people thinking about, influencing, and relating to one another. It pays to discern what that facial expression predicts, how to get someone to do something, or whether to regard another as friend or foe. For centuries, philosophers, novelists, and poets have observed and commented on social behavior. Social psychology is everybody's business.

So, is social psychology only common sense in different words? Social psychology faces two contradictory criticisms: One is that it is trivial because it documents the obvious; the second is that it is dangerous because its findings could be used to manipulate people. Is the first objection valid—does social psychology simply formalize what any amateur already knows intuitively?

Writer Cullen Murphy (1990) thought so: "Day after day social scientists go out into the world. Day after day they discover that people's behavior is pretty much what you'd expect." Nearly a half-century earlier, historian Arthur Schlesinger, Jr. (1949) reacted with similar scorn to social scientists' studies of American World War II soldiers.

What did these studies find? Another reviewer, sociologist Paul Lazarsfeld (1949), offered a sample with interpretive comments, a few of which I paraphrase:

1. Better-educated soldiers suffered more adjustment problems than did less-educated soldiers. (Intellectuals were less prepared for battle stresses than street-smart people.)

2. Southern soldiers coped better with the hot South Sea Island climate than did Northern soldiers. (Southerners are more accustomed to hot weather.)

3. White privates were more eager for promotion than were Black privates. (Years of oppression take a toll on achievement motivation.)

4. Southern Blacks preferred Southern to Northern White officers (because Southern officers were more experienced and skilled in interacting with Blacks).

One problem with common sense, however, is that we invoke it after we know the facts. Events are far more "obvious" and predictable in hindsight than beforehand. Experiments reveal that when people learn the outcome of an experiment, that outcome suddenly seems unsurprising—certainly less surprising than it is to people who are simply told about the experimental procedure and the possible outcomes (Slovic & Fischhoff, 1977). With new knowledge at hand, our efficient memory system purges its outdated presumption (Hoffrage & others, 2000).

You perhaps experienced this phenomenon when reading Lazarsfeld's summary of findings, for Lazarsfeld went on to say, *"Every one of these statements is the direct opposite of what was actually found."* In reality, the book reported that less-educated soldiers adapted more poorly. Southerners were not more likely than Northerners to adjust to a tropical climate. Blacks were more eager than Whites for promotion, and so forth. "If we had mentioned the actual results of the investigation first [as Schlesinger experienced], the reader would have labeled these 'obvious' also."

Likewise, in everyday life we often do not expect something to happen until it does. *Then* we suddenly see clearly the forces that brought about the event and feel unsurprised. After elections or stock market shifts, most commentators find the turn of events unsurprising: "The market was due for a correction."

After the 2003 invasion of Iraq, the result—for Coalition forces victory came swiftly, but not civility and democracy—seemed obvious. Some argued that with the United States' $330 billion to $1.6 billion annual military spending advantage over Iraq, anyone could have predicted the rout, but the American forces should have foreseen the need to protect Baghdad's museums, libraries, and schools from looters. As the Danish philosopher-theologian Søren Kierkegaard put it, "Life is lived forwards, but understood backwards."

Activity
2.1

If this **hindsight bias** (also called the I-knew-it-all-along phenomenon) is pervasive, you may now be feeling that you already knew about it. Indeed, almost any conceivable result of a psychological experiment can seem like common sense—*after* you know the result.

You can demonstrate the phenomenon. Give half a group one psychological finding and the other half the opposite result. For example, tell half as follows:

> Social psychologists have found that, whether choosing friends or falling in love, we are most attracted to people whose traits are different from our own. There seems to be wisdom in the old saying, "Opposites attract."

Tell the other half:

> Social psychologists have found that, whether choosing friends or falling in love, we are most attracted to people whose traits are similar to our own. There seems to be wisdom in the old saying, "Birds of a feather flock together."

Ask the people first to explain the result. Then ask them to say whether it is "surprising" or "not surprising." Virtually all will find whichever result they were given "not surprising."

Indeed, we can draw on our stockpile of proverbs to make almost any result seem to make sense. If a social psychologist reports that separation intensifies romantic attraction, Joe Public responds, "You get paid for this? Everybody knows that 'absence makes the heart grow fonder.'" Should it turn out that separation weakens attraction, Judy Public may say, "My grandmother could have told you, 'Out of sight, out of mind.'"

Karl Teigen (1986) must have had a few chuckles when he asked University of Leicester (England) students to evaluate actual proverbs and their opposites. When given the proverb "Fear is stronger than love," most rated it as true. But so did students who were given its reversed form, "Love is stronger than fear." Likewise, the genuine proverb "He that is fallen cannot help him who is down" was rated highly; but so too was "He that is fallen can help him who is down." My favorites, however, were two highly rated proverbs: "Wise men make proverbs and fools repeat them" (authentic) and its made-up counterpart, "Fools make proverbs and wise men repeat them."

The hindsight bias creates a problem for many psychology students. Sometimes results are genuinely surprising (for example, that Olympic *bronze* medalists take more joy in their achievement than do silver medalists). More often, when you read the results of experiments in your textbooks, the material seems easy, even obvious. When you later take a multiple-choice test on which you must choose among several plausible conclusions, the task may become surprisingly difficult. "I don't know what happened," the befuddled student later moans. "I thought I knew the material."

The I-knew-it-all-along phenomenon can have pernicious consequences. It is conducive to arrogance—an overestimation of our own intellectual powers. Moreover, because outcomes seem as if they should have been foreseeable, we are more likely to blame decision makers for what are in retrospect "obvious" bad choices than to praise them for good choices, which also seem "obvious." Starting *after* the morning of 9/11 and working backward, signals pointing to the impending disaster seemed obvious. A U.S. Senate investigative report listed the missed or misinterpreted clues (Gladwell, 2003). The CIA knew that al Qaeda operatives had entered the country. An FBI agent sent a memo to headquarters that began by warning "the Bureau and New York of the possibility of a coordinated effort by Osama bin Laden to send students to the United States to attend civilian aviation universities and colleges." The FBI ignored this accurate warning and failed to relate it to other reports that terrorists were planning to use planes as weapons. "The dumb fools!" it seemed to hindsight critics. "Why couldn't they connect the dots?"

But what seems clear in hindsight is seldom clear on the front side of history. The intelligence community is overwhelmed with "noise"— the piles of useless information surrounding the shreds of useful information. Analysts must therefore be selective in deciding which to pursue. In the six years prior to 9/11, the FBI's counterterrorism unit had 68,000 uninvestigated leads. In hindsight, the few useful ones are now obvious.

Likewise, we sometimes blame ourselves for "stupid mistakes"— perhaps for not having handled a person or a situation better. Looking back, we see how we should have handled it. "I should have known how busy I would be at the semester's end and started that paper earlier." But sometimes we are too hard on ourselves. We forget that what is obvious to us *now* was not nearly so obvious at the time.

Physicians who are told both a patient's symptoms and the cause of death (as determined by autopsy) sometimes wonder how an incorrect diagnosis could have been made. Other physicians, given only the symptoms, don't find the diagnosis nearly so obvious (Dawson & others, 1988). (Would juries be slower to assume malpractice if they were forced to take a foresight rather than a hindsight perspective?)

Activity
2.2

So what do we conclude—that common sense is usually wrong? Sometimes it is. Common sense and medical experience assured doctors that bleeding was an effective treatment for typhoid fever, until someone in the middle of the nineteenth century bothered to experiment—to divide patients into two groups, one bled, the other given mere bed rest.

Other times, conventional wisdom is right—or it falls on both sides of an issue: Does happiness come from knowing the truth or preserving illusions? From being with others or living in peaceful solitude? Opinions are a dime a dozen; no matter what we find, there will be someone who foresaw it. (Mark Twain jested that Adam was the only person who, when saying a good thing, knew that nobody had said it before.) But which of the many competing ideas best fit reality?

The point is not that common sense is predictably wrong. Rather, common sense usually is right *after the fact*. We therefore easily deceive ourselves into thinking that we know and knew more than we do and did. And this is precisely why we need science—to help us sift reality from illusion and genuine predictions from easy hindsight.

CONCEPT TO REMEMBER

hindsight bias The tendency to exaggerate, *after* learning an outcome, one's ability to have foreseen how something turned out. Also known as the *I-knew-it-all-along phenomenon*.

PART TWO

❖

Social Thinking

This book unfolds around its definition of social psychology: the scientific study of how we *think about* (Part Two), *influence* (Part Three), and *relate to* (Part Four) one another.

These modules on social thinking examine the interplay between our sense of self and our social worlds, for example by showing how self-interest colors our social judgments.

Succeeding modules explore the amazing and sometimes rather amusing ways in which we form beliefs about our social worlds. We have quite remarkable powers of intuition (or what social psychologists call *automatic information processing*), yet in at least a half-dozen ways our intuition often fails us. Knowing these ways not only beckons us to humility; it can help us sharpen our thinking, keeping it more closely in touch with reality.

We will explore the links between attitudes and behaviors: Do our attitudes determine our behaviors? Do our behaviors determine our attitudes? Or does it work both ways?

Finally, we will apply these concepts and findings to clinical psychology, by showing where clinical intuition may go astray but also how social psychologists might assist a clinician's explanation and treatment of depression, loneliness, and anxiety.

MODULE

3

❖

Self-Concept: Who Am I?

No topic in psychology today is more researched than the self. In 2004 the word "self" appeared in 12,703 book and article summaries in *Psychological Abstracts*—more than eight times the number that appeared in 1970. Our sense of self organizes our thoughts, feelings, and actions.

Whatever we do in our fourscore years on this global spaceship, whatever we observe and interpret, whatever we conceive and create, whomever we meet and greet will be filtered through our selves. How, and how accurately, do we know ourselves? What determines our self-concept?

AT THE CENTER OF OUR WORLDS: OUR SENSE OF SELF

Activity
3.1

As a unique and complex creature, you have many ways to complete the sentence "I am _____." (What five answers might you give?) Taken together, your answers define your **self-concept.**

The elements of your self-concept, the specific beliefs by which you define yourself, are your **self-schemas** (Markus & Wurf, 1987). *Schemas* are mental templates by which we organize our worlds. Our *self*-schemas— our perceiving ourselves as athletic, overweight, smart, or whatever— powerfully affect how we process social information. They influence how we perceive, remember, and evaluate both other people and ourselves. If athletics is a central part of your self-concept (if being an athlete is one of your self-schemas), then you will tend to notice others' bodies and skills. You will quickly recall sports-related experiences. And you will welcome information that is consistent with your self-schema (Kihlstrom & Cantor, 1984). The self-schemas that make up our self-concepts help us catalog and retrieve our experiences.

Consider how the self influences memory, a phenomenon known as the **self-reference effect:** *When information is relevant to our self-concepts, we process it quickly and remember it well* (Higgins & Bargh, 1987; Kuiper & Rogers, 1979; Symons & Johnson, 1997). If asked whether a specific word, such as "outgoing," describes us, we later remember that word better than if asked whether it describes someone else. If asked to compare ourselves with a character in a short story, we remember that character better. Two days after a conversation with someone, our recall is best for what the person said about us (Kahan & Johnson, 1992). Thus, memories form around our primary interest: ourselves. When we think about something in relation to ourselves, we remember it better.

The self-reference effect illustrates a basic fact of life: Our sense of self is at the center of our worlds. Because we tend to see ourselves on center stage, we overestimate the extent to which others' behavior is aimed at us. We often see ourselves as responsible for events in which we played only a small part (Fenigstein, 1984). When judging someone else's performance or behavior, we often spontaneously compare it with our own (Dunning & Hayes, 1996). And if, while talking to one person, we overhear our name spoken by another in the room, our auditory radar instantly shifts our attention.

From our self-focused perspective, we presume that others are noticing and evaluating us. Thomas Gilovich, Victoria Medvec, and Kenneth Savitsky (2000) demonstrated this by having individual Cornell University students don embarrassing Barry Manilow T-shirts before entering a room with other students. The self-conscious T-shirt wearers guessed that nearly half their peers would notice the shirt. But only 23 percent actually did. This "spotlight effect" is not only true of our dorky clothes and bad hair but of our anxiety, irritation, disgust, deceit, or attraction as well: Fewer people notice than we presume (Gilovich & others, 1998). Keenly aware of our own emotions, we often have an illusion that they are transparent to others. The same goes for our social blunders and public mental slips. What we agonize over, others may hardly notice and soon forget (Savitsky & others, 2001). The more self-conscious we are, the more we believe this "illusion of transparency" (Vorauer & Ross, 1999).

SELF AND CULTURE

How did you complete the "I am _____" statement on page 25? Did you give information about your personal traits, such as "I am honest," "I am tall," or "I am outgoing"? Or did you also describe your social identity, such as "I am a Pisces," "I am a MacDonald," or "I am a Muslim"?

For some people, especially those in industrialized Western cultures, **individualism** prevails. Identity is pretty much self-contained. Adolescence is a time of separating from parents, becoming self-reliant, and defining one's personal, *independent self*. Uprooted and placed in a foreign land, one's identity—as a unique individual with particular abilities, traits, values, and dreams—would remain intact. The psychology of Western cultures assumes that your life will be enriched by defining your possible selves and believing in your power of personal control. By the last century's end, individualism had become the dominant voice in popular culture.

Western literature, from the *Iliad* to *The Adventures of Huckleberry Finn*, celebrates the self-reliant individual more than the person who fulfills others' expectations. Movie plots feature rugged heroes who buck the establishment. Songs proclaim "I Did It My Way" and "I Gotta Be Me" and, they revere "The Greatest Love of All"—loving oneself (Schoeneman, 1994). Individualism flourishes when people experience affluence, mobility, urbanism, and mass media (Freeman, 1997; Marshall, 1997; Triandis, 1994).

Cultures native to Asia, Africa, and Central and South America place a greater value on **collectivism.** They nurture what Shinobu Kitayama and Hazel Markus (1995) call the *interdependent self*. People are more self-critical and have less need for positive self-regard (Heine & others, 1999). Identity is defined more in relation to others. Malaysians, Indians, Japanese, and traditional Kenyans such as the Maasai, for example, are much more likely than Australians, Americans, and the British to complete the "I am" statement with their group identities (Kanagawa & others, 2001; Ma & Schoeneman, 1997). When speaking, people using the languages of collectivist countries say "I" less often (Kashima & Kashima, 1998, 2003).

Pigeonholing cultures as individualist or collectivist oversimplifies, however, because within any culture individualism varies from person to person (Oyserman & others, 2002a, 2002b). It also varies across a country's regions and political views. In the United States, Hawaiians and those living in the deep South exhibit greater collectivism than do those in Mountain West states such as Oregon and Montana (Vandello & Cohen, 1999). Conservatives tend to be economic individualists ("don't tax or regulate me") and moral collectivists ("do legislate against immorality"). Liberals tend to be economic collectivists and moral individualists.

With an *inter*dependent self one has a greater sense of belonging. Uprooted and cut off from family, colleagues, and loyal friends, interdependent people would lose the social connections that define who they are. They have not one self but many selves: self-with-parents, self-at-work, self-with-friends (Cross & others, 1992). As Figure 3-1 and

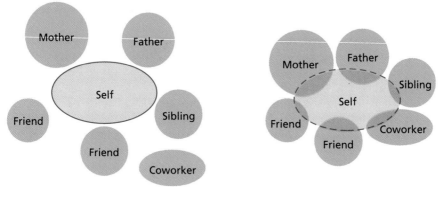

Independent view of self   Interdependent view of self

FIGURE 3-1

Self-construal as independent or interdependent. The independent self acknowledges relationships with others. But the interdependent self is more deeply embedded in others.   **Source:** From Markus & Kitayama, 1991.

Video
3.1

Table 3-1 suggest, the interdependent self is embedded in social memberships. Conversation is less direct and more polite (Holtgraves, 1997). The goal of social life is not so much to enhance one's individual self as to harmonize with and support one's communities. The individualized latte—"decaf, single shot, skinny, extra hot"—that seems just right at a North American espresso shop would seem a bit weird in Seoul, note Heejung Kim and Hazel Markus (1999). In Korea, people place less value on expressing their uniqueness and more on tradition and shared

TABLE 3-1 SELF-CONCEPT: INDEPENDENT OR INTERDEPENDENT.

	Independent	*Interdependent*
Identity is	Personal, defined by individual traits and goals	Social, defined by connections with others
What matters	Me—personal achievement and fulfillment; my rights and liberties	We—group goals and solidarity; our social responsibilities and relationships
Disapproves of	Conformity	Egotism
Illustrative motto	"To thine own self be true"	"No one is an island"
Cultures that support	Individualistic Western	Collectivistic Asian and Third World

practices (Choi & Choi, 2002). Korean advertisements less often highlight personal choice and freedom and more often feature people together (Markus & Kitayama, 2001).

Self-esteem in collectivist cultures correlates closely with what others think of me and their groups. Self-concept is malleable (context-specific) rather than stable (enduring across situations). In one study, four in five Canadian students but only one in three Chinese and Japanese students agreed that "the beliefs that you hold about who you are (your inner self) remain the same across different activity domains" (Tafarodi & others, 2004).

For those in individualistic cultures, and especially for minorities who have learned to discount others' prejudices, "outside" appraisals of one-self and one's group matter somewhat less (Crocker, 1994; Kwan & others, 1997). Self-esteem is more personal and less relational. Threaten our *personal* identity and we'll feel angrier and gloomier than when someone threatens our collective identity (Gaertner & others, 1999).

So when, do you suppose, are university students in collectivist Japan and individualist United States most likely to report positive emo-tions such as happiness and elation? For Japanese students, report Kitayama and Markus (2000), happiness comes with positive social engagement—with feeling close, friendly, and respectful. For American students, it more often comes with disengaged emotions—with feeling effective, superior, and proud. Conflict in collectivist cultures often is between groups; individualist cultures breed more crime and divorce between individuals (Triandis, 2000).

When Kitayama (1999), after 10 years of teaching and researching in America, visited his Japanese alma mater, Kyoto University, graduate students were "astounded" when he explained the Western idea of the independent self. "I persisted in explaining this Western notion of self-concept—one that my American students understood intuitively—and finally began to persuade them that, indeed, many Americans do have such a disconnected notion of self. Still, one of them, sighing deeply, said at the end, 'Could this *really* be true?'"

S ELF-KNOWLEDGE

"Know thyself," admonished the Greek philosopher Socrates. We cer-tainly try. We readily form beliefs about ourselves, and we don't hesitate to explain why we feel and act as we do. But how well do we actually know ourselves?

"There is one thing, and only one in the whole universe which we know more about than we could learn from external observation," noted C. S. Lewis (1952, pp. 18–19). "That one thing is [ourselves]. We have, so to speak, inside information; we are in the know." Indeed. Yet sometimes we *think* we know, but our inside information is wrong. This is the unavoidable conclusion of some fascinating research.

Explaining Our Behavior

Why did you choose your college? Why did you lash out at your room-mate? Why did you fall in love with that special person? Sometimes we know. Sometimes we don't. Asked why we have felt or acted as we have, we produce plausible answers. Yet, when causes are subtle, our self-explanations are often wrong. We may dismiss factors that matter and inflate others that don't. In studies, people have misattributed their rainy-day gloom to life's emptiness and their excitement while crossing a suspension bridge to their attraction to a passerby (Dutton & Aron, 1974; Schwarz & Clore, 1983). And people routinely deny being influenced by the media, which, they acknowledge, affects *others*.

Richard Nisbett and Stanley Schachter (1966) demonstrated people's misreading of their own mind after asking Columbia University students to endure a series of electric shocks of steadily increasing intensity. Before-hand, some took a fake pill that, they were told, would produce heart palpitations, breathing irregularities, and butterflies in the stomach—the very typical reactions to being shocked. Nisbett and Schachter antici-pated that people would attribute the shock symptoms to the pill and thus should tolerate more shock than people not given the pill. Indeed, the effect was enormous. People given the fake pill took four times as much shock. When asked why they withstood so much shock, they didn't mention the fake pill. When told the predicted pill effect, they granted that others might be influenced but denied its influence on them. "I didn't even think about the pill," was a typical reply.

Also thought provoking are studies in which people recorded their moods—every day for two or three months (Stone & others, 1985; Weiss & Brown, 1976; Wilson & others, 1982). They also recorded factors that might affect their moods: the day of the week, the weather, the amount they slept, and so forth. At the end of each study, the people judged how much each factor had affected their moods. Remarkably (given that their attention was being drawn to their daily moods), there was little relationship between their perceptions of how well a factor predicted their mood and how well it actually did so. These findings raise a disconcerting question: How much insight do we really have into what makes us happy or unhappy?

Predicting Our Behavior

People also err when predicting their behavior. If asked whether they would obey demands to deliver severe electric shocks or would hesitate to help a victim if several other people were present, people overwhelmingly deny their vulnerability to such influences. But as we will see, experiments have shown that many of us are vulnerable. Moreover, consider what Sidney Shrauger (1983) discovered when he had college students predict the likelihood that they would experience dozens of different events during the ensuing two months (becoming romantically involved, being sick, and so forth): Their self-predictions were hardly more accurate than predictions based on the average person's experience.

People also err frequently when predicting the fate of their relationships. Dating couples predict the longevity of their relationships through rose-colored glasses. Focusing on the positives, lovers may feel sure they will always be lovers. Their friends and family often know better, report Tara MacDonald and Michael Ross (1997) from studies with University of Waterloo students. The less optimistic predictions of their parents and roommates tend to be more accurate. (Many parents, having seen their child lunge confidently into an ill-fated relationship against all advice, nod yes.)

When predicting negative behaviors such as crying or lying, self-predictions are more accurate than predictions by one's mother and friends (Shrauger & others, 1996). Nevertheless, the surest thing we can say about your individual future is that it is sometimes hard for even you to predict. When predicting behavior, the best advice is to consider past behavior in similar situations (Osberg & Shrauger, 1986, 1990). Observing such, the people who know you can probably predict your behavior better than you can (for example, how nervous and chatty you will be when meeting someone new [Kenny, 1994]). So, to predict your future, consider your past.

Nicholas Epley and David Dunning (2000) discovered that we can sometimes better predict people's behavior by asking them to predict *others'* actions rather than their own. Five weeks ahead of Cornell University's annual "Daffodil Days" charity event, Epley and Dunning asked students to predict whether they would buy at least one daffodil for charity and also to predict what proportion of their fellow students would do so. More than four in five predicted they would buy a daffodil. But only 43 percent actually did, which was close to their prediction that 56 percent of others would buy one. In a laboratory game played for money, 84 percent predicted they would cooperate with another for their mutual gain, though only 61 percent did (again, close to their prediction of 64 percent cooperation by others.) If Lao-tzu was right that "He who knows others is learned. He who knows himself is enlightened," then most people, it would seem, are more learned than enlightened.

Predicting Our Feelings

Many of life's big decisions involve predicting our future feelings. Would marrying this person lead to lifelong contentment? Would entering this profession make for satisfying work? Would going on this vacation produce a happy experience? Or would the likelier results be divorce, job burnout, and holiday disappointment?

Sometimes we know how we will feel—if we fail that exam, win that big game, or soothe our tensions with a half-hour jog. We know what exhilarates us and what makes us anxious or bored. Other times we may mispredict our responses. Asked how they would feel if asked sexually harassing questions on a job interview, most women studied by Julie Woodzicka and Marianne LaFrance (2001) said they would feel angry. When actually asked such questions, however, women more often experienced fear. Studies of "affective forecasting" reveal that people nevertheless have greatest difficulty predicting the *intensity* and the *duration* of their future emotions (Wilson & Gilbert, 2003). People have mispredicted how they would feel for some time after a romantic breakup, receiving a gift, losing an election, winning a game, and being insulted (Gilbert & Ebert, 2002; Loewenstein & Schkade, 1999). Some examples:

- When male youths are shown sexually arousing photographs, then exposed to a passionate date scenario in which their date asks them to "stop," they admit that they might not stop. If not shown sexually arousing pictures first, they more often deny the possibility of being sexually aggressive. When not aroused, one easily mispredicts how one will feel and act when aroused—a phenomenon that leads to professions of love during lust, to unintended pregnancies, and to repeat offenses among sex abusers who have sincerely vowed "never again."

- Hungry shoppers do more impulse buying ("Those doughnuts would be delicious!") than when shopping after scarfing a quarter-pound blueberry muffin (Gilbert & Wilson, 2000). When hungry, one mispredicts how gross those deep-fried doughnuts will seem when sated. When stuffed, one mispredicts how yummy a doughnut might be with a late-night glass of milk.

- Only one in seven occasional smokers (of less than a cigarette per day) predict they will be smoking in five years. But they underestimate the power of their drug cravings, for nearly half will still be smoking (Lynch & Bonnie, 1994).

- People overestimate how much their well-being would be affected by warmer winters, losing weight, more television channels, or more free time. Even extreme events, such as winning a state lottery or suffering a paralyzing accident, affect long-term happiness less than most people suppose.

Our intuitive theory seems to be: We want. We get. We are happy. If that were true, this module would have fewer words. In reality, note

Daniel Gilbert and Timothy Wilson (2000), we often "miswant." People who imagine an idyllic desert island holiday with sun, surf, and sand may be disappointed when they discover "how much they require daily structure, intellectual stimulation, or regular infusions of Pop Tarts." We think that if our candidate or team wins we will be delighted for a long while. But study after study reveals that the emotional traces of such good tidings evaporate more rapidly than we expect.

It's after *negative* events that we're especially prone to "impact bias"—to overestimating the enduring impact of emotion-causing events. When people being tested for HIV predict how they will feel five weeks after getting the results, they expect to be feeling misery over bad news and elation over good news. Yet five weeks later, the bad news recipients are less distraught and the good news recipients are less elated than they anticipated (Sieff & others, 1999). And when Gilbert and his colleagues (1998) asked assistant professors to predict their happiness a few years after achieving tenure or not, most believed a favorable outcome was important for their future happiness. "Losing my job would crush my life's ambitions. It would be terrible." Yet when surveyed several years after the event, those denied tenure were about as happy as those who received it.

Let's make this personal. Gilbert and Wilson invite us to imagine how we might feel a year after losing our nondominant hands. Compared with today, how happy would you be?

Thinking about this, you perhaps focused on what the calamity would mean: no clapping, no shoe tying, no competitive basketball, no speedy keyboarding. Although you likely would forever regret the loss, your general happiness some time after the event would be influenced by "two things: (a) the event, and (b) everything else." In focusing on the negative event, we discount the importance of everything else that contributes to happiness and so overpredict our enduring misery. "Nothing that you focus on will make as much difference as you think," concur researchers David Schkade and Daniel Kahneman (1998).

Moreover, say Wilson and Gilbert (2003), people neglect the speed and power of their psychological immune system, which includes their strategies for rationalizing, discounting, forgiving, and limiting emotional trauma. Being largely ignorant of our "psychological immune system" (a phenomenon Gilbert and Wilson call *immune neglect*), we accommodate to disabilities, romantic breakups, exam failures, tenure denials, and personal and team defeats more readily than we would expect. Ironically, Gilbert and his colleagues report (2004), major negative events (which activate our psychological defenses) can be less enduringly distressing than minor irritations (which don't activate our defenses). In other words, we are resilient.

The Wisdom and Illusions of Self-Analysis

So, to a striking extent, our intuitions are often dead wrong about what has influenced us and what we will feel and do. But let's not overstate the case. When the causes of our behavior are conspicuous and the correct explanation fits our intuition, our self-perceptions will be accurate (Gavanski & Hoffman, 1987). Peter Wright and Peter Rip (1981) found that California high school juniors *could* discern how such features of a college as its size, tuition, and distance from home influenced their reactions to it. But when the causes of behavior are not obvious to an observer, they are not obvious to the person, either.

We are unaware of much that goes on in our minds. Studies of perception and memory show that we are more aware of the *results* than the process of our thinking. Gazing across our mental sea, we behold little below its conscious surface. We do, however, experience the results of our mind's unconscious workings when we set a mental clock to record the passage of time and to awaken us at an appointed hour, or when we somehow achieve a spontaneous creative insight after a problem has unconsciously "incubated." Creative scientists and artists, for example, often cannot report the thought processes that produced their insights.

Timothy Wilson (1985, 2002) offers a bold idea: The mental processes that *control* our social behavior are distinct from the mental processes through which we *explain* our behavior. Our rational explanations may therefore omit the gut-level attitudes that actually guide our behavior. In nine experiments, Wilson and his co-workers (1989) found that expressed attitudes toward things or people usually predicted later behavior reasonably well. If they first asked the participants to *analyze* their feelings, however, their attitude reports became useless. For example, dating couples' happiness with their relationship predicted whether they would still be dating several months later. But other participants first listed all the *reasons* they could think of why their relationship was good or bad before rating their happiness. After doing so, their attitude reports were useless in predicting the future of the relationship! Apparently the process of dissecting the relationship drew attention to easily verbalized factors that actually were less important than aspects of the relationship that were harder to verbalize. We are often "strangers to ourselves," says Wilson (2002).

Activity
3.2

Such findings illustrate that we have a **dual attitude system,** say Wilson and his colleagues (2000). Our automatic *implicit* attitudes regarding someone or something often differ from our consciously controlled, *explicit* attitudes. From childhood, for example, we may retain a habitual, automatic fear or dislike of people for whom we now verbalize respect and appreciation. Although explicit attitudes may change with relative ease, notes Wilson, "implicit attitudes, like old habits, change more slowly." With repeated practice—acting on the new attitude—new habitual attitudes can, however, replace old ones.

Murray Millar and Abraham Tesser (1992) believe that Wilson over-states our ignorance of self. Their research suggests that, yes, drawing people's attention to *reasons* diminishes the usefulness of attitude reports in predicting behaviors that are driven by *feelings*. If, instead of having people analyze their romantic relationships, Wilson had first asked them to get more in touch with their feelings ("How do you feel when you are with and apart from your partner?"), the attitude reports might have been more insightful. Other behavior domains—say, choosing which school to attend based on considerations of cost, career advancement, and so forth—seem more cognitively driven. For these, an analysis of reasons rather than feelings may be most useful. Although the heart has its reasons, sometimes the mind's own reasons are decisive.

This research on the limits of our self-knowledge has two practical implications. The first is for psychological inquiry. *Self-reports are often untrustworthy.* Errors in self-understanding limit the scientific usefulness of subjective personal reports.

The second implication is for our everyday lives. The sincerity with which people report and interpret their experiences is no guarantee of the validity of these reports. Personal testimonies are powerfully per-suasive. But they may also be wrong. Keeping this potential for error in mind can help us feel less intimidated by others and be less gullible.

CONCEPTS TO REMEMBER

self-concept   A person's answers to the question, "Who am I?"

self-schema   Beliefs about self that organize and guide the processing of self-relevant information.

self-reference effect   The ten-dency to process efficiently and remember well informa-tion related to oneself.

individualism   The concept of giving priority to one's own goals over group goals and defining one's identity in terms of personal attributes rather than group identifications.

collectivism   Giving priority to the goals of one's groups (often one's extended family or work group) and defining one's identity accordingly.

dual attitudes   Differing im-plicit (automatic) and explicit (consciously controlled) attitudes toward the same object. Verbalized explicit attitudes may change with education and persuasion; implicit attitudes change slowly, with practice that forms new habits.

4

Self-Serving Bias

A s we process self-relevant information, a potent bias intrudes. We readily excuse our failures, accept credit for our successes, and in many ways see ourselves as better than average. Such self-enhancing perceptions enable most people to enjoy the bright side of high self-esteem, while occasionally suffering the dark side.

It is widely believed that most of us suffer low self-esteem. A generation ago, humanistic psychologist Carl Rogers (1958) concluded that most people he knew "despise themselves, regard themselves as worthless and unlovable." Many popularizers of humanistic psychology concurred. "All of us have inferiority complexes," contended John Powell (1989). "Those who seem not to have such a complex are only pretending." As Groucho Marx (1960) lampooned, "I don't want to belong to any club that would accept me as a member."

Activity
4.1

Actually, most of us have a good reputation with ourselves. In studies of self-esteem, even low-scoring people respond in the midrange of possible scores. (A low-self-esteem person responds to statements such as "I have good ideas" with a qualifying adjective, such as "somewhat" or "sometimes.") Moreover, one of social psychology's most provocative yet firmly established conclusions concerns the potency of **self-serving bias**—a tendency to perceive oneself favorably.

*E*XPLAINING POSITIVE AND NEGATIVE EVENTS

Dozens of experiments have found that people accept credit when told they have succeeded. They attribute the success to their ability and effort, but they attribute failure to external factors such as bad luck or the problem's inherent "impossibility" (Campbell & Sedikides, 1999). Similarly, in explaining their victories, athletes commonly credit themselves, but they attribute losses to something else: bad breaks, bad referee calls, or the other team's super effort or dirty play (Grove & others, 1991; Lalonde, 1992; Mullen & Riordan, 1988). And how much responsibility do you suppose car drivers tend to accept for their accidents? On insurance forms, drivers have described their accidents in words such as these: "An invisible car came out of nowhere, struck my car, and vanished"; "As I reached an intersection, a hedge sprang up, obscuring my vision, and I did not see the other car"; "A pedestrian hit me and went under my car" (*Toronto News*, 1977).

Michael Ross and Fiore Sicoly (1979) observed a marital version of self-serving bias. They found that young married Canadians usually believed they took more responsibility for such activities as cleaning the house and caring for the children than their spouses credited them for. In one national survey, 91 percent of wives but only 76 percent of husbands credited the wife with doing most of the food shopping (Burros, 1988). In other studies, wives estimated they did proportionally more of the housework than their husbands credited them with (Bird, 1999; Fiebert, 1990). Every night, my wife and I used to pitch our laundry at the foot of our bedroom clothes hamper. In the morning, one of us would put it in. When she suggested that I should take more responsibility for this, I thought, "Huh? I already do it 75 percent of the time." So I asked her how often she thought she picked up the clothes. "Oh," she replied, "about 75 percent of the time."

Such biases in allocating responsibility contribute to marital discord, dissatisfaction among workers, and impasses when bargaining (Kruger & Gilovich, 1999). Small wonder that divorced people usually blame their partner for the breakup (Gray & Silver, 1990), or that managers often blame poor performance on workers' lack of ability or effort (Imai, 1994; Rice, 1985). (Workers are more likely to blame something external—inadequate supplies, excessive workload, difficult co-workers, ambiguous assignments.)

Students also exhibit self-serving bias. After receiving an exam grade, those who do well tend to accept personal credit. They judge the exam to be a valid measure of their competence (Arkin & Maruyama, 1979; Davis & Stephan, 1980; Gilmor & Reid, 1979; Griffin & others, 1983). Those who do poorly are much more likely to criticize the exam.

Reading this research, I couldn't resist a satisfied "knew-it-all-along" feeling. But consider teachers' ways of explaining students' good and bad performances. When there is no need to feign modesty, those assigned the role of teacher tend to take credit for positive outcomes and blame failure on the student (Arkin & others, 1980; Davis, 1979). Teachers, it seems, are likely to think, "With my help, Maria graduated with honors. Despite all my help, Melinda flunked out."

CAN WE ALL BE BETTER THAN AVERAGE?

Self-serving bias also appears when people compare themselves with others. If the sixth-century B.C. Chinese philosopher Lao-tzu was right that "at no time in the world will a man who is sane over-reach himself, over-spend himself, overrate himself," then most of us are a little insane. For on most *subjective* and *socially desirable* dimensions, most people see themselves as better than the average person. Compared with people in general, most people see themselves as more ethical, more competent at their job, friend-lier, more intelligent, better looking, less prejudiced, healthier, and even more insightful and less biased in their self-assessments (see "Focus On: Self-Serving Bias—*How Do I Love Me? Let Me Count the Ways*," page 40).

Every community, it seems, is like Garrison Keillor's fictional Lake Wobegon, where "all the women are strong, all the men are good-looking, and all the children are above average." Perhaps one reason for this opti-mism is that although 12 percent of people feel old for their age, many more—66 percent—think they are young for their age (*Public Opinion*, 1984). All of which calls to mind Freud's joke about the husband who told his wife, "If one of us should die, I think I would go live in Paris."

Subjective behavior dimensions (such as "disciplined") trigger greater self-serving bias than objective behavioral dimensions (such as "punctual"). Students are more likely to rate themselves superior in "moral goodness" than in "intelligence" (Allison & others, 1989; Van Lange, 1991). And community residents overwhelmingly see themselves as *caring* more than most others about the environment, hunger, and other social issues, though they don't see themselves as *doing* more, such as contributing time or money to those issues (White & Plous, 1995). Education doesn't eliminate self-serving bias; even social psychologists exhibit it, by believing themselves more ethical than most social psy-chologists (Van Lange & others, 1997).

Subjective qualities give us leeway in constructing our own defini-tions of success (Dunning & others, 1989, 1991). Rating my "athletic abil-ity," I ponder my basketball play, not the agonizing weeks I spent as a Little League baseball player hiding in right field. Assessing my "leadership ability," I conjure up an image of a great leader whose style is similar to mine. By defining ambiguous criteria in our own terms, each of us can see ourselves as relatively successful. In one College Entrance

Examination Board survey of 829,000 high school seniors, 0 percent rated themselves below average in "ability to get along with others" (a subjective, desirable trait), 60 percent rated themselves in the top 10 percent, and 25 percent saw themselves among the top 1 percent!

We also support our self-images by assigning importance to the things we're good at. Over a semester, those who ace an introductory computer science course come to place a higher value on being a computer-literate person in today's world. Those who do poorly are more likely to scorn computer geeks and to exclude computer skills as pertinent to their self-images (Hill & others, 1989).

Activity
4.2

Focus On: Self-Serving Bias – How do I love me? Let me count the ways

"The one thing that unites all human beings, regardless of age, gender, religion, economic status or ethnic background," notes Dave Barry (1998), "is that deep down inside, we all believe that we are above average drivers." We also believe we are above average on most any other subjective and desirable trait. Among the many faces of self-serving bias are these:

- *Ethics.* Most businesspeople see themselves as more ethical than the average businessperson (Baumhart, 1968; Brenner & Molander, 1977). One national survey asked, "How would you rate your own morals and values on a scale from 1 to 100 (100 being perfect)?" Fifty percent of people rated themselves 90 or above; only 11 percent said 74 or less (Lovett, 1997).

- *Professional competence.* Ninety percent of business managers rate their performance as superior to their average peer (French, 1968). In Australia, 86 percent of people rate their job performance as above average and 1 percent as below average (Headey & Wearing, 1987). Most surgeons believe their patients' mortality rate to be lower than average (Gawande, 2002).

- *Virtues.* In the Netherlands, most high school students rate themselves as more honest, persistent, original, friendly, and reliable than the average high school student (Hoorens, 1993, 1995).

- *Driving.* Most drivers—even most drivers who have been hospitalized for accidents—believe themselves to be safer and more skilled than the average driver (Guerin, 1994; McKenna & Myers, 1997; Svenson, 1981).

- *Intelligence.* Most people perceive themselves as more intelligent, better looking, and much less prejudiced than their average peer (*Public Opinion,* 1984; Wylie, 1979). When someone outperforms them, people tend to think of the other as a genius (Lassiter & Munhall, 2001).
- *Tolerance.* In a 1997 Gallup Poll, only 14 percent of White Americans rated their prejudice against Blacks as 5 or higher on a 0 to 10 scale. Yet Whites perceived high prejudice (5 or above) among 44 percent of *other* Whites.
- *Parental support.* Most adults believe they support their aging parents more than do their siblings (Lerner & others, 1991).
- *Health.* Los Angeles residents view themselves as healthier than most of their neighbors, and most college students believe they will outlive their actuarially predicted age of death by about 10 years (Larwood, 1978; C. R. Snyder, 1978).
- *Insight.* Others' words and deeds reveal their natures, we presume. Our *private* thoughts do the same. Thus, most of us believe we know and understand others better than they know and understand us. We also believe we know ourselves better than others know themselves (Pronin & others, 2001). Few college students see themselves as more naïve or more gullible than others; many more think they're less naïve and gullible (Levine, 2003).
- *Freedom from bias.* People see themselves as less vulnerable to various biases than most others (Pronin & others, 2002). They even think themselves less subject to self-serving bias than most others!

*U*NREALISTIC OPTIMISM

Optimism predisposes a positive approach to life. "The optimist," notes H. Jackson Brown (1990, p. 79), "goes to the window every morning and says, 'Good morning, God.' The pessimist goes to the window and says, 'good god, morning.'" Many of us, however, have what researcher Neil Weinstein (1980, 1982) terms "an unrealistic optimism about future life events." Due partly to their relative pessimism about others' fates (Shepperd, 2003), students perceive themselves as far more likely than their classmates to get a good job, draw a good salary, and own a home, and as far less likely to experience negative events, such as developing a drinking problem, having a heart attack before age 40, or being fired. In Scotland and the United States, most older teens think they are much less likely than their peers to become infected by HIV (Abrams, 1991; Pryor & Reeder, 1993). After experiencing the 1989 earthquake, San Francisco Bay area students did lose their optimism. They felt as vulnerable as their school classmates to injury in a natural disaster, but within three months their illusory optimism had rebounded (Burger & Palmer, 1991).

Linda Perloff (1987) notes how illusory optimism increases our vulnerability. Believing ourselves immune to misfortune, we do not take sensible precautions. In one survey, 137 marriage license applicants accurately estimated that half of marriages end in divorce, yet most assessed their chance of divorce as 0 percent (Baker & Emery, 1993). Sexually active undergraduate women who don't consistently use contraceptives perceive themselves, compared with other women at their university, as much *less* vulnerable to unwanted pregnancy (Burger & Burns, 1988).

Those who cheerfully shun seat belts, deny the effects of smoking, and stumble into ill-fated relationships remind us that blind optimism, like pride, may go before a fall. When gambling, optimists more than pessimists persist, even when piling up losses (Gibson & Sanbonmatsu, 2004). If those who deal in the stock market or in real estate perceive their business intuition to be superior to that of their competitors, they, too, may be in for severe disappointment. Even the seventeenth-century economist Adam Smith, a defender of human economic rationality, foresaw that people would overestimate their chances of gain. This "absurd presumption in their own good fortune," he said, arises from "the overweening conceit which the greater part of men have of their own abilities" (Spiegel, 1971, p. 243).

Optimism definitely beats pessimism in promoting self-efficacy, health, and well-being (Armor & Taylor, 1996; Segerstrom, 2001). Being natural optimists, most people believe they will be happier with their lives in the future—a belief that surely helps create happiness in the present (Robinson & Ryff, 1999). Half of 18- to 19-year-old Americans cheer themselves with the thought that they are "somewhat" or "very" likely to "be rich" (a belief shared by progressively fewer people with age (Moore, 2003a). Yet a dash of realism—or what Julie Norem (2000) calls *defensive pessimism*—can save us from the perils of unrealistic optimism. Students who enter university with inflated assessments of their academic ability often suffer deflating self-esteem and well-being (Robins & Beer, 2001). Defensive pessimism anticipates problems and motivates effective coping. As a Chinese proverb says, "Be prepared for danger while staying in peace." Students who exhibit excess optimism (as do many students destined for low grades) can benefit from having some self-doubt, which motivates study (Prohaska, 1994; Sparrell & Shrauger, 1984). (Such illusory optimism often disappears as the time approaches for receiving the exam back—Taylor & Shepperd, 1998.) Students who are overconfident tend to underprepare. Their equally able but more anxious peers, fearing that they are going to bomb on the upcoming exam, study furiously and get higher grades (Goodhart, 1986; Norem & Cantor, 1986; Showers & Ruben, 1987).

The moral: Success in school and beyond requires enough optimism to sustain hope and enough pessimism to motivate concern.

FALSE CONSENSUS AND UNIQUENESS

We have a curious tendency to further enhance our self-images by over-estimating or underestimating the extent to which others think and act as we do. On matters of *opinion*, we find support for our positions by overestimating the extent to which others agree—a phenomenon called the **false consensus effect** (Krueger & Clement, 1994; Marks & Miller, 1987; Mullen & Goethals, 1990). If we favor a Canadian referendum or support New Zealand's National Party, we wishfully overestimate the extent to which others agree (Babad & others, 1992; Koestner, 1993). The sense we make of the world seems like common sense.

When we behave badly or fail in a task, we reassure ourselves by thinking that such lapses also are common. After one person lies to another, the liar begins to perceive the other as dishonest (Sagarin & others, 1998). They guess that others think and act as they do: "I lie, but doesn't everyone?" If we cheat on our income taxes or smoke, we are likely to overestimate the number of other people who do likewise. If we feel sexual desire toward another, we may overestimate the other's reciprocal desire. People who harbor negative ideas about another racial group presume that many others also have negative stereotypes (Krueger, 1996). Thus our perceptions of others' stereotypes may reveal something of our own. "We don't see things as they are," says the Talmud. "We see things as we are."

False consensus may occur because we generalize from a limited sample, which prominently includes ourselves (Dawes, 1990). Lacking other information, why not "project" ourselves; why not impute our own knowledge to others and use our responses as a clue to their likely responses? Also, we're more likely to associate with people who share our attitudes and behaviors and then to judge the world from the people we know.

On matters of *ability* or when we behave well or successfully, a **false uniqueness effect** more often occurs (Goethals & others, 1991). We serve our self-image by seeing our talents and moral behaviors as relatively unusual. Thus those who drink heavily but use seat belts will *over*estimate (false consensus) the number of other heavy drinkers and *under*estimate (false uniqueness) the commonality of seat belt use (Suls & others, 1988). Thus we may see our failings as relatively normal and our virtues as less commonplace than they are.

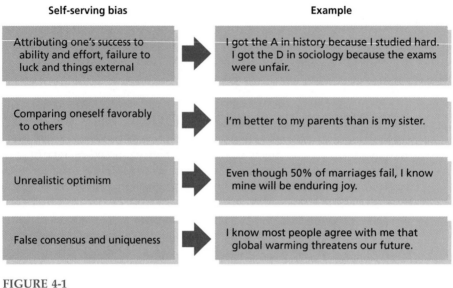

Self-serving bias | **Example**

Attributing one's success to ability and effort, failure to luck and things external ➡ I got the A in history because I studied hard. I got the D in sociology because the exams were unfair.

Comparing oneself favorably to others ➡ I'm better to my parents than is my sister.

Unrealistic optimism ➡ Even though 50% of marriages fail, I know mine will be enduring joy.

False consensus and uniqueness ➡ I know most people agree with me that global warming threatens our future.

FIGURE 4-1
How self-serving bias works.

To sum up, these tendencies toward self-serving attributions, self-congratulatory comparisons, illusory optimism, and false consensus for our failings are major sources of self-serving bias (Figure 4-1).

S ELF-ESTEEM MOTIVATION

Why do people perceive themselves in self-enhancing ways? One explanation sees the self-serving bias as a by-product of how we process and remember information about ourselves. Recall the study in which married people gave themselves credit for doing more housework than their spouses did. Might this be due, as Michael Ross and Fiore Sicoly (1979) believe, to our greater recall for what we've actively done and our lesser recall for what we've not done or merely observed others doing? I can easily picture myself picking up the laundry, but I am less aware of the times when I absentmindedly overlooked it.

Are the biased perceptions, then, simply a perceptual error, an unemotional bent in how we process information? Or are self-serving *motives* also involved? It's now clear from research that we have multiple motives. Questing for self-knowledge, we're eager to assess our competence (Dunning, 1995). Questing for self-confirmation, we're eager to *verify* our self-conceptions (Sanitioso & others, 1990; Swann, 1996, 1997). Questing for self-affirmation, we're especially motivated to *enhance* our self-image (Sedikides, 1993). Self-esteem motivation helps power self-serving bias.

A motivational engine powers our cognitive machinery (Dunning, 1999; Kunda, 1990). For example, Abraham Tesser (1988) at the University of Georgia reports that a "self-esteem maintenance" motive predicts a variety of interesting findings, even friction among brothers and sisters. Do you have a sibling of the same gender who is close to you in age? If so, people probably compared the two of you as you grew up. Tesser presumes that people's perceiving one of you as more capable than the other will motivate the less able one to act in ways that maintain his or her self-esteem. (Tesser thinks the threat to self-esteem is greatest for an older child with a highly capable younger sibling.) Men with a brother with markedly different ability typically recall not getting along well with him; men with a similarly able brother are more likely to recall very little friction.

Self-esteem threats occur among friends, whose success can be more threatening than that of strangers (Zuckerman & Jost, 2001). And it can occur among married partners, too. Although shared interests are healthy, *identical* career goals may produce tension or jealousy (Clark & Bennett, 1992). Similarly, people feel greater jealousy toward a romantic rival whose achievements are in the domain of their own aspirations (DeSteno & Salovey, 1996).

What underlies the motive to maintain or enhance self-esteem? Mark Leary (1998, 1999) believes that our self-esteem feelings are like a fuel gauge. Relationships enable surviving and thriving. Thus, the self-esteem gauge alerts us to threatened social rejection, motivating us to act with greater sensitivity to others' expectations. Studies confirm that social rejection lowers our self-esteem, strengthening our eagerness for approval. Spurned or jilted, we feel unattractive or inadequate. Like a blinking dashboard light, this pain can motivate action—self-improvement and a search for acceptance and inclusion elsewhere.

REFLECTIONS ON SELF-SERVING BIAS

No doubt many readers are finding the self-serving bias either depressing or contrary to their own occasional feelings of inadequacy. To be sure, the people who exhibit the self-serving bias may feel inferior to specific individuals, especially those who are a step or two higher on the ladder of success, attractiveness, or skill. And not everyone operates with a self-serving bias. Some people *do* suffer from low self-esteem.

In experiments, people whose self-esteem is temporarily bruised—by being told they did miserably on an intelligence test, for example—are more likely to disparage others (Beauregard & Dunning, 1998). Those whose egos have recently been wounded also are more prone to self-serving explanations of success or failure than are those whose egos have recently received a boost (McCarrey & others, 1982). So threats to self-esteem may provoke self-protective defensiveness. When they feel unaffirmed, people may offer self-affirming boasts, excuses, and put-downs of others. More generally, people who are down on themselves tend also to be overly reactive to slights—they see rejection where none exists and tend to get down on others (Murray & others, 2002; Wills, 1981). Mockery says as much about the mocker as the one mocked.

Nevertheless, high self-esteem goes hand in hand with self-serving perceptions. Those who score highest on self-esteem tests (who say nice things about themselves) also say nice things about themselves when explaining their successes and failures, when evaluating their group, and when comparing themselves with others (Brown, 1986; Brown & others, 1988; Schlenker & others, 1990).

The Self-Serving Bias as Adaptive

Self-esteem has its dark side, but also its bright side. When good things happen, high-more than low-self-esteem people tend to savor and sustain the good feelings (Wood & others, 2003). Even illusory self-enhancement correlates with many mental health indicators. "Believing one has more talents and positive qualities than one's peers allows one to feel good about oneself and to enter the stressful circumstances of daily life with the resources conferred by a positive sense of self," note Shelley Taylor and her co-researchers (2003). Self-serving bias and its accompanying excuses also help protect people from depression and the biological costs of stress (Snyder & Higgins, 1988; Taylor & others, 2003). Nondepressed people excuse their failures on laboratory tasks or perceive themselves as being more in control than they are. Depressed people's self-appraisals and their appraisals of how others really view them are not inflated.

In their *terror management theory*, Jeff Greenberg, Sheldon Solomon, and Tom Pyszczynski (1997) propose another reason why positive self-esteem is adaptive—it buffers anxiety, including anxiety related to our certain death. In childhood we learn that when we meet the standards taught us by our parents, we are loved and protected; when we don't, love and protection may be withdrawn. We therefore come to associate viewing ourselves as good with feeling secure. Greenberg and colleagues argue that positive self-esteem—viewing oneself as good and secure—even protects us from feeling terror over our eventual death. Their research shows that reminding people of their mortality (say, by writing a short essay on dying) motivates them to affirm their self-worth. Moreover, when facing threats, increased self-esteem leads to decreased anxiety.

As this new research on depression and anxiety suggests, there may be some practical wisdom in self-serving perceptions. It may be strategic to believe we are smarter, stronger, and more socially successful than we are. Cheaters may give a more convincing display of honesty if they believe themselves honorable. Belief in our superiority can also motivate us to achieve—creating a self-fulfilling prophecy—and can sustain a sense of hope in difficult times.

The Self-Serving Bias as Maladaptive

Although self-serving pride may help protect us from depression, it can at times be maladaptive. People who blame others for their social difficulties are often unhappier than people who can acknowledge their mistakes (C. A. Anderson & others, 1983; Newman & Langer, 1981; Peterson & others, 1981).

Research by Barry Schlenker (1976; Schlenker & Miller, 1977a, 1977b) has also shown how self-serving perceptions can poison a group. As a rock band guitarist during his college days, Schlenker noted that "rock band members typically overestimated their contributions to a group's success and underestimated their contributions to failure. I saw many good bands disintegrate from the problems caused by these self-glorifying tendencies." In his later life as a University of Florida social psychologist, Schlenker explored group members' self-serving perceptions. In nine experiments, he had people work together on some task. He then falsely informed them that their group had done either well or poorly. In every one of these studies, the members of successful groups claimed more responsibility for their group's performance than did members of groups that supposedly failed at the task. Most presented themselves as contributing more than the others in their group when the group did well; few said they contributed less.

If most group members believe they are underpaid and underappreciated relative to their better-than-average contributions, disharmony and envy are likely. College presidents and academic deans will readily recognize the phenomenon. Ninety percent or more of college faculty members rate themselves as superior to their average colleague (Blackburn & others, 1980; Cross, 1977). It is therefore inevitable that when merit salary raises are announced and half receive an average raise or less, many will feel themselves victims of injustice.

Self-serving biases also inflate people's judgments of their groups. When groups are comparable, most people consider their own group superior (Codol, 1976; Jourden & Heath, 1996; Taylor & Doria, 1981). Thus:

- Most university sorority members perceive those in their sorority as far less likely to be conceited and snobby than those in other sororities (Biernat & others, 1996).
- Fifty-three percent of Dutch adults rate their marriage or partnership as better than that of most others; only 1 percent rate it as worse than most (Buunk & van der Eijnden, 1997).

- Sixty-six percent of Americans give their oldest child's public schools a grade of A or B. But nearly as many—64 percent—give the *nation's* public schools a grade of C or D (Whitman, 1996).
- Most corporation presidents and production managers over-predict their own firms' productivity and growth (Kidd & Morgan, 1969; Larwood & Whittaker, 1977).

That people see themselves and their groups with a favorable bias is hardly new. The tragic flaw portrayed in ancient Greek drama was *hubris*, or pride. Like the subjects of our experiments, the Greek tragic figures were not self-consciously evil; they merely thought too highly of themselves. In literature, the pitfalls of pride are portrayed again and again. In theology, pride has long been first among the "seven deadly sins."

If pride is akin to the self-serving bias, then what is humility? Is it self-contempt? Or can we be self-affirming and self-accepting without a self-serving bias? To paraphrase the English scholar-writer C. S. Lewis, humility is not handsome people trying to believe they are ugly and clever people trying to believe they are fools. False modesty can actually be a cover for pride in one's better-than-average humility. (James Friedrich [1996] reports that most students congratulate themselves on being better than average at not thinking themselves better than average!) True humility is more like self-forgetfulness than false modesty. It leaves people free to rejoice in their special talents and, with the same honesty, to recognize the talents of others.

CONCEPTS TO REMEMBER

self-serving bias The tendency to perceive oneself favorably.

false consensus effect The tendency to overestimate the commonality of one's opinions and one's undesirable or unsuccessful behaviors.

false uniqueness effect The tendency to underestimate the commonality of one's abilities and one's desirable or successful behaviors.

MODULE

5

❖

The Power of Positive Thinking

We have considered the potent self-serving bias uncovered by social psychologists. When most people see themselves as more moral and deserving than others, conflict among people and nations is a natural result.

Studies of the self-serving bias expose deep truths about human nature. But single truths seldom tell the whole story, because the world is complex. Indeed, there is an important complement to these truths. High self-esteem—a sense of self-worth—is adaptive. Compared to those with low self-esteem, people with high self-esteem are happier, less neurotic, less troubled by ulcers and insomnia, and less prone to drug and alcohol addictions (Brockner & Hulton, 1978; Brown, 1991). Many clinical psychologists report that underneath much human despair is an impoverished self-acceptance.

Additional research on "locus of control," optimism, and "learned helplessness" confirms the benefits of seeing oneself as competent and effective. Albert Bandura (1986) merges much of this research into a concept called **self-efficacy,** a scholarly version of the wisdom behind the power of positive thinking. An optimistic belief in our own competence and effectiveness pays dividends (Bandura & others, 1999; Maddux and Gosselin, 2003). Children and adults with strong feelings of self-efficacy are more persistent, less anxious, and less depressed. They also live healthier lives and are more academically successful.

Your self-efficacy is how competent you feel to do something. If you believe you can do something, will this belief necessarily make a difference? That depends on a second factor: Do you have *control* over your outcomes? You may, for example, feel like an effective driver (high

49

self-efficacy), yet feel endangered by drunken drivers (low control). You may feel like a competent student or worker but, fearing discrimination based on your age, gender, or appearance, you may think your prospects are dim.

L OCUS OF CONTROL

Activity
5.1

"I have no social life," complained a 40-something single man to student therapist Jerry Phares. At Phares's urging, the patient went to a dance, where several women danced with him. "I was just lucky," he later reported; "it would never happen again." When Phares reported this to his mentor, Julian Rotter, it crystallized an idea he had been forming. In Rotter's experiments and in his clinical practice, some people seemed to persistently "feel that what happens to them is governed by external forces of one kind or another, while others feel that what happens to them is governed largely by their own efforts and skills" (quoted by Hunt, 1993, p. 334).

What do you think? Are people more often captains of their destinies or victims of their circumstances? Are they the playwrights, directors, and actors of their own lives or prisoners of their situations? Rotter called this dimension **locus of control**. With Phares, he developed 29 paired statements to measure a person's locus of control. Imagine yourself taking their test. Which do you more strongly believe?

In the long run, people get the respect they deserve in this world.	or	Unfortunately, people's worth passes unrecognized no matter how hard they try.
What happens to me is my own doing.	or	Sometimes I feel that I don't have enough control over the direction my life is taking.
The average person can have an influence in government decisions.	or	This world is run by the few people in power, and there is not much the little guy can do about it.

Do your answers to such questions from Rotter (1973) indicate that you believe you control your own destiny (*internal* locus of control)? Or that chance or outside forces determine your fate (*external* locus of control)? Those who see themselves as internally controlled are more likely to do well in school, successfully stop smoking, wear seat belts, deal with marital problems directly, make lots of money, and delay instant gratification in order to achieve long-term goals (Findley & Cooper, 1983; Lefcourt, 1982; Miller & others, 1986). How much control we feel depends on how we explain setbacks.

L EARNED HELPLESSNESS VERSUS SELF-DETERMINATION

The benefits of feelings of control also appear in animal research. Dogs taught that they cannot escape shocks while confined will learn a sense of helplessness. Later these dogs cower passively in other situations when they could escape punishment. Dogs that learn personal control (by escaping their first shocks successfully) adapt easily to a new situation. Researcher Martin Seligman (1975, 1991) has noted similarities to this **learned helplessness** in human situations. Depressed or oppressed people, for example, become passive because they believe their efforts have no effect. Helpless dogs and depressed people both suffer paralysis of the will, passive resignation, even motionless apathy (Figure 5-1).

Here is a clue to how institutions—whether malevolent, like concentration camps, or benevolent, like hospitals—can dehumanize people. In hospitals, "good patients" don't ring bells, don't ask questions, don't try to control what's happening (Taylor, 1979). Such passivity may be good for hospital efficiency, but it is bad for people's health and survival. Losing control over what you do and what others do to you can make unpleasant events profoundly stressful (Pomerleau & Rodin, 1986). Several diseases are associated with feelings of helplessness and diminished choice. So is the rapidity of decline and death in concentration camps and nursing homes. Hospital patients who are trained to believe they can control stress require fewer pain relievers and sedatives and exhibit less anxiety (Langer & others, 1975).

Ellen Langer and Judith Rodin (1976) tested the importance of personal control by treating elderly patients in a highly rated Connecticut nursing home in one of two ways. With one group the benevolent caregivers stressed "our responsibility to make this a home you can be proud of and happy in." They gave the passive patients their normal well-intentioned, sympathetic care. Three weeks later, most were rated by themselves, by interviewers, and by nurses as further debilitated. Langer and Rodin's other treatment promoted personal control. It stressed opportunities for choice, the possibilities for influencing nursing-home policy, and the person's responsibility "to make of your life whatever

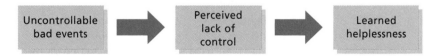

FIGURE 5-1
Learned helplessness. When animals and people experience uncontrollable bad events, they learn to feel helpless and resigned.

you want." These patients were given small decisions to make and responsibilities to fulfill. Over the ensuing three weeks, 93 percent of this group showed improved alertness, activity, and happiness.

The experience of the first group must have been similar to that of James MacKay (1980), an 87-year-old psychologist:

> I became a nonperson last summer. My wife had an arthritic knee which put her in a walker, and I chose that moment to break my leg. We went to a nursing home. It was all nursing and no home. The doctor and the head nurse made all decisions; we were merely animate objects. Thank heavens it was only two weeks. . . . The top man of the nursing home was very well trained and very compassionate; I considered it the best home in town. But we were nonpersons from the time we entered until we left.

Studies confirm that systems of governing or managing people that promote personal control will indeed promote health and happiness (Deci & Ryan, 1987).

- Prisoners given some control over their environments—by being able to move chairs, control TV sets, and operate the lights— experience less stress, exhibit fewer health problems, and commit less vandalism (Ruback & others, 1986; Wener & others, 1987).
- Workers given leeway in carrying out tasks and making decisions experience improved morale (Miller & Monge, 1986).
- Institutionalized residents allowed choice in matters such as what to eat for breakfast, when to go to a movie, whether to sleep late or get up early, may live longer and certainly are happier (Timko & Moos, 1989).
- Homeless shelter residents who perceive little choice in when to eat and sleep, and little control over their privacy, are more likely to have a passive, helpless attitude regarding finding housing and work (Burn, 1992).

Can there ever be too much of a good thing like freedom and self-determination? Swarthmore College psychologist Barry Schwartz (2000, 2004) contends that individualistic modern cultures indeed have "an excess of freedom," causing decreased life satisfaction and increased clinical depression. Too many choices can lead to paralysis, or what Schwartz calls "the tyranny of freedom." After choosing between 30 kinds of jams or chocolates, people express less satisfaction with their choices than those choosing among 6 options (Iyengar & Lepper, 2000). With more choice comes information overload and more opportunities for regret.

In other experiments, people have expressed greater satisfaction with irrevocable choices (like those made in an "all purchases final" sale) than with reversible choices (as when allowing refunds or exchanges). Ironically, people like and will pay for the freedom to reverse their choices. Yet that freedom "can inhibit the psychological processes that manufacture satisfaction" (Gilbert & Ebert, 2002). Owning something irreversibly makes it feel better. This principle may help explain a curious social phenomenon (Myers, 2000a): National surveys show that people expressed more satisfaction with their marriages back when marriage was more irrevocable ("all purchases final"). Today, despite greater freedom to escape bad marriages and try new ones, people tend to express somewhat less satisfaction with the marriage that they have.

R EFLECTIONS ON SELF-EFFICACY

The Power of Positive Thinking

Although psychological research on perceived self-control is relatively new, the emphasis on taking charge of one's life and realizing one's potential is not. The you-can-do-it theme of Horatio Alger's rags-to-riches books is an enduring idea. We find it in Norman Vincent Peale's 1950s best-seller, *The Power of Positive Thinking*—"If you think in positive terms you will get positive results. That is the simple fact." We find it in the many self-help books and videos that urge people to succeed through positive mental attitudes.

Research on self-control gives us greater confidence in traditional virtues such as perseverance and hope. Yet Bandura emphasizes that self-efficacy does not grow primarily by self-persuasion ("I think I can, I think I can") or by puffing people up like hot-air balloons ("You're terrific!"). Its chief source is the experience of success. If your initial efforts to lose weight, stop smoking, or improve your grades succeed, your self-efficacy increases. After mastering the physical skills needed to repel a sexual assault, women feel less vulnerable, less anxious, and more in control (Ozer & Bandura, 1990). After experiencing academic success, students develop higher appraisals of their academic ability, which often stimulate them to work harder and achieve more (Felson, 1984; Marsh & Young, 1997). To do one's best and achieve is to feel more confident and empowered. A team of researchers led by Roy Baumeister (2003) concurs. "Praising all the children just for being themselves," they contend, "simply devalues praise." Better to praise and bolster self-esteem "in recognition of good performance. . . . As the person performs or behaves better, self-esteem is encouraged to rise, and the net effect will be to reinforce both good behavior and improvement. Those outcomes are conducive to both the happiness of the individual and the betterment of society."

So there is a power to positive thinking. But let us remember the point at which we began our consideration of self-efficacy: Any truth, separated from its complementary truth, is a half-truth. The truth embodied in the concept of self-efficacy can encourage us to not resign ourselves to bad situations, to persist despite initial failures, to exert effort without being overly distracted by self-doubts. But lest the pendulum swing too far toward *this* truth, we had best remember that it, too, is not the whole story. If positive thinking can accomplish *anything,* then if we are unhappily married, poor, or depressed, we have only ourselves to blame. For shame! If only we had tried harder, been more disciplined, less stupid. Failing to appreciate that difficulties sometimes reflect the oppressive power of social situations can tempt us to blame people for their problems and failures, or even to blame ourselves too harshly for our own. Ironically, life's greatest disappointments, as well as its highest achievements, are born of the highest expectations. The bigger we dream, the more we might attain—and the more we risk falling short.

The Dark Side of Self-Esteem

Low self-esteem predicts increased risk of depression, drug abuse, and some forms of delinquency. High self-esteem fosters initiative, resilience, and pleasant feelings (Baumeister & others, 2003). Yet teen males who engage in sexual activity at an "inappropriately young age" tend to have *higher* than average self-esteem. So do teen gang leaders, extreme ethnocentrists, and terrorists, notes Robyn Dawes (1994, 1998).

Finding their favorable self-esteem threatened, people often react by putting others down, sometimes with violence. A youth who develops a big ego, which then gets threatened or deflated by social rejection, is potentially dangerous. In one experiment, Todd Heatherton and Kathleen Vohs (2000) threatened some undergraduate men, but not those in a control condition, with a failure experience on an aptitude test. In response to the failure, only high-self-esteem men became considerably more antagonistic (Figure 5-2).

In another experiment, Brad Bushman and Roy Baumeister (1998) had 540 undergraduate volunteers write a paragraph, in response to which another supposed student gave them either praise ("great essay!") or stinging criticism ("one of the worst essays I have read!"). Then each essay writer played a reaction time game against the other student. When the opponent lost, the writer could assault him or her with noise of any intensity and for any duration. After criticism, the people with the biggest egos—those who agreed with "narcissistic" statements such as "I am more capable than other people"—were "exceptionally aggressive." They delivered three times the auditory torture of those with normal self-esteem. Wounded pride motivates retaliation.

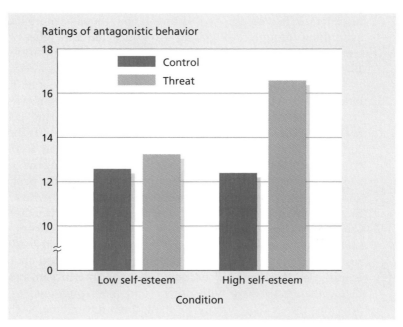

FIGURE 5-2
When big egos get challenged. When feeling threatened, only high-self-esteem people became significantly more antagonistic—arrogant, rude, and unfriendly. **Source:** From Heatherton & Vohs, 2000.

"The enthusiastic claims of the self-esteem movement mostly range from fantasy to hogwash," says Baumeister (Baumeister and others, 1996), who suspects he has "probably published more studies on self-esteem than anybody else." "The effects of self-esteem are small, limited, and not all good." High-self-esteem folks, he reports, are more likely to be obnoxious, to interrupt, and to talk *at* people rather than *with* them (in contrast to the more shy, modest, self-effacing folks with low self-esteem). "My conclusion is that self-control is worth 10 times as much as self-esteem."

Do the big egos of people who sometimes do bad things conceal inner insecurity and low self-esteem? Do assertive, narcissistic people actually have weak egos that are hidden by a self-inflating veneer? Many researchers have tried to find low self-esteem beneath such an outer crust. But studies of bullies, gang members, genocidal dictators, and obnoxious narcissists have turned up no sign of it. "Hitler had very high self-esteem," note Baumeister and his co-authors (2003).

The dark side of high self-esteem exists in tension with the findings that people expressing low self-esteem are somewhat more vulnerable to assorted clinical problems, including anxiety, loneliness, and eating disorders. When feeling bad or threatened, they are more likely to view everything through dark glasses—to notice and remember others' worst behaviors and to think their partners don't love them (Murray & others, 1998, 2002; Ybarra, 1999).

Unlike a fragile self-esteem, a secure self-esteem—one rooted more in feeling good about who one is than on grades, looks, money, or others' approval—is conducive to long-term well-being (Kernis, 2003; Schimel & others, 2001). Jennifer Crocker and her colleagues (2002, 2003, 2004) confirmed this in studies with University of Michigan students. Those whose self-worth was most fragile—most contingent on external sources—experienced more stress, anger, relationship problems, drug and alcohol use, and eating disorders than did those whose worth was rooted more on internal sources, such as personal virtues. Ironically, note Crocker and Lora Park (2004), those who pursue self-esteem, perhaps by seeking to become beautiful, rich, or popular, may lose sight of what really makes for quality of life. Moreover, if feeling good about ourselves is our goal, then we may become less open to criticism, more likely to blame than empathize with others, and more pressured to succeed at activities rather than simply to enjoy them. Over time, such pursuit of self-esteem can fail to satisfy our deep needs for competence, relationship, and autonomy, note Crocker and Park. To focus less on one's self-image, and more on developing one's talents and relationships, eventually leads to greater well-being.

CONCEPTS TO REMEMBER

self-efficacy   A sense that one is competent and effective, distinguished from self-esteem, one's sense of self-worth. A bombardier might feel high self-efficacy and low self-esteem.

locus of control   The extent to which people perceive outcomes as internally controllable by their own efforts and actions or as externally controlled by chance or outside forces.

learned helplessness   The hopelessness and resignation learned when a human or animal perceives no control over repeated bad events.

6

❖

The Fundamental Attribution Error

As later modules will reveal, social psychology's most important lesson concerns the influence of our social environment. At any moment, our internal state, and therefore what we say and do, depends on the situation (as well as on what we bring to the situation). In experiments, a slight difference between two situations sometimes greatly affects how people respond. I have seen this when teaching classes at both 8:30 A.M. and 7:00 P.M. Silent stares would greet me at 8:30; at 7:00 I had to break up a party. In each situation some individuals were more talkative than others, but the difference between the two situations exceeded the individual differences.

Attribution researchers have found a common problem with our attributions. When explaining someone's behavior, we often underestimate the impact of the situation and overestimate the extent to which it reflects the individual's traits and attitudes. Thus, even knowing the effect of the time of day on classroom conversation, I found it terribly tempting to assume that the people in the 7:00 P.M. class were more extraverted than the "silent types" who come at 8:30 A.M.

Video
6.1

This discounting of the situation, dubbed by Lee Ross (1977) the **fundamental attribution error,** appears in many experiments. In the first such study, Edward Jones and Victor Harris (1967) had Duke University students read debaters' speeches supporting or attacking Cuba's leader, Fidel Castro. When the position taken was said to have been chosen by the debater, the students logically enough assumed it reflected the person's own attitude. But what happened when the students were told that the debate coach had assigned the position? People who are merely feigning a position write more forceful statements

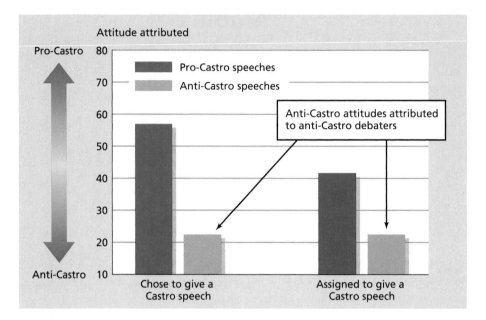

Attitude attributed

FIGURE 6-1
The fundamental attribution error. When people read a debate speech supporting or attacking Fidel Castro, they attributed corresponding attitudes to the speech writer, even when the debate coach assigned the writer's position. **Source:** Data from Jones & Harris, 1967.

than you'd expect (Allison & others, 1993; Miller & others, 1990). Thus, even knowing that the debater had been told to take a pro-Castro position did not prevent students from inferring that the debater in fact had some pro-Castro leanings (Figure 6-1). People seemed to think, "Yeah, I know he was assigned that position, but to some extent I think he really believes it."

We commit the fundamental attribution error when we explain *other people's* behavior. Our *own* behavior we often explain in terms of the situation. So Ian might attribute his behavior to the situation ("I was angry because everything was going wrong"), whereas Rosa might think, "Ian was hostile because he is an angry person." When referring to ourselves, we typically use verbs that describe our actions and reactions ("I get annoyed when . . ."). Referring to someone else, we more often describe what that person *is* ("He is nasty") (Fiedler & others, 1991; McGuire & McGuire, 1986; White & Younger, 1988). Husbands who attribute their wives' criticisms to her being "mean and cold" are more likely to become violent (Schweinle & others, 2002). When she expresses distress about their relationship, he hears the worst and reacts angrily.

THE FUNDAMENTAL ATTRIBUTION ERROR IN EVERYDAY LIFE

If we know the checkout cashier is taught to say, "Thank you and have a nice day," do we nevertheless automatically conclude that the cashier is a friendly, grateful person? We certainly know how to discount behavior that we attribute to ulterior motives (Fein & others, 1990). Yet consider what happened when Williams College students talked with a supposed clinical psychology graduate student who acted either warm and friendly or aloof and critical. Researchers David Napolitan and George Goethals (1979) told half the students beforehand that her behavior would be spontaneous. They told the other half that for purposes of the experiment she had been instructed to feign friendly (or unfriendly) behavior. The effect of the information? None. If she acted friendly, they assumed she was really a friendly person; if she acted unfriendly, they assumed she was an unfriendly person. As when viewing a dummy on the ventriloquist's lap or a movie actor playing a "good-guy" or "bad-guy" role, we find it difficult to escape the illusion that the scripted behavior reflects an inner disposition. Perhaps this is why Leonard Nimoy, who played Mr. Spock on the original *Star Trek*, entitled his book, *I Am Not Spock*.

The discounting of social constraints was evident in a thought-provoking experiment by Lee Ross and his collaborators (Ross & others, 1977). The experiment re-created Ross's firsthand experience of moving from graduate student to professor. His doctoral oral exam had proved a humbling experience as his apparently brilliant professors quizzed him on topics they specialized in. Six months later, *Dr.* Ross was himself an examiner, now able to ask penetrating questions on *his* favorite topics. Ross's hapless student later confessed to feeling exactly as Ross had a half-year before—dissatisfied with his ignorance and impressed with the apparent brilliance of the examiners.

In the experiment, with Teresa Amabile and Julia Steinmetz, Ross set up a simulated quiz game. He randomly assigned some Stanford University students to play the role of questioner, some to play the role of contestant, and others to observe. The researchers invited the questioners to make up difficult questions that would demonstrate their wealth of knowledge. Any one of us can imagine such questions using one's own domain of competence: "Where is Bainbridge Island?" "How did Mary, Queen of Scots, die?" "Which has the longer coastline, Europe or Africa?" If even these few questions have you feeling a little uninformed, then you will appreciate the results of this experiment.*

---

* Bainbridge Island is across Puget Sound from Seattle. Mary was ordered beheaded by her cousin, Queen Elizabeth I. Although the African continent is more than double the area of Europe, Europe's coastline is longer. (It is more convoluted, with lots of harbors and inlets, a geography fact that contributed to its role in the history of maritime trade.)

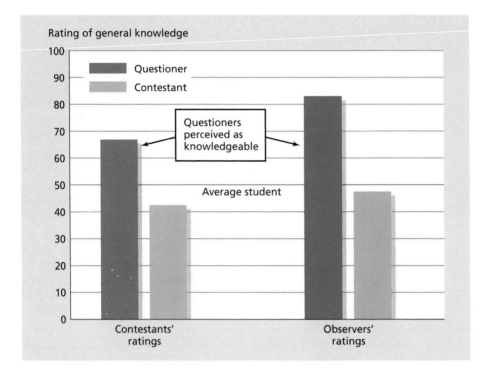

Rating of general knowledge

FIGURE 6-2
Both contestants and observers of a simulated quiz game assumed that a person who had been randomly assigned the role of questioner was far more knowledgeable than the contestant. Actually, the assigned roles of questioner and contestant simply made the questioner seem more knowledgeable. The failure to appreciate this illustrates the fundamental attribution error. **Source:** Data from Ross, Amabile, & Steinmetz, 1977.

Everyone had to know that the questioner would have the advantage. Yet both contestants and observers (but not the questioners) came to the erroneous conclusion that the questioners *really were* more knowledgeable than the contestants (Figure 6-2). Follow-up research shows that these misimpressions are hardly a reflection of low social intelligence. If anything, intelligent and socially competent people are *more* likely to make the attribution error (Block & Funder, 1986).

In real life, those with social power usually initiate and control conversations, which often leads underlings to overestimate their knowledge and intelligence. Medical doctors, for example, are often presumed to be experts on all sorts of questions unrelated to medicine. Similarly, students often overestimate the brilliance of their teachers. (As in the experiment, teachers are questioners on subjects of their special expertise.) When some of these students later become teachers, they are usually amazed to discover that teachers are not so brilliant after all.

To illustrate the fundamental attribution error, most of us need look no further than our own experiences. Determined to make some new friends, Bev plasters a smile on her face and anxiously plunges into a party. Everyone else seems quite relaxed and happy as they laugh and talk with one another. Bev wonders to herself, "Why is everyone always so at ease in groups like this while I'm feeling shy and tense?" Actually, everyone else is feeling nervous, too, and making the same attribution error in assuming that Bev and the others *are* as they *appear*—confidently convivial.

Attributions of responsibility are at the heart of many judicial decisions (Fincham & Jaspars, 1980). During the week following O. J. Simpson's 1994 arrest for the alleged murders of his ex-wife and her friend, a UCLA research team led by Sandra Graham (1997) questioned a sample of Los Angeles people who believed Simpson committed the crimes. Those who perceived his alleged act as an uncontrollable response to the situation advocated a relatively mild punishment. Those who believed he committed a self-initiated act advocated more severe punishment. The case exemplifies many judicial controversies: The prosecution argues, "You are to blame, for you could have done otherwise"; the defendant replies, "It wasn't my fault; I was a victim of the situation" or, " Under the circumstance I did no wrong."

WHY DO WE MAKE THE ATTRIBUTION ERROR?

So far we have seen a bias in the way we explain other people's behavior: We often ignore powerful situational determinants. Why do we tend to underestimate the situational determinants of others' behavior but not of our own?

Perspective and Situational Awareness

Differing Perspectives

Attribution theorists point out that we observe others from a different perspective than we observe ourselves (Jones, 1976; Jones & Nisbett, 1971). When we act, the *environment* commands our attention. When we watch another person act, that *person* occupies the center of our attention and the environment becomes relatively invisible.

To use the perceptual analogy of figure and ground, the person is the figure that stands out from the surrounding environmental ground. So the person seems to cause whatever happens. If this theory is true, what might we expect if the perspectives were reversed? What if we could see ourselves as others see us and if we saw the world through their eyes? Shouldn't this eliminate or reverse the typical attribution error?

See if you can predict the result of a clever experiment conducted by Michael Storms (1973). Picture yourself as a participant in Storms's experiment. You are seated facing another student with whom you are to talk for a few minutes. Beside you is a TV camera that shares your view of the other student. Facing you from alongside the other student are an observer and another TV camera. Afterward, both you and the observer judge whether your behavior was caused more by your personal characteristics or by the situation.

Question: Which of you—participant or observer—will attribute the least importance to the situation? Storms found it was the observer (another demonstration of the fundamental attribution tendency). What if we reverse points of view by having you and the observer each watch the videotape recorded from the other's perspective? (You now view yourself, while the observer views what you saw.) This reverses the attributions: The observer now attributes your behavior mostly to the situation you faced, while you now attribute it to your person. *Remembering* an experience from an observer's perspective—by "seeing" oneself from the outside—has the same effect (Frank & Gilovich, 1989).

In some experiments, people have viewed a videotape of a suspect confessing during a police interview. If they viewed the confession through a camera focused on the suspect, they perceived the confession as genuine. If they viewed it through a camera focused on the detective, they perceived it as more coerced (Lassiter & others, 1986, 2001). The camera perspective influenced people's guilt judgments even when the judge instructed them not to allow it to (Lassiter & others, 2002).

In courtrooms, most confession videotapes focus on the confessor. As we might expect, noted Daniel Lassiter and Kimberly Dudley (1991), such tapes yield a nearly 100 percent conviction rate when played by prosecutors. Aware of this research, reports Lassiter, New Zealand has made it a national policy that police interrogations be filmed with equal focus on the officer and suspect, such as by filming the side profiles of both.

Perspectives Change with Time

As the once-visible person recedes in their memory, observers often give more and more credit to the situation. Immediately after hearing someone argue an assigned position, people assume that's how the person really felt. A week later they are much more ready to credit the situational constraints (Burger, 1991). The day after a presidential election, Jerry Burger and Julie Pavelich (1994) asked voters why the election turned out as it did. Most attributed the outcome to the candidates' personal traits and positions (the winner from the incumbent party was likable). When they asked other voters the same question a year later, only a third attributed the verdict to the candidates. More people now credited circumstances, such as the country's good mood and the robust economy.

Editorial reflections on the six U.S. presidential elections between 1964 and 1988 show the same growth in situational explanations with time (Burger & Pavelich, 1994). Just after the 1978 election, editorial pundits focused on the candidates' campaigns and personalities. Two years later the situation loomed larger: "The shadows of Watergate . . . cleared the way for [Carter's] climb to the Presidency," noted one editorial in the *New York Times*.

Circumstances can also shift our perspective on ourselves. Seeing ourselves on television redirects our attention to ourselves. Seeing ourselves in a mirror, hearing our tape-recorded voices, having our pictures taken, or filling out biographical questionnaires similarly focus our attention inward, making us *self*-conscious instead of *situation*-conscious. Looking back on ill-fated relationships that once seemed like the unsinkable *Titanic*, people can see the icebergs (Berscheid, 1999). All these experiments point to a reason for the attribution error: *We find causes where we look for them.*

To see this in your own experience, consider: Would you say your social psychology instructor is a quiet or a talkative person?

My guess is you inferred that he or she is fairly outgoing. But consider the situation further: Your attention focuses on your instructor while he or she behaves in a public context that demands speaking. The instructor also observes his or her own behavior in many different situations—in the classroom, in meetings, at home. "Me talkative?" your instructor might say. "Well, it all depends on the situation. When I'm in class or with good friends, I'm rather outgoing. But at conventions and in unfamiliar situations I feel and act rather shy." Because we are acutely aware of how our behavior varies with the situation, we see ourselves as more variable than other people (Baxter & Goldberg, 1987; Kammer, 1982; Sande & others, 1988). "Nigel is uptight, Fiona is relaxed. With me it varies."

The less opportunity we have to observe people's behavior in contexts, the more we attribute to their personalities. Thomas Gilovich (1987) explored this by showing people a videotape of someone and then having them describe the person's actions to other people. The secondhand impressions were more extreme, partly because retellings focus attention on the person rather than on the situation (Baron & others, 1997). Similarly, people's impressions of someone they have heard about from a friend are typically more extreme than their friend's firsthand impressions (Prager & Cutler, 1990). Observing someone directly, or better yet, knowing them really well and seeing them in different situations, makes us more sensitive to their context (Idson & Mischel, 2001). Trait labels get applied most readily when describing strangers.

Activity
6.2

Cultural Differences

Cultures also influence the attribution error (Ickes, 1980; Watson, 1982). A Western worldview predisposes people to assume that people, not situations, cause events. Internal explanations are more socially approved (Jellison & Green, 1981). "You can do it!" we are assured by the pop psychology of positive-thinking Western culture.

The assumption here is that, with the right disposition and attitude, anyone can surmount almost any problem: You get what you deserve and deserve what you get. Thus we often explain bad behavior by labeling a person "sick," "lazy," or "sadistic." As children grow up in Western culture, they learn to explain behavior in terms of the other's personal characteristics (Rholes & others, 1990; Ross, 1981). As a first-grader, one of my sons brought home an example. He unscrambled the words "gate the sleeve caught Tom on his" into "The gate caught Tom on his sleeve." His teacher, applying the Western cultural assumptions of the curriculum materials, marked this wrong. The "right" answer located the cause within Tom: "Tom caught his sleeve on the gate."

The fundamental attribution error occurs across all cultures studied (Krull & others, 1999). Yet people in Eastern Asian cultures are somewhat more sensitive to the importance of situations. Thus, when aware of the social context, they are less inclined to assume that others' behavior corresponds to their traits (Choi & others, 1999; Farwell & Weiner, 2000; Masuda & Kitayama, 2004).

Some languages promote external attributions. Instead of "I was late," Spanish idiom allows one to say, "The clock caused me to be late." In collectivist cultures, people less often perceive others in terms of personal dispositions (Lee & others, 1996; Zebrowitz-McArthur, 1988). They are less likely to spontaneously interpret a behavior as reflecting an inner trait (Newman, 1993). When told of someone's actions, Hindus in India are less likely than Americans to offer dispositional explanations ("She is kind") and more likely to offer situational explanations ("Her friends were with her") (Miller, 1984).

*H*OW FUNDAMENTAL IS THE FUNDAMENTAL ATTRIBUTION ERROR?

Like most provocative ideas, the presumption that we're all prone to a fundamental attribution error has its critics. Granted, say some, there is an attribution *bias*. But in any given instance, this may or may not produce an "error," just as parents who are biased to believe their child does not use drugs may or may not be correct (Harvey & others, 1981). We can be biased to believe what is true.

Moreover, some everyday circumstances, such as being in church or on a job interview, are like the experiments we have been considering: They involve clear constraints. Actors realize the constraints more than observers—hence the attribution error. But in other settings—in one's room, at a park—people exhibit their individuality. In such settings, people may see their own behavior as *less* constrained than do observers (Monson & Snyder, 1977; Quattrone, 1982; Robins & others, 1996). So it's an overstatement to say that at all times and in all settings observers underestimate situational influences. For this reason, some social psychologists follow Edward Jones in referring to the fundamental attribution error—seeing behavior as corresponding to an inner disposition—as the *correspondence bias.*

Nevertheless, experiments reveal that the bias occurs even when we are aware of the situational forces: when we know that an assigned debate position is not a good basis for inferring someone's real attitudes (Croxton & Miller, 1987; Croxton & others, 1984; Reeder & others, 1987) or that the questioners' role in the quiz game gives the questioners an advantage (Johnson & others, 1984). It is sobering to think that you and I can know about a social process that distorts our thinking and still be susceptible to it. Perhaps that's because it takes more mental effort to assess social effects on people's behavior than it does merely to attribute the behavior to their dispositions (Gilbert & others, 1988, 1992; Webster, 1993). It's as if the busy person thinks, "This isn't a very good basis for making a judgment, but it's easy and all I've got time to look at."

The attribution error is, however, *fundamental* because it colors our explanations in basic and important ways. Researchers in Britain, India, Australia, and the United States have found that people's attributions predict their attitudes toward the poor and employed (Furnham, 1982; Pandey & others, 1982; Skitka, 1999; Wagstaff, 1983; Zucker & Weiner, 1993). Those who attribute poverty and unemployment to personal dispositions ("They're just lazy and undeserving") tend to adopt political positions unsympathetic to such people (Figure 6-3). Their views differ from those who make external attributions ("If you or I were to live with the same overcrowding, poor education, and discrimination, would we be any better off?"). French investigators Jean-Leon Beauvois and Nicole Dubois (1988) report that "relatively privileged" middle-class people are more likely than less-advantaged people to assume that people's behaviors have internal explanations. (Those who have achieved success tend to assume that you get what you deserve.)

Can we benefit from being aware of the attribution error? I once assisted with some interviews for a faculty position. One candidate was interviewed by six of us at once; each of us had the opportunity to ask two or three questions. I came away thinking, "What a stiff, awkward person he is." The second candidate I met privately over coffee, and we immediately discovered we had a close, mutual friend. As we talked,

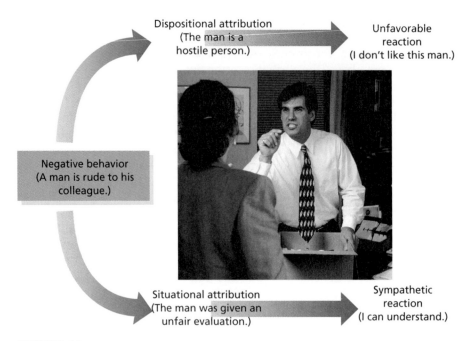

FIGURE 6-3
Attributions and reactions. How we explain someone's negative behavior determines how we feel about it.

I became increasingly impressed by what a "warm, engaging, stimulating person she is." Only later did I remember the fundamental attribution error and reassess my analysis. I had attributed his stiffness and her warmth to their dispositions; in fact, I later realized, such behavior resulted partly from the difference in their interview situations.

*C*ONCEPT TO REMEMBER

fundamental attribution error
The tendency for observers to underestimate situational influences and overestimate dispositional influences upon others' behavior. (Also called *correspondence bias* because we so often see behavior as corresponding to a disposition.)

7

❖

The Powers and Perils of Intuition

What are our powers of intuition—of immediately knowing something without reasoning or analysis? Advocates of "intuitive management" believe we should tune into our hunches. When judging others, they say, we should plug into the nonlogical smarts of our "right brain." When hiring, firing, and investing, we should listen to our premonitions. In making judgments, we should follow the example of *Star Wars'* Luke Skywalker by switching off our computer guidance systems and trusting the force within.

Activity
7.1

Are the intuitionists correct that important information is immediately available apart from our conscious analysis? Or are the skeptics right in saying that intuition is "our knowing we are right, whether we are or not"?

Research suggests that the unconscious indeed controls much of our behavior. As John Bargh and Tanya Chartrand (1999) explain, "Most of a person's everyday life is determined not by their conscious intentions and deliberate choices but by mental processes that are put into motion by features of the environment and that operate outside of conscious awareness and guidance." For example, people quickly recognize that "beautiful" is a good word. But after viewing an imperceptible flashed puppy image (rather than a cockroach) they make that classification more instantly (Giner-Sorolla & others, 1999). Such priming is routine in daily life. When the light turns red, we react and hit the brake before consciously deciding to do so. Indeed, reflect Neil Macrae and Lucy Johnston (1998), "to be able to do just about anything at all (e.g., driving, dating, dancing), action initiation needs to be decoupled from the inefficient (i.e., slow, serial, resource consuming) workings of the conscious mind, otherwise inaction inevitably would prevail."

THE POWERS OF INTUITION

"The heart has its reasons which reason does not know," observed seventeenth-century philosopher-mathematician Blaise Pascal. Three centuries later, scientists have proved Pascal correct. We know more than we know we know. Studies of our unconscious information processing confirm our limited access to what's going on in our minds (Bargh, 1997; Greenwald & Banaji, 1995; Strack & Deutsch, 2004). Our thinking is partly *controlled* (reflective, deliberate, and conscious) and—more than most of us once supposed—partly *automatic* (impulsive, effortless, and without our awareness). Automatic thinking occurs not "on-screen" but off-screen, out of sight, where reason does not go. Consider these examples of automatic thinking, or what we often call intuition:

- *Schemas*—mental templates—automatically, intuitively guide our perceptions and interpretations of our experience. Whether we hear someone speaking of religious *sects* or *sex* depends not only on the word spoken but on how we automatically interpret the sound.

- *Emotional reactions* are often nearly instantaneous, before there is time for deliberate thinking. One neural shortcut takes information from the eye or ear to the brain's sensory switchboard (the thalamus) and out to its emotional control center (the amygdala) before the thinking cortex has had any chance to intervene (LeDoux, 1994, 1996).

  Simple likes, dislikes, and fears typically involve little analysis. Although our intuitive reactions sometimes defy logic, they may still be adaptive. Our ancestors who intuitively feared a sound in the bushes were usually fearing nothing, but they were more likely to survive to pass their genes down to us than their more deliberative cousins.

- Given sufficient *expertise*, people may intuitively know the answer to a problem. A situation cues information stored in our memory. Without knowing quite how we do it, we recognize a friend's voice after the first spoken word of a phone conversation. Master chess players intuitively recognize meaningful patterns that novices miss and often make their next move with only a glance at the board.

- Some things—facts, names, and past experiences—we remember explicitly (consciously). But other things—skills and conditioned dispositions—we remember *implicitly*, without consciously knowing and declaring that we know. It's true of us all, but most strikingly evident in people with brain damage who cannot form new explicit memories. One such person never could learn to recognize her physician, who would need to reintroduce himself with a handshake each day. One day the physician affixed a tack to his hand, causing the patient to jump with pain. When the physician next returned, he was still unrecognized (explicitly). But the patient, retaining an implicit memory, would not shake his hand (LeDoux, 1996).

- Equally dramatic are the cases of *blindsight*. Having lost a portion of the visual cortex to surgery or stroke, people may be functionally blind in part of their field of vision. Shown a series of sticks in the blind field, they report seeing nothing. After correctly guessing whether the sticks are vertical or horizontal, the patients are astounded when told, "You got them all right." Again, these people know more than they know they know. There are, it seems, little minds—parallel processing units—operating unseen.

- Consider your own taken-for-granted capacity to recognize a face intuitively. As you look at a scene, your brain breaks the visual information into subdimensions such as color, depth, movement, and form and works on each aspect simultaneously before reassembling the components. Finally, somehow, your brain compares the perceived image with previously stored images. Voilà! Instantly and effortlessly, you recognize your grandmother. If intuition is immediately knowing something without reasoned analysis, then perceiving is intuition par excellence.

So, many routine cognitive functions occur automatically, unintentionally, without awareness. Our minds function rather like big corporations. Our CEO—our controlled consciousness—attends to the most important or novel issues and assigns routine affairs to subordinates. This delegation of resources enables us to react to many situations quickly, efficiently, intuitively. Such is the "automaticity of everyday life."

THE LIMITS OF INTUITION

Although today's researchers affirm that unconscious information processing can produce flashes of intuition, they have their doubts about its reliable brilliance. Elizabeth Loftus and Mark Klinger (1992) speak for other cognitive scientists in reporting "a general consensus that the unconscious may not be as smart as previously believed." For example, although subliminal stimuli can trigger a weak, fleeting response—enough to evoke a feeling if not conscious awareness—there is no evidence that commercial subliminal tapes can "reprogram your unconscious mind" for success. (A significant body of evidence indicates that they can't [Greenwald, 1992].)

Social psychologists have explored our error-prone hindsight judgments (our intuitive sense, after the fact, that we knew-it-all-along). Other domains of psychology have explored our capacity for illusion—perceptual misinterpretations, fantasies, and constructed beliefs. Michael Gazzaniga (1992) reports that patients whose brain hemispheres have been surgically separated will instantly fabricate—and believe—explanations of their own puzzling behaviors. If the patient gets up and takes a few steps after the experimenter flashes the instruction "walk" to the patient's nonverbal right hemisphere, the verbal left hemisphere will instantly invent a plausible explanation ("I felt like getting a drink").

Illusory thinking also appears in the vast new literature on how we take in, store, and retrieve *social* information. Whereas perception researchers study visual illusions for what they reveal about our normal perceptual mechanisms, social psychologists study illusory thinking for what it reveals about normal information processing. These researchers want to give us a map of everyday social thinking, with the hazards clearly marked.

As we examine some of these efficient thinking patterns, remember this: Demonstrations of how people create counterfeit beliefs do not prove that all beliefs are counterfeit. Still, to recognize counterfeiting, it helps to know how it's done. So let's explore how efficient information processing can go awry, beginning with our self-knowledge.

WE OVERESTIMATE THE ACCURACY OF OUR JUDGMENTS

So far we have seen that our cognitive systems process a vast amount of information efficiently and automatically. But our efficiency has a trade-off; as we interpret our experiences and construct memories, our automatic intuitions often err. Usually, we are unaware of our flaws. The "intellectual conceit" evident in judgments of past knowledge ("I knew it all along") extends to estimates of current knowledge and predictions of future behavior. Although we know we've muffed up in the past, we have more positive expectations for the future—how well we'll meet deadlines, manage relationships, follow an exercise routine (Ross & Newby-Clark, 1998). As we consider our past and our future we construe different selves.

To explore this **overconfidence phenomenon**, Daniel Kahneman and Amos Tversky (1979) gave people factual questions and asked them to fill in the blanks, as in the following: "I feel 98 percent certain that the air distance between New Delhi and Beijing is more than _____ miles but less than _____ miles."* Most individuals were overconfident: About 30 percent of the time, the correct answers lay outside the range they felt 98 percent confident about.

To find out whether overconfidence extends to social judgments, David Dunning and his associates (1990) created a little game show. They asked Stanford University students to guess a stranger's answers to a series of questions, such as "Would you prepare for a difficult exam alone or with others?" and "Would you rate your lecture notes as neat or messy?" Knowing the type of question but not the actual questions, the participants first interviewed their target person about background, hobbies, academic interests, aspirations, astrological sign—anything they thought might be helpful. Then, while the targets privately answered 20 of the two-choice questions, the interviewers predicted their target's answers and rated their own confidence in the predictions.

The interviewers guessed right 63 percent of the time, beating chance by 13 percent. But, on average, they *felt* 75 percent sure of their predictions. When guessing their own roommates' responses, they were 68 percent correct and 78 percent confident. Moreover, the most confident people were most likely to be *over*confident. People also are markedly overconfident when judging whether someone is telling the truth or when estimating things such as the sexual history of their dating partner or the activity preferences of their roommates (DePaulo & others, 1997; Swann & Gill, 1997).

Ironically, incompetence feeds overconfidence. It takes competence to recognize what competence is, note Justin Kruger and David Dunning (1999). Students who score at the bottom on tests of grammar, humor, and logic are most prone to overestimating their gifts at such. Those who don't know what good logic or grammar is are often unaware that they lack it. If ignorance can beget confidence, then—yikes!—where, we may ask, are we unknowingly deficient?

Activity
7.2

Are people better at predicting their own behavior? To find out, Robert Vallone and his colleagues (1990) had college students predict in September whether they would drop a course, declare a major, elect to live off campus next year, and so forth. Although the students felt, on average, 84 percent sure of these self-predictions, they were wrong nearly twice as often as they expected to be. Even when feeling 100 percent sure of their predictions, they erred 15 percent of the time.

* The air distance between New Delhi and Beijing is 2,500 miles.

In estimating their chances for success on a task, such as a major exam, people's confidence runs highest when removed in time from the moment of truth. By exam day, the possibility of failure looms larger and confidence typically drops (Gilovich & others, 1993). Roger Buehler and his colleagues (1994, 2002, 2003) report that most students also confidently underestimate how long it will take them to complete papers and other major assignments. They are not alone:

- Planners routinely underestimate the time and expense of projects. In 1969, Montreal Mayor Jean Drapeau proudly announced that a $120 million stadium with a retractable roof would be built for the 1976 Olympics. The roof was completed in 1989 and cost $120 million by itself. In 1985, officials estimated that Boston's "Big Dig" highway project would cost $2.6 billion and take until 1998. By 2003, the cost had ballooned to $14.6 billion and the project was still unfinished.

- Investment experts market their services with the confident presumption that they can beat the stock market average, forgetting that for every stockbroker or buyer saying "Sell!" at a given price there is another saying "Buy!" A stock's price is the balance point between these mutually confident judgments. Thus, incredible as it may seem, economist Burton Malkiel (1999) reports that mutual fund portfolios selected by investment analysts have not outperformed randomly selected stocks.

- Overconfident decision makers can wreak havoc. It was a confident Adolf Hitler who from 1939 to 1945 waged war against the rest of Europe. It was a confident Lyndon Johnson who in the 1960s invested U.S. weapons and soldiers in the effort to salvage democracy in South Vietnam. It was a confident Saddam Hussein who in 1990 marched his army into Kuwait and in 2003 promised to defeat invading armies. It was a confident George W. Bush who proclaimed that peaceful democracy would soon prevail in a liberated Iraq, with its alleged weapons of mass destruction newly destroyed.

What produces overconfidence? Why doesn't experience lead us to a more realistic self-appraisal? There are several reasons. For one thing, people tend to recall their mistaken judgments as times when they were almost right. Phillip Tetlock (1998, 1999) observed this after inviting various academic and government experts to project—from their viewpoint in the late 1980s—the future governance of the Soviet Union, South Africa, and Canada. Five years later Communism collapsed, South Africa had become a multiracial democracy, and Canada continued undivided. Experts who had felt more than 80 percent confident were right in predicting these turns of events less than 40 percent of the time. Yet, reflecting on their judgments, those who erred believed they were still basically right. I was "almost right," said many. "The hardliners almost succeeded in their coup attempt against Gorbachev." "The Quebeçois separatists almost won the secessionist referendum." "But for the coincidence of de Klerk and Mandela, there would have been a lot bloodier transition to black majority rule in South Africa." Among political experts—and stock market forecasters, mental health workers, and sports prognosticators—overconfidence is hard to dislodge.

People also tend not to seek information that might disprove what they believe. P. C. Wason (1960) demonstrated this, as you can, by giving people a sequence of three numbers (2, 4, 6) that conformed to a rule he had in mind (the rule was simply *any three ascending numbers*). To enable the people to discover the rule, Wason invited each person to generate sets of three numbers. Each time Wason told the person whether or not the set conformed to his rule. When they were sure they had discovered the rule, the people were to stop and announce it.

The result? Seldom right but never in doubt: 23 of the 29 people convinced themselves of a wrong rule. They typically formed some erroneous belief about the rule (for example, counting by twos) and then searched for *confirming* evidence (for example, by testing 8, 10, 12) rather than attempting to *disconfirm* their hunches. We are eager to verify our beliefs but less inclined to seek evidence that might disprove them, a phenomenon called the **confirmation bias.**

Remedies for Overconfidence

What lessons can we draw from research on overconfidence? One lesson is to be wary of other people's dogmatic statements. Even when people seem sure they are right, they may be wrong. Confidence and competence need not coincide.

Two techniques have successfully reduced the overconfidence bias. One is prompt feedback (Lichtenstein & Fischhoff, 1980). In everyday life, weather forecasters and those who set the odds in horse racing both receive clear, daily feedback. Experts in both groups, therefore, do quite well at estimating their probable accuracy (Fischhoff, 1982).

When people think about why an idea *might* be true, it begins to seem true (Koehler, 1991). Thus, another way to reduce overconfidence is to get people to think of one good reason *why their judgments might be wrong;* that is, force them to consider disconfirming information (Koriat & others, 1980). Managers might foster more realistic judgments by insisting that all proposals and recommendations include reasons why they might not work.

Still, we should be careful not to undermine people's self-confidence to a point where they spend too much time in self-analysis or where self-doubts begin to cripple decisiveness. In times when their wisdom is needed, those lacking self-confidence may shrink from speaking up or making tough decisions. Overconfidence can cost us, but realistic self-confidence is adaptive.

CONSTRUCTING MEMORIES

Do you agree or disagree with this statement?

Activity
7.3

Memory can be likened to a storage chest in the brain into which we deposit material and from which we can withdraw it later if needed. Occasionally, something is lost from the "chest," and then we say we have forgotten.

About 85 percent of college students have agreed (Lamal, 1979). As one magazine ad put it, "Science has proven the accumulated experience of a lifetime is preserved perfectly in your mind."

Actually, psychological research has proved the opposite. Many memories are not copies of experiences that remain on deposit in a memory bank. Rather, we construct memories at the time of withdrawal. Like a paleontologist inferring the appearance of a dinosaur from bone fragments, we reconstruct our distant past by using our current feelings and expectations to combine information fragments (Hirt, 1990; Ross & Buehler, 1994). Thus we can easily (though unconsciously) revise our memories to suit our current knowledge. When one of my sons complained, "The June issue of *Cricket* never came," and was then shown where it was, he delightedly responded, "Oh good, I knew I'd gotten it."

Reconstructing Our Past Attitudes

Activity
7.4

Five years ago, how did you feel about nuclear power? About President George W. Bush, or Prime Minister Paul Martin, or Tony Blair? About your parents? If your attitudes have changed, do you know the extent of the change?

Experimenters have explored such questions, and the results have been unnerving. People whose attitudes have changed often insist that they have always felt much as they now feel. Daryl Bem and Keith McConnell (1970) took a survey among Carnegie-Mellon University students. Buried in it was a question concerning student control over the university curriculum. A week later the students agreed to write an essay opposing student control. After doing so, their attitudes shifted toward greater opposition to student control. When asked to recall how they had answered the question before writing the essay, they "remembered" holding the opinion that they *now* held and denied that the experiment had affected them. After observing Clark University students similarly denying their former attitudes, researchers D. R. Wixon and James Laird (1976) commented, "The speed, magnitude, and certainty" with which the students revised their own histories "was striking." As George Vaillant (1977, p. 197) noted after following adults through time, "It is all too common for caterpillars to become butterflies and then to maintain that in their youth they had been little butterflies. Maturation makes liars of us all."

The construction of positive memories brightens our recollections. Terence Mitchell, Leigh Thompson, and their colleagues (1994, 1997) report that people often exhibit *rosy retrospection*—they recall mildly pleasant events more favorably than they experienced them. College students on a three-week bike trip, older adults on a guided tour of Austria, and undergraduates on vacation all reported enjoying their experiences as they were having them. But they later *recalled* such experiences even more fondly, minimizing the unpleasant or boring aspects and remembering the high points. Thus, the pleasant times during which I have sojourned in Scotland I now (back in my office facing deadlines and interruptions) romanticize as pure bliss. The mist and midges are but dim memories. The beauty and fresh sea air are still with me. With any positive experience, some of the pleasure resides in the anticipation, some in the actual experience, and some in the rosy retrospection.

Cathy McFarland and Michael Ross (1985) found that we also revise our recollections of other people as our relationships with them change. They had university students rate their steady dating partners. Two months later, they rated them again. Students who were more in love than ever had a tendency to recall love at first sight. Those who had broken up were more likely to recall having recognized the partner as somewhat selfish and bad-tempered.

Diane Holmberg and John Holmes (1994) discovered the same phenomenon among 373 newlywed couples, most of whom reported being very happy. When resurveyed two years later, those whose marriages had soured recalled that things had always been bad. The results are "frightening," say Holmberg and Holmes: "Such biases can lead to a dangerous downward spiral. The worse your current view of your partner is, the worse your memories are, which only further confirms your negative attitudes."

It's not that we are totally unaware of how we used to feel, just that when memories are hazy, current feelings guide our recall. Parents of every generation bemoan the values of the next generation, partly because they misrecall their youthful values as being closer to their current values. Teens of every generation, depending on their current mood, describe their parents as wonderful or woeful.

Reconstructing Past Behavior

Memory construction enables us to revise our own histories. Michael Ross, Cathy McFarland, and Garth Fletcher (1981) exposed some University of Waterloo students to a message convincing them of the desirability of tooth-brushing. Later, in a supposedly different experiment, these students recalled brushing their teeth more often during the preceding two weeks than did students who had not heard the message. Likewise, projecting from surveys, people report smoking many fewer cigarettes than are actually sold (Hall, 1985). And they recall casting more votes than were actually recorded (Bureau of the Census, 1993).

Social psychologist Anthony Greenwald (1980) noted the similarity of such findings to happenings in George Orwell's novel *1984*—in which it was "necessary to remember that events happened in the desired manner." Indeed, argued Greenwald, we all have "totalitarian egos" that revise the past to suit our present views. Thus, we underreport bad behavior and overreport good behavior.

Sometimes our present view is that we've improved—in which case we may misrecall our past as more unlike the present than it actually was. This tendency resolves a puzzling pair of consistent findings: Those who participate in psychotherapy and self-improvement programs for weight control, antismoking, and exercise show only modest improvement on average. Yet they often claim considerable benefit (Myers, 2004). Michael Conway and Michael Ross (1985, 1986) explain why: Having expended so much time, effort, and money on self-improvement, people may think, "I may not be perfect now, but I was worse before; this did me a lot of good."

CONCEPTS TO REMEMBER

overconfidence phenomenon
   The tendency to be more
   confident than correct—to
   overestimate the accuracy of
   one's beliefs.

confirmation bias   A tendency to
   search for information that
   confirms one's preconceptions.

Reasons for Unreason

What good fortune for those in power that people do not think.

Adolph Hitler

The mixed picture of our intuitive self-knowledge that we saw in Module 7 is paralleled by a mixed picture of our rationality. On the one hand, what species better deserves the name *Homo sapiens*—wise humans? Our cognitive powers outstrip the smartest computers in recognizing patterns, handling language, and processing abstract information. Our information processing is also wonderfully efficient. With such precious little time to process so much information, we specialize in mental shortcuts. Scientists marvel at the speed and ease with which we form impressions, judgments, and explanations. In many situations, our snap generalizations—"That's dangerous!"—are adaptive. They promote our survival.

But our adaptive efficiency has a trade-off; snap generalizations sometimes err. Our helpful strategies for simplifying complex information can lead us astray. To enhance our own powers of critical thinking, let's consider four reasons for unreason—common ways in which people form or sustain false beliefs:

1. Our preconceptions control our interpretations.
2. We often are swayed more by anecdotes than by statistical facts.
3. We misperceive correlation and control.
4. Our beliefs can generate their own conclusions.

OUR PRECONCEPTIONS CONTROL OUR INTERPRETATIONS

It is a significant fact about the human mind—that our preconceptions guide how we perceive and interpret information. We construe the world through theory-tinted glasses. "Sure, preconceptions matter," people will agree, yet they fail to realize how great the effect is.

Let's consider some provocative experiments. The first group examines how prejudgments affect the way people perceive and interpret information. The second group plants a judgment in people's minds *after* they have been given information to see how after-the-fact ideas bias recall. The overarching point: *We respond not to reality as it is but to reality as we construe it.*

An experiment by Robert Vallone, Lee Ross, and Mark Lepper (1985) reveals just how powerful preconceptions can be. They showed pro-Israeli and pro-Arab students six network news segments describing the 1982 killing of civilian refugees at two camps in Lebanon. As Figure 8-1

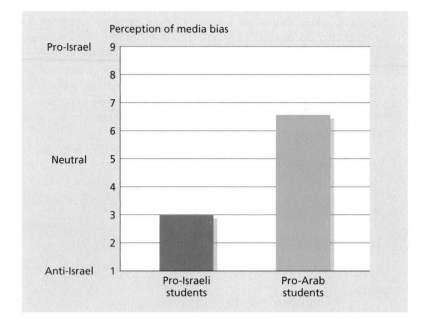

FIGURE 8-1
Pro-Israeli and pro-Arab students who viewed network news descriptions of the "Beirut massacre" believed the coverage was biased against their point of view.   **Source:** Data from Vallone, Ross, & Lepper, 1985.

illustrates, each group perceived the networks as hostile to its side. The phenomenon is commonplace:

- Presidential candidates and their supporters nearly always view the news media as unsympathetic to their cause.
- Sports fans perceive referees as partial to the other side.
- People in conflict (married couples, labor and management, opposing racial groups) see impartial mediators as biased against them.

Our assumptions about the world can even make contradictory evidence seem supportive. For example, Ross and Lepper assisted Charles Lord (1979) in asking students to evaluate the results of two supposedly new research studies. Half the students favored capital punishment and half opposed it. One study confirmed and the other disconfirmed the students' beliefs about the deterrent effect of the death penalty. The results: Both proponents and opponents of capital punishment readily accepted evidence that confirmed their belief but were sharply critical of disconfirming evidence. Showing the two sides an *identical* body of mixed evidence had not lessened their disagreement but *increased* it.

Is this why, in politics, religion, and science, ambiguous information often fuels conflict? U.S. presidential debates have mostly reinforced pre-debate opinions. By nearly a 10-to-1 margin, those who already favored one candidate or the other perceived their candidate as having won (Kinder & Sears, 1985).

Other experiments have manipulated preconceptions, with astonishing effects upon how people interpret and recall what they observe. Myron Rothbart and Pamela Birrell (1977) had University of Oregon students assess the facial expression of a man (Figure 8-2). Those told he was a Gestapo leader responsible for barbaric medical experiments on concentration camp inmates during World War II intuitively judged his expression as cruel. Those told he was a leader in the anti-Nazi underground movement whose courage saved thousands of Jewish lives judged his facial expression as warm and kind.

Filmmakers can control people's perceptions of emotion by manipulating the setting in which they see a face. They call this the "Kulechov effect," after a Russian film director who would skillfully guide viewers' inferences by manipulating their assumptions. Kulechov demonstrated the phenomenon by creating three short films that presented the face of an actor with a neutral expression after viewers had first been shown a dead woman, a dish of soup, or a girl playing—making the actor seem sad, thoughtful, or happy. The moral: There is a reality out there, but our minds actively construe it. Other people may construe reality differently and may therefore behave differently.

FIGURE 8-2
Judge for yourself: Is this person's expression cruel or kind? If told he was a Nazi, would your reading of his face differ?

WE ARE MORE SWAYED BY MEMORABLE EVENTS THAN BY FACTS

Consider the following: Question 1—Does the letter *k* appear in print more often as the first letter of a word or as the third letter? Question 2—Do more people live in Cambodia or in Tanzania? (See end of module for answers.)

You probably answered in terms of how readily *k*'s, Cambodians, and Tanzanians come to mind. If examples are readily *available* in our memory—as letters beginning with *k* and as Cambodians tend to be—then we presume that such are commonplace. Usually it is, so we are often well served by this cognitive rule, called the **availability heuristic.**

But sometimes the rule deludes us. If people hear a list of famous people of one sex (Mother Teresa, Madonna, Hillary Clinton) intermixed with an equal size list of unfamous people of the other sex (Donald Scarr, William Wood, Mel Jasper), the famous names will later be more cognitively available. Most people will therefore recall having heard more (in this instance) women's names (McKelvie, 1995, 1997; Tversky & Kahneman, 1973). Vivid, easy-to-imagine events, such as diseases with easy-to-picture symptoms, may likewise seem more likely than harder-to-picture events

(MacLeod & Campbell, 1992; Sherman & others, 1985). Even fictional happenings in novels, television, and movies leave images that later penetrate our judgments (Gerrig & Prentice, 1991; Green & others, 2002).

Our use of the availability heuristic highlights a basic principle of social thinking: People are slow to deduce particular instances from a general truth, but they are remarkably quick to infer general truth from a vivid instance. No wonder that after hearing and reading stories of rapes, robberies, and beatings, 9 out of 10 Canadians overestimate—usually by a considerable margin—the percentage of crimes that involve violence (Doob & Roberts, 1988).

The availability heuristic explains why powerful anecdotes can nevertheless be more compelling than statistical information and why perceived risk is therefore often badly out of joint with real risks (Allison & others, 1992). Because news footage of airplane crashes is a readily available memory for most of us, especially since 9/11, we often suppose we are more at risk traveling in commercial airplanes than in cars. Actually, U.S. travelers during the last half of the 1990s were more likely to die in a car crash than on a commercial flight covering the same distance (National Safety Council, 2001). For most air travelers, the most dangerous part of the journey is the drive to the airport.

WE MISPERCEIVE CORRELATION AND CONTROL

Another influence on everyday thinking is our search for order in random events, a tendency that can lead us down all sorts of wrong paths.

Illusory Correlation

It's easy to see a correlation where none exists. When we expect to find significant relationships, we easily associate random events, perceiving an **illusory correlation.** William Ward and Herbert Jenkins (1965) showed people the results of a hypothetical 50-day cloud-seeding experiment. They told their subjects which of the 50 days the clouds had been seeded and which days it rained. This information was nothing more than a random mix of results: Sometimes it rained after seeding; sometimes it didn't. People nevertheless became convinced—in conformity with their ideas about the effects of cloud seeding—that they really had observed a relationship between cloud seeding and rain.

Other experiments confirm that people easily misperceive random events as confirming their beliefs (Crocker, 1981; Jennings & others, 1982; Trolier & Hamilton, 1986). If we believe a correlation exists, we are more likely to notice and recall confirming instances. If we believe that premonitions correlate with events, we notice and remember the joint occurrence of the premonition and the event's later occurrence. We seldom notice or remember all the times unusual events do not coincide. If, after we think about a friend, the friend calls us, we notice and remember this coincidence. We don't notice all the times we think of a friend without any ensuing call or receive a call from a friend about whom we've not been thinking.

Illusion of Control

Our tendency to perceive random events as related feeds an **illusion of control**—*the idea that chance events are subject to our influence.* This keeps gamblers going and makes the rest of us do all sorts of unlikely things.

Gambling

Ellen Langer (1977) demonstrated the illusion of control with experiments on gambling. Compared with those given an assigned lottery number, people who chose their own number demanded four times as much money when asked if they would sell their ticket. When playing a game of chance against an awkward and nervous person, they bet significantly more than when playing against a dapper, confident opponent. Throwing the dice or spinning the wheel increases peoples' confidence (Wohl & Enzle, 2002). In these and other ways, more than 50 experiments have consistently found people acting as if they can predict or control chance events (Presson & Benassi, 1996; Thompson & others, 1998).

Observations of real-life gamblers confirm these experimental findings. Dice players may throw softly for low numbers and hard for high numbers (Henslin, 1967). The gambling industry thrives on gamblers' illusions. Gamblers attribute wins to their skill and foresight. Losses become "near misses" or "flukes," or for the sports gambler, a bad call by the referee or a freakish bounce of the ball (Gilovich & Douglas, 1986).

Stock traders also like the "feeling of empowerment" that comes from being able to choose and control their own stock trades, as if their being in control can enable them to outperform the "efficient market." One ad declared that online investing "is about control." Alas, the illusion of control breeds overconfidence, and frequent losses after trading costs are factored in (Barber & Odean, 2001).

Regression Toward the Average

Tversky and Kahneman (1974) noted another way by which an illusion of control may arise: We fail to recognize the statistical phenomenon of **regression toward the average.** Because exam scores fluctuate partly by chance, most students who get extremely high scores on an exam will get lower scores on the next exam. Because their first score is at the ceiling, their second score is more likely to fall back ("regress") toward their own average than to push the ceiling even higher. (This is why a student who does consistently good work, even if never the best, will sometimes end a course at the top of the class.) Conversely, the lowest-scoring students on the first exam are likely to improve. If those who scored lowest go for tutoring after the first exam, the tutors are likely to feel effective when the student improves, even if the tutoring had no effect.

Indeed, when things reach a low point, we will try anything, and whatever we try—going to a psychotherapist, starting a new diet-exercise plan, reading a self-help book—is more likely to be followed by improvement than by further deterioration. Sometimes we recognize that events are not likely to continue at an unusually good or bad extreme. (When we're extremely high or low, we tend to fall back toward our normal average.)

OUR BELIEFS CAN GENERATE THEIR OWN CONFIRMATION

There's one additional reason why our intuitive beliefs resist reality: They sometimes lead us to act in ways that produce their apparent confirmation. Our beliefs about other people can therefore become **self-fulfilling prophecies.**

In his well-known studies of "experimenter bias," Robert Rosenthal (1985) found that research participants sometimes live up to what is expected of them. In one study, experimenters asked individuals to judge the success of people in various photographs. The experimenters read the same instructions to all their participants and showed them the same photos. Nevertheless, experimenters led to expect high ratings obtained higher ratings than did those who expected their participants to see the photographed people as failures. Even more startling—and controversial—are reports that teachers' beliefs about their students similarly serve as self-fulfilling prophecies. If a teacher believes a student is good at math, will the student do well in the class? Let's examine this.

Do Teacher Expectations Affect Student Performance?

Teachers do have higher expectations for some students than for others. Perhaps you have detected this after having a brother or sister precede you in school, or after receiving a label such as "gifted" or "learning disabled," or after being tracked with "high-ability" or "average-ability" students. Perhaps conversation in the teachers' lounge sent your reputation ahead of you. Or perhaps your new teacher scrutinized your school file or discovered your family's social status. Do such teacher expectations affect student performance? It's clear that teachers' evaluations correlate with student achievement: Teachers think well of students who do well. That's mostly because teachers typically perceive their students' abilities and achievements accurately (Jussim & others, 1996; Smith & others, 1998, 1999; Trouilloud & others, 2002).

By Rosenthal's own count, in only about 4 in 10 of the nearly 500 published experiments did expectations significantly affect performance (Rosenthal, 1991, 2002). Low expectations do not doom a capable child, nor do high expectations magically transform a slow learner into a valedictorian. Human nature is not so pliable.

High expectations do seem to boost low achievers, for whom a teacher's positive attitude may be a hope-giving breath of fresh air (Madon & others, 1997). How are such expectations transmitted? Rosenthal and other investigators report that teachers look, smile, and nod more at "high-potential students." Teachers also may teach more to their "gifted" students, set higher goals for them, call on them more, and give them more time to answer (Cooper, 1983; Harris & Rosenthal, 1985, 1986; Jussim, 1986).

Reading the experiments on teacher expectations makes me wonder about the effect of *students'* expectations upon their teachers. You no doubt begin many of your courses having heard "Professor Smith is interesting" and "Professor Jones is a bore." Robert Feldman and Thomas Prohaska (1979; Feldman & Theiss, 1982) found that such expectations can affect both student and teacher. Students in a learning experiment who expected to be taught by an excellent teacher perceived their teacher (who was unaware of their expectations) as more competent and interesting than did students with low expectations. Furthermore, the students actually learned more. In a follow-up experiment, Feldman and Prohaska videotaped teachers and had observers rate their performances. Teachers were judged most capable when assigned a student who nonverbally conveyed positive expectations.

To see whether such effects might also occur in actual classrooms, a research team led by David Jamieson (1987) experimented with four Ontario high school classes taught by a newly transferred teacher. During individual interviews, they told students in two of the classes that both other students and the research team rated the teacher very highly. Compared with the control classes, the students given positive expectations paid better attention during class. At the end of the teaching unit, they also got better grades and rated the teacher as clearer in her teaching. The attitudes that a class has toward its teacher are as important, it seems, as the teacher's attitude toward the students.

Do We Get What We Expect from Others?

So the expectations of experimenters and teachers, though usually reasonably accurate assessments, occasionally act as self-fulfilling prophecies. How widespread are self-fulfilling prophecies? Do we get from others what we expect of them? Studies show that self-fulfilling prophecies also operate in work settings (with managers who have high or low expectations), in courtrooms (as judges instruct juries), and in simulated police contexts (as interrogators with guilty or innocent expectations interrogate and pressure suspects) (Kassin & others, 2003; Rosenthal, 2003).

Do self-fulfilling prophecies color our personal relationships? There are times when negative expectations of someone lead us to be extra nice to that person, which induces them to be nice in return—thus *dis*confirming our expectations. But a more common finding in studies of social interaction is that, yes, we do to some extent get what we expect (Olson & others, 1996).

In laboratory games, hostility nearly always begets hostility: People who perceive their opponents as noncooperative will readily induce them to be noncooperative (Kelley & Stahelski, 1970). Each party's perception of the other as aggressive, resentful, and vindictive induces the other to display these behaviors in self-defense, thus creating a vicious self-perpetuating circle. Whether I expect my wife to be in a bad mood or in a warm, loving mood may affect how I relate to her, thereby inducing her to confirm my belief.

So do intimate relationships prosper when partners idealize one another? Are positive illusions of the other's virtues self-fulfilling? Or are they more often self-defeating, by creating expectations that can't be met and that ultimately spell doom? Among University of Waterloo dating couples followed by Sandra Murray and her associates (1996a, 2000), positive ideals of one's partner were good omens. Idealization helped buffer conflict, bolster satisfaction, and turn self-perceived frogs into princes or princesses. When someone loves and admires us, it helps us become more the person he or she imagines us to be.

Among married couples, too, those who worry that their partner doesn't love and accept them interpret slight hurts as rejections, which motivates them to devalue the partner and distance themselves. Those who presume their partner's love and acceptance respond less defensively, and even may be closer to their partner (Murray & others, 2003). Love helps create its presumed reality.

Several experiments conducted by Mark Snyder (1984) at the University of Minnesota show how, once formed, erroneous beliefs about the social world can induce others to confirm those beliefs, a phenomenon called **behavioral confirmation**. In a now-classic study, Snyder, Elizabeth Tanke, and Ellen Berscheid (1977) had men students talk on the telephone with women they thought (from having been shown a picture) were either attractive or unattractive. Analysis of just the women's comments during the conversations revealed that the supposedly attractive women spoke more warmly than the supposedly unattractive women. The men's erroneous beliefs had become a self-fulfilling prophecy by leading them to act in a way that influenced the women to fulfill the men's stereotype that beautiful people are desirable people.

Expectations influence children's behavior, too. After observing the amount of litter in three classrooms, Richard Miller and his colleagues (1975) had the teacher and others repeatedly tell one class that they should be neat and tidy. This persuasion increased the amount of litter placed in wastebaskets from 15 to 45 percent, but only temporarily.

Another class, which also had been placing only 15 percent of its litter in wastebaskets, was repeatedly congratulated for being so neat and tidy. After eight days of hearing this, and still two weeks later, these children were fulfilling the expectation by putting more than 80 percent of their litter in wastebaskets. Tell children they are hardworking and kind (rather than lazy and mean), and they may live up to their labels.

These experiments help us understand how social beliefs, such as stereotypes about people with disabilities or about people of a particular race or sex, may be self-confirming. We help construct our own social realities. How others treat us reflects how we and others have treated them.

CONCLUSIONS

We have reviewed some reasons why people sometimes come to believe what may be untrue. We cannot easily dismiss these experiments: Most of their participants were intelligent people, often students at leading universities. Moreover, these predictable distortions and biases occurred even when payment for right answers motivated people to think optimally. As one researcher concluded, the illusions "have a persistent quality not unlike that of perceptual illusions" (Slovic, 1972).

Research in cognitive social psychology thus mirrors the mixed review given humanity in literature, philosophy, and religion. Many research psychologists have spent lifetimes exploring the awesome capacities of the human mind. We are smart enough to have cracked our own genetic code, to have invented talking computers, to have sent people to the moon. Three cheers for human reason.

Well, two cheers—because the mind's premium on efficient judgment makes our intuition more vulnerable to misjudgment than we suspect. With remarkable ease, we form and sustain false beliefs. Led by our preconceptions, overconfident, persuaded by vivid anecdotes, perceiving correlations and control even where none may exist, we construct our social beliefs and then influence others to confirm them. "The naked intellect," observed novelist Madeleine L'Engle, "is an extraordinarily inaccurate instrument."

****

Answer to Question 1:   The letter k appears in print two to three times more often as the third letter. Yet most people judge that k appears more often at the beginning of a word. Words beginning with k are more readily available to memory, surmise Amos Tversky and Daniel Kahneman (1974), and ease of recall—availability—is our heuristic for judging the frequency of events.

Answer to Question 2:   Tanzania's 35 million people greatly outnumber Cambodia's 12 million. Most people, having more vivid images of Cambodians, guess wrong.

****

CONCEPTS TO REMEMBER

availability heuristic   A cognitive rule that judges the likelihood of things in terms of their availability in memory. If instances of something come readily to mind, we presume it to be commonplace.

illusory correlation   Perception of a relationship where none exists, or perception of a stronger relationship than actually exists.

illusion of control   Perception of uncontrollable events as subject to one's control or as more controllable than they are.

regression toward the average   The statistical tendency for extreme scores or extreme behavior to return toward one's average.

self-fulfilling prophecy   A belief that leads to its own fulfillment.

behavioral confirmation   A type of self-fulfilling prophecy whereby people's social expectations lead them to behave in ways that cause others to confirm their expectations.

MODULE

9

❖

Behavior and Belief

W hich comes first, belief or behavior? Inner attitude or outer action? Character or conduct? What is the relationship between who we *are* (on the inside) and what we *do* (on the outside)? Opinions on this chicken-and-egg question vary. "The ancestor of every action is a thought," wrote American essayist Ralph Waldo Emerson in 1841. To the contrary, said British Prime Minister Benjamin Disraeli, "Thought is the child of Action." Most people side with Emerson. Underlying our teaching, preaching, and counseling is the assumption that private beliefs determine public behavior: If we want to alter people's actions, we therefore need to change their hearts and minds.

*D*O ATTITUDES INFLUENCE BEHAVIOR?

Attitudes are beliefs and feelings that can influence our reactions. If we *believe* that someone is threatening, we might *feel* dislike and therefore *act* unfriendly. "Change the way people think," said South African civil rights martyr Steve Biko (echoing Emerson), "and things will never be the same."

Believing this, social psychologists during the 1940s and 1950s studied factors that influence attitudes. Thus they were shocked when dozens of studies during the 1960s revealed that what people say they think and feel often has little to do with how they act (Wicker, 1971). In these studies, students' attitudes toward cheating bore little relation to the likelihood of their actually cheating. People's attitudes toward the church were only modestly linked with church attendance on any given Sunday.

Self-described racial attitudes predicted little of the variation in behavior that occurred when people faced an actual interracial situation. People, it seemed, weren't walking the talk.

This realization stimulated more studies during the 1970s and 1980s, which revealed that our attitudes *do* influence our actions in some circumstances:

- *When external influences on our words and actions are minimal.* Sometimes we adjust our attitude reports to please our listeners. This was vividly demonstrated when the U.S. House of Representatives once overwhelmingly passed a salary increase for itself in an off-the-record vote, and then moments later overwhelmingly defeated the same bill on a roll-call vote. Other times social pressure diverts our behavior from the dictates of our attitudes (leading good people sometimes to harm people they do not dislike). When external pressures do not blur the link between our attitudes and actions, we can see that link more clearly.

- *When the attitude is specific to the behavior.* People readily profess honesty while cheating in reporting their taxes, cherish a clean environment while not recycling, or applaud good health while smoking and not exercising. But their more specific attitudes toward jogging better predict whether they jog (Olson & Zanna, 1981), their attitudes toward *recycling* do predict whether they recycle (Oskamp, 1991), and their attitudes toward contraception predict their contraceptive use (Morrison, 1989).

- *When we are conscious of our attitudes.* Attitudes can lie dormant as we act out of habit or as we flow with the crowd. For our attitudes to guide our actions, we must pause to consider them. Thus, when we are self-conscious, perhaps after looking in a mirror, or reminded of how we feel, we act truer to our convictions (Fazio, 1990). Likewise, attitudes formed through a significant experience are more often remembered and acted upon.

So, an attitude will influence our behavior *if* other influences are minimal, *if* the attitude specifically relates to the behavior, and *if* the attitude is potent, perhaps because something brings it to mind. Under these conditions, we *will* stand up for what we believe.

DOES BEHAVIOR INFLUENCE ATTITUDES?

Do we also come to believe in what we've stood up for? Indeed. One of social psychology's big lessons is that we are likely not only to think ourselves into a way of acting but also to act ourselves into a way of thinking. Many streams of evidence confirm that *attitudes follow behavior*.

Role-Playing

The word **role** is borrowed from the theater and, as in the theater, refers to actions expected of those who occupy a particular social position. When enacting new social roles, we may at first feel phony. But our unease seldom lasts.

Think of a time when you stepped into some new role—perhaps your first days on a job, or at college, or in a sorority or fraternity. That first week on campus, for example, you may have been supersensitive to your new social situation and tried valiantly to act appropriately and to root out your high school behavior. At such times you may have felt self-conscious. You observed your new speech and actions because they weren't natural to you. Then one day you noticed something amazing: Your enthusiasm for a sorority or your pseudo-intellectual talk no longer feels forced. The role has begun to fit as comfortably as your old jeans and T-shirt.

Activity
9.1

In one study, college men volunteered to spend time in a simulated prison constructed in Stanford's psychology department by Philip Zimbardo (1971; Haney & Zimbardo, 1998). Zimbardo was wondering: Is prison brutality a product of evil prisoners and malicious guards? Or do the institutional roles of guard and prisoner embitter and harden even compassionate people? Do the people make the place violent? Or does the place make the people violent?

So, by a flip of a coin, Zimbardo designated some students as guards. He gave them uniforms, billy clubs, and whistles and instructed them to enforce the rules. The other half, the prisoners, were locked in cells and made to wear humiliating outfits. After a jovial first day of "playing" their roles, the guards and prisoners, and even the experimenters, got caught up in the situation. The guards began to disparage the prisoners, and some devised cruel and degrading routines. The prisoners broke down, rebelled, or became apathetic. There developed, reported Zimbardo (1972), a "growing confusion between reality and illusion, between role-playing and self-identity. . . . This prison which we had created . . . was absorbing us as creatures of its own reality." Observing the emerging social pathology, Zimbardo was forced to call off the planned two-week simulation after only six days.

The deeper lesson of role-playing studies concerns how what is unreal (an artificial role) can subtly evolve into what is real. In a new career, as teacher, soldier, or businessperson, we enact a role that shapes our attitudes. Imagine playing the role of slave—not just for six days but for decades. If a few days altered the behavior of those in Zimbardo's "prison," then imagine the corrosive effects of decades of subservient behavior. The master may be even more profoundly affected, because the

After the degradation of Iraqi prisoners by some U.S. military personnel, Philip Zimbardo (2004b) noted "direct and sad parallels between similar behavior of the 'guards' in the Stanford Prison Experiment." Such behavior, he contends, is attributable to a toxic situation that can make good people into perpetrators of evil. "It's not that we put bad apples in a good barrel. We put good apples in a bad barrel. The barrel corrupts anything that it touches."

master's role is chosen. Frederick Douglass, a former slave, recalls his slave mistress's transformation as she absorbed her role:

> My new mistress proved to be all she appeared when I first met her at the door—a woman of the kindest heart and finest feelings. . . . I was utterly astonished at her goodness. I scarcely knew how to behave towards her. She was entirely unlike any other white woman I had ever seen. . . . The meanest slave was put fully at ease in her presence, and none left without feeling better for having seen her. Her face was made of heavenly smiles, and her voice of tranquil music. But, alas! this kind heart had but a short time to remain such. The fatal poison of irresponsible power was already in her hands, and soon commenced its infernal work. That cheerful eye, under the influence of slavery, soon became red with rage; that voice, made all of sweet accord, changed to one of harsh and horrid discord; and that angelic face gave place to that of a demon. (Douglass, 1845, pp. 57–58)

Saying Becomes Believing

People often adapt what they say to please their listeners. They are quicker to tell people good news than bad, and they adjust their message toward their listener's position (Manis & others, 1974; Tesser & others, 1972; Tetlock, 1983). When induced to give spoken or written witness to something they doubt, people will often feel bad about their deceit. Nevertheless, they begin to believe what they are saying—*provided* they weren't bribed or coerced into doing so. When there is no compelling external explanation for one's words, saying becomes believing (Klaas, 1978).

Tory Higgins and his colleagues (Higgins & McCann, 1984; Higgins & Rholes, 1978) illustrated how saying becomes believing. They had university students read a personality description of someone and then summarize it for someone else, who was believed either to like or dislike this person. The students wrote a more positive description when the recipient liked the person. Having said positive things, they also then liked the person more themselves. Asked to recall what they had read, they remembered the description as more positive than it was. In short, it seems that we are prone to adjust our messages to our listeners, and, having done so, to believe the altered message.

The Foot-in-the-Door Phenomenon

Activity
9.2

Most of us can recall times when, after agreeing to help out with a project or an organization, we ended up more involved than we ever intended, vowing that in the future we would say no to such requests. How does this happen? Experiments suggest that if you want people to do a big favor for you, an effective strategy is this: Get them to do a small favor first. In the best-known demonstration of this **foot-in-the-door phenomenon,** researchers posing as drive-safely volunteers asked Californians to permit the installation of huge, poorly lettered "Drive Carefully" signs in their front yards. Only 17 percent consented. Others were first approached with a small request: Would they display three-inch "Be a safe driver" window signs? Nearly all readily agreed. When approached two weeks later to allow the large, ugly signs in their front yards, 76 percent consented (Freedman & Fraser, 1966). One project helper who went from house to house later recalled that, not knowing who had been previously visited, "I was simply stunned at how easy it was to convince some people and how impossible to convince others" (Ornstein, 1991).

Other researchers have confirmed the foot-in-the-door phenomenon with altruistic behaviors.

- Patricia Pliner and her collaborators (1974) found 46 percent of Toronto suburbanites willing to give to the Cancer Society when approached directly. Others, asked a day ahead to wear a lapel pin publicizing the drive (which all agreed to do), were nearly twice as likely to donate.

- Anthony Greenwald and his co-researchers (1987) approached a sample of registered voters the day before the 1984 U.S. presidential election and asked them a small question: "Do you expect that you will vote or not?" All said yes. Compared with other voters not asked their intentions, they were 41 percent more likely to vote.

- Angela Lipsitz and others (1989) report that ending blood-drive reminder calls with, "We'll count on seeing you then, OK? [pause for response]," increased the show-up rate from 62 to 81 percent.

- In Internet chatrooms, Paul Markey and his colleagues (2002) requested help ("I can't get my e-mail to work. Is there any way I can get you to send me an e-mail?"). Help increased—from 2 to 16 percent—by including a smaller prior request ("I am new to this whole computer thing. Is there any way you can tell me how to look at someone's profile?"). Nicolas Guéguen and Céline Jacob (2001) tripled the rate of French Internet users contributing to child landmine victims organizations (from 1.6 to 4.9 percent) by first inviting them to sign a petition against landmines.

Note that in these, as in many of the 100+ foot-in-the-door experiments, the initial compliance—signing a petition, wearing a lapel pin, stating one's intention—was voluntary (Burger & Guadagno, 2003). We will see again and again that when people commit themselves to public behaviors *and* perceive these acts to be their own doing, they come to believe more strongly in what they have done.

Social psychologist Robert Cialdini [chal-DEE-nee] is a self-described "patsy." "For as long as I can recall, I've been an easy mark for the pitches of peddlers, fund-raisers, and operators of one sort or another." To better understand why one person says yes to another, he spent three years as a trainee in various sales, fund-raising, and advertising organizations, discovering how they exploit "the weapons of influence." He also put these weapons to the test in simple experiments. In one, Cialdini and his collaborators (1978) explored a variation of the foot-in-the-door phenomenon by experimenting with the **low-ball technique,** a tactic reportedly used by some car dealers. After the customer agrees to buy a new car because of its great price and begins completing the sales forms, the salesperson removes the price advantage by charging for options the customer thought were included or by checking with a boss who disallows the deal because, "We'd be losing money." Folklore has it that more customers now stick with the higher-priced purchase than would have agreed to it at the outset.

Marketing researchers and salespeople have found that the principle works even when we are aware of a profit motive (Cialdini, 1988). A harmless initial commitment—returning a card for more information and a gift, agreeing to listen to an investment possibility—often moves us toward a larger commitment. Salespeople sometimes exploit the power of small commitments by trying to bind people to purchase agreements. Many states now have laws that allow customers of door-to-door salespeople a few days to think over their purchases and cancel. To combat the effect of these laws, many companies use what the sales-training program of one encyclopedia company calls "a very important psychological aid in preventing customers from backing out of their con-tracts" (Cialdini, 1988, p. 78). They simply have the customer, rather than the salesperson, fill out the agreement. Having written it themselves, people usually live up to their commitment.

The foot-in-the-door phenomenon is well worth learning about. Someone trying to seduce us—financially, politically, or sexually—usually will try to create a momentum of compliance. The practical lesson: Before agreeing to a small request, think about what may follow.

Evil Acts and Attitudes

The attitudes-follow-behavior principle works with immoral acts as well. Evil sometimes results from gradually escalating commitments. A trifling evil act can make a worse act easier. Evil acts gnaw at the actor's moral sensitivity. To paraphrase La Rochefoucauld's *Maxims* (1665), it is not as difficult to find a person who has never succumbed to a given tempta-tion as to find a person who has succumbed only once.

For example, cruel acts corrode the consciences of those who perform them. Harming an innocent victim—by uttering hurtful com-ments or delivering electric shocks—typically leads aggressors to dis-parage their victims, thus helping them justify their behavior (Berscheid & others, 1968; Davis & Jones, 1960; Glass, 1964). We tend not only to hurt those we dislike but to dislike those we hurt. In studies establish-ing this, people would justify an action especially when coaxed into it, not coerced. When we agree to a deed voluntarily, we take more respon-sibility for it.

The phenomenon appears in wartime. Concentration camp guards would sometimes display good manners to inmates in their first days on the job, but not for long. Soldiers ordered to kill may initially react with revulsion to the point of sickness over their act, but not for long (Waller, 2002). Often they will denigrate their enemies with dehuman-izing nicknames.

Attitudes also follow behavior in peacetime. A group that holds another in slavery will likely come to perceive the slaves as having traits that justify their oppression. Actions and attitudes feed one another, sometimes to the point of moral numbness. The more one harms another and adjusts one's attitudes, the easier harm-doing becomes. Conscience mutates.

Evil acts shape the self, but so, thankfully, do moral acts. Character, it is said, is reflected in what we do when we think no one is looking. Researchers have tested character by giving children temptations when it seems no one is watching. Consider what happens when children resist the temptation. In a dramatic experiment, Jonathan Freedman (1965) introduced elementary school children to an enticing battery-controlled robot, instructing them not to play with it while he was out of the room. Freedman used a severe threat with half the children and a mild threat with the others. Both were sufficient to deter the children.

Several weeks later a different researcher, with no apparent relation to the earlier events, left each child to play in the same room with the same toys. Of the 18 children who had been given the severe threat, 14 now freely played with the robot; but two-thirds of those who had been given the mild deterrent still resisted playing with it. Having earlier chosen consciously *not* to play with the toy, the mildly deterred children apparently internalized their decisions. This new attitude controlled their subsequent actions. So they internalized the conscientious act if the deterrent was strong enough to elicit the desired behavior yet mild enough to leave them with a sense of choice. Moral action, especially when chosen rather than coerced, affects moral thinking.

Interracial Behavior and Racial Attitudes

If moral action feeds moral attitudes, will positive interracial behavior reduce racial prejudice—much as mandatory seat belt use has produced more favorable seat belt attitudes? This was part of social scientists' testimony before the U.S. Supreme Court's 1954 decision to desegregate schools. Their argument ran like this: If we wait for the heart to change—through preaching and teaching—we will wait a long time for racial justice. But if we legislate moral action, we can, under the right conditions, indirectly affect heartfelt attitudes.

This idea runs counter to the presumption that "you can't legislate morality." Yet attitude change has, in fact, followed desegregation. Consider some correlational findings from this mammoth social experiment:

- Following the Supreme Court decision, the percentage of White Americans favoring integrated schools more than doubled and now includes nearly everyone. (For other examples of old and current racial attitudes, see Module 23.)
- In the 10 years after the Civil Rights Act of 1964, the percentage of White Americans who described their neighborhoods, friends, co-workers, or other students as all-White declined by about

20 percent for each of these measures. Interracial behavior was increasing. During the same period, the percentage of White Americans who said that Blacks should be allowed to live in any neighborhood increased from 65 percent to 87 percent (*ISR Newsletter*, 1975). Attitudes were changing, too.

- More uniform national standards against discrimination were followed by decreasing differences in racial attitudes among people of differing religions, classes, and geographic regions. As Americans came to act more alike, they came to think more alike (Greeley & Sheatsley, 1971; Taylor & others, 1978).

Experiments confirm that positive behavior toward someone fosters liking for that person. Doing a favor for an experimenter or another subject, or tutoring a student, usually increases liking of the person helped (Blanchard & Cook, 1976). It is a lesson worth remembering: If you wish to love someone more, act as if you do.

In 1793, Benjamin Franklin tested the idea that doing a favor engenders liking. As clerk of the Pennsylvania General Assembly, he was disturbed by opposition from another important legislator. So Franklin set out to win him over:

> I did not . . . aim at gaining his favour by paying any servile respect to him but, after some time, took this other method. Having heard that he had in his library a certain very scarce and curious book I wrote a note to him expressing my desire of perusing that book and requesting he would do me the favour of lending it to me for a few days. He sent it immediately and I return'd it in about a week, expressing strongly my sense of the favour. When we next met in the House he spoke to me (which he had never done before), and with great civility; and he ever after manifested a readiness to serve me on all occasions, so that we became great friends and our friendship continued to his death. (Quoted by Rosenzweig, 1972, p. 769)

B RAINWASHING

Many people assume that the most potent social indoctrination comes through *brainwashing*, a term coined to describe what happened to American prisoners of war (POWs) during the 1950s Korean War. Although the "thought-control" program was not nearly as irresistible as this term suggests, the results still were disconcerting. Hundreds of prisoners cooperated with their captors. Twenty-one chose to remain after being granted permission to return to America. And many of those who did return came home believing "although communism won't work in America, I think it's a good thing for Asia" (Segal, 1954).

Edgar Schein (1956) interviewed many of the POWs during their journey home and reported that the captors' methods included a gradual escalation of demands. The captors always started with trivial requests and gradually worked up to more significant ones. "Thus after a prisoner had once been 'trained' to speak or write out trivia, statements on more important issues were demanded." Moreover, they always expected active participation, be it just copying something or participating in group discussions, writing self-criticism, or uttering public confessions. Once a prisoner had spoken or written a statement, he felt an inner need to make his beliefs consistent with his acts. This often drove prisoners to persuade themselves of what they had done. The "start-small-and-build" tactic was an effective application of the foot-in-the-door technique, as it continues to be today in the socialization of terrorists and torturers.

Now let me ask you, before reading further, to play theorist. Ask yourself: Why in these studies and real-life examples did attitudes follow behavior? Why might playing a role or making a speech influence how you feel about something?

The effect of a society's behavior on its racial attitudes suggests the possibility, and the danger, of employing the same idea for political socialization on a mass scale. For many Germans during the 1930s, participation in Nazi rallies, wearing uniforms, demonstrating, and especially the public greeting "Heil Hitler" established a profound inconsistency between behavior and belief. Historian Richard Grunberger (1971) reports that for those who had their doubts about Hitler, "The 'German greeting' was a powerful conditioning device. Having once decided to intone it as an outward token of conformity, many experienced . . . discomfort at the contradiction between their words and their feelings. Prevented from saying what they believed, they tried to establish their psychic equilibrium by consciously making themselves believe what they said" (p. 27).

From these observations—of the effects of role-playing, the foot-in-the-door experience, moral and immoral acts, interracial behavior, and brainwashing—there is a powerful practical lesson: If we want to change ourselves in some important way, it's best not to wait for insight or inspiration. Sometimes we need to act—to begin writing that paper, to make those phone calls, to see that person—even if we don't feel like acting. To strengthen our convictions, it helps to enact them. In this way, faith and love are alike: If we keep them to ourselves, they shrivel. If we enact and express them, they grow.

WHY DOES BEHAVIOR AFFECT OUR ATTITUDES?

Social psychologists agree: Our actions influence our attitudes, sometimes turning foes into friends, captives into collaborators, and doubters into believers. Social psychologists debate: Why?

One idea is that, wanting to make a good impression, people might merely express attitudes that *appear* consistent with their actions. Let's be honest with ourselves. We do care about appearances—why else would we spend so much on clothes, cosmetics, and weight control? To manage the impression we're creating, we might adjust what we say to please rather than offend. To appear consistent we might at times feign attitudes that harmonize with our actions.

But this isn't the whole story. Experiments suggest that some genuine attitude change follows our behavior commitments. Cognitive dissonance theory and self-perception theory offer two explanations.

Activity 9.3

Cognitive dissonance theory, developed by the late Leon Festinger (1957), proposes we feel tension ("dissonance") when two simultaneously accessible thoughts or beliefs ("cognitions") are psychologically inconsistent—as when we decide to say or do something we have mixed feelings about. Festinger argued that to reduce this unpleasant arousal, we often adjust our thinking. This simple idea, and some surprising predictions derived from it, have spawned more than 2,000 studies (Cooper, 1999).

Dissonance theory pertains mostly to discrepancies between behavior and attitudes. We are aware of both. Thus, if we sense some inconsistency, perhaps some hypocrisy, we feel pressure for change. That helps explain why, in a British survey, half of cigarette smokers therefore disagreed with nonsmokers, who nearly all believed that smoking is "really as dangerous as people say" (Eiser & others, 1979). In the United States, too, 40 percent of smokers—and 13 percent of nonsmokers—judge smoking as not very harmful (Saad, 2002).

After the 2003 Iraq War, noted the director of the Program of International Policy Attitudes, some Americans struggled to reduce their "experience of cognitive dissonance" (Kull, 2003). The war's main premise had been that Saddam Hussein, unlike most other brutal dictators whom the world was tolerating, had weapons of mass destruction that threatened U.S. and British security. As the war began, only 38 percent of Americans said the war was justified even if Iraq did not have weapons of mass destruction (Gallup, 2003). Nearly four in five Americans believed their invading troops would find such, and a similar percentage supported the just-launched war (Duffy, 2003; Newport & others, 2003).

When no such weapons were used during the war or found in sufficient quantity to pose a threat, the war-supporting majority experienced dissonance, which was heightened by their awareness of the war's financial and human costs, by scenes of Iraqi chaos in the war's aftermath, by surging anti-American attitudes in Europe and in Muslim countries, and by inflamed pro-terrorist attitudes. (In Indonesia, Jordan, and the Palestinian Authority, majorities now expressed confidence in Osama bin Laden to "do the right thing in world affairs" [Pew, 2003].)

To reduce such dissonance, noted the Program of International Policy Attitudes, some Americans revised their memories of their government's primary rationale for going to war. The reasons now became construed as liberating an oppressed people from tyrannical and genocidal rule, and laying the groundwork for a more peaceful and democratic Middle East. A month after the war, the once-minority opinion was now the majority view: 58 percent of Americans now supported the war even if there were none of the proclaimed weapons of mass destruction (Gallup, 2003). "Whether or not they find weapons of mass destruction doesn't matter," suggested Republican pollster Frank Luntz (2003), "because the rationale for the war changed."

So if we can persuade others to adopt a *new* attitude, their behavior should change accordingly; that's common sense. Or if we can induce people to behave differently, their attitude should change (that's the self-persuasion effect we have been reviewing).

Cognitive dissonance theory assumes that our need to maintain a consistent and positive self-image motivates us to adopt attitudes that justify our actions. Assuming no such motive, **self-perception theory** says simply that when our attitudes are unclear to us, we observe our behaviors and then infer our attitudes from them. As Anne Frank wrote in her diary, "I can watch myself and my actions just like an outsider." Having done so—having noted how we acted toward that person knocking at our door—we infer how we felt about them.

Dissonance theory best explains what happens when our actions openly contradict our well-defined attitudes. When, say, we hurt someone we like, we feel tension, which we might reduce by viewing the other as a jerk. Self-perception theory best explains what happens when we are unsure of our attitudes: We infer them by observing ourselves. If we lend our new neighbors, whom we neither like nor dislike, a cup of sugar, our helpful behavior can lead us to infer that we like them.

In proposing self-perception theory, Daryl Bem (1972) assumed that when we're unsure of our attitudes, we infer them, much as we make inferences about others' attitudes. So it goes as we observe our own behavior. What we freely say and do can be self-revealing. To paraphrase an old saying, How do I know what I think until I hear what I say or see what I do?

The debate over how to explain the attitudes-follow-behavior effect has inspired hundreds of experiments that reveal the conditions under which dissonance and self-perception processes operate. As often happens in science, each theory provides a partial explanation of a complex reality. If only human nature were simple, one simple theory could describe it. Alas, but thankfully, we are not simple creatures, and that is why there are many miles to go before psychological researchers can sleep.

CONCEPTS TO REMEMBER

attitude A belief and feeling that can predispose our response to something or someone.

role A set of norms that defines how people in a given social position ought to behave.

foot-in-the-door phenomenon The tendency for people who have first agreed to a small request to comply later with a larger request.

low-ball technique A tactic for getting people to agree to something. People who agree to an initial request will often still comply when the requester ups the ante. People who receive only the costly request are less likely to comply with it.

cognitive dissonance Tension that arises when one is simultaneously aware of two inconsistent cognitions. For example, dissonance may occur when we realize that we have, with little justification, acted contrary to our attitudes or made a decision favoring one alternative despite reasons favoring another.

self-perception theory The theory that when unsure of our attitudes, we infer them much as would someone observing us—by looking at our behavior and the circumstances under which it occurs.

10

❖

Clinical Intuition

Is Susan suicidal? Should John be committed to a mental hospital? If released, will Tom be a homicide risk? Facing such questions, clinical psychologists struggle to make accurate judgments, recommendations, and predictions.

Such clinical judgments are also *social* judgments and thus vulnerable to illusory correlations, overconfidence bred by hindsight, and self-confirming diagnoses (Maddux, 1993). Let's see why alerting mental health workers to how people form impressions (and *mis*impressions) might help avert serious misjudgments.

*I*LLUSORY CORRELATIONS

Consider the following court transcript in which a seemingly confident psychologist (PSY) is being questioned by an attorney (ATT):

ATT: You asked the defendant to draw a human figure?

PSY: Yes.

ATT: And this is the figure he drew for you? What does it indicate to you about his personality?

PSY: You will note this is a rear view of a male. This is very rare, statistically. It indicates hiding guilt feelings, or turning away from reality.

ATT: And this drawing of a female figure, does it indicate anything to you; and, if so, what?

PSY: It indicates hostility toward women on the part of the subject. The pose, the hands on the hips, the hard-looking face, the stern expression.

ATT: Anything else?

PSY: The size of the ears indicates a paranoid outlook, or hallucinations. Also, the absence of feet indicates feelings of insecurity. (Jeffery, 1964)

The assumption here, as in so many clinical judgments, is that test results reveal something important. Do they? There is a simple way to find out. Have one clinician administer and interpret the test. Have another clinician assess the same person's symptoms. Repeat this process with many people. The proof is in the pudding: Are test outcomes in fact correlated with reported symptoms? Some tests are indeed predictive. Others, such as the preceding Draw-a-Person test, have correlations far weaker than their users suppose (Lilienfeld & others, 2000). Why, then, do clinicians continue to express confidence in uninformative or ambiguous tests?

Pioneering experiments by Loren Chapman and Jean Chapman (1969, 1971) helped us see why. They invited both college students and professional clinicians to study some test performances and diagnoses. If the students or clinicians *expected* a particular association they generally *perceived* it, regardless of whether the data were supportive. For example, clinicians who believed that suspicious people draw peculiar eyes on the Draw-a-Person test perceived such a relationship—even when shown cases in which suspicious people drew peculiar eyes less often than nonsuspicious people. Believing that a relationship existed between two things, they were more likely to notice confirming instances. To believe is to see.

H INDSIGHT

If someone we know commits suicide, how do we react? One common reaction is to think that we, or those close to the person, should have been able to predict and therefore to prevent the suicide: "We should have known!" In hindsight, we can see the suicidal signs and the pleas for help. One experiment gave people a description of a depressed person who later committed suicide. Compared with those not informed of the suicide, those told the person committed suicide were more likely to say they "would have expected" it (Goggin & Range, 1985). Moreover, those told of the suicide viewed the victim's family more negatively. After a tragedy, the I-should-have-known-it-all-along phenomenon can leave family, friends, and therapists feeling guilty.

David Rosenhan (1973) and seven associates provided a striking example of potential error in after-the-fact explanations. To test mental health workers' clinical insights, they each made an appointment with a different mental hospital admissions office and complained of "hearing voices." Apart from giving false names and vocations, they reported their life histories and emotional states honestly and exhibited no further symptoms. Most were diagnosed as schizophrenic and remained hospitalized for two to three weeks. Hospital clinicians then searched for early incidents in the pseudopatients' life histories and hospital behavior that "confirmed" and "explained" the diagnosis. Rosenhan tells of one pseudopatient who truthfully explained to the interviewer that he had a close relationship with his mother but was rather remote from his father during his early childhood. During adolescence and beyond, however, his father became a close friend, while his relationship with his mother cooled. His present relationship with his wife was characteristically close and warm. Apart from occasional angry exchanges, friction was minimal. The children had rarely been spanked.

The interviewer, "knowing" the person suffered from schizophrenia, explained the problem this way:

> This white 39-year-old male . . . manifests a long history of considerable ambivalence in close relationships, which begins in early childhood. A warm relationship with his mother cools during his adolescence. A distant relationship to his father is described as becoming very intense. Affective stability is absent. His attempts to control emotionality with his wife and children are punctuated by angry outbursts and, in the case of the children, spankings. And while he says that he has several good friends, one senses considerable ambivalence embedded in those relationships also.

Rosenhan later told some staff members (who had heard about his controversial experiment but doubted such mistakes could occur in their hospital) that during the next three months one or more pseudopatients would seek admission to their hospital. After the three months, he asked the staff to guess which of the 193 patients admitted during that time were really pseudopatients. Of the 193 new patients, 41 were accused by at least one staff member of being pseudopatients. Actually, there were none.

SELF-CONFIRMING DIAGNOSES

So far we've seen that mental health workers sometimes perceive illusory correlations and that hindsight explanations are often questionable. A third problem with clinical judgment is that people may also supply information that fulfills clinicians' expectations. In a clever series of experiments at the University of Minnesota, Mark Snyder (1984), in collaboration with William Swann and others, gave interviewers some hypotheses to test concerning individuals' traits. To get a feel for their experiments, imagine yourself on a blind date with someone who has been told that you are an uninhibited, outgoing person. To see whether this is true, your date slips questions into the conversation, such as, "Have you ever done anything crazy in front of other people?" As you answer such questions, will your date meet a different "you" than if you were probed for instances when you were shy and retiring?

Snyder and Swann found that people often test for a trait by look-ing for information that confirms it. If they are trying to find out if someone is an extravert, they often solicit instances of extraversion ("What would you do if you wanted to liven things up at a party?"). Testing for introversion, they are more likely to ask, "What factors make it hard for you to really open up to people?" In response, those probed for extraversion seem more sociable, and those probed for introversion seem more shy. Our assumptions help create the kind of people we expect to see.

At Indiana University, Russell Fazio and his colleagues (1981) repro-duced this finding and also discovered that those asked the "extraverted questions" later perceived themselves as actually more outgoing than those asked the introverted questions. Moreover, they really became noticeably more outgoing. An accomplice of the experimenter later met each participant in a waiting room and 70 percent of the time guessed correctly from the person's behavior which condition the person had come from. Likewise, the framing of questions asked of an alleged rape victim—"Did you dance with Peter?" versus "Did Peter dance with you?"—can subtly influence who is perceived as responsible (Semin & De Poot, 1997).

Activity
10.1

In other experiments, Snyder and his colleagues (1982) tried to get people to search for behaviors that would *disconfirm* the trait they were testing. In one experiment, they told the interviewers, "It is relevant and informative to find out ways in which the person . . . may not be like the stereotype." In another experiment Snyder (1981) offered "$25 to the person who develops the set of questions that tell the most about . . . the interviewee." Still, confirmation bias persisted: People resisted choos-ing "introverted" questions when testing for extraversion.

Based on Snyder's experiments, can you see why the behaviors of people undergoing psychotherapy come to fit the theories of their ther-apists (Whitman & others, 1963)? When Harold Renaud and Floyd Estess (1961) conducted life-history interviews of 100 healthy, successful adult men, they were startled to discover that their subjects' childhood expe-riences were loaded with "traumatic events," tense relations with certain people, and bad decisions by their parents—the very factors usually used to explain psychiatric problems. When Freudian therapists go fishing for traumas in early childhood experiences, they often find their hunches confirmed. Thus, surmises Snyder (1981):

The psychiatrist who believes (erroneously) that adult gay males had bad childhood relationships with their mothers may meticulously probe for recalled (or fabricated) signs of tension between their gay clients and their mothers, but neglect to so carefully interrogate their heterosexual clients about their maternal relationships. No doubt, any individual could recall some friction with his or her mother, however minor or isolated the incidents.

Nineteenth-century poet Robert Browning anticipated Snyder's conclusion:

> As is your sort of mind,
> So is your sort of search:
> You'll find
> What you desire.

CLINICAL VERSUS STATISTICAL PREDICTION

Given these hindsight- and diagnosis-confirming tendencies, it will come as no surprise that most clinicians and interviewers express more confidence in their intuitive assessments than in statistical data (such as using past grades and aptitude scores to predict success in graduate or professional school). Yet when researchers pit statistical prediction against intuitive prediction, the statistics usually win. Statistical predictions are indeed unreliable, but human intuition—even expert intuition—is even more unreliable (Faust & Ziskin, 1988; Meehl, 1954; Swets & others, 2000).

Three decades after demonstrating the superiority of statistical over intuitive prediction, Paul Meehl (1986) found the evidence stronger than ever:

> There is no controversy in social science which shows [so many] studies coming out so uniformly in the same direction as this one. . . . When you are pushing 90 investigations, predicting everything from the outcome of football games to the diagnosis of liver disease and when you can hardly come up with a half dozen studies showing even a weak tendency in favor of the clinician, it is time to draw a practical conclusion.

Why then do so many clinicians continue to interpret Rorschach inkblot tests and offer intuitive predictions about parolees, suicide risks, and likelihood of child abuse? Partly out of sheer ignorance, says Meehl, but also partly out of "mistaken conceptions of ethics":

> If I try to forecast something important about a college student, or a criminal, or a depressed patient by inefficient rather than efficient means, meanwhile charging this person or the taxpayer 10 times as much money as I would need to achieve greater predictive accuracy, that is not a sound

ethical practice. That it feels better, warmer, and cuddlier to me as predictor is a shabby excuse indeed.

Such words are shocking. Do Meehl and the other researchers underestimate our intuition? To see why their findings are apparently true, consider the assessment of human potential by graduate admissions interviewers. Dawes (1976) explained why statistical prediction is so often superior to an interviewer's intuition when predicting certain outcomes such as graduate school success:

Activity
10.2

What makes us think that we can do a better job of selection by interviewing (students) for a half hour, than we can by adding together relevant (standardized) variables, such as undergraduate GPA, GRE score, and perhaps ratings of letters of recommendation? The most reasonable explanation to me lies in our overevaluation of our cognitive capacity. And it is really cognitive conceit. Consider, for example, what goes into a GPA. Because for most graduate applicants it is based on at least 3 1/2 years of undergraduate study, it is a composite measure arising from a minimum of 28 courses and possibly, with the popularity of the quarter system, as many as 50. . . . Yet you and I, looking at a folder or interviewing someone for a half hour, are supposed to be able to form a better impression than one based on 3 1/2 years of the cumulative evaluations of 20–40 different professors. . . . Finally, if we do wish to ignore GPA, it appears that the only reason for doing so is believing that the candidate is particularly brilliant even though his or her record may not show it. What better evidence for such brilliance can we have than a score on a carefully devised aptitude test? Do we really think we are better equipped to assess such aptitude than is the Educational Testing Service, whatever its faults?

*I*MPLICATIONS

Professional clinicians are "vulnerable to insidious errors and biases," concludes James Maddux (1993). They

- are frequently the victims of illusory correlation;
- are too readily convinced of their own after-the-fact analyses;
- often fail to appreciate that erroneous diagnoses can be self-confirming; and
- often overestimate the predictive powers of their clinical intuition.

The implications for mental health workers are more easily stated than practiced: Be mindful that clients' verbal agreement with what you say does not prove its validity. Beware of the tendency to see relationships that you expect to see or that are supported by striking examples readily available in your memory. Rely on your notes more than your memory. Recognize that hindsight is seductive: It can lead you to feel overconfident and sometimes to judge yourself too harshly for not having foreseen outcomes. Guard against the tendency to ask questions that assume your preconceptions are correct; consider opposing ideas and test them, too (Garb, 1994).

Research on illusory thinking has implications not only for mental health workers but for all psychologists. What Lewis Thomas (1978) said of biology may as justly be said of psychology:

> The solidest piece of scientific truth I know of, the one thing about which I feel totally confident, is that we are profoundly ignorant about nature. Indeed, I regard this as the major discovery of the past 100 years of biology. . . . It is this sudden confrontation with the depth and scope of ignorance that represents the most significant contribution of 20th century science to the human intellect. We are, at last, facing up to it. In earlier times, we either pretended to understand how things worked or ignored the problem, or simply made up stories to fill the gaps.

Psychology has crept only a little way across the edge of insight into our human condition. Ignorant of their ignorance, some psychologists invent theories to fill gaps in their understanding. Intuitive observation seems to support these theories, even if they are mutually contradictory. Research on illusory thinking therefore leads us to a new humility: It reminds research psychologists why they must test their preconceptions before presenting them as truth. To seek the hard facts, even if they threaten cherished illusions, is the goal of every science.

I am *not* arguing that the scientific method can answer all human questions. There are questions that it cannot address and ways of knowing that it cannot capture. But science *is* one means for examining claims about nature, human nature included. Propositions that imply observable results are best evaluated by systematic observation and experiment— which is the whole point of social psychology. We also need inventive genius, or we may test only trivialities. But whatever unique and enduring insights psychology can offer will be hammered out by research psychologists sorting through competing claims. Science always involves an interplay between intuition and rigorous test, between creative hunch and skepticism.

11

❖

Clinical Therapy: The Powers of Social Cognition

Activity 11.1

If you are a typical college student, you may occasionally feel mildly depressed. Perhaps you have at times felt dissatisfied with your life, discouraged about the future, sad, lacking appetite and energy, unable to concentrate, perhaps even wondering if life is worth it. Maybe disappointing grades have seemed to jeopardize your career goals. Perhaps the breakup of a relationship has left you in despair. At such times, your self-focused brooding only worsens your feelings. For some 10 percent of men and nearly twice that many women, life's down times are not just temporary blue moods but one or more major depressive episodes that last for weeks without any obvious cause.

One of psychology's most intriguing research frontiers concerns the cognitive processes that accompany psychological disorders. What are the memories, attributions, and expectations of depressed, lonely, shy, or illness-prone people? In the case of depression, the most heavily researched disorder, dozens of new studies are providing some answers.

SOCIAL COGNITION AND DEPRESSION

As we all know from experience, depressed people are negative thinkers. They view life through dark-colored glasses. With seriously depressed people—those who are feeling worthless, lethargic, uninterested in friends and family, and unable to sleep or eat normally—the negative thinking becomes self-defeating. Their intensely pessimistic outlook leads them to magnify bad experiences and minimize good ones. A depressed young woman illustrates, "The real me is worthless and inadequate. I can't move forward with my work because I become frozen with doubt" (Burns, 1980, p. 29).

Distortion or Realism?

Are all depressed people unrealistically negative? To find out, Lauren Alloy and Lyn Abramson (1979) studied college students who were either mildly depressed or not depressed. They had the students observe whether their pressing a button was linked with a light coming on. Surprisingly, the depressed students were quite accurate in estimating their degree of control. It was the nondepressives whose judgments were distorted, who exaggerated the extent of their control.

This surprising phenomenon of **depressive realism,** nicknamed the "sadder-but-wiser effect," shows up in various judgments of one's control or skill (Ackermann & DeRubeis, 1991; Alloy & others, 1990). Shelley Taylor (1989, p. 214) explains:

> Normal people exaggerate how competent and well liked they are. Depressed people do not. Normal people remember their past behavior with a rosy glow. Depressed people [unless severely depressed] are more evenhanded in recalling their successes and failures. Normal people describe themselves primarily positively. Depressed people describe both their positive and negative qualities. Normal people take credit for successful outcomes and tend to deny responsibility for failure. Depressed people accept responsibility for both success and failure. Normal people exaggerate the control they have over what goes on around them. Depressed people are less vulnerable to the illusion of control. Normal people believe to an unrealistic degree that the future holds a bounty of good things and few bad things. Depressed people are more realistic in their perceptions of the future. In fact, on virtually every point on which normal people show enhanced self-regard, illusions of control, and unrealistic visions of the future, depressed people fail to show the same biases. "Sadder but wiser" does indeed appear to apply to depression.

Underlying the thinking of depressed people are their attributions of responsibility. Consider: If you fail an exam and blame yourself, you may conclude that you are stupid or lazy and feel depressed. If you attribute the failure to an unfair exam or to other circumstances beyond your control, you may feel angry. In over 100 studies involving 15,000 subjects, depressed people have been more likely than nondepressed people to exhibit a negative **explanatory style** (Figure 11-1; Peterson & Steen, 2002; Sweeney & others, 1986). They are more likely to attribute failure and setbacks to causes that are *stable* ("It's going to last forever"), *global* ("It's going to affect everything I do"), and *internal* ("It's all my fault"). The result of

FIGURE 11-1
Depressive explanatory style. Depression is linked with a negative, pessimistic way of explaining and interpreting failures.

this pessimistic, overgeneralized, self-blaming thinking, say Abramson and her colleagues (1989), is a depressing sense of hopelessness.

Is Negative Thinking a Cause or a Result of Depression?

The cognitive accompaniments of depression raise a chicken-and-egg question: Do depressed moods cause negative thinking, or does negative thinking cause depression?

Depressed Moods Cause Negative Thinking

Without a doubt, our moods definitely color our thinking. When we *feel* happy, we *think* happy. We see and recall a good world. But let our mood turn gloomy, and our thoughts switch to a different track. Off come the rose-colored glasses; on come the dark glasses. Now the bad mood primes our recollections of negative events (Bower, 1987; Johnson & Magaro, 1987). Our relationships seem to sour, our self-images dive, our hopes for the future dim, people's behavior seems more sinister (Brown & Taylor, 1986; Mayer & Salovey, 1987). As depression increases, memories and expectations plummet; when depression lifts, thinking brightens (Barnett & Gotlib, 1988; Kuiper & Higgins, 1985). Thus, *currently* depressed people recall their parents as having been rejecting and punitive. But *formerly* depressed people recall their parents in the same positive terms as do never-depressed people (Lewinsohn & Rosenbaum, 1987). (When you hear depressed people trashing their parents, remember: Moods modify memories.)

Edward Hirt and his colleagues (1992) demonstrated, in a study of Indiana University basketball fans, that even a temporary bad mood induced by defeat can darken our thinking. After the fans were either depressed by watching their team lose or elated by a victory, the researchers asked them to predict the team's future performance, and their own. After a loss, people offered bleaker assessments not only of the team's future but also of their own likely performance at throwing darts, solving anagrams, and getting a date. When things aren't going our way, it may seem as though they never will.

A depressed mood also affects behavior. The person who is withdrawn, glum, and complaining does not elicit joy and warmth in others. Stephen Strack and James Coyne (1983) found that depressed people were realistic in thinking that others didn't appreciate their behavior. Their pessimism and bad moods trigger social rejection (Carver & others, 1994). Depressed behavior can also trigger reciprocal depression in others. College students who have depressed roommates tend to become a little depressed themselves (Burchill & Stiles, 1988; Joiner, 1994; Sanislow & others, 1989). In dating couples, too, depression is often contagious (Katz & others, 1999).

Depressed people are at risk for being divorced, fired, or shunned, thus magnifying their depression (Coyne & others, 1991; Gotlib & Lee, 1989; Sacco & Dunn, 1990). They may also seek out those whose unfavorable views of them verify, and further magnify, their low self-images (Lineham, 1997; Swann & others, 1991).

Negative Thinking Causes Depressed Moods

Depression is natural when experiencing severe stress—losing a job, getting divorced or rejected, suffering physical trauma—anything that disrupts our sense of who we are and why we are worthy human beings (Hamilton & others, 1993; Kendler & others, 1993). Such brooding can be adaptive; insights gained during times of depressed inactivity may later result in better strategies for interacting with the world. But depression-prone people respond to bad events with self-focused rumination and self-blame (Mor & Winquist, 2002; Pyszczynski & others, 1991). Their self-esteem fluctuates more rapidly up with boosts and down with threats (Butler & others, 1994).

Why are some people so affected by *minor* stresses? Evidence suggests that when stress-induced rumination is filtered through a negative explanatory style, the frequent outcome is depression (Robinson & Alloy, 2003). Colin Sacks and Daphne Bugental (1987) asked some young women to get acquainted with a stranger who sometimes acted cold and unfriendly, creating an awkward social situation. Unlike optimistic women, those with a pessimistic explanatory style—who characteristically offer stable, global, and internal attributions for bad events—reacted to the social failure by feeling depressed. Moreover, they then behaved more antagonistically toward the next people they met. Their negative thinking led to a negative mood response, which then led to negative behavior.

Outside the laboratory, studies of children, teenagers, and adults confirm that those with the pessimistic explanatory style are more likely to become depressed when bad things happen. One study monitored university students every six weeks for two and a half years (Alloy & others, 1999). Only 1 percent of those who began college with optimistic thinking styles had a first depressive episode, but 17 percent of those with pessimistic thinking styles did. "A recipe for severe depression is preexisting pessimism encountering failure," notes Martin Seligman (1991, p. 78). Moreover, patients who end therapy no longer feeling depressed but retaining a negative explanatory style tend to relapse as bad events occur (Seligman, 1992). If those with a more optimistic explanatory style relapse, they often recover quickly (Metalsky & others, 1993; Needles & Abramson, 1990).

Researcher Peter Lewinsohn and his colleagues (1985) have assembled these findings into a coherent psychological understanding of depression. In their view, the negative self-image, attributions, and expectations of a depressed person are an essential link in a vicious cycle that is triggered by negative experience—perhaps academic or vocational failure or family conflict or social rejection (Figure 11-2). In those vulnerable to depression, such stresses trigger brooding, self-focused, self-blaming thoughts (Pyszczynski & others, 1991; Wood & others, 1990a, 1990b). Such ruminations create a depressed mood that alters drastically the way a person thinks and acts, which then fuels further negative experiences, self-blame, and depressed mood. In experiments, mildly depressed people's moods brighten when a task diverts their attention to something external (Nix & others, 1995). (Happiness seems best pursued by focusing not on oneself but beyond oneself.) Depression is therefore *both* a cause and a consequence of negative cognitions.

Martin Seligman (1991, 1998, 2002) believes that self-focus and self-blame help explain the near-epidemic levels of depression in the

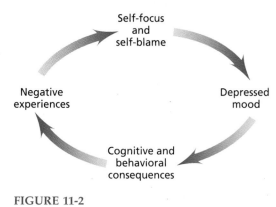

FIGURE 11-2
The vicious cycle of depression.

Western world today. In North America, for example, young adults today are three times as likely as their grandparents to have suffered depression—despite their grandparents' greater years at risk (Cross-National Collaborative Group, 1992; Swindle & others, 2000). Seligman believes that the decline of religion and family, plus the growth of individualism, breeds hopelessness and self-blame when things don't go well. Failed courses, careers, and marriages produce despair when we stand alone, with nothing and no one to fall back on. If, as a macho *Fortune* ad declared, you can "make it on your own," on "your own drive, your own guts, your own energy, your own ambition," then whose fault is it if you *don't* make it? In non-Western cultures, where close-knit relationships and cooperation are the norm, major depression is less common and less tied to guilt and self-blame over perceived personal failure. In Japan, for example, depressed people instead tend to report feeling shame over letting down their family or co-workers (Draguns, 1990).

These insights into the thinking style linked with depression have prompted social psychologists to study thinking patterns associated with other problems. How do those who are plagued with excessive loneliness, shyness, or substance abuse view themselves? How well do they recall their successes and their failures? To what do they attribute their ups and downs? Where is their attention focused—on themselves or on others?

SOCIAL COGNITION AND LONELINESS

If depression is the common cold of psychological disorders, then loneliness is the headache. Loneliness, whether chronic or temporary, is a painful awareness that our social relationships are less numerous or meaningful than we desire. Jenny de Jong-Gierveld (1987) observed in her study of Dutch adults that unmarried and unattached people are more likely to feel lonely. This prompted her to speculate that the modern emphasis on individual fulfillment and the depreciation of marriage and family life may be "loneliness-provoking" (as well as depression-provoking). Job-related mobility also makes for fewer long-term family and social ties and increased loneliness (Dill & Anderson, 1999).

But loneliness need not coincide with aloneness. One can feel lonely in the middle of a party. "In America, there is loneliness but no solitude," lamented Mary Pipher (2002). "There are crowds but no community." In Los Angeles, observed her daughter, "There are 10 million people around me but nobody knows my name." And one can be utterly alone—as I am while writing these words in the solitude of an isolated turret office at a British university 5,000 miles from home—

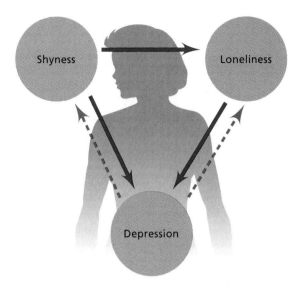

FIGURE 11-3
The interplay of chronic shyness, loneliness, and depression. Solid arrows indicate primary cause-effect direction. **Source:** Summarized by Jody Dill & Craig Anderson (1999).

without feeling lonely. To feel lonely is to feel excluded from a group, unloved by those around you, unable to share your private concerns, or different and alienated from those in your surroundings (Beck & Young, 1978; Davis & Franzoi, 1986).

Like depressed people, chronically lonely people seem caught in a vicious cycle of self-defeating social cognitions and social behaviors. They have some of the negative explanatory style of the depressed; they perceive their interactions as making a poor impression, blame themselves for their poor social relationships, and see most things as beyond their control (Anderson & others, 1994; Christensen & Kashy, 1998; Snodgrass, 1987). Moreover, they perceive others in negative ways. When paired with a stranger of the same gender or with a first-year college roommate, lonely students are more likely to perceive the other person negatively (Jones & others, 1981; Wittenberg & Reis, 1986). As Figure 11-3 illustrates, loneliness, depression, and shyness sometimes feed one another.

These negative views may both reflect and color the lonely person's experience. Believing in their social unworthiness and feeling pessimistic about others inhibit lonely people from acting to reduce their loneliness. Lonely people often find it hard to introduce themselves, make phone calls, and participate in groups (Nurmi & others, 1996, 1997; Rook, 1984;

Spitzberg & Hurt, 1987). Being slow to self-disclose, they disdain those who disclose too much too soon (Rotenberg, 1997). They tend to be self-conscious and low in self-esteem (Check & Melchior, 1990; Vaux, 1988). When talking with a stranger, they spend more time talking about themselves and take less interest in their conversational partners than do nonlonely people (Jones & others, 1982). After such conversations, the new acquaintances often come away with more negative impressions of the lonely people (Jones & others, 1983).

SOCIAL COGNITION AND ANXIETY

Being interviewed for a much-wanted job, dating someone for the first time, stepping into a roomful of strangers, performing before an important audience, or (the most common phobia) giving a speech can make almost anyone feel anxious. Some people, especially those who are shy or easily embarrassed, feel anxious in almost any situation in which they might be evaluated. For these people, anxiety is more a trait than a temporary state.

What causes us to feel anxious in social situations? Why are some people shackled in the prison of their own shyness? Barry Schlenker and Mark Leary (1982, 1985; Leary & Kowalski, 1995) answer these questions by applying self-presentation theory. *Self-presentation theory* assumes that we are eager to present ourselves in ways that make a good impression. The implications for social anxiety are straightforward: *We feel anxious when we are motivated to impress others but doubt our ability to do so.* This simple principle helps explain a variety of research findings, each of which may ring true in your own experience. We feel most anxious when we are

- with powerful, high-status people—people whose impressions of us matter; in an evaluative context, such as when making a first impression on the parents of one's fiancé;
- self-conscious (as shy people often are) and our attention is focused on ourselves and how we are coming across;
- focused on something central to our self-image, as when a college professor presents ideas before peers at a professional convention; or
- in novel or unstructured situations, such as a first school dance or first formal dinner, where we are unsure of the social rules.

The natural tendency in all such situations is to be cautiously self-protective: to talk less; to avoid topics that reveal one's ignorance; to be guarded about oneself; to be unassertive, agreeable, and smiling.

Shyness is a form of social anxiety characterized by self-consciousness and worry about what others think (Anderson & Harvey, 1988; Asendorpf, 1987; Carver & Scheier, 1986). Compared with unshy people, shy, self-conscious people (whose numbers include many adolescents) see incidental events as somehow relevant to themselves (Fenigstein, 1984; Fenigstein & Vanable, 1992). Shown someone they think is interviewing them live (actually a videotaped interviewer), they perceive the interviewer as less accepting and interested in them (Pozo & others, 1991).

Shy, anxious people also overpersonalize situations, a tendency that breeds anxious concern and, in extreme cases, paranoia. They also overestimate the extent to which other people are watching and evaluating them. If their hair won't comb right or they have a facial blemish, they assume everyone else notices and judges them accordingly.

To reduce social anxiety, some people turn to alcohol. Alcohol lowers anxiety as it reduces self-consciousness (Hull & Young, 1983). Thus, chronically self-conscious people are especially likely to drink following a failure. If recovering from alcoholism, they are more likely than those low in self-consciousness to relapse when they again experience stress or failure.

Symptoms as diverse as anxiety and alcohol abuse can also serve a self-handicapping function. Labeling oneself as anxious, shy, depressed, or under the influence of alcohol can provide an excuse for failure (Snyder & Smith, 1986). Behind a barricade of symptoms, the person's ego stands secure. "Why don't I date? Because I'm shy, so people don't easily get to know the real me." The symptom is an unconscious strategic ploy to explain away negative outcomes.

What if we were to remove the need for such a ploy by providing people with a handy alternative explanation for their anxiety and therefore for possible failure? Would a shy person no longer need to be shy? That is precisely what Susan Brodt and Philip Zimbardo (1981) found when they brought shy and not-shy college women to the laboratory and had them converse with a handsome male who posed as another participant. Before the conversation, the women were cooped up in a small chamber and blasted with loud noise. Some of the shy women (but not others) were told that the noise would leave them with a pounding heart, a common symptom of social anxiety. Thus when these women later talked with the man, they could attribute their pounding hearts and any conversational difficulties to the noise, not to their shyness or social inadequacy. Compared with the shy women who were not given this handy explanation for their pounding hearts, these women were no longer so shy. They talked fluently once the conversation got going and asked questions of the man. In fact, unlike the other shy women (whom the man could easily spot as shy), these women were to him indistinguishable from the not-shy women.

S OCIAL-PSYCHOLOGICAL APPROACHES TO TREATMENT

So far, we have considered patterns of thinking that are linked with problems in living, ranging from serious depression to extreme shyness to physical illness. Do these maladaptive thought patterns suggest any treatments? There is no social-psychological therapy. But therapy is a social encounter, and social psychologists have suggested how their principles might be integrated into existing treatment techniques (Forsyth & Leary, 1997; Strong & others, 1992). Consider two approaches.

Inducing Internal Change Through External Behavior

In Module 9, we reviewed a broad range of evidence for a simple but powerful principle: Our actions affect our attitudes. The roles we play, the things we say and do, and the decisions we make influence who we are.

Consistent with this attitudes-follow-behavior principle, several psychotherapy techniques prescribe action. Behavior therapists try to shape behavior and assume that inner dispositions will tag along after the behavior changes. Assertiveness training employs the foot-in-the-door procedure. The individual first role-plays assertiveness in a supportive context, then gradually becomes assertive in everyday life. Rational-emotive therapy assumes that we generate our own emotions; clients receive "homework" assignments to talk and act in new ways that will generate new emotions, such as to challenge an overbearing relative or to stop telling yourself you're an unattractive person and ask someone out. Self-help groups subtly induce participants to behave in new ways in front of the group—to express anger, cry, act with high self-esteem, express positive feelings.

Experiments confirm that what we say about ourselves can affect how we feel. In one experiment, students were induced to write self-laudatory essays (Mirels & McPeek, 1977). These students, more than others who wrote essays about a current social issue, later expressed higher self-esteem when rating themselves privately for a different experimenter. In several more experiments, Edward Jones and his associates (1981; Rhodewalt & Agustsdottir, 1986) influenced students to present themselves to an interviewer in either self-enhancing or self-deprecating ways. Again, the public displays—whether upbeat or downbeat—carried over to later private responses on a test of actual self-esteem. Saying is believing, even when we talk about ourselves. This was especially true when the students were made to feel responsible for how they presented themselves. So, the most therapeutic commitments are both uncoerced and effortful.

Breaking Vicious Cycles

If depression, loneliness, and social anxiety maintain themselves through a vicious cycle of negative experiences, negative thinking, and self-defeating behavior, it should be possible to break the cycle at any of several points—by changing the environment, by training the person to behave more constructively, by reversing negative thinking. And it is. Several different therapy methods help free people from depression's vicious cycle.

Social Skills Training

Depression, loneliness, and shyness are not just problems in someone's mind. To be around a depressed person for any length of time can be irritating and depressing. As lonely and shy people suspect, they may indeed come across poorly in social situations. In these cases, social skills training may help. By observing and then practicing new behaviors in safe situations, the person may develop the confidence to behave more effectively in other situations.

As the person begins to enjoy the rewards of behaving more skillfully, a more positive self-perception develops. Frances Haemmerlie and Robert Montgomery (1982, 1984, 1986) demonstrated this in several heartwarming studies with shy, anxious college students. Those who are inexperienced and nervous around those of the other sex may say to themselves, "I don't date much, so I must be socially inadequate, so I shouldn't try reaching out to anyone." To reverse this negative sequence, Haemmerlie and Montgomery enticed such students into pleasant interactions with people of the other sex.

In one experiment, college men completed social anxiety questionnaires and then came to the laboratory on two different days. Each day they enjoyed 12-minute conversations with each of six young women. The men thought the women were also participants. Actually, the women were confederates who had been asked to carry on a natural, positive, friendly conversation with each of the men.

The effect of these two and a half hours of conversation was remarkable. As one participant wrote afterward, "I had never met so many girls that I could have a good conversation with. After a few girls, my confidence grew to the point where I didn't notice being nervous like I once did." Such comments were supported by a variety of measures. Unlike men in a control condition, those who experienced the conversations reported considerably less female-related anxiety when retested one week and six months later. Placed alone in a room with an attractive female stranger, they also became much more likely to start a conversation. Outside the laboratory they actually began occasional dating.

Haemmerlie and Montgomery note that not only did all this occur without any counseling but it may very well have occurred *because* there was no counseling. Having behaved successfully on their own, the men could now perceive themselves as socially competent. Although seven months later the researchers did debrief the participants, by that time the men had presumably enjoyed enough social success to maintain their internal attributions for success. "Nothing succeeds like success," concluded Haemmerlie (1987)—"as long as there are no external factors present that the client can use as an excuse for that success!"

Explanatory Style Therapy

The vicious cycles that maintain depression, loneliness, and shyness can be broken by social skills training, by positive experiences that alter self-perceptions, *and* by changing negative thought patterns. Some people have social skills, but their experiences with hypercritical friends and family have convinced them they do not. For such people it may be enough to help them reverse their negative beliefs about themselves and their futures. Among the cognitive therapies with this aim is an *explanatory style therapy* proposed by social psychologists (Abramson, 1988; Gillham & others, 2000; Greenberg & others, 1992).

One such program taught depressed college students to change their typical attributions. Mary Anne Layden (1982) first explained the advantages of making attributions more like those of the typical nondepressed person (by accepting credit for successes and seeing how circumstances can make things go wrong). After assigning a variety of tasks, she helped the students see how they typically interpreted success and failure. Then came the treatment phase: Layden instructed them to keep a diary of daily successes and failures, noting how they contributed to their own successes and noting external reasons for their failures. When retested after a month of this attributional retraining and compared with an untreated control group, their self-esteem had risen and their attributional style had become more positive. The more their explanatory style improved, the more their depression lifted. By changing their attributions, they had changed their emotions.

Having emphasized what changed behavior and thought patterns can accomplish, we do well to remind ourselves of their limits. Social skills training and positive thinking cannot transform us into consistent winners who are loved and admired by everyone. Furthermore, temporary depression, loneliness, and shyness are perfectly appropriate responses to profoundly sad events. It is when such feelings exist chronically and without any discernible cause that there is reason for concern and a need to change the self-defeating thoughts and behaviors.

CONCEPTS TO REMEMBER

depressive realism The tendency of mildly depressed people to make accurate rather than self-serving judgments, attributions, and predictions.

explanatory style One's habitual way of explaining life events. A negative, pessimistic, depressive explanatory style attributes failure to stable, global, and internal causes.

PART THREE

❖

Social Influence

Social psychologists study not only how we think about one another—our topic in the preceding modules—but also how we influence and relate to one another. In Modules 12 through 21 we therefore probe social psychology's central concern: the powers of social influence.

What are these unseen social forces that push and pull us? How powerful are they? Research on social influence helps illuminate the invisible strings by which our social worlds move us about. This unit reveals these subtle powers, especially the cultural sources of gender attitudes, the forces of social conformity, the routes to persuasion, and the consequences of being with others and participating in groups.

When we see how these influences operate in everyday situations, we can better understand why people feel and act as they do. And we can ourselves become less vulnerable to unwanted manipulation and more adept at pulling our own strings.

MODULE

12

❖

Human Nature and Cultural Diversity

How do we humans differ? How are we alike? These questions are central to a world where social diversity has become, as historian Arthur Schlesinger (1991) said, "the explosive problem of our times." In a world ripped apart by ethnic, cultural, and gender differences, can we learn to accept our diversity, value our cultural identities, *and* recognize the extent of our human kinship? I believe we can. To see why, let's consider the evolutionary and cultural roots of our humanity.

*E*VOLUTION AND BEHAVIOR

In many important ways, we are more alike than different. As members of one great family with common ancestors, we share not only a common biology but also common behavior tendencies. Each of us perceives the world, feels thirst, and develops language through identical mechanisms. We prefer sweet tastes to sour and divide the visual spectrum into similar colors. We and our kin across the globe all know how to read one another's frowns and smiles.

Humans everywhere are intensely social creatures. We join groups, conform, and recognize distinctions of social status. We return favors, punish offenses, and grieve a child's death. As children, beginning at about 8 months of age, we displayed fear of strangers, and as adults we favor members of our own groups. Confronted by those with dissimilar attitudes or attributes, we react warily or negatively. Alien scientists

127

could drop in anywhere and find humans feasting and dancing, laughing and crying, singing and worshiping. Everywhere, humans prefer living with others—in families and communal groups—to living alone. Anthropologist Donald Brown (1991, 2000) has, in fact, identified several hundred such universal behavior and language patterns. To sample among just those beginning with *v*, all human societies have verbs, violence, visiting, and vowels. Such commonalities define our shared human nature. We're indeed all kin beneath the skin.

The universal behaviors that define human nature arise from our biological similarity. Some 100,000 years ago, most anthropologists believe, we humans were all Africans. Feeling the urge to "be fruitful and multiply, and fill the earth," many of our ancestors moved out of Africa, displacing cousins such as Europe's Neanderthals. In adapting to their new environments, these early humans developed differences that, measured on anthropological scales, are relatively recent and superficial. Those who stayed in Africa had darker skin pigment— "sunscreen for the tropics" (Pinker, 2002). Those who went far north of the equator, for example, evolved lighter skins capable of synthesizing vitamin D in less direct sunlight. Still, historically, we all are Africans.

Indeed, we were Africans recently enough, when our ancestors had dwindled to a small number, that "there has not been much time to accumulate many new versions of the genes," notes Steven Pinker (2002, p. 143). Thus, we humans are strikingly similar, like members of one tribe. We are more numerous than chimpanzees, but chimps are more genetically varied.

To explain the traits of our species, and all species, the British naturalist Charles Darwin (1859) proposed an evolutionary process. Follow the genes, he advised. As organisms vary, nature selects those best equipped to survive and reproduce in particular environments. Genes that predisposed traits that increased the odds of leaving descendants became more abundant. In the snowy Arctic environment, for example, polar bear genes programming a thick coat of camouflaging white fur have won the genetic competition and now predominate. This process of **natural selection,** long an organizing principle of biology, recently has become an important principle for psychology as well.

Evolutionary psychology studies how natural selection predisposes not just physical traits suited to particular contexts—polar bear coats, bats' sonar, humans' color vision—but psychological traits and social behaviors that enhance the preservation and spread of one's genes. We humans are the way we are, say evolutionary psychologists, because among our ancestors' descendants, nature selected those who had our traits—those who, for example, preferred nutritious, energy-providing foods and who disliked bitter, sour, often toxic tastes. Those who lacked such preferences were less likely to survive to contribute their genes to posterity. As mobile gene machines, we carry the legacy of our ancestors' adaptive preferences. We long for whatever helped them survive, reproduce, and nurture their offspring to survive and reproduce. Biologically speaking, one major purpose of life is to leave grandchildren. "The purpose of the heart is to pump blood," notes evolutionary psychologist David Barash (2003). "The brain's purpose," he adds, is to direct our organs and our behavior "in a way that maximizes our evolutionary success. That's it."

The evolutionary perspective highlights our universal human nature. We not only maintain certain food preferences, we also share answers to social questions such as: Whom should I trust, and fear? Whom should I help? When, and with whom, should I mate? To whom should I defer, and whom may I control? Evolutionary psychologists contend that our emotional and behavioral answers to these questions are the same answers that worked for our ancestors.

Because these social tasks are common to people everywhere, humans everywhere tend to agree on the answers. For example, all humans rank others by authority and status. And all have ideas about economic justice (Fiske, 1992). Evolutionary psychologists highlight these universal characteristics that have evolved through natural selection. Cultures, however, provide the specific rules for working out these elements of social life.

CULTURE AND BEHAVIOR

Perhaps our most important similarity, the hallmark of our species, is our capacity to learn and adapt. Evolution has prepared us to live creatively in a changing world and to adapt to environments from equatorial jungles to arctic icefields. Compared with bees, birds, and bulldogs, nature has us on a looser genetic leash. Ironically, therefore, our shared human biology enables our cultural diversity. It enables those in one **culture** to value promptness, welcome frankness, or accept premarital sex, while those in another culture do not. Whether we equate beauty with slimness or shapeliness depends on when and where we live. Whether we define social justice as equality (all receive the same) or as equity (those who produce more receive more) depends on whether Marxism or capitalism shapes our ideology. Whether we tend to be expressive or reserved, casual or formal, hinges partly on whether we have spent our lives in an African, a European, or an Asian culture.

Evolutionary psychology incorporates environmental influences. We humans have been selected not only for big brains and biceps but also for social competence. We come prepared to learn language and to bond and cooperate with others in securing food, caring for young, and protecting ourselves. Nature therefore predisposes us to learn, whatever culture we are born into (Fiske & others, 1998). The cultural perspective, while acknowledging that all behavior requires our evolved genes, highlights human adaptability.

Cultural Diversity

The diversity of our languages, customs, and expressive behaviors suggests that much of our behavior is socially programmed, not hardwired. Genes are not fixed blueprints: their expression depends on the environment (Lickliter & Honeycutt, 2003). Thus, the genetic leash is long. As sociologist Ian Robertson (1987) has noted:

> Americans eat oysters but not snails. The French eat snails but not locusts. The Zulus eat locusts but not fish. The Jews eat fish but not pork. The Hindus eat pork but not beef. The Russians eat beef but not snakes. The Chinese eat snakes but not people. The Jalé of New Guinea find people delicious. (p. 67)

If we all lived as homogeneous ethnic groups in separate regions of the world, as some people still do, cultural diversity would be less relevant to our daily living. In Japan, where there are 127 million people, of whom 126 million are Japanese, internal cultural differences are minimal compared with those found in Los Angeles, where the public schools have coped with 82 different languages (Iyer, 1993).

Increasingly, cultural diversity surrounds us. More and more we live in a global village, connected to our fellow villagers by e-mail, jumbo jets, and international trade. Cultural diversity exists within nations, too. The United Kingdom, Canada, the United States, and Australia each offer a national culture, with a prevalent language, national media, national holidays, and a democratic political system. But they also offer distinct regional cultures marked by clustered immigrant populations, various languages, and distinct climates, dialects, and values. In the United States, for example, New Englanders' valuing of broadmindedness and autonomy ("Live Free or Die" is the New Hampshire motto) differs from Southerners' greater valuing of warmth, cooperation, and honor (Plaut & others, 2002).

Migration and refugee evacuations are mixing cultures more than ever. "East is East and West is West, and never the twain shall meet," wrote the nineteenth-century British author Rudyard Kipling. But today, East and West, and North and South, meet all the time. Italy is home to many Albanians, Germany to Turks, England to Pakistanis, and the result is both friendship and hate crimes. For North Americans and Australians, too, one's country is more and more a mingling of cultures.

One in six Canadians is an immigrant. As we work, play, and live with people from diverse cultural backgrounds, it helps to understand how our cultures influence us and to appreciate important ways in which cultures differ. In a world divided by conflicts, genuine peace requires respect for differences and appreciation for similarities.

To realize the impact of our own culture, we need only confront another one. American males may feel uncomfortable when Middle Eastern heads of state greet the U.S. president with a kiss on the cheek. A German student, accustomed to speaking rarely to "Herr Professor," considers it strange that at my institution most faculty office doors are open and students stop by freely. An Iranian student on her first visit to an American McDonald's restaurant fumbles around in her paper bag looking for the eating utensils until she sees the other customers eating their french fries with, of all things, their hands. In many areas of the globe, your best manners and mine are serious breaches of etiquette. Foreigners visiting Japan often struggle to master the rules of the social game— when to take their shoes off, how to pour the tea, when to give and open gifts, how to act toward someone higher or lower in the social hierarchy.

As etiquette rules illustrate, all cultures have their accepted ideas about appropriate behavior. We often view these social expectations, or **norms,** as a negative force that imprisons people in a blind effort to perpetuate tradition. Norms do restrain and control us—so successfully and so subtly that we hardly sense their existence. Like fish in the ocean, each of us is so immersed in our cultures that we must leap out of them to understand their influence. "When we see other Dutch people behaving in what foreigners would call a Dutch way," note Dutch psychologists Willem Koomen and Anton Dijker (1997), "we often do not realize that the behavior is typically Dutch."

There is no better way to learn the norms of our culture than to visit another culture and see that its members do things *that* way, whereas we do them *this* way. When living in Scotland, I acknowledged to my children that, yes, Europeans eat meat with the fork facing down in the left hand. "But we Americans consider it good manners to cut the meat and then transfer the fork to the right hand. I admit it's inefficient. But it's the way *we* do it."

To those who don't accept them, such norms may seem arbitrary and confining. To most in the Western world, the Muslim woman's veil seems arbitrary and confining, but not to most in Muslim cultures. But just as a play moves smoothly when the actors know their lines, so social behavior occurs smoothly when people know what to expect. Norms grease the social machinery. In unfamiliar situations, when the norms may be unclear, we monitor others' behavior and adjust our own accordingly. An individualist visiting a collectivist culture, or vice versa, may at first feel anxious and self-conscious (see Module 12). In familiar situations, our words and acts come effortlessly.

Cultures also vary in their norms for expressiveness and personal space. To someone from a relatively formal northern European culture, a person whose roots are in an expressive Mediterranean culture may seem "warm, charming, inefficient, and time-wasting." To the Mediterranean person, the northern European may seem "efficient, cold, and overconcerned with time" (Triandis, 1981). Latin American business executives who arrive late for a dinner engagement may be mystified by how obsessed their North American counterparts are with punctuality.

Personal space is a sort of portable bubble or buffer zone that we like to maintain between ourselves and others. As the situation changes, the bubble varies in size. With strangers we maintain a fairly large personal space, keeping a distance of 4 feet or more between us. On uncrowded buses, or in restrooms or libraries, we protect our space and respect others' space. We let friends come closer, often within 2 or 3 feet.

Individuals differ: Some people prefer more personal space than others (Smith, 1981; Sommer, 1969; Stockdale, 1978). Groups differ, too: Adults maintain more distance than children. Men keep more distance from one another than do women. For reasons unknown, cultures near the equator prefer less space and more touching and hugging. Thus the British and Scandinavians prefer more distance than the French and Arabs; North Americans prefer more space than Latin Americans.

To see the effect of encroaching on another's personal space, play space invader. Stand or sit a foot or so from a friend and strike up a conversation. Does the person fidget, look away, back off, show other signs of discomfort? These are the signs of arousal noted by space-invading researchers (Altman & Vinsel, 1978).

Cultural Similarity

Thanks to human adaptability, cultures differ. Yet beneath the veneer of cultural differences, cross-cultural psychologists see "an essential universality" (Lonner, 1980). As members of one species, the processes that underlie our differing behaviors are much the same everywhere. Humans even have cross-cultural norms for conducting war. In the midst of killing one's enemy, there are agreed-upon rules. You are to wear identifiable uniforms, surrender with a gesture of submission, and humanely treat prisoners. (If you can't kill them before they surrender, you should feed them thereafter.) When Iraqi forces violated these norms by showing surrender flags and then attacking and by dressing soldiers as liberated civilians to set up ambushes, a U.S. military spokesperson complained that "Both of these actions are among the most serious violations of the laws of war" (Clarke, 2003).

Although norms vary by culture, humans hold some norms in common. Best known is the taboo against incest: Parents are not to have sexual relations with their children, nor siblings with one another. Although the taboo apparently is violated more often than psychologists once believed, the norm is still universal. Every society disapproves of incest. Given the biological penalties for inbreeding, evolutionary psychologists can easily understand why people everywhere are predisposed against incest.

Roger Brown (1965, 1987; Kroger & Wood, 1992) noticed another universal norm. Wherever people form status hierarchies, they also talk to higher-status people in the respectful way they often talk to strangers. And they talk to lower-status people in the more familiar, first-name way they speak to friends. Patients call their physician "Dr. So and So"; the physician often replies using the patients' first names. Students and professors typically address one another in a similarly non-mutual way.

Most languages have two forms of the English pronoun "you": a respectful form and a familiar form (for example, *Sie* and *du* in German, *vous* and *tu* in French, *usted* and *tu* in Spanish). People typically use the familiar form with intimates and subordinates (not only with close friends and family members but also in speaking to children and dogs). A German child receives a boost when strangers begin addressing the child as "Sie" instead of "du."

This first aspect of Brown's universal norm—that *forms of address communicate not only social distance but also social status*—correlates with a second aspect: *Advances in intimacy are usually suggested by the higher-status person.* In Europe, where most twosomes begin a relationship with the polite, formal "you" and may eventually progress to the more intimate "you," someone obviously has to initiate the increased intimacy. Whom do you suppose does so? On some congenial occasion, the elder or richer or more distinguished of the two may say, "Why don't we say du to one another?"

This norm extends beyond language to every type of advance in intimacy. It is more acceptable to borrow a pen from or put a hand on the shoulder of one's intimates and subordinates than to behave in such a casual way with strangers or superiors. Similarly, the president of my college invites faculty to his home before they invite him to theirs. In general, then, the higher-status person is the pacesetter in the progression toward intimacy.

So, some norms are culture-specific, others are universal. The force of culture appears in varying norms and also in the roles that people play. Cultures everywhere influence people by engaging them in playing certain roles. Module 9 illustrated a powerful phenomenon: Playing a role often leads people to internalize their behavior. Acting becomes believing. So let's consider how roles vary within and across cultures.

*C*ONCEPTS TO REMEMBER

natural selection   The evolutionary process by which nature selects traits that best enable organisms to survive and reproduce in particular environmental niches.

evolutionary psychology   The study of the evolution of behavior using principles of natural selection.

culture   The enduring behaviors, ideas, attitudes, and traditions shared by a large group of people and transmitted from one generation to the next.

norms   Rules for accepted and expected behavior. Norms *prescribe* "proper" behavior. (In a different sense of the word, norms also *describe* what most others do—what is *normal*.)

personal space   The buffer zone we like to maintain around our bodies. Its size depends on our familiarity with whoever is near us.

MODULE

13

❖

Gender, Genes, and Culture

There are many obvious dimensions of human diversity—height, weight, hair color, to name just a few. But for people's self-concepts and social relationships, the two dimensions that matter most, and that people first attune to, are race and, especially, sex (Stangor & others, 1992).

Later, we will consider how race and sex affect the way others regard and treat us. For now, let's consider **gender**—the characteristics people associate with male and female. What behaviors *are* universally characteristic and expected of males? Of females?

"Of the 46 chromosomes in the human genome, 45 are unisex," notes Judith Rich Harris (1998). Females and males are therefore similar in many physical traits, such as age of sitting, teething, and walking. They also are alike in many psychological traits, such as overall vocabulary, creativity, intelligence, self-esteem, and happiness. So shall we conclude that men and women are essentially the same, except for a few anatomical oddities that hardly matter apart from special occasions?

Actually, there are some differences, and it is these differences, not the many similarities, that capture attention and make news. In both science and everyday life, differences excite interest. Compared with males, the average female

- has 70 percent more fat, 40 percent less muscle, and is five inches shorter;
- is more sensitive to smells and sounds; and
- is doubly vulnerable to anxiety disorders and depression.

Compared with females, the average male is

- slower to enter puberty (by two years) but quicker to die (by five years);
- three times more likely to commit suicide, four times more likely to be taking Ritalin for ADHD, five times more likely to become alcoholic, and six times more likely to be killed by lightning; and
- more likely to be capable of wiggling the ears.

During the 1970s, many scholars worried that studies of such gender differences might reinforce stereotypes. Although the findings confirm some stereotypes of women—as less physically aggressive, more nurturant, and more socially sensitive—those are traits that many feminists celebrate and most people prefer (Prentice & Carranza, 2002; Swim, 1994). Small wonder, then, that most people rate their beliefs and feelings regarding "women" as more *favorable* than their feelings regarding "men" (Eagly, 1994; Haddock & Zanna, 1994).

GENDER DIFFERENCES

Let's compare men's and women's social connections, dominance, aggressiveness, and sexuality. Having described these differences, we can then consider how the evolutionary and cultural perspectives might explain them. Do gender differences reflect tendencies predisposed by natural selection? Are they culturally constructed—a reflection of the roles that men and women often play and the situations in which they act? Or do both genes and culture bend the genders?

Independence Versus Connectedness

Individual men display outlooks and behavior that vary from fierce competitiveness to caring nurturance. So do individual women. Without denying that, psychologists Nancy Chodorow (1978, 1989), Jean Baker Miller (1986), and Carol Gilligan and her colleagues (1982, 1990) have contended that women more than men give priority to close, intimate relationships.

Compared with boys, girls talk more intimately and play less aggressively, notes Eleanor Maccoby (2002) from her decades of research on gender development. And as they each interact with their own gender, their differences grow.

As adults, women in individualist cultures describe themselves in more relational terms, welcome more help, experience more relationship-linked emotions, and are more attuned to others' relationships (Addis & Mahalik, 2003; Gabriel & Gardner, 1999; Tamres & others, 2002; Watkins

& others, 1998, 2003). In conversation, men more often focus on tasks and on connections with large groups, women on personal relationships (Tannen, 1990). When on the phone, women's conversations with friends last longer (Smoreda & Licoppe, 2000). When on the computer, women spend more time sending e-mails, in which they express more emotion (Crabtree, 2002; Thomson & Murachver, 2001). When in groups, women share more of their lives and offer more support (Dindia & Allen, 1992; Eagly, 1987). When facing stress, men tend to respond with "fight or flight"; often, their response to a threat is combat. In nearly all studies, notes Shelley Taylor (2002), stressed women more often "tend and befriend"; they turn to friends and family for support. Among first-year college students, 5 in 10 males and 7 in 10 females say it is *very* important to "help others who are in difficulty" (Sax & others, 2002).

In general, report Felicia Pratto and her colleagues (1997), men gravitate disproportionately to jobs that enhance inequalities (prosecuting attorney, corporate advertising); women gravitate to jobs that reduce inequalities (public defender, advertising work for a charity). Studies of 640,000 people's job preferences reveal some tendency for men more than women to value earnings, promotion, challenge, and power, and for women more than men to value good hours, personal relationships, and opportunities to help others (Konrad & others, 2000). Indeed, in most of the North American caregiving professions, such as social worker, teacher, and nurse, women outnumber men. Women also seem more charitable: Among individuals leaving estates worth more than $5 million, 48 percent of women and 35 percent of men make a charitable bequest, and women's colleges have unusually supportive alumni (National Council for Research on Women, 1994).

Women's connections as mothers, daughters, sisters, and grandmothers bind families (Rossi & Rossi, 1990). Women spend more time caring for both preschoolers and aging parents (Eagly & Crowley, 1986). Compared with men, they buy three times as many gifts and greeting cards, write two to four times as many personal letters, and make 10 to 20 percent more long distance calls to friends and family (Putnam, 2000). Asked to provide photos that portray who they are, women include more photos of parents and of themselves with others (Clancy & Dollinger, 1993). For women, especially, a sense of mutual support is crucial to marital satisfaction (Acitelli & Antonucci, 1994).

When surveyed, women are far more likely to describe themselves as having **empathy,** or being able to feel what another feels—to rejoice with those who rejoice and weep with those who weep. Although to a lesser extent, the empathy difference extends to laboratory studies. Shown slides or told stories, girls react with more empathy (Hunt, 1990). Given upsetting experiences in the laboratory or in real life, women more than men express empathy for others enduring similar experiences (Batson & others, 1996). Women are more likely to cry or report feeling distressed at another's distress (Eisenberg & Lennon, 1983). Twelve percent of American men, and 43 percent of women, report having cried as a result of the war in Iraq (Gallup Organization, 2003). Autism, which is a deficiency in empathy, is mostly a disorder of males.

All this helps explain why, compared to friendships with men, both men and women report friendships with women to be more intimate, enjoyable, and nurturing (Rubin, 1985; Sapadin, 1988). When they want empathy and understanding, someone to whom they can disclose their joys and hurts, both men and women usually turn to women.

One explanation for this male-female empathy difference is that women tend to outperform men at reading others' emotions. In her analysis of 125 studies of men's and women's sensitivity to nonverbal cues, Judith Hall (1984) discerned that women are generally superior at decoding others' emotional messages. For example, shown a 2-second silent film clip of the face of an upset woman, women guess more accurately whether she is criticizing someone or discussing her divorce.

Women also are more skilled at *expressing* emotions nonverbally, reports Hall. This is especially so for positive emotion, report Erick Coats and Robert Feldman (1996). They had people talk about times they had been happy, sad, and angry. When shown 5-second silent video clips of these reports, observers could much more accurately discern women's than men's emotions when recalling happiness. Men, however, were slightly more successful in conveying anger.

SOCIAL DOMINANCE

Imagine two people: One is "adventurous, autocratic, coarse, dominant, forceful, independent, and strong." The other is "affectionate, dependent, dreamy, emotional, submissive, and weak." If the first person sounds more to you like a man and the second like a woman, you are not alone, report John Williams and Deborah Best (1990a, p. 15). From Asia to Africa and Europe to Australia, people rate men as more dominant, driven, and aggressive.

These perceptions and expectations correlate with reality. In essentially every society, men *are* socially dominant. In no known societies do women dominate men (Pratto, 1996). As we will see, gender differences vary greatly by culture, and gender differences are shrinking over time as women assume more managerial and leadership positions. Yet consider:

- Women in 2005 were but 16 percent of the world's legislators and 5 percent of prime ministers and presidents (IPU, 2005). Women are 1 percent of the chief executives of the world's 500 largest corporations (Eagly & others, 2003).

- Men more than women are concerned with social dominance and are more likely to favor conservative political candidates and programs that preserve group inequality (Eagly & others, 2003; Sidanius & Pratto, 1999).

- Men have been half of all jurors but 90 percent of elected jury leaders and most of the leaders of ad hoc laboratory groups (Davis & Gilbert, 1989; Kerr & others, 1982).

As is typical of those in higher-status positions, men still initiate most of the inviting for first dates, do most of the driving, and pick up most of the tabs (Laner & Ventrone, 1998, 2000).

Men's style of communicating undergirds their social power. In situations where roles aren't rigidly scripted, men tend to be directive, women to be democratic (Eagly & Johnson, 1990). In leadership roles, men tend to excel as directive, task-focused leaders; women excel more often in the "transformational" leadership that is favored by more and more organizations, with inspirational and social skills that build team spirit (Eagly & others, 2003). Men more than women place priority on winning, getting ahead, and dominating others (Sidanius & others, 1994). They also take more risks (Byrnes & others, 1999). When they lead democratically, women leaders are evaluated as favorably as men. When they lead autocratically, women are evaluated less favorably than men (Eagly & others, 1992). People will accept a man's "strong, assertive" leadership more readily than a woman's "pushy, aggressive" leadership.

In writing, women tend to use more communal prepositions ("with"), fewer quantitative words, and more present tense. One computer program, which taught itself to recognize gender differences in word usage and sentence structure, successfully identified the author's gender of 80 percent of 920 British fiction and nonfiction works (Koppel & others, 2002).

In conversation, men's style reflects their concern for independence, women's for connectedness. Men are more likely to act as powerful people often do—talking assertively, interrupting intrusively, touching with the hand, staring more, smiling less (Anderson & Leaper, 1998; Carli, 1991; Ellyson & others, 1991). Stating the results from a female perspective, women's influence style tends to be more indirect—less interruptive, more sensitive, more polite, less cocky.

So is it right to declare (in the title words of one 1990 best-seller) *Men Are from Mars, Women Are from Venus*? Actually, note Kay Deaux and Marianne LaFrance (1998), men's and women's conversational styles vary with the social context. Much of the style we attribute to men is typical of people (men and women) in positions of status and power. Moreover, individuals vary; some men are characteristically hesitant and deferential, some women direct and assertive. Clearly, it oversimplifies to suggest that women and men are from different emotional planets.

Aggression

By **aggression,** psychologists mean behavior intended to hurt. Throughout the world, hunting, fighting, and warring are primarily male activities. In surveys, men admit to more aggression than do women. In laboratory experiments, men indeed exhibit more physical aggression, for example, by administering what they believe are hurtful electric shocks (Knight & others, 1996). In Canada, the male-to-female arrest ratio is 8 to 1 for murder (Statistics Canada, 2001). In the United States, where 92 percent of prisoners are male, it is 10 to 1 (FBI, 2001). But once again, the gender difference fluctuates with the context. When there is provocation, the gender gap shrinks (Bettencourt & Miller, 1996). And within less assaultive forms of aggression—say, slapping a family member, throwing something, or verbally attacking someone—women are no less aggressive than men (Björkqvist, 1994; White & Kowalski, 1994). Indeed, says John Archer (2000, 2002) from his statistical digests of dozens of studies, women may be slightly more likely to commit an aggressive act. But men are more likely to inflict an injury; 62 percent of those injured by a partner are women.

Sexuality

There is also a gender gap in sexual attitudes and assertiveness. It's true that, in their physiological and subjective responses to sexual stimuli, women and men are "more similar than different" (Griffitt, 1987). Yet consider:

- "I can imagine myself being comfortable and enjoying 'casual' sex with different partners," agreed 48 percent of men and 12 percent of women in an Australian survey (Bailey & others, 2000).

Activity
13.1

- The American Council on Education's recent survey of a quarter million first-year college students offers a similar finding. "If two people really like each other, it's all right for them to have sex even if they've known each other for only a very short time," agreed 53 percent of men but only 30 percent of women (Sax & others, 2002).

- In a survey of 3,400 randomly selected 18- to 59-year-old Americans, half as many men (25 percent) as women (48 percent) cited affection for the partner as a reason for first intercourse. How often do they think about sex? "Every day" or "several times a day," said 19 percent of women and 54 percent of men (Laumann & others, 1994).

The gender difference in sexual attitudes carries over to behavior. "With few exceptions anywhere in the world," report cross-cultural psychologist Marshall Segall and his colleagues (1990, p. 244), "males are more likely than females to initiate sexual activity." Compared with lesbians, gay men also report more interest in uncommitted sex, more responsiveness to visual stimuli, and more concern with partner attractiveness (Bailey & others, 1994). "It's not that gay men are oversexed," observes Steven Pinker (1997). "They are simply men whose male desires bounce off other male desires rather than off female desires."

Indeed, observe Roy Baumeister and Kathleen Vohs (2004; Baumeister & others, 2001), men not only fantasize more about sex, have more permissive attitudes, and seek more partners, they also are more quickly aroused, desire sex more often, masturbate more frequently, are less successful at celibacy, refuse sex less often, take more risks, expend more resources to gain sex, and prefer more sexual variety. One survey asked 16,288 people from 52 nations how many sexual partners they desired in the next month. Among those unattached, 29 percent of men and 6 percent of women wanted more than one partner (Schmitt, 2003). These results were nearly identical for both straight and gay people (29 percent of gay men and 6 percent of lesbians desired more than one partner).

"Everywhere sex is understood to be something females have that males want," offered anthropologist Donald Symons (1979, p. 253). Small wonder, say Baumeister and Vohs, that cultures everywhere attribute greater value to female than male sexuality, as indicated in gender asymmetries in prostitution and courtship, where men generally offer money, gifts, praise, or commitment in implicit exchange for a woman's sexual engagement. In human sexual economics, they note, women rarely if ever pay for sex. Like labor unions opposing "scab labor," which undermines the value of their own labor, most women oppose other women's offering "cheap sex," which reduces the value of their own sexuality. Across 185 countries, the more scarce are available men, the *higher* is the teen pregnancy rate—because when men are scarce "women compete against each other by offering sex at a lower price in terms of commitment" (Barber, 2000; Baumeister & Vohs, 2004). When women are scarce, the market value of their sexuality rises and they demand greater commitment.

Sexual fantasies express the gender difference (Ellis & Symons, 1990). In male-oriented erotica, women are unattached and lust driven. In romance novels, whose primary market is women, a tender male is emotionally consumed by his devoted passion for the heroine. Social scientists aren't the only ones to have noticed. "Women can be fascinated by a four-hour movie with subtitles wherein the entire plot consists of a man and a woman yearning to have, but never actually having a relationship," observes humorist Dave Barry (1995). "Men HATE that. Men can take maybe 45 seconds of yearning, and they want everybody to get naked. Followed by a car chase. A movie called 'Naked People in Car Chases' would do really well among men."

EVOLUTION AND GENDER: DOING WHAT COMES NATURALLY?

"What do you think is the main reason men and women have different personalities, interests, and abilities?" asked the Gallup Organization (1990) in a national survey. "Is it mainly because of the way men and women are raised, or are the differences part of their biological makeup?" Among the 99 percent who answered the question (apparently without questioning its assumptions), nearly equal numbers answered "upbringing" and "biology."

There are, of course, those salient biological sex differences. Men have the muscle mass to hunt game; women can breast-feed. Are biological sex differences limited to such obvious distinctions in reproduction and physique? Or do men's and women's genes, hormones, and brains differ in ways that also contribute to behavioral differences?

Gender and Mating Preferences

Noting the worldwide persistence of gender differences in aggressiveness, dominance, and sexuality, evolutionary psychologist Douglas Kenrick (1987) suggested, as have many others since, that "we cannot change the evolutionary history of our species, and some of the differences between us are undoubtedly a function of that history." Evolutionary psychology predicts no sex differences in all those domains in which the sexes faced similar adaptive challenges (Buss, 1995b). Both sexes regulate heat with sweat, have similar taste preferences to nourish their bodies, and grow calluses where the skin meets friction. But evolutionary psychology does predict sex differences in behaviors relevant to dating, mating, and reproduction.

Consider, for example, the male's greater sexual initiative. The average male produces many trillions of sperm in his lifetime, making sperm cheap compared with eggs. Moreover, whereas a female brings one fetus to term and then nurses it, a male can spread his genes by fertilizing many females. Thus, say evolutionary psychologists, females invest their reproductive opportunities carefully, by looking for signs of health and resources. Males compete with other males for chances to win the genetic sweepstakes by sending their genes into the future. Women seek to reproduce wisely, men widely. Men seek fertile soil in which to plant their seed. Women seek men who will help them tend the garden—resourceful and monogamous dads rather than wandering cads. Or so the theory goes.

Video
13.1

Moreover, evolutionary psychology suggests, physically dominant males gained more access to females, which over generations enhanced male aggression and dominance. Whatever genetically influenced traits enabled Montezuma II to become Aztec king were also perpetuated through offspring from some of his 4,000 women (Wright, 1998). If our ancestral mothers benefited from being able to read their infants' and suitors' emotions, then natural selection may have similarly favored emotion-detecting ability in females. Underlying all these presumptions is a principle: *Nature selects traits that help send one's genes into the future.*

Little of this process is conscious. Few people in the throes of passion stop to think, "I want to give my genes to posterity" (much less, "Oh, how I want to have and raise a baby and have grandchildren!"). Men are not, having done the calculations, driven to line up outside sperm banks. Rather, say evolutionary psychologists, our natural yearnings are our genes' way of making more genes. Emotions execute evolution's dispositions, much as hunger executes the body's need for nutrients.

Evolutionary psychology also predicts that men will strive to offer what women will desire—external resources and physical protection. Male peacocks strut their feathers, and male humans, their abs, Audis, and assets. In one experiment, teen males rated "having lots of money" as more important if put alone in a room with a teen female (Roney, 2003). "Male achievement is ultimately a courtship display," says Glenn Wilson (1994). Women may balloon their breasts, Botox their wrinkles, and liposuction their fat to offer men the youthful, healthy appearance (connoting fertility) that men desire. Sure enough, note Buss (1994a) and Alan Feingold (1992), women's and men's mate preferences confirm these predictions. Studies in 37 cultures, from Australia to Zambia, reveal that men everywhere feel attracted to women whose physical features, such as youthful faces and forms, suggest fertility. Women everywhere feel attracted to men whose wealth, power, and ambition promise resources for protecting and nurturing offspring. Men's greater interest in physical form also makes them the consumers of most of the world's visual pornography. But there are gender similarities, too: Whether residing on an Indonesian island or in urban São Paulo, both women and men desire kindness, love, and mutual attraction.

Reflecting on these findings, Buss (1999) reports feeling somewhat astonished "that men and women across the world differ in their mate preferences in precisely the ways predicted by the evolutionists. Just as our fears of snakes, heights, and spiders provide a window for viewing the survival hazards of our evolutionary ancestors, our mating desires provide a window for viewing the resources our ancestors needed for reproduction. We all carry with us today the desires of our successful forebearers."

Gender and Hormones

If genes predispose gender-related traits, they must do so by their effects on our bodies. In male embryos, the genes direct the formation of testes, which begin to secrete testosterone, the male sex hormone that influences masculine appearance (Berenbaum & Hines, 1992; Hines & Green,

1991). Do hormone differences also predispose psychological gender differences?

The gender gap in aggression does seem influenced by testosterone. In various animals, administering testosterone heightens aggressiveness. In humans, violent male criminals have higher than normal testosterone levels; so do National Football League players and boisterous fraternity members (Dabbs, 2000). Moreover, for both humans and monkeys, the gender difference in aggression appears early in life (before culture has much effect) and wanes as testosterone levels decline during adulthood. No one of these lines of evidence is conclusive. Taken together, they convince many scholars that sex hormones matter. But so, as we will see, does culture.

REFLECTIONS ON EVOLUTIONARY PSYCHOLOGY

Without disputing natural selection—nature's process of selecting physical and behavioral traits that enhance gene survival—critics see two problems with evolutionary explanations. First, evolutionary psychologists sometimes start with an effect (such as the male-female difference in sexual initiative) and then work backward to construct an explanation for it. This approach is reminiscent of functionalism, a dominant theory in psychology during the 1920s. "Why does that behavior occur? Because it serves such and such a function." The theorist can hardly lose at this hindsight explanation, note biologists Paul Ehrlich and Marcus Feldman (2003). It is, scorned paleontologist Stephen Jay Gould (1997), mere "speculation [and] guesswork in the cocktail-party mode."

The way to prevent the hindsight bias is to imagine things turning out otherwise. Let's try it. Imagine that women were stronger and more physically aggressive. "But of course!" someone might say, "all the better for protecting their young." And if human males were never known to have extramarital affairs, might we not see the evolutionary wisdom behind their fidelity? After all, argues Dorothy Einon (1994), women will mate throughout the menstrual cycle and while pregnant or lactating—which means that a faithful married man is hardly less likely to fertilize a woman than is a similarly sexually active unfaithful man. Moreover, because there is more to bringing offspring to maturity than merely depositing sperm, men and women both gain by investing jointly in their children. Males who are loyal to their mates and offspring are more apt to ensure that their young will survive to perpetuate their genes. Monogamy also increases men's certainty of paternity. (These are, in fact, evolutionary explanations for why humans, and certain other species whose young require a heavy parental investment, tend to pair off and be monogamous. Love between man and woman is universal because of its genetic payoffs: The offspring of devoted males were less vulnerable to predators.)

Evolutionary psychologists reply that such criticisms are "flat out wrong." Hindsight, they say, plays no less a role in cultural explanations: Why do women and men differ? Because their culture *socializes* their behavior! When people's roles vary across time and place, "culture" *describes* those roles better than it explains them. And far from being mere hindsight conjecture, say evolutionary psychologists, their field is an empirical science that tests evolutionary predictions with data from animal behavior, cross-cultural observations, and hormonal and genetic studies. As in many scientific fields, observations inspire a theory that generates new, testable predictions. The predictions alert us to unnoticed phenomena and allow us to confirm, refute, or revise the theory.

Evolutionary psychology's critics acknowledge that evolution helps explain both our commonalities and our differences (a certain amount of diversity aids survival). But they contend our common evolutionary heritage does not, by itself, predict the enormous cultural variation in human marriage patterns (from one spouse to a succession of spouses to multiple wives to multiple husbands to spouse swapping). Nor does it explain cultural changes in behavior patterns over mere decades of time. The most significant trait that nature has endowed us with, it seems, is the capacity to adapt—to learn and to change. Therein lies what all agree is culture's shaping power.

CULTURE AND GENDER

Culture, as we noted earlier, is what's shared by a large group and transmitted across generations—ideas, attitudes, behaviors, and traditions. We can see the shaping power of culture in ideas about how men and women should behave—and in the scorn that they endure when violating expectations (Kite, 2001). In countries everywhere, girls spend more time helping with housework and child care, whereas boys spend more time in unsupervised play (Edwards, 1991). Even in contemporary, dual-career, North American marriages, men do most of the household repairs and women arrange the child care (Bianchi & others, 2000; Biernat & Wortman, 1991). And "everywhere, cooking and dishwashing are the least shared household chores." Such behavior expectations for males and females define **gender roles.**

In an experiment with Princeton University undergraduate women, Mark Zanna and Susan Pack (1975) showed the impact of gender-role expectations. The women answered questionnaires on which they described themselves to a tall, unattached, male senior student whom they expected to meet. Those led to believe the man's ideal woman was home oriented and deferential to her husband presented themselves as more traditionally feminine than did women expecting to meet a man who liked strong, ambitious women. Moreover, given a problem-solving test, those expecting to meet the nonsexist man behaved more intelligently: They solved 18 percent more problems than those expecting to meet the man with the traditional views. This adapting of themselves to fit the man's image was much less pronounced if the man was less desirable—a short, already attached freshman. In a companion experiment by Dean Morier and Cara Seroy (1994), men similarly adapted their self-presentations to meet desirable women's gender-role expectations.

Does culture construct gender roles? Or do gender roles merely reflect behavior naturally appropriate for men and women? The variety of gender roles across cultures and over time shows that culture indeed constructs our gender roles.

Gender Roles Vary with Culture and Time

Is life more satisfying when both spouses work and share child care, or when women stay home and care for the children while the husband provides? When the Pew Global Attitudes (2003) survey posed that question to 38,000 people, majorities in 41 of 44 countries said the more satisfying way of life was when both spouses worked in both domains. But as Figure 13-1 shows, the country-to-country differences were considerable. Egyptians disagreed with the world majority opinion by 2 to 1, whereas Vietnamese concurred by 11 to 1. In industrialized societies, roles vary enormously. Women fill 1 in 10 managerial positions in Japan and Germany and nearly 1 in 2 in Australia and the United States (ILO, 1997; Wallace, 2000). In North America, most doctors and dentists are men; in Russia most doctors are women, as are most dentists in Denmark.

In the last half-century—a thin slice of our long history—gender roles have changed dramatically. In 1938, one in five Americans approved "of a married woman earning money in business or industry if she has a husband capable of supporting her." By 1996, four in five approved (Niemi & others, 1989; NORC, 1996). In 1967, 57 percent of first-year American collegians agreed that "the activities of married women are best confined to the home and family." In 2002, only 22 percent agreed (Astin & others, 1987; Sax & others, 2002).

Behavioral changes have accompanied this attitude shift. Between 1960 and 1998, the proportion of 40-year-old married U.S. women in the workforce doubled—from 38 to 75 percent (Bureau of the Census, 1999). A similar influx of women in the workforce has occurred in Canada, Australia, and Britain.

In 1965, the Harvard Business School had never graduated a woman. At the turn of the century, 30 percent of its graduates were women. From 1960 to the end of the century, women as a proportion of graduates rose

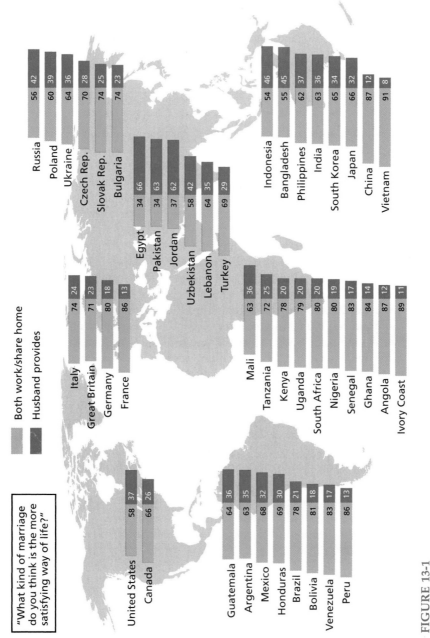

"What kind of marriage do you think is the more satisfying way of life?"

■ Both work/share home
■ Husband provides

	Both work/share home	Husband provides
Russia	56	42
Poland	60	39
Ukraine	64	36
Czech Rep.	70	28
Slovak Rep.	74	25
Bulgaria	74	23

	Both work/share home	Husband provides
Italy	74	24
Great Britain	71	23
Germany	80	18
France	86	13

	Both work/share home	Husband provides
Egypt	34	66
Pakistan	34	63
Jordan	37	62
Uzbekistan	58	42
Lebanon	64	35
Turkey	69	29

	Both work/share home	Husband provides
Indonesia	54	46
Bangladesh	55	45
Philippines	62	37
India	63	36
South Korea	65	34
Japan	66	32
China	87	12
Vietnam	91	8

	Both work/share home	Husband provides
Mali	63	36
Tanzania	72	25
Kenya	78	20
Uganda	79	20
South Africa	80	20
Nigeria	80	19
Senegal	83	17
Ghana	84	14
Angola	87	12
Ivory Coast	89	11

	Both work/share home	Husband provides
United States	58	37
Canada	66	26

	Both work/share home	Husband provides
Guatemala	64	36
Argentina	63	35
Mexico	68	32
Honduras	69	30
Brazil	78	21
Bolivia	81	18
Venezuela	83	17
Peru	86	13

FIGURE 13-1

Approved gender roles vary with culture.   **Source:** Data from the 2003 Pew Global Attitudes survey.

from 6 to 43 percent in American medical schools and from 3 to 45 percent in law schools (Hunt, 2000). In the mid-1960s, American married women devoted *seven times* as many hours to housework as did their husbands; by the mid-1990s this was down to twice as many hours. This striking variation of roles across cultures and over time signals that evolution and biology do not fix gender roles: Culture also bends the genders.

*C*ONCLUSIONS: BIOLOGY *AND* CULTURE

We needn't think of evolution and culture as competitors. Cultural norms subtly but powerfully affect our attitudes and behavior, but they don't do so independent of biology. Everything social and psychological is ultimately biological. If others' expectations influence us, that is part of our biological programming. Moreover, what our biological heritage initiates, culture may accentuate. If genes and hormones predispose males to be more physically aggressive than females, culture may amplify this difference through norms that expect males to be tough and females to be the kinder, gentler sex.

Biology and culture may also **interact.** Today's genetic science indicates how experience uses genes to change the brain (Quartz & Sejnowski, 2002). Environmental stimuli can turn on genes that produce new brain cell branching receptors. Visual experience turns on genes that develop the brain's visual area. Parental touch turns on genes that help offspring cope with future stressful events. Genes don't just constrain us; they respond adaptively to our experiences.

Biology and experience interact as biological traits influence how the environment reacts. People respond differently to a David Beckham than to a Woody Allen. Men, being 8 percent taller and averaging almost double the proportion of muscle mass, may likewise have different experiences than women. Or consider this: A very strong cultural norm dictates that males should be taller than their female mates. In one study, only 1 in 720 married couples violated this norm (Gillis & Avis, 1980). With hindsight, we can speculate a psychological explanation: Perhaps being taller (and older) helps men perpetuate their social power over women. But we can also speculate evolutionary wisdom that might underlie the cultural norm: If people preferred partners of the same height, tall men and short women would often be without partners. As it is, evolution dictates that men tend to be taller than women, and culture dictates the same for couples. So the height norm might well be a result of biology *and* culture.

Video
13.2

Alice Eagly and Wendy Wood (1999; Eagly, 1987) theorize how biology and culture interact (Figure 13-2). They believe that a variety of factors, including biological influences and childhood socialization,

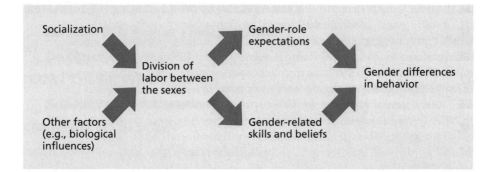

FIGURE 13-2
A social-role theory of gender differences in social behavior. Various influences, including childhood experiences and factors, bend males and females toward differing roles. It is the expectations and the skills and beliefs associated with these differing roles that affect men's and women's behavior. **Source:** Adapted from Eagly, 1987; Eagly & Wood, 1991.

predispose a sexual division of labor. In adult life the immediate causes of gender differences in social behavior are the *roles* that reflect this sexual division of labor. Men, because of their strength and speed, tend to be found in roles demanding physical power. Women's capacity for childbearing and nursing inclines them to more nurturant roles. Each sex then tends to exhibit the behaviors expected of those who fill such roles and to have their skills and beliefs shaped accordingly. Nature and nurture are a "tangled web."

CONCEPTS TO REMEMBER

gender   In psychology, the characteristics, whether biological or socially influenced, by which people define male and female.

empathy   The vicarious experience of another's feelings; putting oneself in another's shoes.

aggression   Physical or verbal behavior intended to hurt someone. In laboratory experiments, this might mean

delivering electric shocks or saying something likely to hurt another's feelings.

gender role   A set of behavior expectations (norms) for males and females.

interaction   The effect of one factor (such as biology) depends on another factor (such as environment).

14

❖

How Nice People Get Corrupted

You have surely experienced the phenomenon: As a controversial speaker or music concert finishes, the adoring fans near the front stand to applaud. The approving folks just behind them follow their example and join the standing ovation. Now the wave of people standing reaches people who, unprompted, would merely be giving polite applause from their comfortable seats. Seated among them, part of you wants to stay seated ("this speaker doesn't represent my views at all"). But as the wave of standing people sweeps by, will you alone stay seated? It's not easy, being a minority of one.

Researchers who study **conformity** construct miniature social worlds—laboratory microcultures that simplify and simulate important features of everyday social influence. Consider three noted sets of experiments. Each provides a method for studying conformity—and some startling findings.

ASCH'S STUDIES OF CONFORMITY

From his boyhood, Solomon Asch (1907–1996) recalls a traditional Jewish seder at Passover:

> I asked my uncle, who was sitting next to me, why the door was being opened. He replied, "The prophet Elijah visits this evening every Jewish home and takes a sip of wine from the cup reserved for him."
> I was amazed at this news and repeated, "Does he really come? Does he really take a sip?"

My uncle said, "If you watch very closely, when the door is opened you will see—you watch the cup—you will see that the wine will go down a little."

And that's what happened. My eyes were riveted upon the cup of wine. I was determined to see whether there would be a change. And to me it seemed it was tantalizing, and of course, it was hard to be absolutely sure—that indeed something was happening at the rim of the cup, and the wine did go down a little. (Aron & Aron, 1989, p. 27)

Years later, social psychologist Asch re-created his boyhood experience in his laboratory. Imagine yourself as one of Asch's volunteer subjects. You are seated sixth in a row of seven people. After explaining that you will be taking part in a study of perceptual judgments, the experimenter asks you to say which of the three lines in Figure 14-1 matches the standard line. You can easily see that it's line 2. So it's no surprise when the five people responding before you all say, "Line 2."

The next comparison proves as easy, and you settle in for what seems a simple test. But the third trial startles you. Although the correct answer seems just as clear-cut, the first person gives a wrong answer. When the second person gives the same wrong answer, you sit up in your chair and stare at the cards. The third person agrees with the first two. Your jaw drops; you start to perspire. "What is this?" you ask yourself. "Are they blind? Or am I?" The fourth and fifth people agree with the others. Then the experimenter looks at you. Now you are experiencing an epistemological dilemma: "How am I to know what is true? Is it what my peers tell me or what my eyes tell me?"

Activity
14.1

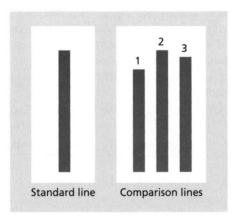

Standard line   Comparison lines

FIGURE 14-1
Sample comparison from Solomon Asch's conformity procedure. The participants judged which of three comparison lines matched the standard.

In one of Asch's conformity experiments, subject number 6 experienced uneasiness and conflict after hearing five people before him give a wrong answer.

Dozens of college students experienced this conflict during Asch's experiments. Those in a control condition who answered alone were correct more than 99 percent of the time. Asch wondered: If several others (confederates coached by the experimenter) gave identical wrong answers, would people declare what they would otherwise have denied? Although some people never conformed, three-quarters did so at least once. All told, 37 percent of the responses were conforming (or should we say "*trusting* of others"?). Of course, that means 63 percent of the time people did not conform. Despite the independence shown by many of his participants, Asch's (1955) feelings about the conformity were as clear as the correct answers to his questions: "That reasonably intelligent and well-meaning young people are willing to call white black is a matter of concern. It raises questions about our ways of education and about the values that guide our conduct."

Asch's results are startling because they involved no obvious pressure to conform—there were no rewards for "team play," no punishments for individuality. If people are this conforming in response to such minimal pressure, how compliant will they be if they are directly coerced? Could someone force the average American or British Commonwealth citizen to perform cruel acts? I would have guessed not: Their humane, democratic, individualistic values would make them resist such pressure. Besides, the easy verbal pronouncements of these experiments are a giant step away from actually harming someone; you and I would never yield to coercion to hurt another. Or would we? Social psychologist Stanley Milgram wondered.

MILGRAM'S OBEDIENCE EXPERIMENTS

Milgram's (1965, 1974) experiments tested what happens when the demands of authority clash with the demands of conscience. These have become social psychology's most famous and controversial experiments. "Perhaps more than any other empirical contributions in the history of social science," notes Lee Ross (1988), "they have become part of our society's shared intellectual legacy—that small body of historical incidents, biblical parables, and classic literature that serious thinkers feel free to draw on when they debate about human nature or contemplate human history."

Video
14.1

Here is the scene staged by Milgram, a creative artist who wrote stories and stage plays: Two men come to Yale University's psychology laboratory to participate in a study of learning and memory. A stern experimenter in a gray technician's coat explains that this is a pioneering study of the effect of punishment on learning. The experiment requires one of them to teach a list of word pairs to the other and to punish errors by delivering shocks of increasing intensity. To assign the roles, they draw slips out of a hat. One of the men, a mild-mannered, 47-year-old accountant who is the experimenter's confederate, pretends that his slip says "learner" and is ushered into an adjacent room. The "teacher" (who has come in response to a newspaper ad) takes a mild sample shock and then looks on as the experimenter straps the learner into a chair and attaches an electrode to his wrist.

Teacher and experimenter then return to the main room (see Figure 14-2), where the teacher takes his place before a "shock generator" with switches ranging from 15 to 450 volts in 15-volt increments. The switches are labeled "Slight Shock," "Very Strong Shock," "Danger: Severe Shock," and so forth. Under the 435- and 450-volt switches appears "XXX." The experimenter tells the teacher to "move one level higher on the shock generator" each time the learner gives a wrong answer. With each flick

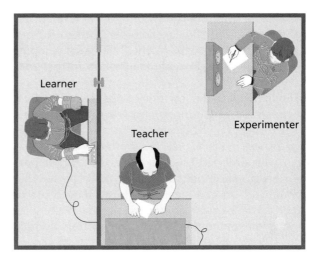

FIGURE 14-2
Milgram's obedience experiment.   Source: Milgram,
1974.

of a switch, lights flash, relay switches click, and an electric buzz sounds.

If the participant complies with the experimenter's requests, he hears the learner grunt at 75, 90, and 105 volts. At 120 volts the learner shouts that the shocks are painful. And at 150 volts he cries out, "Experimenter, get me out of here! I won't be in the experiment anymore! I refuse to go on!" By 270 volts his protests have become screams of agony, and he continues to insist to be let out. At 300 and 315 volts, he screams his refusal to answer. After 330 volts he falls silent. In answer to the "teacher's" inquiries and pleas to end the experiment, the experimenter states that the nonresponses should be treated as wrong answers. To keep the participant going, he uses four verbal prods:

Prod 1: Please continue (or Please go on).

Prod 2: The experiment requires that you continue.

Prod 3: It is absolutely essential that you continue.

Prod 4: You have no other choice; you must go on.

How far would you go? Milgram described the experiment to 110 psychiatrists, college students, and middle-class adults. People in all three groups guessed that they would disobey by about 135 volts; none expected to go beyond 300 volts. Recognizing that self-estimates may reflect self-serving bias, Milgram asked them how far they thought *other* people would go. Virtually no one expected anyone to proceed to XXX on the shock panel. (The psychiatrists guessed about 1 in 1,000.)

But when Milgram conducted the experiment with 40 men—a vocational mix of 20- to 50-year-olds—26 of them (65 percent) progressed to 450 volts. In fact, all who reached 450 volts complied with a command to *continue* the procedure until, after two further trials, the experimenter called a halt.

Having expected a low rate of **obedience,** and with plans to replicate the experiment in Germany and assess the culture difference, Milgram was disturbed (A. Milgram, 2000). So instead of going to Germany, Milgram next made the learner's protests even more compelling. As the learner was strapped into the chair, the teacher heard him mention his "slight heart condition" and heard the experimenter's reassurance that "although the shocks may be painful, they cause no permanent tissue damage." The learner's anguished protests were to little avail; of 40 new men in this experiment, 25 (63 percent) fully complied with the experimenter's demands (Figure 14-3).

The obedience of his subjects disturbed Milgram. The procedures he used disturbed many social psychologists (Miller, 1986). The "learner" in these experiments actually received no shock (he disengaged himself from the electric chair and turned on a tape recorder that delivered the protests). Nevertheless, some critics said that Milgram did to his participants what they did to their victims: He stressed them against their will. Indeed, many of the "teachers" did experience agony.

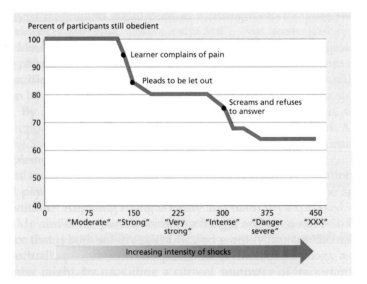

FIGURE 14-3
The Milgram obedience experiment. Percentage of participants complying despite the learner's cries of protest and failure to respond. **Source:** From Milgram, 1965.

They sweated, trembled, stuttered, bit their lips, groaned, or even broke into uncontrollable nervous laughter. A *New York Times* reviewer complained that the cruelty inflicted by the experiments "upon their unwitting subjects is surpassed only by the cruelty that they elicit from them" (Marcus, 1974).

Critics also argued that the participants' self-concepts may have been altered. One participant's wife told him, "You can call yourself Eichmann" (referring to Nazi death camp administrator Adolf Eichmann). CBS television depicted the results and the controversy in a two-hour dramatization starring William Shatner, of *Star Trek* fame, as Milgram. "A world of evil so terrifying no one dares penetrate its secret. Until Now!" declared a *TV Guide* ad for the program (Elms, 1995).

In his own defense, Milgram pointed to the lessons taught by his nearly two dozen experiments with a diverse sample of more than 1,000 participants. He also reminded critics of the support he received from the participants after the deception was revealed and the experiment explained. When surveyed afterward, 84 percent said they were glad to have participated; only 1 percent regretted volunteering. A year later, a psychiatrist interviewed 40 of those who had suffered most and concluded that, despite the temporary stress, none was harmed.

The ethical controversy was "terribly overblown," Milgram believed:

> There is less consequence to subjects in this experiment from the standpoint of effects on self-esteem, than to university students who take ordinary course examinations, and who do not get the grades they want. . . . It seems that [in giving exams] we are quite prepared to accept stress, tension, and consequences for self-esteem. But in regard to the process of generating new knowledge, how little tolerance we show. (quoted by Blass, 1996)

What Breeds Obedience?

Milgram did more than reveal the extent to which people will obey an authority; he also examined the conditions that breed obedience. In further experiments, he varied the social conditions and got compliance ranging from 0 to 93 percent fully obedient. Four factors that determined obedience were the victim's emotional distance, the authority's closeness and legitimacy, whether or not the authority was institutionalized, and the liberating effects of a disobedient fellow participant.

Emotional Distance of the Victim

Milgram's participants acted with least compassion when the "learners" could not be seen (and could not see them). When the victim was remote and the "teachers" heard no complaints, nearly all obeyed calmly to the end. This situation minimized the learner's influence relative to the experimenter's. But what if we made the learner's pleas and the experimenter's pleas more equally visible? When the learner was in the same room, "only" 40 percent obeyed to 450 volts. Full compliance dropped to 30 percent when teachers were required to force the learner's hand into contact with a shock plate.

In everyday life, too, it is easiest to abuse someone who is distant or depersonalized. People will be unresponsive even to great tragedies. Executioners often depersonalize those being executed by placing hoods over their heads. The ethics of war allow one to bomb a helpless village from 40,000 feet but not to shoot an equally helpless villager. In combat with an enemy they can see, many soldiers either do not fire or do not aim. Such disobedience is rare among those given orders to kill with the more distant artillery or aircraft weapons (Padgett, 1989).

On the positive side, people act most compassionately toward those who are personalized. That is why appeals for the unborn, for the hungry, or for animal rights are nearly always personalized with a compelling photograph or description. Perhaps even more compelling is an ultrasound picture of one's own developing fetus. When queried by John Lydon and Christine Dunkel-Schetter (1994), expectant women expressed more commitment to their pregnancies if they had seen ultrasound pictures of their fetuses that clearly displayed body parts.

Closeness and Legitimacy of the Authority
The physical presence of the experimenter also affected obedience. When Milgram gave the commands by telephone, full obedience dropped to 21 percent (although many lied and said they were obeying). Other studies confirm that when the one making the request is physically close, compliance increases. Given a light touch on the arm, people are more likely to lend a dime, sign a petition, or sample a new pizza (Kleinke, 1977; Smith & others, 1982; Willis & Hamm, 1980).

The authority, however, must be perceived as legitimate. In another twist on the basic experiment, the experimenter received a rigged telephone call that required him to leave the laboratory. He said that since the equipment recorded data automatically, the "teacher" should just go ahead. After the experimenter left, another person, who had been assigned a clerical role (actually a second confederate), assumed command. The clerk "decided" that the shock should be increased one level for each wrong answer and instructed the teacher accordingly. Now 80 percent of the teachers refused to comply fully. The confederate, feigning disgust at this defiance, sat down in front of the shock generator and tried to take over the teacher's role. At this point most of the defiant participants protested. Some tried to unplug the generator. One large man lifted the zealous confederate from his chair and threw him across the room. This rebellion against an illegitimate authority contrasted sharply with the deferential politeness usually shown the experimenter.

It also contrasts with the behavior of hospital nurses who in one study were called by an unknown physician and ordered to administer an obvious drug overdose (Hofling & others, 1966). The researchers told one group of nurses and nursing students about the experiment and asked how they would react. Nearly all said they would not have followed the order. One said she would have replied, "I'm sorry, sir, but I am not authorized to give any medication without a written order, especially one so large over the usual dose and one that I'm unfamiliar with. If it were possible, I would be glad to do it, but this is against hospital policy and my own ethical standards." Nevertheless, when 22 other nurses were actually given the phoned-in overdose order, all but one obeyed without delay (until being intercepted on their way to the patient). Although not all nurses are so compliant (Krackow & Blass, 1995; Rank & Jacobson, 1977), these nurses were following a familiar script: Doctor (a legitimate authority) orders; nurse obeys.

Compliance with legitimate authority was also apparent in the strange case of the "rectal ear ache" (Cohen & Davis, 1981). A doctor ordered ear drops for a patient suffering infection in the right ear. On the prescription, the doctor abbreviated "place in right ear" as "place in R ear." Reading the order, the compliant nurse put the required drops in the compliant patient's rectum.

Institutional Authority

If the prestige of the authority is this important, then perhaps the institutional prestige of Yale University legitimized the Milgram experiment commands. In postexperimental interviews, many participants said that had it not been for Yale's reputation, they would not have obeyed. To see whether this was true, Milgram moved the experiment to Bridgeport, Connecticut. He set himself up in a modest commercial building as the "Research Associates of Bridgeport." When the usual "heart disturbance" experiment was run with the same personnel, what percentage of the men do you suppose fully obeyed? Though reduced, the rate remained remarkably high—48 percent.

The Liberating Effects of Group Influence
These classic experiments give us a negative view of conformity. But conformity can also be constructive. Perhaps you can recall a time you felt justifiably angry at an unfair teacher but you hesitated to object. Then one or two other students spoke up about the unfair practices, and you followed their example which had a liberating effect. Milgram captured this liberating effect of conformity by placing the teacher with two confederates who were to help conduct the procedure. During the experiment, both confederates defied the experimenter, who then ordered the real participant to continue alone. Did he? No. Ninety percent liberated themselves by conforming to the defiant confederates.

REFLECTIONS ON THE CLASSIC STUDIES

The common response to Milgram's results is to note their counterparts in recent history: the "I was only following orders" defenses of Adolf Eichmann in Nazi Germany; of Lieutenant William Calley, who in 1968 directed the unprovoked slaughter of hundreds of Vietnamese in the village of My Lai; and of the "ethnic cleansing" occurring more recently in Iraq, Rwanda, Bosnia, and Kosovo.

Soldiers are trained to obey superiors. Thus one participant in the My Lai massacre recalled:

> [Lieutenant Calley] told me to start shooting. So I started shooting, I poured about four clips into the group. . . . They were begging and saying, "No, no." And the mothers were hugging their children and. . . . Well, we kept right on firing. They was waving their arms and begging. (Wallace, 1969)

The "safe" scientific contexts of the obedience experiments differ from the wartime contexts. Moreover, much of the mockery and brutality of war and genocide goes beyond obedience (Miller, 2004). The obedience experiments also differ from the other conformity experiments in the strength of the social pressure: Compliance is explicitly commanded. Without the coercion, people did not act cruelly. Yet both the Asch and Milgram experiments share certain commonalities. They showed how compliance can take precedence over moral sense. They succeeded in pressuring people to go against their own consciences. They did more than teach an academic lesson; they sensitized us to moral conflicts in our own lives. And they illustrated and affirmed some familiar social psychological principles: the link between behavior and attitudes, the power of the situation, and the strength of the fundamental attribution error.

Behavior and Attitudes

In Module 9 we noted that attitudes fail to determine behavior when external influences override inner convictions. These experiments vividly illustrate this principle. When responding alone, Asch's participants nearly always gave the correct answer. It was another matter when they stood alone against a group.

In the obedience experiments, a powerful social pressure (the experimenter's commands) overcame a weaker one (the remote victim's pleas). Torn between the pleas of the victim and the orders of the experimenter, between the desire to avoid doing harm and the desire to be a good participant, a surprising number of people chose to obey.

Why were the participants unable to disengage themselves? How had they become trapped? Imagine yourself as the teacher in yet another version of Milgram's experiment, one he never conducted. Assume that when the learner gives the first wrong answer, the experimenter asks you to zap him with 330 volts. After flicking the switch, you hear the learner scream, complain of a heart disturbance, and plead for mercy. Do you continue?

I think not. Recall the step-by-step entrapment of the foot-in-the-door phenomenon (Module 9) as we compare this hypothetical experiment to what Milgram's participants experienced. Their first commitment was mild—15 volts—and it elicited no protest. You, too, would agree to do that much. By the time they delivered 75 volts and heard the learner's first groan, they already had complied five times. On the next trial, the experimenter asked them to commit an act only slightly more extreme than what they had already repeatedly committed. By the time they delivered 330 volts, after 22 acts of compliance, the participants had reduced some of their dissonance. They were therefore in a different psychological state from that of someone beginning the experiment at that point. As we saw in Module 9, external behavior and internal disposition can feed one another, sometimes in an escalating spiral. Thus, reported Milgram (1974, p. 10):

> Many subjects harshly devalue the victim *as a consequence* of acting against him. Such comments as, "He was so stupid and stubborn he deserved to get shocked," were common. Once having acted against the victim, these subjects found it necessary to view him as an unworthy individual, whose punishment was made inevitable by his own deficiencies of intellect and character.

During the early 1970s, the military junta then in power in Greece used this "blame-the-victim" process to train torturers (Haritos-Fatouros, 1988, 2002; Staub, 1989, 2003). There, as in the earlier training of SS officers in Nazi Germany, the military selected candidates based on their respect for and submission to authority. But such tendencies alone do not a torturer make. Thus they would first assign the trainee to guard prisoners, then to participate in arrest squads, then to hit prisoners, then to observe torture, and only then to practice it. Step by step, an obedient but otherwise decent person evolved into an agent of cruelty. Compliance bred acceptance.

As a Holocaust survivor, University of Massachusetts social psychologist Ervin Staub knows too well the forces that can transform citizens into agents of death. From his study of human genocide across the world, Staub (2003) shows where this process can lead. Too often, criticism produces contempt, which licenses cruelty, which, when justified, leads to brutality, then killing, then systematic killing. Evolving attitudes both follow and justify actions. Staub's disturbing conclusion: "Human beings have the capacity to come to experience killing other people as nothing extraordinary" (1989, p. 13).

Humans also have a capacity for heroism. During the Nazi Holocaust, 3,500 French Jews and 1,500 other refugees destined for deportation to

Germany were sheltered by the villagers of Le Chambon. The villagers were mostly Protestants, descendants of a persecuted group, and people whose own authorities, their pastors, had taught them to "resist whenever our adversaries will demand of us obedience contrary to the orders of the Gospel" (Rochat, 1993; Rochat & Modigliani, 1995). Ordered to divulge the sheltered Jews, the head pastor modeled disobedience: "I don't know of Jews, I only know of human beings." Without knowing how terrible the war would be or how much they would suffer, the resisters made an initial commitment and then—supported by their beliefs, by their own authorities, and by one another—remained defiant to the war's end. Here and elsewhere, the ultimate response to Nazi occupation usually came early. The first acts of compliance or resistance bred attitudes that influenced behavior, which strengthened attitudes. Initial helping heightened commitment, leading to more helping.

The Power of the Situation

The most important lesson of Module 13—that culture is a powerful shaper of lives—and this module's most important lesson—that immediate situational forces are just as powerful—reveal the strength of the social context. To feel this for yourself, imagine violating some minor norms: standing up in the middle of a class; singing out loud in a restaurant; playing golf in a suit. In trying to break with social constraints, we suddenly realize how strong they are.

Some of Milgram's own students learned this lesson when he and John Sabini (1983) asked their help in studying the effects of violating a simple social norm: asking riders on the New York City subway system for their seats. To their surprise, 56 percent gave up their seats, even when no justification was given. The students' own reactions to making the request were as interesting: Most found it extremely difficult. Often, the words got stuck in their throats, and they had to withdraw. Once having made their requests and gotten seats, they sometimes justified their norm violation by pretending to be sick. Such is the power of the unspoken rules governing our public behavior.

The students in a recent Pennsylvania State University experiment found it similarly difficult to get challenging words out of their mouths. Some students imagined themselves discussing with three others whom to select for survival on a desert island. They were asked to imagine one of the others, a man, injecting three sexist comments, such as, "I think we need more women on the island to keep the men satisfied." How would they react to such sexist remarks? Only 5 percent predicted they would ignore each of the comments or wait to see how others reacted. But when Janet Swim and Lauri Hyers (1999) engaged other students in discussions where such comments were actually made by a male confederate, 55 percent (not 5 percent) said nothing. This once again demonstrates the power of normative pressures and how hard it is to predict behavior, even our own behavior.

Milgram's experiments also offer a lesson about evil. Evil sometimes results from a few bad apples. That's the image of evil symbolized by depraved killers in suspense novels and horror movies. In real life we think of Hitler's extermination of Jews, of Saddam Hussein's extermination of Kurds, of Osama bin Laden's plotting terror. But evil also results from social forces—from the heat, humidity, and disease that help make a whole barrel of apples go bad. As these experiments show, situations can induce ordinary people to agree to falsehoods or to capitulate to cruelty.

German civil servants surprised Nazi leaders with their willingness to handle the paperwork of the Holocaust. They were not killing Jews, of course; they were merely pushing paper (Silver & Geller, 1978). When fragmented, evil becomes easier. Milgram studied this compartmentalization of evil by involving yet another 40 men more indirectly. With someone else triggering the shock, they had only to administer the learning test. Now, 37 of the 40 fully complied.

So it is in our everyday lives: The drift toward evil usually comes in small increments, without any conscious intent to do evil. Procrastination involves a similar unintended drift, toward self-harm (Sabini & Silver, 1982). A student knows the deadline for a term paper weeks ahead. Each diversion from work on the paper—a video game here, a TV program there—seems harmless enough. Yet gradually the student veers toward not doing the paper without ever consciously deciding not to do it.

The Fundamental Attribution Error

Why do the results of these classic experiments so often startle people? Is it because we expect people to act in accord with their dispositions? It doesn't surprise us when a surly person is nasty, but we expect those with pleasant dispositions to be kind. Bad people do bad things; good people do good things. The "senseless" 9/11 horror was perpetrated, we heard over and again, by "madmen," by "evil cowards," by "demonic" monsters.

When you read about Milgram's experiments, what impressions did you form of the obedient participants? Most people when told about one or two of the obedient persons, judge them to be aggressive, cold, and unappealing—even after learning that their behavior was typical (Miller & others, 1973). Cruelty, we presume, is inflicted by the cruel at heart.

Günter Bierbrauer (1979) tried to eliminate this underestimation of social forces (the fundamental attribution error). He had university students observe a vivid reenactment of the experiment or play the role of obedient teacher themselves. They still predicted that, in a repeat of Milgram's experiment, their friends would be only minimally compliant. Bierbrauer concluded that although social scientists accumulate evidence that our behavior is a product of our social histories and current environments, most people continue to believe that people's inner qualities reveal themselves—that good people do good and that evil people do evil.

It is tempting to assume that Eichmann and the Auschwitz death camp commanders were uncivilized monsters. But after a hard day's work, the commanders would relax by listening to Beethoven and Schubert. Of the 14 men who attended the January 1942 Wannsee Conference and formulated the Final Solution leading to the Nazi Holocaust, 8 had European university doctorates (Patterson, 1996). Like most other Nazis, Eichmann himself was outwardly indistinguishable from common people with ordinary jobs (Arendt, 1963; Zillmer & others, 1995). Mohamed Atta, the leader of the 9/11 attacks, reportedly had been a "good boy" and an excellent student from a healthy family. Zacarias Moussaoui, the alleged would-be 20th 9/11 attacker, had been very polite when applying for flight lessons and buying knives. He called women "ma'am." If these men had lived next door to us, they would hardly have fit our image of evil monsters.

Or consider the German police battalion responsible for shooting nearly 40,000 Jews in Poland, many of them women, children, and elderly people who were shot in the backs of their heads, gruesomely spraying their brains. Christopher Browning (1992) portrays the "normality" of these men. Like the many others who ravaged Europe's Jewish ghettos, operated the deportation trains, and administered the death camps, they were not Nazis, SS members, or racial fanatics. They were laborers, salesmen, clerks, and artisans—family men who were too old for military service, but who, when directly ordered to kill, did not refuse.

Milgram's conclusion also makes it hard to attribute the Nazi Holocaust to unique character traits in the German people: "The most fundamental lesson of our study," he noted, is that "ordinary people, simply doing their jobs, and without any particular hostility on their part, can become agents in a terrible destructive process" (Milgram, 1974, p. 6). As Mister Rogers often reminded his preschool television audience, "Good people sometimes do bad things." Perhaps then, we should be more wary of political leaders whose charming dispositions lull us into supposing they would never do evil. Under the sway of evil forces, even nice people are sometimes corrupted as they construct moral rationalizations for immoral behavior (Tsang, 2002).

CONCEPTS TO REMEMBER

Conformity   A change in behavior or belief to accord with others.

Obedience   Acting in accord with a direct order.

MODULE

15

❖

Two Routes to Persuasion

Persuasion is everywhere—at the heart of politics, marketing, courtship, parenting, negotiation, evangelism, and courtroom decision making. Social psychologists therefore seek to understand what leads to effective, long-lasting attitude change. What factors affect persuasion? And how, as persuaders, can we most effectively "educate" others?

Imagine that you are a marketing or advertising executive. Or imagine that you are a preacher, trying to increase love and charity among your parishioners. Or imagine that you want to promote energy conservation, to encourage breastfeeding, or to campaign for a political candidate. What could you do to make yourself and your message persuasive? If you are wary of being manipulated by such appeals, to what tactics should you be alert?

To answer such questions, social psychologists usually study persuasion the way some geologists study erosion—by observing the effects of various factors in brief, controlled experiments. The effects are small and are most potent on weak attitudes that don't touch our values (Johnson & Eagly, 1989; Petty & Krosnick, 1995). Yet they enable us to understand how, given enough time, such factors could produce big effects.

*T*HE TWO ROUTES

In choosing tactics, you must first decide: Should you focus mostly on building strong *central arguments*? Or should you make your message appealing by associating it with favorable *peripheral cues,* such as sex

165

appeal? Persuasion researchers Richard Petty and John Cacioppo (Cass-ee-OH-poh) (1986; Petty & Wegener, 1999) and Alice Eagly and Shelly Chaiken (1993) report that persuasion is likely to occur via either a central or peripheral route. When people are motivated and able to think systematically about an issue, they are likely to take the **central route to persuasion**—focusing on the arguments. If those arguments are strong and compelling, persuasion is likely. If the message contains only weak arguments, thoughtful people will notice that the arguments aren't very compelling and will counterargue.

Video
15.1

But sometimes the strength of the arguments doesn't matter. Sometimes we're not all that motivated or able to think carefully. If we're distracted, uninvolved, or just plain busy, we may not take the time to think carefully about the message content. Rather than noticing whether the arguments are particularly compelling, we might follow the **peripheral route to persuasion**—focusing on cues that trigger acceptance without much thinking. Billboards and television commercials—media that consumers are able to take in for only brief amounts of time—typically use visual images as peripheral cues. Our opinions regarding products such as food and drink, cigarettes, and clothing are often based more on feelings than on logic. Ads for such products often use visual peripheral cues. Instead of providing arguments in favor of smoking, cigarette ads associate the product with images of beauty and pleasure. So do soft-drink ads that promote "the real thing" with images of youth, vitality, and happy polar bears. On the other hand, computer ads, which interested, logical consumers may pore over for some time, seldom feature Hollywood stars or great athletes; instead they offer customers information on competitive features and prices. Matching the type of message to the route that message recipients are likely to follow also increases their attention to it (Petty, Wheeler, & Bizer, 2000; Shavitt, 1990).

Even thinking people sometimes form tentative opinions using the peripheral route to persuasion. Sometimes it's just easier for us to use simple rule-of-thumb heuristics, such as "trust the experts" or "long messages are credible" (Chaiken & Maheswaran, 1994). Residents of my community once voted on a complicated issue involving the legal ownership of our local hospital. I didn't have the time or interest to study this question myself (I had this book to write). But I noted that referendum supporters were all people I either liked or regarded as experts. So I used a simple heuristic—friends and experts can be trusted—and voted accordingly. We all make snap judgments using other heuristics: If a speaker is articulate and appealing, has apparently good motives, and has several arguments (or better, if the different arguments come from different sources), we usually take the

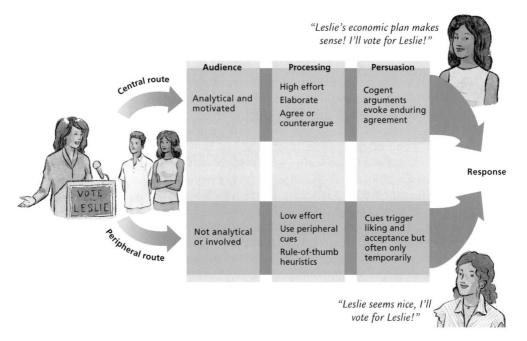

"Leslie's economic plan makes sense! I'll vote for Leslie!"

Audience	Processing	Persuasion
Analytical and motivated	High effort Elaborate Agree or counterargue	Cogent arguments evoke enduring agreement
Not analytical or involved	Low effort Use peripheral cues Rule-of-thumb heuristics	Cues trigger liking and acceptance but often only temporarily

Central route

Peripheral route

Response

"Leslie seems nice, I'll vote for Leslie!"

FIGURE 15-1
The central and peripheral routes to persuasion. Computer ads typically take the central route by assuming their audience wants to systematically compare features and prices. Soft-drink ads usually take the peripheral route, by merely associating their product with glamour, pleasure, and good moods. Central route processing more often produces enduring attitude change.

easy peripheral route and accept the message without much thought (Figure 15-1).

*T*HE ELEMENTS OF PERSUASION

Among the primary ingredients of persuasion explored by social psychologists are these four: (1) the communicator, (2) the message, (3) how the message is communicated, and (4) the audience. In other words, *who* says *what* by *what means* to *whom?*

Who Says? The Communicator

Imagine the following scene: I. M. Wright, a middle-aged American, is watching the evening news. In the first segment, a small group of radicals are shown burning an American flag. As they do, one shouts through a bullhorn that whenever any government becomes oppressive, "it is the

Right of the People to alter or to abolish it. . . . It is their right, it is their duty, to throw off such government!" Angered, Mr. Wright mutters to his wife, "It's sickening to hear them spouting that Communist line." In the next segment, a presidential candidate speaking before an antitax rally declares, "Thrift should be the guiding principle in our government expenditure. It should be made clear to all government workers that corruption and waste are very great crimes." An obviously pleased Mr. Wright relaxes and smiles: "Now that's the kind of good sense we need. That's my kinda guy."

Now switch the scene. Imagine Mr. Wright hearing the same revolutionary line about "the Right of the People" at a July 4 oration of the Declaration of Independence (from which the line comes) and hearing a Communist speaker read the thrift sentence from *Quotations from Chairman Mao Zedong* (from which it comes). Would he now react differently?

Social psychologists have found that who is saying something affects how an audience receives it. In one experiment, when the Socialist and Liberal leaders in the Dutch parliament argued identical positions using the same words, each was most effective with members of his own party (Wiegman, 1985). It's not just the message that matters, but also who says it. What makes one communicator more persuasive than another?

Credibility

Any of us would find a statement about the benefits of exercise more believable if it came from the Royal Society or National Academy of Sciences rather than from a tabloid newspaper. But the effects of source **credibility** (perceived expertise and trustworthiness) diminish after a month or so. If a credible person's message is persuasive, its impact may fade as its source is forgotten or dissociated from the message. The impact of a noncredible person may correspondingly increase over time (if people remember the message better than the reason for discounting it) (Cook & Flay, 1978; Gruder & others, 1978; Pratkanis & others, 1988). This delayed persuasion, after people forget the source or its connection with the message, is called the **sleeper effect.**

Attractiveness

Most people deny that endorsements by star athletes and entertainers affect them. Most people know that stars are seldom knowledgeable about the product they endorse. Besides, we know the intent is to persuade us; we don't just accidentally eavesdrop on Tiger Woods discussing clothes or cars. Such ads are based on another characteristic of an effective communicator: attractiveness. We may think we are not influenced by attractiveness or likability, but researchers have found otherwise. We're more likely to respond to those we like, a phenomenon well known to those organizing charitable solicitations, candy sales, and Tupperware parties. Even a mere fleeting conversation with someone is enough to increase our liking for someone and our responsiveness to their influence (Burger & others, 2001). Our liking may open us up to the communicator's arguments (central route persuasion), or it may trigger positive associations when we see the product later (peripheral route persuasion).

Attractiveness varies in several ways. *Physical appeal* is one. Arguments, especially emotional ones, are often more influential when they come from beautiful people (Chaiken, 1979; Dion & Stein, 1978; Pallak & others, 1983). *Similarity* is another. As Module 26 will emphasize, we tend to like people who are like us. We also are influenced by them. For example, Theodore Dembroski, Thomas Lasater, and Albert Ramirez (1978) gave African American junior high students a taped appeal for proper dental care. When a dentist assessed the cleanliness of their teeth the next day, those who heard the appeal from an African American dentist had cleaner teeth. As a general rule, people respond better to a message that comes from someone in their group (Van Knippenberg & Wilke, 1992; Wilder, 1990).

What Is Said? The Message Content

It matters not only who says something, but *what* that person says. If you were to help organize an appeal to get people to vote for school taxes or to stop smoking or to give money to world hunger relief, you might wonder how to concoct a recipe for central route persuasion. Common sense could lead you to either side of these questions:

- Is a purely logical message most persuasive—or one that arouses emotion?

- Will you get more opinion change by advocating a position only slightly discrepant from the listeners' existing opinions or by advocating an extreme point of view?

- Should the message express your side only, or should it acknowledge and refute the opposing views?

- If people are to present both sides—say, in successive talks at a community meeting—is there an advantage to going first or last?

As an example of how persuasion researchers address such questions, let's explore the first one.

Reason Versus Emotion
Suppose you were campaigning in support of world hunger relief. Would you best itemize your arguments and cite an array of impressive statistics? Or would you be more effective presenting an emotional approach—perhaps the compelling story of one starving child? Of

course, an argument can be both reasonable and emotional. You can marry passion and logic. Still, which is *more* influential—reason or emotion? Was Shakespeare's Lysander right: "The will of man is by his reason sway'd"? Or was Lord Chesterfield's advice wiser: "Address yourself generally to the senses, to the heart, and to the weaknesses of mankind, but rarely to their reason"?

The answer: It depends on the audience. Well-educated or analytical people are more responsive to rational appeals than are less educated or less analytical people (Cacioppo & others, 1983, 1996; Hovland & others, 1949). Thoughtful, involved audiences travel the central route; they are most responsive to reasoned arguments. Disinterested audiences travel the peripheral route; they are more affected by how much they like the communicator (Chaiken, 1980; Petty & others, 1981).

To judge from interviews before major elections, many voters are uninvolved. Americans' voting preferences have been more predictable from emotional reactions to the candidates than from their beliefs about the candidates' traits and likely behaviors (Abelson & others, 1982).

The Effect of Good Feelings

Messages also become more persuasive through association with good feelings. Irving Janis and his colleagues (1965; Dabbs & Janis, 1965) found that Yale students were more convinced by persuasive messages if they were allowed to enjoy peanuts and Pepsi while reading the messages. Similarly, Mark Galizio and Clyde Hendrick (1972) found that Kent State University students were more persuaded by folk-song lyrics accompanied by pleasant guitar music than they were by unaccompanied lyrics. Those who like conducting business over sumptuous lunches with soft background music can celebrate these results.

Good feelings often enhance persuasion—partly by enhancing positive thinking (if people are motivated to think) and partly by linking good feelings with the message (Petty & others, 1993). As noted previously, in a good mood, people view the world through rose-colored glasses. But they also make faster, more impulsive decisions; they rely more on peripheral cues (Bodenhausen, 1993; Schwarz & others, 1991). Unhappy people ruminate more before reacting, so they are less easily swayed by weak arguments. Thus, if you can't make a strong case, you might want to put your audience in a good mood and hope they'll feel good about your message without thinking too much about it.

The Effect of Arousing Fear

Messages can also be effective by evoking negative emotions. When trying to convince people to cut down on smoking, brush their teeth more often, get a tetanus shot, or drive carefully, a fear-arousing message can be potent (Muller & Johnson, 1990). The Canadian government is counting on the fact that showing cigarette smokers the horrible things that can happen to people who smoke adds to persuasiveness by requiring cigarette makers to include graphic representations of the hazards of smoking on each new pack of cigarettes (Newman, 2001). But how much fear should you arouse? Should you evoke just a little fear, lest people become so frightened that they tune out your painful message? Or should you try to scare the daylights out of them? Experiments by Howard Leventhal (1970) and his collaborators at the University of Wisconsin and by Ronald Rogers and his collaborators at the University of Alabama (Robberson & Rogers, 1988) show that, often, the more frightened people are, the more they respond.

The effectiveness of fear-arousing communications is being applied in ads discouraging not only smoking, but also risky sexual behaviors and drinking and driving. When Claude Levy-Leboyer (1988) found that attitudes toward alcohol and drinking habits among French youth were changed effectively by fear-arousing pictures, the French government incorporated such pictures into its TV spots. To have one's fears aroused is to become more intensely interested in information about a disease and in ways to prevent it (Das & others, 2003; Ruiter & others, 2001a).

Fear-arousing communications are increasing people's detection behaviors, such as getting mammograms, doing breast or testicular self-exams, and checking for signs of skin cancer. Sara Banks, Peter Salovey, and their colleagues (1995) had women, aged 40–66 who had not obtained mammograms, view an educational video on mammography. Of those who received a positively framed message (emphasizing that getting a mammogram can save your life through early detection), only half got a mammogram within 12 months. Of those who received a fear-framed message (emphasizing that not getting a mammogram can cost you your life), two-thirds got a mammogram within 12 months.

People may engage in denial because, when they aren't told how to avoid the danger, frightening messages can be overwhelming (Leventhal, 1970; Rogers & Mewborn, 1976). Fear-arousing messages are more effective if you lead people not only to fear the severity and likelihood of a threatened event but also to perceive a solution and to feel capable of implementing it (Devos-Comby & Salovey, 2002; Maddux & Rogers, 1983; Ruiter & others, 2001b). Many ads aimed at reducing sexual risks aim both to arouse fear—"AIDS kills"—and to offer a protective strategy: Abstain or wear a condom or save sex for a committed relationship. During the 1980s, fear of AIDS did persuade many men to alter their behavior. One study of 5,000 gay men found that, as the AIDS crisis mushroomed between 1984 and 1986, the number saying they were celibate or monogamous rose from 14 to 39 percent (Fineberg, 1988).

To Whom Is It Said?

It also matters who *receives* a message. Let's consider two other characteristics of those who receive a message: age and thoughtfulness.

How Old Are They?

People tend to have different social and political attitudes depending on their age. Social psychologists give two explanations for the difference. One is a *life cycle explanation:* Attitudes change (for example, become more conservative) as people grow older. The other is a *generational explanation:* The attitudes older people adopted when they were young persist largely unchanged; because these attitudes are different from those being adopted by young people today, a generation gap develops.

The evidence mostly supports the generational explanation. In surveys and resurveys of groups of younger and older people over several years, the attitudes of older people usually show less change than do those of young people. As David Sears (1979, 1986) puts it, researchers have "almost invariably found generational rather than life cycle effects."

Older adults are not inflexible; most people in their fifties and sixties have more liberal sexual and racial attitudes than they had in their thirties and forties (Glenn, 1980, 1981). Few of us are utterly uninfluenced by changing cultural norms. Moreover, research by Penny Visser and Jon Krosnick (1998) suggests that older adults, near the end of the life cycle, may again become more susceptible to attitude change, perhaps due to a decline in the strength of their attitudes.

Nevertheless, the teens and early twenties are important formative years (Krosnick & Alwin, 1989), and the attitudes formed then tend to remain stable through middle adulthood. Young people might therefore be advised to choose their social influences—the groups they join, the media they imbibe, the roles they adopt—carefully.

Adolescent and early adult experiences are formative partly because they make deep and lasting impressions. When Howard Schuman and Jacqueline Scott (1989) asked people to name the one or two most important national or world events of the previous half-century, most recalled events from their teens or early twenties. For those who experienced the Great Depression or World War II as 16- to 24-year-olds, those events overshadowed the civil rights movement and the Kennedy assassination of the early sixties, the Vietnam War and moon landing of the late sixties, and the women's movement of the seventies—all of which were imprinted on the minds of those who experienced them as 16- to 24-year-olds. We may therefore expect that today's young adults will include phenomena such as e-mail, the Web, and 9/11 as the memorable turning points in world history.

What Are They Thinking?
The crucial aspect of central route persuasion is not the message but the responses it evokes in a person's mind. Our minds are not sponges that soak up whatever pours over them. If the message summons favorable thoughts, it persuades us. If it provokes us to think of contrary arguments, we remain unpersuaded.

Forewarned is forearmed—if you care enough to counterargue. What circumstances breed counterargument? One is a warning that someone is going to try to persuade you. If you had to tell your family that you wanted to drop out of school, you would likely anticipate their pleading with you to stay. So you might develop a list of arguments to counter every conceivable argument they might make.

Jonathan Freedman and David Sears (1965) demonstrated the difficulty of trying to persuade people under such circumstances. They warned one group of California high schoolers that they were going to hear a talk: "Why Teenagers Should Not Be Allowed to Drive." Those forewarned did not budge in their opinions. Others, not forewarned, did. In courtrooms, too, defense attorneys sometimes forewarn juries about prosecution evidence to come. With mock juries, such "stealing thunder" neutralizes its negative impact (Dolnik & others, 2003).

Sneak attacks on attitudes are especially useful with involved people. Given several minutes' forewarning, involved people will prepare defenses (Chen & others, 1992; Petty & Cacioppo, 1977, 1979). When forewarned people regard an issue as trivial, however, they may agree even before receiving the message, to avoid later seeming gullible (Wood & Quinn, 2003).

Distraction disarms counterarguing. Verbal persuasion is also enhanced by distracting people with something that attracts their attention just enough to inhibit counterarguing (Festinger & Maccoby, 1964; Keating & Brock, 1974; Osterhouse & Brock, 1970). Political ads often use this technique. The words promote the candidate, and the visual images keep us occupied so we don't analyze the words. Distraction is especially effective when the message is simple (Harkins & Petty, 1981; Regan & Cheng, 1973).

Uninvolved audiences use peripheral cues. Recall the two routes to persuasion—the central route of systematic thinking and the peripheral route of heuristic cues. Like the road through town, the central route has starts and stops as the mind analyzes arguments and formulates responses. Like the freeway around town, the peripheral route zips people to their destination. Analytical people—those with a high *need for cognition*—enjoy thinking carefully and prefer central routes (Cacioppo & others, 1996). People who like to conserve their mental resources—

those with a low need for cognition—are quicker to respond to such peripheral cues as the communicator's attractiveness and the pleasantness of the surroundings.

But the issue matters, too. All of us actively struggle with issues that involve us while making snap judgments about things that matter little (Johnson & Eagly, 1990). As we mentally elaborate on an important issue, the strength of the arguments and of our own thoughts determine our attitudes.

This simple theory—*that what we think in response to a message is crucial*, especially if we are motivated and able to think about it—helps us understand several findings. For example, we more readily believe trustworthy, expert communicators if we're following the peripheral route. When we trust the source, we think favorable thoughts and are less likely to counterargue. Mistrusting the source makes us more likely to follow the central route. If we don't trust those who sell, we'll probably think critically about their sales pitch.

The theory has also generated many predictions, most of which have been confirmed by Petty, Cacioppo, and others (Axsom & others, 1987; Harkins & Petty, 1987; Leippe & Elkin, 1987). Many experiments have explored ways to stimulate people's thinking—by using *rhetorical questions,* by presenting *multiple speakers* (for example, having each of three speakers give one argument instead of one speaker giving three), by making people *feel responsible* for evaluating or passing along the message, by using *relaxed postures* rather than standing ones, by *repeating* the message, and by getting people's *undistracted attention*. Their consistent finding with each of these techniques: *Stimulating thinking makes strong messages more persuasive and* (because of counterarguing) *weak messages less persuasive.*

The theory also has practical implications. Effective communicators care not only about their images and their messages but also about how their audience is likely to react. The best instructors tend to get students to think actively. They ask rhetorical questions, provide intriguing examples, and challenge students with difficult problems. All these techniques are likely to foster a process that moves information through the central route to persuasion. In classes where the instruction is less engaging, you can provide your own central processing. If you think about the material and elaborate on the arguments, you are likely to do better in the course.

During the final days of a closely contested 1980 presidential campaign, Ronald Reagan effectively used rhetorical questions to stimulate desired thoughts in voters' minds. His summary statement in the presidential debate began with two potent rhetorical questions that he repeated often during the campaign's remaining week: "Are you better off than you were four years ago? Is it easier for you to go and buy things in the stores than it was four years ago?" Most people answered no, and Reagan, thanks partly to the way he prodded people to take the central route, won by a bigger-than-expected margin.

THE TWO ROUTES TO PERSUASION IN THERAPY

One constructive use of persuasion is in counseling and psychotherapy, which social-counseling psychologist Stanley Strong views "as a branch of applied social psychology" (1978, p. 101). By the 1990s, more and more psychologists had accepted the idea that social influence, one person affecting another, is at the heart of therapy.

Early analyses of psychotherapeutic influence focused on how therapists establish credible expertise and trustworthiness and how their credibility enhances their influence (Strong, 1968). More recent analyses have focused less on the therapist than on how the interaction affects the client's thinking (Cacioppo & others, 1991; McNeill & Stoltenberg, 1988; Neimeyer & others, 1991). Peripheral cues, such as therapist credibility, may open the door for ideas that the therapist can now get the client to think about. But the thoughtful central route to persuasion provides the most enduring attitude and behavior change. Therapists should therefore aim not to elicit a client's superficial agreement with their expert judgment but to change the client's own thinking.

Fortunately, most clients entering therapy are motivated to take the central route, to think deeply about their problems under the therapist's guidance. The therapist's task is to offer arguments and raise questions calculated to elicit favorable thoughts. The therapist's insights matter less than the thoughts they evoke in the client. The therapist needs to put things in ways that a client can hear and understand, ways that will prompt agreement rather than counterargument and that will allow time and space for the client to reflect. Questions such as "How do you respond to what I just said?" can stimulate the client's thinking.

Martin Heesacker (1989) illustrates with the case of Dave, a 35-year-old male graduate student. Having seen what Dave denied—an underlying substance abuse problem—the counselor drew on his knowledge of Dave, an intellectual person who liked hard evidence, in persuading him to accept the diagnosis and join a treatment-support group. The counselor said, "OK, if my diagnosis is wrong, I'll be glad to change it. But let's go through a list of the characteristics of a substance abuser to check out my accuracy." The counselor then went through each criterion slowly, giving Dave time to think about each point. As he finished, Dave sat back and exclaimed, "I don't believe it: I'm a damned alcoholic."

In an experiment, John Ernst and Heesacker (1993) showed the effectiveness of escorting participants in an assertion training workshop through the central route to persuasion. Some participants experienced the typical assertiveness workshop by learning and rehearsing concepts of assertiveness. Others learned the same concepts but also recalled a time when they had hurt themselves by being unassertive. Then they heard arguments that Ernst and Heesacker knew were likely to trigger favorable thoughts (for example, "By failing to assert yourself, you train others to mistreat you"). At the workshop's end, Ernst and Heesacker asked the people to stop and reflect on how they now felt about all they had learned. Compared with those in the first group, those who went through the thought-evoking workshop left the experience with more favorable attitudes and intentions regarding assertiveness. Moreover, their roommates noticed greater assertiveness during the ensuing two weeks.

In his 1620 *Pensées*, the philosopher Pascal foresaw this principle: "People are usually more convinced by reasons they discover themselves than by those found by others." It's a principle worth remembering.

CONCEPTS TO REMEMBER

persuasion   The process by which a message induces change in beliefs, attitudes, or behaviors.

central route to persuasion   Occurs when interested people focus on the arguments and respond with favorable thoughts.

peripheral route to persuasion   Occurs when people are influenced by incidental cues, such as a speaker's attractiveness.

credibility   Believability. A credible communicator is perceived as both expert and trustworthy.

sleeper effect   A delayed impact of a message occurs when an initially discounted message becomes effective, as we remember the message but forget the reason for discounting it.

attractiveness   Having qualities that appeal to an audience. An appealing communicator (often someone similar to the audience) is most persuasive on matters of subjective preference.

MODULE

16

❖

Indoctrination and Inoculation

Joseph Goebbels, Germany's minister of "popular enlightenment" and propaganda from 1933 to 1945, understood the power of persuasion. Given control of publications, radio programs, motion pictures, and the arts, he undertook to persuade Germans to accept Nazi ideology. Julius Streicher, another member of the Nazi group, published *Der Stürmer*, a weekly anti-Semitic (anti-Jewish) newspaper with a circulation of 500,000 and the only paper read cover to cover by his intimate friend, Adolf Hitler. Streicher also published anti-Semitic children's books and, with Goebbels, spoke at the mass rallies that became part of the Nazi propaganda machine.

How effective were Goebbels, Streicher, and other Nazi propagandists? Did they, as the Allies alleged at Streicher's Nuremberg trial, "inject poison into the minds of millions and millions" (Bytwerk, 1976)? Most Germans were not persuaded to feel raging hatred for the Jews. But many were. Others became sympathetic to anti-Semitic measures. And most of the rest became either sufficiently uncertain or sufficiently intimidated to staff the huge genocidal program, or at least to allow it to happen. Without the complicity of millions of people, there would have been no Holocaust (Goldhagen, 1996).

The powers of persuasion were more recently apparent in what a Pew survey (2003) called the "rift between Americans and Western Europeans" over the Iraq War. Surveys shortly before the war, for example, revealed that Europeans (and Canadians) opposed military action against Iraq by about two to one, while Americans favored it by the same margin (Burkholder, 2003; Moore, 2003b; Pew, 2003). Once the war began, Americans' support for the war rose to more than three to one

(Newport & others, 2003). Except for Israel, people surveyed in all other countries were opposed to the attack.

Without taking sides regarding the wisdom of the war—that debate we can leave to history—the huge rift between Americans and their distant cousins in other countries points to persuasion at work. What persuaded Americans to favor the war? What persuaded most people elsewhere to oppose it? (Tell me where you live and I will guess whether you view the United States more as protector or predator.)

In addition to possible rationalization of "my country's" actions, attitudes were also being shaped by persuasive messages that led half of Americans to believe that Saddam was directly involved in the 9/11 attacks and four in five to believe that weapons of mass destruction would be found (Duffy, 2003; Gallup, 2003c; Newport & others, 2003). Sociologist James Davison Hunter (2002) notes that culture-shaping usually occurs top-down, as cultural elites control the dissemination of information and ideas. Thus, Americans and people elsewhere learned about and watched a different war (della Cava, 2003; Friedman, 2003b; Goldsmith, 2003; Krugman, 2003; Tomorrow, 2003). Depending on where you lived, you may have heard and read about

- "America's liberation of Iraq" or "America's invasion of Iraq."
- "Operation Iraqi Freedom" or "The War in Iraq."
- the Iraqi "death squads" or the "Fedayeen" irregulars.
- headlines such as "Tense Standoff Between Troops and Iraqis Erupts in Bloodshed" (ambiguous passive voice headline of *Los Angeles Times*) or "U.S. Troops Fire on Iraqis; 13 Reported Dead" (active voice headline of the same incident by Canada's CBC).
- scenes of captured and dead Iraqis or scenes of captured and dead Americans.
- brief clips of "the usual protestors" (Fox News) or features on massive antiwar rallies.

To many Americans, the media of other nations appeared to combine a pervasive anti-American bias with a blindness to the threat posed by Saddam. To many people elsewhere, the "embedded" American war journalists seemed to feel it their patriotic duty to sell the war. Regardless of where bias lay or whose perspective was better informed, this much seems clear: Depending on where they lived, people were fed (and discussed and believed) somewhat differing information. Persuasion matters.

Persuasive forces also have been harnessed to promote healthier living. Thanks partly to health promotion campaigns, the Centers for Disease Control and Prevention reports that the American cigarette smoking rate has plunged to 23 percent, barely more than half the rate of 40 years ago. *Statistics Canada* reports a similar smoking decline in Canada. And the rate of new U.S. collegians reporting abstinence from beer has increased—from 25 percent in 1981 to 46 percent in 2004 (Sax & others, 2004). More than at any time in recent decades, health- and safety-conscious educated adults are shunning cigarettes and beer.

CULT INDOCTRINATION

On March 22, 1997, Marshall Herff Applewhite and 37 of his disciples decided the time had come to shed their bodies—mere "containers"— and be whisked up to a UFO trailing the Hale-Bopp Comet, en route to heaven's gate. So they put themselves to sleep by mixing phenobarbital into pudding or applesauce, washing it down with vodka, and then fixing plastic bags over their heads so they would suffocate in their slumber. On that same day, a cottage in the French Canadian village of St. Casimir exploded in an inferno, consuming five people—the latest of 74 members of the Order of the Solar Temple to have committed suicide in Canada, Switzerland, and France. All were hoping to be transported to the star Sirius, nine light-years away.

The question on many minds: What persuades people to leave behind their former beliefs and join these mental chain gangs? Shall we attribute their strange behaviors to strange personalities? Or do their experiences illustrate the common dynamics of social influence and persuasion?

Bear two things in mind. First, this is hindsight analysis. It uses persuasion principles as categories for explaining, after the fact, a fascinating and sometimes disturbing social phenomenon. Second, explaining *why* people believe something says nothing about the *truth* of their beliefs. That is a logically separate issue. A psychology of religion might tell us *why* a theist believes in God and an atheist disbelieves, but it cannot tell us who is right. Explaining either belief does not explain it away. So if someone tries to discount your beliefs by saying, "You just believe that because . . . ," you might recall Archbishop William Temple's reply to a questioner who challenged: "Well, of course, Archbishop, the point is that you believe what you believe because of the way you were brought up." To which the archbishop replied: "That is as it may be. But the fact remains that you believe I believe what I believe because of the way I was brought up, because of the way you were brought up."

In recent decades, several **cults**—which some social scientists prefer to call *new religious movements*—have gained much publicity: Sun Myung Moon's Unification Church, Jim Jones's People's Temple, David Koresh's Branch Davidians, and Marshall Applewhite's Heaven's Gate.

Sun Myung Moon's mixture of Christianity, anticommunism, and glorification of Moon himself as a new messiah attracted a worldwide following. In response to Moon's declaration, "What I wish must be your wish," many people committed themselves and their incomes to the Unification Church.

In 1978 in Guyana, 914 disciples of Jim Jones, who had followed him there from San Francisco, shocked the world when they died by following his order to down a suicidal grape drink laced with tranquilizers, painkillers, and a lethal dose of cyanide.

In 1993, high-school dropout David Koresh used his talent for memorizing Scripture and mesmerizing people to seize control of a faction of a sect called the Branch Davidians. Over time, members were gradually relieved of their bank accounts and possessions. Koresh also persuaded the men to live celibately while he slept with their wives and daughters, and he convinced his 19 "wives" that they should bear his children. Under siege after a shootout that killed six members and four federal agents, Koresh told his followers they would soon die and go with him straight to heaven. Federal agents rammed the compound with tanks, hoping to inject tear gas, and, by the end of the assault, 86 people were consumed in a fire that engulfed the compound.

Marshall Applewhite was not similarly tempted to command sexual favors. Having been fired from two music teaching jobs for homosexual affairs with students, he sought sexless devotion by castration, as had 7 of the other 17 Heaven's Gate men who died with him (Chua-Eoan, 1997; Gardner, 1997). While in a psychiatric hospital in 1971, Applewhite had linked up with nurse and astrology dabbler Bonnie Lu Nettles, who gave the intense and charismatic Applewhite a cosmological vision of a route to "the next level." Preaching with passion, he persuaded his followers to renounce families, sex, drugs, and personal money with promises of a spaceship voyage to salvation.

How could these things happen? What persuaded these people to give such total allegiance? Shall we make dispositional explanations— by blaming the victims? Shall we dismiss them as gullible kooks or dumb weirdos? Or can familiar principles of conformity, compliance, dissonance, persuasion, and group influence explain their behavior—putting them on common ground with the rest of us who in our own ways are shaped by such forces?

Attitudes Follow Behavior

Compliance Breeds Acceptance

As we saw in Module 9's discussion of behavior and belief, people usually internalize commitments made voluntarily, publicly, and repeatedly. Cult leaders seem to know this. New converts soon learn that membership is no trivial matter. They are quickly made active members of the team. Rituals within the cult community, and public canvassing and fund-raising, strengthen the initiates' identities as members. As those in social-psychological experiments come to believe in what they bear witness to (Aronson & Mills, 1959; Gerard & Mathewson, 1966), so cult initiates become committed advocates. The greater the personal commitment, the more the need to justify it.

The Foot-in-the-Door Phenomenon
How are we induced to make commitments? Seldom by an abrupt, conscious decision. One does not just decide, "I'm through with mainstream religion. I'm gonna find a cult." Nor do cult recruiters approach people on the street with, "Hi. I'm a Moonie. Care to join us?" Rather, the recruitment strategy exploits the foot-in-the-door principle. Unification Church recruiters would invite people to a dinner and then to a weekend of warm fellowship and discussions of philosophies of life. At the weekend retreat, they would encourage the attenders to join them in songs, activities, and discussion. Potential converts were then urged to sign up for longer training retreats. Eventually the activities would become more arduous—soliciting contributions and attempting to convert others.

Jim Jones also used this foot-in-the-door technique. At first, monetary offerings were voluntary. Jones next inaugurated a required 10-percent-of-income contribution, which soon increased to 25 percent. Finally, he ordered members to turn over to him everything they owned. Workloads also became progressively more demanding. Former cult member Grace Stoen recalls the gradual progress:

> Nothing was ever done drastically. That's how Jim Jones got away with so much. You slowly gave up things and slowly had to put up with more, but it was always done very gradually. It was amazing, because you would sit up sometimes and say, wow, I really have given up a lot. I really am putting up with a lot. But he did it so slowly that you figured, I've made it this far, what the hell is the difference? (Conway & Siegelman, 1979, p. 236)

Persuasive Elements

We can also analyze cult persuasion using the factors discussed in Module 15: *Who* (the communicator) said *what* (the message) to *whom* (the audience)?

The Communicator
Successful cults have a charismatic leader—someone who attracts and directs the members. As in experiments on persuasion, a credible communicator is someone the audience perceives as expert and trustworthy—for example, as "Father" Moon.

Jim Jones used "psychic readings" to establish his credibility. Newcomers were asked to identify themselves as they entered the church before services. Then one of his aides would quickly call the person's home and say, "Hi. We're doing a survey, and we'd like to ask you some questions." During the service, one ex-member recalled, Jones would call out the person's name and say

> Have you ever seen me before? Well, you live in such and such a place, your phone number is such and such, and in your living room you've got this, that, and the other, and on your sofa you've got such and such a pillow. . . . Now do you remember me ever being in your house? (Conway & Siegelman, 1979, p. 234)

Trust is another aspect of credibility. Cult researcher Margaret Singer (1979) noted that middle-class Caucasian youths are more vulnerable to recruitment because they are more trusting. They lack the "street smarts" of lower-class youths (who know how to resist a hustle) and the wariness of upper-class youths (who have been warned of kidnappers since child-hood). Many cult members have been recruited by friends or relatives, people they trust (Stark & Bainbridge, 1980).

The Message
The vivid, emotional messages and the warmth and acceptance with which the group showers lonely or depressed people can be strikingly appealing: Trust the master, join the family; we have the answer, the "one way." The message echoes through channels as varied as lectures, small-group discussions, and direct social pressure.

The Audience
Recruits are often young—people under 25 and still at that compara-tively open age before attitudes and values stabilize. Some, such as the followers of Jim Jones, are less-educated people who like the simplicity of the message and find it difficult to counterargue. But most are educated, middle-class people who, taken by the ideals, overlook the contradictions in those who profess selflessness and practice greed, who pretend concern and behave indifferently.

Potential converts are often at turning points in their lives, facing personal crises, or vacationing or living away from home. They have needs; the cult offers them an answer (Lofland & Stark, 1965; Singer, 1979). Gail Maeder joined Heaven's Gate after her T-shirt shop had failed. David Moore joined when he was 19, just out of high school, and searching for direction. Times of social and economic upheaval are espe-cially conducive to someone who can make apparent simple sense out of the confusion (O'Dea, 1968; Sales, 1972).

Group Effects

Cults also illustrate the next module's theme: the power of a group to shape members' views and behavior. The cult typically separates mem-bers from their previous social support systems and isolates them with other cultists. There may then occur what Rodney Stark and William Bainbridge (1980) call a "social implosion": External ties weaken until the group collapses inward socially, each person engaging only with other group members. Cut off from families and former friends, they lose access to counterarguments. The group now offers identity and defines reality. Because the cult frowns on or punishes disagreements, the apparent consensus helps eliminate any lingering doubts. Moreover, stress and emotional arousal narrow attention, making people "more susceptible to poorly supported arguments, social pressure, and the temptation to derogate nongroup members" (Baron, 2000).

Marshall Applewhite and Bonnie Nettles (who died of cancer in 1985) at first formed their own group of two, reinforcing each other's aberrant thinking—a phenomenon that psychiatrists call *folie à deux* (French for "insanity of two"). As others joined them, the group's social isolation facilitated more peculiar thinking. As Internet conspiracy theory discussion groups illustrate (Heaven's Gate was skilled in Internet recruiting), virtual groups can likewise foster paranoia.

Contrary to the idea that cults turn hapless people into mindless robots, these techniques—increasing behavioral commitments, persuasion, and group isolation—do not have unlimited power. The Unification Church has successfully recruited fewer than 1 in 10 people who attend its workshops (Ennis & Verrilli, 1989). Most who joined Heaven's Gate had left before that fateful day. David Koresh ruled with a mix of persuasion, intimidation, and violence. As Jim Jones made his demands more extreme, he, too, increasingly had to control people with intimidation. He used threats of harm to those who fled the community, beatings for noncompliance, and drugs to neutralize disagreeable members. By the end, he was as much an arm twister as a mind bender.

Moreover, cult influence techniques are in some ways similar to techniques used by groups more familiar to us. Fraternity and sorority members have reported that the initial "love bombing" of potential cult recruits is not unlike their own "rush" period. Members lavish prospective pledges with attention and make them feel special. During the pledge period, new members are somewhat isolated, cut off from old friends who did not pledge. They spend time studying the history and rules of their new group. They suffer and commit time on its behalf. They are expected to comply with all its demands. The result is usually a committed new member.

Much the same is true for recovering drug and alcohol abusers in some therapeutic communities. Zealous self-help groups form a cohesive "social cocoon," have intense beliefs, and exert a profound influence on members' behavior (Galanter, 1989, 1990).

I chose the examples of fraternities, sororities, and self-help groups not to disparage them but to illustrate two concluding observations. First, if we attribute new religious movements to the leader's mystical force or to the followers' peculiar weaknesses, we may delude ourselves into thinking we are immune to social control techniques. In truth, our own groups—and countless political leaders, educators, and other persuaders—successfully use many of these tactics on us. Between education and indoctrination, enlightenment and propaganda, conversion and coercion, therapy and mind control, there is but a blurry line.

Second, the fact that Jim Jones and other cult leaders abused the power of persuasion does not mean persuasion is intrinsically bad. Nuclear power enables us to light up homes or wipe out cities. Sexual power enables us to express and celebrate committed love or exploit people for selfish gratification. Persuasive power enables us to enlighten or deceive. Knowing that these powers can be harnessed for evil purposes should alert us, as scientists and citizens, to guard against their immoral use. But the powers themselves are neither inherently evil nor inherently good; how we use them determines whether their effect is destructive or constructive. Condemning persuasion because of deceit is like condemning eating because of gluttony.

R ESISTING PERSUASION: ATTITUDE INOCULATION

This consideration of persuasive influences has perhaps made you wonder if it is possible to resist unwanted persuasion.

Blessed with logic, information, and motivation, we do resist falsehoods. If, because of an aura of credibility, the repair person's uniform and doctor's title have intimidated us into unquestioning agreement, we can rethink our habitual responses to authority. We can seek more information before committing time or money. We can question what we don't understand.

Stimulate Commitment

There is another way to resist: Before encountering others' judgments, make a public commitment to your position. Having stood up for your convictions, you will become less susceptible (or should we say less "open"?) to what others have to say.

Challenging Beliefs

How might we stimulate people to commit themselves? From his experiments, Charles Kiesler (1971) offered one possible way: Mildly attack their position. Kiesler found that when committed people were attacked strongly enough to cause them to react, but not so strongly as to overwhelm them, they became even more committed. Kiesler explained: "When you attack committed people and your attack is of inadequate strength, you drive them to even more extreme behaviors in defense of their previous commitment. Their commitment escalates, in a sense, because the number of acts consistent with their belief increases" (p. 88). Perhaps you can recall a time when this happened in an argument, as those involved escalated their rhetoric, committing themselves to increasingly extreme positions.

Develop Counterarguments
There is a second reason a mild attack might build resistance. When someone attacks one of our cherished attitudes, we typically feel some irritation and contemplate counterarguments. Counterarguing helps people resist persuasion (Jacks & Cameron, 2003). Refute someone's persuasion, and know that you have done so, and you will feel more certain than ever (Tormala & Petty, 2002).

Like inoculations against disease, even weak arguments will prompt counterarguments, which are then available for a stronger attack. William McGuire (1964) documented this in a series of experiments. McGuire wondered: Could we inoculate people against persuasion much as we inoculate them against a virus? Is there such a thing as **attitude inoculation?** Could we take people raised in a "germ-free ideological environment"—people who hold some unquestioned belief—and stimulate their mental defenses? And would subjecting them to a small dose of belief-threatening material inoculate them against later persuasion?

That is what McGuire did. First, he found some cultural truisms, such as, "It's a good idea to brush your teeth after every meal if at all possible." He then showed that people were vulnerable to a massive, credible assault upon these truisms (for example, prestigious authorities were said to have discovered that too much toothbrushing can damage one's gums). If, however, before having their belief attacked, they were "immunized" by first receiving a small challenge to their belief, *and* if they read or wrote an essay in refutation of this mild attack, then they were better able to resist the powerful attack.

Robert Cialdini and his colleagues (2003) agree that appropriate counterarguments are a great way to resist persuasion but wondered how to bring them to mind in response to an opponents' ads, especially when the opponent (like most political incumbents) has a huge spending advantage. The answer, they suggest, is a "poison parasite" defense—one that combines a poison (strong counterarguments) with a parasite (retrieval cues that bring those arguments to mind when seeing the opponent's ads). In their studies, participants who viewed a familiar political ad were least persuaded by it when they had earlier seen counterarguments overlaid on a replica of the ad. Seeing the ad again thus also brought to mind the puncturing counterarguments. Antismoking ads have effectively done this, for example, by re-creating a "Marlboro Man" commercial set in the rugged outdoors but now showing a coughing, decrepit cowboy.

A *"poison parasite"* ad.

Real-Life Applications: Inoculation Programs

Inoculating Children Against Peer Pressure to Smoke

In a clear demonstration of how laboratory research findings can lead to practical applications, a research team led by Alfred McAlister (1980) had high school students "inoculate" seventh-graders against peer pressures to smoke. The seventh-graders were taught to respond to advertisements implying that liberated women smoke by saying, "She's not really liberated if she is hooked on tobacco." They also acted in role plays in which, after being called "chicken" for not taking a cigarette, they answered with statements like, "I'd be a real chicken if I smoked just to impress you." After several of these sessions during the seventh and eighth grades, the inoculated students were half as likely to begin smoking as were uninoculated students at another junior high school that had an identical parental smoking rate (Figure 16-1).

Other research teams have confirmed that inoculation procedures, sometimes supplemented by other life skill training, reduce teen smoking (Botvin & others, 1995; Evans & others, 1984; Flay & others, 1985). Most newer efforts emphasize strategies for resisting social pressure. One study exposed sixth- to eighth-graders to antismoking films or to information about smoking, together with role plays of student-generated ways of refusing a cigarette (Hirschman & Leventhal, 1989). A year and a half later, 31 percent of those who watched the antismoking films had taken up smoking. Among those who role-played refusing, only 19 percent had begun smoking.

Antismoking and drug education programs apply other persuasion principles, too. They use attractive peers to communicate information. They trigger the students' own cognitive processing ("Here's something

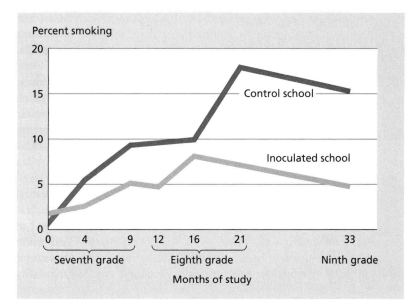

FIGURE 16-1
The percentage of cigarette smokers at an "inoculated" junior high school was much less than at a matched control school using a more typical smoking education program. **Source:** Data from McAlister & others, 1980; Telch & others, 1981.

you might want to think about"). They get the students to make a public commitment (by making a rational decision about smoking and then announcing it, along with their reasoning, to their classmates). Some of these smoking-prevention programs require only two to six hours of class, using prepared printed materials or videotapes. Today any school district or teacher wishing to use the social-psychological approach to smoking prevention can do so easily, inexpensively, and with the hope of significant reductions in future smoking rates and associated health costs.

Inoculating Children Against the Influence of Advertising
Sweden, Italy, Greece, Belgium, Denmark, and Ireland all restrict advertising that targets children, and other European countries have been discussing doing the same (McGuire, 2002). In the United States, notes Robert Levine in *The Power of Persuasion: How We're Bought and Sold*, the average child sees over 10,000 commercials a year. "Two decades ago," he notes, "children drank twice as much milk as soda. Thanks to advertising, the ratio is now reversed" (2003, p. 16). Smokers often develop an "initial brand choice" in their teens, said a 1981 report from researchers at Philip Morris, a major player in the $11.2 billion spent

annually on tobacco advertising and promotion (FTC, 2003). "Today's teenager is tomorrow's potential regular customer, and the overwhelming majority of smokers first begin to smoke while still in their teens" (Lichtblau, 2003).

In response, researchers have studied how to immunize young children against the effects of television commercials. This research was prompted partly by studies showing that children, especially those under 8 years old, (1) have trouble distinguishing commercials from programs and fail to grasp their persuasive intent, (2) trust television advertising rather indiscriminately, and (3) desire and badger their parents for advertised products (Adler & others, 1980; Feshbach, 1980; Palmer & Dorr, 1980). Children, it seems, are an advertiser's dream: gullible, vulnerable, an easy sell.

Armed with this data, citizens' groups have given the advertisers of such products a chewing out (Moody, 1980): "When a sophisticated advertiser spends millions to sell unsophisticated, trusting children an unhealthy product, this can only be called exploitation." In "Mothers' Statement to Advertisers" (Motherhood Project, 2001), a broad coalition of American women echoed this outrage:

> For us, our children are priceless gifts. For you, our children are customers, and childhood is a "market segment" to be exploited. . . . The line between *meeting* and *creating* consumer needs and desire is increasingly being crossed, as your battery of highly trained and creative experts study, analyze, persuade, and manipulate our children. . . . The driving messages are "You deserve a break today," "Have it your way," "Follow your instincts. Obey your thirst," "Just Do It," "No Boundaries," "Got the Urge?" These [exemplify] the dominant message of advertising and marketing: that life is about selfishness, instant gratification, and materialism.

On the other side are those who have commercial interests and claim that ads allow parents to teach their children consumer skills and, more important, finance children's television programs. In the United States, the Federal Trade Commission has been in the middle, pushed by research findings and political pressures while trying to decide whether to place new constraints on TV ads for unhealthy foods and for R-rated movies aimed at underage youth.

Meanwhile, researchers have wondered whether children can be taught to resist deceptive ads. In one such effort, a team of investigators led by Norma Feshbach (1980; Cohen, 1980) gave small groups of Los Angeles–area elementary school children three half-hour lessons in analyzing commercials. The children were inoculated by viewing ads and discussing them. For example, after viewing a toy ad, they were immediately given the toy and challenged to make it do what they had just seen in the commercial. Such experiences helped breed a more realistic understanding of commercials.

Implications

The best way to build resistance to brainwashing probably isn't stronger indoctrination into one's current beliefs. If parents are worried that their children might become members of a cult, they might better teach their children about the various cults and prepare them to counter persuasive appeals.

For the same reason, religious educators should be wary of creating a "germfree ideological environment" in their churches and schools. An attack, if refuted, is more likely to solidify one's position than to undermine it, particularly if the threatening material can be examined with like-minded others. Cults apply this principle by forewarning members of how families and friends will attack the cult's beliefs. When the expected challenge comes, the member is armed with counterarguments.

Another implication is that, for the persuader, an ineffective appeal can be worse than none. Can you see why? Those who reject an appeal are inoculated against further appeals. Consider an experiment in which Susan Darley and Joel Cooper (1972) invited students to write essays advocating a strict dress code. Because this was against the students' own positions and the essays were to be published, all chose *not* to write the essay—even those offered money to do so. After turning down the money, they became even more extreme and confident in their anti-dress-code opinions. Having made an overt decision against the dress code, they became even more resistant to it. Those who have rejected initial appeals to quit smoking may likewise become immune to further appeals. Ineffective persuasion, by stimulating the listener's defenses, may be counterproductive. It may "harden the heart" against later appeals.

Activity
16.1

To be critical thinkers, we might take a cue from inoculation research. Do you want to build your resistance to persuasion without becoming closed to valid messages? Be an active listener and a critical thinker. Force yourself to counterargue. After hearing a political speech, discuss it with others. In other words, don't just listen; react. If the message cannot withstand careful analysis, so much the worse for it. If it can, its effect on you will be that much more enduring.

*C*ONCEPTS TO REMEMBER

cult (also called new religious movement)   A group typically characterized by (1) distinctive ritual and beliefs related to its devotion to a god or a person, (2) isolation from the surrounding "evil" culture, and (3) a charismatic leader.

(A sect, by contrast, is a spin-off from a major religion.)

attitude inoculation   Exposing people to weak attacks upon their attitudes so that when stronger attacks come, they will have refutations available.

17

❖

The Mere Presence of Others

Our world contains not only 6.4 billion individuals, but 200 nation-states, 4 million local communities, 20 million economic organizations, and hundreds of millions of other formal and informal groups—couples on dates, families, churches, housemates in bull sessions. How do these groups influence individuals?

Let's begin with social psychology's most elementary question: Are we affected by the mere presence of another person? "Mere presence" means people are not competing, do not reward or punish, and in fact do nothing except be present as a passive audience or as **co-actors.** Would the mere presence of others affect a person's jogging, eating, typing, or exam performance? The search for the answer is a scientific mystery story.

THE PRESENCE OF OTHERS

More than a century ago, Norman Triplett (1898), a psychologist interested in bicycle racing, noticed that cyclists' times were faster when racing together than when racing alone against the clock. Before he peddled his hunch (that others' presence boosts performance), Triplett conducted one of social psychology's first laboratory experiments. Children told to wind string on a fishing reel as rapidly as possible wound faster when they worked with co-actors than when they worked alone.

Ensuing experiments found that others' presence improves the speed with which people do simple multiplication problems and cross out designated letters. It also improves the accuracy with which people perform simple motor tasks, such as keeping a metal stick in contact with a dime-sized disk on a moving turntable (F. H. Allport, 1920; Dashiell, 1930; Travis, 1925). This **social facilitation** effect also occurs with animals. In the presence of others of their species, ants excavate more sand, chickens eat more grain, and sexually active rat pairs mate more often (Bayer, 1929; Chen, 1937; Larsson, 1956).

But wait: Other studies revealed that on some tasks the presence of others *hinders* performance. In the presence of others, cockroaches, parakeets, and green finches learn mazes more slowly (Allee & Masure, 1936; Gates & Allee, 1933; Klopfer, 1958). This disruptive effect also occurs with people. Others' presence diminishes efficiency at learning nonsense syllables, completing a maze, and performing complex multiplication problems (Dashiell, 1930; Pessin, 1933; Pessin & Husband, 1933).

Saying that the presence of others sometimes facilitates performance and sometimes hinders it is about as satisfying as the typical Scottish weather forecast—predicting that it might be sunny but then again it might rain. By 1940, research activity in this area had ground to a halt, and it lay dormant for 25 years until awakened by the touch of a new idea.

Social psychologist Robert Zajonc (pronounced *Zy-ence,* rhymes with *science*) wondered whether these seemingly contradictory findings could be reconciled. As often happens at creative moments in science, Zajonc (1965) used one field of research to illuminate another. In this case the illumination came from a well-established principle in experimental psychology: Arousal enhances whatever response tendency is dominant. Increased arousal enhances performance on easy tasks for which the most likely—"dominant"—response is the correct one. People solve easy anagrams, such as *akec,* fastest when they are aroused. On complex tasks, for which the correct answer is not dominant, increased arousal promotes *incorrect* responding. On harder anagrams people do worse when anxious.

Could this principle solve the mystery of social facilitation? It seemed reasonable to assume what evidence now confirms—that others' presence will arouse or energize people (Mullen & others, 1997). (We can all recall feeling more tense or excited in front of an audience.) If social arousal facilitates dominant responses, it should *boost performance on easy tasks* and *hurt performance on difficult tasks.* Now the confusing results made sense. Winding fishing reels, doing simple multiplication problems, and eating were all easy tasks for which the responses were well learned or naturally dominant. Sure enough, having others around boosted performance. Learning new material, doing a maze, and solving complex math problems were more difficult tasks for which the correct responses were initially less probable. In these cases, the presence of others increased the number of *incorrect* responses on these tasks. The same general rule—*arousal facilitates dominant responses*—worked in both cases (see Figure 17-1). Suddenly, what had looked like contradictory results no longer seemed contradictory.

Zajonc's solution, so simple and elegant, left other social psychologists thinking what Thomas H. Huxley thought after first reading Darwin's *Origin of the Species:* "How extremely stupid not to have thought of that!" It seemed obvious—once Zajonc had pointed it out. Perhaps, however, the pieces appeared to merge so neatly only through the spectacles of hindsight. Would the solution survive direct experimental tests? After almost 300 studies, conducted with the help of more than 25,000 volunteers, the solution has survived (Bond & Titus, 1983; Guerin, 1993, 1999).

In various ways, later experiments confirmed that social arousal facilitates dominant responses, whether right or wrong. Peter Hunt and Joseph Hillery (1973) found that in others' presence, students took less time to learn a simple maze and more time to learn a complex one (just as the cockroaches do!). And James Michaels and his collaborators (1982) found that good pool players in a student union (who had made 71 percent of their shots while being unobtrusively observed) did even better (80 percent) when four observers came up to watch them play. Poor shooters (who had previously averaged 36 percent) did even worse (25 percent) when closely observed.

Athletes perform well-practiced skills, which helps explain why they often perform best when energized by the responses of a supportive crowd. Studies of more than 80,000 college and professional athletic events in Canada, the United States, and England reveal that home teams win about 6 in 10 games (somewhat fewer for baseball and football, somewhat more for basketball and soccer). The home advantage may, however, also stem from the players' familiarity with their home

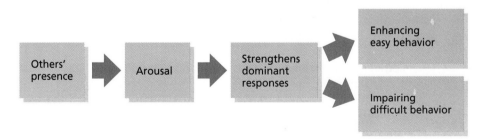

FIGURE 17-1
The effects of social arousal. Robert Zajonc reconciled apparently conflicting findings by proposing that arousal from others' presence strengthens dominant responses (the correct responses only on easy or well-learned tasks).

environment, less travel fatigue, feelings of dominance derived from territorial control, or increased team identity when cheered by fans (Zillmann & Paulus, 1993).

CROWDING: THE PRESENCE OF MANY OTHERS

So people do respond to others' presence. But does the presence of observers really arouse people? In times of stress, a comrade can be comforting. But with others present, people perspire more, breathe faster, tense their muscles more, and have higher blood pressure and a faster heart rate (Geen & Gange, 1983; Moore & Baron, 1983). Even a supportive audience may elicit poorer performance on challenging tasks (Butler & Baumeister, 1998). Having your extended family at your first piano recital likely won't boost your performance.

The effect of other people increases with their number (Jackson & Latané, 1981; Knowles, 1983). Sometimes the arousal and self-conscious attention created by a large audience interferes even with well-learned, automatic behaviors, such as speaking. Given *extreme* pressure, we're vulnerable to choking. Stutterers tend to stutter more in front of larger audiences than when speaking to just one or two people (Mullen, 1986). College basketball players become slightly *less* accurate in their free-throw shooting when very highly aroused by a packed rather than a near empty fieldhouse (Sokoll & Mynatt, 1984).

Being *in* a crowd also intensifies positive or negative reactions. When they sit close together, friendly people are liked even more, and *un*friendly people are *dis*liked even more (Schiffenbauer & Schiavo, 1976; Storms & Thomas, 1977). In experiments with Columbia University students and with Ontario Science Center visitors, Jonathan Freedman and his co-workers (1979, 1980) had an accomplice listen to a humorous tape or watch a movie with other participants. When they all sat close together, the accomplice could more readily induce the individuals to laugh and clap. As theater directors and sports fans know, and as researchers have confirmed, a "good house" is a full house (Aiello & others, 1983; Worchel & Brown, 1984).

Perhaps you've noticed that a class of 35 students feels more warm and lively in a room that seats just 35 than when spread around a room that seats 100. This occurs partly because when others are close by, we are more likely to notice and join in their laughter or clapping. But crowding also enhances arousal, as Gary Evans (1979) found. He tested 10-person groups of University of Massachusetts students, either in a room 20 by 30 feet or in one 8 by 12 feet. Compared with those in the large room, those densely packed had higher pulse rates and blood pressure (indicating arousal). On difficult tasks they made more errors, an effect of crowding replicated by Dinesh Nagar and Janak Pandey (1987) with university students in India. So, crowding enhances arousal, which facilitates dominant responses.

WHY ARE WE AROUSED IN THE PRESENCE OF OTHERS?

What you do well, you will be energized to do best in front of others (unless you become hyperaroused and self-conscious). What you find difficult may seem impossible in the same circumstances. What is it about other people that causes arousal? There is evidence to support at least three possible factors (Aiello & Douthitt, 2001): evaluation apprehension, distraction, and mere presence.

Evaluation Apprehension

Nickolas Cottrell surmised that observers make us apprehensive because we wonder how they are evaluating us. To test whether **evaluation apprehension** exists, Cottrell and his associates (1968) blindfolded observers, supposedly in preparation for a perception experiment. In contrast to the effect of the watching audience, the mere presence of these blindfolded people did *not* boost well-practiced responses.

Other experiments confirmed Cottrell's conclusion: The enhancement of dominant responses is strongest when people think they are being evaluated. In one experiment, joggers on a University of California at Santa Barbara jogging path sped up as they came upon a woman seated on the grass—*if* she was facing them rather than sitting with her back turned (Worringham & Messick, 1983).

Evaluation apprehension also helps explain

- why people perform best when their co-actor is slightly superior (Seta, 1982).
- why arousal lessens when a high-status group is diluted by adding people whose opinions don't matter to us (Seta & Seta, 1992).
- why people who worry most about what others think are the ones most affected by their presence (Gastorf & others, 1980; Geen & Gange, 1983).
- why social facilitation effects are greatest when the others are unfamiliar and hard to keep an eye on (Guerin & Innes, 1982).

The self-consciousness we feel when being evaluated can also interfere with behaviors that we perform best automatically (Mullen &

Baumeister, 1987). If self-conscious basketball players analyze their body movements while shooting critical free throws, they are more likely to miss.

Driven by Distraction

Glenn Sanders, Robert Baron, and Danny Moore (1978; Baron, 1986) carried evaluation apprehension a step further. They theorized that when we wonder how co-actors are doing or how an audience is reacting, we get distracted. This *conflict* between paying attention to others and paying attention to the task overloads our cognitive system, causing arousal. We are "driven by distraction." This response facilitation comes not just from the presence of another person but even from a nonhuman distraction, such as bursts of light (Sanders, 1981a, 1981b).

Mere Presence

Activity
17.1

Zajonc, however, believes that the mere presence of others produces some arousal even without evaluation apprehension or arousing distraction. For example, people's color preferences are stronger when they make judgments with others present (Goldman, 1967). On such a task, there is no "good" or "right" answer for others to evaluate and thus no reason to be concerned with their reactions. Still, others' presence is energizing.

Recall that facilitation effects also occur with nonhuman animals. This hints at an innate social arousal mechanism common to much of the zoological world. (Animals probably are not consciously worrying about how other animals are evaluating them.) At the human level, most joggers are energized when jogging with someone else, even one who neither competes nor evaluates.

This is a good time to remind ourselves of the purpose of a theory. A good theory is a scientific shorthand: It simplifies and summarizes a variety of observations. Social facilitation theory does this well. It is a simple summary of many research findings. A good theory also offers clear predictions that (1) help confirm or modify the theory, (2) guide new exploration, and (3) suggest practical applications. Social facilitation theory has definitely generated the first two types of prediction: (1) The basics of the theory (that the presence of others is arousing and that this social arousal enhances dominant responses) have been confirmed, and (2) the theory has brought new life to a long dormant field of research.

Are there (3) some practical applications? We can make some educated guesses. Many new office buildings have replaced private offices with large, open areas divided by low partitions. Might the resulting awareness of others' presence help boost the performance of well-learned tasks, but disrupt creative thinking on complex tasks? Can you think of other possible applications?

CONCEPTS TO REMEMBER

co-actors   Co-participants working individually on a noncompetitive activity.

social facilitation   (1) Original meaning—the tendency of people to perform simple or well-learned tasks better when others are present.

(2) Current meaning—the strengthening of dominant (prevalent, likely) responses in the presence of others.

evaluation apprehension   Concern for how others are evaluating us.

18

❖

Many Hands Make Diminished Responsibility

In a team tug-of-war, will eight people on a side exert as much force as the sum of their best efforts in individual tugs-of-war? If not, why not? And what level of individual effort can we expect from members of work groups?

Social facilitation usually occurs when people work toward individual goals and when their efforts, whether winding fishing reels or solving math problems, can be individually evaluated. These situations parallel some everyday work situations, but not those in which people pool their efforts toward a *common* goal and where individuals are *not* accountable for their efforts. A team tug-of-war provides one such example. Organizational fund-raising—pooling candy sale proceeds to pay for the class trip—provides another. So does a class project where all get the same grade. On such "additive tasks"—tasks where the group's achievement depends on the sum of the individual efforts—will team spirit boost productivity? Will bricklayers lay bricks faster when working as a team than when working alone? One way to attack such questions is with laboratory simulations.

MANY HANDS MAKE LIGHT WORK

Nearly a century ago, French engineer Max Ringelmann (reported by Kravitz & Martin, 1986) found that the collective effort of tug-of-war teams was but half the sum of the individual efforts. This suggests, contrary to the presumption "in unity there is strength," that

199

FIGURE 18-1
The rope-pulling apparatus. People in the first position pulled less hard when they thought people behind them were also pulling. **Source:** Data from Ingham, Levinger, Graves, & Peckham, 1974. Photo by Alan G. Ingham.

group members may actually be less motivated when performing additive tasks. Maybe, though, poor performance stemmed from poor coordination—people pulling a rope in slightly different directions at slightly different times. A group of Massachusetts researchers led by Alan Ingham (1974) cleverly eliminated this problem by making individuals think others were pulling with them, when in fact they were pulling alone. Blindfolded participants were assigned the first position in the apparatus shown in Figure 18-1 and told, "Pull as hard as you can." They pulled 18 percent harder when they knew they were pulling alone than when they believed that behind them two to five people were also pulling.

Researchers Bibb Latané, Kipling Williams, and Stephen Harkins (1979; Harkins & others, 1980) kept their ears open for other ways to investigate this phenomenon, which they labeled **social loafing.** They observed that the noise produced by six people shouting or clapping "as loud as you can" was less than three times that produced by one person alone. Like the tug-of-war task, however, noisemaking is vulnerable to group inefficiency. So Latané and his associates followed Ingham's example by leading their Ohio State University participants to believe others were shouting or clapping with them, when in fact they were doing so alone.

Their method was to blindfold six people, seat them in a semicircle, and have them put on headphones, over which they were blasted with the sound of people shouting or clapping. People could not hear their own shouting or clapping, much less that of others. On various trials they were instructed to shout or clap either alone or along with the group. People who were told about this experiment guessed the participants would shout louder when with others, because they would be less inhibited (Harkins, 1981). The actual result? Social loafing: When the participants believed five others were also either shouting or clapping, they produced one-third less noise than when they thought themselves alone. Social loafing occurred even when the participants were high school cheerleaders who believed themselves to be cheering together or alone (Hardy & Latané, 1986).

John Sweeney (1973), a political scientist interested in the policy implications of social loafing, observed the phenomenon in an experiment at the University of Texas. Students pumped exercise bicycles more energetically (as measured by electrical output) when they knew they were being individually monitored than when they thought their output was being pooled with that of other riders. In the group condition, people were tempted to **free-ride** on the group effort.

In this and 160 other studies (Karau & Williams, 1993), we see a twist on one of the psychological forces that makes for social facilitation: evaluation apprehension. In the social loafing experiments, individuals believed they were evaluated only when they acted alone. The group situation (rope pulling, shouting, and so forth) *decreased* evaluation apprehension. When people are not accountable and cannot evaluate their own efforts, responsibility is diffused across all group members (Harkins & Jackson, 1985; Kerr & Bruun, 1981). By contrast, the social facilitation experiments *increased* exposure to evaluation. When made the center of attention, people self-consciously monitor their behavior (Mullen & Baumeister, 1987). So the principle is the same: When being observed *increases* evaluation concerns, social facilitation occurs; when being lost in a crowd *decreases* evaluation concerns, social loafing occurs (Figure 18-2).

To motivate group members, one strategy is to make individual performance identifiable. Some football coaches do this by filming and evaluating each player individually. Whether in a group or not, people exert more effort when their outputs are individually identifiable: University swim team members swim faster in intrasquad relay races when someone monitors and announces their individual times (Williams & others, 1989). Even without pay consequences, actual assembly line workers in

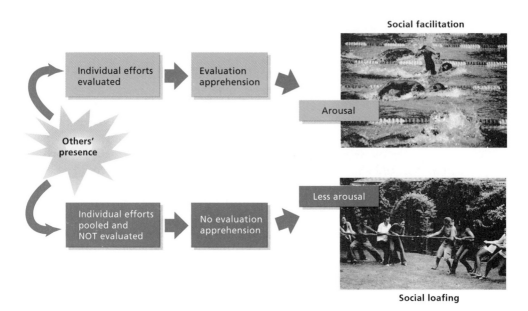

FIGURE 18-2
Social facilitation or social loafing? When individuals cannot be evaluated or held accountable, loafing becomes more likely. An individual swimmer is evaluated on her ability to win the race. In tug-of-war, no single person on the team is held accountable, so any one member might relax or loaf.

one small experiment produced 16 percent more product when their individual output was identified (Faulkner & Williams, 1996).

SOCIAL LOAFING IN EVERYDAY LIFE

Activity
18.1

How widespread is social loafing? In the laboratory, the phenomenon occurs not only among people who are pulling ropes, cycling, shouting, and clapping but also among those who are pumping water or air, evaluating poems or editorials, producing ideas, typing, and detecting signals. Do these results generalize to everyday worker productivity?

On their collective farms under communism, Russian peasants worked one field one day, another field the next, with little direct responsibility for any given plot. For their own use, they were given small private plots. One analysis found that the private plots occupied 1 percent of the agricultural land, yet produced 27 percent of the Soviet farm output (H. Smith, 1976). In Hungary, private plots accounted for only 13 percent of the farmland but produced one-third of the output (Spivak, 1979). When China began allowing farmers to sell food grown in excess of that owed to the state, food production jumped 8 percent per year—2.5 times the annual increase in the preceding 26 years (Church, 1986).

In North America, workers who do not pay dues or volunteer time to their unions or professional associations nevertheless are usually happy to accept its benefits. So, too, are public television viewers who don't respond to their station's fund drives. This hints at another possible explanation of social loafing. When rewards are divided equally, regardless of how much one contributes to the group, any individual gets more reward per unit of effort by free-riding on the group. So people may be motivated to slack off when their efforts are not individually monitored and rewarded. Situations that welcome free riders can therefore be, in the words of one commune member, a "paradise for parasites."

In a pickle factory, for example, the key job is picking the right size dill pickle halves off the conveyor belt and stuffing them in jars. Unfortunately, workers are tempted to stuff any size pickle in, because their output is not identifiable (the jars go into a common hopper before reaching the quality-control section). Williams, Harkins, and Latané (1981) note that research on social loafing suggests "making individual production identifiable, and raises the question: 'How many pickles could a pickle packer pack if pickle packers were only paid for properly packed pickles?'"

But surely collective effort does not always lead to slacking off. Sometimes the goal is so compelling and maximum output from everyone is so essential that team spirit maintains or intensifies effort. In an Olympic crew race, will the individual rowers in an eight-person crew pull their oars with less effort than those in a one- or two-person crew?

The evidence assures us they will not. People in groups loaf less when the task is *challenging, appealing,* or *involving* (Karau & Williams, 1993). On challenging tasks, people may perceive their efforts as indispensable (Harkins & Petty, 1982; Kerr, 1983; Kerr & Bruun, 1983). When people see others in their group as unreliable or as unable to contribute much, they work harder (Plaks & Higgins, 2000; Williams & Karau, 1991). Adding incentives or challenging a group to strive for certain standards also promotes collective effort (Harkins & Szymanski, 1989; Shepperd & Wright, 1989).

Groups also loaf less when their members are *friends* or identified with their group, rather than strangers (Davis & Greenlees, 1992; Karau & Williams, 1997; Worchel & others, 1998). Even just expecting to interact with someone again serves to increase effort on team projects (Groenenboom & others, 2001). Collaborate on a class project with others whom you will be seeing often and it is likely that you will feel more motivated than if you never expect to see them again. Latané notes that Israel's communal kibbutz farms have actually outproduced Israel's noncollective farms (Leon, 1969). Cohesiveness intensifies effort. So will there be social loafing in group-centered cultures? To find out, Latané and his co-researchers (Gabrenya & others, 1985) headed for Asia, where they repeated their sound production experiments in Japan, Thailand, Taiwan, India, and Malaysia. Their findings? Social loafing was evident in all these countries, too.

Seventeen later studies in Asia reveal that people in collectivist cultures do, however, exhibit less social loafing than do people in individualist cultures (Karau & Williams, 1993; Kugihara, 1999). As we noted earlier, loyalty to family and work groups runs strong in collectivist cultures. Likewise, women tend to be less individualistic than men—and to exhibit less social loafing.

Some of these findings parallel those from studies of everyday work groups. When groups are given challenging objectives, when they are rewarded for group success, and when there is a spirit of commitment to the "team," group members work hard (Hackman, 1986). Keeping work groups small and forming them with equally competent people can also help members believe their contributions are indispensable (Comer, 1995). So while social loafing is a common occurrence when group members work collectively and without individual accountability, many hands need not always make light work.

*C*ONCEPTS TO REMEMBER

social loafing The tendency for people to exert less effort when they pool their efforts toward a common goal than when they are individually accountable.

free riders People who benefit from the group but give little in return.

19

❖

Doing Together What We Would Never Do Alone

I n April 2003, in the wake of American troops entering Iraq's cities, looters—"liberated" from the scrutiny of Saddam Hussein's police—ran rampant. In "frenzied looting," hospitals lost beds. The National Library lost tens of thousands of old manuscripts and lay in smoldering ruins. Universities lost computers, chairs, even lightbulbs. The National Museum in Baghdad lost thousands of artifacts within 48 hours—most of what had previously been removed to safekeeping (Burns, 2003a, 2003b; Lawler, 2003c). "Not since the Spanish conquistadors ravaged the Aztec and Inca cultures has so much been lost so quickly," reported *Science* (Lawler, 2003a). "They came in mobs: A group of 50 would come, then would go, and another would come," explained one university dean (Lawler, 2003b). Such reports had the rest of the world wondering: What happened to the looters' sense of morality? Why did such behavior erupt?

D EINDIVIDUATION

Social facilitation experiments show that groups can arouse people. Social loafing experiments show that groups can diffuse responsibility. When arousal and diffused responsibility combine and normal inhibitions diminish, the results may be startling. People may commit acts that range from a mild lessening of restraint (throwing food in the dining hall, snarling at a referee, screaming during a rock concert) to impulsive self-gratification (group vandalism, orgies, thefts) to destructive social

Apparently acting without their normal conscience, people looted Iraqi institutions after the toppling of Saddam Hussein's regime.

explosions (police brutality, riots, lynchings). In a 1967 incident, 200 University of Oklahoma students gathered to watch a disturbed fellow student threatening to jump from a tower. They began to chant "Jump. Jump. . . ." The student jumped to his death (UPI, 1967).

These unrestrained behaviors have something in common: They are somehow provoked by the power of a group. Groups can generate a sense of excitement, of being caught up in something bigger than one's self. It is harder to imagine a single rock fan screaming deliriously at a private rock concert, a single Oklahoma student trying to coax someone to suicide, or even a single police officer beating a defenseless motorist. In certain kinds of group situations, people are more likely to abandon normal restraints, to lose their sense of individual identity, to become responsive to group or crowd norms—in a word, to become what Leon Festinger, Albert Pepitone, and Theodore Newcomb (1952) labeled **deindividuated.** What circumstances elicit this psychological state?

Group Size

A group has the power not only to arouse its members but also to render them unidentifiable. The snarling crowd hides the snarling basketball fan. A lynch mob enables its members to believe they will not be prosecuted; they perceive the action as the *group's*. Looters, made faceless by the mob, are freed to loot. In an analysis of 21 instances in which crowds were present as someone threatened to jump from a building or bridge, Leon Mann (1981) found that when the crowd was small and exposed by daylight, people usually did not try to bait the person. But when a large crowd or the cover of night gave people anonymity, the crowd usually baited and jeered.

Brian Mullen (1986a) reports a similar effect of lynch mobs: The bigger the mob, the more its members lose self-awareness and become willing to commit atrocities, such as burning, lacerating, or dismembering the victim. In each of these examples, from sports crowds to lynch mobs, evaluation apprehension plummets. Because "everyone is doing it," all can attribute their behavior to the situation rather than to their own choices.

Philip Zimbardo (1970) speculated that the mere immensity of crowded cities produces anonymity and thus norms that permit vandalism. He purchased two 10-year-old cars and left them with the hoods up and license plates removed, one on a street near the old Bronx campus of New York University and one near the Stanford University campus in Palo Alto, a much smaller city. In New York the first auto strippers arrived within 10 minutes; they took the battery and radiator. After three days and 23 incidents of theft and vandalism (by neatly dressed White people), the car was reduced to a battered, useless hulk of metal. By contrast, the only person observed to touch the Palo Alto car in over a week was a passerby who lowered the hood when it began to rain.

Physical Anonymity

How can we be sure that the crucial difference between the Bronx and Palo Alto experiments is greater anonymity in the Bronx? We can't. But we can experiment with anonymity to see if it actually lessens inhibitions. Zimbardo (1970, 2002) got the idea for such an experiment from his undergraduate students, who questioned how good boys in William Golding's *Lord of the Flies* could so suddenly become monsters after painting their faces. To experiment with such anonymity, he dressed New York University women in identical white coats and hoods, rather like Ku Klux Klan members (Figure 19-1). Asked to deliver electric shocks to a woman, they pressed the shock button twice as long as did women who were visible and wearing large name tags.

The Internet offers similar anonymity. Millions of those who were aghast at the looting by the Baghdad mobs were on those very days anonymously pirating music tracks using file-sharing software. With so many doing it, and with so little concern about being caught, downloading someone's copyright-protected property and then offloading it to an MP3 player just didn't seem terribly immoral.

FIGURE 19-1
Anonymous women delivered more shock to helpless victims than did
identifiable women.

Testing deindividuation on the streets, Patricia Ellison, John Govern,
and their colleagues (1995) had a confederate driver stop at a red light
and wait for 12 seconds whenever she was followed by a convertible or
4 × 4 vehicle. While enduring the wait, she recorded any horn-honking
(a mild aggressive act) by the car behind. Compared with drivers of con-
vertibles and 4 × 4s with the tops down, those who were relatively
anonymous (with the tops up) honked one-third sooner, twice as often,
and for nearly twice as long.

A research team led by Ed Diener (1976) cleverly demonstrated the
effect both of being in a group *and* being physically anonymous. At
Halloween, they observed 1,352 Seattle children trick-or-treating. As the
children, either alone or in groups, approached 1 of 27 homes scattered
throughout the city, an experimenter greeted them warmly, invited them
to "take *one* of the candies," and then left the room. Hidden observers
noted that children in groups were more than twice as likely to take extra
candy as solo children. Also, those who were left anonymous were more
than twice as likely to transgress as children who had been asked their
names and where they lived. As Figure 19-2 shows, the transgression
rate varied dramatically with the situation. When they were deindividuated by group immersion combined with anonymity, most children
stole extra candy.

These experiments make me wonder about the effect of wearing uniforms. Preparing for battle, warriors in some tribal cultures (like rabid

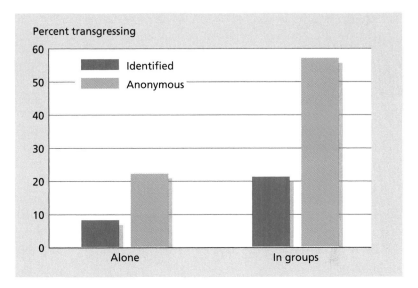

FIGURE 19-2
Children were more likely to transgress by taking extra Halloween candy when in a group, when anonymous, and especially, when deindividuated by the combination of group immersion and anonymity.
Source: Data from Diener & others, 1976.

fans of some sports teams) depersonalize themselves with body and face paints or special masks. After the battle, some cultures kill, torture, or mutilate any remaining enemies; other cultures take prisoners alive. Robert Watson (1973) scrutinized anthropological files and discovered that the cultures with depersonalized warriors were also the cultures that brutalized their enemies. The uniformed Los Angeles police officers who beat Rodney King were angered and aroused by his defiant refusal to stop his car. They were enjoying one another's camaraderie and unaware that outsiders would view their actions. Thus, forgetting their normal standards, they were swept away by the situation.

In Northern Ireland, 206 of 500 violent attacks studied by Andrew Silke (2003) were conducted by attackers who wore masks, hoods, or other face disguises. Compared with undisguised attackers, these anonymous attackers inflicted more serious injuries, attacked more people, and committed more vandalism.

Does becoming physically anonymous *always* unleash our worst impulses? Fortunately, no. In all these situations, people were responding to clear antisocial cues. Robert Johnson and Leslie Downing (1979) point out that the Klan-like outfits worn by Zimbardo's participants may have encouraged hostility. In an experiment at the University of Georgia, women put on nurses' uniforms before deciding how much shock someone should receive. When those wearing the nurses' uniforms were made anonymous, they became *less* aggressive in administering shocks than when their names and personal identities were stressed. From their analysis of 60 deindividuation studies, Tom Postmes and Russell Spears (1998; Reicher & others, 1995) conclude that being anonymous makes one less self-conscious, more group-conscious, and more responsive to cues present in the situation, whether negative (Klan uniforms) or positive (nurses' uniforms). Given altruistic cues, deindividuated people even give more money (Spivey & Prentice-Dunn, 1990).

Arousing and Distracting Activities

Aggressive outbursts by large groups often are preceded by minor actions that arouse and divert people's attention. Group shouting, chanting, clapping, or dancing serve both to hype people up and to reduce self-consciousness. One Moonie observer recalls how the "choo-choo" chant helped deindividuate:

> All the brothers and sisters joined hands and chanted with increasing intensity, choo-choo-choo, Choo-choo-choo, CHOO-CHOO-CHOO! YEA! YEA! POWW!!! The act made us a group, as though in some strange way we had all experienced something important together. The power of the choo-choo frightened me, but it made me feel more comfortable and there was something very relaxing about building up the energy and releasing it. (Zimbardo & others, 1977, p. 186)

Ed Diener's experiments (1976, 1979) have shown that activities such as throwing rocks and group singing can set the stage for more disinhibited behavior. There is a self-reinforcing pleasure in acting impulsively while observing others doing likewise. When we see others act as we are acting, we think they feel as we do, which reinforces our own feelings (Orive, 1984). Moreover, impulsive group action absorbs our attention. When we yell at the referee, we are not thinking about our values; we are reacting to the immediate situation. Later, when we stop to think about what we have done or said, we sometimes feel chagrined. Sometimes. At other times we seek deindividuating group experiences—dances, worship experiences, group encounters—where we can enjoy intense positive feelings and closeness to others.

DIMINISHED SELF-AWARENESS

Group experiences that diminish self-consciousness tend to disconnect behavior from attitudes. Experiments by Ed Diener (1980) and Steven Prentice-Dunn and Ronald Rogers (1980, 1989) reveal that unself-conscious, deindividuated people are less restrained, less self-regulated, more likely to act without thinking about their own values, and more responsive to the situation. These findings complement and reinforce the experiments on *self-awareness*.

Self-awareness is the opposite of deindividuation. Those made self-aware, by acting in front of a mirror or TV camera, exhibit *increased* self-control, and their actions more clearly reflect their attitudes. In front of a mirror, people taste-testing cream cheese varieties eat less of the high-fat variety (Sentyrz & Bushman, 1998). Perhaps dieters should put mirrors in the kitchen.

People made self-aware are also less likely to cheat (Beaman & others, 1979; Diener & Wallbom, 1976). So are those who generally have a strong sense of themselves as distinct and independent (Nadler & others, 1982). People who are self-conscious, or who are temporarily made so, exhibit greater consistency between their words outside a situation and their deeds in it. Circumstances that decrease self-awareness, as alcohol consumption does, therefore increase deindividuation (Hull & others, 1983). And deindividuation decreases in circumstances that increase self-awareness: mirrors and cameras, small towns, bright lights, large name tags, undistracted quiet, individual clothes and houses (Ickes & others, 1978). When a teenager leaves for a party, a parent's parting advice could well be, "Have fun, and remember who you are." In other words, enjoy being with the group, but be self-aware; maintain your personal identity; don't become deindividuated.

CONCEPT TO REMEMBER

deindividuation Loss of self-awareness and evaluation apprehension; occurs in group situations that foster responsiveness to group norms, good or bad.

20

❖

How Groups Intensify Decisions

W hich effect—good or bad—does group interaction more often have? Police brutality and mob violence demonstrate its destructive potential. Yet support-group leaders, management consultants, and educational theorists proclaim its benefits, and social and religious movements urge their members to strengthen their identities by fellowship with like-minded others.

Studies of people in small groups have produced a principle that helps explain both bad and good outcomes: Group discussion often strengthens members' initial inclinations. The unfolding of this research on *group polarization* illustrates the process of inquiry—how an interesting discovery often leads researchers to hasty and erroneous conclusions, which ultimately get replaced with more accurate conclusions. This is one scientific mystery I can discuss firsthand, having been one of the detectives.

*T*HE CASE OF THE "RISKY SHIFT"

Activity
20.1

A research literature of more than 300 studies began with a surprising finding by James Stoner (1961), then an MIT graduate student. For his master's thesis in industrial management, Stoner tested the commonly held belief that groups are more cautious than individuals. He posed decision dilemmas in which the participant's task was to advise imagined characters how much risk to take. Put yourself in the participant's shoes: What advice would you give the character in this situation?

Helen is a writer who is said to have considerable creative talent but who so far has been earning a comfortable living by writing cheap westerns. Recently she has come up with an idea for a potentially significant novel. If it could be written and accepted, it might have considerable literary impact and be a big boost to her career. On the other hand, if she cannot work out her idea or if the novel is a flop, she will have expended considerable time and energy without remuneration.

Imagine that you are advising Helen. Please check the *lowest* probability that you would consider acceptable for Helen to attempt to write the novel.

Helen should attempt to write the novel if the chances that the novel will be a success are at least

_____1 in 10	_____7 in 10
_____2 in 10	_____8 in 10
_____3 in 10	_____9 in 10
_____4 in 10	_____10 in 10 (Place a check here if you think
_____5 in 10	Helen should attempt the novel only if it is
_____6 in 10	certain that the novel will be a success.)

After making your decision, guess what this book's average reader would advise.

Having marked their advice on a dozen such items, five or so individuals would then discuss and reach agreement on each item. How do you think the group decisions compared with the average decision before the discussions? Would the groups be likely to take greater risks, be more cautious, or stay the same?

To everyone's amazement, the group decisions were usually riskier. Dubbed the "risky shift phenomenon," this finding set off a wave of group risk-taking studies. These revealed that risky shift occurs not only when a group decides by consensus; after a brief discussion, individuals, too, will alter their decisions. What is more, researchers successfully repeated Stoner's finding with people of varying ages and occupations in a dozen nations.

During discussion, opinions converged. Curiously, however, the point toward which they converged was usually a lower (riskier) number than their initial average. Here was a delightful puzzle. The small risky shift effect was reliable, unexpected, and without any immediately obvious explanation. What group influences produce such an effect? And how widespread is it? Do discussions in juries, business committees, and military organizations also promote risk taking? Does this explain why teenage reckless driving, as measured by death rates, nearly doubles when a 16- or 17-year-old driver has two passengers rather than none (Chen & others, 2000)?

After several years of study, we discovered that the risky shift was not universal. We could write decision dilemmas on which people became more *cautious* after discussion. One of these featured "Roger," a young married man with two school-age children and a secure but low-paying job. Roger can afford life's necessities but few of its luxuries. He hears that the stock of a relatively unknown company may soon triple in value if its new product is favorably received or decline considerably if it does not sell. Roger has no savings. To invest in the company, he is considering selling his life insurance policy.

Can you see a general principle that predicts both the tendency to give riskier advice after discussing Helen's situation and more cautious advice after discussing Roger's?

If you are like most people, you would advise Helen to take a greater risk than Roger, even before talking with others. It turns out there is a strong tendency for discussion to accentuate these initial leanings.

DO GROUPS INTENSIFY OPINIONS?

Realizing that this group phenomenon was not a consistent shift to risk, we reconceived the phenomenon as a tendency for group discussion to enhance group members' initial leanings. This idea led investigators to propose what French researchers Serge Moscovici and Marisa Zavalloni (1969) called **group polarization:** *Discussion typically strengthens the average inclination of group members.*

Group Polarization Experiments

This new view of the changes induced by group discussion prompted experimenters to have people discuss attitude statements that most of them favored or most of them opposed. Would talking in groups enhance their initial inclinations as it did with the decision dilemmas? In groups, would risk takers not only become riskier, but bigots become despisers, and givers become more philanthropic? That's what the group polarization hypothesis predicts (Figure 20-1).

Dozens of studies confirm group polarization.

- Moscovici and Zavalloni (1969) observed that discussion enhanced French students' initially positive attitude toward their president and negative attitude toward Americans.
- Mititoshi Isozaki (1984) found that Japanese university students gave more pronounced judgments of "guilty" after discussing a traffic case.

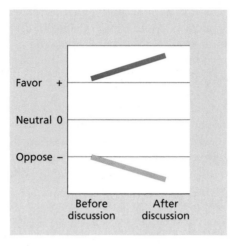

FIGURE 20-1
Group polarization. The group polarization hypothesis predicts that discussion
will strengthen an attitude shared by
group members.

- And Glen Whyte (1993) reported that groups exacerbate the
  "too much invested to quit" phenomenon that has cost many
  businesses huge sums of money. Canadian business students
  imagined themselves having to decide whether to invest more
  money in the hope of preventing losses in various failing
  projects (for example, whether to make a high-risk loan to protect an earlier investment). They exhibited the typical effect:
  Seventy-two percent reinvested money they would seldom have
  invested if they were considering it as a new investment on its
  own merits. When making the same decision in groups,
  94 percent opted for reinvestment.

Another research strategy has been to pick issues on which opinions
are divided and then isolate people who hold the same view. Does discussion with like-minded people strengthen shared views? Does it magnify the attitude gap that separates the two sides?

George Bishop and I wondered. So we set up groups of relatively
prejudiced and unprejudiced high school students and asked them to
respond—before and after discussion—to issues involving racial attitudes, such as property rights versus open housing (Myers & Bishop,
1970). We found that the discussions among like-minded students did
indeed increase the initial gap between the two groups (Figure 20-2).

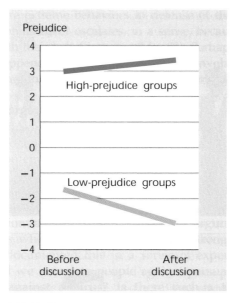

FIGURE 20-2
Discussion increased polarization
between homogeneous groups of high-
and low-prejudice high school students.
Talking over racial issues increased
prejudice in a high-prejudice group and
decreased it in a low-prejudice group.
Source: Data from Myers & Bishop, 1970.

Group Polarization in Everyday Life

In everyday life people associate mostly with others whose attitudes are
similar to their own. (Look at your own circle of friends.) Does everyday group interaction with like-minded friends intensify shared attitudes? Do nerds become nerdier and jocks jockier?

It happens. The self-segregation of boys into all-male groups and of
girls into all-female groups accentuates over time their initially modest
gender differences, notes Eleanor Maccoby (2002). Boys with boys
become gradually more competitive and action oriented in their play and
fictional fare, while girls with girls become more relationally oriented.
On U.S. federal appellate court cases, "Republican-appointed judges
tend to vote like Republicans and Democratic-appointed judges tend to
vote like Democrats," David Schkade and Cass Sunstein (2003) have
observed. But such tendencies are accentuated when among like-minded
judges. "A Republican appointee sitting with two other Republicans
votes far more conservatively than when the same judge sits with at least

one Democratic appointee. A Democratic appointee, meanwhile, shows the same tendency in the opposite ideological direction."

Group Polarization in Schools
Another real-life parallel to the laboratory phenomenon is what educa- tion researchers have called the "accentuation phenomenon": Over time, initial differences among groups of college students become accentuated. If the students at college X are initially more intellectual than the stu- dents at college Y, that gap is likely to grow during college. Likewise, compared with fraternity and sorority members, independents tend to have more liberal political attitudes, a difference that grows with time in college (Pascarella & Terenzini, 1991). Researchers believe this results partly from group members reinforcing shared inclinations.

Group Polarization in Communities
During community conflicts, like-minded people associate increasingly with one another, amplifying their shared tendencies. Gang delinquency emerges from a process of mutual reinforcement within neighborhood gangs, whose members share attributes and hostilities (Cartwright, 1975). If, on your block, "a second out-of-control 15-year-old moves in," surmises David Lykken (1997), "the mischief they get into as a team is likely to be more than merely double what the first would do on his own. . . . A gang is more dangerous than the sum of its individual parts." Indeed, "unsupervised peer groups" are "the strongest predictor" of a neighborhood's crime victimization rate, report Bonita Veysey and Steven Messner (1999). Moreover, experimental interventions grouping delinquent adolescents with other delinquents actually—no surprise to any group polarization researcher—*increase* the rate of problem behavior (Dishion & others, 1999).

From their analysis of terrorist organizations around the world, Clark McCauley and Mary Segal (1987; McCauley, 2002) note that terrorism does not erupt suddenly. Rather, it arises among people whose shared grievances bring them together. As they interact in isolation from mod- erating influences, they become progressively more extreme. The social amplifier brings the signal in stronger. The result is violent acts that the individuals, apart from the group, would never have committed.

For example, the 9/11 terrorists were bred by a long process that engaged the polarizing effect of the interaction among the like-minded. The process of becoming a terrorist, noted a National Research Council panel, isolates individuals from other belief systems, dehumanizes potential targets, and tolerates no dissent (Smelser & Mitchell, 2002). Ariel Merari (2002), an investigator of Middle Eastern and Sri Lankan suicide terrorism, believes the key to creating a suicide terrorist is the group process. "To the best of my knowledge, there has not been a sin- gle case of suicide terrorism which was done on a personal whim."

Massacres are likewise group phenomena, enabled by the killers egging each other on (Zajonc, 2000).

Group Polarization on the Internet
E-mail and electronic chat rooms offer a potential new medium for group interaction. By the beginning of the new century, 85 percent of Canadian teens were using the Internet for an average of 9.3 hours weekly (TGM, 2000). Its countless virtual groups enable peacemakers and neo-Nazis, geeks and goths, conspiracy theorists, and cancer survivors to isolate themselves with one another and find support for their shared concerns, interests, and suspicions (Gerstenfeld and others, 2003; McKenna & Bargh, 1998, 2000; Sunstein, 2001). Without the nonverbal nuances of face-to-face contact, will such discussions produce group polarization? Will peacemakers become more pacifistic and militia members more terror prone? E-mail, Google, and chat rooms "make it much easier for small groups to rally like-minded people, crystallize diffuse hatreds and mobilize lethal force," observes Robert Wright (2003a). As broadband spreads, Internet-spawned polarization will increase, he speculates. "Ever seen one of Osama bin Laden's recruiting videos? They're very effective, and they'll reach their targeted audience much more efficiently via broadband."

EXPLAINING GROUP POLARIZATION

Why do groups adopt stances that are more exaggerated than the average opinions of their individual members? Researchers hoped that solving the mystery of group polarization might provide some insights. Solving small puzzles sometimes provides clues for solving larger ones.

Among several proposed theories of group polarization, two survived scientific scrutiny. One deals with the arguments presented during a discussion, the other with how members of a group view themselves vis-à-vis the other members. The first idea is an example of informational influence (influence that results from accepting evidence about reality). The second is an example of normative influence (influence based on a person's desire to be accepted or admired by others).

Informational Influence

According to the best-supported explanation, group discussion elicits a pooling of ideas, most of which favor the dominant viewpoint. Ideas that were common knowledge to group members will often be brought up in discussion or, even if unmentioned, will jointly influence their discussion (Gigone & Hastie, 1993; Larson & others, 1994; Stasser, 1991). Other ideas may include persuasive arguments that some group members had not previously considered. When discussing Helen the writer, someone may say, "Helen should go for it, because she has little to lose. If her novel flops, she can always go back to writing cheap westerns." Such statements often entangle information about the person's *arguments* with cues concerning the person's *position* on the issue. But when people hear relevant arguments without learning the specific stands other people assume, they still shift their positions (Burnstein & Vinokur, 1977; Hinsz & others, 1997). *Arguments,* in and of themselves, matter.

Normative Influence

A second explanation of polarization involves comparison with others. As Leon Festinger (1954) argued in his influential theory of **social comparison,** we humans want to evaluate our opinions and abilities, something we can do by comparing our views with others'. We are most persuaded by people in our "reference groups"—groups we identify with (Abrams & others, 1990; Hogg & others, 1990). Moreover, wanting people to like us, we may express stronger opinions after discovering that others share our views.

When we ask people (as I asked you earlier) to predict how others would respond to items such as the "Helen" dilemma, they typically exhibit pluralistic ignorance: They don't realize how much others support the socially preferred tendency (in this case, writing the novel). A typical person will advise writing the novel even if its chance of success is only 4 in 10 but will estimate that most other people would require 5 or 6 in 10. (This finding is reminiscent of the self-serving bias: People tend to view themselves as better-than-average embodiments of socially desirable traits and attitudes.) When the discussion begins, most people discover they are not outshining the others as they had supposed. In fact, some others are ahead of them, having taken an even stronger position for writing the novel. No longer restrained by a misperceived group norm, they are liberated to voice their preferences more strongly.

Perhaps you can recall a time when you and others were guarded and reserved in a group, until someone broke the ice and said, "Well, to be perfectly honest, I think . . ." Soon you were all surprised to discover strong support for your shared views.

This social comparison theory prompted experiments that exposed people to others' positions but not to their arguments. This is roughly the experience we have when reading the results of an opinion poll or of exit polling on election day. When people learn others' positions—without prior commitment or discussion—will they adjust their responses to maintain a socially favorable position? When people have made no prior commitment to a particular response, seeing others' responses does stimulate a small polarization (Goethals & Zanna, 1979; Sanders & Baron, 1977). This comparison-based polarization is usually less than that produced by a lively discussion. Still, it's surprising that, instead of simply conforming to the group average, people often go it one better.

Group polarization research illustrates the complexity of social-psychological inquiry. As much as we like our explanations of a phenomenon to be simple, one explanation seldom accounts for all the data. Because people are complex, more than one factor frequently influences an outcome. In group discussions, persuasive arguments predominate on issues that have a factual element ("Is she guilty of the crime?"). Social comparison sways responses on value-laden judgments ("How long a sentence should she serve?") (Kaplan, 1989). On the many issues that have both factual and value-laden aspects, the two factors work together. Discovering that others share one's feelings (social comparison) unleashes arguments (informational influence) supporting what everyone secretly favors.

GROUPTHINK

Do the social-psychological phenomena we have been considering in these first 20 modules occur in sophisticated groups like corporate boards or the president's cabinet? Is there likely to be self-justification? Self-serving bias? A cohesive "we feeling" provoking conformity and rejection of dissent? Public commitment producing resistance to change? Group polarization? Social psychologist Irving Janis (1971, 1982) wondered whether such phenomena might help explain good and bad group decisions made by some twentieth-century American presidents and their advisers. To find out, he analyzed the decision-making procedures that led to several major fiascos:

Pearl Harbor. In the weeks preceding the December 1941 Pearl Harbor attack that put the United States into World War II, military commanders in Hawaii received a steady stream of information about Japan's preparations for an attack on the United States somewhere in the Pacific. Then military intelligence lost radio contact with Japanese aircraft carriers, which had begun moving straight for Hawaii. Air reconnaissance could have spotted the carriers or at least provided a few minutes' warning. But complacent commanders decided against such precautions. The result: No alert was sounded until the attack on a virtually defenseless base was under way. The loss: 18 ships, 170 planes, and 2,400 lives.

The Bay of Pigs Invasion. In 1961 President John Kennedy and his advisers tried to overthrow Fidel Castro by invading Cuba with 1,400 CIA-trained Cuban exiles. Nearly all the invaders were soon killed or captured, the United States was humiliated, and Cuba allied itself more closely with the former U.S.S.R. After learning the outcome, Kennedy wondered aloud, "How could we have been so stupid?"

The Vietnam War. From 1964 to 1967 President Lyndon Johnson and his "Tuesday lunch group" of policy advisers escalated the war in Vietnam on the assumption that U.S. aerial bombardment, defoliation, and search-and-destroy missions would bring North Vietnam to the peace table with the appreciative support of the South Vietnamese populace. They continued the escalation despite warnings from government intelligence experts and nearly all U.S. allies. The resulting disaster cost more than 58,000 American and 1 million Vietnamese lives, polarized Americans, drove the president from office, and created huge budget deficits that helped fuel inflation in the 1970s.

Janis believed these blunders were bred by the tendency of decision-making groups to suppress dissent in the interests of group harmony, a phenomenon he called **groupthink.** In work groups, camaraderie boosts productivity (Mullen & Copper, 1994). Moreover, team spirit is good for morale. But when making decisions, close-knit groups may pay a price. Janis believed that the soil from which groupthink sprouts includes

- an amiable, *cohesive* group;
- relative *isolation* of the group from dissenting viewpoints;
- and a *directive leader* who signals what decision he or she favors.

When planning the ill-fated Bay of Pigs invasion, the newly elected President Kennedy and his advisers enjoyed a strong esprit de corps. Arguments critical of the plan were suppressed or excluded, and the president soon endorsed the invasion.

SYMPTOMS OF GROUPTHINK

From historical records and the memoirs of participants and observers, Janis identified eight groupthink symptoms. These symptoms are a collective form of dissonance reduction that surface as group members try to maintain their positive group feeling when facing a threat (Turner & others, 1992, 1994).

The first two groupthink symptoms lead group members to *overestimate their group's might and right.*

- **An illusion of invulnerability.** The groups Janis studied all developed an excessive optimism that blinded them to warnings of danger. Told that his forces had lost radio contact with the Japanese carriers, Admiral Kimmel, the chief naval officer at Pearl Harbor, joked that maybe the Japanese were about to round Honolulu's Diamond Head. They were, but Kimmel's laughing at the idea dismissed the very possibility of its being true.

- **Unquestioned belief in the group's morality.** Group members assume the inherent morality of their group and ignore ethical and moral issues. The Kennedy group knew that adviser Arthur Schlesinger, Jr., and Senator J. William Fulbright had moral reservations about invading a small, neighboring country. But the group never entertained or discussed these moral qualms.

Group members also become *closed-minded:*

- **Rationalization.** The groups discount challenges by collectively justifying their decisions. President Johnson's Tuesday lunch group spent far more time rationalizing (explaining and justifying) than reflecting upon and rethinking prior decisions to escalate. Each initiative became an action to defend and justify.
- **Stereotyped view of opponent.** Participants in these groupthink tanks consider their enemies too evil to negotiate with or too weak and unintelligent to defend themselves against the planned initiative. The Kennedy group convinced itself that Castro's military was so weak and his popular support so shallow that a single brigade could easily overturn his regime.

Finally, the group suffers from pressures toward *uniformity:*

- **Conformity pressure.** Group members rebuffed those who raised doubts about the group's assumption and plans, at times not by argument but by personal sarcasm. Once, when President Johnson's assistant Bill Moyers arrived at a meeting, the president derided him with, "Well, here comes Mr. Stop-the-Bombing." Faced with such ridicule, most people fall into line.
- **Self-censorship.** Because disagreements were often uncomfortable and the groups seemed in consensus, members withheld or discounted their misgivings. In the months following the Bay of Pigs invasion, Arthur Schlesinger (1965, p. 255) reproached himself "for having kept so silent during those crucial discussions in the Cabinet Room, though my feelings of guilt were tempered by the knowledge that a course of objection would have accomplished little save to gain me a name as a nuisance."
- **Illusion of unanimity.** Self-censorship and pressure not to puncture the consensus create an illusion of unanimity. What is more, the apparent consensus confirms the group's decision. This appearance of consensus was evident in these three fiascos and in other fiascos before and since. Albert Speer (1971), an adviser to Adolf Hitler, described the atmosphere around Hitler as one where pressure to conform suppressed all deviation. The absence of dissent created an illusion of unanimity:

In normal circumstances people who turn their backs on reality are soon set straight by the mockery and criticism of those around them, which makes them aware they have lost credibility. In the Third Reich there were no such correctives, especially for those who belonged to the upper stratum. On the contrary, every self-deception was multiplied as in a hall of distorting mirrors, becoming a repeatedly confirmed picture of a fantastical dream world which no longer bore any relationship to the grim outside world. In those mirrors I could see nothing but my own face reproduced many times over. No external factors disturbed the uniformity of hundreds of unchanging faces, all mine. (p. 379)

- **Mindguards.** Some members protect the group from information that would call into question the effectiveness or morality of its decisions. Before the Bay of Pigs invasion, Robert Kennedy took Schlesinger aside and told him, "Don't push it any further." Secretary of State Dean Rusk withheld diplomatic and intelligence experts' warnings against the invasion. They thus served as the president's "mindguards," protecting him from disagreeable facts rather than physical harm.

Groupthink in Action

Groupthink symptoms can produce a failure to seek and discuss contrary information and alternative possibilities (Figure 20-3). When a leader promotes an idea and when a group insulates itself from dissenting views, groupthink may produce defective decisions (McCauley, 1989).

British psychologists Ben Newell and David Lagnado (2003) believe groupthink symptoms may have also contributed to the Iraq War. They and others contended that both Saddam Hussein and George W. Bush surrounded themselves with like-minded advisers, intimidated opposing

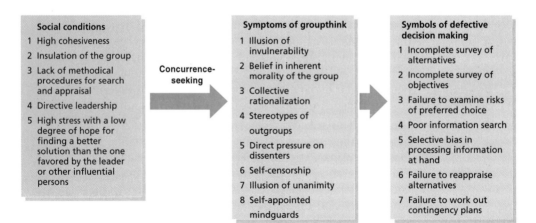

FIGURE 20-3
Theoretical analysis of groupthink.   **Source:** Janis & Mann, 1977, p. 132.

voices into silence, and received filtered information that mostly supported their assumptions—Iraq's expressed assumption that the invading force could be resisted and the United States' assumption that a successful invasion would be followed by a short, peaceful occupation and a soon-thriving democracy.

Preventing Groupthink

Flawed group dynamics help explain many failed decisions; sometimes too many cooks spoil the broth. However, given open leadership, a cohesive team spirit can improve decisions. Sometimes two or more heads are better than one.

In search of conditions that breed good decisions, Janis also analyzed two seemingly successful ventures: the Truman administration's formulation of the Marshall Plan for getting Europe back on its feet after World War II and the Kennedy administration's handling of the former U.S.S.R.'s attempts to install missile bases in Cuba in 1962. Janis's (1982) recommendations for preventing groupthink incorporate many of the effective group procedures used in both cases:

- Be impartial—do not endorse any position.
- Encourage critical evaluation; assign a "devil's advocate." Better yet, welcome the input of a genuine dissenter, which does even more to stimulate original thinking and to open a group to opposing views, report Charlan Nemeth and her colleagues (2001a, 2001b).
- Occasionally subdivide the group, then reunite to air differences.
- Welcome critiques from outside experts and associates. Before implementing, call a "second-chance" meeting to air any lingering doubts.

When such steps are taken, group decisions may take longer to make yet ultimately prove less defective and more effective.

CONCEPTS TO REMEMBER

group polarization Group-produced enhancement of members' preexisting tendencies; a strengthening of the members' *average* tendency, not a split within the group.

social comparison Evaluating one's opinions and abilities by comparing oneself to others.

groupthink "The mode of thinking that persons engage in when concurrence-seeking becomes so dominant in a cohesive in-group that it tends to override realistic appraisal of alternative courses of action" (Irving Janis [1971]).

MODULE

21

❖

Power to the Person

"There are trivial truths and great truths," declared the physicist Niels Bohr. "The opposite of a trivial truth is plainly false. The opposite of a great truth is also true." Each module in this unit on social influence teaches a great truth: the power of the social situation. This great truth about the power of external pressures would sufficiently explain our behavior if we were passive, like tumbleweeds. But unlike tumbleweeds, we are not just blown here and there by the environment. We act; we react. We respond, and we get responses. We can resist the social situation and sometimes even change it. Thus each of these "social influence" modules concludes by calling attention to the opposite of the great truth: the power of the person.

Perhaps stressing the power of culture leaves you somewhat uncomfortable. Most of us resent any suggestion that external forces determine our behavior; we see ourselves as free beings, as the originators of our actions (well, at least of our good actions). We sense that believing in social determinism can lead to what philosopher Jean-Paul Sartre called "bad faith"—evading responsibility by blaming something or someone for one's fate.

Actually, social control (the power of the situation) and personal control (the power of the person) no more compete with one another than do biological and cultural explanations. Social and personal explanations of our social behavior are both valid, for at any moment we are both the creatures and the creators of our social worlds. We may well be the products of the interplay of our genes and environment. But it is also true that the future is coming, and it is our job to decide where it is going. Our choices today determine our environment tomorrow.

*I*NTERACTING PERSONS AND SITUATIONS

Social situations do profoundly influence individuals. But individuals also influence social situations. The two *interact*. Asking whether external situations or inner dispositions (or culture or evolution) determine behavior is like asking whether length or width determines the area of a field.

The interaction occurs in at least three ways (Snyder & Ickes, 1985). First, a given social situation often *affects different people differently*. Because our minds do not see reality identically, each of us responds to a situation as we construe it. And some people are more sensitive and responsive to social situations than others (Snyder, 1983). The Japanese, for example, are more responsive to social expectations than the British (Argyle & others, 1978).

Second, interaction between persons and situations occurs because people often *choose their situations* (Ickes & others, 1997). Given a choice, sociable people elect situations that evoke social interaction. When you chose your college, you were also choosing to expose yourself to a specific set of social influences. Ardent political liberals are unlikely to settle in Orange County, California, and join the Chamber of Commerce. They are more likely to live in San Francisco or Toronto and join Greenpeace (or to read the *Manchester Guardian* rather than the *Times of London*)—in other words, to choose a social world that reinforces their inclinations.

Third, people often *create their situations*. Recall again that our preconceptions can be self-fulfilling: If we expect someone to be extraverted, hostile, feminine, or sexy, our actions toward the person may induce the very behavior we expect. What, after all, makes a social situation but the people in it? A liberal environment is created by liberals. What takes place in the sorority is created by the members. The social environment is not like the weather—something that just happens to us. It is more like our homes—something we make for ourselves.

The reciprocal causation between situations and persons allows us to see people as either *reacting to* or *acting upon* their environment. Each perspective is correct, for we are both the products and the architects of our social worlds. Is one perspective wiser, however? In one sense, it is wise to see ourselves as the creatures of our environments (lest we become too proud of our achievements and blame ourselves too much for our problems) and to see others as free actors (lest we become paternalistic and manipulative).

Perhaps we would do well more often to assume the reverse, however—to view ourselves as free agents and to view others as influenced by their environments. We would then assume self-efficacy as we view ourselves, and we would seek understanding and social reform as we relate to others. (If we view others as influenced by their situations, we are more likely to empathize than smugly to judge unpleasant behavior as freely chosen by "immoral," "sadistic," or "lazy" persons.)

Most religions encourage us to take responsibility for ourselves but to refrain from judging others. Is this because our natural inclination is to excuse our own failures while blaming others for theirs?

RESISTING SOCIAL PRESSURE

Social psychology offers other reminders of the power of the person. We are not just billiard balls moving where pushed; we act in response to the forces that push upon us. Knowing that someone is trying to coerce us may even prompt us to react in the *opposite* direction.

Reactance

Activity
21.1

Individuals value their sense of freedom and self-efficacy. So when social pressure becomes so blatant that it threatens their sense of freedom, they often rebel. Think of Romeo and Juliet, whose love was intensified by their families' opposition. Or think of children asserting their freedom and independence by doing the opposite of what their parents ask. Savvy parents therefore offer their children choices instead of commands: "It's time to clean up: Do you want a bath or a shower?"

The theory of psychological **reactance**—that people do indeed act to protect their sense of freedom—is supported by experiments showing that attempts to restrict a person's freedom often produce an anticonformity "boomerang effect" (Brehm & Brehm, 1981; Nail & others, 2000). After today's Western university women give thought to how traditional culture expects women to behave, they become less likely to exhibit traditional feminine modesty (Cialdini & others, 1998). Or suppose someone stops you on the street and asks you to sign a petition advocating something you mildly support. While considering the petition, you are told someone else believes "people absolutely should not be allowed to distribute or sign such petitions." Reactance theory predicts that such blatant attempts to limit freedom will actually increase the likelihood of your signing. When Madeline Heilman (1976) staged this experiment on the streets of New York City, that is precisely what she found.

Reactance may contribute to underage drinking. A survey of 18- to 24-year-olds by the Canadian Centre on Substance Abuse (1997) revealed that 69 percent of those over the legal drinking age (21) had been drunk in the last year, as had 77 percent of those *under* 21. In the United States, a survey of students on 56 campuses revealed a 25 percent rate of abstinence among students of legal drinking age (21) but only a 19 percent abstinence rate among students under 21 (Engs & Hanson, 1989). Reactance may also contribute to rape and sexual coercion, suggest Roy Baumeister, Kathleen Catanese, and Henry Wallace (2002). When a woman refuses to comply with a man's desire for sex, he may react with frustration over his restricted freedom and increased desire for the forbidden activity. Mix reactance with narcissism—a self-serving sense of entitlement and low empathy for others—and the unfortunate result can be forced sex.

Asserting Uniqueness

Imagine a world of complete conformity, where there were no differences among people. Would such a world be a happy place? If nonconformity can create discomfort, can sameness create comfort?

People feel uncomfortable when they appear too different from others. But, at least in Western cultures, they also feel uncomfortable when they appear exactly like everyone else. As experiments by C. R. Snyder and Howard Fromkin (1980) have shown, people feel better when they see themselves as moderately unique. Moreover, they act in ways that will assert their individuality. In one experiment, Snyder (1980) led Purdue University students to believe that their "10 most important attitudes" were either distinct from or nearly identical to the attitudes of 10,000 other students. Then, when they participated in a conformity experiment, those deprived of their feeling of uniqueness were most likely to assert their individuality by nonconformity. In another experiment, people who heard others express attitudes identical to their own altered their positions to maintain their sense of uniqueness.

Both social influence and the desire for uniqueness appear in popular baby names. People seeking less commonplace names often hit upon the same ones at the same time. Among the top 10 U.S. girls' names for 2002 were Madison (2), Alexis (5), and Olivia (10). Those who, in the 1960s, broke out of the pack by naming their baby Rebecca, thinking they were bucking convention, soon discovered their choice was part of a new pack, notes Peggy Orenstein (2003). Hillary, a popular late '80s, early '90s name, became less original-seeming and less frequent (even among her admirers) after Hillary Clinton became famous. Although the popularity of such names then fades, observes Orenstein, it may resurface with a future generation. Max, Rose, and Sophie sound like the roster of a retirement home—or a play group.

Seeing oneself as unique also appears in people's "spontaneous self-concepts." William McGuire and his Yale University colleagues (McGuire & others, 1979; McGuire & Padawer-Singer, 1978) report that when children are invited to "tell us about yourself," they are most likely to mention their distinctive attributes. Foreign-born children are more likely than others to mention their birthplace. Redheads are more likely than black- and brown-haired children to volunteer their hair color. Light and heavy children are the most likely to refer to their body weight. Minority children are the most likely to mention their race.

Likewise, we become more keenly aware of our gender when we are with people of the other gender (Cota & Dion, 1986). When I attended an American Psychological Association meeting with 10 others—all women as it happened—I immediately was aware of my gender. As we took a break at the end of the second day, I joked that the line would be short at my bathroom, triggering the woman sitting next to me to notice what hadn't crossed her mind—the group's gender makeup.

The principle, says McGuire, is that "one is conscious of oneself insofar as, and in the ways that, one is different." Thus, "If I am a Black woman in a group of White women, I tend to think of myself as a Black; if I move to a group of Black men, my blackness loses salience and I become more conscious of being a woman" (McGuire & others, 1978). This insight helps us understand why any minority group tends to be conscious of its distinctiveness and how the surrounding culture relates to it. The majority group, being less conscious of race, may see the minority group as hypersensitive. When occasionally living in Scotland, where my American accent marks me as a foreigner, I am conscious of my national identity and sensitive to how others react to it. For those of us in Western cultures, our distinctiveness is central to our identity (Vignoles & others, 2000).

When the people of two cultures are nearly identical, they still will notice their differences, however small. Even trivial distinctions may provoke scorn and conflict. Jonathan Swift satirized the phenomenon in *Gulliver's Travels* with the story of the Little-Endians' war against the Big-Endians. Their difference: The Little-Endians preferred to break their eggs on the small end, the Big-Endians on the large end. On a world scale, the differences may not seem great between Scots and English, Serbs and Croatians, or Catholic and Protestant Northern Irish. But small differences can mean big conflicts (Rothbart & Taylor, 1992). Rivalry is often most intense when the other group most closely resembles you.

It seems that, while we do not like being greatly deviant, we are, ironically, all alike in wanting to feel distinctive and in noticing how we are distinctive. But as research on the self-serving bias (Module 4) makes clear, it is not just any kind of distinctiveness we seek but distinctiveness in the right direction. Our quest is not merely to be different from the average, but *better* than average.

*M*INORITY INFLUENCE

We have seen that

- cultural situations mold us, but we also help create and choose these situations;
- pressures to conform sometimes overwhelm our better judgment, but blatant pressure can motivate us to assert our individuality and freedom;

- persuasive forces are indeed powerful, but we can resist persuasion by making public commitments and by anticipating persuasive appeals.

Consider, finally, how individuals can influence their groups.

At the beginning of most social movements, a small minority will sometimes sway, and then even become, the majority. "All history," wrote Ralph Waldo Emerson, "is a record of the power of minorities, and of minorities of one." Think of Copernicus and Galileo, of Martin Luther King, Jr., of Susan B. Anthony. The American civil rights movement was ignited by the refusal of one African American woman, Rosa Parks, to relinquish her seat on a Montgomery, Alabama, bus. Technological history has also been made by innovative minorities. As Robert Fulton developed his steamboat—"Fulton's Folly"—he endured constant derision: "Never did a single encouraging remark, a bright hope, a warm wish, cross my path" (Cantril & Bumstead, 1960).

What makes a minority persuasive? What might Arthur Schlesinger have done to get the Kennedy group to consider his doubts about the Bay of Pigs invasion? Experiments initiated by Serge Moscovici in Paris have identified several determinants of minority influence: consistency, self-confidence, and defection. Keep in mind that "minority influence" refers to minority *opinions*, not to ethnic minorities.

Consistency

More influential than a minority that wavers is a minority that sticks to its position. Moscovici and his associates (1969, 1985) found that if a minority consistently judges blue slides as green, members of the majority will occasionally agree. But if the minority wavers, saying "blue" to one-third of the blue slides and "green" to the rest, virtually no one in the majority will ever agree with "green."

Experiments show—and experience confirms—that nonconformity, especially persistent nonconformity, is often painful (Levine, 1989). That helps explain a *minority slowness effect*—a tendency for people with minority views to express them less quickly than do people in the majority (Bassili, 2003). If you set out to be Emerson's minority of one, prepare yourself for ridicule—especially when you argue an issue that's personally relevant to the majority and when the group wants to settle an issue by reaching consensus (Kameda & Sugimori, 1993; Kruglanski & Webster, 1991; Trost & others, 1992). People may attribute your dissent to psychological peculiarities (Papastamou & Mugny, 1990). When Charlan Nemeth (1979) planted a minority of two within a simulated jury and had them oppose the majority's opinions, the duo was inevitably disliked. Nevertheless, the majority acknowledged that the persistence of the two did more than anything else to make them rethink their positions.

In so doing, a minority may stimulate creative thinking (Martin, 1996; Mucchi-Faina & others, 1991; Peterson & Nemeth, 1996). With dissent from within one's own group, people take in more information, think about it in new ways, and often make better decisions. Believing that one need not win friends to influence people, Nemeth quotes Oscar Wilde: "We dislike arguments of any kind; they are always vulgar, and often convincing."

Some successful companies have recognized the creativity and innovation sometimes stimulated by minority perspectives, which may contribute new ideas and stimulate colleagues to think in fresh ways. 3M, which has been famed for valuing "respect for individual initiative," has welcomed employees spending time on wild ideas. The Post-it Notes adhesive was a failed attempt by Spencer Silver to develop a super strong glue. Art Fry, after having trouble marking his church choir hymnal with pieces of paper, thought "What I need is a bookmark with Spence's adhesive along the edge." Even so, this was a minority view that eventually won over a skeptical marketing department (Nemeth, 1997).

Self-Confidence

Consistency and persistence convey self-confidence. Furthermore, Nemeth and Joel Wachtler (1974) reported that any behavior by a minority that conveys self-confidence—for example, taking the head seat at the table—tends to raise self-doubts among the majority. By being firm and forceful, the minority's apparent self-assurance may prompt the majority to reconsider its position. This is especially so on matters of opinion rather than fact. In her research at Italy's University of Padova, Anne Maass and her colleagues (1996) report that minorities are less persuasive when answering a question of fact ("from which country does Italy import most of its raw oil?") than of attitude ("from which country should Italy import most of its raw oil?").

Defections from the Majority

A persistent minority punctures any illusion of unanimity. When a minority consistently doubts the majority wisdom, majority members become freer to express their own doubts and may even switch to the minority position. In research with University of Pittsburgh students, John Levine (1989) found that a minority person who had defected from the majority was more persuasive than a consistent minority voice. In her jury-simulation experiments, Nemeth found that once defections begin, others often soon follow, initiating a snowball effect.

Are these factors that strengthen minority influence unique to minorities? Sharon Wolf and Bibb Latané (1985; Wolf, 1987) and Russell Clark (1995) believe not. They argue that the same social forces work for both majorities and minorities. Informational and normative influence fuels both group polarization and minority influence. And if consistency, self-confidence, and defections from the other side strengthen the minority, such variables also strengthen a majority. The social impact of any position depends on the strength, immediacy, and number of those who support it. Minorities have less influence than majorities simply because they are smaller.

Anne Maass and Russell Clark (1984, 1986) agree with Moscovici, however, that minorities are more likely to convert people to *accepting* their views. And from their analyses of how groups evolve over time, John Levine and Richard Moreland (1985) conclude that new recruits to a group exert a different type of minority influence than do longtime members. Newcomers exert influence through the attention they receive and the group awareness they trigger in the old-timers. Established members feel freer to dissent and to exert leadership.

There is a delightful irony in this new emphasis on how individuals can influence the group. Until recently, the idea that the minority could sway the majority was itself a minority view in social psychology. Nevertheless, by arguing consistently and forcefully, Moscovici, Nemeth, Maass, Clark, and others have convinced the majority of group influence researchers that minority influence is a phenomenon worthy of study. And the way that several of these minority-influence researchers came by their interests should, perhaps, not surprise us. Anne Maass (1998) became interested in how minorities could effect social change after growing up in postwar Germany and hearing her grandmother's personal accounts of fascism. Charlan Nemeth (1999) developed her interest while she was a visiting professor in Europe "working with Henri Tajfel and Serge Moscovici. The three of us were 'outsiders'—I an American Roman Catholic female in Europe, they having survived World War II as Eastern European Jews. Sensitivity to the value and the struggles of the minority perspective came to dominate our work."

*I*S LEADERSHIP MINORITY INFLUENCE?

Activity
21.2

In 1910, the Norwegians and English engaged in an epic race to the South Pole. The Norwegians, effectively led by Roald Amundsen, made it. The English, ineptly led by Robert Falcon Scott, did not; Scott and three team members died. Amundsen illustrated the power of **leadership,** the process by which certain individuals mobilize and guide groups. The presidency of George W. Bush illustrates "the power of one," observes Michael Kinsley (2003). "Before Bush brought it up [there was] no popular passion" for the idea "that Saddam was a terrible threat and had to go. . . . You could call this many things, but one of them is leadership.

If real leadership means leading people where they don't want to go, George W. Bush has shown himself to be a real leader."

Some leaders are formally appointed or elected; others emerge informally as the group interacts. What makes for good leadership often depends on the situation—the best person to lead the engineering team may not make the best leader of the sales force. Some people excel at *task leadership*—at organizing work, setting standards, and focusing on goal attainment. Others excel at *social leadership*—at building teamwork, mediating conflicts, and being supportive.

Task leaders often have a directive style—one that can work well if the leader is bright enough to give good orders (Fiedler, 1987). Being goal oriented, such leaders also keep the group's attention and effort focused on its mission. Experiments show that the combination of specific, challenging goals and periodic progress reports helps motivate high achievement (Locke & Latham, 1990).

Social leaders often have a democratic style—one that delegates authority, welcomes input from team members, and, as we have seen, helps prevent groupthink. Many experiments reveal that social leadership is good for morale. Group members usually feel more satisfied when they participate in making decisions (Spector, 1986; Vanderslice & others, 1987). Given control over their tasks, workers also become more motivated to achieve (Burger, 1987).

The once-popular "great person" theory of leadership—that all great leaders share certain traits—has fallen into disrepute. Effective leadership styles, we now know, vary with the situations. People who know what they are doing may resent task leadership, while those who don't may welcome it. Recently, however, social psychologists have again wondered if there might be qualities that mark a good leader in many situations (Hogan & others, 1994). British social psychologists Peter Smith and Monir Tayeb (1989) report that studies done in India, Taiwan, and Iran have found that the most effective supervisors in coal mines, banks, and government offices score high on tests of *both* task and social leadership. They are actively concerned with how work is progressing *and* sensitive to the needs of their subordinates.

Studies also reveal that many effective leaders of laboratory groups, work teams, and large corporations exhibit the behaviors that help make a minority view persuasive. Such leaders engender trust by *consistently* sticking to their goals. And they often exude a *self-confident* charisma that kindles the allegiance of their followers (Bennis, 1984; House & Singh, 1987). Charismatic leaders typically have a compelling *vision* of some desired state of affairs, an ability to *communicate* this to others in clear and simple language, and enough optimism and faith in their group to *inspire* others to follow.

To be sure, groups also influence their leaders. Sometimes those at the front of the herd have simply sensed where it is already heading.

Political candidates know how to read the opinion polls. Someone who typifies the group's views is more likely to be selected as a leader; a leader who deviates too radically from the group's standards may be rejected (Hogg & others, 1998). Smart leaders usually remain with the majority and spend their influence prudently. In rare circumstances, the right traits matched with the right situation yield history-making greatness, notes Dean Keith Simonton (1994). To have a Winston Churchill or a Margaret Thatcher, a Thomas Jefferson or a Karl Marx, a Napoleon or an Adolph Hitler, an Abraham Lincoln or a Martin Luther King, Jr., appear takes the right person in the right place at the right time. When an apt combination of intelligence, skill, determination, self-confidence, and social charisma meets a rare opportunity, the result is sometimes a championship, a Nobel Prize, or a social revolution. Just ask Rosa Parks.

CONCEPTS TO REMEMBER

reactance   A motive to protect or restore one's sense of freedom. Reactance arises when someone threatens our freedom of action.

leadership   The process by which certain group members motivate and guide the group.

PART FOUR

❖

Social Relations

aving explored how we do social psychology (Part One), and
how we think about (Part Two) and influence (Part Three) one
another, we come to social psychology's fourth facet—how
we relate to one another. Our feelings and actions toward other people
are sometimes negative, sometimes positive.

The upcoming modules on prejudice, aggression, and conflict
examine the unpleasant aspects of human relations: Why do we dislike,
even despise, one another? Why and when do we hurt one another?

Then in the modules on conflict resolution, liking, loving, and
helping, we explore the more pleasant aspects: How can social conflicts
be justly and amicably resolved? Why do we like or love particular
people? When will we offer help to others?

Finally, Module 31 asks what social psychological principles might
contribute to help avert an ecological holocaust, triggered by increasing
population, consumption, and global warming.

The Dislike of Diversity[1]

Prejudices come in many forms—for our own group and against some other group: against "northeastern liberals" or "southern hillbillies," Arab "terrorists" or American "infidels," people who are short or fat or homely.

The 9/11 attacks and their aftermath illustrate the power of hatred and prejudice:

"Our terrorism is against America. Our terrorism is a blessed terrorism."

—Osama bin Laden in a video after the 9/11 attacks.

"If I see someone that comes in [an airport] that's got a diaper on his head and a fan belt wrapped around that diaper on his head, that guy needs to be pulled over."

—U.S. Congressman John Cooksey in a radio interview after the 9/11 attacks.

Shortly after 9/11, hostilities flared against people perceived to be of Arab descent. In suburban New York City, a man tried to run down a Pakistani woman while shouting that he was "doing this for my country" (Brown, 2001). In Denton, Texas, a mosque was firebombed (Thompson, 2001). At Boston University, a Middle Eastern student was stabbed, and

---

[1] Modules 22 and 23 were co-authored by Steven J. Spencer, associate professor and chair of the Social Psychology Department program at the University of Waterloo.

at the University of Colorado, students spray-painted the library with "Arabs Go Home." These were not isolated events. The American Arab Anti-Discrimination Committee cataloged more than 250 acts of violence against Arab American students on college campuses in the week following the 9/11 attacks (cnn.com, 2001). Negative views of Middle Eastern immigrants have persisted. In one U.S. survey six months after the 9/11 attacks, Pakistanis and Palestinians were rated as negatively as drug dealers (Fiske, 2002).

Other groups face profound prejudice too. When seeking love and employment, overweight people—especially overweight White women—face slim prospects. In correlational studies, overweight people marry less often, gain entry to less desirable jobs, and make less money. In experiments (in which some people are made to appear overweight) they are perceived as less attractive, intelligent, happy, self-disciplined, and successful (Gortmaker & others, 1993; Hebl & Heatherton, 1998; Pingitore & others, 1994). People have even denigrated those just standing or seated next to an obese person (Hebl & Mannix, 2003). Weight discrimination, in fact, notably exceeds race or gender discrimination and occurs at every employment stage—hiring, placement, promotion, compensation, discipline, and discharge (Roehling, 2000).

WHAT IS PREJUDICE?

www.mhhe.com/myersssp

Activity
22.1

Prejudice, stereotyping, discrimination, racism, sexism—the terms often overlap. Let's clarify them. Each of the situations just described involved a negative evaluation of some group. And that is the essence of **prejudice:** a negative prejudgment of a group and its individual members. Prejudice biases us against a person based on the person's perceived group.

Prejudice is an attitude. An attitude is a distinct combination of feelings, inclinations to act, and beliefs. This combination is the ABC of attitudes: *a*ffect (feelings), *b*ehavior tendency (inclination to act), and cognition (beliefs). A prejudiced person might *dislike* those different from self and *behave* in a discriminatory manner, *believing* them ignorant and dangerous. Like many attitudes, prejudice is complex and may include a component of patronizing affection that serves to keep the target disadvantaged.

The negative evaluations that mark prejudice can stem from emotional associations, from the need to justify behavior, or from negative beliefs, called **stereotypes.** To stereotype is to generalize. To simplify the world, we generalize: The British are reserved. Americans are outgoing. Professors are absentminded.

A problem with stereotypes arises when they are *overgeneralized* or just plain wrong. To presume that most American welfare clients are

African American is to overgeneralize, because it just isn't so. University students' stereotypes of members of particular fraternities (as preferring foreign language courses to economics, or softball to tennis) contain a germ of truth but are overblown. Individuals within the stereotyped group vary more than expected (Brodt & Ross, 1998).

Prejudice is a negative *attitude;* **discrimination** is negative *behavior.* Discriminatory behavior often has its source in prejudicial attitudes (Dovidio & others, 1996). As Module 9 emphasized, however, attitudes and behavior are often loosely linked. Prejudiced attitudes need not breed hostile acts, nor does all oppression spring from prejudice. **Racism** and **sexism** are institutional practices that discriminate, even when there is no prejudicial intent. If word-of-mouth hiring practices in an all-White business have the effect of excluding potential non-White employees, the practice could be called racist—even if an employer intended no discrimination.

*H*OW PERVASIVE IS PREJUDICE?

Is prejudice inevitable? Let's look at the most heavily studied examples— racial and gender prejudice.

Racial Prejudice

In the context of the world, every race is a minority. Non-Hispanic Whites, for example, are only one-fifth of the world's people and will be one-eighth within another half-century. Thanks to mobility and migration during the past two centuries, the world's races now intermingle, in relations that are sometimes hostile, sometimes amiable.

To a molecular biologist, skin color is a trivial human characteristic, one controlled by a minuscule genetic difference between races. Moreover, nature doesn't cluster races in neatly defined categories. It is people, not nature, who sometimes label Tiger Woods "African American" (his ancestry is 25 percent African) or "Asian American" (he is also 25 percent Thai and 25 percent Chinese)—or even as Native American or Dutch (he is one-eighth each).

Is Racial Prejudice Disappearing?

In 1942, most Americans agreed, "There should be separate sections for Negroes on streetcars and buses" (Hyman & Sheatsley, 1956). Today, the question would seem bizarre, because such blatant prejudice has nearly disappeared. In 1942, fewer than a third of all Whites (only 1 in 50 in the South) supported school integration; by 1980, support for it was 90 percent. Considering what a thin slice of history is covered by the years since 1942, or even since slavery was practiced, the changes are dramatic.

In Canada, too, acceptance of ethnic diversity and various immigrant groups has increased in recent decades (Berry & Kalin, 1995).

African Americans' attitudes also have changed since the 1940s, when Kenneth Clark and Mamie Clark (1947) demonstrated that many held anti-Black prejudices. In making its historic 1954 decision declaring segregated schools unconstitutional, the Supreme Court found it note-worthy that when the Clarks gave African American children a choice between Black dolls and White dolls, most chose the White. In studies from the 1950s through the 1970s, Black children were increasingly likely to prefer Black dolls. And adult Blacks came to view Blacks and Whites as similar in traits such as intelligence, laziness, and dependability (Jackman & Senter, 1981; Smedley & Bayton, 1978).

People of different races also now share many of the same attitudes and aspirations, notes Amitai Etzioni (1999). More than 9 in 10 Blacks and Whites say they could vote for a Black presidential candidate. More than 8 in 10 in both groups agree that "to graduate from high school, students should be required to understand the common history and ideas that tie all Americans together." Similar proportions in both groups seek "fair treatment for all, without prejudice or discrimination." And about 2 in 3 in both groups agree that moral and ethical standards have been in decline. Thanks to such shared ideals, notes Etzioni, the United States and most Western democracies have been spared the ethnic trib-alism that has torn apart Kosovo and Rwanda.

Questions concerning intimate interracial contacts still detect preju-dice. "I would probably feel uncomfortable dancing with a Black person in a public place" detects more racial feeling in Whites than "I would probably feel uncomfortable riding a bus with a Black person." Many people who welcome diverse people as co-workers or classmates still socialize, date, and marry within their own race. This helps explain why, in a survey of students at 390 colleges and universities, 53 percent of African American students felt excluded from social activities (Hurtado & others, 1994). Such majority-minority relationships transcend race. On NBA basketball teams minority players (in this case, Whites) feel simi-larly detached from their group's socializing (Schoenfeld, 1995).

This phenomenon of *greatest prejudice in the most intimate social realms* seems universal. In India, people who accept the caste system will typically allow someone from a lower caste into their homes but would not consider marrying such a person (Sharma, 1981). In a national survey of Americans, 75 percent said they would "shop at a store owned by a homosexual," but only 39 percent would "see a homosexual doctor" (Henry, 1994).

Subtle Forms of Prejudice

Much prejudice remains hidden, until evoked by circumstance. When White students indicate racial attitudes and men indicate their sympa-thy for women's rights while hooked up to a supposed lie detector,

Activity
22.2

they admit to prejudice. Other experiments have assessed people's *behavior* toward Blacks and Whites. Whites are equally helpful to any person in need—except when the needy person is remote (say, a wrong-number caller with an apparent Black accent who needs a message relayed). Likewise, when asked to use electric shocks to "teach" a task, White people give no more (if anything less) shock to a Black than to a White person—except when they are angered or when the recipient can't retaliate or know who did it (Crosby & others, 1980; Rogers & Prentice-Dunn, 1981).

As blatant prejudice subsides, automatic emotional reactions linger. Recent research indicates that conscious prejudice can affect our instant reactions. But Patricia Devine and her colleagues (1989, 2000) report that people low and high in prejudice sometimes have similar automatic prejudicial responses.

Try as we might to suppress unwanted thoughts—thoughts about food, thoughts about romance with a friend's partner, judgmental thoughts about another group—they sometimes refuse to go away (Macrae & others, 1994; Wegner & Erber, 1992). This is especially so for older adults, who lose some of their ability to inhibit unwanted thoughts and therefore to suppress old stereotypes (von Hippel & others, 2000). The result for all of us: Unwanted (dissonant) thoughts and feelings often persist. Breaking the prejudice habit is not easy.

All of this illustrates again our *dual attitude* system (Module 2). We can have differing explicit (conscious) and implicit (automatic) attitudes toward the same target. Thus we may retain from childhood a habitual, automatic fear or dislike of people for whom we now express respect and appreciation. Although explicit attitudes may change dramatically with education, implicit attitudes may linger, changing only as we form new habits through practice (Kawakami & others, 2000).

A raft of experiments by researchers at Yale University (Banaji & Bhaskar, 2000), Indiana University (Fazio & others, 1995), the University of Colorado (Wittenbrink & others, 1997), the University of Washington (Greenwald & others, 2000), and New York University (Bargh & Chartrand, 1999) have confirmed the phenomenon of automatic stereotyping and prejudice. These studies briefly flash words or faces that "prime" (automatically activate) stereotypes of some racial, gender, or age group. Without their awareness, the participants' activated stereotypes may then bias their behavior. Having been primed with images associated with African Americans, for example, they may then react with more hostility to an experimenter's annoying request. In clever experiments by Anthony Greenwald and his colleagues (1998, 2000), 9 in 10 White people took longer to identify pleasant words (such as *peace* and *paradise*) as "good" when associated with Black rather than White faces. The participants, mind you, typically expressed little or no prejudice, only an unconscious, unintended response. Moreover, report Kurt Hugenberg

Automatic prejudice. When Joshua Correll and his colleagues invited people to react quickly to people holding either a gun or a harmless object, race influenced perceptions and reactions.

and Galen Bodenhausen (2003), the more strongly people exhibit such implicit prejudice, the readier they are to perceive anger in Black faces.

In separate experiments, Joshua Correll and his co-workers (2002) and Anthony Greenwald and his co-workers (2003) invited people to press buttons quickly to "shoot" or "not shoot" men who suddenly appeared on-screen holding either a gun or a harmless object such as a flashlight or bottle. The participants (both Blacks and Whites, in one of the studies) more often mistakenly shot targets who were Black. In a related series of studies, Keith Payne (2001), and Charles Judd and colleagues (2004), found that when primed with a Black rather than a White face, people think guns: They more quickly recognize a gun and they more often mistake tools, such as a wrench, for a gun. These studies help explain why Amadou Diallo (a Black immigrant in New York City) was shot 41 times by police officers for removing his wallet from his back pocket.

Gender Prejudice

How pervasive is prejudice against women? In Module 13, we examined gender-role norms—people's ideas about how women and men *ought* to behave. Here we consider gender *stereotypes*—people's beliefs about how women and men *do* behave. Norms are *pre*scriptive, stereotypes are *de*scriptive.

Gender Stereotypes

From research on stereotypes, two conclusions are indisputable: Strong gender stereotypes exist, and, as often happens, members of the stereotyped group accept the stereotypes. Men and women agree that you *can*

FIGURE 22-1
Which one of these people would you guess is the group's strongest contributor?
When shown this picture, college students from the early 1980s usually guessed
one of the two men, although those shown photos of same-sex groups most
commonly guessed the person at the head of the table.

judge the book by its sexual cover. In one survey, Mary Jackman and
Mary Senter (1981) found that gender stereotypes were much stronger
than racial stereotypes. For example, only 22 percent of men thought the
two sexes equally "emotional." Of the remaining 78 percent, those who
believed females were more emotional outnumbered those who thought
males were by 15 to 1. And what did the women believe? To within 1
percentage point, their responses were identical.

Consider, too, a study by Natalie Porter, Florence Geis, and Joyce
Jennings Walstedt (1983). They showed students pictures of "a group of
graduate students working as a team on a research project" (Figure 22-1).
Then they gave them a test of "first impressions," asking them to guess
who contributed most to the group. Ignoring the woman at the head of
the table, each of the men in Figure 22-1 received more of the leadership
choices than all three women combined! This stereotype of men as leaders was true not only of women as well as men but also of feminists as
well as nonfeminists. Newer research reveals that behaviors associated
with leadership are perceived less favorably when enacted by a woman
(Eagly & Karau, 2000). Assertiveness can seem less becoming in a woman

than in a man (making it harder for women to become and succeed as leaders). How pervasive are gender stereotypes? Very pervasive.

Remember that stereotypes are generalizations about a group of people and may be true, false, or overgeneralized from a kernel of truth. (They may also be self-fulfilling.) In Module 13, we noted that the average man and woman do differ somewhat in social connectedness, empathy, social power, aggressiveness, and sexual initiative (though not in intelligence). Do we then conclude that gender stereotypes are accurate? Sometimes stereotypes exaggerate differences. But not always, observed Janet Swim (1994). She found that Pennsylvania State University students' stereotypes of men's and women's restlessness, nonverbal sensitivity, aggressiveness, and so forth, were reasonable approximations of actual gender differences. Moreover, such stereotypes have persisted across time and culture. Averaging data from 27 countries, John Williams and his colleagues (1999, 2000) found that folks everywhere perceive women as more agreeable, men as more outgoing. The persistence and omnipresence of gender stereotypes leads some evolutionary psychologists to believe they reflect innate, stable reality (Lueptow & others, 1995).

Stereotypes (beliefs) are not prejudices (attitudes). Stereotypes may support prejudice. Yet one might believe, without prejudice, that men and women are "different yet equal." Let us therefore see how researchers probe for gender prejudice.

Gender Attitudes

Judging from what people tell survey researchers, attitudes toward women have changed as rapidly as racial attitudes. In 1937, one-third of Americans said they would vote for a qualified woman whom their party nominated for president; by 2003, 87 percent said they would (Jones & Moore, 2003). In 1967, 56 percent of first-year American college students agreed that "the activities of married women are best confined to the home and family"; by 2002, only 22 percent agreed (Astin & others, 1987; Sax & others, 2002).

Alice Eagly and her associates (1991) and Geoffrey Haddock and Mark Zanna (1994) also report that people don't respond to women with gut-level negative emotions as they do to certain other groups. Most people like women more than men. They perceive women as more understanding, kind, and helpful. A *favorable* stereotype, which Eagly (1994) dubs the *women-are-wonderful effect*, results in a favorable attitude.

Is gender bias fast becoming extinct in Western countries? Has the women's movement nearly completed its work? As with racial prejudice, blatant gender prejudice is dying, but subtle bias lives. The bogus-pipeline method, for example, exposes bias: Men who believe an experimenter can read their true attitudes with a sensitive lie detector express less sympathy toward women's rights. Even on paper-and-pencil questionnaires, Janet Swim and her co-researchers (1995, 1997) have found a subtle ("modern") sexism that parallels subtle ("modern") racism. Both forms appear in denials of discrimination and in antagonism toward efforts to promote equality (as in "Blacks are getting too demanding in their push for equal rights").

We can also detect bias in behavior. That's what a research team led by Ian Ayres (1991) did. Team members visited 90 Chicago-area car dealers, using a uniform strategy to negotiate the lowest price on a new car that cost the dealer about $11,000. White males were given a final price that averaged $11,362; White females were given an average price of $11,504; Black males were given an average price of $11,783; and Black females were given an average price of $12,237. To test for possible labor market discrimination, M.I.T. researchers sent 5,000 résumés out in response to 1,300 varied employment ads (Bertrand & Mullainathan, 2003). Applicants randomly assigned White names (Emily, Greg) received one callback for every 10 résumés sent. Those given Black names (Lakisha, Jamal) received one callback for every 15 résumés sent.

In the world beyond democratic Western countries, gender discrimination looms even larger:

- Two-thirds of the world's unschooled children are girls (United Nations, 1991).

- In Saudi Arabia, women are forbidden to drive (Beyer, 1990).

- Around the world, people tend to prefer having baby boys. In the United States in 1941, 38 percent of expectant parents said they preferred a boy if they could only have one child; 24 percent preferred a girl; and 23 percent said they didn't care. In 2003, the answers were virtually unchanged with 38 percent still preferring a boy (Lyons, 2003; Simmons, 2000). With the widespread use of ultrasound to determine the sex of a fetus and the growing availability of abortion, these preferences are affecting the number of boys and girls. The 2000 China census revealed 119 newborn boys for every 100 girls (Walfish, 2001). The 2001 India census reported that Punjab Province had 126 newborn boys for every 100 girls (Dugger, 2001). The net result is tens of millions of "missing women."

To conclude, overt prejudice against people of color and against women is far less common today than it was four decades ago. The same is true of prejudice against homosexual people. Nevertheless, techniques that are sensitive to subtle prejudice still detect widespread bias. And in parts of the world, gender prejudice is literally deadly. Therefore, we need to look carefully and closely at the social, emotional, and cognitive sources of prejudice.

CONCEPTS TO REMEMBER

prejudice   A negative prejudgment of a group and its individual members.

stereotype   A belief about the personal attributes of a group of people. Stereotypes are sometimes overgeneralized, inaccurate, and resistant to new information.

discrimination   Unjustifiable negative behavior toward a group or its members.

racism   (1) An individual's prejudicial attitudes and discriminatory behavior toward people of a given race, or (2) institutional practices (even if not motivated by prejudice) that subordinate people of a given race.

sexism   (1) An individual's prejudicial attitudes and discriminatory behavior toward people of a given sex, or (2) institutional practices (even if not motivated by prejudice) that subordinate people of a given sex.

MODULE

23

❖

The Roots of Prejudice

rejudice springs from several sources. It may arise from differences in social status and people's desires to justify and maintain these differences. It may also be learned at our parent's knee as we are socialized about what differences matter between people. Finally, our social institutions may function to maintain and support prejudice. Consider first how prejudice can function to defend self-esteem and social position.

SOCIAL SOURCES OF PREJUDICE

Unequal Status

A principle to remember: *Unequal status breeds prejudice*. Masters view slaves as lazy, irresponsible, lacking ambition—as having just those traits that justify the slavery. Historians debate the forces that create unequal status. But once these inequalities exist, prejudice helps justify the economic and social superiority of those who have wealth and power. Tell me the economic relationship between two groups and I'll predict the intergroup attitudes. Stereotypes rationalize unequal status (Yzerbyt & others, 1997).

In times of conflict, attitudes adjust easily to behavior. People often view enemies as subhuman and depersonalize them with labels. During World War II, the Japanese people became "the Japs." After the war was over, they became "the intelligent, hardworking Japanese." Attitudes are amazingly adaptable. As we have noted in previous modules, cruel acts breed cruel attitudes.

Gender stereotypes, too, help rationalize gender roles. After studying these stereotypes worldwide, John Williams and Deborah Best (1990b) noted that if women provide most of the care to young children, it is reassuring to think women are naturally nurturant. If males run the businesses, hunt, and fight wars, it is comforting to suppose that men are aggressive, independent, and adventurous. In experiments, people perceive members of unknown groups as having traits that suit their roles (Hoffman & Hurst, 1990).

Discrimination's Impact: The Self-Fulfilling Prophecy

Attitudes may coincide with the social hierarchy not only as a rationalization for it but also because discrimination affects its victims. "One's reputation," wrote Gordon Allport, "cannot be hammered, hammered, hammered into one's head without doing something to one's character" (1958, p. 139). If we could snap our fingers and end all discrimination, it would be naive then to say, "The tough times are all over, folks! You can now put on suits or dresses and be attaché-carrying executives and professionals." When the oppression ends, its effects linger, like a societal hangover.

In *The Nature of Prejudice*, Allport cataloged 15 possible effects of victimization. Allport believed these reactions were reducible to two basic types—those that involve blaming oneself (withdrawal, self-hate, aggression against one's own group) and those that involve blaming external causes (fighting back, suspiciousness, increased group pride). If the net results are negative—say, higher rates of crime—people can use them to justify the discrimination that helps maintain them: "If we let those people in our nice neighborhood, property values will plummet."

Does discrimination affect its victims in this way? We must be careful not to overstate the point. The soul and style of Black culture is for many a proud heritage, not just a response to victimization (Jones, 2004). Thus, while White youth are learning to de-emphasize ethnic differences and avoid stereotypes, African American youth "are increasingly taking pride in their ethnicity and positively valuing ethnic differences," noted Charles Judd and his co-researchers (1995). Cultural differences need not imply social deficits.

Nevertheless, social beliefs *can* be self-confirming, as demonstrated in a clever pair of experiments by Carl Word, Mark Zanna, and Joel Cooper (1974). In the first experiment, Princeton University White men interviewed White and Black research assistants posing as job applicants. When the applicant was Black, the interviewers sat farther away, ended the interview 25 percent sooner, and made 50 percent more speech errors than when the applicant was White. Imagine being interviewed by someone who sat at a distance, stammered, and ended the interview rather quickly. Would it affect your performance or your feelings about the interviewer?

To find out, the researchers conducted a second experiment in which trained interviewers treated students the way the interviewers in the first experiment had treated either the White or Black applicants. When videotapes of the interviews were later rated, those who were treated like the Blacks in the first experiment seemed more nervous and less effective. Moreover, the interviewees could themselves sense a difference; those treated the way the Blacks were treated judged their interviewers to be less adequate and less friendly. The experimenters concluded that part of "the 'problem' of Black performance resides . . . within the interaction setting itself." As with other self-fulfilling prophecies, prejudice affects its targets (Swim & Stangor, 1998). One vehicle for its doing so is "stereotype threat."

Stereotype Threat

Video
23.1

Placed in a situation where others expect you to perform poorly, your anxiety may cause you to confirm the belief. I am a short guy in my early 60s. When I join a pickup basketball game with bigger, younger players, I often suspect that they expect me to be a detriment to their team and that tends to undermine my confidence and performance. Claude Steele and his colleagues call this phenomenon **stereotype threat**—a self-confirming apprehension that one will be evaluated based on a negative stereotype (Steele, 1997; Steele & others, 2002).

In several experiments, Steven Spencer, Steele, and Diane Quinn (1999) gave a very difficult math test to men and women students who had similar math backgrounds. When told that there were *no* gender differences on the test and no evaluation of any group stereotype, the women's performance consistently equaled the men's. Told that there *was* a gender difference, the women dramatically confirmed the stereotype (Figure 23-1). Frustrated by the extremely difficult test questions, they apparently felt added apprehension, which undermined their performances.

The media can provoke stereotype threat. Paul Davies and his colleagues (2002) had women and men watch a series of commercials expecting that they would be tested for their memory of details. For half the participants, the commercials contained only neutral stimuli; for the other half, some of the commercials contained images of "airheaded" women. After seeing the stereotypic images, women not only performed worse than men on a math test, they also reported less interest in obtaining a math or science major or entering a math or science career.

Might racial stereotypes be similarly self-fulfilling? Steele and Joshua Aronson (1995) confirmed that they are when giving difficult verbal

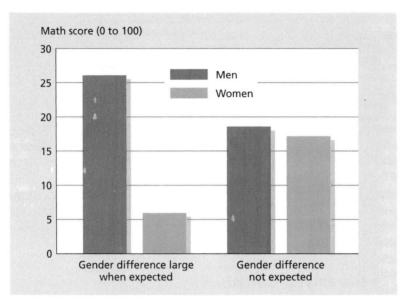

FIGURE 23-1
Stereotype vulnerability and women's math performance. Steven Spencer,
Claude Steele, and Diane Quinn (1999) gave equally capable men and
women a difficult math test. When participants were led to believe there
were gender differences on the test, women scored lower than men.
When the threat of confirming the stereotype was removed (when gender differences were not expected), women did just as well as men.

abilities tests to Whites and Blacks. Blacks underperformed Whites only
when taking the tests under conditions high in stereotype threat. Jeff
Stone and his colleagues (1999) report that stereotype threat affects athletic performance, too. Blacks did worse than usual when a golf task was
framed as a test of "sports intelligence," and Whites did worse when it
was a test of "natural athletic ability." "When people are reminded
of a negative stereotype about themselves—'White men can't jump' or
'Black men can't think'—it can adversely affect performance," Stone (2000)
surmised.

If you tell students they are at risk of failure (as is often suggested
by minority support programs), the stereotype may erode their performance, says Steele (1997), and cause them to "disidentify" with school and
seek self-esteem elsewhere (Figure 23-2). Indeed, as African American
students move from eighth to tenth grade, there is a weakening connection between their school performance and self-esteem (Osborne, 1995).
Moreover, students led to think they have benefited from gender- or race-
based preferences in gaining admission to a college or an academic group
tend to underperform compared to those who are led to feel competent

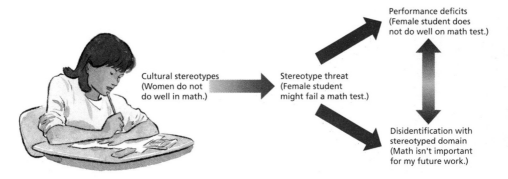

FIGURE 23-2
Stereotype threat. Threat from facing a negative stereotype can produce performance deficits and disidentification.

(Brown & others, 2000). Better, therefore, to challenge students to believe in their potential, observes Steele.

But how does stereotype threat undermine performance? One rout is cognitive. Stereotype threat is distracting: The effort it takes to dismiss its allegations increases mental demands and decreases working memory (Croizet & others, 2004; Schmader & Johns, 2003; Steele & others, 2002). Another effect is motivational: Worrying about mistakes under stereotype threat can impair a person's performance (Keller & Dauenheimer, 2003; Seibt & Forster, 2004), and the physiological arousal that accompanies stereotype threat can impair performance on hard tests (Ben-Zeev, Fein, & Inzlicht, 2004; O'Brien & Crandall, 2003). (Recall from Module 17 the effect of arousal from others: Presence tends to strengthen performance on easy tasks and disrupt performance on hard tasks.)

If stereotype threats can disrupt performance, could *positive* stereotypes enhance it? Margaret Shih, Todd Pittinsky, and Nalini Ambady (1999) confirmed this possibility. When Asian American females were asked biographical questions that reminded them of their gender identity before taking a math test, their performance plunged (compared with a control group). When similarly reminded of their Asian identity, their performance rose. Negative stereotypes disrupt performance, and positive stereotypes, it seems, facilitate performance.

SOCIAL IDENTITY

Humans are a group-bound species. Our ancestral history prepares us to feed and protect ourselves—to live—in groups. Humans cheer for their groups, kill for their groups, die for their groups. Not surprisingly, we also define ourselves by our groups, note Australian social psychologists

John Turner (1981, 1987, 1991, 2001), Michael Hogg (1992, 1996, 2003), and their colleagues. Self-concept—our sense of who we are—contains not just a *personal identity* (our sense of our personal attributes and attitudes) but a **social identity.** Fiona identifies herself as a woman, an Aussie, a Labourite, a University of New South Wales student, a member of the MacDonald family. We carry such social identities like playing cards, playing them when appropriate.

Working with the late British social psychologist Henri Tajfel [pronounced TOSH-fel], Turner proposed *social identity theory.* Turner and Tajfel observed the following:

- We *categorize:* We find it useful to put people, ourselves included, into categories. To label someone as a Hindu, a Scot, or a bus driver is a shorthand way of saying some other things about the person.
- We *identify:* We associate ourselves with certain groups (our **ingroups**) and gain self-esteem by doing so.
- We *compare:* We contrast our groups with other groups (**outgroups**), with a favorable bias toward our own group.

We evaluate ourselves partly by our group memberships. Having a sense of "we-ness" strengthens our self-concepts. It *feels* good. We seek not only *respect* for ourselves but *pride* in our groups (Smith & Tyler, 1997). Moreover, seeing our groups as superior helps us feel even better. It's as if we all think, "I am an X [name your group]. X is good. Therefore, I am good."

Lacking a positive personal identity, people often seek self-esteem by identifying with a group. Thus, many youths find pride, power, and identity in gang affiliations. Many superpatriots define themselves by their national identities (Staub, 1997). And many people at loose ends find identity in their associations with new religious movements, self-help groups, or fraternal clubs.

Ingroup Bias

The group definition of who you are—your race, religion, gender, academic major—implies a definition of who you are not. The circle that includes "us" (the ingroup) excludes "them" (the outgroup). Thus, the mere experience of being formed into groups may promote **ingroup bias.** Ask children, "Which are better, the children in your school or the children at [another school nearby]?" Virtually all will say their own school has the better children. For adults, too, the closer to home, the better things seem. More than 80 percent of both Whites and Blacks say race relations are generally good in their neighborhoods, but fewer than 60 percent see relations as generally good in the country as a whole (Sack & Elder, 2000). Merely sharing a birthday with someone creates enough of a bond to evoke heightened cooperation in a laboratory experiment (Miller & others, 1998).

Ingroup bias is one more example of the human quest for a positive self-concept. We are so group conscious that given any excuse to think of ourselves as a group we will do so—and will then exhibit ingroup bias. Cluster people into groups defined by nothing more than their driver's license number's last digit, and they'll feel a certain kinship with their number mates. In a series of experiments, Tajfel and Michael Billig (1974; Tajfel, 1970, 1981, 1982) discovered how little it takes to provoke favoritism toward *us* and unfairness toward *them*. In one study, Tajfel and Billig had British teenagers evaluate modern abstract paintings and then told them that they and some others had favored the art of Paul Klee over that of Wassily Kandinsky. Finally, without ever meeting the other members of their group, the teens divided some money among members of both groups.

In this and other experiments, defining groups even in this trivial way produced ingroup favoritism. David Wilder (1981) summarized the typical result: "When given the opportunity to divide 15 points [worth money], subjects generally award 9 or 10 points to their own group and 5 or 6 points to the other group." This bias occurs with both sexes and with people of all ages and nationalities, though especially with people from individualist cultures (Gudykunst, 1989). (People in communal cultures identify more with all their peers and so treat everyone more the same.)

We also are more prone to ingroup bias when our group is small and lower in status relative to the outgroup (Ellemers & others, 1997; Mullen & others, 1992). When we're part of a small group surrounded by a larger group, we are also conscious of our group membership; when our ingroup is the majority, we think less about it. To be a foreign student, to be gay or lesbian, or to be of a minority race or gender at some social gathering is to feel one's social identity more keenly and to react accordingly.

Even forming conspicuous groups on *no* logical basis—say, merely by composing groups X and Y with the flip of a coin—will produce some ingroup bias (Billig & Tajfel, 1973; Brewer & Silver, 1978; Locksley & others, 1980). In Kurt Vonnegut's novel *Slapstick,* computers gave everyone a new middle name; all "Daffodil-11s" then felt unity with one another and distance from "Raspberry-13s." The self-serving bias (Module 4) rides again, enabling people to achieve a more positive social identity: "We" are better than "they," even when "we" and "they" are defined randomly!

Conformity

Once established, prejudice is maintained largely by inertia. If prejudice is socially accepted, many people will follow the path of least resistance and conform to the fashion. They will act not so much out of a need to hate as out of a need to be liked and accepted.

Thomas Pettigrew's (1958) studies of Whites in South Africa and the American South revealed that, during the 1950s, those who conformed most to other social norms were also most prejudiced; those who were less conforming mirrored less of the surrounding prejudice. The price of nonconformity was painfully clear to the ministers of Little Rock, Arkansas, where the U.S. Supreme Court's 1954 school desegregation decision was implemented. Most ministers favored integration but usually only privately; they feared that advocating it openly would lose them members and contributions (Campbell & Pettigrew, 1959). Or consider the Indiana steel workers and West Virginia coal miners of the same era. In the mills and the mines, the workers accepted integration. In the neighborhoods, the norm was rigid segregation (Minard, 1952; Reitzes, 1953). Prejudice was clearly *not* a manifestation of "sick" personalities but simply of the social norms.

Conformity also maintains gender prejudice. "If we have come to think that the nursery and the kitchen are the natural sphere of a woman," wrote George Bernard Shaw in an 1891 essay, "we have done so exactly as English children come to think that a cage is the natural sphere of a parrot—because they have never seen one anywhere else." Children who *have* seen women elsewhere—children of employed women—have less stereotyped views of men and women (Hoffman, 1977).

In all this, there is a message of hope. If prejudice is not deeply ingrained in personality, then as fashions change and new norms evolve, prejudice can diminish. And so it has.

EMOTIONAL SOURCES OF PREJUDICE

Prejudice may be bred by social situations, but emotional factors often add fuel to the fire: Frustration can feed prejudice, as can personality factors like status needs and authoritarian tendencies. Let's see how.

Frustration and Aggression: The Scapegoat Theory

Pain and frustration (the blocking of a goal) often evoke hostility. When the cause of our frustration is intimidating or unknown, we often redirect our hostility. This phenomenon of "displaced aggression" may have contributed to the lynchings of African Americans in the South after the Civil War. Between 1882 and 1930, more lynchings occurred in years when cotton prices were low and economic frustration was therefore presumably high (Hepworth & West, 1988; Hovland & Sears, 1940). Hate crimes seem not to have fluctuated with unemployment in recent decades (Green & others, 1998). However, when living standards are rising, societies tend to be more open to diversity and to antidiscrimination laws (Frank, 1999). Ethnic peace is easier to maintain during prosperity.

Targets for this displaced aggression vary. Following their defeat in World War I and their country's subsequent economic chaos, many Germans saw Jews as villains. Long before Hitler came to power, one German leader explained: "The Jew is just convenient. . . . If there were no Jews, the anti-Semites would have to invent them" (quoted by G. W. Allport, 1958, p. 325). In earlier centuries people vented their fear and hostility on witches, whom they sometimes burned or drowned in public. Passions provoke prejudice.

One source of frustration is competition. When two groups compete for jobs, housing, or social prestige, one group's goal fulfillment can become the other group's frustration. Thus the **realistic group conflict theory** suggests that prejudice arises when groups compete for scarce resources (Esses & others, 1998). A corresponding ecological principle, Gause's law, states that maximum competition will exist between species with identical needs. In Western Europe, for example, some people agree, "Over the last five years people like yourself have been economically worse off than most [name of country's minority group]." These frustrated people express relatively high levels of blatant prejudice (Pettigrew & Meertens, 1995). In Canada, opposition to immigration since 1975 has gone up and down with the unemployment rate (Palmer, 1996). In America, the strongest anti-Black prejudice occurs among Whites who are closest to Blacks on the socioeconomic ladder (Greeley & Sheatsley, 1971; Pettigrew, 1978; Tumin, 1958). When interests clash, prejudice—for some people—pays.

Personality Dynamics

Any two people with equal reason to feel frustrated or threatened will often not be equally prejudiced. This suggests that prejudice serves other functions besides advancing competitive self-interest.

Need for Status, Self-Regard, and Belonging

Status is relative: To perceive ourselves as having status, we need people below us. Thus one psychological benefit of prejudice, or of any status system, is a feeling of superiority. Most of us can recall a time when we took secret satisfaction in another's failure—perhaps seeing a brother or sister punished or a classmate failing a test. In Europe and North America, prejudice is often greater among those low or slipping on the socioeconomic ladder and among those whose positive self-image is being threatened (Lemyre & Smith, 1985; Pettigrew & others, 1998; Thompson & Crocker, 1985). In one study, members of lower-status sororities were more disparaging of other sororities than were members of higher-status sororities (Crocker & others, 1987). Perhaps people whose status is secure have less need to feel superior.

But other factors associated with low status could also account for prejudice. Imagine yourself as one of the Arizona State University students who took part in an experiment by Robert Cialdini and Kenneth Richardson (1980). You are walking alone across campus. Someone approaches you and asks your help with a five-minute survey. You agree. After the researcher gives you a brief "creativity test," he deflates you with the news that "you have scored relatively low on the test." The researcher then completes the survey by asking you some evaluative questions about either your school or its traditional rival, the University of Arizona. Would your feelings of failure affect your ratings of either school? Compared with those in a control group whose self-esteem was not threatened, the students who experienced failure gave higher ratings to their own school and lower ratings to their rival. Apparently, asserting one's social identity by boasting about one's own group and denigrating outgroups can boost one's ego.

James Meindl and Melvin Lerner (1984) found that a humiliating experience—accidentally knocking over a stack of someone's important computer cards—provoked English-speaking Canadian students to express increased hostility toward French-speaking Canadians. And Teresa Amabile and Ann Glazebrook (1982) found that Dartmouth College men who were made to feel insecure judged others' work more harshly.

The Authoritarian Personality

In the 1940s, University of California Berkeley researchers—two of whom had fled Nazi Germany—set out on an urgent research mission: to uncover the psychological roots of an anti-Semitism so poisonous that it caused the slaughter of millions of Jews and turned many millions of Europeans into indifferent spectators. In studies of American adults, Theodor Adorno and his colleagues (1950) discovered that hostility toward Jews often coexisted with hostility toward other minorities. Prejudice appeared to be less an attitude specific to one group than a way of thinking about those who are different. Moreover, these judgmental, **ethnocentric** people shared authoritarian tendencies—an intolerance for weakness, a punitive attitude, and a submissive respect for their ingroup's authorities, as reflected in their agreement with such statements as, "Obedience and respect for authority are the most important virtues children should learn."

As children, authoritarian people often faced harsh discipline. This supposedly led them to repress their hostilities and impulses and to "project" them onto outgroups. The insecurity of authoritarian children seemed to predispose them toward an excessive concern with power and status and an inflexible right-wrong way of thinking that made ambiguity difficult to tolerate. Such people therefore tended to be submissive to those with power over them and aggressive or punitive toward those beneath them.

Scholars criticized the research for focusing on right-wing authoritarianism and overlooking dogmatic authoritarianism of the Left. Still, its main conclusion has survived: Authoritarian tendencies, sometimes reflected in ethnic tensions, surge during threatening times of economic recession and social upheaval (Doty & others, 1991; Sales, 1973). In contemporary Russia, individuals scoring high in authoritarianism have tended to support a return to Marxist-Leninist ideology and to oppose democratic reform (McFarland & others, 1992, 1996).

Moreover, contemporary studies of right-wing authoritarians by University of Manitoba psychologist Bob Altemeyer (1988, 1992) confirm that there *are* individuals whose fears and hostilities surface as prejudice. Feelings of moral superiority may go hand in hand with brutality toward perceived inferiors.

Different forms of prejudice—toward Blacks, gays and lesbians, women, old people, fat people, AIDS victims, the homeless—*do* tend to coexist in the same individuals (Bierly, 1985; Crandall, 1994; Peterson & others, 1993; Snyder & Ickes, 1985). As Altemeyer concludes, right-wing authoritarians tend to be "equal opportunity bigots."

Particularly striking are people high in social dominance orientation and authoritarian personality. Altemeyer (2004) reports that these "Double Highs" are, not surprisingly, "among the most prejudiced persons in our society." What is perhaps most surprising and more troubling is that they seem to display the worst qualities of each type of personality, striving for status often in manipulative ways while being dogmatic and ethnocentric. Altemeyer argues that although these people are relatively rare, they are predisposed to be leaders of hate groups.

COGNITIVE SOURCES OF PREJUDICE

Much of the explanation of prejudice so far could have been written in the 1960s—but not what follows. This new look at prejudice, fueled in the 1990s by more than 2,100 articles on stereotyping, applies the new research on social thinking. The basic point is this: Stereotyped beliefs and prejudiced attitudes exist not only because of social conditioning and because they enable people to displace hostilities, but also as by-products of normal thinking processes. Many stereotypes spring less from malice of the heart than the machinery of the mind. Like perceptual illusions, which are by-products of our knack for interpreting the world, stereotypes can be by-products of how we simplify our complex worlds.

Categorization

One way we simplify our environment is to *categorize*—to organize the world by clustering objects into groups (Macrae & Bodenhausen, 2000). A biologist classifies plants and animals. A human classifies people. Having done so, we think about them more easily. If persons in a group share some similarities—if most MENSA members are smart, most basketball players are tall—knowing their group memberships can provide useful information with minimal effort (Macrae & others, 1994). Stereotypes sometimes offer "a beneficial ratio of information gained to effort expended" (Sherman & others, 1998). Customs inspectors and airplane antihijack personnel are therefore given "profiles" of suspicious individuals (Kraut & Poe, 1980).

We find it especially easy and efficient to rely on stereotypes when

- pressed for time (Kaplan & others, 1993),
- preoccupied (Gilbert & Hixon, 1991),
- tired (Bodenhausen, 1990),
- emotionally aroused (Esses & others, 1993b; Stroessner & Mackie, 1993), and
- too young to appreciate diversity (Biernat, 1991).

Ethnicity and sex are, in our current world, powerful ways of categorizing people. Imagine Tom, a 45-year-old, African American New Orleans real estate agent. I suspect that your image of "Black male" predominates over the categories "middle-aged," "businessperson," and "American southerner." Moreover, when shown pictures of Black or White individuals, our brains respond differently, beginning within about one-tenth of a second (Ito & Urland, 2003).

Experiments expose our spontaneous categorization of people by race. Much as we organize what is actually a color continuum into what we perceive as distinct colors, so we cannot resist categorizing people into groups. We label people of widely varying ancestry as simply "Black" or "White," as if such categories were black and white. When individuals view different people making statements, they often forget who said what, yet they remember the race of the person who made each statement (Hewstone & others, 1991; Stroessner & others, 1990; Taylor & others, 1978). By itself, such categorization is not prejudice, but it does provide a foundation for prejudice.

Perceived Similarities and Differences
Picture the following objects: apples, chairs, pencils.

There is a strong tendency to see objects within a group as being more uniform than they really are. Were your apples all red? Your chairs all straight-backed? Your pencils all yellow? It's the same with people. Once we assign people to groups—athletes, drama majors, math professors—we are likely to exaggerate the similarities within the groups and the differences between them (S. E. Taylor, 1981; Wilder, 1978). Mere division into groups can create an **outgroup homogeneity effect**—a sense that they are "all alike" and different from "us" and "our" group (Ostrom & Sedikides, 1992). Because we generally like people we think are similar to us and dislike those we perceive as different, the natural result is ingroup bias (Byrne & Wong, 1962; Rokeach & Mezei, 1966; Stein & others, 1965).

When the group is our own, we are more likely to see diversity:

- Many non-Europeans see the Swiss as a fairly homogeneous people. But to the people of Switzerland, the Swiss are diverse, encompassing French-, German-, and Italian-speaking groups.

- Many Anglo-Americans lump "Latinos" together. Mexican Americans, Cuban Americans, and Puerto Ricans see important differences (Huddy & Virtanen, 1995).

- Sorority sisters perceive the members of any other sorority as less diverse than the mix in their own (Park & Rothbart, 1982).

In general, the greater our familiarity with a social group, the more we see its diversity (Brown & Wootton-Millward, 1993; Linville & others, 1989). The less our familiarity, the more we stereotype. Also, the smaller and less powerful the group, the less we attend to them and the more we stereotype (Fiske, 1993; Mullen & Hu, 1989). To those in power, we pay attention.

Perhaps you have noticed: *They*—the members of any racial group other than your own—even *look* alike. Many of us can recall embarrassing ourselves by confusing two people of another racial group, prompting the person we've misnamed to say, "You think we all look alike." Experiments by John Brigham, June Chance, Alvin Goldstein, and Roy Malpass in the United States and by Hayden Ellis in Scotland reveal that people of other races do in fact *seem* to look more alike than do people of one's own race (Chance & Goldstein, 1981, 1996; Ellis, 1981; Meissner & Brigham, 2001). When White students are shown faces of a few White and a few Black individuals and then asked to pick these individuals out of a photographic lineup, they more accurately recognize the White faces than the Black, and they often falsely recognize Black faces never before seen.

Blacks more easily recognize another Black than they do a White (Bothwell & others, 1989). And Hispanics more readily recognize another Hispanic whom they saw a couple of hours earlier than they do an Anglo (Platz & Hosch, 1988).

It's true outside the laboratory as well, as Daniel Wright and his colleagues (2001) found after either a Black or a White researcher approached

Black and White people in South African and English shopping malls. When later asked to identify the researcher from lineups, people better recognized those of their own race. It's not that we cannot perceive differences among faces of another race. Rather, when looking at a face from another racial group we often attend first to race ("that man is Black"), rather than to individual features. When viewing someone of our own race, we are less race conscious and more attentive to individual details (Levin, 2000).

Distinctiveness

Other ways we perceive our worlds also breed stereotypes. Distinctive people and vivid or extreme occurrences often capture attention and distort judgments. As with the outgroup homogeneity effect, this innocent-seeming phenomenon sometimes breeds stereotypes.

Distinctive People Draw Attention

Have you ever found yourself in a situation where you were the only person of your gender, race, or nationality? If so, your difference from the others probably made you more noticeable and the object of more attention. A Black in an otherwise White group, a man in an otherwise female group, or a woman in an otherwise male group seems more prominent and influential and to have exaggerated good and bad qualities (Crocker & McGraw, 1984; S. E. Taylor & others, 1979). When someone in a group is made salient (conspicuous), we tend to see that person as causing whatever happens (Taylor & Fiske, 1978). If we are positioned to look at Joe, an average group member, Joe will seem to have a greater than average influence on the group. People who capture our attention seem more responsible for what happens.

Have you noticed that people also define you by your most distinctive traits and behaviors? Tell people about someone who is a skydiver and a tennis player, report Lori Nelson and Dale Miller (1995), and they will think of the person as a skydiver. Asked to choose a gift book for the person, they will pick a skydiving book over a tennis book. A person who has both a pet snake and a pet dog is seen more as a snake owner than a dog owner. People also take note of those who violate expectations (Bettencourt & others, 1997). "Like a flower blooming in winter, intellect is more readily noticed where it is not expected," reflected Stephen Carter (1993, p. 54) on his experience as an African American intellectual. Such perceived distinctiveness makes it easier for highly capable job applicants from low-status groups to get noticed, though they also must work harder to prove that their abilities are genuine (Biernat & Kobrynowicz, 1997).

Ellen Langer and Lois Imber (1980) cleverly demonstrated the attention paid to distinctive people. They asked Harvard students to watch a video of a man reading. The students paid closer attention when they were led to think he was out of the ordinary—a cancer patient, a homosexual, or a millionaire. They detected characteristics that other viewers ignored, and their evaluation of him was more extreme. Those who thought the man was a cancer patient noticed distinctive facial characteristics and bodily movements and thus perceived him to be much more "different from most people" than did the other viewers. The extra attention we pay to distinctive people creates an illusion that they differ from others more than they really do. If people thought you had the IQ of a genius, they would probably notice things about you that otherwise would pass unnoticed.

When surrounded by Whites, Blacks sometimes detect people reacting to their distinctiveness. Many report being stared or glared at, being subject to insensitive comments, and receiving bad service (Swim & others, 1998). Sometimes we misperceive others as reacting to our distinctiveness. At Dartmouth College, researchers Robert Kleck and Angelo Strenta (1980) discovered this when they led college women to feel disfigured. The women thought the purpose of the experiment was to assess how someone would react to a facial scar created with theatrical makeup; the scar was on the right cheek, running from the ear to the mouth. Actually, the purpose was to see how the women themselves, when made to feel deviant, would perceive others' behavior toward them. After applying the makeup, the experimenter gave each woman a small hand mirror so she could see the authentic-looking scar. When she put the mirror down, he then applied some "moisturizer" to "keep the makeup from cracking." What the "moisturizer" really did was remove the scar.

The scene that followed was poignant. A young woman, feeling terribly self-conscious about her supposedly disfigured face, talked with another woman who sees no such disfigurement and knows nothing of what has gone on before. If you have ever felt similarly self-conscious—perhaps about a physical disability, acne, even just a bad hair day—then perhaps you can sympathize with the self-conscious woman. Compared with women who were led to believe their conversational partners merely thought they had an allergy, the "disfigured" women became acutely sensitive to how their partners were looking at them. They rated their partners as more tense, distant, and patronizing. In fact, observers who later analyzed videotapes of how the partners treated "disfigured" persons could find no such differences in treatment. Self-conscious about being different, the "disfigured" women misinterpreted mannerisms and comments they would otherwise not have noticed.

Vivid Cases
Our minds also use distinctive cases as a shortcut to judging groups. Are Blacks good athletes? "Well, there's Venus and Serena Williams and Shaquille O'Neal. Yeah, I'd say so." Note the thought processes at work

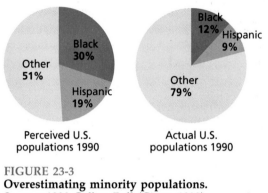

Perceived U.S.
populations 1990

Actual U.S.
populations 1990

FIGURE 23-3
Overestimating minority populations.
Source: 1990 Gallup Poll (Gates, 1993).

here: Given limited experience with a particular social group, we recall examples of it and generalize from those (Sherman, 1996). Moreover, encountering exemplars of negative stereotypes (say, a hostile Black) can prime such stereotypes, leading us to minimize contact with the group (Hendersen-King & Nisbett, 1996).

Generalizing from single cases can cause problems. Vivid instances, though more available in memory, are seldom representative of the larger group. Exceptional athletes, though distinctive and memorable, are not the best basis for judging the distribution of athletic talent among an entire group.

Those in a numerical minority, being more distinctive, also may be numerically overestimated by the majority. What proportion of your country's population would you say is Muslim? People in non-Muslim countries often overestimate this proportion. In the United States, for example, less than 0.5 percent declared themselves Muslim in a 2002 Gallup survey (Strausberg, 2003).

Or consider a 1990 Gallup poll report that the average American greatly overestimated the U.S. Black population and Hispanic populations (Figure 23-3). A 2002 Gallup poll found the average American thinking 21 percent of men were gay and 22 percent of women were lesbian (Robinson, 2002). Repeated surveys suggest that about 3 or 4 percent of men and 1 or 2 percent of women have a same-sex orientation (National Center for Health Statistics, 1991; Smith, 1998; Tarmann, 2002).

Myron Rothbart and his colleagues (1978) showed how distinctive cases also fuel stereotypes. They had University of Oregon students view 50 slides, each of which stated a man's height. For one group of students, 10 of the men were slightly over 6 feet (up to 6 feet, 4 inches). For other students, these 10 men were well over 6 feet (up to 6 feet, 11 inches). When asked later how many of the men were over 6 feet, those given the moderately tall examples recalled 5 percent too many. Those given the extremely tall examples recalled 50 percent too many. In a follow-up experiment, students read descriptions of the actions of 50 men, 10 of whom had committed either nonviolent crimes, such as forgery, or violent crimes, such as rape. Of those shown the list with the violent crimes, most overestimated the number of criminal acts.

The attention-getting power of distinctive, extreme cases helps explain why middle-class people so greatly exaggerate the dissimilarities between themselves and the underclass. The less we know about a group, the more we are influenced by a few vivid cases (Quattrone & Jones, 1980). Contrary to stereotypes of "welfare queens" driving Cadillacs, people living in poverty generally share the aspirations of the middle class and would rather provide for themselves than accept public assistance (Cook & Curtin, 1987).

Attribution: Is It a Just World?

In explaining others' actions, we frequently commit the fundamental attribution error: We attribute their behavior so much to their inner dispositions that we discount important situational forces. The error occurs partly because our attention focuses on the persons, not the situation. A person's race or sex is vivid and gets attention; the situational forces working upon that person are usually less visible. Slavery was often overlooked as an explanation for slave behavior; the behavior was instead attributed to the slaves' own nature. Until recently, the same was true of how we explained the perceived differences between women and men. Because gender-role constraints were hard to see, we attributed men's and women's behavior solely to their innate dispositions. The more people assume that human traits are fixed dispositions, the stronger are their stereotypes (Levy & others, 1998).

In a series of experiments conducted at the Universities of Waterloo and Kentucky, Melvin Lerner (Lerner, 1980; Lerner & Miller, 1978) discovered that merely *observing* another innocent person being victimized is enough to make the victim seem less worthy. Imagine that you, along with some others, are participating in one of Lerner's studies—supposedly on the perception of emotional cues (Lerner & Simmons, 1966). One of the participants, a confederate, is selected by lottery to perform a memory task. This person receives painful shocks whenever she gives a wrong answer. You and the others note her emotional responses.

After watching the victim receive these apparently painful shocks, the experimenter asks you to evaluate her. How would you respond? With compassionate sympathy? We might expect so. As Ralph Waldo Emerson wrote, "The martyr cannot be dishonored." On the contrary, the experiments revealed that martyrs *can* be dishonored. When observers were powerless to alter the victim's fate, they often rejected and devalued the victim. Juvenal, the Roman satirist, anticipated these results: "The

Roman mob follows after Fortune . . . and hates those who have been condemned."

Linda Carli and her colleagues (1989, 1999) report that this **just-world phenomenon** colors our impressions of rape victims. Carli had people read detailed descriptions of interactions between a man and a woman. For example, a woman and her boss meet for dinner, go to his home, and each have a glass of wine. Some read a scenario that has a happy ending: "Then he led me to the couch. He held my hand and asked me to marry him." In hindsight, people find the ending unsurprising and admire the man's and woman's character traits. Others read the same scenario with a different ending: "But then he became very rough and pushed me onto the couch. He held me down on the couch and raped me." Given this ending, people see it as inevitable and blame the woman for behavior that seems faultless in the first scenario.

Lerner (1980) noted that such disparaging of hapless victims results from the human need to believe that, "I am a just person living in a just world, a world where people get what they deserve." From early childhood, he argues, we are taught that good is rewarded and evil punished. Hard work and virtue pay dividends; laziness and immorality do not. From this it is but a short leap to assuming that those who flourish must be good and those who suffer must deserve their fate. The classic illustration is the Old Testament story of Job, a good person who suffers terrible misfortune. Job's friends surmise that, this being a just world, Job must have done something wicked to elicit such terrible suffering.

This suggests that people are indifferent to social injustice not because they lack concern for justice but because they see no injustice. Those who assume a just world believe that rape victims must have behaved seductively (Borgida & Brekke, 1985), that battered spouses must have provoked their beatings (Summers & Feldman, 1984), that poor people don't deserve better (Furnham & Gunter, 1984), and that sick people are responsible for their illnesses (Gruman & Sloan, 1983). Such beliefs enable successful people to reassure themselves that they, too, deserve what they have. The wealthy and healthy can see their own good fortune, and others' misfortune, as justly deserved. Linking good fortune with virtue and misfortune with moral failure enables the fortunate to feel pride and to avoid responsibility for the unfortunate.

Social psychologists have been more successful in explaining prejudice than in alleviating it. Because prejudice results from many interrelated factors, there is no simple remedy. Nevertheless, we can now anticipate techniques for reducing prejudice (discussed further in modules to come): If unequal status breeds prejudice, then we can seek to create cooperative, equal-status relationships. If prejudice often rationalizes discriminatory behavior, then we can mandate nondiscrimination. If outgroups seem more unlike one's own group than they really are, then we can make efforts to personalize their members. These are some of the antidotes for the poison of prejudice.

Since the end of World War II in 1945 a number of these antidotes have been applied, and racial and gender prejudices have indeed diminished. It now remains to be seen whether, during the next century, progress will continue . . . or whether, as could easily happen in a time of increasing population and diminishing resources, antagonisms will again erupt into open hostility.

CONCEPTS TO REMEMBER

stereotype threat A disruptive concern, when facing a negative stereotype, that one will be evaluated based on a negative stereotype. Unlike self-fulfilling prophecies that hammer one's reputation into one's self-concept, stereotype threat situations have immediate effects.

social identity The "we" aspect of our self-concept; the part of our answer to "Who am I?" that comes from our group memberships.

ingroup "Us"—a group of people who share a sense of belonging, a feeling of common identity.

outgroup "Them"—a group that people perceive as distinctively different from or apart from their ingroup.

ingroup bias The tendency to favor one's own group.

realistic group conflict theory The theory that prejudice arises from competition between groups for scarce resources.

ethnocentric Believing in the superiority of one's own ethnic and cultural group, and having a corresponding disdain for all other groups.

outgroup homogeneity effect Perception of outgroup members as more similar to one another than are ingroup members. Thus "they are alike; we are diverse."

just-world phenomenon The tendency of people to believe the world is just and that people therefore get what they deserve and deserve what they get.

MODULE

24

❖

The Nature and Nurture of Aggression

Although Woody Allen's tongue-in-cheek prediction that "by 1990 kidnapping will be the dominant mode of social interaction" went unfulfilled, the years since have hardly been serene. The horror of 9/11 may have been the most dramatic violence, but in terms of human lives, it was not the most catastrophic. About the same time, the human carnage from tribal warfare in the Congo was claiming an estimated 3 million lives, some hacked to death with machetes, many others dying of starvation and disease after fleeing in terror from their villages (Sengupta, 2003). Neighboring Rwandans, where some 750,000 people—including half the Tutsi population—were slaughtered in the genocidal summer of 1994, understood this human capacity for carnage (Staub, 1999b).

Such hatred and destruction is hardly peculiar to the post-2000 Middle Eastern and African worlds. Worldwide, more than $2 billion per day is spent on arms and armies—$2 billion that could feed, educate, and protect the environment of the world's impoverished millions. During the last century, some 250 wars killed 110 million people, enough to populate a "nation of the dead" with more than the combined population of France, Belgium, the Netherlands, Denmark, Finland, Norway, and Sweden (Figure 24-1). The tolls came not only from the world wars, but also from genocides, including the 1915 to 1923 genocide of Armenians by the Ottoman Empire, the 1971 Pakistani genocide of 3 million Bangladeshis, and the 1.5 million Cambodians murdered in a reign of terror starting in 1975 (Sternberg, 2003). As Hitler's genocide of millions of Jews, Stalin's genocide of millions of Russians, Mao's genocide of millions of Chinese, and the early Americans' genocide of millions of Native

269

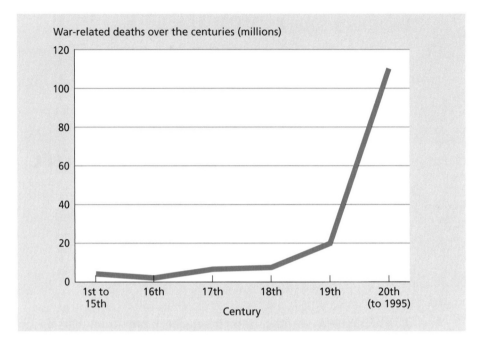

FIGURE 24-1
The bloodiest century. Twentieth-century humanity was the most educated, and homicidal, in history (data from Renner, 1999). Adding in genocides and human-made famines, there were approximately 182 million "deaths by mass unpleasant-ness" (White, 2000).

Americans makes plain, the human potential for extraordinary cruelty crosses the globe.

Activity 24.1

To a social psychologist, **aggression** is any *physical or verbal behavior intended to hurt someone.* This excludes accidents, dental treatments, and sidewalk collisions. It includes slaps, direct insults, even gossipy "digs."

Instrumental aggression aims to hurt only as a means to some other end. Most terrorism is instrumental aggression. "What nearly all suicide terrorist campaigns have in common is a specific secular and strategic goal," concludes Robert Pape (2003) after studying all suicide bombings from 1980 to 2001. That goal is "to compel liberal democracies to withdraw military forces from territory that the terrorists consider to be their homeland." In 2003, American and British leaders justified attacking Iraq not as a hostile effort to kill Iraqis, but as an instrumental act of liberation and of self-defense against presumed weapons of mass destruction. Hostile aggression is "hot"; instrumental aggression is "cool."

THEORIES OF AGGRESSION

Is Aggression an Instinct?

Philosophers have debated whether our human nature is fundamentally that of a benign, contented, "noble savage" or that of a brute. The first view, argued by the eighteenth-century French philosopher Jean-Jacques Rousseau (1712–1778), blames society, not human nature, for social evils. The second idea, associated with the English philosopher Thomas Hobbes (1588–1679), sees society's laws as necessary to restrain and control the human brute. In the twentieth century, the "brutish" view—that aggressive drive is inborn and thus inevitable—was argued by Sigmund Freud in Vienna and Konrad Lorenz in Germany.

Freud speculated that human aggression springs from a self-destructive impulse. It redirects toward others the energy of a primitive death urge (which, loosely speaking, he called the "death instinct"). Lorenz, an animal behavior expert, saw aggression as adaptive rather than self-destructive. Both agreed that aggressive energy is instinctual (unlearned and universal). If not discharged, it supposedly builds up until it explodes or until an appropriate stimulus "releases" it, like a mouse releasing a mousetrap. Although Lorenz (1976) also argued that we have innate mechanisms for inhibiting aggression (such as making ourselves defenseless), he feared the implications of arming our "fighting instinct" without arming our inhibitions. The imbalanced focus on releasing aggressive tendencies helps explain why more people were killed in twentieth-century wars than in all prior wars.

The idea that aggression is an instinct collapsed as the list of supposed human instincts grew to include nearly every conceivable human behavior, and scientists became aware how much behavior varies from person to person and culture to culture. Yet, biology clearly does influence behavior just as nurture works upon nature. Our experiences interact with the nervous system engineered by our genes.

Neural Influences

Because aggression is a complex behavior, no one spot in the brain controls it. But researchers have found neural systems in both animals and humans that facilitate aggression. When the scientists activate these areas in the brain, hostility increases; when they deactivate them, hostility decreases. Docile animals can thus be provoked into rage and raging animals into submission.

In one experiment, researchers placed an electrode in an aggression-inhibiting area of a domineering monkey's brain. A smaller monkey, given a button that activated the electrode, learned to push it every time the tyrant monkey became intimidating. Brain activation works with humans, too. After receiving painless electrical stimulation in her amygdala (a part of the brain core), one woman became enraged and smashed her guitar against the wall, barely missing her psychiatrist's head (Moyer, 1976, 1983).

So, are violent people's brains in some way abnormal? To find out, Adrian Raine and his colleagues (1998, 2000) used brain scans to measure brain activity in murderers and to measure the amount of gray matter in men with antisocial conduct disorder. They found that the prefrontal cortex, which acts like an emergency brake on deeper brain areas involved in aggressive behavior, was 14 percent less active than normal in nonabused murderers and 15 percent smaller in the antisocial men. As other studies of murderers and death-row inmates confirm, abnormal brains can contribute to abnormally aggressive behavior (Davidson & others, 2000; Lewis, 1998; Pincus, 2001). Did the brain abnormality by itself predispose violence? Possibly not, but for some violent people it likely is a factor (Davidson & others, 2000).

Genetic Influences

Heredity influences the neural system's sensitivity to aggressive cues. It has long been known that animals can be bred for aggressiveness. Sometimes this is done for practical purposes (the breeding of fighting cocks). Sometimes, breeding is done for research. Finnish psychologist Kirsti Lagerspetz (1979) took normal albino mice and bred the most aggressive ones together and the least aggressive ones together. After repeating the procedure for 26 generations, she had one set of fierce mice and one set of placid mice.

Aggressiveness varies among primates and humans (Asher, 1987; Olweus, 1979). Our temperaments—how intense and reactive we are—are partly brought with us into the world, influenced by our sympathetic nervous system's reactivity (Kagan, 1989). A person's temperament, observed in infancy, usually endures (Larsen & Diener, 1987; Wilson & Matheny, 1986). A child who is nonaggressive at age 8 will very likely still be a nonaggressive person at age 48 (Huesmann & others, 2003).

Blood Chemistry

Blood chemistry also influences neural sensitivity to aggressive stimulation. Both laboratory experiments and police data indicate that when people are provoked, alcohol unleashes aggression (Bushman, 1993; Taylor & Chermack, 1993; Testa, 2002). Violent people are more likely (1) to drink, and (2) to become aggressive when intoxicated (White & others, 1993). Consider:

- In experiments, intoxicated people administer stronger shocks and feel angrier when thinking back on relationship conflicts (MacDonald & others, 2000).

- In 65 percent of homicides and 55 percent of in-home fights and assaults, the assailant and/or the victim had been drinking (American Psychological Association, 1993).
- If spouse-battering alcoholics cease their problem drinking after treatment, their violent behavior typically ceases (Murphy & O'Farrell, 1996).

Alcohol enhances aggressiveness by reducing people's self-awareness and by reducing their ability to consider consequences (Hull & Bond, 1986; Ito & others, 1996; Steele & Southwick, 1985). Alcohol deindividuates, and it disinhibits.

Aggressiveness also correlates with the male sex hormone, testosterone. Hormonal influences appear much stronger in lower animals than in humans. But drugs that diminish testosterone levels in violent human males will subdue their aggressive tendencies.

After people reach age 25, their testosterone levels and rates of violent crime decrease together. Testosterone levels tend to be higher among prisoners convicted of planned and unprovoked violent crimes than of nonviolent crimes (Dabbs, 1992; Dabbs & others, 1995, 1997, 2001). And among the normal range of teen boys and adult men, those with high testosterone levels are more prone to delinquency, hard drug use, and aggressive responses to provocation (Archer, 1991; Dabbs & Morris, 1990; Olweus & others, 1988). Testosterone, says James Dabbs (2000), "is a small molecule with large effects." Injecting a man with testosterone won't automatically make him aggressive, yet men with low testosterone are somewhat less likely to react aggressively when provoked (Geen, 1998). Testosterone is roughly like battery power. Only if the battery levels are very low will things noticeably slow down.

*P*SYCHOLOGICAL INFLUENCES ON AGGRESSION

There exist important neural, genetic, and biochemical influences on aggression. Biological influences predispose some people more than others to react aggressively to conflict and provocation. But there is more to the story.

Frustration and Aggression

It is a warm evening. Tired and thirsty after two hours of studying, you borrow some change from a friend and head for the nearest soft-drink machine. As the machine devours the change, you can almost taste the cold, refreshing cola. But when you push the button, nothing happens. You push it again. Then you flip the coin return button. Still nothing.

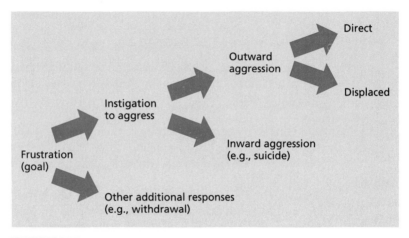

FIGURE 24-2
The classic frustration-aggression theory. Frustration creates a motive
to aggress. Fear of punishment or disapproval for aggressing against
the source of frustration may cause the aggressive drive to be displaced
against some other target or even redirected against oneself.
Source: Based on Dollard & others, 1939; and Miller, 1941.

Again, you hit the buttons. You slam them. And finally you shake and
whack the machine. You stomp back to your studies, empty-handed and
shortchanged. Should your roommate beware? Are you now more likely
to say or do something hurtful?

One of the first psychological theories of aggression, the popular
frustration-aggression theory, answered yes. "Frustration always leads to
some form of aggression," said John Dollard and his colleagues (1939, p. 1).
Frustration is anything (such as the malfunctioning vending machine)
that blocks our attaining a goal. Frustration grows when our motivation
to achieve a goal is very strong, when we expected gratification, and
when the blocking is complete. When Rupert Brown and his colleagues
(2001) surveyed British ferry passengers heading to France, they found
much higher aggressive attitudes on a day when French fishing boats
blockaded the port, preventing their travel. Blocked from obtaining their
goal, the passengers became more likely (in responding to various
vignettes) to agree with, for example, an insult toward a French person
who had spilled coffee.

As Figure 24-2 suggests, the aggressive energy need not explode
directly against its source. We learn to inhibit direct retaliation, especially
when others might disapprove or punish; instead, we *displace* our hostilities to safer targets. **Displacement** occurs in the old anecdote about a
man who, humiliated by his boss, berates his wife, who yells at their
son, who kicks the dog, which bites the mail carrier. In experiments and

in real life, however, displaced aggression is most likely when the target shares some similarity to the instigator and does some minor irritating act that unleashes the displaced aggression (Marcus-Newhall & others, 2000; Miller & others, 2003; Pedersen & others, 2000). When a person is harboring anger from a prior provocation, even a trivial offense—one that would normally produce no response—may elicit an explosive overreaction.

Various commentators have observed that the understandably intense American anger over 9/11 contributed to the eagerness to attack Iraq. Americans were looking for an outlet for their rage and found one in an evil tyrant, Saddam Hussein, who was once their ally. "The 'real reason' for this war," noted Thomas Friedman (2003b), "was that after 9/11 America needed to hit someone in the Arab-Muslim world. . . . We hit Saddam for one simple reason: because we could, and because he deserved it, and because he was right in the heart of that world." One of the war's advocates, Vice President Richard Cheney (2003), seemed to concur. When asked why most others in the world disagreed with America's launching war, he replied, "They didn't experience 9/11."

Laboratory tests of the frustration-aggression theory produced mixed results: Sometimes frustration increased aggressiveness, sometimes not. For example, if the frustration was understandable—if, as in one experiment, a confederate disrupted a group's problem solving because his hearing aid malfunctioned (rather than just because he paid no attention)—then frustration led to irritation, not aggression (Burnstein & Worchel, 1962).

Leonard Berkowitz (1978, 1989) realized that the original theory overstated the frustration-aggression connection, so he revised it. Berkowitz theorized that frustration produces *anger*, an emotional readiness to aggress. Anger arises when someone who frustrates us could have chosen to act otherwise (Averill, 1983; Weiner, 1981). A frustrated person is especially likely to lash out when aggressive cues pull the cork, releasing bottled-up anger. Sometimes the cork will blow without such cues. But, as we will see, cues associated with aggression amplify aggression (Carlson & others, 1990).

Berkowitz (1968, 1981, 1995) and others have found that the sight of a weapon is such a cue, especially when perceived as an instrument of violence rather than recreation. In one experiment, children who had just played with toy guns became more willing to knock down another child's blocks. In another, angered University of Wisconsin men gave more electric shocks to their tormenter when a rifle and a revolver (supposedly left over from a previous experiment) were nearby than when badminton rackets had been left behind (Berkowitz & LePage, 1967). Guns prime hostile thoughts and punitive judgments (Anderson & others, 1998; Dienstbier & others, 1998). What's within sight is within mind. Thus, Berkowitz was not surprised that half of all U.S. murders are committed with handguns and that handguns in homes are far more likely to kill household members than intruders. "Guns not only permit violence," he reported, "they can stimulate it as well. The finger pulls the trigger, but the trigger may also be pulling the finger."

Berkowitz is further unsurprised that countries that ban handguns have lower murder rates. Compared with the United States, Britain has one-fourth as many people and one-sixteenth as many murders. The United States has 10,000 handgun homicides a year; Australia has about a dozen, Britain two dozen, and Canada 100. When Washington, D.C., adopted a law restricting handgun possession, the numbers of gun-related murders and suicides each abruptly dropped about 25 percent. No changes occurred in other methods of murder and suicide, nor did adjacent areas outside the reach of this law experience any such declines (Loftin & others, 1991).

Guns not only serve as aggression cues, they also put psychological distance between aggressor and victim. As Milgram's obedience studies taught us, remoteness from the victim facilitates cruelty. A knife can kill someone, but a knife attack is more difficult than pulling a trigger from a distance.

The Learning of Aggression

Theories of aggression based on instinct and frustration assume that hostile urges erupt from inner emotions, which naturally "push" aggression from within. Social psychologists contend that learning also "pulls" aggression out of us.

The Rewards of Aggression

By experience and by observing others, we learn that aggression often pays. Experiments have transformed animals from docile creatures into ferocious fighters. Severe defeats, on the other hand, create submissiveness (Ginsburg & Allee, 1942; Kahn, 1951; Scott & Marston, 1953).

People, too, can learn the rewards of aggression. A child whose aggressive acts successfully intimidate other children will likely become increasingly aggressive (Patterson & others, 1967). Aggressive hockey players—the ones sent most often to the penalty box for rough play— score more goals than nonaggressive players (McCarthy & Kelly, 1978a, 1978b). Canadian teenage hockey players whose fathers applaud physically aggressive play show the most aggressive attitudes and style of play (Ennis & Zanna, 1991). In these cases, aggression is instrumental in achieving certain rewards.

Collective violence can also pay. After the 1967 Detroit riot, the Ford Motor Company accelerated its efforts to hire minority workers, prompting comedian Dick Gregory to joke, "Last summer the fire got too close to the Ford plant. Don't scorch the Mustangs, baby."

The same is true of terrorist acts, which enable powerless people to garner widespread attention. "Kill one, frighten ten thousand," asserts an ancient Chinese proverb. Deprived of what Margaret Thatcher called "the oxygen of publicity," terrorism would surely diminish, concluded Jeffrey Rubin (1986). It's like the 1970s incidents of naked spectators "streaking" onto football fields for a few seconds of television exposure. Once the networks decided to ignore the incidents, the phenomenon ended.

Observational Learning

Albert Bandura (1997) proposed a **social learning theory** of aggression. He believes that we learn aggression not only by experiencing its payoffs but also by observing others. As with most social behaviors, we acquire aggression by watching others act and noting the consequences.

Picture this scene from one of Bandura's experiments (Bandura & others, 1961). A Stanford nursery school child is put to work on an interesting art activity. An adult is in another part of the room, where there are Tinker Toys, a mallet, and a big, inflated "Bobo" doll. After a minute of working with the Tinker Toys, the adult gets up and for almost 10 minutes attacks the inflated doll. She pounds it with the mallet, kicks it, and throws it, while yelling, "Sock him in the nose. . . . Knock him down. . . . Kick him."

After observing this outburst, the child goes to a different room with many very attractive toys. But after two minutes the experimenter interrupts, saying these are her best toys and she must "save them for the other children." The frustrated child now goes into another room with various toys for aggressive and nonaggressive play, two of which are a Bobo doll and a mallet.

Children who were not exposed to the aggressive adult model seldom displayed any aggressive play or talk. Although frustrated, they nevertheless played calmly. Those who had observed the aggressive adult were many times more likely to pick up the mallet and lash out at the doll. Watching the adult's aggressive behavior lowered their inhibitions. Moreover, the children often reproduced the model's acts and said her words. Observing aggressive behavior had both lowered their inhibitions and taught them ways to aggress.

Bandura (1979) believes that everyday life exposes us to aggressive models in the family, the subculture, and the mass media. Physically aggressive children tend to have had physically punitive parents, who disciplined them by modeling aggression with screaming, slapping, and beating (Patterson & others, 1982). These parents often had parents who were physically punitive (Bandura & Walters, 1959; Straus & Gelles, 1980). Although most abused children do not become criminals or abusive parents, 30 percent do later abuse their own children—four times the general population rate (Kaufman & Zigler, 1987; Widom, 1989). Violence often begets violence.

The social environment outside the home also provides models. In communities where "macho" images are admired, aggression is readily transmitted to new generations (Cartwright, 1975; Short, 1969). The violent subculture of teenage gangs, for instance, provides its junior members with aggressive models.

The broader the culture also matters. Show social psychologists a man from a nondemocratic culture that is economically underdeveloped, that has great economic inequality, and that prepares men to be warriors and has engaged in war, and they will show you someone who is likely to be predisposed to support and engage in aggressive behavior (Bond, 2004).

Richard Nisbett (1990, 1993) and Dov Cohen (1996, 1998) have explored the subculture effect. Within the United States, they report, the sober, cooperative White folk who settled New England and the Middle Atlantic region produced a different culture than the swashbuckling, honor-preserving White folk (many of them my Scots-Irish ancestral cousins) who settled much of the South. The former were farmer-artisans; the latter, more aggressive hunters and herders. To the present, American cities and areas populated by southerners have much higher White homicide rates than those populated by northerners.

So, people learn aggressive responses both by experience and by observing aggressive models. But when will aggressive responses actually occur? Bandura (1979) contended that aggressive acts are motivated by a variety of aversive experiences—frustration, pain, insults. Such experiences arouse us emotionally. But whether we act aggressively depends on the consequences we anticipate. Aggression is most likely when we are aroused and it seems safe *and* rewarding to aggress.

Environmental Influences

Social learning theory offers a perspective from which we can examine specific influences on aggression. Under what conditions do we aggress? What environmental influences pull our trigger?

Painful Incidents

Researcher Nathan Azrin wanted to know if switching off foot shocks would reinforce two rats' positive interactions with each other. Azrin planned to turn on the shock and then, once the rats approached each other, cut off the pain. To his great surprise, the experiment proved impossible. As soon as the rats felt pain, they attacked each other, before the experimenter could switch off the shock. The greater the shock (and pain), the more violent the attack.

Is this true of rats alone? The researchers found that with a wide variety of species, the cruelty the animals imposed on each other matched zap for zap the cruelty imposed on them. As Azrin (1967) explained, the pain-attack response occurred in many different strains of rats. Then we found that shock produced attack when pairs of the following species were caged together: some kinds of mice, hamsters, opossums, raccoons, marmosets, foxes, nutria, cats, snapping turtles, squirrel monkeys, ferrets, red squirrels, bantam roosters, alligators, crayfish, amphiuma (an amphibian), and several species of snakes including the boa constrictor, rattlesnake, brown rat-snake, cottonmouth, copperhead, and black snake. The shock-attack reaction was clearly present in many very different kinds of creatures. In all the species in which shock produced attack it was fast and consistent, in the same "push-button" manner as with the rats.

The animals were not choosy about their targets. They would attack animals of their own species and also those of a different species, or stuffed dolls, or even tennis balls.

The researchers also varied the source of pain. They found that not just shocks induced attack; intense heat and "psychological pain"—for example, suddenly not rewarding hungry pigeons that have been trained to expect a grain reward after pecking at a disk—brought the same reaction as shocks. This "psychological pain" is, of course, frustration.

Pain heightens aggressiveness in humans, also. Many of us can recall such a reaction after stubbing a toe or suffering a headache. Leonard Berkowitz and his associates demonstrated this by having University of Wisconsin students hold one hand in lukewarm water or painfully cold water. Those whose hands were submerged in the cold water reported feeling more irritable and more annoyed, and they were more willing to blast another person with unpleasant noise. In view of such results, Berkowitz (1983, 1989, 1998) proposed that aversive stimulation rather than frustration is the basic trigger of hostile aggression. Frustration is certainly one important type of unpleasantness. But any aversive event, whether a dashed expectation, a personal insult, or physical pain, can incite an emotional outburst. Even the torment of a depressed state increases the likelihood of hostile aggressive behavior.

Heat

An uncomfortable environment also heightens aggressive tendencies. Offensive odors, cigarette smoke, and air pollution have all been linked with aggressive behavior (Rotton & Frey, 1985). But the most-studied environmental irritant is heat. William Griffitt (1970; Griffitt & Veitch, 1971) found that compared with students who answered questionnaires in a room with a normal temperature, those who did so in an uncomfortably hot room (over 90°F) reported feeling more tired and aggressive and expressed more hostility toward a stranger. Follow-up experiments revealed that heat also triggers retaliative actions (Bell, 1980; Rule & others, 1987).

Does uncomfortable heat increase aggression in the real world as well as in the laboratory? Consider:

- In heat-stricken Phoenix, Arizona, drivers without air conditioning have been more likely to honk at a stalled car (Kenrick & MacFarlane, 1986).
- During the 1986 to 1988 major league baseball seasons, the number of batters hit by a pitch was two-thirds greater for games played above 90°F than for games played below 80°F (Reifman & others, 1991). Pitchers weren't wilder on hot days—they had no more walks and wild pitches. They just clobbered more batters.
- The riots occurring in 79 U.S. cities between 1967 and 1971 were more likely on hot than on cool days.
- Studies in six cities have found that when the weather is hot, violent crimes are more likely (Anderson & Anderson, 1984; Cohn, 1993; Cotton, 1981, 1986; Harries & Stadler, 1988; Rotton & Frey, 1985).
- Across the Northern Hemisphere, not only do hotter days have more violent crimes, so do hotter seasons of the year, hotter summers, hotter years, hotter cities, and hotter regions (Anderson & Anderson, 1998, 2000). If a 4°F (about 2°C) global warming occurs, Anderson and his colleagues project that the United States alone would annually see at least 50,000 more serious assaults.

Attacks
Being attacked or insulted by another is especially conducive to aggression. Several experiments, including one at Osaka University by Kennichi Ohbuchi and Toshihiro Kambara (1985), confirm that intentional attacks breed retaliatory attacks. In most of these experiments, one person competes with another in a reaction-time contest. After each test trial, the winner chooses how much shock to give the loser. Actually, each person is playing a programmed opponent, who steadily escalates the amount of shock. Do the real participants respond charitably? Hardly. Extracting "an eye for an eye" is the more likely response.

Crowding
Crowding—the subjective feeling of not having enough space—is stressful. Crammed in the back of a bus, trapped in slow-moving freeway traffic, or living three to a small room in a college dorm diminishes one's sense of control (Baron & others, 1976; McNeel, 1980). Might such experiences also heighten aggression?

The stress experienced by animals allowed to overpopulate a confined environment does heighten aggressiveness (Calhoun, 1962; Christian & others, 1960). But it is a rather large leap from rats in an enclosure or deer on an island to humans in a city. Nevertheless, it's true that dense urban areas do experience higher rates of crime and emotional distress (Fleming & others, 1987; Kirmeyer, 1978). Even when they don't suffer higher crime rates, residents of crowded cities may *feel* more fearful. Toronto's crime rate has been four times higher than Hong Kong's. Yet compared to Toronto people, people from safer Hong Kong—which is four times more densely populated—have reported feeling more fearful on their city's streets (Gifford & Peacock, 1979).

R EDUCING AGGRESSION

We have examined instinct, frustration-aggression, and social learning theories of aggression, and we have scrutinized influences on aggression. How, then, can we reduce aggression? Do theory and research suggest ways to control aggression?

Catharsis?

"Youngsters should be taught to vent their anger." So advised Ann Landers (1969). If a person "bottles up his rage, we have to find an outlet. We have to give him an opportunity of letting off steam." So asserted the prominent psychiatrist Fritz Perls (1973). "Some expression of prejudice . . . lets off steam . . . it can siphon off conflict through words, rather than actions." So argued Andrew Sullivan (1999) in a *New York Times Magazine* article on hate crimes. Such statements assume the "hydraulic model"—accumulated aggressive energy, like dammed-up water, needs a release.

The concept of catharsis is usually credited to Aristotle. Although Aristotle actually said nothing about aggression, he did argue that we can purge emotions by experiencing them and that viewing the classic tragedies therefore enabled a **catharsis** ("purgation") of pity and fear. To have an emotion excited, he believed, is to have that emotion released (Butcher, 1951). The catharsis hypothesis has been extended to include the emotional release supposedly obtained not only by observing drama but also through recalling and reliving past events, through expressing emotions, and through various actions.

The near consensus among social psychologists is that contrary to what Freud, Lorenz, and their followers supposed, catharsis also fails to occur with violence (Geen & Quanty, 1977). For example, Robert Arms and his associates report that Canadian and American spectators of football, wrestling, and hockey games exhibit *more* hostility after viewing the event than before (Arms & others, 1979; Goldstein & Arms, 1971; Russell, 1983). Not even war seems to purge aggressive feelings. After a war, a nation's murder rate tends to jump (Archer & Gartner, 1976).

In laboratory tests of catharsis, Brad Bushman (2002) invited angered participants to hit a punching bag while either ruminating about the person who angered them or thinking about becoming physically fit. A third group did not hit the punching bag. Then, when given a chance to administer loud blasts of noise to the person who angered them, people in the punching bag plus rumination condition felt angrier and were most aggressive. Doing nothing at all more effectively reduced aggression than "blowing off steam."

In some real-life experiments, too, aggressing has led to heightened aggression. Ebbe Ebbesen and his co-researchers (1975) interviewed 100 engineers and technicians shortly after they were angered by layoff notices. Some were asked questions that gave them an opportunity to express hostility against their employer or supervisors—for example, "What instances can you think of where the company has not been fair with you?" Afterward, they answered a questionnaire assessing attitudes toward the company and the supervisors. Did the previous opportunity to "vent" or "drain off" their hostility reduce it? To the contrary, their hostility increased. Expressing hostility bred more hostility.

Sound familiar? Recall from Module 9 that cruel acts beget cruel attitudes. Furthermore, as we noted in analyzing Stanley Milgram's obedience experiments, little aggressive acts can breed their own justification. People derogate their victims, rationalizing further aggression. Even if retaliation sometimes (in the short run) reduces tension, in the long run it reduces inhibitions. Even when provoked people hit a punching bag *believing* it will be cathartic, the effect is the opposite—leading them to exhibit *more* cruelty, report Bushman and his colleagues (1999, 2000, 2001). "It's like the old joke," reflected Bushman (1999). "How do you get to Carnegie Hall? Practice, practice, practice. How do you become a very angry person? The answer is the same. Practice, practice, practice."

Should we therefore bottle up anger and aggressive urges? Silent sulking is hardly more effective, because it allows us to continue reciting our grievances as we conduct conversations in our head. Fortunately, there are nonaggressive ways to express our feelings and to inform others how their behavior affects us. Across cultures, those who reframe accusatory "you" messages as "I" messages—"I'm angry," or, "When you leave dirty dishes I get irritated"—communicate their feelings in a way that better enables the other person to make a positive response (Kubany & others, 1995). We can be assertive without being aggressive.

A Social Learning Approach

If aggressive behavior is learned, then there is hope for its control. Let us briefly review factors that influence aggression and speculate how to counteract them.

Aversive experiences such as frustrated expectations and personal attacks predispose hostile aggression. So it is wise to refrain from planting false, unreachable expectations in people's minds. Anticipated rewards and costs influence instrumental aggression. This suggests that we should reward cooperative, nonaggressive behavior. In experiments, children become less aggressive when caregivers ignore their aggressive behavior and reinforce their nonaggressive behavior (Hamblin & others, 1969).

Moreover, there are limits to punishment's effectiveness. Most mortal aggression is impulsive, hot aggression—the result of an argument, an insult, or an attack. Thus, we must *prevent* aggression before it happens. We must teach nonaggressive conflict-resolution strategies. If mortal aggression were cool and instrumental we could hope that waiting till it happens and severely punishing the criminal afterward would deter such acts. In that world, states that impose the death penalty might have a lower murder rate than states without the death penalty. But in our world of hot homicide, that is not so (Costanzo, 1998).

To foster a gentler world, we could model and reward sensitivity and cooperation from an early age, perhaps by training parents how to discipline without violence. Training programs encourage parents to reinforce desirable behaviors and to frame statements positively ("When you finish cleaning your room you can go play," rather than, "If you don't clean your room, you're grounded"). One "aggression-replacement program" has reduced re-arrest rates of juvenile offenders and gang members by teaching the youths and their parents communication skills, training them to control anger, and raising their level of moral reasoning (Goldstein & others, 1998).

If observing aggressive models lowers inhibitions and elicits imitation, then we might also reduce brutal, dehumanizing portrayals in films and on television—steps comparable to those already taken to reduce racist and sexist portrayals. We can also inoculate children against the effects of media violence. Wondering if the TV networks would ever "face the facts and change their programming," Eron and Huesmann (1984) taught 170 Oak Park, Illinois, children that television portrays the world unrealistically, that aggression is less common and less effective than TV suggests, and that aggressive behavior is undesirable. (Drawing upon attitude research, Eron and Huesmann encouraged children to draw these inferences themselves and to attribute their expressed criticisms of television to their own convictions.) When restudied two years later, these children were less influenced by TV violence than were untrained children. In a more recent study, Stanford University used 18 classroom lessons to persuade children to simply reduce their TV watching and video game playing (Robinson & others, 2001). They reduced their TV viewing by a third—and the children's aggressive behavior at school dropped 25 percent compared with children in a control school.

Aggressive stimuli also trigger aggression. This suggests reducing the availability of weapons such as handguns. Jamaica in 1974 implemented a sweeping anticrime program that included strict gun control and censorship of gun scenes from television and movies (Diener & Crandall, 1979). In the following year, robberies dropped 25 percent, nonfatal shootings 37 percent. In Sweden, the toy industry has discontinued the sale of war toys. The Swedish Information Service (1980) states the national attitude: "Playing at war means learning to settle disputes by violent means."

Activity
24.2

Suggestions such as these can help us minimize aggression. But given the complexity of aggression's causes and the difficulty of controlling them, who can feel the optimism expressed by Andrew Carnegie's forecast that, in the twentieth century, "To kill a man will be considered as disgusting as we in this day consider it disgusting to eat one." Since Carnegie uttered those words in 1900, some 200 million human beings have been killed. It is a sad irony that although today we understand human aggression better than ever before, humanity's inhumanity endures. Nevertheless, cultures can change. "The Vikings slaughtered and plundered," notes Natalie Angier. "Their descendants in Sweden haven't fought a war in nearly 200 years."

CONCEPTS TO REMEMBER

aggression   Physical or verbal behavior intended to hurt someone.

instrumental aggression   Aggression that is a means to some other end.

frustration   The blocking of goal-directed behavior.

displacement   The redirection of aggression to a target other than the source of the frustration. Generally, the new target is a safer or more socially acceptable target.

social learning theory   The theory that we learn social behavior by observing and imitating and by being rewarded and punished.

crowding   A subjective feeling that there is not enough space per person.

catharsis   Emotional release. The catharsis view of aggression is that aggressive drive is reduced when one "releases" aggressive energy, either by acting aggressively or by fantasizing aggression.

25

❖

Does the Media Influence Social Behavior?

The increase in violent crime reported between 1960 and the early 1990s, especially among juveniles, prompts us to wonder: Why the change? What social forces have caused the mushrooming violence?

Alcohol contributes to aggression, but alcohol use has not dramatically changed since 1960. Other biological factors (testosterone, genes, neurotransmitters) also influence aggression but cannot explain the large cultural changes. Might the surging violence instead be fueled by the growth in individualism and materialism? By the growing gap between the powerful rich and the powerless poor? By the decline in two-parent families and the increase in absent fathers? By the media's increasing modeling of violence and unrestrained sexuality? The last question arises because increased rates of violence and sexual coercion have coincided with increases in media mayhem and sexual suggestion. Is the historical correlation a coincidence? To find out, researchers have explored the social consequences of pornography (which *Webster's* defines as *erotic depictions intended to excite sexual arousal*) and the effects of modeling violence in movies and on television.

PORNOGRAPHY AND SEXUAL VIOLENCE

Repeated exposure to fictional eroticism has several effects. It can decrease one's attraction to one's less exciting real-life partner (Kenrick & others, 1989). It can also increase one's acceptance of extramarital sex and of women's sexual submission to men (Zillmann, 1989). Rock video images of macho men and sexually acquiescent women similarly color viewers' perceptions of men and women (Hansen, 1989; Hansen & Hansen, 1988, 1990; St. Lawrence & Joyner, 1991).

In the United States, pornography has become a bigger business than professional football, basketball, and baseball combined, thanks to some $10 billion a year spent on the industry's cable and satellite networks, on its theaters and pay-per-view movies, on in-room hotel movies, phone sex, and sex magazines, and on the estimated 400,000 for-profit websites (National Research Council, 2002; Rich, 2001; Schlosser, 2003). In one survey of university students, 57 percent of men and 35 percent of women reported having sought out sex-related websites, though only 6 percent of men and 1 percent of women did so "frequently" (Banfield & McCabe, 2001).

Social-psychological research on pornography has focused mostly on depictions of sexual violence. A typical sexually violent episode finds a man forcing himself upon a woman. She at first resists and tries to fight off her attacker. Gradually she becomes sexually aroused, and her resistance melts. By the end she is in ecstasy, pleading for more. We have all viewed or read nonpornographic versions of this sequence: She resists, he persists. Dashing man grabs and forcibly kisses protesting woman. Within moments, the arms that were pushing him away are clutching him tight, her resistance overwhelmed by her unleashed passion. In *Gone with the Wind*, Scarlett O'Hara is carried to bed protesting and kicking and wakes up singing.

Social psychologists report that viewing such fictional scenes of a man overpowering and arousing a woman can distort one's perceptions of how women actually respond to sexual coercion and increase men's aggression against women, at least in laboratory settings.

Distorted Perceptions of Sexual Reality

Does viewing sexual violence reinforce the "rape myth"—that some women would welcome sexual assault—that "no doesn't really mean no"? To find out, Neil Malamuth and James Check (1981) showed University of Manitoba men either two nonsexual movies or two movies depicting a man sexually overcoming a woman. A week later, when surveyed by a different experimenter, those who saw the films with mild sexual violence were more accepting of violence against women. Other studies confirm that exposure to pornography increases acceptance of the rape myth (Oddone-Paolucci & others, 2000). For example, while spending three evenings watching sexually violent movies, male viewers in an experiment by Charles Mullin and Daniel Linz (1995) also became progressively less bothered by the raping and slashing. Compared with others not exposed to the films, they also, three days later, expressed less sympathy for domestic violence victims, and they rated the victims' injuries as less severe. In fact, said researchers Edward Donnerstein, Daniel Linz, and Steven Penrod (1987), what better way for an evil character to get people to react calmly to the torture and mutilation of women than to show a gradually escalating series of such films?

Aggression Against Women

Evidence also suggests that pornography contributes to men's actual aggression toward women. Correlational studies raise that possibility. John Court (1985) noted that across the world, as pornography became more widely available during the 1960s and 1970s, the rate of reported rapes sharply increased—except in countries and areas where pornography was controlled. (The examples that counter this trend, such as Japan, where violent pornography is available but the rape rate is low, remind us that other factors are also important.) In Hawaii, the number of reported rapes rose ninefold between 1960 and 1974, dropped when restraints on pornography were temporarily imposed, and rose again when the restraints were lifted.

In another correlational study, Larry Baron and Murray Straus (1984) discovered that the sales of sexually explicit magazines (such as *Hustler* and *Playboy*) in the 50 states correlated with state rape rates, even after controlling for other factors, such as the percentage of young males in each state. Alaska ranked first in sex magazine sales and first in rape. Nevada was second on both measures.

When interviewed, Canadian and American sexual offenders commonly acknowledge pornography use. For example, William Marshall (1989) reported that Ontario rapists and child molesters used pornography much more than men who were not sexual offenders. An FBI study also reported considerable exposure to pornography among serial killers, as did the Los Angeles Police Department among most child sex abusers (Bennett, 1991; Ressler & others, 1988).

Although limited to the sorts of short-term behaviors that can be studied in the laboratory, controlled experiments reveal what correlational studies cannot—cause and effect. A consensus statement by 21 leading social scientists summed up the results: "Exposure to violent pornography increases punitive behavior toward women" (Koop, 1987). One of these social scientists, Edward Donnerstein (1980), had shown 120 University of Wisconsin men a neutral, an erotic, or an aggressive-erotic (rape) film. Then, the men, supposedly as part of another experiment, "taught" a male or female confederate some nonsense syllables by choosing how much shock to administer for incorrect answers. The men who had watched the rape film administered markedly stronger shocks, especially when angered and with a female victim.

If the ethics of conducting such experiments trouble you, rest assured that these researchers appreciate the controversial and powerful

experience they are giving participants. Only after giving their knowing consent do people participate. Moreover, after the experiment,
researchers effectively debunk any myths the films communicated
(Check & Malamuth, 1984).

Justification for this experimentation is not only scientific but also
humanitarian:

- In one careful national survey, 22 percent of women reported having been forced by a man to do something sexual (Laumann &
  others, 1994).

- In another, 18 percent of women reported an experience that
  met the definition of rape (Tjaden & Thoennes, 2000). Six times
  in seven the perpetrator was someone they knew.

- Surveys in other industrialized countries offer similar results.
  Three in four stranger rapes and nearly all acquaintance rapes
  went unreported to police. Thus, the known rape rate *greatly*
  underestimates the actual rape rate.

Media Awareness Education

As most Germans quietly tolerated the degrading anti-Semitic images
that fed the Holocaust, so most people today tolerate media images of
women that feed sexual harassment, abuse, and rape. So, should portrayals that demean or violate women be restrained?

Activity
25.1

In the contest of individual versus collective rights, people in most
Western nations side with individual rights. As an alternative to censorship, many psychologists favor "media awareness training." Recall that
pornography researchers have successfully resensitized and educated
participants to women's actual responses to sexual violence. Could educators similarly promote critical viewing skills? By sensitizing people to
the view of women that predominates in pornography and to issues of
sexual harassment and violence, it should be possible to counter the
myth that women enjoy being coerced. "Our utopian and perhaps naive
hope," say Edward Donnerstein, Daniel Linz, and Steven Penrod (1987,
p. 196), "is that in the end the truth revealed through good science will
prevail and the public will be convinced that these images not only
demean those portrayed but also those who view them."

Is such a hope naive? Consider: Without banning cigarettes, the number of U.S. smokers dropped from 42 percent in 1965 to 23 percent in the
early twenty-first century. Without censoring racism, once-common media
images of African Americans as childlike, superstitious buffoons have
nearly disappeared. As public consciousness changed, script writers, pro-
ducers, and media executives decided that exploitative images of minorities were not good. More recently they have decided that drugs are not
glamorous, as many films and songs from the 1960s and 1970s implied,

but dangerous—and high school seniors' marijuana use during the previous month has dropped from 37 percent in 1979 to 12 percent in 1992, before rebounding to more than 20 percent for most years since 1996, as the cultural anti-drug voice softened and drug use became reglamorized in some music and films (Johnston & others, 2005). Will we one day look back with embarrassment on the time when movies entertained people with scenes of exploitation, mutilation, and sexual coercion?

TELEVISION

We have seen that watching an aggressive model can unleash children's aggressive urges and teach them new ways to aggress. And we have seen that after viewing sexual violence, many angry men will act more violently toward women. Does television have any similar effects?

Consider these few facts about watching television. In 1945, the Gallup poll asked Americans, "Do you know what television is?" (Gallup, 1972, p. 551). Today, in much of the industrialized world, nearly all households (99.2 percent in Australia, for example) have a TV set, more than have telephones (Trewin, 2001). Most homes have more than one set, which helps explain why parents' reports of what their children watch correlate minimally with children's reports of what they watch (Donnerstein, 1998). With MTV in 140 countries and CNN spanning the globe, television is creating a global pop culture (Gundersen, 2001).

In the average home, the set is on seven hours a day, with individual household members averaging three to four hours which means that someone living to age 80 would have spent a decade watching television. Women watch more than men, non-Whites more than Whites, preschoolers and retired people more than those in school or working, and the less educated more than the highly educated (Comstock & Scharrer, 1999).

During all those hours, what social behaviors are modeled? From 1994 to 1997, bleary-eyed employees of the National Television Violence Study (1997) analyzed some 10,000 programs from the major networks and cable channels. Their findings? Six in 10 programs contained violence ("physically compelling action that threatens to hurt or kill, or actual hurting or killing").

What does it add up to? All told, television beams its electromagnetic waves into children's eyeballs for more growing-up hours than they spend in school. More hours, in fact, than they spend in any other waking activity. By the end of elementary school, the average child views some 8,000 TV murders and 100,000 other violent acts (Huston & others, 1992). Reflecting on his 22 years of cruelty counting, media researcher George Gerbner (1994) lamented: "Humankind has had more bloodthirsty eras but none as filled with *images* of violence as the present. We are awash in a tide of violent representations the world has never seen . . . drenching every home with graphic scenes of expertly choreographed brutality."

Does prime-time crime stimulate the behavior it depicts? Or, as viewers vicariously participate in aggressive acts, do the shows drain off aggressive energy? The latter idea, a variation on the catharsis hypothesis, maintains that watching violent drama enables people to release their pent-up hostilities. Defenders of the media cite this theory frequently and remind us that violence predates television. In an imaginary debate with one of television's critics, the medium's defender might argue, "Television played no role in the genocides of Jews and Native Americans. Television just reflects and caters to our tastes." "Agreed," responds the critic, "but it's also true that during America's TV age, reported violent crime increased several times faster than the population rate. Surely you don't mean the popular arts are mere passive reflections, without any power to influence public consciousness, or that advertisers' belief in the medium's power is an illusion." The defender replies: "The violence epidemic results from many factors. TV may even reduce aggression by keeping people off the streets and by offering them a harmless opportunity to vent their aggression."

Television's Effects on Behavior

Do viewers imitate violent models? Examples abound of people reenacting television crimes. In one survey of 208 prison convicts, 9 of 10 admitted that they learned new criminal tricks by watching crime programs. Four out of 10 said they had attempted specific crimes seen on television (*TV Guide*, 1977).

Correlating TV Viewing and Behavior

Crime stories are not scientific evidence. Researchers therefore use correlational and experimental studies to examine the effects of viewing violence. One technique, commonly used with schoolchildren, asks whether their TV watching predicts their aggressiveness. To some extent it does. The more violent the content of the child's TV viewing, the more aggressive the child (Eron, 1987; Turner & others, 1986). The relationship is modest but consistently found in North America, Europe, and Australia.

So can we conclude that a diet of violent TV fuels aggression? Perhaps you are already thinking that because this is a correlational study, the cause-effect relation could also work in the opposite direction. Maybe aggressive children prefer aggressive programs. Or maybe some underlying third factor, such as lower intelligence, predisposes some children both to prefer aggressive programs and to act aggressively.

Researchers have developed two ways to test these alternative explanations. They test the "hidden third factor" explanation by statistically pulling out the influence of some of these possible factors. For example, William Belson (1978; Muson, 1978) studied 1,565 London boys. Compared with those who watched little violence, those who watched a great deal (especially realistic rather than cartoon violence) admitted to 50 percent more violent acts during the preceding six months (for example, "I busted the telephone in a telephone box"). Belson also examined 22 likely third factors, such as family size. The heavy and light viewers still differed after equating them with respect to potential third factors. So Belson surmised that the heavy viewers were indeed more violent *because* of their TV exposure.

Similarly, Leonard Eron and Rowell Huesmann (1980, 1985) found that violence viewing among 875 8-year-olds correlated with aggressiveness even after statistically pulling out several obvious possible third factors. Moreover, when they restudied these individuals as 19-year-olds, they discovered that viewing violence at age 8 modestly predicted aggressiveness at age 19, but that aggressiveness at age 8 did *not* predict viewing violence at age 19. Aggression followed viewing, not the reverse. Moreover, by age 30, the children who had watched the most violence had become adults who were more likely to have been convicted of a crime (Figure 25-1).

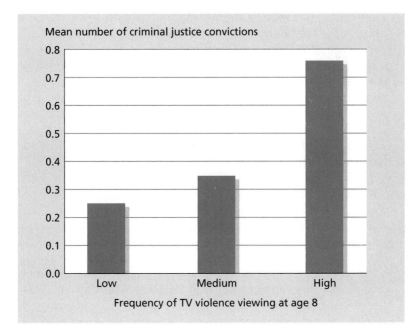

FIGURE 25-1
Children's television viewing and later criminal activity. Violence viewing at age 8 was a predictor of a serious criminal offense by age 30.
Source: Data from Eron and Huesmann, 1984.

Huesmann and his colleagues (1984, 2003) confirmed these findings in follow-up studies of Chicago-area youngsters. Boys who as 8-year-olds had been in the top 20 percent of violence watchers were, 15 years later, twice as likely as others to acknowledge pushing, grabbing, or shoving their wives, and their violence-viewing female counterparts were twice as likely, as young women, to have thrown something at their husbands.

Adolescent viewing also clues us to future adult behaviors, as Jeffrey Johnson and his co-workers (2002) found when they followed more than 700 lives through time. Among 14-year-olds who watched less than an hour of TV daily, 6 percent were involved in aggressive acts (such as assault, robbery, or threats of injury) at ages 16 to 22, as were five times as many—29 percent—of those who had watched more than three hours a day.

Another fact to ponder: Where television goes, increased violence follows. Even murder rates increase when and where television comes. In Canada and the United States, the homicide rate doubled between 1957 and 1974 as violent television spread. In census regions where television came later, the homicide rate jumped later, too. In White South Africa, where television was not introduced until 1975, a similar near doubling of the homicide rate did not begin until after 1975 (Centerwall, 1989). And in a closely studied rural Canadian town where television came late, playground aggression doubled soon after (Williams, 1986).

Notice that these studies illustrate how researchers are now using correlational findings to *suggest* cause and effect. Yet an infinite number of possible third factors could be creating a merely coincidental relation between viewing violence and aggression. Fortunately, the experimental method can control these extraneous factors. If we randomly assign some children to watch a violent film and others a nonviolent film, any later aggression difference between the two groups will be due to the only factor that distinguishes them: what they watched.

TV Viewing Experiments

Video
25.1

The trailblazing experiments by Albert Bandura and Richard Walters (1963) sometimes had young children view the adult pounding the inflated doll on film instead of observing it live—with much the same effect. Then Leonard Berkowitz and Russell Geen (1966) found that angered college students who viewed a violent film acted more aggressively than did similarly angered students who viewed nonaggressive films. These laboratory experiments, coupled with growing public concern, were sufficient to prompt the U.S. surgeon general to commission 50 new research studies during the early 1970s. By and large, these studies, and more than 100 later ones, confirmed that viewing violence amplifies aggression (Anderson & Bushman, 2002; Bushman & Anderson, 2001).

For example, research teams led by Ross Parke (1977) in the United States and Jacques Leyens (1975) in Belgium showed institutionalized American and Belgian delinquent boys a series of either aggressive or nonaggressive commercial films. Their consistent finding: "Exposure to movie violence . . . led to an increase in viewer aggression." Compared with the week preceding the film series, physical attacks increased sharply in cottages where boys were viewing violent films. Dolf Zillmann and James Weaver (1999) similarly exposed men and women, on four consecutive days, to violent or nonviolent feature films. When participating in a different project on the fifth day, those exposed to the violent films were more hostile to the research assistant.

The aggression provoked in these experiments is not assault and battery; it's more on the scale of a shove in the lunch line, a cruel comment, a threatening gesture. Nevertheless, the convergence of evidence is striking. "The irrefutable conclusion," said a 1993 American Psychological Association youth violence commission, is "that viewing violence increases violence." This is especially so among people with aggressive tendencies (Bushman, 1995). The violence viewing effect also is strongest when an attractive person commits justified, realistic violence that goes unpunished and that shows no pain or harm (Donnerstein, 1998).

All in all, conclude researchers Brad Bushman and Craig Anderson (2001), violence-viewing's effect on aggression surpasses the effect of passive smoking on lung cancer, calcium intake on bone mass, and homework on academic achievement. As with smoking and cancer, not everyone shows the effect—other factors matter as well. The cumulative long-term effects are what's worrisome, and corporate interests pooh-pooh the evidence. But the evidence is now "overwhelming," say Bushman and Anderson: "Exposure to media violence causes significant increases in aggression." The research base is large, the methods diverse, and the overall findings consistent, echo a National Institute of Mental Health task force of leading media violence researchers (Anderson & others, 2003). "Our in-depth review . . . reveals unequivocal evidence that exposure to media violence can increase the likelihood of aggressive and violent behavior in both immediate and long-term contexts."

Why Does TV Viewing Affect Behavior?
The conclusion drawn by the surgeon general and by these researchers is *not* that television and pornography are primary causes of social violence, any more than asbestos is a primary cause of cancer. Rather they say television is *a* cause. Even if it is just one ingredient in a complex recipe for violence, it is one that, like cyclamates, is potentially controllable.

Given the convergence of correlational and experimental evidence, researchers have explored *why* viewing violence has this effect. Consider three possibilities (Geen & Thomas, 1986). One is that it is not the violent content that causes social violence but the *arousal* it produces (Mueller & others, 1983; Zillmann, 1989a). As we noted earlier, arousal tends to spill over: One type of arousal energizes other behaviors.

Other research shows that viewing violence *disinhibits*. In Bandura's experiment, the adult's punching of the Bobo doll seemed to make these outbursts legitimate and to lower the children's inhibitions. Viewing violence primes the viewer for aggressive behavior by activating violence-related thoughts (Berkowitz, 1984; Bushman & Geen, 1990; Josephson, 1987). Listening to music with sexually violent lyrics seems to have a similar effect (Barongan & Hall, 1995; Johnson & others, 1995; Pritchard, 1998).

Media portrayals also evoke *imitation*. The children in Bandura's experiments reenacted the specific behaviors they had witnessed. The commercial television industry is hard-pressed to dispute that television leads viewers to imitate what they have seen: Its advertisers model consumption. Are media executives right, however, to argue that TV merely holds a mirror to a violent society? That art imitates life? And that the "reel" world therefore shows us the real world? Actually, on TV programs, acts of assault have outnumbered affectionate acts four to one.

But there is good news here, too. If the ways of relating and problem solving modeled on television do trigger imitation, especially among young viewers, then modeling **prosocial behavior** should be socially beneficial. Module 30 contains good news: Television's subtle influence can indeed teach children positive lessons in behavior.

In one study, researchers Lynette Friedrich and Aletha Stein (1973; Stein & Friedrich, 1972) showed preschool children *Mister Rogers' Neighborhood* episodes each day for four weeks as part of their nursery school program. (*Mister Rogers' Neighborhood* aims to enhance young children's social and emotional development.) During this viewing period, children from less-educated homes became more cooperative, helpful, and likely to state their feelings. In a follow-up study, kindergartners who viewed four *Mister Rogers'* programs were able to state its prosocial content, both on a test and in puppet play (Friedrich & Stein, 1975; also Coates & others, 1976).

*M*EDIA INFLUENCES: VIDEO GAMES

"The scientific debate over *whether* media violence has an effect is basically over," contend Douglas Gentile and Craig Anderson (2003). Researchers are now shifting their attention to video games, which have exploded in popularity and are exploding with increasing brutality. Educational research shows that "video games are excellent teaching tools," note Gentile and Anderson. "If health video games can successfully teach health behaviors, and flight simulator video games can teach people how to fly, then what should we expect violent murder-simulating games to teach?"

The Games Kids Play

In 2002, the video game industry celebrated its 30th birthday. Since the first video game in 1972 we have moved from electronic Ping-Pong to splatter games (Anderson, 2004; Gentile & Anderson, 2003).

Today's mass murder simulators are not obscure games. By the turn of the century, some 200 million games a year were being purchased, and the average 2- to 17-year-old was playing video games seven hours a week. In one survey of fourth-graders, 59 percent of girls and 73 percent of boys reported their favorite games as violent ones (Anderson, 2003, 2004). Games rated "M" (mature) are supposedly intended for sale only to those 17 and older but often get marketed to those younger. The Federal Trade Commission found that in four out of five attempts, underage children could easily purchase them (Pereira, 2003).

Effects of the Games Kids Play

Concerns about violent video games heightened after teen assassins in Kentucky, Arkansas, and Colorado enacted the horrific violence they had so often played on-screen. People wondered: When youth role-play attacking and dismembering people, do they learn anything that stays with them?

Most smokers don't die of heart disease. Most abused children don't become abusive. And most people who spend hundreds of hours rehearsing human slaughter live gentle lives. This enables video game defenders, like tobacco and TV interests, to say their products are harmless. "There is absolutely no evidence, none, that playing a violent game leads to aggressive behavior," contended Doug Lowenstein (2000), president of the Interactive Digital Software Association. Gentile and Anderson nevertheless offer some reasons why violent game playing *might* have a more toxic effect than watching violent television. With game playing, players

- identify with, and play the role of, a violent character.
- actively rehearse violence, not just passively watch it.
- engage in the whole sequence of enacting violence—selecting victims, acquiring weapons and ammunition, stalking the victim, aiming the weapon, pulling the trigger.
- are engaged with continual violence and threats of attack.
- repeat violent behaviors over and over.
- are rewarded for effective aggression.

For such reasons, military organizations often prepare soldiers to fire in combat (which many in World War II reportedly were hesitant to do) by engaging them with attack simulation games.

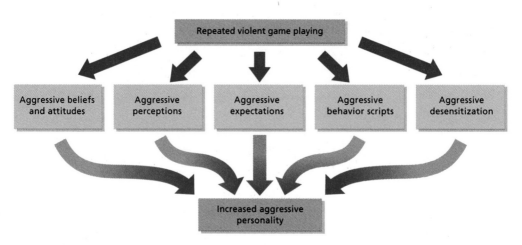

FIGURE 25-2
Violent video game influences on aggressive tendencies.   Source: Adapted from
Craig A. Anderson and Brad J. Bushman (2001).

But what does the available research actually find? Craig Anderson
(2003, 2004; Anderson & others, 2004) offers statistical digests of three
dozen available studies that reveal five consistent effects. Playing violent
video games, more than playing nonviolent games

- *increases arousal*—heart rate and blood pressure rise.
- *increases aggressive thinking*—for example, Brad Bushman and
  Anderson (2002) found that after playing games such as *Duke
  Nukem* and *Mortal Kombat*, university students became more likely
  to guess that a man whose car was just rear-ended would respond
  aggressively, by using abusive language, kicking out a window, or
  starting a fight. Anderson and his colleagues (2003) find that violent music lyrics also prime aggressive thinking, making students
  more likely to complete "h_t" as "hit" rather than "hat."
- *increases aggressive feelings*—frustration levels rise, as does
  expressed hostility.
- *increases aggressive behaviors*—after violent game play, children
  and youth play more aggressively with their peers, get into
  more arguments with their teachers, and participate in more
  fights. The effect occurs inside and outside the laboratory, across
  self-reports, teacher reports, and parent reports, and for reasons
  illustrated in Figure 25-2.
- *decreases prosocial behaviors*—after violent video game playing,
  people become slower to help a person whimpering in the
  hallway outside and slower to offer help to peers.

Moreover, the more violent the games played, the bigger the effects. Video games *have* become more violent, which helps explain why newer studies find the biggest effects. Although much remains to be learned, these studies indicate that, contrary to the catharsis hypothesis, practicing violence breeds rather than releases violence.

As a concerned scientist, Anderson (2003, 2004) therefore encourages parents to discover what their kids are ingesting and to ensure that their media diet, as least in their own home, is healthy. Parents may not be able to control what their child watches, plays, and eats in someone else's home, but they can oversee consumption in their own home and provide increased time for alternative activities. Networking with other parents can build a kid-friendly neighborhood. And schools can help by providing media awareness education.

CONCEPT TO REMEMBER

prosocial behavior   Positive, constructive, helpful social behavior; the opposite of anti-social behavior.

MODULE

26

❖

Who Likes Whom?

In the beginning there was attraction—the attraction between a particular man and a particular woman to which we each owe our existence.

What predisposes one person to like, or to love, another? So much has been written about liking and loving that almost every conceivable explanation—and its opposite—has already been proposed. For most people—and for you—what factors nurture liking and loving? Does absence make the heart grow fonder? Or is someone who is out of sight also out of mind? Is it likes that attract? Or opposites?

Consider a simple but powerful *reward theory of attraction:* Those who reward us, or whom we associate with rewards, we like. Friends reward each other. Without keeping score, they do favors for one another. Likewise, we develop a liking for those whom we associate with pleasant happenings and surroundings. Thus, surmised Elaine Hatfield and William Walster (1978), "romantic dinners, trips to the theatre, evenings at home together, and vacations never stop being important. . . . If your relationship is to survive, it's important that you *both* continue to associate your relationship with good things."

But as with most sweeping generalizations, the reward theory of attraction leaves many questions unanswered. What, precisely, *is* rewarding? Is it usually more rewarding to be with someone who differs from us or someone who is similar to us? To be lavishly flattered or constructively criticized? What factors have fostered *your* close relationships?

PROXIMITY

One powerful predictor of whether any two people are friends is sheer **proximity.** Proximity can also breed hostility; most assaults and murders involve people living close together. But far more often, proximity kindles liking. Though it may seem trivial to those pondering the mysterious origins of romantic love, sociologists have found that most people marry someone who lives in the same neighborhood, or works at the same company or job, or sits in the same class (Bossard, 1932; Burr, 1973; Clarke, 1952; Katz & Hill, 1958). Look around. If you marry, it will likely be to someone who has lived or worked or studied within walking distance.

Interaction

Actually, it is not geographic distance that is critical but "functional distance"—how often people's paths cross. We frequently become friends with those who use the same entrances, parking lots, and recreation areas. Randomly assigned college roommates, who of course can hardly avoid frequent interaction, are far more likely to become good friends than enemies (Newcomb, 1961). Such interaction enables people to explore their similarities, to sense one another's liking, and to perceive themselves as a social unit (Arkin & Burger, 1980).

At my college the men and women once lived on opposite sides of the campus. They understandably bemoaned the lack of cross-sex friendships. Now that they occupy different areas of the same dormitories and share common sidewalks, lounges, and laundry facilities, friendships between men and women are far more frequent. So if you're new in town and want to make friends, try to get an apartment near the mailboxes, a desk near the coffeepot, a parking spot near the main buildings. Such is the architecture of friendship.

Why does proximity breed liking? One factor is availability; obviously there are fewer opportunities to get to know someone who attends a different school or lives in another town. But there is more to it than that. Most people like their roommates, or those one door away, better than those two doors away. Those just a few doors away, or even a floor below, hardly live at an inconvenient distance. Moreover, those close by are potential enemies as well as friends. So why does proximity encourage affection more often than animosity?

Anticipation of Interaction

Already we have noted that proximity enables people to discover commonalities and exchange rewards. What is more, merely *anticipating* interaction boosts liking. John Darley and Ellen Berscheid (1967) discovered this when they gave University of Minnesota women ambiguous information about two other women, one of whom they expected to talk with intimately. Asked how much they liked each one, the women preferred the person they expected to meet. Expecting to date someone similarly boosts liking (Berscheid & others, 1976). Even voters on the losing side of an election will find their opinions of the winning candidate—whom they are now stuck with—rising (Gilbert & others, 1998).

The phenomenon is adaptive. Anticipatory liking—expecting that someone will be pleasant and compatible—increases the chance of forming a rewarding relationship (Klein & Kunda, 1992; Knight & Vallacher, 1981; Miller & Marks, 1982). And how good it is that we are biased to like those we often see. Our lives are filled with relationships with people whom we may not have chosen but with whom we need to have continuing interactions—roommates, siblings, grandparents, teachers, classmates, co-workers. Liking such people is surely conducive to better relationships with them, which in turn makes for happier, more productive living.

Mere Exposure

Proximity leads to liking not only because it enables interaction and anticipatory liking, but also for another reason: More than 200 experiments reveal that, contrary to an old proverb, familiarity does not foster contempt. Rather it breeds fondness (Bornstein, 1989, 1999). **Mere exposure** to all sorts of novel stimuli—nonsense syllables, Chinese characters, musical selections, faces—boosts people's ratings of them. Do the supposed Turkish words *nansoma*, *saricik*, and *afworbu* mean something better or something worse than the words *iktitaf*, *biwojni*, and *kadirga*? University of Michigan students tested by Robert Zajonc (1968, 1970) preferred whichever of these words they had seen most frequently. The more times they had seen a meaningless word or a Chinese ideograph, the more likely they were to say it meant something good (Figure 26-1). This, I have found, makes a nifty class demonstration. Periodically flash certain nonsense words on a screen. By the end of the semester, students will rate those "words" more positively than other nonsense words they have never before seen.

Or consider: What are your favorite letters of the alphabet? People of differing nationalities, languages, and ages prefer the letters appearing in their own names and those that frequently appear in their own languages (Hoorens & others, 1990, 1993; Kitayama & Karasawa, 1997; Nuttin, 1987). French students rate capital *W*, the least frequent letter in French, as their least favorite letter. Japanese students not only prefer letters from their names, but numbers corresponding to their birth dates. This "name letter effect" reflects more than mere exposure, however (see "Focus On: Liking Things Associated with Oneself" on pages 303–304).

The mere-exposure effect violates the commonsense prediction of boredom—*decreased* interest in repeated stimuli, for example, repeatedly

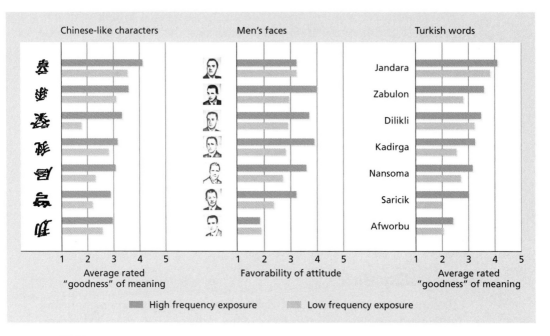

FIGURE 26-1
The mere-exposure effect. Students rated stimuli—a sample of which is shown here—more positively after being shown them repeatedly. **Source:** From Zajonc, 1968.

heard music or tasted foods (Kahneman & Snell, 1992). Unless the repetitions are incessant ("Even the best song becomes tiresome if heard too often," says a Korean proverb), liking usually increases. When completed in 1889, the Eiffel Tower in Paris was mocked as grotesque (Harrison, 1977). Today it is the beloved symbol of Paris.

The mere-exposure effect has "enormous adaptive significance," notes Zajonc (1998). It is a "hardwired" phenomenon that predisposes our attractions and attachments. It helped our ancestors categorize things and people as either familiar and safe, or unfamiliar and possibly dangerous. Of course, the phenomenon's darker side is our wariness of the unfamiliar—which may explain the primitive, automatic prejudice people often feel when confronting those who are different. Fearful or prejudicial feelings are not always expressions of stereotyped beliefs; sometimes the beliefs arise later as justifications for intuitive feelings.

We even like ourselves better when we are the way we're used to seeing ourselves. In a delightful experiment, Theodore Mita, Marshall Dermer, and Jeffrey Knight (1977) photographed women students at the University of Wisconsin–Milwaukee and later showed each one her actual picture along with a mirror image of it. Asked which picture they liked better, most preferred the mirror image—the image they were used to seeing. (No wonder our photographs never look quite right.) When close friends of the women were shown the same two pictures, they preferred the true picture—the image *they* were used to seeing.

Focus On: Liking Things Associated with Oneself

We humans love to feel good about ourselves, and generally we do. Not only are we prone to self-serving bias (Module 4), we exhibit what Brett Pelham, Matthew Mirenberg, and John Jones (2002) call *implicit egotism*: We like what we associate with ourselves. This includes the letters of our name, but also the people, places, and things that we unconsciously connect with ourselves (Jones & others, 2002; Koole & others, 2001).

Such preferences appear to subtly influence major life decisions, including our locations and careers, report Pelham and his colleagues. Philadelphia, being larger than Jacksonville, has 2.2 times as many men named Jack. But it has 10.4 times as many people named Philip. Likewise, Virginia Beach has a disproportionate number of people named Virginia.

Does this merely reflect the influence of one's place when naming one's baby? Are people in Georgia, for example, more likely to name their babies George or Georgia? That may be so, but it doesn't explain why states tend to have a relative excess of people whose *last* names are similar to the state names. California, for example, has a disproportionate number of people whose names begin with Cali (as in Califano). Likewise, major Canadian cities tend to have larger-than-expected numbers of people whose last names overlap with the city names. Toronto has a marked excess of people whose names begin with Tor.

Moreover, women named "Georgia" are disproportionately likely to *move* to Georgia, as do Virginias to Virginia. Such mobility could help explain why St. Louis has a 49 percent excess (relative to the national proportion) of men named Louis, and why people named Hill, Park, Beach, Lake, or Rock are disproportionately likely to live in cities with names such as Park City that include their names. "People are attracted to places that resemble their names," surmise Pelham, Mirenberg, and Jones.

Weirder yet—I am not making this up—people seem to prefer careers related to their names. Across the United States, Jerry, Dennis, and Walter are equally popular names (0.42 percent of people carry each of these names). Yet America's dentists are almost twice as likely to be named Dennis as Jerry or Walter. There also are 2.5 times as

(Continued)

many dentists named Denise as there are with the equally popular names, Beverly or Tammy. People named George or Geoffrey are overrepresented among geoscientists (geologists, geophysicists, and geochemists). And in the 2000 presidential campaign, people with last names beginning with *B* and *G* were more likely to contribute to the campaigns of Bush and Gore, respectively.

Reading about implicit egotism-based preferences gives me pause: Has this anything to do with why I enjoyed that trip to Fort Myers? Why I've written about moods, the media, and marriage? Why I collaborated with Professor Murdoch?

Advertisers and politicians exploit this phenomenon. When people have no strong feelings about a product or a candidate, repetition alone can increase sales or votes (McCullough & Ostrom, 1974; Winter, 1973). After endless repetition of a commercial, shoppers often have an unthinking, automatic, favorable response to the product. If candidates are relatively unknown, those with the most media exposure usually win (Patterson, 1980; Schaffner & others, 1981). Political strategists who understand the mere-exposure effect have replaced reasoned argument with brief ads that hammer home a candidate's name and sound-bite message.

The respected chief of the Washington State Supreme Court, Keith Callow, learned this lesson when in 1990 he lost to a nominal opponent, Charles Johnson. Johnson, an unknown attorney who handled minor criminal cases and divorces, filed for the seat on the principle that judges "need to be challenged." Neither man campaigned, and the media ignored the race. On election day, the two candidates' names appeared without any identification—just one name next to the other. The result: a 53 percent to 47 percent Johnson victory. "There are a lot more Johnsons out there than Callows," offered the ousted judge afterward to a stunned legal community. Indeed, the state's largest newspaper counted 27 Charlie Johnsons in its local phone book. There was Charles Johnson, the local judge. And, in a nearby city, there was television anchor Charles Johnson, whose broadcasts were seen on statewide cable TV. Forced to choose between two unknown names, many voters preferred the comfortable, familiar name of Charlie Johnson.

*P*HYSICAL ATTRACTIVENESS

What do (or did) you look for in a potential date? Sincerity? Good looks? Character? Humor? Conversational ability? Sophisticated, intelligent people are unconcerned with such superficial qualities as good looks;

they know "beauty is only skin deep" and "you can't judge a book by its cover." At least they know that's how they *ought* to feel. As Cicero counseled, "Resist appearance."

The belief that looks matter little may be another instance of how we deny real influences upon us, for there is now a file cabinet full of research studies showing that appearance *does* matter. The consistency and pervasiveness of this effect is disconcerting. Good looks are a great asset.

Attractiveness and Dating

Like it or not, a young woman's physical attractiveness is a moderately good predictor of how frequently she dates. A young man's attractiveness is slightly less a predictor of how frequently he dates (Berscheid & others, 1971; Krebs & Adinolfi, 1975; Reis & others, 1980, 1982; Walster & others, 1966). Moreover, women more than men say they would prefer a mate who's homely and warm over one who's attractive and cold (Fletcher & others, 2003). Does this imply, as many have surmised, that women are better at following Cicero's advice? Or does it merely reflect the fact that men more often do the inviting? If women were to indicate their preferences among various men, would looks be as important to them as to men? Philosopher Bertrand Russell (1930, p. 139) thought not: "On the whole women tend to love men for their character while men tend to love women for their appearance."

To see whether men are indeed more influenced by looks, researchers have provided male and female students with information about someone of the other sex, including a picture of the person. Or they have briefly introduced a man and a woman and later asked each about their interest in dating the other. In such experiments, men do put somewhat more value on opposite-sex physical attractiveness (Feingold, 1990, 1991; Sprecher & others, 1994). Perhaps sensing this, women worry more about their appearance and constitute nearly 90 percent of cosmetic surgery patients (ASAPS, 2003). But women, too, respond to a man's looks.

In one ambitious study, Elaine Hatfield and her co-workers (1966) matched 752 University of Minnesota first-year students for a "Welcome Week" computer dance. The researchers gave each student personality and aptitude tests but then matched the couples randomly. On the night of the dance, the couples danced and talked for two and one-half hours and then took a brief intermission to evaluate their dates. How well did the personality and aptitude tests predict attraction? Did people like someone better who was high in self-esteem, or low in anxiety, or different from themselves in outgoingness? The researchers examined a long list of possibilities. But so far as they could determine, only one thing mattered: how physically attractive the person was (as previously rated by the researchers). The more attractive a woman was, the more the man liked her and wanted to date her again. And the more attractive the man was, the more the woman liked him and wanted to date him again. Pretty pleases.

To say that attractiveness is important, other things being equal, is not to say that physical appearance always outranks other qualities. Some people more than others judge people by their looks (Livingston, 2001). Moreover, attractiveness probably most affects first impressions. But first impressions are important—and are becoming more so as societies become increasingly mobile and urbanized and as contacts with people become more fleeting (Berscheid, 1981).

Though interviewers may deny it, attractiveness and grooming affect first impressions in job interviews (Cash & Janda, 1984; Mack & Rainey, 1990; Marvelle & Green, 1980). This helps explain why attractive people have more prestigious jobs and make more money (Umberson & Hughes, 1987). Patricia Roszell and her colleagues (1990) looked at the attractiveness of a national sample of Canadians whom interviewers had rated on a 1 (homely) to 5 (strikingly attractive) scale. They found that for each additional scale unit of rated attractiveness, people earned, on average, an additional $1,988 annually. Irene Hanson Frieze and her associates (1991) did the same analysis with 737 MBA graduates after rating them on a similar 1 to 5 scale using student picture book photos. For each additional scale unit of rated attractiveness, men earned an added $2,600 and women earned an added $2,150.

The Matching Phenomenon

Not everyone can end up paired with someone stunningly attractive. So how do people pair off? Judging from research by Bernard Murstein (1986) and others, they pair off with people who are about as attractive as they are. Several studies have found a strong correspondence between the attractiveness of husbands and wives, of dating partners, and even of those within particular fraternities (Feingold, 1988). People tend to select as friends and especially to marry those who are a "good match" not only to their level of intelligence but also to their level of attractiveness.

Experiments confirm this **matching phenomenon.** When choosing whom to approach, knowing the other is free to say yes or no, people often approach someone whose attractiveness roughly matches (or not too greatly exceeds) their own (Berscheid & others, 1971; Huston, 1973; Stroebe & others, 1971). Good physical matches may also be conducive to good relationships, as Gregory White (1980) found in a study of UCLA dating couples. Those who were most similar in physical attractiveness were most likely, nine months later, to have fallen more deeply in love.

So who might we expect to be most closely matched for attractiveness—married couples or couples casually dating? White found, as have other researchers, that married couples are better matched.

Perhaps this research prompts you to think of happy couples who are not equally attractive. In such cases, the less attractive person often has compensating qualities. Each partner brings assets to the social marketplace, and the value of the respective assets creates an equitable match. Personal advertisements exhibit this exchange of assets (Cicerello & Sheehan, 1995; Koestner & Wheeler, 1988; Rajecki & others, 1991). Men typically offer wealth or status and seek youth and attractiveness; women more often do the reverse: "Attractive, bright woman, 26, slender, seeks warm, professional male." Men who advertise their income and education, and women who advertise their youth and looks, receive more responses to their ads (Baize & Schroeder, 1995). The asset-matching process helps explain why beautiful young women often marry older men of higher social status (Elder, 1969).

The Physical-Attractiveness Stereotype

Does the attractiveness effect spring entirely from sexual attractiveness? Clearly not, as Vicky Houston and Ray Bull (1994) discovered when they used a makeup artist to give an accomplice an apparently scarred, bruised, or birth-marked face. When riding on a Glasgow commuter rail line, people of *both* sexes avoided sitting next to the accomplice when she appeared facially disfigured. Moreover, much as adults are biased toward attractive adults, young children are biased toward attractive children (Dion, 1973; Dion & Berscheid, 1974; Langlois & others, 2000). To judge from how long they gaze at someone, even babies prefer attractive faces (Langlois & others, 1987), and at three months, infants have not yet been brainwashed by *Baywatch* or *The Bachelor*.

Adults show a similar bias when judging children. Margaret Clifford and Elaine Hatfield (Clifford & Walster, 1973) gave Missouri fifth-grade teachers identical information about a boy or girl, but with the photograph of an attractive or unattractive child attached. The teachers perceived the attractive child as more intelligent and successful in school. Think of yourself as a playground supervisor having to discipline an unruly child. Might you, like the women studied by Karen Dion (1972), show less warmth and tact to an unattractive child? The sad truth is that most of us assume what we might call a "Bart Simpson effect"—that homely children are less able and socially competent than their beautiful peers.

What is more, we assume that beautiful people possess certain desirable traits. Other things being equal, we guess beautiful people are happier, sexually warmer, and more outgoing, intelligent, and successful—

though not more honest or concerned for others (Eagly & others, 1991; Feingold, 1992b; Jackson & others, 1995). In collectivist Korea, honesty and concern for others are highly valued and *are* traits people associate with attractiveness (Wheeler & Kim, 1997).

Added together, the findings define a **physical-attractiveness stereotype:** What is beautiful is good. Children learn the stereotype quite early. Snow White and Cinderella are beautiful—and kind. The witch and the stepsisters are ugly—and wicked. "If you want to be loved by somebody who isn't already in your family, it doesn't hurt to be beautiful," surmised one 8-year-old girl. Or as one kindergarten girl put it when asked what it means to be pretty, "It's like to be a princess. Everybody loves you" (Dion, 1979). Think Princess Diana.

If physical attractiveness is this important, then permanently changing people's attractiveness should change the way others react to them. But is it ethical to alter someone's looks? Such manipulations are performed millions of times a year by plastic surgeons and orthodontists. With teeth and nose straightened, hair replaced and dyed, face lifted, fat liposuctioned, and breasts enlarged, lifted, or reduced, can a self-dissatisfied person now find happiness?

To examine the effect of such alterations, Michael Kalick (1977) had Harvard students rate their impressions of eight women based on profile photographs taken before or after cosmetic surgery. Not only did they judge the women as more physically attractive after the surgery but also as kinder, more sensitive, more sexually warm and responsive, more likable, and so on. Ellen Berscheid (1981) noted that although such cosmetic improvements can boost self-image, they can also be temporarily disturbing:

> Most of us—at least those of us who have *not* experienced swift alterations of our physical appearance—can continue to believe that our physical attractiveness level plays a minor role in how we are treated by others. It is harder, however, for those who have actually experienced swift changes in appearance to continue to deny and to minimize the influence of physical attractiveness in their own lives—and the fact of it may be disturbing, even when the changes are for the better.

Do beautiful people indeed have desirable traits? Or was Leo Tolstoy correct when he wrote that it's "a strange illusion . . . to suppose that beauty is goodness"? There is some truth to the stereotype. Attractive children and young adults are somewhat more relaxed, outgoing, and socially polished (Feingold, 1992b; Langlois & others, 2000). William Goldman and Philip Lewis (1977) demonstrated this by having 60 University of Georgia men call and talk for five minutes with each of three women students. Afterward the men and women rated the most attractive of their unseen telephone partners as somewhat more socially skillful and likable. Physically attractive individuals tend also to be more popular, more outgoing, and more gender typed (more traditionally masculine if male, more feminine if female) (Langlois & others, 1996).

These small average differences between attractive and unattractive people probably result from self-fulfilling prophecies. Attractive people are valued and favored, and so many develop more social self-confidence. (Recall from Module 8 an experiment in which men evoked a warm response from unseen women they *thought* were attractive.) By this analysis, what's crucial to your social skill is not how you look but how people treat you and how you feel about yourself—whether you accept yourself, like yourself, feel comfortable with yourself.

Despite all the advantages of being beautiful, attraction researchers Elaine Hatfield and Susan Sprecher (1986) report there is also an ugly truth about beauty. Exceptionally attractive people may suffer unwelcome sexual advances and resentment from those of their own sex. They may be unsure whether others are responding to their performance, inner qualities, or just to their looks, which in time will fade (Satterfield & Muehlenhard, 1997). Moreover, if they can coast on their looks, they may be less motivated to develop themselves in other ways. Ellen Berscheid wonders whether we might still be lighting our houses with candles if Charles Steinmetz, the homely and exceptionally short genius of electricity, had instead been subjected to the social enticements experienced by a Denzel Washington.

Who Is Attractive?

I have described attractiveness as if it were an objective quality like height, which some people have more of, some less. Strictly speaking, attractiveness is whatever the people of any given place and time find attractive. This, of course, varies. The beauty standards by which Miss Universe is judged hardly apply evenly to the whole planet. People in various places and times have pierced noses, lengthened necks, dyed hair, painted skin, gorged themselves to become voluptuous, starved to become thin, and bound themselves with leather garments to make their breasts seem small and used silicone and padded bras to make them seem big.

Despite such variations, there remains "strong agreement both within and across cultures about who is and who is not attractive," notes Judith Langlois and her colleagues (2000). People's agreement about others' attractiveness is especially high when men rate women, and less so for men rating men (Marcus & Miller, 2003).

To be really attractive is, ironically, to be perfectly average. Research teams led by Judith Langlois and Lorri Roggman (1990, 1994) at the University of Texas and Anthony Little and David Perrett (2002), working with Ian Penton-Voak at the University of St. Andrews, have digitized multiple faces and averaged them using a computer. Inevitably, people find the composite faces more appealing than almost all the actual faces.

Computer-averaged faces also tend to be perfectly symmetrical—another characteristic of strikingly attractive people (Gangestad & Thornhill, 1997; Mealey & others, 1999; Shackelford & Larsen, 1997). Research teams led by Gillian Rhodes (1999) and by Ian Penton-Voak (2001) have shown that if you could merge either half of your face with its mirror image—thus forming a perfectly symmetrical new face—you would boost your looks a tad. Averaging a number of such symmetrical faces produces an even better looking face. So, in some respects, perfectly average is quite attractive. It's even true for dogs, birds, and wristwatches, report Jamin Halberstadt and Rhodes (2000). For example, what people perceive as your average dog they also rate as attractive.

Evolution and Attraction

Activity
26.1

Psychologists working from the evolutionary perspective explain these gender differences in terms of reproductive strategy (Module 13). They assume that beauty signals biologically important information: health, youth, and fertility. Over time, men who preferred fertile-looking women out-reproduced those who were as happy to mate with prepubescent or postmenopausal females. They also assume evolution predisposes women to favor male traits that signify an ability to provide and protect resources. That, David Buss (1989) believes, explains why the males he studied in 37 cultures—from Australia to Zambia—did indeed prefer female characteristics that signify reproductive capacity. And it explains why physically attractive females tend to marry high-status males and why men compete with such determination to display status by achieving fame and fortune. In screening potential mates, report Norman Li and his fellow researchers (2002), men require a modicum of physical attractiveness, women require status and resources, and both welcome kindness and intelligence.

Video
26.1

So, in every culture the beauty business is a big and growing business. Asians, Britains, Germans, and Americans are all seeking cosmetic surgery in rapidly increasing numbers (Wall, 2002). In the United States, for example, cosmetic procedures such as liposuction, breast augmentation, and Botox injections rose 228 percent between 1997 and 2002 (ASAPS, 2003). Beverly Hills now has twice as many plastic surgeons as pediatricians (*People*, 2003). Modern, affluent people with cracked or discolored teeth fix them. More and more, so do people with wrinkles and flab.

We are, evolutionary psychologists suggest, driven by primal attractions. Like eating and breathing, attraction and mating are too important to leave to the whims of culture.

The Contrast Effect

Although our mating psychology has biological wisdom, attraction is not all hardwired. What's attractive to you also depends on your comparison standards.

Douglas Kenrick and Sara Gutierres (1980) had male confederates interrupt Montana State University men in their dormitory rooms and explain, "We have a friend coming to town this week and we want to fix him up with a date, but we can't decide whether to fix him up with her or not, so we decided to conduct a survey. . . . We want you to give us your vote on how attractive you think she is . . . on a scale of 1 to 7." Shown a picture of an average young woman, those who had just been watching *Charlie's Angels*, a television show featuring three beautiful women, rated her less attractive than those who hadn't.

Laboratory experiments confirm this "contrast effect." To men who have recently been gazing at centerfolds, average women or even their own wives tend to seem less attractive (Kenrick & others, 1989). Viewing pornographic films simulating passionate sex similarly decreases satisfaction with one's own partner (Zillmann, 1989b). Being sexually aroused may *temporarily* make a person of the other sex seem more attractive. But the lingering effect of exposure to perfect "10s," or of unrealistic sexual depictions, is to make one's own partner seem less appealing—more like a "6" than an "8."

It works the same way with our self-perceptions. After viewing a super-attractive person of the same gender, people feel *less* attractive than after viewing a homely person (Brown & others, 1992; Thornton & Maurice, 1997).

The Attractiveness of Those We Love

Let's conclude our discussion of attractiveness on an upbeat note. Not only do we perceive attractive people as likable, we also perceive likable people as attractive. Perhaps you can recall individuals who, as you grew to like them, became more attractive. Their physical imperfections were no longer so noticeable. Alan Gross and Christine Crofton (1977) had students view someone's photograph after reading a favorable or unfavorable description of the person's personality. Those portrayed as warm, helpful, and considerate also *looked* more attractive. Discovering someone's similarities to us also makes the person seem more attractive (Beaman & Klentz, 1983; Klentz & others, 1987).

Moreover, love sees loveliness: The more in love a woman is with a man, the more physically attractive she finds him (Price & others, 1974). And the more in love people are, the less attractive they find all others of the opposite sex (Johnson & Rusbult, 1989; Simpson & others, 1990). "The grass may be greener on the other side," note Rowland Miller and Jeffry Simpson (1990), "but happy gardeners are less likely to notice." To paraphrase Benjamin Franklin, when Jill's in love, she finds Jack more handsome than his friends.

SIMILARITY VERSUS COMPLEMENTARITY

From our discussion so far, one might surmise Leo Tolstoy was entirely correct: "Love depends . . . on frequent meetings, and on the style in which the hair is done up, and on the color and cut of the dress." As people get to know one another, however, other factors influence whether acquaintance develops into friendship.

Do Birds of a Feather Flock Together?

Activity
26.2

Of this much we may be sure: Birds that flock together are of a feather. Friends, engaged couples, and spouses are far more likely than people randomly paired to share common attitudes, beliefs, and values. Furthermore, the greater the similarity between husband and wife, the happier they are and the less likely they are to divorce (Byrne, 1971; Caspi & Herbener, 1990). Such correlational findings are intriguing. But cause and effect remain an enigma. Does similarity lead to liking? Or does liking lead to similarity?

Likeness Begets Liking
To discern cause and effect, we experiment. Imagine that at a campus party Laura gets involved in a long discussion of politics, religion, and personal likes and dislikes with Les and Larry. She and Les discover they agree on almost everything, she and Larry on few things. Afterward, she reflects: "Les is really intelligent . . . and so likable . . . hope we meet again." In experiments, Donn Byrne (1971) and his colleagues captured the essence of Laura's experience. Over and over again, they found that the more similar someone's attitudes are to your own, the more likable you will find the person. Likeness produces liking not only for college students but also for children and the elderly, for people of various occupations, and for those in various cultures.

The likeness-leads-to-liking effect has been tested in real-life situations by noting who comes to like whom. At the University of Michigan, Theodore Newcomb (1961) studied two groups of 17 unacquainted male transfer students. After 13 weeks of boardinghouse life, those whose agreement was initially highest were most likely to have formed close friendships. One group of friends was composed of five liberal arts students, each a political liberal with strong intellectual interests. Another was made up of three conservative veterans who were all enrolled in the engineering college.

William Griffitt and Russell Veitch (1974) compressed the getting-to-know-you process by confining 13 unacquainted men in a fallout shelter.

(The men were paid volunteers.) Knowing the men's opinions on various issues, the researchers could predict with better-than-chance accuracy those each man would most like and most dislike. As in the boarding-house, the men liked best those most like themselves. Similarity breeds content. Birds of a feather *do* flock together. Surely you have noticed this upon discovering a special someone who shares your ideas, values, and desires, a soul mate who likes the same music, the same activities, even the same foods you do.

Do Opposites Attract?

Are we not also attracted to people who in some ways *differ* from our-selves, in ways that complement our own characteristics? Researchers have explored this question by comparing not only friends' and spouses' attitudes and beliefs but also their ages, religions, races, smoking behav-iors, economic levels, educations, height, intelligence, and appearance. In all these ways and more, similarity still prevails (Buss, 1985; Kandel, 1978). Smart birds flock together. So do rich birds, Protestant birds, tall birds, pretty birds.

Still we resist: Are we not attracted to people whose needs and personalities complement our own? Would a sadist and a masochist find true love? Even the *Reader's Digest* has told us that "opposites attract. . . . Socializers pair with loners, novelty-lovers with those who dislike change, free spenders with scrimpers, risk-takers with the very cautious" (Jacoby, 1986). Sociologist Robert Winch (1958) reasoned that the needs of an outgoing and domineering person would natu-rally complement those of someone who is shy and submissive. The logic seems compelling, and most of us can think of couples who view their differences as complementary: "My husband and I are perfect for each other. I'm Aquarius—a decisive person. He's Libra—can't make decisions. But he's always happy to go along with arrangements I make."

Some **complementarity** may evolve as a relationship progresses (even a relationship between two identical twins). Yet people are slightly more prone to like and to marry those whose needs and per-sonalities are *similar* (Botwin & others, 1997; Buss, 1984; Fishbein & Thelen, 1981a, 1981b; Nias, 1979). Perhaps one day we will discover some ways (other than heterosexuality) in which differences commonly breed liking. Dominance/submissiveness may be one such way (Dryer & Horowitz, 1997). And we tend not to feel attracted to those who show our own worst traits (Schimel & others, 2000). But researcher David Buss (1985) doubts complementarity: "The tendency of opposites to marry, or mate . . . has never been reliably demonstrated, with the sin-gle exception of sex."

*L*IKING THOSE WHO LIKE US

With hindsight, the reward principle explains our conclusions so far:

- *Proximity* is rewarding. It costs less time and effort to receive friendship's benefits with someone who lives or works close by.
- We like *attractive* people because we perceive that they offer other desirable traits and because we benefit by associating with them.
- If others have *similar* opinions, we feel rewarded because we presume that they like us in return. Moreover, those who share our views help validate them. We especially like people if we have successfully converted them to our way of thinking (Lombardo & others, 1972; Riordan, 1980; Sigall, 1970).
- We like to be liked and love to be loved. Thus, liking is usually mutual. We like those who like us.

But does liking a person *cause* that person to return the appreciation? People's reports of how they fell in love suggest yes (Aron & others, 1989). Discovering that an appealing someone really likes you seems to awaken romantic feelings. Experiments confirm it: Those told that certain others like or admire them usually feel a reciprocal affection (Berscheid & Walster, 1978).

And consider this finding by Ellen Berscheid and her colleagues (1969): Students like another student who says eight positive things about them better than one who says seven positive things and one negative thing. We are sensitive to the slightest hint of criticism. Writer Larry L. King speaks for many in noting, "I have discovered over the years that good reviews strangely fail to make the author feel as good as bad reviews make him feel bad." Whether we are judging ourselves or others, negative information carries more weight because, being less usual, it grabs more attention (Yzerbyt & Leyens, 1991). People's votes are more influenced by their impressions of presidential candidates' weaknesses than by their impressions of strengths (Klein, 1991), a phenomenon that has not been lost on those who design negative campaigns.

That we like those we perceive as liking us was recognized long ago. Observers from the ancient philosopher Hecato ("If you wish to be loved, love") to Ralph Waldo Emerson ("The only way to have a friend is to be one") to Dale Carnegie ("Dole out praise lavishly") anticipated the findings. What they did not anticipate was the precise conditions under which the principle works.

Self-Esteem and Attraction

Elaine Hatfield (Walster, 1965) wondered if another's approval is especially rewarding after we have been deprived of approval, much as eating is most rewarding after fasting. To test this idea, she gave some Stanford University women either very favorable or very unfavorable analyses of their personalities, affirming some and wounding others. Then she asked them to evaluate several people, including an attractive male confederate who just before the experiment had struck up a warm conversation with each woman and had asked each for a date. (Not one turned him down.) Which women do you suppose most liked the man? It was those whose self-esteem had been temporarily shattered and who were presumably hungry for social approval. (After this experiment Hatfield spent almost an hour explaining the experiment and talking with each woman. She reports that in the end, none remained disturbed by the temporary ego blow or the broken date.)

Proximity, attractiveness, similarity, being liked—these are the factors known to influence our friendship formation. Sometimes friendship deepens into the passion and intimacy of love. What is love? And why does it sometimes flourish and sometimes fade? But to answer these questions, first we need to understand our deep need to belong.

OUR NEED TO BELONG

Aristotle called humans "the social animal." Indeed, we have an intense **need to belong**—to connect with others in enduring, close relationships.

Social psychologists Roy Baumeister and Mark Leary (1995) illustrate the power of social attractions bred by our need to belong.

- For our ancestors, mutual attachments enabled group survival. When hunting game or erecting shelter, 10 hands were better than 2.

- For a woman and a man, the bonds of love can lead to children, whose survival chances are boosted by the nurturing of two bonded parents who support each other.

- For children and their caregivers, social attachments enhance survival. Unexplainably separated from each other, parent and toddler may each panic, until reunited in a tight embrace. Reared under extreme neglect or in institutions without belonging to anybody, children become pathetic, anxious creatures.

- For people everywhere, actual and hoped-for close relationships preoccupy thinking and color emotions. Finding a supportive soul mate in whom we can confide, we feel accepted and prized. Falling in love, we feel irrepressible joy. Longing for acceptance and love, we spend billions on cosmetics, clothes, and diets.

- Exiled, imprisoned, or in solitary confinement, people ache for their own people and places. Rejected, we are at risk for depression (Nolan & others, 2003). Time goes slower and life seems more meaningless (Twenge & others, 2003).

- For the jilted, the widowed, and the sojourner in a strange place, the loss of social bonds triggers pain, loneliness, or withdrawal. Losing a soul-mate relationship, adults feel jealous, distraught, or bereaved, as well as more mindful of death and the fragility of life.

- Reminders of death in turn heighten our need to belong, to be with others and hold close those we love (Mikulincer & others, 2003; Wisman & Koole, 2003). Facing the terror of 9/11, millions of Americans called and connected with loved ones. Likewise, the shocking death of a classmate, co-worker, or family member brings people together, their differences no longer mattering.

We are, indeed, social animals. We need to belong. When we do belong—when we feel supported by close, intimate relationships—we tend to be healthier and happier.

Kipling Williams (2002) has explored what happens when our need to belong is thwarted by *ostracism* (acts of excluding or ignoring). Humans in all cultures, whether in schools, workplaces, or homes, use ostracism to regulate social behavior. So what is it like to be shunned—to be avoided, met with averted eyes, or given the silent treatment? People (women especially) respond to ostracism with depressed mood, anxiety, hurt feelings, efforts to restore relationship, and eventual withdrawal. The silent treatment is "emotional abuse" and "a terrible, terrible weapon to use" say those who have experienced it from a family member or co-worker. In experiments, people who are left out of a simple game of ball tossing feel deflated and stressed.

Sometimes deflation turns nasty. In several studies, Jean Twenge and her collaborators (2001, 2002; Baumeister & others, 2002) gave some people an experience of being socially included. Others experienced exclusion: They were either told (based on a personality test) that they "were likely to end up alone later in life" or that others whom they'd met didn't want them in their group. Those led to feel excluded became more likely to disparage or deliver a blast of noise to someone who had insulted them. If a small laboratory experience could produce such aggression, noted the researchers, one wonders what aggressive tendencies "might arise from a series of important rejections or chronic exclusion."

Williams and his colleagues (2000) were surprised to discover that even "cyber-ostracism" by faceless people whom one will never meet takes a toll. (Perhaps you have experienced this when feeling ignored in a chat room or when your e-mail is not answered.) The researchers had

1,486 participants from 62 countries play a Web-based game of throwing a flying disc with two others (actually computer-generated fellow players). Those ostracized by the other players experienced poorer moods and became more likely to conform to others' wrong judgments on a subsequent perceptual task. They also, in a follow-up experiment, exhibited heightened activity in a brain cortex area that also is activated in response to physical pain. Ostracism, it seems, is a real pain.

Williams and four of his colleagues (2000) even found ostracism stressful when each of them was ignored for an agreed-upon day by the unresponsive four others. Contrary to their expectations that this would be a laughter-filled role-playing game, the simulated ostracism disrupted work, interfered with pleasant social functioning, and "caused temporary concern, anxiety, paranoia, and general fragility of spirit." To thwart our deep need to belong is to unsettle our life.

CONCEPTS TO REMEMBER

proximity   Geographical nearness. Proximity (more precisely, "functional distance") powerfully predicts liking.

mere-exposure effect   The tendency for novel stimuli to be liked more or rated more positively after the rater has been repeatedly exposed to them.

matching phenomenon   The tendency for men and women to choose as partners those who are a "good match" in attractiveness and other traits.

physical-attractiveness stereotype   The presumption that physically attractive people possess other socially desirable traits as well: What is beautiful is good.

complementarity   The popularly supposed tendency, in a relationship between two people, for each to complete what is missing in the other.

need to belong   A motivation to bond with others in relationships that provide ongoing, positive interactions.

27

❖

The Ups and Downs of Love

W hat is this thing called "love"? Can passionate love endure? If not, what can replace it? Loving is more complex than liking and thus more difficult to measure, more perplexing to study. People yearn for it, live for it, die for it. Yet only in the last few years has loving become a serious topic in social psychology.

Most attraction researchers have studied what is most easily studied—responses during brief encounters between strangers. The influences on our initial liking of another—proximity, attractiveness, similarity, being liked, and other rewarding traits—also influence our long-term, close relationships. The impressions that dating couples quickly form of each other therefore provide a clue to their long-term future (Berg, 1984; Berg & McQuinn, 1986). Indeed, if North American romances flourished *randomly*, without regard to proximity and similarity, then most Catholics (being a minority) would marry Protestants, most Blacks would marry Whites, and college graduates would be as apt to marry high school dropouts as fellow graduates.

So first impressions are important. Nevertheless, long-term loving is not merely an intensification of initial liking. Social psychologists have therefore shifted their attention from the mild attraction experienced during first encounters to the study of enduring, close relationships.

*P*ASSIONATE LOVE

The first step in scientifically studying romantic love, as in studying any variable, is to decide how to define and measure it. We have ways to measure aggression, altruism, prejudice, and liking—but how do we measure love?

"How do I love thee? Let me count the ways" wrote Elizabeth Barrett Browning. Social scientists have counted various ways. Psychologist Robert Sternberg (1998) views love as a triangle, whose three sides (of varying lengths) are passion, intimacy, and commitment (Figure 27-1). Drawing from ancient philosophy and literature, sociologist John Alan Lee (1988) and psychologists Clyde Hendrick and Susan Hendrick (1993, 2003) identify three primary love styles: *eros* (self-disclosing passion), *ludus* (uncommitted game playing), and *storge* (friendship), which, like the primary colors, combine to form secondary love styles. Some love styles, notably eros and storge, predict high relationship satisfaction; others, such as ludus, predict low satisfaction.

Some elements are common to all loving relationships: mutual understanding, giving and receiving support, enjoying the loved one's company. Some elements are distinctive. If we experience passionate love, we express it physically, we expect the relationship to be exclusive, and we are intensely fascinated with our partner. You can see it in our eyes. Zick Rubin confirmed this. He administered a love scale to hundreds of University of Michigan dating couples. Later, from behind

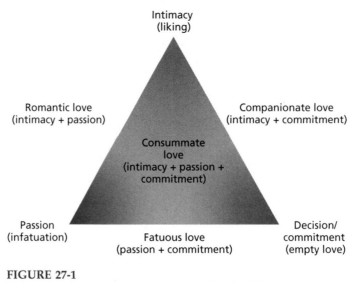

FIGURE 27-1
Robert Sternberg's (1988) conception of kinds of loving as combinations of three basic components of love.

a one-way mirror in a laboratory waiting room, he clocked eye contact among "weak-love" and "strong-love" couples. His result will not surprise you: The strong-love couples gave themselves away by gazing long into one another's eyes. When talking, Gian Gonzaga and others (2001) have observed, they also nod their head, smile naturally, and lean forward.

Activity
27.1

Passionate love is emotional, exciting, intense. Elaine Hatfield (1988) defined it as *"a state of intense longing for union with another"* (p. 193). If reciprocated, one feels fulfilled and joyous; if not, one feels empty or despairing. Like other forms of emotional excitement, passionate love involves a roller coaster of elation and gloom, tingling exhilaration and dejected misery.

A Theory of Passionate Love

To explain passionate love, Hatfield notes that a given state of arousal can be steered into any of several emotions, depending on how we attribute the arousal. An emotion involves both body and mind—both arousal and how we interpret and label the arousal. Imagine yourself with pounding heart and trembling hands: Are you experiencing fear, anxiety, joy? Physiologically, one emotion is quite similar to another. You may therefore experience the arousal as joy if you are in a euphoric situation, anger if your environment is hostile, and passionate love if the situation is romantic. In this view, passionate love is the psychological experience of being biologically aroused by someone we find attractive.

If indeed passion is a revved-up state that's labeled "love," then whatever revs one up should intensify feelings of love. In several experiments, college men aroused sexually by reading or viewing erotic materials had a heightened response to a woman—for example, by scoring much higher on a love scale when describing their girlfriend (Carducci & others, 1978; Dermer & Pyszczynski, 1978; Stephan & others, 1971). Proponents of the **two-factor theory of emotion,** developed by Stanley Schachter and Jerome Singer (1962), argue that when the revved-up men responded to a woman, they easily misattributed some of their arousal to her.

According to this theory, being aroused by *any* source should intensify passionate feelings, providing the mind is free to attribute some of the arousal to a romantic stimulus. In a dramatic demonstration of this phenomenon, Donald Dutton and Arthur Aron (1974) had an attractive young woman approach individual young men as they crossed a narrow, wobbly, 450-foot-long suspension walkway hanging 230 feet above British Columbia's rocky Capilano River. The woman asked each man to help her fill out a class questionnaire. When he had finished, she scribbled her name and phone number and invited him to call if he wanted to hear more about the project. Most accepted the phone number, and half who did so called. By contrast, men approached by the woman on a low, solid bridge, and men approached on the high bridge by a *male* interviewer, rarely called. Once again, physical arousal accentuated romantic responses. As you perhaps have noticed after scary movies, roller-coaster rides, and physical exercise, adrenaline makes the heart grow fonder.

Variations in Love

Time and Culture

There is always a temptation to assume that most others share our feelings and ideas. We assume, for example, that love is a precondition for marriage. Most cultures—89 percent in one analysis of 166 cultures—do have a concept of romantic love, as reflected in flirtation or couples running off together (Jankowiak & Fischer, 1992). But in some cultures, notably those practicing arranged marriages, love tends to follow rather than to precede marriage. Until recently in North America, marital choices, especially those by women, were strongly influenced by considerations of economic security, family background, and professional status.

Gender

Do males and females differ in how they experience passionate love? Studies of men and women falling in and out of love reveal some surprises. Most people, including the writer of the following letter to a newspaper advice columnist, suppose that women fall in love more readily:

> Dear Dr. Brothers:
> Do you think it's effeminate for a 19-year-old guy to fall in love so hard it's like the whole world's turned around? I think I'm really crazy because this has happened several times now and love just seems to hit me on the head from nowhere. . . . My father says this is the way girls fall in love and that it doesn't happen this way with guys—at least it's not supposed to. I can't change how I am in this way but it kind of worries me.—P.T. (quoted by Dion & Dion, 1985)

P.T. would be reassured by the repeated finding that it is actually *men* who tend to fall more readily in love (Dion & Dion, 1985; Peplau & Gordon, 1985). Men also seem to fall out of love more slowly and are less likely than women to break up a premarital romance. Women in love, however, are typically as emotionally involved as their partners, or more so. They are more likely to report feeling euphoric and "giddy and carefree," as if they were "floating on a cloud." Women are also somewhat more likely than men to focus on the intimacy of the friendship and on their concern for their partner. Men are more likely than women to think about the playful and physical aspects of the relationship (Hendrick & Hendrick, 1995).

COMPANIONATE LOVE

Although passionate love burns hot, it inevitably simmers down. The longer a relationship endures, the fewer its emotional ups and downs (Berscheid & others, 1989). The high of romance may be sustained for a few months, even a couple of years. But no high lasts forever. "When you're in love it's the most glorious two-and-a-half days of your life," jests comedian Richard Lewis. The novelty, the intense absorption in the other, the thrill of the romance, the giddy "floating on a cloud" feeling, fades. After two years of marriage, spouses express affection about half as often as when they were newlyweds (Huston & Chorost, 1994). About four years after marriage, the divorce rate peaks in cultures worldwide (Fisher, 1994). If a close relationship is to endure, it will settle to a steadier but still warm afterglow that Hatfield calls **companionate love.**

Activity
27.2

Unlike the wild emotions of passionate love, companionate love is lower key; it's a deep, affectionate attachment. And it is just as real. Nisa, a !Kung San woman of the African Kalahari Desert, explains: "When two people are first together, their hearts are on fire and their passion is very great. After a while, the fire cools and that's how it stays. They continue to love each other, but it's in a different way—warm and dependable" (Shostak, 1981).

The cooling of passionate love over time and the growing importance of other factors, such as shared values, can be seen in the feelings of those who enter arranged versus love-based marriages in India. Usha Gupta and Pushpa Singh (1982) asked 50 couples in Jaipur, India, to complete a love scale. They found that those who married for love reported diminishing feelings of love if they had been married more than five years. By contrast, those in arranged marriages reported *more* love if they were not newlyweds (Figure 27-2).

The cooling of intense romantic love often triggers a period of disillusion, especially among those who regard that intensity of love as essential both for a marriage and for its continuation. Jeffry Simpson, Bruce Campbell, and Ellen Berscheid (1986) suspect "the sharp rise in the divorce rate in the past two decades is linked, at least in part, to the growing importance of intense positive emotional experiences (e.g., romantic love) in people's lives, experiences that may be particularly difficult to sustain over time." Compared with North Americans, Asians tend to focus less on personal feelings and more on the practical aspects

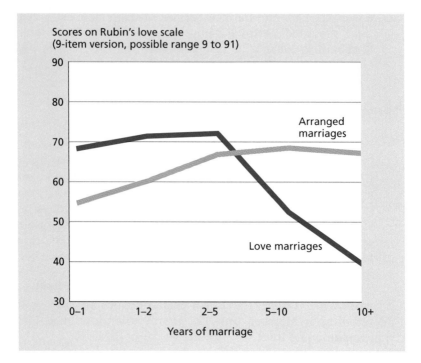

FIGURE 27-2
Romantic love between partners in arranged or love marriages in Jaipur,
India. **Source:** Data from Gupta & Singh, 1982.

of social attachments (Dion & Dion, 1988; Sprecher & others, 1994, 2002).
Thus, they are less vulnerable to disillusionment. Asians are also less
prone to the self-focused individualism that in the long run can undermine a relationship and lead to divorce (Dion & Dion, 1991, 1996; Triandis
& others, 1988).

The decline in intense mutual fascination may be natural and adaptive for species survival. The result of passionate love frequently is children, whose survival is aided by the parents' waning obsession with
each other (Kenrick & Trost, 1987). Nevertheless, for those married more
than 20 years, some of the lost romantic feeling is often renewed as the
family nest empties and the parents are once again free to focus their
attention on each other (Hatfield & Sprecher, 1986). "No man or woman
really knows what love is until they have been married a quarter of a
century," said Mark Twain. If the relationship has been intimate and
mutually rewarding, companionate love rooted in a rich history of
shared experiences deepens. But what is intimacy? And what is mutually rewarding?

MAINTAINING CLOSE RELATIONSHIPS

What factors influence the ups and downs of our close relationships? Let's consider two: equity and intimacy.

Equity

If both partners in a relationship pursue their personal desires willy-nilly, the friendship will die. Therefore, our society teaches us to exchange rewards by what Elaine Hatfield, William Walster, and Ellen Berscheid (1978) have called an **equity** principle of attraction: What you and your partner get out of a relationship should be proportional to what you each put into it. If two people receive equal outcomes, they should contribute equally; otherwise one or the other will feel it is unfair. If both feel their outcomes correspond to the assets and efforts each contributes, then both perceive equity.

Strangers and casual acquaintances maintain equity by exchanging benefits: You lend me your class notes; later, I'll lend you mine. I invite you to my party; you invite me to yours. Those in an enduring relationship, including roommates and those in love, do not feel bound to trade similar benefits—notes for notes, parties for parties (Berg, 1984). They feel freer to maintain equity by exchanging a variety of benefits ("When you drop by to lend me your notes, why don't you stay for dinner?") and eventually to stop keeping track of who owes whom.

Long-Term Equity

Is it crass to suppose that friendship and love are rooted in an equitable exchange of rewards? Don't we sometimes give in response to a loved one's need, without expecting any sort of return? Indeed, those involved in an equitable, long-term relationship are unconcerned with short-term equity. Margaret Clark and Judson Mills (1979, 1993; Clark, 1984, 1986) argue that people even take pains to *avoid* calculating any exchange benefits. When we help a good friend, we do not want instant repayment. If someone has us for dinner, we wait before reciprocating, lest the person attribute the motive for our return invitation to be merely paying off a social debt. True friends tune into one another's needs even when reciprocation is impossible (Clark & others, 1986, 1989). As people observe their partners sacrificing self-interest, their sense of trust grows (Wieselquist & others, 1999). One clue that an acquaintance is becoming a close friend is that the person shares when sharing is unexpected (Miller & others, 1989). Happily married people tend *not* to keep score of how much they are giving and getting (Buunk & Van Yperen, 1991).

Previously we noted an equity rule at work in the matching phenomenon: People usually bring equal assets to romantic relationships. Recall that often they are matched for attractiveness, status, and so forth.

If they are mismatched in one area, such as attractiveness, they tend to be mismatched in some other area, such as status. But in total assets, they are an equitable match. No one says, and few even think, "I'll trade you my good looks for your big income." But especially in relationships that last, equity is the rule.

Perceived Equity and Satisfaction

Those in an equitable relationship are more content (Fletcher & others, 1987; Hatfield & others, 1985; Van Yperen & Buunk, 1990). Those who perceive their relationship as *in*equitable feel discomfort: The one who has the better deal may feel guilty and the one who senses a raw deal may feel strong irritation. (Given the self-serving bias—most husbands perceive themselves as contributing more housework than their wives credit them for—the person who is "overbenefited" is less sensitive to the inequity.)

Robert Schafer and Patricia Keith (1980) surveyed several hundred married couples of all ages, noting those who felt their marriages were somewhat unfair because one spouse contributed too little to the cooking, housekeeping, parenting, or providing. Inequity took its toll: Those who perceived inequity also felt more distressed and depressed. During the child-rearing years, when wives often feel underbenefited and husbands feel overbenefited, marital satisfaction tends to dip. During the honeymoon and empty-nest stages, spouses are more likely to perceive equity and to feel satisfaction with their marriages (Feeney & others, 1994). When both partners freely give and receive, and make decisions together, the odds of sustained, satisfying love are good.

Self-Disclosure

Deep, companionate relationships are intimate. They enable us to be known as we truly are and to feel accepted. We discover this delicious experience in a good marriage or a close friendship—a relationship where trust displaces anxiety and where we are free to open ourselves without fear of losing the other's affection (Holmes & Rempel, 1989). Such relationships are characterized by what the late Sidney Jourard called **self-disclosure** (Derlega & others, 1993). As a relationship grows, self-disclosing partners reveal more and more of themselves to each other; their knowledge of each other penetrates to deeper and deeper levels until it reaches an appropriate depth.

Experiments have probed both the *causes* and the *effects* of self-disclosure. When are people most willing to disclose intimate information concerning "what you like and don't like about yourself" or "what you're most ashamed and most proud of"? And what effects do such revelations have on both those who reveal and those who receive them?

The most reliable finding is the **disclosure reciprocity** effect: Disclosure begets disclosure (Berg, 1987; Miller, 1990; Reis & Shaver, 1988). We reveal more to those who have been open with us. But intimacy is seldom instant. (If it is, the person may seem indiscreet and unstable.) Appropriate intimacy progresses like a dance: I reveal a little, you reveal a little—but not too much. You then reveal more, and I reciprocate.

For those in love, deepening intimacy is exciting. "Rising intimacy will create a strong sense of passion," note Roy Baumeister and Ellen Bratslavsky (1999). When intimacy is stable, passion is less. This helps explain why those who remarry after the loss of a spouse tend to begin the new marriage with an increased frequency of sex, and why passion often rides highest when intimacy is restored following severe conflict. "Passion and friendship [are] the two major predictors for relationship satisfaction," observe love researchers Susan Hendrick and Clyde Hendrick (1997). As it happens, the two can ride together: Deepening friendship feeds passion.

Some people—most of them women—are especially skilled "openers"; they easily elicit intimate disclosures from others, even from those who normally don't reveal very much of themselves (Miller & others, 1983; Pegalis & others, 1994; Shaffer & others, 1996). Such people tend to be good listeners. During conversation they maintain attentive facial expressions and appear to be comfortably enjoying themselves (Purvis & others, 1984). They may also express interest by uttering supportive phrases while their conversational partner is speaking. They are what psychologist Carl Rogers (1980) called "growth-promoting" listeners— people who are *genuine* in revealing their own feelings, *accepting* of others' feelings, and *empathic*, sensitive, reflective listeners.

What are the effects of such self-disclosure? Jourard (1964) argued that dropping our masks, letting ourselves be known as we are, nurtures love. He presumed that it is gratifying to open up to another and then to receive the trust another implies by being open with us. For example, having an intimate friend with whom we can discuss threats to our self-image seems to help us survive such stresses (Swann & Predmore, 1985). A true friendship is a special relationship that helps us cope with our other relationships. "When I am with my friend," reflected the Roman playwright Seneca, "methinks I am alone, and as much at liberty to speak anything as to think it." At its best, marriage is such a friendship, sealed by commitment.

Intimate self-disclosure is also one of companionate love's delights. Dating and married couples who most reveal themselves to one another express most satisfaction with their relationship and are more likely to endure in it (Berg & McQuinn, 1986; Hendrick & others, 1988; Sprecher, 1987). Married partners who mostly strongly agree that "I try to share my most intimate thoughts and feelings with my partner" tend to have the most satisfying marriages (Sanderson & Cantor, 2001). In a Gallup national marriage survey, 75 percent of those who prayed with their spouses (and 57 percent of those who didn't) reported their marriages as very happy (Greeley, 1991). Among believers, shared prayer from the heart is a humbling, intimate, soulful exposure. Those who pray together also more often say they discuss their marriages together, respect their spouses, and rate their spouses as skilled lovers.

Researchers have also found that women are often more willing to disclose their fears and weaknesses than are men (Cunningham, 1981). As Kate Millett (1975) put it, "Women express, men repress." Nevertheless, men today, particularly men with egalitarian gender-role attitudes, seem increasingly willing to reveal intimate feelings and to enjoy the satisfactions that accompany a relationship of mutual trust and self-disclosure. And that, say Arthur Aron and Elaine Aron (1994), is the essence of love—two selves connecting, disclosing, and identifying with each other; two selves, each retaining their individuality, yet sharing activities, delighting in similarities, and mutually supporting.

Does the Internet Create Intimacy or Isolation?

As a reader of this college text, you are almost surely one of the world's 650 million people (as of 2006) with Internet access. It took the telephone seven decades to go from 1 percent to 75 percent penetration of North American households. Internet access reached 75 percent penetration in about seven years (Putnam, 2000). You and a billion others now enjoy e-mail, Web surfing, and perhaps participating in listservs, news groups, or chat rooms.

Activity
27.3

What do you think: Is computer-mediated communication within virtual communities a poor substitute for in-person relationships? Or is it a wonderful way to widen our social circles? Does the Internet do more to connect people or to drain time from face-to-face relationships? Consider the emerging debate.

Point: The Internet, like the printing press and telephone, expands communication, and communication enables relationships. Printing reduced face-to-face storytelling and the telephone reduced face-to-face chats, but both enable us to reach and be reached by people without limitations of time and distance. Social relations involve networking, and the Net is the ultimate network. It enables efficient networking with family, friends, and kindred spirits—including people we otherwise never would have found, be they fellow MS patients, St. Nicholas collectors, or Harry Potter fans.

Counterpoint: True, but computer communication is impoverished. It lacks the nuances of eye-to-eye contact punctuated with nonverbal cues and physical touches. Except for simple emoticons—such as a :-) for an unnuanced smile—electronic messages are devoid of gestures, facial expressions, and tones of voice. No wonder it's so easy to misread them. The absence of expressive e-motion makes for ambiguous emotion.

For example, vocal nuances can signal whether a statement is serious, kidding, or sarcastic. Research by Justin Kruger and his colleagues

(1999) shows that communicators often think their "just kidding" intent is equally clear, whether e-mailed or spoken, when it isn't when e-mailed. Thanks also to one's anonymity in virtual discussions, the occasional result is a hostile "flame war."

The Internet, like television, diverts time from real relationships. Internet romances are not the developmental equivalent of real dating. Cybersex is artificial intimacy. Individualized Web-based entertainment displaces getting together for bridge. Such artificiality and isolation are regrettable, because our ancestral history predisposes our needing real-time relationships, replete with smirks and smiles. No wonder that a Stanford University survey found that 25 percent of more than 4,000 adults surveyed reported that their time online had reduced time spent in person and on the phone with family and friends (Nie & Erbring, 2000).

Point: But most folks don't perceive the Internet to be isolating. Another national survey found that "Internet users in general—and online women in particular—believe that their use of e-mail has strengthened their relationships and increased their contact with relatives and friends" (Pew, 2000). Internet use may displace in-person intimacy, but it also displaces television watching. If one-click cyber-shopping is bad for your local bookstore, it frees time for relationships. Telecommuting does the same, enabling people to work from home and to have time for their families.

Why say that computer-formed relationships are unreal? On the Internet your looks and location cease to matter. Your appearance, age, and race don't deter people from relating to you based on what's more genuinely important—your shared interests and values. In workplace and professional networks, computer-mediated discussions are less influenced by status and are therefore more candid and equally participatory. Computer-mediated communication fosters more spontaneous self-disclosure than face-to-face conversation (Joinson, 2001).

By 2003, online dating sites were receiving 45 million visits per month (Harmon, 2003). Americans alone, in the first half of 2003, spent $214 million on Internet dating sites—almost triple their spending in all of 2001 (Egan, 2003).

Most Internet flirtations go nowhere. "Everyone I know who has tried online dating . . . agrees that we loathe spending (wasting?) hours gabbing to someone and then meeting him and realizing that he is a creep," observed one Toronto woman (Dicum, 2003). But friendships and romantic relationships that form on the Internet are *more* likely to last for at least two years, report Katelyn McKenna and John Bargh, and their colleagues (Bargh & others, 2002; McKenna & Bargh, 1998, 2000; McKenna & others, 2002). In one experiment, they found that people disclosed more, with greater honesty and less posturing, when they met people online. They also felt more liking for people whom they conversed with online for 20 minutes than for those met for the same time face-to-face. This was even true when they unknowingly met the *same* person in both contexts. People surveyed similarly feel that Internet friendships are as real, important, and close as offline relationships.

Counterpoint: The Internet allows people to be who they really are, but also to feign who they really aren't, sometimes in the interests of sexual exploitation. Internet sexual media, like other forms of pornography, likely serve to distort people's perceptions of sexual reality, decrease the attractiveness of their real-life partner, prime men to perceive women in sexual terms, make sexual coercion seem more trivial, provide mental scripts for how to act in sexual situations, increase arousal, and lead to disinhibition and imitation of loveless sexual behaviors.

Finally, suggests Robert Putnam (2000), the social benefits of computer-mediated communication are constrained by two other realities: The "digital divide" accentuates social and educational inequalities between the haves and have nots. While "cyber-balkanization" enables BMW 2002 owners to network, it also, as noted in Module 14, enables White supremacists to find each other. The digital divide may be remedied with lowering prices and increasing public access locations. The balkanization is intrinsic to the medium.

As the debate over the Internet's social consequences continues, "the most important question," says Putnam (p. 180), will be "not what the Internet will do to us, but what we will do with it? . . . How can we harness this promising technology to thicken community ties? How can we develop the technology to enhance social presence, social feedback, and social cues? How can we use the prospect of fast, cheap communication to enhance the now fraying fabric of our real communities?"

E NDING RELATIONSHIPS

Often love dies. What factors predict marital dissolution? How do couples typically detach or renew their relationships?

In 1971, a man wrote a love poem to his bride, slipped it into a bottle, and dropped it into the Pacific Ocean between Seattle and Hawaii. A decade later, a jogger found it on a Guam beach:

> If, by the time this letter reaches you, I am old and gray, I know that our love will be as fresh as it is today.
> It may take a week or it may take years for this note to find you. . . . If this should never reach you, it will still be written in my heart that I will go to extreme means to prove my love for you. Your husband, Bob.

The woman to whom the love note was addressed was reached by phone. When the note was read to her she burst out laughing. And the more she heard, the harder she laughed. "We're divorced," she finally said, and slammed down the phone.

So it often goes. Comparing their unsatisfying relationship with the support and affection they imagine are available elsewhere, people are divorcing more often—at double the 1960 rate. Roughly half of American marriages and 40 percent of Canadian marriages now end in divorce. Enduring relationships are rooted in enduring love and satisfaction, but also in inattention to possible alternative partners, fear of the termination cost, and a sense of moral obligation (Adams & Jones, 1997; Miller, 1997). As economic and social barriers to divorce weakened during the 1960s and 1970s, thanks partly to women's increasing employment, divorce rates rose. "We are living longer, but loving more briefly," quips Os Guiness (1993, p. 309).

Britain's royal House of Windsor knows well the hazards of modern marriage. The fairy-tale marriages of Princess Margaret, Princess Anne, Prince Charles, and Prince Andrew all crumbled, smiles replaced with stony stares. Shortly after her 1986 marriage to Prince Andrew, Sarah Ferguson gushed, "I love his wit, his charm, his looks. I worship him." Andrew reciprocated her euphoria: "She is the best thing in my life." Six years later, Andrew, having decided her friends were "philistines," and Sarah, having derided Andrew's boorish behavior as "terribly gauche," called it quits (*Time*, 1992).

Who Divorces?

Divorce rates have varied widely by country, ranging from 0.01 percent of the population annually in Bolivia, the Philippines, and Spain to 4.7 percent in the world's most divorce-prone country, the United States. To predict a culture's divorce rates, it helps to know its values (Triandis, 1994). Individualistic cultures (where love is a feeling and people ask, "What does my heart say?") have more divorce than do communal cultures (where love entails obligation and people ask, "What will other people say?"). Individualists marry "for as long as we both shall love" and collectivists, more often for life. Individualists expect more passion and personal fulfillment in a marriage, which puts greater pressure on the relationship (Dion & Dion, 1993). "Keeping romance alive" was rated important to a good marriage by 78 percent of American women surveyed and 29 percent of Japanese women (*American Enterprise*, 1992).

Even in Western society, however, those who enter relationships with a long-term orientation and an intention to persist do experience healthier, less turbulent, and more durable partnerships (Arriaga, 2001; Arriaga & Agnew, 2001). Those whose commitment to a union outlasts the desire that gave birth to it will often endure times of conflict and unhappiness. One national survey found that 86 percent of those who were unhappily married but who stayed with the marriage were, when reinterviewed five years later, now mostly "very" or "quite" happy with their marriages (Popenoe, 2002).

Risk of divorce also depends on who marries whom (Fergusson & others, 1984; Myers, 2000a; Tzeng, 1992). People usually stay married if they

- married after age 20.
- both grew up in stable, two-parent homes.
- dated for a long while before marriage.
- are well and similarly educated.
- enjoy a stable income from a good job.
- live in a small town or on a farm.
- did not cohabit or become pregnant before marriage.
- are religiously committed.
- are of similar age, faith, and education.

None of these predictors, by itself, is essential to a stable marriage. But if none of these things is true for someone, marital breakdown is an almost sure bet. If all are true, they are *very* likely to stay together until death. The English perhaps had it right, several centuries ago, when presuming that the temporary intoxication of passionate love was a foolish basis for permanent marital decisions. Better, they felt, to choose a mate based on stable friendship and compatible backgrounds, interests, habits, and values (Stone, 1977).

The Detachment Process

Severing bonds produces a predictable sequence of agitated preoccupation with the lost partner, followed by deep sadness and, eventually, the beginnings of emotional detachment and a return to normal living (Hazan & Shaver, 1994). Even newly separated couples who have long ago ceased feeling affection are often surprised at their desire to be near the former partner. Deep and longstanding attachments seldom break quickly; detaching is a process, not an event.

Among dating couples, the closer and longer the relationship and the fewer the available alternatives, the more painful the breakup (Simpson, 1987). Surprisingly, Roy Baumeister and Sara Wotman (1992) report that, months or years later, people recall more pain over spurning someone's love than over having been spurned. Their distress arises from guilt over hurting someone, from upset over the heartbroken lover's persistence, or from uncertainty over how to respond. Among married couples, breakup has additional costs: shocked parents and friends, guilt over broken vows, possibly restricted parental rights. Still, each year millions of couples are willing to pay such costs to extricate themselves from what they perceive as the greater costs of continuing a painful, unrewarding relationship. Such costs include, in one study of 328 married couples, a tenfold increase in depression symptoms when a marriage is marked by discord rather than satisfaction (O'Leary & others, 1994).

When relationships suffer, those without better alternatives or who feel invested in a relationship (through time, energy, mutual friends, possessions, and perhaps children) will seek alternatives to exiting the relationship. Caryl Rusbult and her colleagues (1986, 1987, 1998) have explored three ways of coping with a failing relationship. Some people exhibit *loyalty*—by waiting for conditions to improve. The problems are too painful to speak of and the risks of separation are too great, so the loyal partner perseveres, hoping the good old days will return. Others (especially men) exhibit *neglect*; they ignore the partner and allow the relationship to deteriorate. When painful dissatisfactions are ignored, an insidious emotional uncoupling ensues as the partners talk less and begin redefining their lives without each other. Still others will *voice* their concerns and take active steps to improve the relationship by discussing problems, seeking advice, and attempting to change.

Study after study—in fact, 115 studies of 45,000 couples—reveal that unhappy couples disagree, command, criticize, and put down. Happy couples more often agree, approve, assent, and laugh (Karney & Bradbury, 1995; Noller & Fitzpatrick, 1990). After observing 2,000 couples, John Gottman (1994, 1998) noted that healthy marriages were not necessarily devoid of conflict. Rather, they were marked by an ability to reconcile differences and to overbalance criticism with affection. In successful marriages, positive interactions (smiling, touching, complimenting, laughing) outnumbered negative interactions (sarcasm, disapproval, insults) by at least a five-to-one ratio.

Successful couples have learned, sometimes aided by communication training, to restrain the cancerous put-downs and gut-level reactions, to fight fair (by stating feelings without insulting), and to depersonalize conflict with comments like, "I know it's not your fault" (Markman & others, 1988; Notarius & Markman, 1993; Yovetich & Rusbult, 1994). Would unhappy relationships get better if the partners agreed to *act* more as happy couples do—by complaining and criticizing less? By affirming and agreeing more? By setting times aside to voice their concerns? By praying or playing together daily? As attitudes trail behaviors, do affections trail actions?

Joan Kellerman, James Lewis, and James Laird (1989) wondered. They knew that among couples passionately in love, eye gazing is typically prolonged and mutual (Rubin, 1973). Would intimate eye gazing similarly stir feelings between those not in love (much as 45 minutes of escalating self-disclosure evoked feelings of closeness among those unacquainted students)? To find out, they asked unacquainted male-female pairs to gaze intently for 2 minutes either at each other's hands or in each other's eyes. When they separated, the eye gazers reported a tingle of attraction and affection toward each other. Simulating love had begun to stir it.

By enacting and expressing love, researcher Robert Sternberg (1988) believes the passion of initial romance can evolve into enduring love:

> "Living happily ever after" need not be a myth, but if it is to be a reality, the happiness must be based upon different configurations of mutual feelings at various times in a relationship. Couples who expect their passion to last forever, or their intimacy to remain unchallenged, are in for disappointment. . . . We must constantly work at understanding, building, and rebuilding our loving relationships. Relationships are constructions, and they decay over time if they are not maintained and improved. We cannot expect a relationship simply to take care of itself, any more than we can expect that of a building. Rather, we must take responsibility for making our relationships the best they can be.

Given the psychological ingredients of marital happiness—kindred minds, social and sexual intimacy, equitable giving and receiving of emotional and material resources—it does, however, become possible to contest the French saying, "Love makes the time pass and time makes love pass." But it takes effort to stem love's decay. It takes effort to carve out time each day to talk over the day's happenings. It takes effort to forgo nagging and bickering and instead to disclose and hear each other's hurts, concerns, and dreams. It takes effort to make a relationship into "a classless utopia of social equality" (Sarnoff & Sarnoff, 1989), in which both partners freely give and receive, share decision making, and enjoy life together.

CONCEPTS TO REMEMBER

passionate love   A state of intense longing for union with another. Passionate lovers are absorbed in one another, feel ecstatic at attaining their partner's love, and are disconsolate on losing it.

two-factor theory of emotion   Emotional experience is a product of physiological arousal and how we cognitively label the arousal.

companionate love   The affection we feel for those with whom our lives are deeply intertwined.

equity   A condition in which the outcomes people receive from a relationship are proportional to what they contribute to it. *Note:* Equitable outcomes needn't always be equal outcomes.

self-disclosure   Revealing intimate aspects of oneself to others.

disclosure reciprocity   The tendency for one person's intimacy of self-disclosure to match that of a conversational partner.

28

❖

Causes of Conflict

There is a speech that has been spoken in many languages by the leaders of many countries. It goes like this: "The intentions of our country are entirely peaceful. Yet, we are also aware that other nations, with their new weapons, threaten us. Thus we must defend ourselves against attack. By so doing, we shall protect our way of life and preserve the peace" (Richardson, 1960). Almost every nation claims concern only for peace but, mistrusting other nations, arms itself in self-defense. The result is a world that has been spending $2 billion per day on arms and armies while hundreds of millions die of malnutrition and untreated disease.

The elements of such **conflict** (a perceived incompatibility of actions or goals) are similar at all levels, from nations in an arms race, to conflicted Middle Easterners, to corporate executives and workers disputing salaries, to a feuding married couple. Let's consider these conflict elements.

SOCIAL DILEMMAS

Several of the problems that most threaten our human future—nuclear arms, global warming, overpopulation, natural resource depletion—arise as various parties pursue their self-interests, ironically, to their collective detriment. Anyone can think, "It would cost me a lot to buy expensive pollution controls. Besides, by itself my pollution is trivial." Many others reason similarly, and the result is unclean air and water.

Thus, choices that are individually rewarding become collectively punishing. We therefore have an urgent dilemma: How can we reconcile the rights of individuals to pursue their personal interests with communal well-being?

To isolate and illustrate this dilemma, social psychologists have used laboratory games that expose the heart of many real social conflicts. By showing us how well-meaning people become trapped in mutually destructive behavior, they illuminate some fascinating, yet troubling, paradoxes.

"Social psychologists who study conflict are in much the same position as the astronomers," noted conflict researcher Morton Deutsch (1999). "We cannot conduct true experiments with large-scale social events. But we can identify the conceptual similarities between the large scale and the small, as the astronomers have between the planets and Newton's apple. That is why the games people play as subjects in our laboratory may advance our understanding of war, peace, and social justice." Consider two examples: the Prisoners' Dilemma and the Tragedy of the Commons.

The Prisoners' Dilemma

One dilemma derives from an anecdote concerning two suspects questioned separately by the district attorney (DA) (Rapoport, 1960). They are jointly guilty; however, the DA has only enough evidence to convict them of a lesser offense. So the DA creates an incentive for each to confess privately:

- If one confesses and the other doesn't, the DA will grant the confessor immunity (and will use the confession to convict the other of a maximum offense).
- If both confess, each will receive a moderate sentence.
- If neither confesses, each will receive a light sentence.

The matrix of Figure 28-1 summarizes the choices. Faced with such a dilemma, would you confess?

To minimize their own sentences, many would confess, despite the fact that mutual confession elicits more severe sentences than mutual nonconfession. Note from the matrix that no matter what the other prisoner decides, each is better off confessing. If the other also confesses, one then gets a moderate sentence instead of a severe one. If the other does not confess, one goes free. Of course, each prisoner understands this. Hence, the social trap.

In some 2,000 studies (Dawes, 1991), university students have faced variations of the Prisoners' Dilemma with the outcomes not being prison terms but chips, money, or course points. On any given decision, a person is better off defecting (because such behavior exploits

Activity
28.1

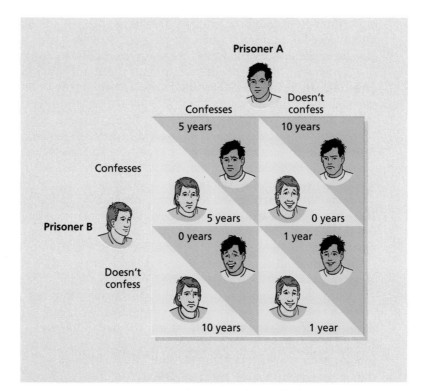

FIGURE 28-1

The Classic Prisoners' Dilemma. In each box, the number above the diagonal is prisoner A's outcome. Thus, if both prisoners confess, both get five years. If neither confesses, each gets a year. If one confesses, that prisoner is set free in exchange for evidence used to convict the other of a crime bringing a 10-year sentence. If you were one of the prisoners, unable to communicate with your fellow prisoner, would you confess?

the other's cooperation or protects against the other's exploitation). However—and here's the rub—by not cooperating, both parties end up far worse off than if they had trusted each other and thus had gained a joint profit. This dilemma often traps each one in a maddening predicament in which both realize they *could* mutually profit. But unable to communicate and mistrusting one another, they become "locked in" to not cooperating.

The Tragedy of the Commons

Many social dilemmas involve more than two parties. Global warming stems from deforestation and from the carbon dioxide emitted by cars, furnaces, and coal-fired power plants. Each gas-guzzling SUV contributes infinitesimally to the problem, and the harm each does is diffused over many people. To model such social predicaments, researchers have developed laboratory dilemmas that involve multiple people.

A metaphor for the insidious nature of social dilemmas is what ecologist Garrett Hardin (1968) called the Tragedy of the Commons. He derived the name from the centrally located pasture in old English towns, but the "commons" can be air, water, whales, cookies, or any shared and limited resource. If all use the resource in moderation, it may replenish itself as rapidly as it's harvested. The grass will grow, the whales will reproduce, and the cookie jar gets restocked. If not, there occurs a tragedy of the commons.

Imagine 100 farmers surrounding a commons capable of sustaining 100 cows. When each grazes one cow, the common feeding ground is optimally used. But then someone reasons, "If I put a second cow in the pasture, I'll double my output, minus the mere 1 percent overgrazing." So this farmer adds a second cow. So do each of the other farmers. The inevitable result? The Tragedy of the Commons—a mud field.

Many real predicaments parallel this story. Internet congestion occurs as individuals, seeking to maximize their own gain, surf the Web, filling its pipelines with graphical information (Huberman & Lukose, 1997). Likewise, environmental pollution is the sum of many minor pollutions, each of which benefits the individual polluters much more than they could benefit themselves (and the environment) if they stopped polluting. We litter public places—dorm lounges, parks, zoos—while keeping our personal spaces clean. We deplete our natural resources because the immediate personal benefits of, say, taking a long, hot shower outweigh the seemingly inconsequential costs. Whalers knew others would exploit the whales if they didn't and that taking a few whales would hardly diminish the species. Therein lies the tragedy. Everybody's business (conservation) becomes nobody's business.

Is such individualism uniquely American? Kaori Sato (1987) gave students in a more collective culture, Japan, opportunities to harvest—for actual money—trees from a simulated forest. When the students shared equally the costs of planting the forest, the result was like those in Western cultures. More than half the trees were harvested before they had grown to the most profitable size.

Sato's forest reminds me of the cookie jar in our home. What we *should* have done is conserve cookies during the interval between weekly restockings, so that each day we could each munch two or three. Lacking regulation and fearing that other family members would soon deplete the resource, what we actually did was maximize our individual cookie consumption by downing one after the other. The result: Within 24 hours the cookie glut would often end, the jar sitting empty.

The Prisoners' Dilemma and the Tragedy of the Commons games have several similar features. First, both tempt people to explain their own behavior situationally ("I had to protect myself against exploitation by my opponent") and to explain their partners' behavior dispositionally ("she was greedy," "he was untrustworthy"). Most never realize that their counterparts are viewing them with the same fundamental attribution error (Gifford & Hine, 1997; Hine & Gifford, 1996).

Second, motives often change. At first, people are eager to make some easy money, then to minimize their losses, and finally to save face and avoid defeat (Brockner & others, 1982; Teger, 1980). These shifting motives are strikingly similar to the shifting motives during the buildup of the 1960s Vietnam War. At first, President Johnson's speeches expressed concern for democracy, freedom, and justice. As the conflict escalated, his concern became protecting America's honor and avoiding the national humiliation of losing a war.

Third, most real-life conflicts, like the Prisoners' Dilemma and the Tragedy of the Commons, are **non-zero-sum games.** The two sides' profits and losses need not add up to zero. Both can win; both can lose. Each game pits the immediate interests of individuals against the well-being of the group. Each is a diabolical social trap that shows how, even when individuals behave "rationally," harm can result. No malicious person planned for the earth's atmosphere to be warmed by a blanket of carbon dioxide.

Not all self-serving behavior leads to collective doom. In a plentiful commons—as in the world of the eighteenth-century capitalist economist Adam Smith (1776, p. 18)—individuals who seek to maximize their own profit may also give the community what it needs: "It is not from the benevolence of the butcher, the brewer, or the baker, that we expect our dinner," he observed, "but from their regard to their own interest."

Resolving Social Dilemmas

In those situations that are indeed social traps, how can we induce people to cooperate for their mutual betterment? Research with the laboratory dilemmas reveals several ways (Gifford & Hine, 1997).

Regulation

If taxes were entirely voluntary, how many would pay their full share? Surely, many would not, which is why modern societies do not depend on charity to pay for schools, parks, and social and military security. We also develop laws and regulations for our common good. An International Whaling Commission sets an agreed-upon "harvest" that enables whales to regenerate.

Small Is Beautiful

There is another way to resolve social dilemmas: Make the group small. In a small commons, each person feels more responsible and effective

(Kerr, 1989). As a group grows larger, people more often think, "I couldn't have made a difference anyway"—a common excuse for noncooperation (Kerr & Kaufman-Gilliland, 1997). In small groups, people also feel more identified with a group's success. Anything else that enhances group identity will also increase cooperation. Even just a few minutes of discussion or just believing that one shares similarities with others in the group can increase "we feeling" and cooperation (Brewer, 1987; Orbell & others, 1988).

On the Pacific Northwest island where I grew up, our small neighborhood shared a communal water supply. On hot summer days when the reservoir ran low, a light came on, signaling our 15 families to conserve. Recognizing our responsibility to one another, and feeling like our conservation really mattered, each of us conserved. Never did the reservoir run dry. In a much larger commons—say, a city—voluntary conservation is less successful.

Communication

To escape a social trap, people must communicate. In the laboratory, group communication sometimes degenerates into threats and name calling (Deutsch & Krauss, 1960). More often, communication enables people to cooperate (Bornstein & others, 1988, 1989). Discussing the dilemma forges a group identity, which enhances concern for everyone's welfare. It devises group norms and consensus expectations and puts pressure on members to follow them. Especially when people are face-to-face, it enables them to commit themselves to cooperation (Bouas & Komorita, 1996; Drolet & Morris, 2000; Kerr & others, 1994, 1997; Pruitt, 1998).

Without communication, those who expect others not to cooperate will usually refuse to cooperate themselves (Messé & Sivacek, 1979; Pruitt & Kimmel, 1977). One who mistrusts almost has to be uncooperative (to protect against exploitation). Noncooperation, in turn, feeds further mistrust ("What else could I do? It's a dog-eat-dog world"). In experiments, communication reduces mistrust, enabling people to reach agreements that lead to their common betterment.

Changing the Payoffs

Cooperation rises when experimenters change the payoff matrix to make cooperation more rewarding and exploitation less rewarding (Komorita & Barth, 1985; Pruitt & Rubin, 1986). Changing payoffs also helps resolve actual dilemmas. In some cities, freeways clog and skies smog because people prefer the convenience of driving themselves directly to work. Each knows that one more car does not add noticeably to the congestion and pollution. To alter the personal cost-benefit calculations, many cities now give carpoolers incentives, such as designated freeway lanes or reduced tolls.

Appeals to Altruistic Norms

When cooperation obviously serves the public good, one can usefully appeal to the social-responsibility norm (Lynn & Oldenquist, 1986). When, for example, people believe public transportation can save time, they will be more likely to use it if they also believe it reduces pollution (Van Vugt & others, 1996). In the struggle for civil rights, many marchers willingly agreed, for the sake of the larger group, to suffer harassment, beatings, and jail. In wartime, people make great personal sacrifices for the good of their group. As Winston Churchill said of the Battle of Britain, the actions of the Royal Air Force pilots were genuinely altruistic: A great many people owed a great deal to those who flew into battle knowing there was a high probability—70 percent for those on a standard tour of duty—they would not return (Levinson, 1950).

To summarize, we can minimize destructive entrapment in social dilemmas by establishing rules that regulate self-serving behavior, by keeping groups small, by enabling people to communicate, by changing payoffs to make cooperation more rewarding, and by invoking altruistic norms.

COMPETITION

In the module on prejudice, we noted that racial hostilities often arise when groups compete for scarce jobs, housing, or resources. When interests clash, conflict erupts.

But does competition by itself provoke hostile conflict? Real-life situations are so complex that it is hard to be sure. If competition is indeed responsible, then it should be possible to provoke in an experiment. We could randomly divide people into two groups, have the groups compete for a scarce resource, and note what happens. This is precisely what Muzafer Sherif (1966) and his colleagues did in a dramatic series of experiments with typical 11- and 12-year-old boys. The inspiration for these experiments dated back to Sherif's witnessing, as a teenager, Greek troops invading his Turkish province in 1919.

> They started killing people right and left. [That] made a great impression on me. There and then I became interested in understanding why these things were happening among human beings. . . . I wanted to learn whatever science or specialization was needed to understand this intergroup savagery. (quoted by Aron & Aron, 1989, p. 131)

After studying the social roots of savagery, Sherif introduced the seeming essentials into several three-week summer camping experiences. In one such study, he divided 22 unacquainted Oklahoma City boys into two groups, took them to a Boy Scout camp in separate buses, and settled them in bunkhouses about a half-mile apart at Oklahoma's Robber's Cave State Park. For most of the first week, they were unaware of the other group's existence. By cooperating in various activities—preparing meals, camping out, fixing up a swimming hole, building a rope bridge—each group soon became close-knit. They gave themselves names: "Rattlers" and "Eagles." Typifying the good feeling, a sign appeared in one cabin: "Home Sweet Home."

Group identity thus established, the stage was set for the conflict. Toward the end of the first week, the Rattlers "discovered the Eagles on 'our' baseball field." When the camp staff then proposed a tournament of competitive activities between the two groups (baseball games, tugs-of-war, cabin inspections, treasure hunts, and so forth), both groups responded enthusiastically. This was win-lose competition. The spoils (medals, knives) would all go to the tournament victor.

The result? The camp gradually degenerated into open warfare. It was like a scene from William Golding's novel *Lord of the Flies*, which depicts the social disintegration of boys marooned on an island. In Sherif's study, the conflict began with each side calling the other names during the competitive activities. Soon it escalated to dining hall "garbage wars," flag burnings, cabin ransackings, even fistfights. Asked to describe the other group, the boys said "they" were "sneaky," "smart alecks," "stinkers," while referring to their own group as "brave," "tough," "friendly."

The win-lose competition had produced intense conflict, negative images of the outgroup, and strong ingroup cohesiveness and pride. Group polarization no doubt exacerbated the conflict. In experiments, groups behave more competitively than individuals in competition-fostering situations (Wildschut & others, 2003). All this occurred without any cultural, physical, or economic differences between the two groups and with boys who were their communities' "cream of the crop." Sherif noted that, had we visited the camp at this point, we would have concluded these "were wicked, disturbed, and vicious bunches of youngsters" (1966, p. 85). Actually, their evil behavior was triggered by an evil situation. Fortunately, as we will see in Module 29, Sherif not only made strangers into enemies; he then made the enemies into friends.

*P*ERCEIVED INJUSTICE

"That's unfair!" "What a ripoff!" "We deserve better!" Such comments typify conflicts bred by perceived injustice. But what is "justice"? According to some social-psychological theorists, people perceive justice as equity—the distribution of rewards in proportion to individuals' contributions (Walster & others, 1978). If you and I have a relationship (employer-employee, teacher-student, husband-wife, colleague-colleague), it is equitable if:

$$\frac{\text{My outcomes}}{\text{My inputs}} = \frac{\text{Your outcomes}}{\text{Your inputs}}$$

If you contribute more and benefit less than I do, you will feel exploited and irritated; I may feel exploitative and guilty. Chances are, though, that you more than I will be sensitive to the inequity (Greenberg, 1986; Messick & Sentis, 1979).

We may agree with the equity principle's definition of justice yet disagree on whether our relationship is equitable. If two people are colleagues, what will each consider a relevant input? The one who is older may favor basing pay on seniority, the other on current productivity. Given such a disagreement, whose definition is likely to prevail? More often than not, those with social power convince themselves and others that they deserve what they're getting (Mikula, 1984). This has been called a "golden" rule: Whoever has the gold makes the rules.

As this suggests, the exploiter can relieve guilt by devaluing others' inputs. Those who inflict harm may blame the victim and thus maintain their belief in a just world.

And how do those who are exploited react? Elaine Hatfield, William Walster, and Ellen Berscheid (1978) detected three possibilities. They can accept and justify their inferior position ("We're poor but we're happy"). They can demand compensation, perhaps by harassing, embarrassing, even cheating their exploiter. If all else fails, they may try to restore equity by retaliating.

An interesting implication of equity theory—an implication that has been confirmed experimentally—is that the more competent and worthy people feel (the more they value their inputs), the more they will feel underbenefitted and thus eager to retaliate (Ross & others, 1971). Intense social protests generally come from those who, perhaps after being educated, believe themselves worthy of more than they are receiving.

Since 1970 professional opportunities for women have increased significantly. Ironically, though understandably to an equity theorist, so have people's feelings that women's status is *in*equitable (Table 28-1). So long as women compared their opportunities and earnings with those of other women, they felt generally satisfied—as they did with their disproportionate share of family labor (Jackson, 1989; Major, 1989, 1993). Now that women are more likely to see themselves as men's equals, their sense of relative deprivation has grown (Desmarais & Curtis, 2001). If secretarial work and truck driving have "comparable worth" (for the skills required), then they deserve comparable pay; that's equity, say advocates of gender equality (Lowe & Wittig, 1989).

TABLE 28-1 GALLUP POLLS REVEAL INCREASED PERCEPTIONS OF
GENDER INEQUALITY

All things considered, who has a better life in this country—men or women?

	1972	*1993*
Men	29%	60%
Women	35%	21%
Same	30%	15%
No opinion	6%	5%

Source: Roper Center for Public Opinion Research, 1997.

MISPERCEPTION

Recall that conflict is a *perceived* incompatibility of actions or goals. Many conflicts contain but a small core of truly incompatible goals; the bigger problem is the misperceptions of the other's motives and goals. The Eagles and the Rattlers did indeed have some genuinely incompatible aims. But their perceptions subjectively magnified their differences (Figure 28-2).

In earlier modules we considered the seeds of such misperception. The *self-serving bias* leads individuals and groups to accept credit for their good deeds and shuck responsibility for bad deeds, without according others the same benefit of the doubt. A tendency to *self-justify* further inclines people to deny the wrong of their evil acts that cannot

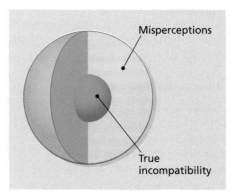

FIGURE 28-2
Many conflicts contain a core of truly incompatible goals surrounded by a larger exterior of misperceptions.

be shucked off. Thanks to the *fundamental attribution error*, each side sees the other's hostility as reflecting an evil disposition. One then filters the information and interprets it to fit one's *preconceptions*. Groups frequently *polarize* these self-serving, self-justifying, biasing tendencies. One symptom of *groupthink* is the tendency to perceive one's own group as moral and strong, the opposition as evil and weak. Terrorist acts that are despicable brutality to most people are "holy war" to others. Indeed, the mere fact of being in a group triggers an *ingroup bias*. And negative *stereotypes*, once formed, are often resistant to contradictory evidence.

So it should not surprise us, though it should sober us, that people in conflict form distorted images of one another. Even the types of misperception are intriguingly predictable.

Mirror-Image Perceptions

To a striking degree, the misperceptions of those in conflict are mutual. People in conflict attribute similar virtues to themselves and vices to the other. When American psychologist Urie Bronfenbrenner (1961) visited the former Soviet Union in 1960 and conversed with many ordinary citizens in Russian, he was astonished to hear them saying the same things about America that Americans were saying about Russia. The Russians said that the U.S. government was militarily aggressive; that it exploited and deluded the American people; that in diplomacy it was not to be trusted. "Slowly and painfully, it forced itself upon one that the Russians' distorted picture of us was curiously similar to our view of them—a mirror image."

When the two sides have clashing perceptions, at least one of the two is misperceiving the other. And when such misperceptions exist, noted Bronfenbrenner, "It is a psychological phenomenon without parallel in the gravity of its consequences . . . for *it is characteristic of such images that they are self-confirming.*" If A expects B to be hostile, A may treat B in such a way that B fulfills A's expectations, thus beginning a vicious circle. Morton Deutsch (1986) explained:

> You hear the false rumor that a friend is saying nasty things about you; you snub him; he then badmouths you, confirming your expectation. Similarly, if the policymakers of East and West believe that war is likely and either attempts to increase its military security vis-à-vis the other, the other's response will justify the initial move.

Negative **mirror-image perceptions** have been an obstacle to peace in many places:

- Both sides of the Arab-Israeli conflict insisted that "we" are motivated by our need to protect our security and our territory, while "they" want to obliterate us and gobble up our land.

"We" are the indigenous people here, "they" are the invaders. "We" are the victims, "they" are the aggressors" (Heradstveit, 1979; Rouhana & Bar-Tal, 1998). Given such intense mistrust, negotiation is difficult.

- At Northern Ireland's University of Ulster, J. A. Hunter and his colleagues (1991) showed Catholic and Protestant students videos of a Protestant attack at a Catholic funeral and a Catholic attack at a Protestant funeral. Most students attributed the other side's attack to "bloodthirsty" motives but its own side's attack to retaliation or self-defense.

- As the United States and Iraq prepared for war, each repeatedly spoke of the other as "evil." To George W. Bush, Saddam Hussein was a "murderous tyrant" and "madman" who was threatening the civilized world with weapons of mass destruction. To Iraq's government, the Bush government was a "gang of evil" that lusted for Middle Eastern oil.

Such conflicts, notes Philip Zimbardo (2004a), engage "a two-category world—of good people, like US, and of bad people, like THEM." Opposing sides in a conflict tend to exaggerate their differences, note David Sherman, Leif Nelson, and Lee Ross (2003). On issues such as abortion, immigration, and affirmative action, proponents aren't as liberal and opponents aren't as conservative as their adversaries suppose. To resolve conflicts, it helps to understand the other's mind. But it isn't easy, notes Robert Wright (2003b): "Putting yourself in the shoes of people who do things you find abhorrent may be the hardest moral exercise there is."

Destructive mirror-image perceptions also operate in conflicts between small groups and between individuals. As we saw in the dilemma games, both parties may say, "We want to cooperate. But their refusal to cooperate forces us to react defensively." In a study of executives, Kenneth Thomas and Louis Pondy (1977) uncovered such attributions. Asked to describe a significant recent conflict, only 12 percent felt the other party was cooperative; 74 percent perceived themselves as cooperative. The executives explained that they had "suggested," "informed," and "recommmended," while their antagonist had "demanded," " disagreed with everything I said," and "refused."

Conflicts are often fueled by an illusion that the enemy's top leaders are evil but their people, though controlled and manipulated, are pro-us. This *evil leader–good people* perception characterized Americans' and Russians' views of each other during the cold war. The United States entered the Vietnam War believing that in areas dominated by the Communist Vietcong "terrorists," many of the people were allies-in-waiting. As suppressed information later revealed, these beliefs were mere wishful thinking. In 2003, the United States began the Iraq War presuming the existence of "a vast underground network that would rise in support of coalition forces to assist security and law enforcement" (Phillips, 2003). Alas, the network didn't materialize, and the resulting postwar security vacuum enabled looting, sabotage, and persistent attacks on American forces.

Another type of mirror-image perception is each side's exaggeration of the other's position. People with opposing views on issues such as abortion, capital punishment, and government budget cuts often differ less than they suppose. Each side overestimates the extremity of the other's views. And each presumes that "our" beliefs follow from the facts while "their" ideology dictates their interpretation of facts (Keltner & Robinson, 1996; Robinson & others, 1995). From such exaggerated perceptions arise culture wars. Ralph White (1996, 1998) reports that the Serbs started the war in Bosnia partly out of an exaggerated fear of the relatively secularized Bosnian Muslims, whose beliefs they wrongly associated with Middle Eastern Islamic fundamentalism and fanatical terrorism.

Shifting Perceptions

If misperceptions accompany conflict, then they should appear and disappear as conflicts wax and wane. They do, with startling regularity. The same processes that create the enemy's image can reverse that image when the enemy becomes an ally. Thus the "bloodthirsty, cruel, treacherous, buck-toothed little Japs" of World War II soon became—in North American minds (Gallup, 1972) and in the media—our "intelligent, hardworking, self-disciplined, resourceful allies."

The Germans, who after two world wars were hated, then admired, and then again hated, were once again admired—apparently no longer plagued by what earlier was presumed to be cruelty in their national character. So long as Iraq was attacking Iran, even while using chemical weapons and massacring its own Kurds, many nations supported it. Our enemy's enemy is our friend. When Iraq ended its war with Iran and invaded oil-rich Kuwait, Iraq's behavior suddenly became "barbaric." Images of our enemies change with amazing ease.

The extent of misperceptions during conflict provides a chilling reminder that people need not be insane or abnormally evil to form these distorted images of their antagonists. When we experience conflict with another nation, another group, or simply a roommate or parent, we readily misperceive our own motives and actions as wholly good and the other's as totally evil. Our antagonists usually form a mirror-image perception of us.

So, trapped in a social dilemma, competing for scarce resources, or perceiving injustice, the conflict continues until something enables both parties to peel away their misperceptions and work at reconciling their actual differences. Good advice, then, is this: When in conflict, do not assume that the other fails to share your values and morality. Rather, compare perceptions, assuming that the other is likely perceiving the situation differently.

CONCEPTS TO REMEMBER

conflict   A perceived incompatibility of actions or goals.

non-zero-sum games   Games in which outcomes need not sum to zero. With cooperation, both can win; with competition, both can lose. (Also called *mixed-motive situations*.)

mirror-image perceptions   Reciprocal views of one another often held by parties in conflict; for example, each may view itself as moral and peace-loving and the other as evil and aggressive.

MODULE

29

❖

Blessed Are the Peacemakers

W e have seen how conflicts are ignited by social traps, competition, perceived injustices, and misperceptions. Although the picture is grim, it is not hopeless. Sometimes closed fists become open arms as hostilities evolve into friendship. Social psychologists have focused on four strategies for helping enemies become comrades. We can remember these as the four Cs of peacemaking: contact, cooperation, communication, conciliation.

*C*ONTACT

Might putting two conflicting individuals or groups into close contact enable them to know and like each other? We have seen why it might. We have seen that proximity—and the accompanying interaction, anticipation of interaction, and mere exposure—boosts liking. We have noted how blatant racial prejudice declined following desegregation, showing that "attitudes follow behavior."

During the last 30 years in the United States, segregation and prejudice have diminished together. Was interracial contact the *cause* of these improved attitudes? Were those who actually experienced desegregation affected by it?

Does Desegregation Improve Racial Attitudes?

School desegregation has produced measurable benefits, such as leading more Blacks to attend and succeed in college (Stephan, 1988). Does desegregation of schools, neighborhoods, and workplaces also produce favorable *social* results? The evidence is mixed.

On the one hand, many studies conducted during and shortly after the desegregation following World War II found Whites' attitudes toward Blacks improving markedly. Whether the people were department store clerks and customers, merchant marines, government workers, police officers, neighbors, or students, racial contact led to diminished prejudice (Amir, 1969; Pettigrew, 1969). For example, near the end of World War II, the U.S. Army partially desegregated some of its rifle companies (Stouffer & others, 1949). When asked their opinions of such desegregation, 11 percent of the White soldiers in segregated companies approved. Of those in desegregated companies, 60 percent approved.

When Morton Deutsch and Mary Collins (1951) took advantage of a made-to-order natural experiment, they observed similar results. In accord with state law, New York City desegregated its public housing units; it assigned families to apartments without regard to race. In a similar development across the river in Newark, Blacks and Whites were assigned to separate buildings. When surveyed, White women in the desegregated development were far more likely to favor interracial housing and to say their attitudes toward Blacks had improved. Exaggerated stereotypes had wilted in the face of reality. As one woman put it, "I've really come to like it. I see they're just as human as we are."

Contact predicts tolerant attitudes in nonracial realms as well. In a painstakingly complete analysis, Linda Tropp and Thomas Pettigrew (2004) assembled data from 515 studies of 250,513 people in 38 nations. In 94 percent of studies, *increased contact predicted decreased prejudice*. The correlation holds not only for interracial contacts, but also contacts with the elderly, psychiatric patients, gays, and children with disabilities, notes Miles Hewstone (2003).

Findings such as these influenced the Supreme Court's 1954 decision to desegregate U.S. schools and helped fuel the civil rights movement of the 1960s (Pettigrew, 1986). Yet studies of the effects of school desegregation have been less encouraging. After reviewing all the available studies, Walter Stephan (1986) concluded that racial attitudes had been little affected by desegregation. For Blacks, the more noticeable consequence of desegregated schooling was their increased likelihood of attending integrated (or predominantly White) colleges, living in integrated neighborhoods, and working in integrated settings.

So sometimes desegregation improves racial attitudes; sometimes it doesn't. Such disagreements excite the scientist's detective spirit. What explains the difference? So far, we've been lumping all kinds of desegregation together. Actual desegregation occurs in many ways and under vastly different conditions.

When Does Desegregation Improve Racial Attitudes?

Might the frequency of interracial contact be a factor? Indeed it seems to be. Researchers have gone into dozens of desegregated schools and observed those with whom children of a given race eat, talk, and loiter. Race influences contact. Whites disproportionately associate with Whites, Blacks with Blacks (Schofield, 1982, 1986). The same self-imposed segregation was evident in a South African desegregated beach, as John Dixon and Kevin Durrheim (2003) discovered when they recorded the location of Black, White, and Indian beachgoers one midsummer (December 30) afternoon (Figure 29-1). Efforts to facilitate contact sometimes help, but sometimes fall flat. "We had one day when some of the Protestant schools came over," explained one Catholic youngster after a Northern Ireland school exchange (Cairns & Hewstone, 2002). "It

FIGURE 29-1
Desegregation needn't mean contact. After this Scottburgh, South Africa, beach became "open" and desegregated in the new South Africa, Blacks (represented by black circles), Whites (grey circles), and Indians (white circles) tended to cluster with their own race. **Source:** From Dixon & Durrheim, 2003.

was supposed to be like . . . mixing, but there was very little mixing. It wasn't because we didn't want to; it was just really awkward."

In contrast, the more encouraging older studies of store clerks, soldiers, and housing project neighbors involved considerable interracial contact, more than enough to reduce the anxiety that marks initial intergroup contact. Other studies involving prolonged, personal contact— between Black and White prison inmates and between Black and White girls in an interracial summer camp—show similar benefits (Clore & others, 1978; Foley, 1976). Among American students who have studied in Germany or Britain, the more their contact with host country people, the more positive their attitudes (Stangor & others, 1996). In experiments, those who form *friendships* with outgroup members develop more positive attitudes toward the outgroup (Pettigrew & Tropp, 2000; Wright & others, 1997). It's not just head knowledge of other people that matters: It's the *emotional* ties that form with intimate friendships and that serve to reduce anxiety (Hewstone, 2003; Pettigrew & Tropp, 2000).

Surveys of nearly 4,000 Europeans reveal that friendship is a key to successful contact: If you have a minority-group friend, you become much more likely to express sympathy and support for the friend's group and even somewhat more support for immigration by that group. It's true of West Germans' attitudes toward Turks, French people's attitudes toward Asians and North Africans, Netherlanders' attitudes toward Surinamers and Turks, and Britishers' attitudes toward West Indians and Asians (Brown & others, 1999; Hamberger & Hewstone, 1997; Pettigrew, 1997). Likewise, antigay feeling is lower among people who know gays personally (Herek, 1993). Additional studies of attitudes toward people who are elderly, mentally ill, living with AIDS, and those with disabilities confirm that contact often predicts positive attitudes (Pettigrew, 1998).

The social psychologists who advocated desegregation never claimed that contact of *any* sort would improve attitudes. They expected poor results when contacts were competitive, unsupported by authorities, and unequal (Pettigrew, 1988; Stephan, 1987). Before 1954, many prejudiced Whites had frequent contacts with Blacks—as shoeshine men and domestic workers. Such unequal contacts breed attitudes that merely justify the continuation of inequality. So it's important that the contact be **equal-status contact,** like that between the store clerks, the soldiers, the neighbors, the prisoners, and the summer campers.

COOPERATION

Although equal-status contact can help, it is sometimes not enough. It didn't help when Muzafer Sherif stopped the Eagles versus Rattlers competition and brought the groups together for noncompetitive activities, such as watching movies, shooting off fireworks, and eating. By this time, their hostility was so strong that mere contact only provided opportunities for taunts and attacks. When an Eagle was bumped by a Rattler, his fellow Eagles urged him to "brush off the dirt." Obviously, desegregating the two groups had hardly promoted their social integration.

Given entrenched hostility, what can a peacemaker do? Think back to successful and unsuccessful desegregation efforts. The army's racial mixing of rifle companies not only brought Blacks and Whites into equal-status contact but also made them interdependent. Together, they were fighting a common enemy, striving toward a shared goal.

Does this suggest a second factor that predicts whether the effect of desegregation will be favorable? Does competitive contact divide and *cooperative* contact unite? Consider what happens to people who together face a common predicament.

Common External Threats

Together with others, have you ever been victimized by the weather; harassed as part of your initiation into a group; punished by a teacher; or persecuted and ridiculed because of your social, racial, or religious identity? If so, you may recall feeling close to those with whom you shared the predicament. Perhaps previous social barriers were dropped as you helped one another dig out of the snow or struggled to cope with your common enemy.

Such friendliness is common among those who experience a shared threat. John Lanzetta (1955) observed this when he put four-man groups of naval ROTC cadets to work on problem-solving tasks and then began informing them over a loudspeaker that their answers were wrong, their productivity inexcusably low, their thinking stupid. Other groups did not receive this harassment. Lanzetta observed that the group members under duress became friendlier to one another, more cooperative, less argumentative, less competitive. They were in it together. And the result was a cohesive spirit.

Having a common enemy unified the groups of competing boys in Sherif's camping experiments—and in many subsequent experiments (Dion, 1979). Times of interracial strife similarly heighten group pride. For Chinese university students in Toronto, facing discrimination heightens a sense of kinship with other Chinese (Pak & others, 1991). Just being reminded of an outgroup (say, a rival school) heightens people's responsiveness to their own group (Wilder & Shapiro, 1984). When keenly conscious of who "they" are, we also know who "we" are.

During wartimes against a well-defined external threat, we-feeling soars. The membership of civic organizations mushrooms (Putnam, 2000). Citizens unite behind their leader and support their troops. This was dramatically evident after the catastrophe of 9/11 and the threats of further terrorist attacks. In New York City, "old racial antagonisms have dissolved," reported the *New York Times*, at least for a while (Sengupta, 2001). "I just thought of myself as Black," said 18-year-old Louis Johnson, reflecting on life before 9/11. "But now I feel like I'm an American, more than ever." One sampling of conversation on 9/11, and another of New York Mayor Giuliani's press conferences before and after 9/11, found a doubled rate of the word "we" (Liehr & others, 2004; Pennebaker & Lay, 2002).

George W. Bush's job performance ratings reflected this threat-bred spirit of unity. Just before 9/11, a mere 51 percent of Americans approved of his presidential performance. Just after, an exceptional 90 percent approved. In the public eye, the mediocre president of 9/10 had become the exalted president of 10/10—"our leader" in the fight against "those who hate us." Thereafter, his ratings gradually declined but then jumped again as the war against Iraq began. When Sheldon Solomon and his colleagues (2004) asked American students to reflect on the events of 9/11 (rather than on an upcoming exam), they become more likely to agree that "I endorse the actions of President Bush and the members of his administration who have taken bold action in Iraq."

Superordinate Goals

Closely related to the unifying power of an external threat is the unifying power of **superordinate goals,** goals that unite all in a group and require cooperative effort. To promote harmony among his warring campers, Sherif introduced such goals. He created a problem with the camp water supply, necessitating both groups' cooperation to restore the water. Given an opportunity to rent a movie, one expensive enough to require the joint resources of both groups, they again cooperated. When a truck "broke down" on a camping trip, a staff member casually left the tug-of-war rope nearby, prompting one boy to suggest that they all pull the truck to get it started. When it started, a backslapping celebration ensued over their victorious "tug-of-war against the truck."

After working together to achieve such superordinate goals, the boys ate together and enjoyed themselves around a campfire. Friendships sprouted across group lines. Hostilities plummeted. On the last day, the boys decided to travel home together on one bus. During the trip they no longer sat by groups. As the bus approached Oklahoma City and home, they, as one, spontaneously sang "Oklahoma" and then bade their friends farewell. With isolation and competition, Sherif made strangers into bitter enemies. With superordinate goals, he made enemies into friends.

Are Sherif's experiments mere child's play? Or can pulling together to achieve superordinate goals be similarly beneficial with adults in conflict? Robert Blake and Jane Mouton (1979) wondered. So in a series of two-week experiments involving more than 1,000 executives in 150 different groups, they re-created the essential features of the situation experienced by the Rattlers and Eagles. Each group first engaged in activities by itself, then competed with another group, and then cooperated with the other group in working toward jointly chosen superordinate goals. Their results provided "unequivocal evidence that adult reactions parallel those of Sherif's younger subjects."

Extending these findings, Samuel Gaertner, John Dovidio, and their collaborators (1993, 2000) report that working cooperatively has especially favorable effects under conditions that lead people to define a new, inclusive group that dissolves their former subgroups. Old feelings of bias against another group diminish when members of the two groups sit alternately around a table (rather than on opposite sides), give their new group a single name, and then work together under conditions that foster a good mood. "Us" and "them" become "we."

Cooperative Learning

So far we have noted the apparently meager social benefits of typical school desegregation (especially if unaccompanied by the emotional bonds of friendship and by equal-status relationships). And we have noted the apparently dramatic social benefits of successful, cooperative contacts between members of rival groups. Could putting these two findings together suggest a constructive alternative to traditional desegregation practices? Several independent research teams speculated yes. Each wondered whether, without compromising academic achievement, we could promote interracial friendships by replacing competitive learning situations with cooperative ones. Given the diversity of their methods—all involving students on integrated study teams, sometimes in competition with other teams—the results are striking and very heartening.

Video
29.1

One research team, led by Elliot Aronson (1978, 2000, 2002; Aronson & Gonzalez, 1988), elicited similar group cooperation with a "jigsaw" technique. In experiments in Texas and California elementary schools, the researchers assigned children to racially and academically diverse six-member groups. The subject was then divided into six parts, with each student becoming the expert on his or her part. In a unit on Chile, one student might be the expert on Chile's history, another on its geography, another on its culture. First, the various " historians," "geographers," and so forth, got together to master their material. Then they returned to the home groups to teach it to their classmates. Each group member held, so to speak, a piece of the jigsaw. The self-confident students therefore had to listen to and learn from the reticent students, who in turn soon realized they had something important to offer their peers.

With cooperative learning, students learn not only the material but other lessons as well. Cross-racial friendships also begin to blossom. The exam scores of minority students improve (perhaps because academic achievement is now peer-supported). After the experiments are over, many teachers continue using cooperative learning (D. W. Johnson & others, 1981; Slavin, 1990). "It is clear," wrote race-relations expert John McConahay (1981), that cooperative learning "is the most effective practice for improving race relations in desegregated schools that we know of to date."

So, cooperative, equal-status contacts exert a positive influence on boy campers, industrial executives, college students, and schoolchildren. Does the principle extend to all levels of human relations? Are families unified by pulling together to farm the land, restore an old house, or sail a sloop? Are communal identities forged by barn raisings, group singing, or cheering on the football team? Is international understanding bred by international collaboration in science and space, by joint efforts to feed the world and conserve resources, by friendly personal contacts between people of different nations? Indications are that the answer to all these questions is yes (Brewer & Miller, 1988; Desforges & others, 1991, 1997; Deutsch, 1985, 1994). Thus an important challenge facing our divided world is to identify and agree on our superordinate goals and to structure cooperative efforts to achieve them.

*C*OMMUNICATION

Conflicting parties have other ways to resolve their differences. When husband and wife, or labor and management, or nation X and nation Y disagree, they can **bargain** with one another directly. They can ask a third party to **mediate** by making suggestions and facilitating their negotiations. Or they can **arbitrate** by submitting their disagreement to someone who will study the issues and impose a settlement.

Bargaining

If you want to buy or sell a new car, are you better off adopting a tough bargaining stance—opening with an extreme offer so that splitting the difference will yield a favorable result? Or are you better off beginning with a sincere "good-faith" offer?

Experiments suggest no simple answer. On the one hand, those who demand more will often get more. Tough bargaining may lower the other party's expectations, making the other side willing to settle for less (Yukl, 1974). But toughness can sometimes backfire. Many a conflict is not over a pie of fixed size but over a pie that shrinks if the conflict continues. Yet often negotiators fail to realize their common interests and about 20 percent of the time negotiate "lose-lose" agreements that are mutually costly (Thompson & Hrebec, 1996).

Delayed agreements can be costly. When a strike is prolonged, both labor and management lose. Being tough can also diminish the chances of actually reaching an agreement. If the other party responds with an equally extreme stance, both may be locked into positions from which neither can back down without losing face. In the weeks before the 1991 Persian Gulf War, President Bush threatened, in the full glare of publicity, to "kick Saddam's ass." Saddam Hussein, no less macho, threatened to make "infidel" Americans "swim in their own blood." After such belligerent statements, it was difficult for each side to evade war and save face. If face-saving had been implemented, perhaps negotiations could have averted war.

Mediation

A third-party mediator may offer suggestions that enable conflicting parties to make concessions and still save face (Pruitt, 1998). If my concession can be attributed to a mediator, who is gaining an equal concession from my antagonist, then neither of us will be viewed as weakly caving in to the other's demands.

Turning Win-Lose into Win-Win

Mediators also help resolve conflicts by facilitating constructive communication. Their first task is to help the parties rethink the conflict and gain information about others' interests (Thompson, 1998). Typically, people on both sides have a competitive "win-lose" orientation: They are successful if their opponent is unhappy with the result, and unsuccessful if their opponent is pleased (Thompson & others, 1995). The mediator aims to replace this win-lose orientation with a cooperative "win-win" orientation, by prodding both sides to set aside their conflicting demands and instead to think about each other's underlying needs, interests, and goals. In experiments, Leigh Thompson (1990a, 1990b) found that, with experience, negotiators become better able to make mutually beneficial trade-offs and thus to achieve win-win resolutions.

A classic story of such a resolution concerns the two sisters who quarreled over an orange (Follett, 1940). Finally they compromised and split the orange in half, whereupon one sister squeezed her half for juice while the other used the peel to make a cake. In experiments at the State University of New York at Buffalo, Dean Pruitt and his associates induced bargainers to search for **integrative agreements** (Johnson & Johnson, 2003; Pruitt & Lewis, 1975, 1977). If the sisters had agreed to split the orange, giving one sister all the juice and the other all the peel, they would have hit on such an agreement, one that integrates both parties' interests. Compared with compromises, in which each party sacrifices something important, integrative agreements are more enduring. Because they are mutually rewarding, they also lead to better ongoing relationships (Pruitt, 1986).

Unraveling Misperceptions with Controlled Communications
Communication often helps reduce self-fulfilling misperceptions. Perhaps you can recall experiences similar to that of this college student:

> Often, after a prolonged period of little communication, I perceive Martha's silence as a sign of her dislike for me. She, in turn, thinks that my quietness is a result of my being mad at her. My silence induces her silence, which makes me even more silent . . . until this snowballing effect is broken by some occurrence that makes it necessary for us to interact. And the communication then unravels all the misinterpretations we had made about one another.

The outcome of such conflicts often depends on *how* people communicate their feelings to one another. Roger Knudson and his colleagues (1980) invited married couples to come to the University of Illinois psychology laboratory and relive, through role-playing, one of their past conflicts. Before, during, and after their conversation (which often generated as much emotion as the actual previous conflict), the couples were observed closely and questioned. Couples who evaded the issue—by failing to make their positions clear or failing to acknowledge their spouse's position—left with the illusion that they were more in harmony and agreement than they really were. Often, they came to believe they now agreed more when actually they agreed less. In contrast, those who engaged the issue—by making their positions clear and by taking one another's views into account—achieved more actual agreement and gained more accurate information about one another's perceptions. That helps explain why couples who communicate their concerns directly and openly are usually happily married (Grush & Glidden, 1987).

Conflict researchers report that a key factor is *trust* (Ross & Ward, 1995). If you believe the other person is well intentioned, you are then more likely to divulge your needs and concerns. Lacking trust, you may fear that being open will give the other party information that might be used against you.

When the two parties mistrust each other and communicate unproductively, a third-party mediator—a marriage counselor, a labor mediator, a diplomat—sometimes helps. Often the mediator is someone trusted by both sides. In the 1980s it took an Algerian Muslim to mediate the conflict between Iran and Iraq, and the pope to resolve a geographical dispute between Argentina and Chile (Carnevale & Choi, 2000).

After coaxing the conflicting parties to rethink their perceived win-lose conflict, the mediator often has each party identify and rank its goals. When goals are compatible, the ranking procedure makes it easier for each to concede on less important goals so that both achieve their chief goals (Erickson & others, 1974; Schulz & Pruitt, 1978). South Africa achieved internal peace when Black and White South Africans granted each other's top priorities—replacing apartheid with majority rule and safeguarding the security, welfare, and rights of Whites (Kelman, 1998).

Once labor and management both believe that management's goal of higher productivity and profit is compatible with labor's goal of better wages and working conditions, they can begin to work for an integrative win-win solution.

When the parties then convene to communicate directly, they are usually *not* set loose in the hope that, eyeball to eyeball, the conflict will resolve itself. In the midst of a threatening, stressful conflict, emotions often disrupt the ability to understand the other party's point of view. Communication may become most difficult just when it is most needed (Tetlock, 1985). The mediator will therefore often structure the encounter to help each party understand and feel understood by the other. The mediator may ask the conflicting parties to restrict their arguments to statements of fact, including statements of how they feel and how they respond when the other acts in a given way: "I enjoy music. But when you play it loud, I find it hard to concentrate. That makes me crabby." Also, the mediator may ask people to reverse roles and argue the other's position or to imagine and explain what the other person is experiencing. (Experiments show that inducing empathy decreases stereotyping and increases cooperation—Batson & Moran, 1999; Galinsky & Moskowitz, 2000.) Or the mediator may have them restate one another's positions before replying with their own: "My turning up the stereo bugs you."

Neutral third parties may also suggest mutually agreeable proposals that would be dismissed—"reactively devalued"—if offered by either side. Constance Stillinger and her colleagues (1991) found that a nuclear disarmament proposal that Americans dismissed when attributed to the former Soviet Union seemed more acceptable when attributed to a neutral third party. Likewise, people will often reactively devalue a concession offered by an adversary ("they must not value it"); the same concession may seem more than a token gesture when suggested by a third party.

These peacemaking principles, based partly on laboratory experiments, partly on practical experience, have helped mediate both international and industrial conflicts (Blake & Mouton, 1962, 1979; Fisher, 1994; Wehr, 1979). One small team of Arab and Jewish Americans, led by social psychologist Herbert Kelman (1997), has conducted workshops bringing together influential Arabs and Israelis. Another social psychologist team, led by Ervin Staub and Laurie Ann Pearlman (2004), worked in Rwanda between 1999 and 2003 by training facilitators and journalists to understand and write about Rwanda's traumas in ways that promote healing and reconciliation. Using methods such as those we've considered, Kelman and colleagues counter misperceptions and have participants seek creative solutions for their common good. Isolated, the participants are free to speak directly to their adversaries without fear that their constituents are second-guessing what they are saying. The result? Those from both sides typically come to understand the other's perspective and how the other side responds to their own group's actions.

Arbitration

Some conflicts are so intractable, the underlying interests so divergent, that a mutually satisfactory resolution is unattainable. In Bosnia and Kosovo, both Serbs and Muslims could not have jurisdiction over the same homelands. In a divorce dispute over custody of a child, both parents cannot enjoy full custody. In these and many other cases (disputes over tenants' repair bills, athletes' wages, and national territories), a third-party mediator may—or may not—help resolve the conflict.

If not, the parties may turn to *arbitration* by having the mediator or another third party *impose* a settlement. Disputants usually prefer to settle their differences without arbitration, so they retain control over the outcome. Neil McGillicuddy and others (1987) observed this preference in an experiment involving disputants coming to a dispute settlement center. When people knew they would face an arbitrated settlement if mediation failed, they tried harder to resolve the problem, exhibited less hostility, and thus were more likely to reach agreement.

In cases where differences seem large and irreconcilable, the prospect of arbitration may cause the disputants to freeze their positions, hoping to gain an advantage when the arbitrator chooses a compromise. To combat this tendency, some disputes, such as those involving salaries of individual baseball players, are settled with "final-offer arbitration" in which the third party chooses one of the two final offers. Final-offer arbitration motivates each party to make a reasonable proposal.

Typically, however, the final offer is not as reasonable as it would be if each party, free of self-serving bias, saw its own proposal through others' eyes. Negotiation researchers report that most disputants are made stubborn by "optimistic overconfidence" (Kahneman & Tversky, 1995). Successful mediation is hindered when, as often happens, both parties believe they have a two-thirds chance of winning a final-offer arbitration (Bazerman, 1986, 1990).

C ONCILIATION

Sometimes tension and suspicion run so high that communication, much less resolution, becomes all but impossible. Each party may threaten, coerce, or retaliate against the other. Unfortunately, such acts tend to be reciprocated, escalating the conflict. So, would a strategy of appeasing the other party by being unconditionally cooperative produce a satisfying result? Often not. In laboratory games, those who are 100 percent cooperative often get exploited. Politically, a one-sided pacifism is usually out of the question anyway.

Social psychologist Charles Osgood (1962, 1980) advocated a third alternative, one that is conciliatory, yet strong enough to discourage exploitation. Osgood called it "graduated and reciprocated initiatives in tension reduction." He nicknamed it **GRIT,** a label that suggests the determination it requires. GRIT aims to reverse the "conflict spiral" by triggering reciprocal de-escalation. GRIT requires one side to initiate a few small de-escalatory actions, after *announcing a conciliatory intent.* The initiator states its desire to reduce tension, declares each conciliatory act prior to making it, and invites the adversary to reciprocate. Such announcements create a framework that helps the adversary correctly interpret what otherwise might be seen as weak or tricky actions. They also bring public pressure on the adversary to follow the reciprocity norm.

Next, the initiator establishes credibility and genuineness by carrying out, exactly as announced, several verifiable *conciliatory acts.* This intensifies the pressure to reciprocate. Making conciliatory acts diverse—perhaps offering medical information, closing a military base, and lifting a trade ban—keeps the initiator from making a significant sacrifice in any one area and leaves the adversary freer to choose its own means of reciprocation. If the adversary reciprocates voluntarily, its own conciliatory behavior may soften its attitudes.

GRIT *is* conciliatory. But it is not "surrender on the installment plan." The remaining aspects of the plan protect each side's self-interest by *maintaining retaliatory capability.* The initial conciliatory steps entail some small risk but do not jeopardize either one's security; rather, they are calculated to begin edging both sides down the tension ladder. If one side takes an aggressive action, the other side reciprocates in kind, making clear it will not tolerate exploitation. Yet the reciprocal act is not an overresponse that would re-escalate the conflict. If the adversary offers its own conciliatory acts, these, too, are matched or even slightly exceeded. Morton Deutsch (1993) captures the spirit of GRIT in advising negotiators to be "'firm, fair, and friendly': *firm* in resisting intimidation, exploitation, and dirty tricks; *fair* in holding to one's moral principles and not reciprocating the other's immoral behavior despite his or her provocations; and *friendly* in the sense that one is willing to initiate and reciprocate cooperation."

Does GRIT really work? In laboratory dilemma games a successful strategy has proved to be simple "tit-for-tat," which similarly begins with a cooperative opening play and thereafter matches the other party's last response (Axelrod & Dion, 1988; Parks & Rumble, 2001; Van Lange & Visser, 1999). Although initially friendly, tit-for-tat immediately punishes noncooperation but also immediately forgives wayward opponents who again cooperate. In a lengthy series of experiments at Ohio University, Svenn Lindskold and his associates (1976 to 1988) found "strong support for the various steps in the GRIT proposal." In laboratory games, announcing cooperative intent *does* boost cooperation. Repeated conciliatory acts *do* breed greater trust (although self-serving biases often make one's own acts seem more conciliatory and less hostile than those of the adversary). Maintaining an equality of power *does* protect against exploitation.

GRIT-like strategies have occasionally been tried outside the laboratory with promising results. To many, the most significant attempt at GRIT was the so-called Kennedy experiment (Etzioni, 1967). On June 10, 1963, President Kennedy gave a major speech, "A Strategy for Peace." He noted that "Our problems are man-made . . . and can be solved by man," and then announced his first conciliatory act: The United States was stopping all atmospheric nuclear tests and would not resume them unless another country did. In the former Soviet Union, Kennedy's speech was published in full. Five days later Premier Khrushchev reciprocated, announcing he had halted production of strategic bombers. There soon followed further reciprocal gestures: The United States agreed to sell wheat to Russia, the Russians agreed to a "hot line" between the two countries, and the two countries soon achieved a test-ban treaty. For a time, these conciliatory initiatives warmed relations between the two countries.

Might conciliatory efforts also help reduce tension between individuals? There is every reason to expect so. When a relationship is strained and communication nonexistent, it sometimes takes only a conciliatory gesture—a soft answer, a warm smile, a gentle touch—for both parties to begin easing down the tension ladder, to a rung where contact, cooperation, and communication again become possible.

C ONCEPTS TO REMEMBER

equal-status contact Contact on an equal basis. Just as a relationship between people of unequal status breeds attitudes consistent with their relationship, so do relationships between those of equal status. Thus, to reduce prejudice, interracial contact should be between persons equal in status.

superordinate goal A shared goal that necessitates cooperative effort; a goal that overrides people's differences from one another.

bargaining Seeking an agreement to a conflict through direct negotiation between parties.

mediation An attempt by a neutral third party to resolve a conflict by facilitating communication and offering suggestions.

arbitration Resolution of a conflict by a neutral third party who studies both sides and imposes a settlement.

integrative agreements Win-win agreements that reconcile both parties' interests to their mutual benefit.

GRIT Acronym for "*g*raduated and *r*eciprocated *i*nitiatives in *t*ension reduction"—a strategy designed to de-escalate international tensions.

30

❖

When Do People Help?

On March 13, 1964, bar manager Kitty Genovese was set upon by a knife-wielding attacker as she returned to her Queens, New York, apartment house at 3:00 A.M. Her screams of terror and pleas for help—"Oh my God, he stabbed me! Please help me! Please help me!"—aroused 38 of her neighbors. Many came to their windows and caught fleeting glimpses as the attacker left and returned to attack again. Not until her attacker finally departed did anyone call the police. Soon after, she died.

Eleanor Bradley tripped and broke her leg while shopping. Dazed and in pain, she pleaded for help. For 40 minutes, the stream of shoppers simply parted and flowed around her. Finally, a cab driver helped her to a doctor (Darley & Latané, 1968). Or would we be heroes, like Everett Sanderson? Hearing the rumble of an approaching New York subway train, Everett Sanderson leapt down onto the tracks and raced toward the approaching headlights to rescue Michelle De Jesus, a 4-year-old who had fallen from the platform. Three seconds before the train would have run her over, Sanderson flung Michelle into the crowd above. As the train roared in, he himself failed in his first effort to jump back to the platform. At the last instant, bystanders pulled him to safety (Young, 1977).

Or consider the hillside in Jerusalem where hundreds of trees form the Garden of the Righteous Among the Nations. Beneath each tree is a plaque with the name of a European Christian who gave refuge to one or more Jews during the Nazi Holocaust. These "righteous Gentiles" knew that if the refugees were discovered, Nazi policy dictated that both host and refugee would suffer a common fate. Many did (Hellman, 1980; Wiesel, 1985).

On 9/11 and in the days that followed, one coordinated act of evil triggered innumerable acts of kindness. Multitudes of people overwhelmed
blood banks, food banks, and clothing banks, hoping to give something
from their hearts that spoke to the hearts and needs of those devastated.
Some were self-sacrificially altruistic. After the World Trade Center's North
Tower was struck, Ed Emery gathered five Fiduciary Trust colleagues on
the South Tower's 90th floor, escorted them down 12 floors, got them on a
packed express elevator, let the door close in front of him, and then headed
back up to the 97th floor, hoping to evacuate six more colleagues who were
backing up the computers. Alas, when moments later his own building was
struck beneath him, his fate was sealed. Nearby, his colleague Edward
McNally was thinking of how, in his last moments, he could help his loved
ones. As the floor began buckling, he called his wife, Liz, and recited life
insurance work policies and bonuses. "He said I meant the world to him,
and he loved me," Mrs. McNally later recalled as they seemingly
exchanged their final goodbyes (*New York Times*, 2002). But her phone rang
one more time. McNally sheepishly reported he had booked them a trip to
Rome for her 40th birthday. "Liz, you have to cancel that."

Less dramatic acts of comforting, caring, and compassion abound:
Without asking anything in return, people offer directions, donate money,
give blood, volunteer time. Why, and when, will people help? What can
be done to lessen indifference and increase helping?

Activity
30.1

Altruism is selfishness in reverse. An altruistic person is concerned
and helpful even when no benefits are offered or expected in return.
Jesus' parable of the Good Samaritan provides the classic illustration:

> A man was going down from Jerusalem to Jericho, and fell into the hands
> of robbers, who stripped him, beat him, and went away, leaving him half
> dead. Now by chance a priest was going down that road; and when he
> saw him, he passed by on the other side. So likewise a Levite, when he
> came to the place and saw him, passed by on the other side. But a Samar-
> itan while traveling came near him; and when he saw him, he was moved
> with pity. He went to him and bandaged his wounds, having poured oil
> and wine on them. Then he put him on his own animal, brought him to
> an inn, and took care of him. The next day he took out two denarii, gave
> them to the innkeeper, and said, "Take care of him; and when I come
> back, I will repay you whatever more you spend." (Luke 10:30–35)

The Samaritan illustrates altruism. Filled with compassion, he is
motivated to give a stranger time, energy, and money while expecting
neither repayment nor appreciation.

WHY DO PEOPLE HELP?

What motivates altruism? One idea, called **social-exchange theory,** is
that we help after doing a cost-benefit analysis. As part of an exchange
of benefits, helpers aim to maximize their rewards and minimize their

costs. When donating blood, we weigh the costs (the inconvenience and discomfort) against the benefits (the social approval and noble feeling). If the anticipated rewards exceed the costs, we help.

You might object: Social-exchange theory takes the selflessness out of altruism. It seems to imply that a helpful act is never genuinely altruistic; we merely call it "altruistic" when the rewards are inconspicuous. If we know people are tutoring only to alleviate guilt or gain social approval, we hardly credit them for a good deed. We laud people for their altruism only when we can't otherwise explain it.

From babyhood onward, however, people sometimes exhibit a natural empathy, by feeling distress when seeing someone in distress and relief when their suffering ends. Loving parents (unlike child abusers and other perpetrators of cruelty) suffer when their children suffer and rejoice over their children's joys (Miller & Eisenberg, 1988). Although some helpful acts are indeed done to gain rewards or relieve guilt, experiments suggest that other helpful acts aim simply to increase another's welfare, producing satisfaction for oneself merely as a by-product (Batson, 1991). In these experiments, empathy often produces helping only when helpgivers believe the other will actually receive the needed help and regardless of whether the recipient knows who helped.

Social norms also motivate helping. They prescribe how we *ought* to behave. We learn the **reciprocity norm**—that we should return help to those who have helped us. Thus we expect that those who receive favors (gifts, invitations, help) should later return them. The reciprocity norm is qualified by our awareness that some people are incapable of reciprocal giving and receiving. Thus we also feel a **social-responsibility norm**—that we should help those who really need it, without regard to future exchanges. When we pick up the dropped books for the person on crutches, we expect nothing in return.

These suggested reasons for helping make biological sense. The empathy that parents feel for their children and other relatives promotes the survival of their shared genes. Likewise, say evolutionary psychologists, reciprocal altruism in small groups boosts everyone's survival.

WHEN DO PEOPLE HELP?

Social psychologists were curious and concerned about bystanders' lack of involvement during such events as the Kitty Genovese murder. So they undertook experiments to identify when people will help in an emergency. Then they broadened the question to, Who is likely to help in nonemergencies—by such deeds as giving money, donating blood, or contributing time? Among their answers: Helping often increases among people who are

- feeling guilty, thus providing a way to relieve the guilt or restore self-image;
- in a good mood; or
- deeply religious (evidenced by higher rates of charitable giving and volunteerism).

Social psychologists also study the *circumstances* that enhance helpfulness. The odds of our helping someone increase in these circumstances:

- We have just observed a helpful model.
- We are not hurried.
- The victim appears to need and deserve help.
- The victim is similar to ourselves.
- We are in a small town or rural area.
- There are few other bystanders.

NUMBER OF BYSTANDERS

Bystander passivity during emergencies has prompted social commentators to lament people's "alienation," "apathy," "indifference," and "unconscious sadistic impulses." By attributing the nonintervention to the bystanders' dispositions, we can reassure ourselves that, as caring people, we would have helped. But were the bystanders such inhuman characters?

Social psychologists Bibb Latané and John Darley (1970) were unconvinced. They staged ingenious emergencies and found that a single situational factor—the presence of other bystanders—greatly decreased intervention. By 1980, four dozen experiments had compared help given by bystanders who perceived themselves to be either alone or with others. In about 90 percent of these comparisons, involving nearly 6,000 people, lone bystanders were more likely to help (Latané & Nida, 1981).

Sometimes, the victim was actually less likely to get help when many people were around. When Latané and Dabbs (1975), and 145 collaborators "accidentally" dropped coins or pencils during 1,497 elevator rides, they were helped 40 percent of the time when one other person was on the elevator and less than 20 percent of the time when there were six passengers. Why do other bystanders sometimes inhibit helping? Latané and Darley surmised that as the number of bystanders increases, any given bystander is less likely to *notice* the incident, less likely to *interpret* the incident as a problem or emergency, and less likely to *assume responsibility* for taking action (Figure 30-1).

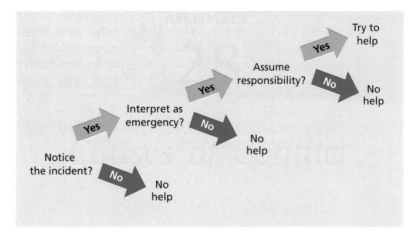

FIGURE 30-1
Latané and Darley's decision tree. Only one path up the tree leads to helping. At each fork of the path, the presence of other bystanders may divert a person down a branch toward not helping. **Source:** Adapted from Darley & Latané, 1968.

Noticing

Twenty minutes after Eleanor Bradley has fallen and broken her leg on a crowded city sidewalk, you come along. Your eyes are on the backs of the pedestrians in front of you (it is bad manners to stare at those you pass) and your private thoughts are on the day's events. Would you therefore be less likely to notice the injured woman than if the sidewalk were virtually deserted?

To find out, Latané and Darley (1968) had Columbia University men fill out a questionnaire in a room, either by themselves or with two strangers. While they were working (and being observed through a one-way mirror), there was a staged emergency: Smoke poured into the room through a wall vent. Solitary students, who often glanced idly about the room while working, noticed the smoke almost immediately—usually in less than 5 seconds. Those in groups kept their eyes on their work. It typically took them about 20 seconds to notice the smoke.

Interpreting

Once we notice an ambiguous event, we must interpret it. Put yourself in the room filling with smoke. Though worried, you don't want to embarrass yourself by appearing flustered. You glance at the others. They look calm, indifferent. Assuming everything must be okay, you shrug it off and go back to work. Then one of the others notices the smoke and, noting your

apparent unconcern, reacts similarly. This is yet another example of informational influence. Each person uses others' behavior as clues to reality.

So it happened in Latané and Darley's experiment. When those working alone noticed the smoke, they usually hesitated a moment, then got up,
walked over to the vent, felt, sniffed, and waved at the smoke, hesitated
again, and then went to report it. In dramatic contrast, those in groups of
three did not move. Among the 24 men in eight groups, only one person
reported the smoke within the first four minutes (Figure 30-2). By the end
of the six-minute experiment, the smoke was so thick it was obscuring
the men's vision and they were rubbing their eyes and coughing. Still,
in only three of the eight groups did even a single person leave to report
the problem.

Equally interesting, the group's passivity affected its members' interpretations. What caused the smoke? "A leak in the air conditioning."
"Chemistry labs in the building." "Steam pipes." "Truth gas." Not one
said, "Fire." The group members, by serving as nonresponsive models,
influenced one another's interpretation of the situation.

This experimental dilemma parallels dilemmas we all face. Are the
shrieks outside merely playful antics or the desperate screams of someone being assaulted? Is the boys' scuffling a friendly tussle or a vicious
fight? Is the person slumped in the doorway sleeping, high on drugs, or

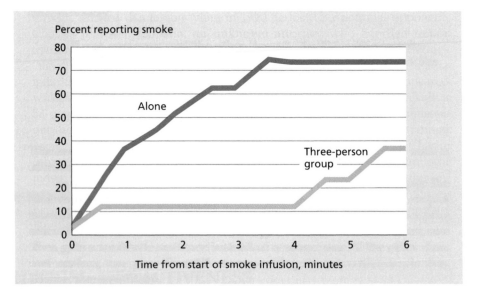

FIGURE 30-2
The smoke-filled room experiment. Smoke pouring into the testing room was much
more likely to be reported by individuals working alone than by three-person
groups. **Source:** Data from Darley & Latané, 1968.

seriously ill, perhaps in a diabetic coma? That surely was the question confronting those who passed by Sidney Brookins (AP, 1993). Brookins, who had suffered a concussion when beaten, died after lying near the door to a Minneapolis apartment house for two days. That may also have been the question for those who in 2003 watched Brandon Vedas overdose and die online. As his life ebbed, his audience, which was left to wonder whether he was putting on an act, failed to decipher available clues to his whereabouts and to contact police (Nichols, 2003).

Assuming Responsibility

Misinterpretation is not the only cause of **bystander effect** (the inaction of strangers faced with ambiguous emergencies). What about those times when an emergency is obvious? Those who saw and heard Kitty Genovese's pleas for help correctly interpreted what was happening. But the lights and silhouetted figures in neighboring windows told them that others were also watching. This diffused the responsibility for action.

Few of us have observed a murder. But all of us have at times been slower to react to a need when others were present. Passing a stranded motorist on a highway, we are less likely to offer help than on a country road. To explore bystander inaction in clear emergencies, Darley and Latané (1968) simulated the Genovese drama. They placed people in separate rooms from which the participants would hear a victim crying for help. To create this situation, Darley and Latané asked some New York University students to discuss their problems with university life over a laboratory intercom. The researchers told the students that to guarantee their anonymity, no one would be visible, nor would the experimenter eavesdrop. During the ensuing discussion, when the experimenter turned his microphone on, the participants heard one person lapse into a seizure. With increasing intensity and speech difficulty, he pleaded for someone to help.

Of those led to believe there were no other listeners, 85 percent left their room to seek help. Of those who believed four others also overheard the victim, only 31 percent went for help. Were those who didn't respond apathetic and indifferent? When the experimenter came in to end the experiment, she did not find this response. Most immediately expressed concern. Many had trembling hands and sweating palms. They believed an emergency had occurred but were undecided whether to act.

After the smoke-filled room, the woman-in-distress, and the seizure experiments, Latané and Darley asked the participants whether the presence of others had influenced them. We know the others had a dramatic effect. Yet the participants almost invariably denied the influence. They typically replied, "I was aware of the others, but I would have reacted just the same if they weren't there." This response reinforces a familiar point: *We often do not know why we do what we do.* That is why experiments are revealing. A survey of uninvolved bystanders following a real emergency would have left the bystander effect hidden.

These experiments raise again the issue of research ethics. Is it right to force hundreds of subway riders to witness someone's apparent collapse? Were the researchers in the seizure experiment ethical when they forced people to decide whether to abort the discussion to report the problem? Would you object to being in such a study? Note that it would have been impossible to get your "informed consent"; doing so would have destroyed the cover for the experiment.

In defense of the researchers, they were always careful to debrief the laboratory participants. After explaining the seizure experiment, probably the most stressful, the experimenter gave the participants a questionnaire. One hundred percent said the deception was justified and that they would be willing to take part in similar experiments in the future. None reported feeling angry at the experimenter. Other researchers confirm that the overwhelming majority of participants in such experiments say that their participation was both instructive and ethically justified (Schwartz & Gottlieb, 1981). In field experiments, such as the one in the subway car, an accomplice assisted the victim if no one else did, thus reassuring bystanders that the problem was being dealt with.

Remember that the social psychologist has a twofold ethical obligation: to protect the participants and to enhance human welfare by discovering influences upon human behavior. Such discoveries can alert us to unwanted influences and show us how we might exert positive influences. The ethical principle seems to be: After protecting participants' welfare, social psychologists fulfill their responsibility to society by doing such research.

Will learning about the factors that inhibit altruism reduce their influence? Sometimes, such "enlightenment" is not our problem but one of our goals.

Experiments with University of Montana students by Arthur Beaman and his colleagues (1978) revealed that once people understand why the presence of bystanders inhibits helping, they become more likely to help in group situations. The researchers used a lecture to inform some students how bystander inaction can affect the interpretation of an emergency and feelings of responsibility. Other students heard either a different lecture or no lecture at all. Two weeks later, as part of a different experiment in a different location, the participants found themselves walking (with an unresponsive confederate) past someone slumped over or past a person sprawled beneath a bicycle. Of those who had not heard the helping lecture, one-fourth paused to offer help; twice as many of those "enlightened" did so.

Having read this module, you, too, perhaps have changed. As you come to understand what influences people's responses, will your attitudes and your behavior be the same? Coincidentally, shortly before I wrote the last paragraph, a former student, now living in Washington, D.C., stopped by. She mentioned that she recently found herself part of a stream of pedestrians striding past a man lying unconscious on the sidewalk. "It took my mind back to our social psych class and the accounts of why people fail to help in such situations. Then I thought, 'Well, if I just walk by, too, who's going to help him?'" So she made a call to an emergency help number and waited with the victim—and other bystanders who now joined her—until help arrived.

So, how will learning about social influences upon good and evil affect you? Will the knowledge you've gained affect your actions? I hope so.

CONCEPTS TO REMEMBER

altruism   A motive to increase another's welfare without conscious regard for one's self-interests.

social-exchange theory   The theory that human interactions are transactions that aim to maximize one's rewards and minimize one's costs.

reciprocity norm   An expectation that people will help, not hurt, those who have helped them.

social-responsibility norm   An expectation that people will help those dependent upon them.

bystander effect   The finding that a person is less likely to provide help when there are other bystanders.

31

❖

The Social Psychology of Sustainability

Can we move nations and people in the direction of sustainability? Such a move would be a modification of society comparable in scale to only two other changes: the Agricultural Revolution and the Industrial Revolution of the past two centuries. Those revolutions were gradual, spontaneous, and largely unconscious. This one will have to be a fully conscious operation. . . . If we actually do it, the undertaking will be absolutely unique in humanity's stay on the Earth.

—William D. Ruckelshaus

Former Environmental Protection Agency director

"Toward a Sustainable World," 1989

Activity
31.1

L ife is good. Today we enjoy luxuries unknown even to royalty in centuries past—hot showers, flush toilets, microwave ovens, jet travel, wintertime fresh fruit, big screen television, e-mail, and Post-it notes. But on the horizon beyond the sunny skies, dark clouds are gathering. In scientific gatherings hosted by the United Nations, Britain's Royal Society, and the U.S. National Academy of Sciences, a consensus has emerged: Increasing population and increasing consumption have combined to overshoot the earth's ecological carrying capacity (Heap & Kent, 2000; Oskamp, 2000). We are spending our environmental capital, not just living off the interest.

In 1950, the earth carried 2.5 billion people and 50 million cars. Today it has more than 6 billion people and 10 times as many cars. If world economic growth enabled all countries to match Americans' present car ownership, the number of cars would multiply yet another 13 times over (N. Myers, 2000). These cars, along with the burning of coal and oil to generate electricity and heat homes, produce greenhouse gases that contribute to global warming. The five warmest years on record have occurred since 1998 (WMO, 2005). The polar icecaps are melting at an accelerating rate. So are mountain glaciers from the Alps to the Andes.

In the Arctic, the air temperature is increasing, the permafrost is thawing, the trees and shrubs are invading the tundra, the icecaps are melting, the glaciers are shrinking, and the sea is encroaching on villages (Sturm & others, 2003). Elsewhere, birds are breeding earlier in the spring, flowering plants are climbing Alpine mountains, and butterflies are migrating northward (Kennedy, 2002). With the changing climate, extreme atmospheric events, including hurricanes, heat waves, droughts, and floods, are becoming more common. As precipitation falls more as rain, and less as snow, the likely result will be more floods in rainy seasons and less melting snow and glaciers for rivers during dry seasons.

With consumption and population both destined to increase (despite falling birthrates), further resource depletion and global warming seems inevitable. Thus, the need for more sustainable consumption has taken on "urgency and global significance" (Heap & Kent, 2000). The simple, stubborn fact is that the earth cannot indefinitely support our present consumption, much less the expected increase in consumption. For our species to survive and flourish, some things must change.

If global warming is occurring, if it is a potential weapon of mass destruction, and if, as most scientists presume, it results primarily from human-produced greenhouse gases, then why is global warming not a hotter topic? Why, ask environmentalists, do we spend $200 billion to protect ourselves against Iraq's presumed weapons of mass destruction but not against more likely and globally consequential ones?

And why do only 28 percent of Americans worry a "great deal" about global warming? Is it, as Gallup researcher Lydia Saad (2003) believes, because on a chilly winter day "'global warming' may sound, well, appealing"? Might people be more concerned about averting "global heating"? Recall from earlier modules that labels matter. Whether we call those resisting the foreign occupation of their country "terrorists," "the guerrilla resistance," or "freedom fighters" colors our attitudes. Whether we describe someone who responds to others as "conforming" or as "sensitive" and "open" shapes our perceptions. Language shapes thought.

Resource depletion will also affect the human future. Most of the world's original forest cover has been taken down, and what remains in the tropics is being cleared for agriculture, livestock grazing, logging, and settlements. With deforestation comes diminished absorption of greenhouse gases and sometimes flooding, soil erosion, changing rainfall and temperature, and the decimation of many animal species.

A growing population's appetite for fish, together with ecosystem destruction, has also led to decreasing annual catches in 11 of 15 major oceanic fishing areas and in 7 in 10 major fish species (Karavellas, 2000; McGinn, 1998). Due in part to overfishing, stocks of wild salmon, Atlantic cod, haddock, herring, and other species have suffered major depletion.

ENABLING SUSTAINABLE LIVING

So, what shall we do? Eat, drink, and be merry for tomorrow is doom? Behave as have so many participants in prisoners' dilemma games, by pursuing self-interest to our collective detriment? ("Heck, on a global scale, my consumption is infinitesimal; it provides me pleasure at but a nominal cost to the world.") Wring our hands and vow never to bring children into a hurting world? Must fertility plus prosperity produce calamity?

Those more optimistic about the future see two routes to sustainable lifestyles: (a) increasing technological efficiency and agricultural productivity, and (b) moderating consumption and decreasing population.

Increasing Efficiency and Productivity

One route to a sustainable future is through improving eco-technologies. Already we have replaced many incandescent bulbs with cool fluorescent bulbs, replaced printed and delivered letters and catalogs with e-mail and e-commerce, and developed environmentally friendlier cars. Today's middle-aged adults drive cars that get twice the mileage and produce a twentieth the pollution of their first cars.

Plausible future technologies include diodes that emit light for 20 years without bulbs; ultrasound washing machines that consume no water, heat, or soap; reusable and compostable plastics; cars running on fuel cells that combine hydrogen and oxygen and produce water exhaust; extra-light materials stronger than steel; and roofs and roads that double as solar energy collectors (N. Myers, 2000).

Given the speed of innovation—who could have imagined today's world a century ago?—the future will surely bring solutions that we aren't yet imagining. Surely, say the optimists, the future will bring increased material well-being for more people requiring many fewer raw materials and much less polluting waste.

Reducing Consumption

The second route to a sustainable future is through reduced consumption. Instead of more people consuming and polluting more, a stable population will need to consume and pollute less.

Thanks to family planning efforts, the world's population growth rate has decelerated, especially in developed nations. Where food security has improved and women have become educated and empowered, birthrates have fallen. But even if birthrates everywhere instantly fell to replacement levels, the lingering momentum of population growth, fed by the bulge of younger humans, would continue for years to come.

Given that we have already overshot the earth's carrying capacity, individual consumption must also moderate. With our material appetites continually swelling—as people seek more CDs, more air conditioning, more holiday travel—what can be done to moderate consumption?

One way is through public policies that harness the motivating power of incentives. As a general rule, what we tax we get less of, what we reward we get more of. If our highways are jammed and our air polluted, we can create fast lanes that reward carpooling and penalize driving solo. We can build bike lanes and subsidize mass transportation, thus encouraging alternatives to cars. We can shift taxes to petrol, and reward recycling with a refundable deposit on soda cans and bottles.

Robert Frank (1999), an economist well-versed in social psychology, suggests how a socially responsible market economy might reward achievement while promoting more sustainable consumption. He proposes a progressive consumption tax that encourages savings and investment while increasing the price on nonessential luxury goods, such as the $18,500 Range Rover child's toy car. His proposal is simple: Tax people not on what they earn but on what they spend—which is their earnings minus their savings and perhaps their charity. The tax could be made progressive with ample exemptions for dependents and higher tax rates for the big spenders. Frank argues that a progressive consumption tax (beginning, say, with a 20 percent tax rate on annual consumption beyond $30,000 for a family of four and rising to 70 percent for consumption over $500,000) promises to moderate consumption. People who would have bought a BMW may now adjust, with no less happiness, down to a Mazda.

Support for such policies will require a shift in public consciousness not unlike that occurring during the 1960s civil rights movement and the 1970s women's movement. As the atmosphere warms and oil and other resources become scarce, such a shift is inevitable, eventually. Is there any hope that, before the crisis becomes acute, human priorities might shift from accumulating money to finding meaning, and from aggressive consumption to nurturing connections? Perhaps social psychology can help, by exposing our *materialism*, by informing people of the disconnect between *economic growth and human morale*, and by helping people understand *why materialism and money fail to satisfy*.

*T*HE SOCIAL PSYCHOLOGY OF MATERIALISM AND WEALTH

www.mhhe.com/myerssp

Activity
31.2

Does money buy happiness? Few of us would answer yes. But ask a different question—"Would a *little* more money make you a *little* happier?"—and many of us will smirk and nod. There is, we believe, some connection between wealth and well-being. That belief feeds what

Juliet Schor (1998) calls the "cycle of work and spend"—working more to buy more.

Increased Materialism

Although the earth asks that we live more lightly upon it, material-ism has surged, most clearly in the United States. According to one Gallup Poll (1990), 1 in 2 women, 2 in 3 men, and 4 in 5 people earn-ing more than $75,000 a year would like to be rich. Think of it as today's American dream: life, liberty, and the purchase of happiness.

Such materialism surged during the 1970s and 1980s. The most dra-matic evidence comes from the UCLA/American Council on Education annual survey of nearly a quarter million entering collegians. The pro-portion considering it "very important or essential" that they become "very well off financially," rose from 39 percent in 1970 to 74 percent in 2004 (Figure 31-1). These proportions virtually flip-flopped with those who considered it very important to "develop a meaningful philosophy of life." Materialism was up, spirituality down.

What a change in values. Among 19 listed objectives, new American collegians in most recent years have ranked becoming "very well off financially" number one. This outranks not only developing a life

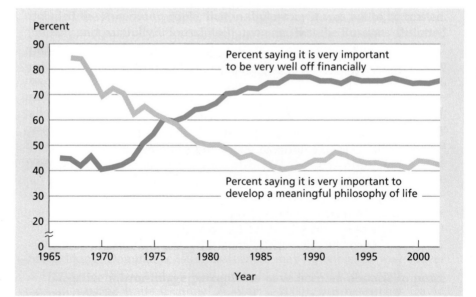

FIGURE 31-1

Changing materialism, from annual surveys of more than 2,000,000 entering U.S. collegians (total sample nearly 7 million students). **Source:** Data from Dey, Astin, & Korn, 1991, and their subsequent annual reports.

philosophy but also "becoming an authority in my own field," "helping others in difficulty," and "raising a family."

Wealth and Well-Being

Does sustainable consumption indeed enable "the good life"? Does being well-off produce—or at least correlate with—psychological well-being? Would people be happier if they could exchange a simple lifestyle for one with palatial surroundings, Alps ski vacations, and executive class travel? Would you be happier if you won a publishers' sweepstake and could choose from its suggested indulgences: a 40-foot yacht, deluxe motor home, designer wardrobe, luxury car, and private housekeeper? Social psychological theory and evidence offer some answers.

We can observe the traffic between wealth and well-being by asking, first, if *rich nations are happier*. There is, indeed, some correlation between national wealth and well-being (indexed as self-reported happiness and life satisfaction). The Scandinavians have been mostly prosperous and satisfied; the Bulgarians are neither. But early 1990s data revealed that once nations reached about $10,000 GNP per person, which was roughly the economic level of Ireland before its recent economic surge, higher levels of national wealth were not predictive of increased well-being. Better to be Irish than Bulgarian. But whether one was an average Irish person or west German (with double the Irish purchasing power) hardly mattered (Inglehart, 1990, 1997).

We can ask, second, whether within any given nation, *rich people are happier*. In poor countries, where low income threatens basic needs, being relatively well-off does predict greater well-being (Argyle, 1999). In affluent countries, where most can afford life's necessities, affluence matters less. Income increases and windfalls temporarily boost happiness, and recessions create short-term psychic losses (Di Tella, MacCulloch, & Oswald, 2001; Gardner & Oswald, 2001). But over time the emotions wane. Once comfortable, more and more money produces diminishing long-term returns. World values researcher Ronald Inglehart (1990, p. 242) therefore found the income-happiness correlation to be "surprisingly weak." David Lykken (1999, p. 17) illustrates: "People who go to work in their overalls and on the bus are just as happy, on the average, as those in suits who drive to work in their own Mercedes."

Even the super rich—the *Forbes* 100 wealthiest Americans—report only slightly greater happiness than average (Diener, Horwitz, and Emmons, 1985). And even winning a state lottery seems not to enduringly elevate well-being (Brickman, Coates, & Janoff-Bulman, 1978). Such jolts of joy have "a short half-life," notes Richard Ryan (1999).

We can ask, third, whether, over time, a culture's *happiness rises with its affluence*. Does our collective well-being float upward with a rising economic tide?

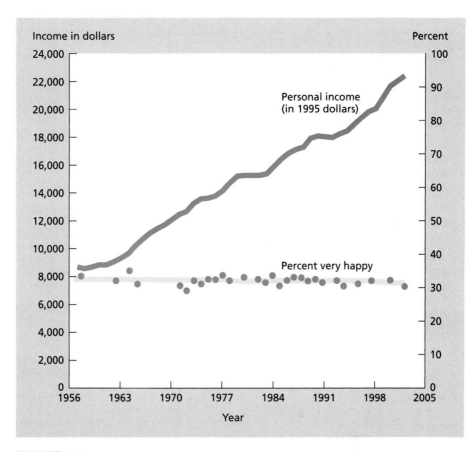

FIGURE 31-2

Has economic growth advanced human morale? While inflation-adjusted income has risen, self-reported happiness has not. **Source:** Happiness data from General Social Surveys, National Opinion Research Center, University of Chicago. Income data from Bureau of the Census (1975) and *Economic Indicators*.

In 1957 as economist John Galbraith was describing the United States as *The Affluent Society*, Americans' per person income was (in 1995 dollars) about $9,000. Today, as Figure 31-2 indicates, the United States is a doubly affluent society. Although this rising tide has lifted the yachts faster than the dinghies, nearly all boats have risen. With double the spending power, thanks partly to the surge in married women's employment, we now own twice as many cars per person, eat out twice as often, and are supported by a whole new world of technology. Since 1960 we have also seen the proportion of households with dishwashers rise from 7 to 50 percent, clothes dryers from 20 to 71 percent, and air conditioning from 15 to

73 percent. Daily showers—a luxury enjoyed by 29 percent of Americans in 1950—had become a necessity for 75 percent of Americans by 1999 (Myers, 2000a).

So, believing that it's "very important" to "be very well-off financially," and having become better off financially, are today's Americans happier? Are we happier with espresso coffee, caller ID, and suitcases on wheels than before?

We are not. Since 1957 the number of Americans who say they are "very happy" has declined ever so slightly from 35 to 34 percent. Twice as rich and apparently no happier. Meanwhile, the divorce rate has doubled, the teen suicide rate has more than doubled, and more people than ever (especially teens and young adults) are depressed.

I call this soaring wealth and shrinking spirit "the American paradox." More than ever, we have big houses and broken homes, high incomes and low morale, secured rights and diminished civility. We excel at making a living but often fail at making a life. We celebrate our prosperity but yearn for purpose. We cherish our freedoms but long for connection. In an age of plenty, we feel spiritual hunger.

It is hard to avoid a startling conclusion: Our becoming much better off over the last four decades has not been accompanied by one iota of increased subjective well-being. The same is true of the European countries and Japan, reports Richard Easterlin (1995). In Britain, for example, sharp increases in the percent of households with cars, central heating, and telephones have not been accompanied by increased happiness. The conclusion is startling because it challenges modern materialism: *Economic growth in affluent countries has provided no apparent boost to human morale.*

Why Materialism Fails to Satisfy

It is striking that economic growth in affluent countries has failed to satisfy. It is further striking that individuals who strive most for wealth tend to live with lower well-being, a finding that "comes through very strongly in every culture I've looked at," reports Richard Ryan (1999). His collaborator, Tim Kasser (2000, 2002), concludes from their studies that those who instead strive for "intimacy, personal growth, and contribution to the community" experience a higher quality of life.

Pause a moment and think: What is the single most personally satisfying event that you experienced in the last month? Kennon Sheldon and his colleagues (2001) put that question (and similar questions about the last week and semester) to samples of university students. Then they asked them to rate the extent to which 10 different needs were met by the satisfying event. The students rated self-esteem, relatedness (feeling connected with others), and autonomy (feeling in control) as the 4 emotional needs that most strongly accompanied the satisfying event. At the bottom of the list of factors predicting satisfaction were money and luxury.

People who identify themselves with expensive possessions experience fewer positive moods, report Emily Solberg, Ed Diener, and Michael Robinson (2003). Such materialists tend to report a relatively large gap between what they want and what they have, and to enjoy fewer close, fulfilling relationships. The challenge for healthy nations, then, is to foster improving standards of living without encouraging a materialism and consumerism that displaces the deep need to belong.

So, why have we not become happier? Why have 41 percent of Americans—up from 13 percent in 1973—come to regard automotive air-conditioning as "a necessity" (Schor, 1998)? Why do yesterday's luxuries so quickly become today's requirements and tomorrow's relics? Two principles drive this psychology of consumption.

Our Human Capacity for Adaptation

The **adaptation-level phenomenon** is our tendency to judge our experience (for example, of sounds, lights, or income) relative to a neutral level defined by our prior experience. We adjust our neutral levels—the points at which sounds seem neither loud nor soft, temperatures neither hot nor cold, events neither pleasant nor unpleasant—based on our experience. We then notice and react to up or down changes from these levels.

Adaptation researcher Allen Parducci (1995) recalls a striking example: "On the Micronesian island of Ponope, which is almost on the equator, I was told of a bitter night back in 1915 when the temperature dropped to a record-breaking 69 degrees [Fahrenheit]!" In the United States, Midwesterners, perhaps after watching too many *Baywatch* episodes, see sunny California as a happy place to live. But contrary to Midwesterners' intuitions, Californians—much as they may prefer their climate—are no happier (Schkade & Kahneman, 1998). Warm sun is just your average day.

Thus, as our achievements rise above past levels we feel successful and satisfied. As our social prestige, income, or in-home technology surges, we feel pleasure. Before long, however, we adapt. What once felt good comes to register as neutral, and what formerly was neutral now feels like deprivation. As the good feelings wane, it takes a higher high to rejuice the joy.

So, could we ever create a social paradise? Donald Campbell (1975) answered no: If you woke up tomorrow to your utopia—perhaps a world with no bills, no ills, someone who loves you unreservedly—you would feel euphoric, for a time. Yet before long, you would recalibrate your adaptation level and again sometimes feel gratified (when achievements surpass expectations), sometimes feel deprived (when they fall below), and sometimes feel neutral.

As you may recall from Module 3, we underestimate our adaptive capacity. People have difficulty predicting the intensity and duration of their future emotions, a phenomenon called "durability bias" (Wilson &

Gilbert, 2003). The elation from getting what we want—riches, top exam scores, the Chicago Cubs winning the World Series—evaporate more rapidly than we expect. We also sometimes "miswant." When first-year university students predicted their satisfaction with various housing possibilities shortly before entering their school's housing lottery, they focused on physical features. "I'll be happiest in a beautiful and well-located dorm," many students seemed to think. But they were wrong. When contacted a year later, it was the social features, such as a sense of community, that predicted happiness, report Elizabeth Dunn and her colleagues (2003). When focused on the short-term and forgetting how quickly we adapt, we may think that the material features of our world predispose our happiness. Actually, report Leaf Van Boven and Thomas Gilovich (2003) from their surveys and experiments, positive *experiences* (often social experiences) leave us happier. The best things in life are not things.

Our Wanting to Compare

Much of life revolves around **social comparison,** a point made by the old joke about two hikers who meet a bear. One reaches into his backpack and pulls out a pair of sneakers. "Why bother putting those on?" asks the other. "You can't outrun a bear." "I don't have to outrun the bear," answers the first. "I just have to outrun you."

Happiness, too, is relative not only to our past experiences but also to our comparisons with others (Lyubomirsky, 2001). Whether we feel good or bad depends on with whom we're comparing ourselves. We are slow-witted or clumsy only when others are smart or agile. Let one baseball player sign a new contract for $15 million a year and his $8 million a year teammate may now feel less satisfied. "Our poverty became a reality. Not because of our having less, but by our neighbors having more," recalled Will Campbell in *Brother to a Dragonfly*.

Further feeding our luxury fever is the tendency to compare upward: As we climb the ladder of success or affluence, we mostly compare ourselves with peers who are at or above our current level. Those living in communities with unequal incomes that are skewed by a very rich class tend to feel less satisfied as they compare upward.

The rich-poor gap has grown, observes Michael Hagerty (2000), and this helps explain why rising affluence has not produced increased happiness. Rising income inequality, notes Hagerty, makes for more people markedly above us in our communities. And that helps explain why those living in communities with a large rich-poor gap tend to feel less satisfied. If you live in a 2,000-square-foot house in a community filled with other 2,000-square-foot houses you likely are happier than if living in the same house amid 4,000-square-foot homes. Television's modeling of the lifestyles of the wealthy also serves to accentuate feelings of "relative deprivation" and desires for more (Schor, 1998).

The adaptation-level and social comparison phenomena give us pause. They imply that the quest for happiness through material achievement requires continually expanding affluence. But the good news is that adaptation to simpler lives can also happen. If choice or necessity shrinks our consumption we will initially feel pain, but it will pass. "Weeping may tarry for the night, but joy comes with the morning," reflected the Psalmist. Indeed, thanks to our capacity to adapt and to adjust comparisons, the emotional impact of significant life events—losing a job, or even a disabling accident—dissipates sooner than most people suppose (Gilbert & others, 1998).

TOWARD SUSTAINABILITY AND SURVIVAL

A shift to postmaterialist values will gain momentum as people

- face the implications of population and consumption growth for climate change, habitat destruction, and resource depletion;
- realize that materialist values mark *less* happy lives; and
- appreciate that economic growth has *not* bred increased well-being and that other things matter more.

"If the world is to change for the better it must have a change in human consciousness," said Czech poet-president Vaclav Havel (1990). We must discover "a deeper sense of responsibility toward the world, which means responsibility toward something higher than self." If people came to believe that stacks of unplayed CDs, closets full of seldom-worn clothes, and garages with luxury cars do not define the good life, then might a shift in consciousness become possible? Instead of being an indicator of social status, might conspicuous consumption become gauche?

Social psychology's contribution to a sustainable and survivable future will come partly through its consciousness-transforming insights into adaptation and comparison. These insights also come from experiments that lower people's comparison standards and thereby cool luxury fever and renew contentment. In two such experiments, Marshall Dermer and his colleagues (1979) put university women through imaginative exercises in deprivation. After viewing depictions of the grimness of Milwaukee life in 1900, or after imagining and writing about being burned and disfigured, the women expressed greater satisfaction with their own lives.

In another experiment, Jennifer Crocker and Lisa Gallo (1985) found that people who five times completed the sentence "I'm glad I'm not a . . ." afterward felt less depressed and more satisfied with their lives than did those who completed sentences beginning "I wish I were a. . . ."

Realizing that others have it worse helps us count our blessings. "I cried because I had no shoes," says a Persian proverb, "until I met a man who had no feet." *Downward* social comparison facilitates contentment.

Social psychology also contributes to a sustainable and survivable future through its explorations of the good life. If materialism does not enhance life quality, what does?

- *Close, supportive relationships.* As we saw in Module 26, our deep need to belong is satisfied by close, supportive relationships. Those supported by intimate friendships or a committed marriage are much more likely to declare themselves "very happy."
- *Faith communities* are often a source of such connections, as well as of meaning and hope. That helps explain a finding from National Opinion Research Center surveys of 42,000 Americans since 1972: Twenty-six percent of those who rarely or never attending religious services declared themselves very happy, as did 47 percent of those attending multiple times weekly.
- *Positive traits.* Optimism, self-esteem, perceived control, and extraversion also mark happy experiences and happy lives.
- *Flow.* Work and leisure experiences that engage one's skills also mark happy lives. Between the anxiety of being overwhelmed and stressed, and the apathy of being underwhelmed and bored, notes Mihaly Csikszentmihalyi (1990, 1999), lies a zone in which people experience *flow,* an optimal state in which, absorbed in an activity, we lose consciousness of self and time. When their experience is sampled using electronic pagers, people report greatest enjoyment not when mindlessly passive, but when unself-consciously absorbed in a mindful challenge. In fact, the less expensive (and generally more involving) a leisure activity, the *happier* people are while doing it. Most people are happier gardening than power boating, talking to friends than watching TV. Low-consumption recreations prove most satisfying.

That is good news indeed. Those things that make for the genuinely good life—close relationships, a hope-filled faith, positive traits, engaging activity—are enduringly sustainable. And that is an idea close to the heart of Jigme Singye Wangchuk, King of Bhutan. "Gross national happiness is more important than gross national product," he believes. Writing from Bhutan's Center of Bhutan Studies, Sander Tideman (2003) explains: "Gross National Happiness . . . aims to promote real progress and sustainability by measuring the quality of life, rather than the mere sum of production and consumption.

CONCEPTS TO REMEMBER

adaptation-level phenomenon
The tendency to adapt to a
given level of stimulation and
thus to notice and react to
changes from that level.

social comparison Evaluating
one's abilities and opinions by
comparing oneself to others.

References

❖

ABELSON, R. P., KINDER, D. R., PETERS, M. D., & FISKE, S. T. (1982). Affective and semantic components in political person perception. *Journal of Personality and Social Psychology, 42,* 619–630.

ABRAMS, D. (1991). AIDS: What young people believe and what they do. Paper presented at the British Association for the Advancement of Science conference.

ABRAMS, D., WETHERELL, M., COCHRANE, S., HOGG, M. A., & TURNER, J. C. (1990). Knowing what to think by knowing who you are: Self-categorization and the nature of norm formation, conformity and group polarization. *British Journal of Social Psychology, 29,* 97–119.

ABRAMSON, L. Y. (ED.). (1988). Social cognition and clinical psychology: A synthesis. New York: Guilford Press.

ABRAMSON, L. Y., METALSKY, G. I., & ALLOY, L. B. (1989). Hopelessness depression: A theory-based subtype. *Psychological Review, 96,* 358–372.

ACITELLI, L. K., & ANTONUCCI, T. C. (1994). Gender differences in the link between marital support and satisfaction in older couples. *Journal of Personality and Social Psychology, 67,* 688–698.

ACKERMANN, R., & DERUBEIS, R. J. (1991). Is depressive realism real? *Clinical Psychology Review, 11,* 565–584.

ADAIR, J. G., DUSHENKO, T. W., & LINDSAY, R. C. L. (1985). Ethical regulations and their impact on research practice. *American Psychologist, 40,* 59–72.

ADAMS, J. M., & JONES, W. H. (1997). The conceptualization of marital commitment: An integrative analysis. *Journal of Personality and Social Psychology, 72,* 1177–1196.

ADDIS, M. E., & MAHALIK, J. R. (2003). Men, masculinity, and the contexts of help seeking. *American Psychologist, 58,* 5–14.

ADLER, N. E., BOYCE, T., CHESNEY, M. A., COHEN, S., FOLKMAN, S., KAHN, R. L., & SYME, S. L. (1993). Socioeconomic inequalities in health: No easy solution. *Journal of the American Medical Association, 269,* 3140–3145.

ADLER, R. P., LESSER, G. S., MERINGOFF, L. K., ROBERTSON, T. S., & WARD, S. (1980). *The effects of television advertising on children.* Lexington, MA: Lexington Books.

ADORNO, T., FRENKEL-BRUNSWIK, E., LEVINSON, D., & SANFORD, R. N. (1950). *The authoritarian personality.* New York: Harper.

AIELLO, J. R., & DOUTHITT, E. Z. (2001). Social facilitation from Triplett to electronic performance monitoring. *Group Dynamics: Theory, Research, and Practice, 5,* 163–180.

AIELLO, J. R., THOMPSON, D. E., & BRODZINSKY, D. M. (1983). How funny is crowding anyway? Effects of room size, group size, and the introduction of humor. *Basic and Applied Social Psychology, 4,* 193–207.

ALLEE, W. C., & MASURE, R. M. (1936). A comparison of maze behavior in paired and isolated shell-parakeets *(Melopsittacus undulatus Shaw)* in a two-alley problem box. *Journal of Comparative Psychology, 22,* 131–155.

ALLISON, S. T., JORDAN, M. R., & YEATTS, C. E. (1992). A cluster-analytic approach toward identifying the structure and content of human decision making. *Human Relations, 45,* 49–72.

ALLISON, S. T., MACKIE, D. M., MULLER, M. M., & WORTH, L. T. (1993). Sequential correspondence biases and perceptions of change: The Castro studies revisited. *Personality and Social Psychology Bulletin, 19,* 151–157.

ALLISON, S. T., MESSICK, D. M., & GOETHALS, G. R. (1989). On being better but not smarter than others: The Muhammad Ali effect. *Social Cognition, 7,* 275–296.

ALLOY, L. B., & ABRAMSON, L. Y. (1979). Judgment of contingency in depressed and nondepressed students: Sadder but wiser? *Journal of Experimental Psychology: General, 108,* 441–485.

ALLOY, L. B., ABRAMSON, L. Y., WHITEHOUSE, W. G., HOGAN, M. E., TASHMAN, N. A., STEINBERG, D. L., ROSE, D. T., & DONOVAN, P. (1999). Depressogenic cognitive styles: Predictive validity, information processing and personality characteristics, and developmental origins. *Behaviour Research and Therapy, 37,* 503–531.

ALLPORT, G. W. (1958). *The nature of prejudice* (abridged). Garden City, NY: Anchor Books.

ALTEMEYER, B. (1988). *Enemies of freedom: Understanding right-wing authoritarianism.* San Francisco: Jossey-Bass.

ALTEMEYER, B. (1992). Six studies of right-wing authoritarianism among American state legislators. Unpublished manuscript, University of Manitoba.

ALTEMEYER, R. (2004). Highly dominating, highly authoritarian personalities. *Journal of Social Psychology, 144,* 421–447.

ALTMAN, I., & VINSEL, A. M. (1978). Personal space: An analysis of E. T. Hall's proxemics framework. In I. Altman & J. Wohlwill (Eds.), *Human behavior and the environment.* New York: Plenum Press.

AMABILE, T. M., & GLAZEBROOK, A. H. (1982). A negativity bias in interpersonal evaluation. *Journal of Experimental Social Psychology, 18,* 1–22.

AMERICAN ENTERPRISE. (1992, January/February). Women, men, marriages & ministers, p. 106.

AMERICAN PSYCHOLOGICAL ASSOCIATION. (1993). *Violence and youth: Psychology's response. Vol. I: Summary report of the American Psychological Association Commission on Violence and Youth.* Washington, DC: Public Interest Directorate, American Psychological Association.

AMERICAN PSYCHOLOGICAL ASSOCIATION. (2002). *Ethical principles of psychologists and code of conduct 2002.* Washington, DC: APA (www.apa.org/ethics/code2002.html).

AMIR, Y. (1969). Contact hypothesis in ethnic relations. *Psychological Bulletin, 71,* 319–342.

ANDERSON, C. A. (2003). Video games and aggressive behavior. In D. Ravitch and J. P. Viteritti (Eds.), *Kids stuff: Marking violence and vulgarity in the popular culture.* Baltimore: Johns Hopkins University Press.

ANDERSON, C. A. (2004). An update on the effects of violent video games. *Journal of Adolescence, 27,* 113–122.

ANDERSON, C. A., & ANDERSON, D. C. (1984). Ambient temperature and violent crime: Tests of the linear and curvilinear hypotheses. *Journal of Personality and Social Psychology, 46,* 91–97.

ANDERSON, C. A., & ANDERSON, K. B. (1998). Temperature and aggression: Paradox, controversy, and a (fairly) clear picture. In R. G. Geen & E. Donnerstein (Eds.), *Human aggression: Theories, research, and implications for social policy.* San Diego, CA: Academic Press.

ANDERSON, C. A., BENJAMIN, A. J., JR., & BARTHOLOW, B. D. (1998). Does the gun pull the trigger? Automatic priming effects of weapon pictures and weapon names. *Psychological Science, 9,* 308–314.

ANDERSON, C. A., BERKOWITZ, L., DONNERSTEIN, E., HUESMANN, R. L., JOHNSON, J., LINZ, D., MALAMUTH, N., & WARTELLA, E. (in press). The influence of media violence on youth. *Psychological Science in the Public Interest.*

ANDERSON, C. A., & BUSHMAN, B. J. (1997). External validity of "trivial" experiments: The case of laboratory aggression. *Review of General Psychology, 1,* 19–41.

ANDERSON, C. A., & BUSHMAN, B. J. (2002). Media violence and the American public revisited. *American Psychologist, 57,* 448–450.

ANDERSON, C. A., CARNAGEY, N. L., & EUBANKS, J. (2003). Exposure to violent media: The effects of songs with violent lyrics on aggressive thoughts and feelings. *Journal of Personality and Social Psychology, 84,* 960–971.

ANDERSON, C. A., & HARVEY, R. J. (1988). Discriminating between problems in living: An examination of measures of depression, loneliness, shyness, and social anxiety. *Journal of Social and Clinical Psychology, 6,* 482–491.

ANDERSON, C. A., HOROWITZ, L. M., & FRENCH, R. D. (1983). Attributional style of lonely and depressed people. *Journal of Personality and Social Psychology, 45,* 127–136.

ANDERSON, C. A., LINDSAY, J. J., & BUSHMAN, B. J. (1999). Research in the psychological laboratory: Truth or triviality? *Current Directions in Psychological Science, 8,* 3–9.

ANDERSON, C. A., MILLER, R. S., RIGER, A. L., DILL, J. C., & SEDIKIDES, C. (1994). Behavioral and characterological attributional styles as predictors of depression and loneliness: Review, refinement, and test. *Journal of Personality and Social Psychology, 66,* 549–558.

ANDERSON, K. J., & LEAPER, C. (1998). Meta-analyses of gender effects on conversational interruption: Who, what, when, where, and how. *Sex Roles, 39,* 225–252.

AP. (1993, June 10). Walking past a dying man. *New York Times* (via Associated Press), 485.

ARCHER, D., & GARTNER, R. (1976). Violent acts and violent times: A comparative approach to postwar homicide rates. *American Sociological Review, 41,* 937–963.

ARCHER, J. (1991). The influence of testosterone on human aggression. *British Journal of Psychology, 82,* 1–28.

ARCHER, J. (2000). Sex differences in aggression between heterosexual partners: A meta-analytic review. *Psychological Bulletin, 126,* 651–680.

ARCHER, J. (2002). Sex differences in physically aggressive acts between heterosexual partners: A meta-analytic review. *Aggression and Violent Behavior, 7,* 313–351.

ARENDT, H. (1963). *Eichmann in Jerusalem: A report on the banality of evil.* New York: Viking Press.

ARGYLE, M. (1999). Causes and correlates of happiness. In D. Kahneman, E. Diener, & N. Schwartz (Eds.), *Foundations of hedonic psychology: Scientific perspectives on enjoyment and suffering.* New York: Russell Sage Foundation.

ARGYLE, M., SHIMODA, K., & LITTLE, B. (1978). Variance due to persons and situations in England and Japan. *British Journal of Social and Clinical Psychology, 17,* 335–337.

ARKIN, R. M., & BURGER, J. M. (1980). Effects of unit relation tendencies on interpersonal attraction. *Social Psychology Quarterly, 43,* 380–391.

ARKIN, R. M., COOPER, H., & KOLDITZ, T. (1980). A statistical review of the literature concerning the self-serving attribution bias in interpersonal influence situations. *Journal of Personality, 48,* 435–448.

ARKIN, R. M., & MARUYAMA, G. M. (1979). Attribution, affect, and college exam performance. *Journal of Educational Psychology, 71,* 85–93.

ARMOR, D. A., & TAYLOR, S. E. (1996). Situated optimism: Specific outcome expectancies and self-regulation. In M. P. Zanna (Ed.), *Advances in experimental social psychology, vol. 30.* San Diego, CA: Academic Press.

ARMS, R. L., RUSSELL, G. W., & SANDILANDS, M. L. (1979). Effects on the hostility of spectators of viewing aggressive sports. *Social Psychology Quarterly, 42,* 275–279.

ARON, A., & ARON, E. (1989). *The heart of social psychology,* 2nd ed. Lexington, MA: Lexington Books.

ARON, A., & ARON, E. N. (1994). Love. In A. L. Weber & J. H. Harvey (Eds.), *Perspective on close relationships.* Boston: Allyn & Bacon.

ARON, A., DUTTON, D. G., ARON, E. N., & IVERSON, A. (1989). Experiences of falling in love. *Journal of Social and Personal Relationships, 6,* 243–257.

ARONSON, E. (2000). *Nobody left to hate: Teaching compassion after Columbine.* New York: Freeman/Worth.

ARONSON, E. (2002). Building empathy, compassion, and achievement in the jigsaw classroom. In J. Aronson (Ed.), *Improving academic achievement: Impact of psychological factors on education.* San Diego, CA: Academic Press.

ARONSON, E., BLANEY, N., STEPHAN, C., SIKES, J., & SNAPP, M. (1978). *The jigsaw classroom*. Beverly Hills, CA: Sage.

ARONSON, E., BREWER, M., & CARLSMITH, J. M. (1985). Experimentation in social psychology. In G. Lindzey & E. Aronson (Eds.), *Handbook of social psychology, vol. 1*. Hillsdale, NJ: Erlbaum.

ARONSON, E., & GONZALEZ, A. (1988). Desegregation, jigsaw, and the Mexican-American experience. In P. A. Katz & D. Taylor (Eds.), *Towards the elimination of racism: Profiles in controversy*. New York: Plenum.

ARONSON, E., & MILLS, J. (1959). The effect of severity of initiation on liking for a group. *Journal of Abnormal and Social Psychology, 59*, 177–181.

ARRIAGA, X. B. (2001). The ups and downs of dating: Fluctuations in satisfaction in newly formed romantic relationships. *Journal of Personality and Social Psychology, 80*, 754–765.

ARRIAGA, X. B., & AGNEW, C. R. (2001). Being committed: Affective, cognitive, and conative components of relationship commitment. *Personality and Social Psychology Bulletin, 27*, 1190–1203.

ASAPS. (2003). Statistics 2002. The American Society for Aesthetic Plastic Surgery (www.surgery.org).

ASCH, S. E. (1955, November). Opinions and social pressure. *Scientific American*, pp. 31–35.

ASENDORPF, J. B. (1987). Videotape reconstruction of emotions and cognitions related to shyness. *Journal of Personality and Social Psychology, 53*, 541–549.

ASHER, J. (1987, April). Born to be shy? *Psychology Today*, pp. 56–64.

ASTIN, A. W., GREEN, K. C., KORN, W. S., & SCHALIT, M. (1987). *The American freshman: National norms for Fall 1987*. Los Angeles: Higher Education Research Institute, UCLA.

AVERILL, J. R. (1983). Studies on anger and aggression: Implications for theories of emotion. *American Psychologist, 38*, 1145–1160.

AXELROD, R., & DION, D. (1988). The further evolution of cooperation. *Science, 242*, 1385–1390.

AXSOM, D., YATES, S., & CHAIKEN, S. (1987). Audience response as a heuristic cue in persuasion. *Journal of Personality and Social Psychology, 53*, 30–40.

AYRES, I. (1991). Fair driving: Gender and race discrimination in retail car negotiations. *Harvard Law Review, 104*, 817–872.

AZRIN, N. H. (1967, May). Pain and aggression. *Psychology Today*, pp. 27–33.

BABAD, E., HILLS, M., & O'DRISCOLL, M. (1992). Factors influencing wishful thinking and predictions of election outcomes. *Basic and Applied Social Psychology, 13*, 461–476.

BACHMAN, J. G., & O'MALLEY, P. M. (1977). Self-esteem in young men: A longitudinal analysis of the impact of educational and occupational attainment. *Journal of Personality and Social Psychology, 35*, 365–380.

BAILEY, J. M., GAULIN, S., AGYEI, Y., & GLADUE, B. A. (1994). Effects of gender and sexual orientation on evolutionary relevant aspects of human mating psychology. *Journal of Personality and Social Psychology, 66*, 1081–1093.

BAILEY, J. M., KIRK, K. M., ZHU, G., DUNNE, M. P., & MARTIN, N. G. (2000). Do individual differences in sociosexuality represent genetic or environmentally contingent strategies? Evidence from the Australian Twin Registry. *Journal of Personality and Social Psychology, 78*, 537–545.

BAIZE, H. R., JR., & SCHROEDER, J. E. (1995). Personality and mate selection in personal ads: Evolutionary preferences in a public mate selection process. *Journal of Social Behavior and Personality, 10*, 517–536.

BAKER, L. A., & EMERY, R. E. (1993). When every relationship is above average: Perceptions and expectations of divorce at the time of marriage. *Law and Human Behavior, 17*, 439–450.

BANAJI, M. R., & BHASKAR, R. (2000). Implicit stereotypes and memory: The bounded rationality of social beliefs. In D. L. Schacter & E. Scarry (Eds.), *Memory, brain, and belief*. Cambridge, MA: Harvard University Press.

BANDURA, A. (1979). The social learning perspective: Mechanisms of aggression. In H. Toch (Ed.), *Psychology of crime and criminal justice*. New York: Holt, Rinehart & Winston.

BANDURA, A. (1986). *Social foundations of thought and action: A social cognitive theory*. Englewood Cliffs, NJ: Prentice Hall.

BANDURA, A. (1997). *Self-efficacy: The exercise of control*. New York: Freeman.

BANDURA, A., PASTORELLI, C., BARBARANELLI, C., & CAPRARA, G. V. (1999). Self-efficacy pathways to childhood depression. *Journal of Personality and Social Psychology, 76,* 258–269.

BANDURA, A., ROSS, D., & ROSS, S. A. (1961). Transmission of aggression through imitation of aggressive models. *Journal of Abnormal and Social Psychology, 63,* 575–582.

BANDURA, A., & WALTERS, R. H. (1959). *Adolescent aggression*. New York: Ronald Press.

BANDURA, A., & WALTERS, R. H. (1963). *Social learning and personality development*. New York: Holt, Rinehart and Winston.

BANFIELD, S., & McCABE, M. P. (2001). Extra relationship involvement among women: Are they different from men? *Archives of Sexual Behavior, 30,* 119–142.

BANKS, S. M., SALOVEY, P., GREENER, S., ROTHMAN, A. J., MOYER, A., BEAUVAIS, J., & EPEL, E. (1995). The effects of message framing on mammography utilization. *Health Psychology, 14,* 178–184.

BARASH, D. P. (2003, November 7). Unreason's seductive charms. *Chronicle of Higher Education* (www.chronicle.com/free/v50/i11/11b00601.htm).

BARBER, B. M., & ODEAN, T. (2001). The Internet and the investor. *Journal of Economic Perspectives, 15,* 41–54.

BARBER, N. (2000). On the relationship between country sex ratios and teen pregnancy rates: A replication. *Cross-Cultural Research, 34,* 327–333.

BARGH, J. A. (1997). The automaticity of everyday life. In R. S. Wyer, Jr. (Ed.), *Advances in social cognition, vol. 10*. Mahwah, NJ: Erlbaum.

BARGH, J. A., & CHARTRAND, T. L. (1999). The unbearable automaticity of being. *American Psychologist, 54,* 462–479.

BARGH, J. A., McKENNA, K. Y. A., & FITZSIMONS, G. M. (2002). Can you see the real me? Activation and expression of the "true self" on the Internet. *Journal of Social Issues, 58,* 33–48.

BARNETT, P. A., & GOTLIB, I. H. (1988). Psychosocial functioning and depression: Distinguishing among antecedents, concomitants, and consequences. *Psychological Bulletin, 104,* 97–126.

BARON, L., & STRAUS, M. A. (1984). Sexual stratification, pornography, and rape in the United States. In N. M. Malamuth & E. Donnerstein (Eds.), *Pornography and sexual aggression*. New York: Academic Press.

BARON, R. M., MANDEL, D. R., ADAMS, C. A., & GRIFFEN, L. M. (1976). Effects of social density in university residential environments. *Journal of Personality and Social Psychology, 34,* 434–446.

BARON, R. S. (1986). Distraction-conflict theory: Progress and problems. In L. Berkowitz (Ed.), *Advances in experimental social psychology*. Orlando, FL: Academic Press.

BARON, R. S. (2000). Arousal, capacity, and intense indoctrination. *Personality and Social Psychology Review, 4,* 238–254.

BARON, R. S., DAVID, J. P., INMAN, M., & BRUNSMAN, B. M. (1997). Why listeners hear less than they are told: Attentional load and the teller-listener extremity effect. *Journal of Personality and Social Psychology, 72,* 826–838.

BARONGAN, C., & HALL, G. C. N. (1995). The influence of misogynous rap music on sexual aggression against women. *Psychology of Women Quarterly, 19,* 195–207.

BARRY, D. (1995, January). Bored stiff. *Funny Times,* p. 5.

BARRY, D. (1998). *Dave Barry turns 50*. New York: Crown.

BASSILI, J. N. (2003). The minority slowness effect: Subtle inhibitions in the expression of views not shared by others. *Journal of Personality and Social Psychology, 84,* 261–276.

BATSON, C. D., & MORAN, T. (1999). Empathy-induced altruism in a prisoner's dilemma. *European Journal of Social Psychology, 29,* 909–924.

BATSON, C. D., SYMPSON, S. C., HINDMAN, J. L., DECRUZ, P., TODD, R. M., JENNINGS, G., & BURRIS, C. T. (1996). "I've been there, too": Effect on empathy of prior experience with a need. *Personality and Social Psychology Bulletin, 22,* 474–482.

BAUMEISTER, R. F., & BRATSLAVSKY, E. (1999). Passion, intimacy, and time: Passionate love as a function of change in intimacy. *Personality and Social Psychology Review, 3,* 49–67.

BAUMEISTER, R. F., CAMPBELL, J. D., KRUEGER, J. I., & VOHS, K. D. (2003). Does high self-esteem cause better performance, interpersonal success, happiness, or healthier lifestyles? *Psychological Science in the Public Interest, 4*(1), 1–44.

BAUMEISTER, R. F., CATANESE, K. R., & VOHS, K. D. (2001). Is there a gender difference in strength of sex drive? Theoretical views, conceptual distinctions, and a review of relevant evidence. *Personality and Social Psychology Review, 5,* 242–273.

BAUMEISTER, R. F., CATANESE, K. R., & WALLACE, H. M. (2002). Conquest by force: A narcissistic reactance theory of rape and sexual coercion. *Review of General Psychology, 6,* 92–135.

BAUMEISTER, R. F., & LEARY, M. R. (1995). The need to belong: Desire for interpersonal attachment as a fundamental human motivation. *Psychological Bulletin, 117,* 497–529.

BAUMEISTER, R. F., & VOHS, K. (2004). Sexual economics: Sex as female resource for social exchange in heterosexual interactions. *Personality and Social Psychology Bulletin, 8,* 339–363.

BAUMEISTER, R. F., & WOTMAN, S. R. (1992). *Breaking hearts: The two sides of unrequited love.* New York: Guilford Press.

BAUMHART, R. (1968). *An honest profit.* New York: Holt, Rinehart & Winston.

BAXTER, T. L., & GOLDBERG, L. R. (1987). Perceived behavioral consistency underlying trait attributions to oneself and another: An extension of the actor-observer effect. *Personality and Social Psychology Bulletin, 13,* 437–447.

BAYER, E. (1929). Beitrage zur zeikomponenten theorie des hungers. *Zeitschrift fur Psychologie, 112,* 1–54.

BAZERMAN, M. H. (1986, June). Why negotiations go wrong. *Psychology Today,* pp. 54–58.

BAZERMAN, M. H. (1990). *Judgment in managerial decision making,* 2nd ed. New York: Wiley.

BEAMAN, A. L., BARNES, P. J., KLENTZ, B., & McQUIRK, B. (1978). Increasing helping rates through information dissemination: Teaching pays. *Personality and Social Psychology Bulletin, 4,* 406–411.

BEAMAN, A. L., & KLENTZ, B. (1983). The supposed physical attractiveness bias against supporters of the women's movement: A meta-analysis. *Personality and Social Psychology Bulletin, 9,* 544–550.

BEAMAN, A. L., KLENTZ, B., DIENER, E., & SVANUM, S. (1979). Self-awareness and transgression in children: Two field studies. *Journal of Personality and Social Psychology, 37,* 1835–1846.

BEAUREGARD, K. S., & DUNNING, D. (1998). Turning up the contrast: Self-enhancement motives prompt egocentric contrast effects in social judgments. *Journal of Personality and Social Psychology, 74,* 606–621.

BEAUVOIS, J. L., & DUBOIS, N. (1988). The norm of internality in the explanation of psychological events. *European Journal of Social Psychology, 18,* 299–316.

BECK, A. T., & YOUNG, J. E. (1978, September). College blues. *Psychology Today,* pp. 80–92.

BELL, P. A. (1980). Effects of heat, noise, and provocation on retaliatory evaluative behavior. *Journal of Social Psychology, 110,* 97–100.

BELSON, W. A. (1978). *Television violence and the adolescent boy.* Westmead, England: Saxon House, Teakfield Ltd.

BEM, D. J. (1972). Self-perception theory. In L. Berkowitz (Ed.), *Advances in experimental social psychology, vol. 6.* New York: Academic Press.

BEM, D. J., & McCONNELL, H. K. (1970). Testing the self-perception explanation of dissonance phenomena: On the salience of premanipulation attitudes. *Journal of Personality and Social Psychology, 14,* 23–31.

BENNETT, R. (1991, February). Pornography and extrafamilial child sexual abuse: Examining the relationship. Unpublished manuscript, Los Angeles Police Department Sexually Exploited Child Unit.

BENNIS, W. (1984). Transformative power and leadership. In T. J. Sergiovani & J. E. Corbally (Eds.), *Leadership and organizational culture.* Urbana: University of Illinois Press.

BEN-ZEEV, T., FEIN, S., & INZLICHT, M. (2005). Arousal and stereotype threat. *Journal of Experimental Social Psychology, 41,* 174–181.

BERENBAUM, S. A., & HINES, M. (1992). Early androgens are related to childhood sex-typed toy preferences. *Psychological Science, 3,* 203–206.

BERG, J. H. (1984). Development of friendship between roommates. *Journal of Personality and Social Psychology, 46,* 346–356.

BERG, J. H. (1987). Responsiveness and self-disclosure. In V. J. Derlega & J. H. Berg (Eds.), *Self-disclosure: Theory, research, and therapy.* New York: Plenum.

BERG, J. H., & McQUINN, R. D. (1986). Attraction and exchange in continuing and noncontinuing dating relationships. *Journal of Personality and Social Psychology, 50,* 942–952.

BERKOWITZ, L. (1968, September). Impulse, aggression and the gun. *Psychology Today,* pp. 18–22.

BERKOWITZ, L. (1978). Whatever happened to the frustration-aggression hypothesis? *American Behavioral Scientists, 21,* 691–708.

BERKOWITZ, L. (1981, June). How guns control us. *Psychology Today,* pp. 11–12.

BERKOWITZ, L. (1983). Aversively stimulated aggression: Some parallels and differences in research with animals and humans. *American Psychologist, 38,* 1135–1144.

BERKOWITZ, L. (1984). Some effects of thoughts on anti- and prosocial influences of media events: A cognitive-neoassociation analysis. *Psychological Bulletin, 95,* 410–427.

BERKOWITZ, L. (1989). Frustration-aggression hypothesis: Examination and reformulation. *Psychological Bulletin, 106,* 59–73.

BERKOWITZ, L. (1995). A career on aggression. In G. G. Brannigan & M. R. Merrens (Eds.), *The social psychologists: Research adventures.* New York: McGraw-Hill.

BERKOWITZ, L. (1998). Affective aggression: The role of stress, pain, and negative affect. In R. G. Geen & E. Donnerstein (Eds.), *Human aggression: Theories, research, and implications for social policy.* San Diego, CA: Academic Press.

BERKOWITZ, L., & GEEN, R. G. (1966). Film violence and the cue properties of available targets. *Journal of Personality and Social Psychology, 3,* 525–530.

BERKOWITZ, L., & LePAGE, A. (1967). Weapons as aggression-eliciting stimuli. *Journal of Personality and Social Psychology, 7,* 202–207.

BERRY, J. W., & KALIN, R. (1995). Multicultural and ethnic attitudes in Canada: An overview of the 1991 national survey. *Canadian Journal of Behavioural Science, 27,* 301–320.

BERSCHEID, E. (1981). An overview of the psychological effects of physical attractiveness and some comments upon the psychological effects of knowledge of the effects of physical attractiveness. In W. Lucker, K. Ribbens, & J. A. McNamera (Eds.), *Logical aspects of facial form (craniofacial growth series).* Ann Arbor: University of Michigan Press.

BERSCHEID, E. (1999). The greening of relationship science. *American Psychologist, 54,* 260–266.

BERSCHEID, E., BOYE, D., & WALSTER (HATFIELD), E. (1968). Retaliation as a means of restoring equity. *Journal of Personality and Social Psychology, 10,* 370–376.

BERSCHEID, E., DION, K., WALSTER (HATFIELD), E., & WALSTER, G. W. (1971). Physical attractiveness and dating choice: A test of the matching hypothesis. *Journal of Experimental Social Psychology, 7,* 173–189.

BERSCHEID, E., GRAZIANO, W., MONSON, T., & DERMER, M. (1976). Outcome dependency: Attention, attribution, and attraction. *Journal of Personality and Social Psychology, 34,* 978–989.

BERSCHEID, E., SNYDER, M., & OMOTO, A. M. (1989). Issues in studying close relationships: Conceptualizing and measuring closeness. In C. Hendrick (Ed.), *Review of personality and social psychology, vol. 10.* Newbury Park, CA: Sage.

BERSCHEID, E., & WALSTER (HATFIELD), E. (1978). *Interpersonal attraction.* Reading, MA: Addison-Wesley.

BERSCHEID, E., WALSTER, G. W., & HATFIELD (was WALSTER), E. (1969). Effects of accuracy and positivity of evaluation on liking for the evaluator. Unpublished manuscript. Summarized by E. Berscheid and E. Walster (Hatfield) (1978), *Interpersonal attraction.* Reading, MA: Addison-Wesley.

BERTRAND, M., & MULLAINATHAN, S. (2003). Are Emily and Greg more employable than Lakisha and Jamal? A field experiment on labor market discrimination. Massachusetts Institute of Technology, Department of Economics, Working Paper 03-22.

BETTENCOURT, B. A., DILL, K. E., GREATHOUSE, S. A., CHARLTON, K., & MULHOLLAND, A. (1997). Evaluations of ingroup and outgroup members: The role of category-based expectancy violation. *Journal of Experimental Social Psychology, 33,* 244–275.

BETTENCOURT, B. A., & MILLER, N. (1996). Gender differences in aggression as a function of provocation: A meta-analysis. *Psychological Bulletin, 119,* 422–447.

BEYER, L. (1990, Fall issue on women). Life behind the veil. *Time,* p. 37.

BIANCHI, S. M., MILKIE, M. A., SAYER, L. C., & ROBINSON, J. P. (2000). Is anyone doing the housework? Trends in the gender division of household labor. *Social Forces, 79,* 191–228.

BIERBRAUER, G. (1979). Why did he do it? Attribution of obedience and the phenomenon of dispositional bias. *European Journal of Social Psychology 9*, 67–84.

BIERLY, M. M. (1985). Prejudice toward contemporary outgroups as a generalized attitude. *Journal of Applied Social Psychology, 15*, 189–199.

BIERNAT, M. (1991). Gender stereotypes and the relationship between masculinity and femininity: A developmental analysis. *Journal of Personality and Social Psychology, 61*, 351–365.

BIERNAT, M., & KOBRYNOWICZ, D. (1997). Gender- and race-based standards of competence: Lower minimum standards but higher ability standards for devalued groups. *Journal of Personality and Social Psychology, 72*, 544–557.

BIERNAT, M., VESCIO, T. K., & THENO, S. A. (1996). Violating American values: A "Value congruence" approach to understanding outgroup attitudes. *Journal of Experimental Social Psychology, 32*, 387–410.

BIERNAT, M., & WORTMAN, C. B. (1991). Sharing of home responsibilities between professionally employed women and their husbands. *Journal of Personality and Social Psychology, 60*, 844–860.

BILLIG, M., & TAJFEL, H. (1973). Social categorization and similarity in intergroup behaviour. *European Journal of Social Psychology, 3*, 27–52.

BIRD, C. E. (1999). Gender, household labor, and psychological distress: The impact of the amount and division of housework. *Journal of Health & Social Behavior, 40*, 32–45.

BJÖRKQVIST, K. (1994). Sex differences in physical, verbal, and indirect aggression: A review of recent research. *Sex Roles, 30*, 177–188.

BLACKBURN, R. T., PELLINO, G. R., BOBERG, A., & O'CONNELL, C. (1980). Are instructional improvement programs off target? *Current Issues in Higher Education, 1*, 31–48.

BLAKE, R. R., & MOUTON, J. S. (1962). The intergroup dynamics of win-lose conflict and problem-solving collaboration in union-management relations. In M. Sherif (Ed.), *Intergroup relations and leadership*. New York: Wiley.

BLAKE, R. R., & MOUTON, J. S. (1979). Intergroup problem solving in organizations: From theory to practice. In W. G. Austin & S. Worchel (Eds.), *The social psychology of intergroup relations*. Monterey, CA: Brooks/Cole.

BLANCHARD, F. A., & COOK, S. W. (1976). Effects of helping a less competent member of a cooperating interracial group on the development of interpersonal attraction. *Journal of Personality and Social Psychology, 34*, 1245–1255.

BLASS, T. (1996). Stanley Milgram: A life of inventiveness and controversy. In G. A. Kimble, C. A. Boneau, & M. Wertheimer (Eds.), *Portraits of pioneers in psychology, vol. 2*. Washington, DC: American Psychological Association.

BLOCK J., & FUNDER, D. C. (1986). Social roles and social perception: Individual differences in attribution and error. *Journal of Personality and Social Psychology, 51*, 1200–1207.

BODENHAUSEN, G. V. (1990). Stereotypes as judgmental heuristics: Evidence of circadian variations in discrimination. *Psychological Science, 1*, 319–322.

BODENHAUSEN, G. V. (1993). Emotions, arousal, and stereotypic judgments: A heuristic model of affect and stereotyping. In D. M. Mackie & D. L. Hamilton (Eds.), *Affect, cognition, and stereotyping: Interactive processes in group perception*. San Diego, CA: Academic Press.

BOND, C. F., JR., & TITUS, L. J. (1983). Social facilitation: A meta-analysis of 241 studies. *Psychological Bulletin, 94*, 265–292.

BOND, M. H. (2004). Culture and aggression: From context to coercion. *Personality and Social Psychology Review, 8*, 62–78.

BORGIDA, E., & BREKKE, N. (1985). Psycholegal research on rape trials. In A. W. Burgess (Ed.), *Rape and sexual assault: A research handbook*. New York: Garland.

BORNSTEIN, G., & RAPOPORT, A. (1988). Intergroup competition for the provision of step-level public goods: Effects of preplay communication. *European Journal of Social Psychology, 18*, 125–142.

BORNSTEIN, G., RAPOPORT, A., KERPEL, L., & KATZ, T. (1989). Within- and between-group communication in intergroup competition for public goods. *Journal of Experimental Social Psychology, 25*, 422–436.

BORNSTEIN, R. F. (1989). Exposure and affect: Overview and meta-analysis of research, 1968–1987. *Psychological Bulletin, 106*, 265–289.

BORNSTEIN, R. F. (1999). Source amnesia, misattribution, and the power of unconscious perceptions and memories. *Psychoanalytic Psychology, 16*, 155–178.

Bossard, J. H. S. (1932). Residential propinquity as a factor in marriage selection. *American Journal of Sociology, 38*, 219–224.

Bothwell, R. K., Brigham, J. C., & Malpass, R. S. (1989). Cross-racial identification. *Personality and Social Psychology Bulletin, 15*, 19–25.

Botvin, G. J., Schinke, S., & Orlandi, M. A. (1995). School-based health promotion: Substance abuse and sexual behavior. *Applied & Preventive Psychology, 4*, 167–184.

Botwin, M. D., Buss, D. M., & Shackelford, T. K. (1997). Personality and mate preferences: Five factors in mate selection and marital satisfaction. *Journal of Personality, 65*, 107–136.

Bouas, K. S., & Komorita, S. S. (1996). Group discussion and cooperation in social dilemmas. *Personality and Social Psychology Bulletin, 22*, 1144–1150.

Bower, G. H. (1987). Commentary on mood and memory. *Behavioral Research and Therapy, 25*, 443–455.

Boyatzis, C. J., Matillo, G. M., & Nesbitt, K. M. (1995). Effects of the "Mighty Morphin Power Rangers" on children's aggression with peers. *Child Study Journal, 25*, 45–55.

Brehm, S., & Brehm, J. W. (1981). *Psychological reactance: A theory of freedom and control.* New York: Academic Press.

Brenner, S. N., & Molander, E. A. (1977, January–February). Is the ethics of business changing? *Harvard Business Review*, pp. 57–71.

Brewer, M. B. (1987). Collective decisions. *Social Science, 72*, 140–143.

Brewer, M. B., & Miller, N. (1988). Contact and cooperation: When do they work? In P. A. Katz & D. Taylor (Eds.), *Towards the elimination of racism: Profiles in controversy.* New York: Plenum.

Brewer, M. B., & Silver, M. (1978). In-group bias as a function of task characteristics. *European Journal of Social Psychology, 8*, 393–400.

Brickman, P., Coates, D., & Janoff-Bulman, R. J. (1978). Lottery winners and accident victims: Is happiness relative? *Journal of Personality and Social Psychology, 36*, 917–927.

British Psychological Society. (2000). *Code of conduct, ethical principles and guidelines.* Leicester, England: British Psychological Society (www.bps.org.uk/documents/Code.pdf).

Brockner, J., & Hulton, A. J. B. (1978). How to reverse the vicious cycle of low self-esteem: The importance of attentional focus. *Journal of Experimental Social Psychology, 14*, 564–578.

Brockner, J., Rubin, J. Z., Fine, J., Hamilton, T. P., Thomas, B., & Turetsky, B. (1982). Factors affecting entrapment in escalating conflicts: The importance of timing. *Journal of Research in Personality, 16*, 247–266.

Brodt, S. E., & Ross, L. D. (1998). The role of stereotyping in overconfident social prediction. *Social Cognition, 16*, 228–252.

Brodt, S. E., & Zimbardo, P. G. (1981). Modifying shyness-related social behavior through symptom misattribution. *Journal of Personality and Social Psychology, 41*, 437–449.

Bronfenbrenner, U. (1961). The mirror image in Soviet-American relations. *Journal of Social Issues, 17*(3), 45–56.

Brown, D. E. (1991). *Human universals.* New York: McGraw-Hill.

Brown, D. E. (2000). Human universals and their implications. In N. Roughley (Ed.), *Being humans: Anthropological universality and particularity in transdisciplinary perspectives.* New York: Walter de Gruyter.

Brown, H. J., Jr. (1990). *P.S. I love you.* Nashville, TN: Rutledge Hill.

Brown, J. (2001, September 13). Anti-Arab passions sweep the U.S. Salon.com (www.salon.com/news/feature/2001/09/13/backlash/print.html).

Brown, J. D. (1986). Evaluations of self and others: Self-enhancement biases in social judgments. *Social Cognition, 4*, 353–376.

Brown, J. D. (1991). Accuracy and bias in self-knowledge: Can knowing the truth be hazardous to your health? In C. R. Snyder & D. F. Forsyth (Eds.), *Handbook of social and clinical psychology: The health perspective.* New York: Pergamon Press.

Brown, J. D., Collins, R. L., & Schmidt, G. W. (1988). Self-esteem and direct versus indirect forms of self-enhancement. *Journal of Personality and Social Psychology, 55*, 445–453.

Brown, J. D., Novick, N. J., Lord, K. A., & Richards, J. M. (1992). When Gulliver travels: Social context, psychological closeness, and self-appraisals. *Journal of Personality and Social Psychology, 62,* 717–727.

Brown, J. D., & Taylor, S. E. (1986). Affect and the processing of personal information: Evidence for mood-activated self-schemata. *Journal of Experimental Social Psychology, 22,* 436–452.

Brown, R. (1965). *Social psychology.* New York: Free Press.

Brown, R. (1987). Theory of politness: An exemplary case. Paper presented to the Society of Experimental Social Psychology meeting. Cited by R. O. Kroker & L. A. Wood, 1992. Are the rules of address universal? IV: Comparison of Chinese, Korean, Greek, and German usage. *Journal of Cross-Cultural Psychology, 23,* 148–162.

Brown, R., Maras, P., Masser, B., Vivian, J., & Hewstone, M. (2001). Life on the ocean wave: Testing some intergroup hypotheses in a naturalistic setting. *Group Processes and Intergroup Relations, 4,* 81–97.

Brown, R., Vivian, J., & Hewstone, M. (1999). Changing attitudes through intergroup contact: The effects of group membership salience. *European Journal of Social Psychology, 29,* 741–764.

Brown, R., & Wootton-Millward, L. (1993). Perceptions of group homogeneity during group formation and change. *Social Cognition, 11,* 126–149.

Brown, R. P., Charnsangavej, T., Keough, K. A., Newman, M. L., & Rentfrom, P. J. (2000). Putting the "affirm" into affirmative action: Preferential selection and academic performance. *Journal of Personality and Social Psychology, 79,* 736–747.

Browning, C. (1992). *Ordinary men: Reserve police battalion 101 and the final solution in Poland.* New York: HarperCollins.

Buehler, R., & Griffin, D. (2003). Planning, personality, and prediction: The role of future focus in optimistic time predictions. *Organizational Behavior and Human Decision Processes, 92,* 80–90.

Buehler, R., Griffin, D., & Ross, M. (1994). Exploring the "planning fallacy": When people underestimate their task completion times. *Journal of Personality and Social Psychology, 67,* 366–381.

Buehler, R., Griffin, D., & Ross, M. (2002). Inside the planning fallacy: The causes and consequences of optimistic time predictions. In T. Gilovich, D. Griffin, & D. Kahneman (Eds.), *Heuristics and biases: The psychology of intuitive judgment.* Cambridge: Cambridge University Press.

Burchill, S. A. L., & Stiles, W. B. (1988). Interactions of depressed college students with their roommates: Not necessarily negative. *Journal of Personality and Social Psychology, 55,* 410–419.

Bureau of the Census. (1975). *Historical abstract of the United States: Colonial times to 1970.* Washington, DC: Superintendent of Documents.

Bureau of the Census. (1993, May 4). Voting survey, reported by Associated Press.

Bureau of the Census. (1999). *Statistical abstract of the United States 1996* (Table 65). Washington, DC: Superintendent of Documents.

Burger, J. M. (1987). Increased performance with increased personal control: A self-presentation interpretation. *Journal of Experimental Social Psychology, 23,* 350–360.

Burger, J. M. (1991). Changes in attributions over time: The ephemeral fundamental attribution error. *Social Cognition, 9,* 182–193.

Burger, J. M., & Burns, L. (1988). The illusion of unique invulnerability and the use of effective contraception. *Personality and Social Psychology Bulletin, 14,* 264–270.

Burger, J. M., & Guadagno, R. E. (2003). Self-concept clarity and the foot-in-the-door procedure. *Basic and Applied Social Psychology, 25,* 79–86.

Burger, J. M., & Palmer, M. L. (1991). Changes in and generalization of unrealistic optimism following experiences with stressful events: Reactions to the 1989 California earthquake. *Personality and Social Psychology Bulletin, 18,* 39–43.

Burger, J. M., & Pavelich, J. L. (1994). Attributions for presidential elections: The situational shift over time. *Basic and Applied Social Psychology, 15,* 359–371.

Burger, J. M., Soroka, S., Gonzago, K., Murphy, E., & Somervell, E. (2001). The effect of fleeting attraction on compliance to requests. *Personality and Social Psychology Bulletin, 27,* 1578–1586.

Burkholder, R. (2003, February 14). Unwilling coalition? Majorities in Britain, Canada oppose military action in Iraq. *Gallup Poll Tuesday Briefing* (www.gallup.com/poll).

BURN, S. M. (1992). Locus of control, attributions, and helplessness in the homeless. *Journal of Applied Social Psychology, 22,* 1161–1174.

BURNS, D. D. (1980). *Feeling good: The new mood therapy.* New York: Signet.

BURNS, J. F. (2003a, April 13). Pillagers strip Iraqi museum of its treasure. *New York Times* (www.nytimes.com).

BURNS, J. F. (2003b, April 14). Baghdad residents begin a long climb to an ordered city. *New York Times* (www.nytimes.com).

BURNSTEIN, E., & VINOKUR, A. (1977). Persuasive argumentation and social comparison as determinants of attitude polarization. *Journal of Experimental Social Psychology, 13,* 315–332.

BURNSTEIN, E., & WORCHEL, P. (1962). Arbitrariness of frustration and its consequences for aggression in a social situation. *Journal of Personality, 30,* 528–540.

BURR, W. R. (1973). *Theory construction and the sociology of the family.* New York: Wiley.

BURROS, M. (1988, February 24). Women: Out of the house but not out of the kitchen. *New York Times.*

BUSHMAN, B. J. (1993). Human aggression while under the influence of alcohol and other drugs: An integrative research review. *Current Directions in Psychological Science, 2,* 148–152.

BUSHMAN, B. J. (1995). Moderating role of trait aggressiveness in the effects of violent media on aggression. *Journal of Personality and Social Psychology, 69,* 950–960.

BUSHMAN, B. J. (2002). Does venting anger feed or extinguish the flame? Catharsis, rumination, distraction, anger, and aggressive responding. *Personality and Social Psychology Bulletin, 28,* 724–731.

BUSHMAN, B. J., & ANDERSON, C. A. (2001). Media violence and the American public: Scientific facts versus media misinformation. *American Psychologist, 56,* 477–489.

BUSHMAN, B. J., & BAUMEISTER, R. (1998). Threatened egotism, narcissism, self-esteem, and direct and displaced aggression: Does self-love or self-hate lead to violence? *Journal of Personality and Social Psychology, 75,* 219–229.

BUSHMAN, B. J., BAUMEISTER, R. F., & PHILLIPS, C. M. (2001). Do people aggress to improve their mood? Catharsis beliefs, affect regulation opportunity, and aggressive responding. *Journal of Personality and Social Psychology, 81,* 17–32.

BUSHMAN, B. J., BAUMEISTER, R. F., & STACK, A. D. (1999). Catharsis, aggression, and persuasive influence: Self-fulfilling or self-defeating prophecies? *Journal of Personality and Social Psychology, 76,* 367–376.

BUSHMAN, B. J., & GEEN, R. G. (1990). Role of cognitive-emotional mediators and individual differences in the effects of media violence on aggression. *Journal of Personality and Social Psychology, 58,* 156–163.

BUSS, D. M. (1984). Toward a psychology of person-environment (PE) correlation: The role of spouse selection. *Journal of Personality and Social Psychology, 47,* 361–377.

BUSS, D. M. (1985). Human mate selection. *American Scientist, 73,* 47–51.

BUSS, D. M. (1989). Sex differences in human mate preferences: Evolutionary hypotheses tested in 37 cultures. *Behavioral and Brain Sciences, 12,* 1–49.

BUSS, D. M. (1994a). *The evolution of desire: Strategies of human mating.* New York: Basic Books.

BUSS, D. M. (1995b). Psychological sex differences: Origins through sexual selection. *American Psychologist, 50,* 164–168.

BUSS, D. M. (1999). Behind the scenes. In D. G. Myers, *Social psychology,* 6th ed. New York: McGraw-Hill.

BUTCHER, S. H. (1951). *Aristotle's theory of poetry and fine art.* New York: Dover.

BUTLER, A. C., HOKANSON, J. E., & FLYNN, H. A. (1994). A comparison of self-esteem liability and low trait self-esteem as vulnerability factors for depression. *Journal of Personality and Social Psychology, 66,* 166–177.

BUTLER, J. L., & BAUMEISTER, R. F. (1998). The trouble with friendly faces: Skilled performance with a supportive audience. *Journal of Personality and Social Psychology, 75,* 1213–1230.

BUUNK, B. P., & VAN DER EIJNDEN, R. J. J. M. (1997). Perceived prevalence, perceived superiority, and relationship satisfaction: Most relationships are good, but ours is the best. *Personality and Social Psychology Bulletin, 23,* 219–228.

BUUNK, B. P., & VAN YPEREN, N. W. (1991). Referential comparisons, relational comparisons, and exchange orientation: Their relation to marital satisfaction. *Personality and Social Psychology Bulletin, 17,* 709–717.

BYRNE, D. (1971). *The attraction paradigm*. New York: Academic Press.

BYRNE, D., & WONG, T. J. (1962). Racial prejudice, interpersonal attraction, and assumed dissimilarity of attitudes. *Journal of Abnormal and Social Psychology, 65,* 246–253.

BYRNES, J. P., MILLER, D. C., & SCHAFER, W. D. (1999). Gender differences in risk taking: A meta-analysis. *Psychological Bulletin, 125,* 367–383.

BYTWERK, R. L. (1976). Julius Streicher and the impact of *Der Stürmer. Wiener Library Bulletin, 29,* 41–46.

CACIOPPO, J. T., CLAIBORN, C. D., PETTY, R. E., & HEESACKER, M. (1991). General framework for the study of attitude change in psychotherapy. In C. R. Snyder & D. R. Forsyth (Eds.), *Handbook of social and clinical psychology.* New York: Pergamon.

CACIOPPO, J. T., PETTY, R. E., FEINSTEIN, J. A., & JARVIS, W. B. G. (1996). Dispositional differences in cognitive motivation: The life and times of individuals varying in need for cognition. *Psychological Bulletin, 119,* 197–253.

CACIOPPO, J. T., PETTY, R. E., & MORRIS, K. J. (1983). Effects of need for cognition on message evaluation, recall, and persuasion. *Journal of Personality and Social Psychology, 45,* 805–818.

CAIRNS, E., & HEWSTONE, M. (2002). The impact of peacemaking in Northern Ireland on intergroup behavior. In S. Gabi & B. Nevo (Eds.), *Peace education: The concept, principles, and practices around the world.* Mahwah, NJ: Erlbaum.

CALLHOUN, J. B. (1962, February). Population density and social pathology. *Scientific American,* 139–148.

CAMPBELL, D. T. (1975). The conflict between social and biological evolution and the concept of original sin. *Zygon, 10,* 234–249.

CAMPBELL, E. Q., & PETTIGREW, T. F. (1959). Racial and moral crisis: The role of Little Rock ministers. *American Journal of Sociology, 64,* 509–516.

CAMPBELL, W. K., & SEDIKIDES, C. (1999). Self-threat magnifies the self-serving bias: A meta-analytic integration. *Review of General Psychology, 3,* 23–43.

CANADIAN CENTRE ON SUBSTANCE ABUSE. (1997). *Canadian profile: Alcohol, tobacco, and other drugs.* Ottawa: Canadian Centre on Substance Abuse.

CANADIAN PSYCHOLOGICAL ASSOCIATION. (2000). *Canadian code of ethics for psychologists.* Ottawa: Canadian Psychological Association (www.cpa.ca/ethics2000.html).

CANTRIL, H., & BUMSTEAD, C. H. (1960). *Reflections on the human venture.* New York: New York University Press.

CARDUCCI, B. J., COSBY, P. C., & WARD, D. D. (1978). Sexual arousal and interpersonal evaluations. *Journal of Experimental Social Psychology, 14,* 449–457.

CARLI, L. L. (1991). Gender, status, and influence. In E. J. Lawler & B. Markovsky (Eds.), *Advances in group processes: Theory and research, vol. 8.* Greenwich, CT: JAI Press.

CARLI, L. L. (1999). Cognitive reconstruction, hindsight, and reactions to victims and perpetrators. *Personality and Social Psychology Bulletin, 25,* 966–979.

CARLI, L. L., & LEONARD, J. B. (1989). The effect of hindsight on victim derogation. *Journal of Social and Clinical Psychology, 8,* 331–343.

CARLSON, M., MARCUS-NEWHALL, A., & MILLER, N. (1990). Effects of situational aggression cues: A quantitative review. *Journal of Personality and Social Psychology, 58,* 622–633.

CARNEVALE, P. J., & CHOI, D-W. (2000). Culture in the mediation of international disputes. *International Journal of Psychology, 35,* 105–110.

CARROLL, D., DAVEY SMITH, G., & BENNETT, P. (1994, March). Health and socio-economic status. *The Psychologist,* pp. 122–125.

CARTER, S. L. (1993). *Reflections of an affirmative action baby.* New York: Basic Books.

CARTWRIGHT, D. S. (1975). The nature of gangs. In D. S. Cartwright, B. Tomson, & H. Schwartz (Eds.), *Gang delinquency.* Monterey, CA: Brooks/Cole.

CARVER, C. S., KUS, L. A., & SCHEIER, M. F. (1994). Effect of good versus bad mood and optimistic versus pessimistic outlook on social acceptance versus rejection. *Journal of Social and Clinical Psychology, 13,* 138–151.

CARVER, C. S., & SCHEIER, M. F. (1986). Analyzing shyness: A specific application of broader self-regulatory principles. In W. H. Jones, J. M. Cheek, & S. R. Briggs (Eds.), *Shyness: Perspectives on research and treatment.* New York: Plenum.

CASH, T. F., & JANDA, L. H. (1984, December). The eye of the beholder. *Psychology Today,* pp. 46–52.

CASPI, A., & HERBENER, E. S. (1990). Continuity and change: Assortative marriage and the consistency of personality in adulthood. *Journal of Personality and Social Psychology, 58,* 250–258.

CENTERWALL, B. S. (1989). Exposure to television as a risk factor for violence. *American Journal of Epidemiology, 129,* 643–652.

CHAIKEN, S. (1979). Communicator physical attractiveness and persuasion. *Journal of Personality and Social Psychology, 37,* 1387–1397.

CHAIKEN, S. (1980). Heuristic versus systematic information processing and the use of source versus message cues in persuasion. *Journal of Personality and Social Psychology, 39,* 752–766.

CHAIKEN, S., & MAHESWARAN, D. (1994). Neuristic processing can bias systematic processing: Effects of source credibility, argument ambiguity, and task importance on attitude judgment. *Journal of Personality and Social Psychology, 66,* 460–473.

CHANCE, J. E., & GOLDSTEIN, A. G. (1981). Depth of processing in response to own- and other-race faces. *Personality and Social Psychology Bulletin, 7,* 475–480.

CHANCE, J. E., & GOLDSTEIN, A. G. (1996). The other-race effect and eyewitness identification. In S. L. Sporer (Ed.), *Psychological issues in eyewitness identification* (pp. 153–176) Mahwah, NJ: Erlbaum.

CHAPMAN, L. J., & CHAPMAN, J. P. (1969). Genesis of popular but erroneous psychodiagnostic observations. *Journal of Abnormal Psychology, 74,* 272–280.

CHAPMAN, L. J., & CHAPMAN, J. P. (1971, November). Test results are what you think they are. *Psychology Today,* pp. 18–22, 106–107.

CHECK, J., & MALAMUTH, N. (1984). Can there be positive effects of participation in pornography experiments? *Journal of Sex Research, 20,* 14–31.

CHECK, J. M., & MELCHIOR, L. A. (1990). Shyness, self-esteem, and self-consciousness. In H. Leitenberg (Ed.), *Handbook of social and evaluation anxiety.* New York: Plenum.

CHEN, H. C., REARDON, R., & REA, C. (1992). Forewarning of content and involvement: Consequences for persuasion and resistance to persuasion. *Journal of Experimental Social Psychology, 28,* 523–541.

CHEN, L-H., BAKER, S. P., BRAVER, E. R., & LI, G. (2000). Carrying passengers as a risk factor for crashes fatal to 16- and 17-year-old drivers. *Journal of the American Medical Association, 283,* 1578–1582.

CHEN, S. C. (1937). Social modification of the activity of ants in nest-building. *Physiological Zoology, 10,* 420–436.

CHENEY, R. (2003, March 16). Comments on *Face the Nation,* CBS News.

CHODOROW, N. J. (1978). *The reproduction of mother: Psychoanalysis and the sociology of gender.* Berkeley: University of California Press.

CHODOROW, N. J. (1989). *Feminism and psychoanalytic theory.* New Haven, CT: Yale University Press.

CHOI, I., & CHOI, Y. (2002). Culture and self-concept flexibility. *Personality and Social Psychology Bulletin, 28,* 1508–1517.

CHOI, I., NISBETT, R. E., & NORENZAYAN, A. (1999). Causal attribution across cultures: Variation and universality. *Psychological Bulletin, 125,* 47–63.

CHRISTENSEN, P. N., & KASHY, D. A. (1998). Perceptions of and by lonely people in initial social interaction. *Personality and Social Psychology Bulletin, 24,* 322–329.

CHRISTIAN, J. J., FLYGER, V., & DAVIS, D. E. (1960). Factors in the mass mortality of a herd of sika deer, *Cervus Nippon. Chesapeake Science, 1,* 79–95.

CHUA-EOAN, H. (1997, April 7). Imprisoned by his own passions. *Time,* pp. 40–42.

CHURCH, G. J. (1986, January 6). China. *Time,* pp. 6–19.

CIALDINI, R. B. (1988). *Influence: Science and practice.* Glenview, IL: Scott, Foresman/Little, Brown.

CIALDINI, R. B., CACIOPPO, J. T., BASSETT, R., & MILLER, J. A. (1978). Lowball procedure for producing compliance: Commitment then cost. *Journal of Personality and Social Psychology, 36,* 463–476.

CIALDINI, R. B., DEMAINE, L. J., BARRETT, D. W., SAGARIN, B. J., & RHOADS, K. L. V. (2003). The poison parasite defense: A strategy for sapping a stronger opponent's persuasive strength. Unpublished manuscript, Arizona State University.

CIALDINI, R. B., & RICHARDSON, K. D. (1980). Two indirect tactics of image management: Basking and blasting. *Journal of Personality and Social Psychology, 39,* 406–415.

CIALDINI, R. B., WOSINSKA, W., DABUL, A. J., WHETSTONE-DION, R., & HESZEN, I. (1998). When social role salience leads to social role rejection: Modest self-presentation among women and men in two cultures. *Personality and Social Psychology Bulletin, 24,* 473–481.

CICERELLO, A., & SHEEHAN, E. P. (1995). Personal advertisements: A content analysis. *Journal of Social Behavior and Personality, 10,* 751–756.

CLANCY, S. M., & DOLLINGER, S. J. (1993). Photographic depictions of the self: Gender and age differences in social connectedness. *Sex Roles, 29,* 477–495.

CLARK, K., & CLARK, M. (1947). Racial identification and preference in Negro children. In T. M. Newcomb & E. L. Hartley (Eds.), *Readings in social psychology.* New York: Holt.

CLARK, M. S. (1984). Record keeping in two types of relationships. *Journal of Personality and Social Psychology, 47,* 549–557.

CLARK, M. S. (1986). Evidence for the effectiveness of manipulations of desire for communal versus exchange relationships. *Personality and Social Psychology Bulletin, 12,* 414–425.

CLARK, M. S., & BENNETT, M. E. (1992). Research on relationships: Implications for mental health. In D. Ruble P. Costanzo (Eds.), *The social psychology of mental health.* New York: Guilford Press.

CLARK, M. S., & MILLS, J. (1979). Interpersonal attraction in exchange and communal relationships. *Journal of Personality and Social Psychology, 37,* 12–24.

CLARK, M. S., & MILLS, J. (1993). The difference between communal and exchange relationships: What it is and is not. *Personality and Social Psychology Bulletin, 19,* 684–691.

CLARK, M. S., MILLS, J., & CORCORAN, D. (1989). Keeping track of needs and inputs of friends and strangers. *Personality and Social Psychology Bulletin, 15,* 533–542.

CLARK, M. S., MILLS, J., & POWELL, M. C. (1986). Keeping track of needs in communal and exchange relationships. *Journal of Personality and Social Psychology, 51,* 333–338.

CLARK, R. D., III. (1995). A few parallels between group polarization and minority influence. In S. Moscovici, H. Mucchi-Faina, & A. Maass (Eds.), *Minority influence.* Chicago: Nelson-Hall.

CLARKE, A. C. (1952). An examination of the operation of residual propinquity as a factor in mate selection. *American Sociological Review, 27,* 17–22.

CLARKE, V. (2003, March 25). Quoted in Street fighting: A volatile enemy. *Wall Street Journal,* pp. A1, A13.

CLIFFORD, M. M., & WALSTER, E. H. (1973). The effect of physical attractiveness on teacher expectation. *Sociology of Education, 46,* 248–258.

CLORE, G. L., BRAY, R. M., ITKIN, S. M., & MURPHY, P. (1978). Interracial attitudes and behavior at a summer camp. *Journal of Personality and Social Psychology, 36,* 107–116.

cnn.com. (2001, September 17). Hate crimes reports up in wake of terrorist attacks. cnn.com/U.S. (www.cnn.com/2001/US/09/16/gen.hate.crimes/).

COATES, B., PUSSER, H. E., & GOODMAN, I. (1976). The influence of "Sesame Street" and "Mister Rogers' Neighborhood" on children's social behavior in the preschool. *Child Development, 47,* 138–144.

COATS, E. J., & FELDMAN, R. S. (1996). Gender differences in nonverbal correlates of social status. *Personality and Social Psychology Bulletin, 22,* 1014–1022.

CODOL, J.-P. (1976). On the so-called superior conformity of the self behavior: Twenty experimental investigations. *European Journal of Social Psychology, 5,* 457–501.

COHEN, D. (1996). Law, social policy, and violence: The impact of regional cultures. *Journal of Personality and Social Psychology, 70,* 961–978.

COHEN, D. (1998). Culture, social organization, and patterns of violence. *Journal of Personality and Social Psychology, 75,* 408–419.

COHEN, M., & DAVIS, N. (1981). *Medication errors: Causes and prevention.* Philadelphia: G. F. Stickley Co. Cited by R. B. Cialdini (1989). Agents of influence: Bunglers, smugglers, and sleuths. Paper presented at the American Psychological Association convention.

COHEN, S. (1980). Training to understand TV advertising: Effects and some policy implications. Paper presented at the American Psychological Association convention.

COHN, E. G. (1993). The prediction of police calls for service: The influence of weather and temporal variables on rape and domestic violence. *Environmental Psychology, 13,* 71–83.

COMER, D. R. (1995). A model of social loafing in real work group. *Human Relations, 48,* 647–667.

COMSTOCK, G., & SCHARRER, E. (1999). *Television: What's on, who's watching and what it means*. San Diego, CA: Academic Press.

CONWAY, F., & SIEGELMAN, J. (1979). *Snapping: America's epidemic of sudden personality change*. New York: Delta Books.

CONWAY, M., & ROSS, M. (1985). Remembering one's own past: The construction of personal histories. In R. Sorrentino & E. T. Higgins (Eds.), *Handbook of motivation and cognition*. New York: Guilford Press.

CONWAY, M., & ROSS, M. (1986). Remembering one's own past: The construction of personal histories. In R. Sorrentino & E. T. Higgins (Eds.), *Handbook of motivation and cognition*. New York: Guilford.

COOK, T. D., & CURTIN, T. R. (1987). The mainstream and the underclass: Why are the differences so salient and the similarities so unobtrusive? In J. C. Masters & W. P. Smith (Eds.), *Social comparison, social justice, and relative deprivation: Theoretical, empirical, and policy perspectives*. Hillsdale, NJ: Erlbaum.

COOK, T. D., & FLAY, B. R. (1978). The persistence of experimentally induced attitude change. In L. Berkowitz (Ed.), *Advances in experimental social psychology, vol. 11*. New York: Academic Press.

COOPER, H. (1983). Teacher expectation effects. In L. Bickman (Ed.), *Applied social psychology annual, vol. 4*. Beverly Hills, CA: Sage.

COOPER, J. (1999). Unwanted consequences and the self: In search of the motivation for dissonance reduction. In E. Harmon-Jones & J. Mills (Eds.), *Cognitive dissonance: Progress on a pivotal theory in social psychology*. Washington, DC: American Psychological Association.

CORRELL, J., PARK, B., JUDD, C. M., & WITTENBRINK, B. (2002). The police officer's dilemma: Using ethnicity to disambiguate potentially threatening individuals. *Journal of Personality and Social Psychology, 83*, 1314–1329.

COSTANZO, M. (1998). *Just revenge*. New York: St. Martin's.

COTA, A. A., & DION, K. L. (1986). Salience of gender and sex composition of ad hoc groups: An experimental test of distinctiveness theory. *Journal of Personality and Social Psychology, 50*, 770–776.

COTTON, J. L. (1981). Ambient temperature and violent crime. Paper presented at the Midwestern Psychological Association convention.

COTTON, J. L. (1986). Ambient temperature and violent crime. *Journal of Applied Social Psychology, 16*, 786–801.

COTTRELL, N. B., WACK, D. L., SEKERAK, G. J., & RITTLE, R. M. (1968). Social facilitation of dominant responses by the presence of an audience and the mere presence of others. *Journal of Personality and Social Psychology, 9*, 245–250.

COURT, J. H. (1985). Sex and violence: A ripple effect. In N. M. Malamuth & E. Donnerstein (Eds.), *Pornography and sexual aggression*. New York: Academic Press.

COYNE, J. C., BURCHILL, S. A. L., & STILES, W. B. (1991). In C. R. Snyder & D. O. Forsyth (Eds.), *Handbook of social and clinical psychology: The health perspective*. New York: Pergamon.

CRABTREE, S. (2002, January 22). Gender roles reflected in teen tech use. *Gallup Tuesday Briefing* (www.gallup.com).

CRANDALL, C. S. (1994). Prejudice against fat people: Ideology and self-interest. *Journal of Personality and Social Psychology, 66*, 882–894.

CROCKER, J. (1981). Judgment of covariation by social perceivers. *Psychological Bulletin, 90*, 272–292.

CROCKER, J. (1994, October 14). Who cares what they think? Reflected and deflected appraisal. Presentation to the Society of Experimental Social Psychology meeting.

CROCKER, J. (2002). The costs of seeking self-esteem. *Journal of Social Issues, 58*, 597–615.

CROCKER, J., & GALLO, L. (1985). The self-enhancing effect of downward comparison. Paper presented at the American Psychological Association convention.

CROCKER, J., & LUHTANEN, R. (2003). Level of self-esteem and contingencies of self-worth: Unique effects on academic, social, and financial problems in college students. *Personality and Social Psychology Bulletin, 29*, 701–712.

CROCKER, J., & MCGRAW, K. M. (1984). What's good for the goose is not good for the gander: Solo status as an obstacle to occupational achievement for males and females. *American Behavioral Scientist, 27*, 357–370.

CROCKER, J., & PARK, L. E. (2004). The costly pursuit of self-esteem. *Psychological Bulletin, 130*, 392–414.

CROCKER, J., THOMPSON, L. L., McGRAW, K. M., & INGERMAN, C. (1987). Downward comparison, prejudice, and evaluations of others: Effects of self-esteem and threat. *Journal of Personality and Social Psychology, 52*, 907–916.

CROIZET, J. C., DESPRES, G., GAUZINS, M. E., HUGUET, P., LEYENS, J. P., & MEOT, A. (2004). Stereotype threat undermines intellectual performance by triggering a disruptive mental load. *Personality and Social Psychology Bulletin, 30*, 721–731.

CROSBY, F., BROMLEY, S., & SAXE, L. (1980). Recent unobtrusive studies of black and white discrimination and prejudice: A literature review. *Psychological Bulletin, 87*, 546–563.

CROSS, P. (1977, Spring). Not can but will college teaching be improved? *New Directions for Higher Education,* No. 17, pp. 1–15.

CROSS, S. E., LIAO, M-H., & JOSEPHS, R. (1992). A cross-cultural test of the self-evaluation maintenance model. Paper presented at the American Psychological Association convention.

CROSS-NATIONAL COLLABORATIVE GROUP. (1992). The changing rate of major depression. *Journal of the American Medical Association, 268*, 3098–3105.

CROXTON, J. S., EDDY, T., & MORROW, N. (1984). Memory biases in the reconstruction of interpersonal encounters. *Journal of Social and Clinical Psychology, 2*, 348–354.

CROXTON, J. S., & MILLER, A. G. (1987). Behavioral disconfirmation and the observer bias. *Journal of Social Behavior and Personality, 2*, 145–152.

CROYLE, R. T., & COOPER, J. (1983). Dissonance arousal: Physiological evidence. *Journal of Personality and Social Psychology, 45*, 782–791.

CSIKSZENTMIHALYI, M. (1990). *Flow: The psychology of optimal experience.* New York: Harper & Row.

CSIKSZENTMIHALYI, M. (1999). If we are so rich, why aren't we happy? *American Psychologist, 54*, 821–827.

CUNNINGHAM, J. D. (1981). Self-disclosure intimacy: Sex, sex-of-target, cross-national, and generational differences. *Personality and Social Psychology Bulletin, 7*, 314–319.

DABBS, J. M., JR. (1992). Testosterone measurements in social and clinical psychology. *Journal of Social and Clinical Psychology, 11*, 302–321.

DABBS, J. M., JR. (2000). *Heroes, rogues, and lovers: Testosterone and behavior.* New York: McGraw-Hill.

DABBS, J. M., JR., CARR, T. S., FRADY, R. L., & RIAD, J. K. (1995). Testosterone, crime, and misbehavior among 692 male prison inmates. *Personality and Individual Differences, 18*, 627–633.

DABBS, J. M., JR., & JANIS, I. L. (1965). Why does eating while reading facilitate opinion change? An experimental inquiry. *Journal of Experimental Social Psychology, 1*, 133–144.

DABBS, J. M., JR., & MORRIS, R. (1990). Testosterone, social class, and antisocial behavior in a sample of 4,462 men. *Psychological Science, 1*, 209–211.

DABBS, J. M., JR., RIAD, J. K., & CHANCE, S. E. (2001). Testosterone and ruthless homicide. *Personality and Individual Differences, 31*, 599–603.

DABBS, J. M., JR., STRONG, R., & MILUN, R. (1997). Exploring the mind of testosterone: A beeper study. *Journal of Research in Personality, 31*, 577–588.

DAMON, W. (1995). *Greater expectations: Overcoming the culture of indulgence in America's Homes and schools.* New York: Free Press.

DARLEY, J. M., & BERSCHEID, E. (1967). Increased liking as a result of the anticipation of personal contact. *Human Relations, 20*, 29–40.

DARLEY, J. M., & LATANÉ, B. (1968). Bystander intervention in emergencies: Diffusion of responsibility. *Journal of Personality and Social Psychology, 8*, 377–383.

DARLEY, S., & COOPER, J. (1972). Cognitive consequences of forced noncompliance. *Journal of Personality and Social Psychology, 24*, 321–326.

DARWIN, C. (1859/1988). *The origin of species. Vol. 15 of The Works of Charles Darwin,* edited by P. H. Barrett & R. B. Freeman. New York: New York University Press.

DAS, E. H. H. J., DE WIT, J. B. F., & STROEBE, W. (2003). Fear appeals motivate acceptance of action recommendations: Evidence for a positive bias in the processing of persuasive messages. *Personality and Social Psychology Bulletin, 29*, 650–664.

DASHIELL, J. F. (1930). An experimental analysis of some group effects. *Journal of Abnormal and Social Psychology, 25*, 190–199.

DAVIDSON, R. J., PUTNAM, K. M., & LARSON, C. L. (2000). Dysfunction in the neural circuitry of emotion regulation—A possible prelude to violence. *Science, 289,* 591–594.

DAVIES, P. G., SPENCER, S. J., QUINN, D. M., & GERHARDSTEIN, R. (2002). Consuming images: How television commercials that elicit stereotype threat can restrain women academically and professionally. *Personality and Social Psychology Bulletin, 28,* 1615–1628.

DAVIS, B. M., & GILBERT, L. A. (1989). Effect of dispositional and situational influences on women's dominance expression in mixed-sex dyads. *Journal of Personality and Social Psychology, 57,* 294–300.

DAVIS, K. E., & JONES, E. E. (1960). Changes in interpersonal perception as a means of reducing cognitive dissonance. *Journal of Abnormal and Social Psychology, 61,* 402–410.

DAVIS, L., & GREENLEES, C. (1992). Social loafing revisited: Factors that mitigate—and reverse—performance loss. Paper presented at the Southwestern Psychological Association convention.

DAVIS, M. H. (1979). The case for attributional egotism. Paper presented at the American Psychological Association convention.

DAVIS, M. H., & FRANZOI, S. L. (1986). Adolescent loneliness, self-disclosure, and private self-consciousness: A longitudinal investigation. *Journal of Personality and Social Psychology, 51,* 595–608.

DAVIS, M. H., & STEPHAN, W. G. (1980). Attributions for exam performance. *Journal of Applied Social Psychology, 10,* 235–248.

DAWES, R. M. (1976). Shallow psychology. In J. S. Carroll & J. W. Payne (Eds.), *Cognition and social behavior.* Hillsdale, NJ: Erlbaum.

DAWES, R. M. (1990). The potential nonfalsity of the false consensus effect. In R. M. Hogarth (Ed.), *Insights in decision making: A tribute to Hillel J. Einhorn.* Chicago: University of Chicago Press.

DAWES, R. M. (1991). Social dilemmas, economic self-interest, and evolutionary theory. In D. R. Brown & J. E. Keith Smith (Eds.), *Frontiers of mathematical psychology: Essays in honor of Clyde Coombs.* New York: Springer-Verlag.

DAWES, R. M. (1994). *House of cards: Psychology and psychotherapy built on myth.* New York: Free Press.

DAWSON, N. V., ARKES, H. R., SICILIANO, C., BLINKHORN, R., LAKSHMANAN, M., & PETRELLI, M. (1988). Hindsight bias: An impediment to accurate probability estimation in clinicopathologic conferences. *Medical Decision Making, 8,* 259–264.

DE CREMER, D. (2002). Charismatic leadership and cooperation in social dilemmas: A matter of transforming motives? *Journal of Applied Social Psychology, 32,* 997–1016.

DE JONG-GIERVELD, J. (1987). Developing and testing a model of loneliness. *Journal of Personality and Social Psychology, 53,* 119–128.

DEAUX, K., & LAFRANCE, M. (1998). Gender. In D. Gilbert, S. Fiske, & G. Lindzey (Eds.), *The handbook of social psychology,* 4th ed. Hillsdale, NJ: Erlbaum.

DECI, E. L., & RYAN, R. M. (1987). The support of autonomy and the control of behavior. *Journal of Personality and Social Psychology, 53,* 1024–1037.

DELLA CAVA, M. R. (2003, April 2). Iraq gets sympathetic press around the world. *USA Today* (www.usatoday.com).

DEMBROSKI, T. M., LASATER, T. M., & RAMIREZ, A. (1978). Communicator similarity, fear arousing communications, and compliance with health care recommendations. *Journal of Applied Social Psychology, 8,* 254–269.

DEPAULO, B. M., CHARLTON, K., COOPER, H., LINDSAY, J. J., & MUHLENBRUCK, L. (1997). The accuracy-confidence correlation in the detection of deception. *Personality and Social Psychology Review, 1,* 346–357.

DERLEGA, V., METTS, S., PETRONIO, S., & MARGULIS, S. T. (1993). *Self-disclosure.* Newbury Park, CA: Sage.

DERMER, M., COHEN, S. J., JACOBSEN, E., & ANDERSON, E. A. (1979). Evaluative judgments of aspects of life as a function of vicarious exposure to hedonic extremes. *Journal of Personality and Social Psychology, 37,* 247–260.

DERMER, M., & PYSZCZYNSKI, T. A. (1978). Effects of erotica upon men's loving and liking responses for women they love. *Journal of Personality and Social Psychology, 36,* 1302–1309.

DESFORGES, D. M., LORD, C. G., PUGH, M. A., SIA, T. L., SCARBERRY, N. C., & RATCLIFF, C. D. (1997). Role of group representativeness in the generalization part of the contact hypothesis. *Basic and Applied Social Psychology, 19,* 183–204.

DESFORGES, D. M., LORD, C. G., RAMSEY, S. L., MASON, J. A., VAN LEEUWEN, M. D., WEST, S. C., & LEPPER, M. R. (1991). Effects of structured cooperative contact on changing negative attitudes toward stigmatized social groups. *Journal of Personality and Social Psychology, 60,* 531–544.

DESMARAIS, S., & CURTIS, J. (2001). Gender and perceived income entitlement among full-time workers: Analyses for Canadian national samples, 1984 and 1994. *Basic and Applied Social Psychology, 23,* 157–168.

DESTENO, D. A., & SALOVEY, P. (1996). Jealousy and the characteristics of one's rival: A self-evaluation maintenance perspective. *Personality and Social Psychology Bulletin, 22,* 920–932.

DEUTSCH, M. (1985). *Distributive justice: A social psychological perspective.* New Haven, CT: Yale University Press.

DEUTSCH, M. (1986). Folie à deux: A psychological perspective on Soviet-American relations. In M. P. Kearns (Ed.), *Persistent patterns and emergent structures in a waving century.* New York: Praeger.

DEUTSCH, M. (1993). Educating for a peaceful world. *American Psychologist, 48,* 510–517.

DEUTSCH, M. (1994). Constructive conflict resolution: Principles, training, and research. *Journal of Social Issues, 50,* 13–32.

DEUTSCH, M. (1999). Behind the scenes. In D. G. Myers, *Social psychology* 6th ed., p. 519. New York: McGraw-Hill.

DEUTSCH, M., & COLLINS, M. E. (1951). *Interracial housing: A psychological evaluation of a social experiment.* Minneapolis: University of Minnesota Press.

DEUTSCH, M., & KRAUSS, R. M. (1960). The effect of threat upon interpersonal bargaining. *Journal of Abnormal and Social Psychology, 61,* 181–189.

DEVINE, P. G. (1989). Stereotypes and prejudice: Their automatic and controlled components. *Journal of Personality and Social Psychology, 56,* 5–18.

DEVINE, P. G., PLANT, E. A., & BUSWELL, B. N. (2000). Breaking the prejudice habit: Progress and obstacles. In S. Oskamp (Ed.), *Reducing prejudice and discrimination.* Mahwah, NJ: Erlbaum.

DEVOS-COMBY, L., & SALOVEY, P. (2002). Applying persuasion strategies to alter HIV-relevant thoughts and behavior. *Review of General Psychology, 6,* 287–304.

DEY, E. L., ASTIN, A. W., & KORN, W. S. (1991). *The American freshman: Twenty-five year trends.* Los Angeles: Higher Education Research Institute, UCLA.

DI Tella, R., MacCulloh, R. J., Oswald, A. J. (2001). Preferences over inflation and unemployment: Evidence from surveys of happiness. *The American Economic Review, 91,* 335.

DICUM, J. (2003, November 11). Letter to the editor. *New York Times,* p. A20.

DIENER, E. (1976). Effects of prior destructive behavior, anonymity, and group presence on deindividuation and aggression. *Journal of Personality and Social Psychology, 33,* 497–507.

DIENER, E. (1979). Deindividuation, self-awareness, and disinhibition. *Journal of Personality and Social Psychology, 37,* 1160–1171.

DIENER, E. (1980). Deindividuation: The absence of self-awareness and self-regulation in group members. In P. Paulus (Ed.), *The psychology of group influence.* Hillsdale, NJ: Erlbaum.

DIENER, E., & CRANDALL, R. (1979). An evaluation of the Jamaican anticrime program. *Journal of Applied Social Psychology, 9,* 135–146.

DIENER, E., HOROWITZ, J., & EMMONS, R. A. (1985). Happiness of the very wealthy. *Social Indicators, 16,* 263–274.

DIENER, E., & WALLBOM, M. (1976). Effects of self-awareness on antinormative behavior. *Journal of Research in Personality, 10,* 107–111.

DIENSTBIER, R. A., ROESCH, S. C., MIZUMOTO, A., HEMENOVER, S. H., LOTT, R. C., & CARLO, G. (1998). Effects of weapons on guilt judgments and sentencing recommendations for criminals. *Basic and Applied Social Psychology, 20,* 93–102.

DILL, J. C., & ANDERSON, C.A. (1999). Loneliness, shyness, and depression: The etiology and interrelationships of everyday problems in living. In T. Joiner and J. C. Coyne (Eds.), *The interactional nature of depression: Advances in interpersonal approaches.* Washington, DC: American Psychological Association.

DINDIA, K., & ALLEN, M. (1992). Sex differences in self-disclosure: A meta-analysis. *Psychological Bulletin, 112,* 106–124.

DION, K. K. (1972). Physical attractiveness and evaluations of children's transgressions. *Journal of Personality and Social Psychology, 24,* 207–213.

DION, K. K. (1973). Young children's stereotyping of facial attractiveness. *Developmental Psychology, 9,* 183–188.

DION, K. K., & BERSCHEID, E. (1974). Physical attractiveness and peer perception among children. *Sociometry, 37,* 1–12.

DION, K. K., & DION, K. L. (1985). Personality, gender, and the phenomenology of romantic love. In P. R. Shaver (Ed.), *Review of personality and social psychology, vol. 6.* Beverly Hills, CA: Sage.

DION, K. K., & DION, K. L. (1991). Psychological individualism and romantic love. *Journal of Social Behavior and Personality, 6,* 17–33.

DION, K. K., & DION, K. L. (1993). Individualistic and collectivistic perspectives on gender and the cultural context of love and intimacy. *Journal of Social Issues, 49,* 53–69.

DION, K. K., & DION, K. L. (1996). Cultural perspectives on romantic love. *Personal Relationships, 3,* 5–17.

DION, K. K., & STEIN, S. (1978). Physical attractiveness and interpersonal influence. *Journal of Experimental Social Psychology, 14,* 97–109.

DION, K. L. (1979). Intergroup conflict and intragroup cohesiveness. In W. G. Austin, & S. Worchel (Eds.), *The social psychology of intergroup relations.* Monterey, CA: Brooks/Cole.

DION, K. L., & DION, K. K. (1988). Romantic love: Individual and cultural perspectives. In R. J. Sternberg & M. L. Barnes (Eds.), *The psychology of love.* New Haven, CT: Yale University Press.

DISHION, T. J., MCCORD, J., & POULIN, F. (1999). When interventions harm: Peer groups and problem behavior. *American Psychologist, 54,* 755–764.

DIXON, J., & DURRHEIM, K. (2003). Contact and the ecology of racial division: Some varieties of informal segregation. *British Journal of Social Psychology, 42,* 1–23.

DOLLARD, J., DOOB, L., MILLER, N., MOWRER, O. H., & SEARS, R. R. (1939). *Frustration and aggression.* New Haven, CT: Yale University Press.

DOLNIK, L., CASE, T. I., & WILLIAMS, K. D. (2003). Stealing thunder as a courtroom tactic revisited: Processes and boundaries. *Law and Human Behavior, 27,* 265–285.

DONNERSTEIN, E. (1980). Aggressive erotica and violence against women. *Journal of Personality and Social Psychology, 39,* 269–277.

DONNERSTEIN, E. (1998). Why do we have those new ratings on television? Invited address to the National Institute on the Teaching of Psychology.

DONNERSTEIN, E., LINZ, D., & PENROD, S. (1987). *The question of pornography.* London: Free Press.

DOOB, A. N., & ROBERTS, J. (1988). Public attitudes toward sentencing in Canada. In N. Walker & M. Hough (Eds.), *Sentencing and the public.* London: Gower.

DOTY, R. M., PETERSON, B. E., & WINTER, D. G. (1991). Threat and authoritarianism in the United States, 1978–1987. *Journal of Personality and Social Psychology, 61,* 629–640.

DOUGLASS, F. (1845/1960). *Narrative of the life of Frederick Douglass, an American slave: Written by himself.* (B. Quarles, Ed.). Cambridge, MA: Harvard University Press.)

DOVIDIO, J. R., BRIGHAM, J. C., JOHNSON, B. T., & GAERTNER, S. L. (1996). Stereotyping, prejudice, and discrimination: Another look. In N. Macrae, M. Hewstone, & C. Stangor (Eds.), *Stereotypes and stereotyping.* New York: Guilford.

DRAGUNS, J. G. (1990). Normal and abnormal behavior in cross-cultural perspective: Specifying the nature of their relationship. *Nebraska Symposium on Motivation 1989, 37,* 235–277.

DROLET, A. L., & MORRIS, M. W. (2000). Rapport in conflict resolution: Accounting for how face-to-face contact fosters mutual cooperation in mixed-motive conflicts. *Journal of Experimental Social Psychology, 36,* 26–50.

DRYER, D. C., & HOROWITZ, L. M. (1997). When do opposites attract? Interpersonal complementarity versus similarity. *Journal of Personality and Social Psychology, 72,* 592–603.

DUFFY, M. (2003, June 9). Weapons of mass disappearance. *Time,* pp. 28–33.

DUGGER, C. W. (2001, April 22). Abortion in India spurred by sex text skew the ratio against girls. *New York Times,* Late edition, p. 12.

DUNN, E. W., WILSON, T. D., & GILBERT, D. T. (2003). Location, location, location: The misprediction of satisfaction in housing lotteries. *Personality and Social Psychology Bulletin, 29,* 1421–1432.

DUNNING, D. (1995). Trait importance and modifiability as factors influencing self-assessment and self-enhancement motives. *Personality and Social Psychology Bulletin, 21,* 1297–1306.

DUNNING, D. (1999). A newer look: Motivated social cognition and the schematic representation of social concepts. *Psychological Inquiry, 10,* 1–11.

DUNNING, D., GRIFFIN, D. W., MILOJKOVIC, J. D., & ROSS, L. (1990). The overconfidence effect in social prediction. *Journal of Personality and Social Psychology, 58,* 568–581.

DUNNING, D., & HAYES, A. F. (1996). Evidence for egocentric comparison in social judgment. *Journal of Personality and Social Psychology, 71,* 213–229.

DUNNING, D., MEYEROWITZ, J. A., & HOLZBERG, A. D. (1989). Ambiguity and self-evaluation. *Journal of Personality and Social Psychology, 57,* 1082–1090.

DUNNING, D., PERIE, M., & STORY, A. L. (1991). Self-serving prototypes of social categories. *Journal of Personality and Social Psychology, 61,* 957–968.

DUTTON, D. G., & ARON, A. P. (1974). Some evidence for heightened sexual attraction under conditions of high anxiety. *Journal of Personality and Social Psychology, 30,* 510–517.

EAGLY, A. H. (1987). *Sex differences in social behavior: A social-role interpretation.* Hillsdale, NJ: Erlbaum.

EAGLY, A. H. (1994). Are people prejudiced against women? Donald Campbell Award invited address, American Psychological Association convention.

EAGLY, A. H., ASHMORE, R. D., MAKHIJANI, M. G., & LONGO, L. C. (1991). What is beautiful is good, but . . . : A meta-analytic review of research on the physical attractiveness stereotype. *Psychological Bulletin, 110,* 109–128.

EAGLY, A. H., & CHAIKEN, S. (1993). *The psychology of attitudes.* San Diego, CA: Harcourt Brace Jovanovich.

EAGLY, A. H., & CROWLEY, M. (1986). Gender and helping behavior: A meta-analytic review of the social psychological literature. *Psychological Bulletin, 100,* 283–308.

EAGLY, A. H., DIEKMAN, A. B., SCHNEIDER, M., & KULESA, P. (2003). Experimental tests of an attitudinal theory of the gender gap in voting. *Personality and Social Psychology Bulletin, 29,* 1245–1258.

EAGLY, A. H., & JOHNSON, B. T. (1990). Gender and leadership style: A meta-analysis. *Psychological Bulletin, 108,* 233–256.

EAGLY, A. H., & KARAU, S. J. (2000). Few women at the top: Is prejudice a cause? Unpublished manuscript, Northwestern University.

EAGLY, A. H., MAKHIJANI, M. G., & KLONSKY, B. G. (1992). Gender and the evaluation of leaders: A meta-analysis. *Psychological Bulletin, 111,* 3–22.

EAGLY, A. H., MLADINIC, A., & OTTO, S. (1991). Are women evaluated more favorably than men? *Psychology of Women Quarterly, 15,* 203–216.

EAGLY, A. H., & WOOD, W. (1991). Explaining sex differences in social behavior: A meta-analytic perspective. *Personality and Social Psychology Bulletin, 17,* 306–315.

EAGLY, A. H., & WOOD, W. (1999). The origins of sex differences in human behavior: Evolved dispositions versus social roles. *American Psychologist, 54,* 408–423.

EASTERLIN, R. (1995). Will raising the incomes of all increase the happiness of all? *Journal of Economic Behavior and Organization, 27,* 35–47.

EBBESEN, E. B., DUNCAN, B., & KONECNI, V. J. (1975). Effects of content of verbal aggression on future verbal aggression: A field experiment. *Journal of Experimental Social Psychology, 11,* 192–204.

EDWARDS, C. P. (1991). Behavioral sex differences in children of diverse cultures: The case of nurturance to infants. In M. Pereira & L. Fairbanks (Eds.), *Juveniles: Comparative socioecology.* Oxford: Oxford University Press.

EGAN, J. (2003, November 23). Love in the time of no time. *New York Times* (www.nytimes.com).

EHRLICH, P., & FELDMAN, M. (2003). Genes and cultures: What creates our behavioral phenome? *Current Anthropology, 44,* 87–95.

EINON, D. (1994). Are men more promiscuous than women? *Ethology and Sociobiology, 15,* 131–143.

EISENBERG, N., & LENNON, R. (1983). Sex differences in empathy and related capacities. *Psychological Bulletin, 94,* 100–131.

EISER, J. R., SUTTON, S. R., & WOBER, M. (1979). Smoking, seat-belts, and beliefs about health. *Addictive Behaviors, 4,* 331–338.

ELDER, G. H., JR. (1969). Appearance and education in marriage mobility. *American Sociological Review, 34,* 519–533.

ELLEMERS, N., VAN RIJSWIJK, W., ROEFS, M., & SIMONS, C. (1997). Bias in intergroup perceptions: Balancing group identity with social reality. *Personality and Social Psychology Bulletin, 23,* 186–198.

ELLIS, B. J., & SYMONS, D. (1990). Sex difference in sexual fantasy: An evolutionary psychological approach. *Journal of Sex Research, 27,* 490–521.

ELLIS, H. D. (1981). Theoretical aspects of face recognition. In G. H. Davies, H. D. Ellis, & J. Shepherd (Eds.), *Perceiving and remembering faces.* London: Academic Press.

ELLISON, P. A., GOVERN, J. M., PETRI, H. L., & FIGLER, M. H. (1995). Anonymity and aggressive driving behavior: A field study. *Journal of Social Behavior and Personality, 10,* 265–272.

ELLYSON, S. L., DOVIDIO, J. F., & BROWN, C. E. (1991). The look of power: Gender differences and similarities in visual dominance behavior. In C. Ridgeway (Ed.), *Gender and interaction: The role of microstructures in inequality.* New York: Springer-Verlag.

ELMS, A. C. (1995). Obedience in retrospect. *Journal of Social Issues, 51,* 21–31.

ENGS, R., & HANSON, D. J. (1989). Reactance theory: A test with collegiate drinking. *Psychological Reports, 64,* 1083–1086.

ENNIS, B. J., & VERRILLI, D. B., JR. (1989). Motion for leave to file brief amicus curiae and brief of Society for the Scientific Study of Religion, American Sociological Association, and others. U.S. Supreme Court Case No. 88–1600, *Holy Spirit Association for the Unification of World Christianity, et al., v. David Molko and Tracy Leal.* On petition for write of certiorari to the Supreme Court of California. Washington, DC: Jenner & Block, 21 Dupont Circle NW.

ENNIS, R., & ZANNA, M. P. (1991). Hockey assault: Constitutive versus normative violations. Paper presented at the Canadian Psychological Association convention.

EPLEY, N., & DUNNING, D. (2000). Feeling "holier than thou": Are self-serving assessments produced by errors in self- or other prediction? *Journal of Personality and Social Psychology 79,* 861–875.

EPLEY, N., & HUFF, C. (1998). Suspicion, affective response, and educational benefit as a result of deception in psychology research. *Personality and Social Psychology Bulletin, 24,* 759–768.

ERICKSON, B., HOLMES, J. G., FREY, R., WALKER, L., & THIBAUT, J. (1974). Functions of a third party in the resolution of conflict: The role of a judge in pretrial conferences. *Journal of Personality and Social Psychology, 30,* 296–306.

ERNST, J. M., & HEESACKER, M. (1993). Application of the elaboration likelihood model of attitude change to assertion training. *Journal of Counseling Psychology, 40,* 37–45.

ERON, L. D. (1987). The development of aggressive behavior from the perspective of a developing behaviorism. *American Psychologist, 42,* 425–442.

ERON, L. D., & HUESMANN, L. R. (1980). Adolescent aggression and television. *Annals of the New York Academy of Sciences, 347,* 319–331.

ERON, L. D., & HUESMANN, L. R. (1984). The control of aggressive behavior by changes in attitudes, values, and the conditions of learning. In R. J. Blanchard & C. Blanchard (Eds.), *Advances in the study of aggression, vol. 1.* Orlando, FL: Academic Press.

ERON, L. D., & HUESMANN, L. R. (1985). The role of television in the development of prosocial and antisocial behavior. In D. Olweus, M. Radke-Yarrow, & J. Block (Eds.), *Development of antisocial and prosocial behavior.* Orlando, FL: Academic Press.

ESSES, V. M., HADDOCK, G., & ZANNA, M. P. (1993). The role of mood in the expression of intergroup stereotypes. In M. P. Zanna & J. M. Olson (Eds.), *The psychology of prejudice: The Ontario symposium, vol. 7.* Hillsdale, NJ: Erlbaum.

ESSES, V. M., JACKSON, L. M., & ARMSTRONG, T. L. (1998). Intergroup competition and attitudes toward immigrants and immigration: An instrumental model of group conflict. *Journal of Social Issues, 54,* 699–724.

ETZIONI, A. (1967). The Kennedy experiment. *The Western Political Quarterly, 20,* 361–380.

ETZIONI, A. (1999, Fall). The monochrome society. *The Public Interest, 137,* pp. 42–55.

EVANS, G. W. (1979). Behavioral and physiological consequences of crowding in humans. *Journal of Applied Social Psychology, 9,* 27–46.

EVANS, R. I., SMITH, C. K., & RAINES, B. E. (1984). Deterring cigarette smoking in adolescents: A psychosocial-behavioral analysis of an intervention strategy. In A. Baum, J. Singer, & S. Taylor (Eds.), *Handbook of psychology and health: Social psychological aspects of health, vol. 4.* Hillsdale, NJ: Erlbaum.

FARWELL, L., & WEINER, B. (2000). Bleeding hearts and the heartless: Popular perceptions of liberal and conservative ideologies. *Personality and Social Psychology Bulletin, 26,* 845–852.

FAULKNER, S. L., & WILLIAMS, K. D. (1996). A study of social loafing in industry. Paper presented to the Midwestern Psychological Association convention.

FAUST, D., & ZISKIN, J. (1988). The expert witness in psychology and psychiatry. *Science, 241,* 31–35.

FAZIO, R. H. (1990). Multiple processes by which attitudes guide behavior: The mode model as an integrative framework. *Advances in Experimental Social Psychology, 23,* 75–109.

FAZIO, R. H., EFFREIN, E. A., & FALENDER, V. J. (1981). Self-perceptions following social interaction. *Journal of Personality and Social Psychology, 41,* 232–242.

FAZIO, R. H., JACKSON, J. R., DUNTON, B. C., & WILLIAMS, C. J. (1995). Variability in automatic activation as an unobtrusive measure of racial attitudes: A bona fide pipeline? *Journal of Personality and Social Psychology, 69,* 1013–1027.

FBI. (2001). *Uniform crime reports for the United States.* Washington, DC: Federal Bureau of Investigation.

FEENEY, J., PETERSON, C., & NOLLER, P. (1994). Equity and marital satisfaction over the family life cycle. *Personality Relationships, 1,* 83–99.

FEIN, S., Hilton, J. L., & Miller, D. T. (1990). Suspicion of ulterior motivation and the correspondence bias. *Journal of Personality and Social Psychology, 58,* 753–764.

FEINGOLD, A. (1988). Matching for attractiveness in romantic partners and same-sex friends: A meta-analysis and theoretical critique. *Psychological Bulletin, 104,* 226–235.

FEINGOLD, A. (1990). Gender differences in effects of physical attractiveness on romantic attraction: A comparison across five research paradigms. *Journal of Personality and Social Psychology, 59,* 981–993.

FEINGOLD, A. (1991). Sex differences in the effects of similarity and physical attractiveness on opposite-sex attraction. *Basic and Applied Social Psychology, 12,* 357–367.

FEINGOLD, A. (1992a). Gender differences in mate selection preferences: A test of the parental investment model. *Psychological Bulletin, 112,* 125–139.

FEINGOLD, A. (1992b). Good-looking people are not what we think. *Psychology Bulletin, 111,* 304–341.

FELDMAN, R. S., & PROHASKA, T. (1979). The student as Pygmalion: Effect of student expectation on the teacher. *Journal of Educational Psychology, 71,* 485–493.

FELDMAN, R. S., & THEISS, A. J. (1982). The teacher and student as Pygmalions: Joint effects of teacher and student expectations. *Journal of Educational Psychology, 74,* 217–223.

FELSON, R. B. (1984). The effect of self-appraisals of ability on academic performance. *Journal of Personality and Social Psychology, 47,* 944–952.

FENIGSTEIN, A. (1984). Self-consciousness and the overperception of self as a target. *Journal of Personality and Social Psychology, 47,* 860–870.

FENIGSTEIN, A., & VANABLE, P. A. (1992). Paranoia and self-consciousness. *Journal of Personality and Social Psychology, 62,* 129–138.

FERGUSSON, D. M., HORWOOD, L. J., & SHANNON, F. T. (1984). A proportional hazards model of family breakdown. *Journal of Marriage and the Family, 46,* 539–549.

FESHBACH, N. D. (1980). The child as "psychologist" and "economist": Two curricula. Paper presented at the American Psychological Association convention.

FESHBACH, S. (1980). Television advertising and children: Policy issues and alternatives. Paper presented at the American Psychological Association convention.

FESTINGER, L. (1954). A theory of social comparison processes. *Human Relations, 7,* 117–140.

FESTINGER, L. (1957). *A theory of cognitive dissonance.* Stanford, CA: Stanford University Press.

FESTINGER, L., & MACCOBY, N. (1964). On resistance to persuasive communications. *Journal of Abnormal and Social Psychology, 68,* 359–366.

FESTINGER, L., PEPITONE, A., & NEWCOMB, T. (1952). Some consequences of deindividuation in a group. *Journal of Abnormal and Social Psychology, 47,* 382–389.

FIEBERT, M. S. (1990). Men, women and housework: The Roshomon effect. *Men's Studies Review, 8,* 6.

FIEDLER, F. E. (1987, September). When to lead, when to stand back. *Psychology Today,* pp. 26–27.

FIEDLER, K., SEMIN, G. R., & KOPPETSCH, C. (1991). Language use and attributional biases in close personal relationships. Personality and Social Psychology Bulletin, 17, 147–155.

FINCHAM, F. D., & JASPARS, J. M. (1980). Attribution of responsibility: From man the scientist to man as lawyer. In L. Berkowitz (Ed.), Advances in experimental social psychology (*Vol. 13*). New York: Academic Press.

FINDLEY, M. J., & COOPER, H. M. (1983). Locus of control and academic achievement: A literature review. Journal of Personality and Social Psychology, 44, 419–427.

FINEBERG, H. V. (1988). Education to prevent AIDS: Prospects and obstacles. Science, 239, 592–596.

FISCHHOFF, B. (1982). Debiasing. In D. Kahneman, P. Slovic, & A. Tversky (Eds.), Judgment under uncertainty: Heuristics and biases. New York: Cambridge University Press.

FISHBEIN, D., & THELEN, M. H. (1981a). Husband-wife similarity and marital satisfaction: A different approach. Paper presented at the Midwestern Psychological Association convention.

FISHBEIN, D., & THELEN, M. H. (1981b). Psychological factors in mate selection and marital satisfaction: A review (Ms. 2374). Catalog of Selected Documents in Psychology, 11, 84.

FISHER, H. (1994, April). The nature of romantic love. Journal of NIH Research, pp. 59–64.

FISHER, R. J. (1994). Generic principles for resolving intergroup conflict. Journal of Social Issues, 50, 47–66.

FISKE, A. P., KITAYAMA, S., MARKUS, H. R., & NISBETT, R. E. (1998). The cultural matrix of social psychology. In D. Gilbert, S. Fiske, and G. Lindzey (Eds.), The handbook of social psychology, 4th edition. Hillsdale, NJ: Erlbaum.

FISKE, S. T. (1992). Thinking is for doing: Portraits of social cognition from Daguerrotype to Laserphoto. Journal of Personality and Social Psychology, 63, 877–889.

FISKE, S. T. (1993). Controlling other people: The impact of power on stereotyping. *American Psychologist, 48,* 621–628.

FISKE, S. T. (2002, June). Envy, contempt, pity, and pride: Dangerous intergroup emotions on September 11th. Talk given at the APS symposium "Psychological science perspectives on September 11th."

FLAY, B. R., RYAN, K. B., BEST, J. A., BROWN, K. S., KERSELL, M. W., D'AVERNAS, J. R., & ZANNA, M. P. (1985). Are social-psychological smoking prevention programs effective? The Waterloo study. *Journal of Behavioral Medicine, 8,* 37–59.

FLEMING, I., Baum, A., & Weiss, L. (1987). Social density and perceived control as mediators of crowding stress in high-density residential neighborhoods. *Journal of Personality and Social Psychology, 52,* 899–906.

FLETCHER, G. J. O., FINCHAM, F. D., CRAMER, L., & HERON, N. (1987). The role of attributions in the development of dating relationships. *Journal of Personality and Social Psychology, 53,* 481–489.

FLETCHER, G. J. O., TITHER, J. M., O'LOUGHLIN, C., FRIESEN, M., & OVERALL, N. (2003). Warm and homely or cold and beautiful? Sex differences in trading off traits in mate selection. Paper presented to the Society for Personality and Social Psychology meeting, Los Angeles.

FOLEY, L. A. (1976). Personality and situational influences on changes in prejudice: A replication of Cook's railroad game in a prison setting. *Journal of Personality and Social Psychology, 34,* 846–856.

FOLLETT, M. P. (1940). Constructive conflict. In H. C. Metcalf & L. Urwick (Eds.), *Dynamic administration: The collected papers of Mary Parker Follett.* New York: Harper.

FORSYTH, D. R., & LEARY, M. R. (1997). Achieving the goals of the scientist-practitioner model: The seven interfaces of social and counseling psychology. *The Counseling Psychologist, 25,* 180–200.

FRANK, M. G., & GILOVICH, T. (1989). Effect of memory perspective on retrospective causal attributions. *Journal of Personality and Social Psychology, 57,* 399–403.

FRANK, R. (1999). *Luxury fever: Why money fails to satisfy in an era of excess.* New York: Free Press.

FREEDMAN, J. L., Birsky, J., & Cavoukian, A. (1980). Environmental determinants of behavioral contagion: Density and number. *Basic and Applied Social Psychology, 1,* 155–161.

FREEDMAN, J. L., & FRASER, S. C. (1966). Compliance without pressure: The foot-in-the-door technique. *Journal of Personality and Social Psychology, 4,* 195–202.

FREEDMAN, J. L., & PERLICK, D. (1979). Crowding, contagion, and laughter. *Journal of Experimental Social Psychology, 15,* 295–303.

FREEDMAN, J. L., & SEARS, D. O. (1965). Warning, distraction, and resistance to influence. *Journal of Personality and Social Psychology, 1,* 262–266.

FREEDMAN, J. S. (1965). Long-term behavioral effects of cognitive dissonance. *Journal of Experimental Social Psychology, 1,* 145–155.

FREEMAN, M. A. (1997). Demographic correlates of individualism and collectivism: A study of social values in Sri Lanka. *Journal of Cross-Cultural Psychology, 28,* 321–341.

FRENCH, J. R. P. (1968). The conceptualization and the measurement of mental health in terms of self-identity theory. In S. B. Sells (Ed.), *The definition and measurement of mental health.* Washington, DC: Department of Health, Education, and Welfare. (Cited by M. Rosenberg, 1979, *Conceiving the self.* New York: Basic Books.)

FRIEDMAN, T. L. (2003a, April 9). Hold your applause. *New York Times* (www.nytimes.com).

FRIEDMAN, T. L. (2003b, June 4). Because we could. *New York Times* (www.nytimes.com).

FRIEDRICH, J. (1996). On seeing oneself as less self-serving than others: The ultimate self-serving bias? *Teaching of Psychology, 23,* 107–109.

FRIEDRICH, L. K., & STEIN, A. H. (1973). Aggressive and prosocial television programs and the natural behavior of preschool children. *Monographs of the Society of Research in Child Development, 38* (4, Serial No. 151).

FRIEDRICH, L. K., & STEIN, A. H. (1975). Prosocial television and young children: The effects of verbal labeling and role playing on learning and behavior. *Child Development, 46,* 27–38.

FRIEZE, I. H., OLSON, J. E., & RUSSELL, J. (1991). Attractiveness and income for men and women in management. *Journal of Applied Social Psychology, 21,* 1039–1057.

FTC. (2003, June 12). Federal Trade Commission cigarette report for 2001 (www.ftc.gov/opa/2003/06/2001cigrpt.htm).

FURNHAM, A. (1982). Explanations for unemployment in Britain. *European Journal of Social Psychology, 12,* 335–352.

FURNHAM, A., & GUNTER. B. (1984). Just world beliefs and attitudes towards the poor. *British Journal of Social Psychology, 23,* 265–269.

GABRENYA, W. K., JR., WANG, Y.-E., & LATANÉ, B. (1985). Social loafing on an optimizing task: Cross-cultural differences among Chinese and Americans. *Journal of Cross-Cultural Psychology, 16,* 223–242.

GABRIEL, S., & GARDNER, W. L. (1999). Are there "his" and "hers" types of interdependence? The implications of gender differences in collective versus relational interdependence for affect, behavior, and cognition. *Journal of Personality and Social Psychology, 77,* 642–655.

GAERTNER, L., SEDIKIDES, C., & GRAETZ, K. (1999). In search of self-definition: Motivational primacy of the individual self, motivational primacy of the collective self, or contextual primacy? *Journal of Personality and Social Psychology, 76,* 5–18.

GAERTNER, S. L., DOVIDIO, J. F., ANASTASIO, P. A., BACHMAN, B. A., & RUST, M. C. (1993). The Common Ingroup Identity Model: Recategorization and the reduction of intergroup bias. In W. Stroebe & M. Hewstone (Eds.), *European Review of Social Psychology, vol. 4.* London: Wiley.

GAERTNER, S. L., DOVIDIO, J. F., NIER, J. A., BANKER, B. S., WARD, C. M., HOULETTE, M., & LOUX, S. (2000). The common ingroup identity model for reducing intergroup bias: Progress and challenges. In D. Capozza & R. Brown (Eds.), *Social identity processes: Trends in theory and research.* London: Sage.

GALANTER, M. (1989). *Cults: Faith, healing, and coercion.* New York: Oxford University Press.

GALANTER, M. (1990). Cults and zealous self-help movements: A psychiatric perspective. *American Journal of Psychiatry, 147,* 543–551.

GALINSKY, A. D., & MOSKOWITZ, G. B. (2000). Perspective-taking: Decreasing stereotype expression, stereotype accessibility, and in-group favoritism. *Journal of Personality and Social Psychology, 78*, 708–724.

GALIZIO, M., & HENDRICK, C. (1972). Effect of musical accompaniment on attitude: The guitar as a prop for persuasion. *Journal of Applied Social Psychology, 2*, 350–359.

GALLUP, G. H. (1972). *The Gallup poll: Public opinion 1935–1971, (vol. 3.* New York: Random House, pp. 551, 1716).

GALLUP ORGANIZATION. (1990). April 19–22 survey reported in *American Enterprise,* September/October, 1990, p. 92.

GALLUP POLL. (1990, July). Reported by G. Gallup, Jr., & F. Newport, Americans widely disagree on what constitutes "rich." *Gallup Poll Monthly,* pp. 28–36.

GANGESTAD, S. W., & THORNHILL, R. (1997). Human sexual selection and developmental stability. In J. A. Simpson & D. T. Kenrick (Eds.), *Evolutionary social psychology.* Mahwah, NJ: Erlbaum.

GARB, H. N. (1994). Judgment research: Implications for clinical practice and testimony in court. *Applied and Preventive Psychology, 3*, 173–183.

GARDNER, J., & OSWALD, A. (2001). Does money buy happiness? A longitudinal study using data on windfalls. Working paper, Department of Economics, Cambridge University.

GARDNER, M. (1997, July/August). Heaven's Gate: The UFO cult of Bo and Peep. *Skeptical Inquirer,* pp. 15–17.

GASTORF, J. W., SULS, J., & SANDERS, G. S. (1980). Type A coronary-prone behavior pattern and social facilitation. *Journal of Personality and Social Psychology, 8*, 773–780.

GATES, D. (1993, March 29). White male paranoia. *Newsweek,* pp. 48–53.

GATES, M. F., & ALLEE, W. C. (1933). Conditioned behavior of isolated and grouped cockroaches on a simple maze. *Journal of Comparative Psychology, 15*, 331–358.

GAVANSKI, I., & HOFFMAN, C. (1987). Awareness of influences on one's own judgments: The roles of covariation detection and attention to the judgment process. *Journal of Personality and Social Psychology, 52*, 453–463.

GAWANDE, A. (2002). *Complications: A surgeon's notes on an imperfect science.* New York: Metropolitan Books, Holt and Company.

GAZZANIGA, M. S. (1992). *Nature's mind: The biological roots of thinking, emotions, sexuality, language, and intelligence.* New York: Basic Books.

GEEN, R. G. (1998). Aggression and antisocial behavior. In D. Gilbert, S. Fiske, & G. Lindzey (Eds.), *Handbook of social psychology,* 4th ed. New York: McGraw-Hill.

GEEN, R. G., & GANGE, J. J. (1983). Social facilitation: Drive theory and beyond. In H. H. Blumberg, A. P. Hare, V. Kent, & M. Davies (Eds.), *Small groups and social interaction, vol. 1.* London: Wiley.

GEEN, R. G., & QUANTY, M. B. (1977). The catharsis of aggression: An evaluation of a hypothesis. In L. Berkowitz (Ed.), *Advances in experimental social psychology, (vol. 10).* New York: Academic Press.

GEEN, R. G., & THOMAS, S. L. (1986). The immediate effects of media violence on behavior. *Journal of Social Issues, 42*(3), 7–28.

GENTILE, D. A., & ANDERSON, C. A. (2003). Violent video games: The newest media violence hazard. In D. A. Gentile (Ed.), *Media violence and children.* Westport, CT: Ablex.

GERARD, H. B., & MATHEWSON, G. C. (1966). The effects of severity of initiation on liking for a group: A replication. *Journal of Experimental Social Psychology, 2*, 278–287.

GERBNER, G. (1994). The politics of media violence: Some reflections. In C. Hamelink & O. Linne (Eds.), *Mass communication research: On problems and policies.* Norwood, NJ: Ablex.

GERRIG, R. J., & PRENTICE, D. A. (1991, September). The representation of fictional information. *Psychological Science, 2*, 336–340.

GERSTENFELD, P. B., GRANT, D. R., & CHIANG, C-P. (2003). Hate online: A content analysis of extremist Internet sites. *Analyses of Social Issues and Public Policy, 3*, 29–44.

GIBSON, B., & SANBONMATSU, D. M. (2004). Optimism, pessimism, and gambling: The downside of optimism. *Personality and Social Psychology Bulletin, 30*, 149–160.

GIFFORD, R., & HINE, D. W. (1997). Toward cooperation in commons dilemmas. *Canadian Journal of Behavioural Science, 29*, 167–179.

GIFFORD, R., & Peacock, J. (1979). Crowding: More fearsome than crime-provoking? Comparison of an Asian city and a North American city. *Psychologia, 22*, 79–83.

GIGONE, D., & HASTIE, R. (1993). The common knowledge effect: Information sharing and group judgment. *Journal of Personality and Social Psychology, 65*, 959–974.

GILBERT, D. T., & EBERT, J. E. J. (2002). Decisions and revisions: The affective forecasting of escapable outcomes. Unpublished manuscript, Harvard University.

GILBERT, D. T., & HIXON, J. G. (1991). The trouble of thinking: Activation and application of stereotypic beliefs. *Journal of Personality and Social Psychology, 60*, 509–517.

GILBERT, D. T., LIEBERMAN, M. D., MOREWEDGE, C. K., & WILSON, T. D. (2004). The peculiar longevity of things not so bad. *Psychological Science, 15*, 14–19.

GILBERT, D. T., McNULTY, S. E., GIULIANO, T. A., & BENSON, J. E. (1992). Blurry words and fuzzy deeds: The attribution of obscure behavior. *Journal of Personality and Social Psychology, 62*, 18–25.

GILBERT, D. T., PELHAM, B. W., & KRULL, D. S. (1988). On cognitive busyness: When person perceivers meet persons perceived. *Journal of Personality and Social Psychology, 54*, 733–740.

GILBERT, D. T., PINEL, E. C., WILSON, T. D., BLUMBERG, S. J., & WHEATLEY, T. P. (1998). Immune neglect: A source of durability bias in affective forecasting. *Journal of Personality and Social Psychology, 75*, 617–638.

GILBERT, D. T., & WILSON, T. D. (2000). Miswanting: Some problems in the forecasting of future affective states. In J. Forgas (Ed.), *Feeling and thinking: The role of affect in social cognition.* Cambridge: Cambridge University Press.

GILLHAM, J. E., Reivich, K. J., & Shatte, A. J. (2000a, b). Building optimism and preventing depressive symptoms in children. In E. C. Change (Ed.), *Optimism and pessimism. Washington,* DC: APA Books.

GILLIGAN, C. (1982). In a different voice: Psychological theory and women's development. Cambridge, MA: Harvard University Press.

GILLIGAN, C., LYONS, N. P., & HANMER, T. J. (Eds.). (1990). Making connections: The relational worlds of adolescent girls at Emma Willard School. Cambridge, MA: Harvard University Press.

GILLIS, J. S., & AVIS, W. E. (1980). The male-taller norm in mate selection. *Personality and Social Psychology Bulletin, 6*, 396–401.

GILMOR, T. M., & REID, D. W. (1979). Locus of control and causal attribution for positive and negative outcomes on university examinations. *Journal of Research in Personality, 13*, 154–160.

GILOVICH, T. (1987). Secondhand information and social judgment. *Journal of Experimental Social Psychology, 23*, 59–74.

GILOVICH, T., & DOUGLAS, C. (1986). Biased evaluations of randomly determined gambling outcomes. *Journal of Experimental Social Psychology, 22*, 228–241.

GILOVICH, T., KERR, M., & MEDVEC, V. H. (1993). Effect of temporal perspective on subjective confidence. *Journal of Personality and Social Psychology, 64*, 552–560.

GILOVICH, T., MEDVEC, V. H., & SAVITSKY, K. (2000). The spotlight effect in social judgment: An egocentric bias in estimates of the salience of one's own actions and appearance. *Journal of Personality and Social Psychology, 78*, 211–222.

GILOVICH, T., SAVITSKY, K., & MEDVEC, V. H. (1998). The illusion of transparency: Biased assessments of others' ability to read one's emotional states. *Journal of Personality and Social Psychology, 75*, 332–346.

GINER-SOROLLA, R., GARCIA, M. T., & BARGH, J. (1999). The automatic evaluation of pictures. *Social Cognition, 17*, 79–96.

GINSBURG, B., & ALLEE, W. C. (1942). Some effects of conditioning on social dominance and subordination in inbred strains of mice. *Physiological Zoology, 15*, 485–506.

GLADWELL, M. (2003, March 10). Connecting the dots: The paradoxes of intelligence reform. *The New Yorker,* pp. 83–88.

GLASS, D. C. (1964). Changes in liking as a means of reducing cognitive discrepancies between self-esteem and aggression. *Journal of Personality, 32*, 531–549.

GLENN, N. D. (1980). Aging and attitudinal stability. In O. G. Brim, Jr. & J. Kagan (Eds.), *Constancy and change in human development.* Cambridge, MA: Harvard University Press.

GLENN, N. D. (1981). Personal communication.

GOETHALS, G. R., MESSICK, D. M., & ALLISON, S. T. (1991). The uniqueness bias: Studies of constructive social comparison. In J. Suls & T. A. Wills (Eds.), *Social comparison: Contemporary theory and research.* Hillsdale, NJ: Erlbaum.

GOETHALS, G. R., & Zanna, M. P. (1979). The rold of social comparison in choice shifts. *Journal of Personality and Social Psychology, 37,* 1469–1476.

GOGGIN, W. C., & RANGE, L. M. (1985). The disadvantages of hindsight in the perception of suicide. *Journal of Social and Clinical Psychology, 3,* 232–237.

GOLDHAGEN, D. J. (1996). *Hitler's willing executioners.* New York: Knopf.

GOLDMAN, J. (1967). A comparison of sensory modality preference of children and adults. Dissertation: Thesis (Ph.D.). Ferkauf Graduate School of Humanities and Social Sciences, Yeshiva University.

GOLDMAN, W., & LEWIS, P. (1977). Beautiful is good: Evidence that the physically attractive are more socially skillful. *Journal of Experimental Social Psychology, 13,* 125–130.

GOLDSMITH, C. (2003, March 25). World media turn wary eye on U.S. *Wall Street Journal,* p. A12.

GOLDSTEIN, A. P., GLICK, B., & GIBBS, J. C. (1998). *Aggression replacement training: A comprehensive intervention for aggressive youth* (rev. ed.). Champaign, IL: Research Press.

GOLDSTEIN, J. H., & ARMS, R. L. (1971). Effects of observing athletic contests on hostility. *Sociometry, 34,* 83–90.

GONZAGA, G., KELTNER, D., LONDAHL, E. A., & SMITH, M. D. (2001). Love and the commitment problem in romantic relations and friendship. *Journal of Personality and Social Psychology, 81,* 247–262.

GOODHART, D. E. (1986). The effects of positive and negative thinking on performance in an achievement situation. *Journal of Personality and Social Psychology, 51,* 117–124.

GORTMAKER, S. L., MUST, A., PERRIN, J. M., SOBOL, A. M., & DIETZ, W. H. (1993). Social and economic consequences of overweight in adolescence and young adulthood. *New England Journal of Medicine, 329,* 1008–1012.

GOTLIB, I. H., & LEE, C. M. (1989). The social functioning of depressed patients: A longitudinal assessment. *Journal of Social and Clinical Psychology, 8,* 223–237.

GOTTMAN, J. (with N. Silver). (1994). *Why marriages succeed or fail.* New York: Simon & Schuster.

GOTTMAN, J. M. (1998). Psychology and the study of marital processes. *Annual Review of Psychology, 49,* 169–197.

GOULD, S. J. (1997, October 20). Quoted by J. M. Nash, Evolutionary pop star. *Time,* p. 92.

GRAHAM, S., WEINER, B., & ZUCKER, G. S. (1997). An attributional analysis of punishment goals and public reactions to O. J. Simpson. *Personality and Social Psychology Bulletin, 23,* 331–346.

GRAY, J. D., & SILVER, R. C. (1990). Opposite sides of the same coin: Former spouses' divergent perspectives in coping with their divorce. *Journal of Personality and Social Psychology, 59,* 1180–1191.

GREELEY, A. M. (1991). *Faithful attraction.* New York: Tor Books.

GREELEY, A. M., & SHEATSLEY, P. B. (1971). Attitudes toward racial integration. *Scientific American, 225*(6), 13–19.

GREEN, D. P., GLASER, J., & RICH, A. (1998). From lynching to gay bashing: The elusive connection between economic conditions and hate crime. *Journal of Personality and Social Psychology, 75,* 82–92.

GREEN, M. C., STRANGE, J. J., & BROCK, T. C. (EDS.). (2002). *Narrative impact: Social and cognitive foundations.* Mahwah, NJ: Erlbaum.

GREENBERG, J. (1986). Differential intolerance for inequity from organizational and individual agents. *Journal of Applied Social Psychology, 16,* 191–196.

GREENBERG, J., PYSZCZYNSKI, T., BURLING, J., & TIBBS, K. (1992). Depression, self-focused attention, and the self-serving attributional bias. *Personality and Individual Differences, 13,* 959–965.

GREENBERG, J., SOLOMON, S., & PYSZCZYNSKI, T. (1997). Terror management theory of self-esteem and cultural worldviews: Empirical assessments and conceptual refinements. *Advances in Experimental Social Psychology, 29,* 61–142.

GREENWALD, A. G. (1980). The totalitarian ego: Fabrication and revision of personal history. *American Psychologist, 35,* 603–618.

GREENWALD, A. G. (1992). New look 3: Unconscious cognition reclaimed. *American Psychologist, 47,* 766–779.

GREENWALD, A. G., & BANAJI, M. R. (1995). Implicit social cognition: Attitudes, self-esteem, and stereotypes. *Psychological Review, 102,* 4–27.

GREENWALD, A. G., BANAJI, M. R., RUDMAN, L. A., FARNHAM, S. D., NOSEK, B. A., & ROSIER, M. (2000). Prologue to a unified theory of attitudes, stereotypes, and self-concept. In J. P. Forgas (Ed.), *Feeling and thinking: The role of affect in social cognition and behavior.* New York: Cambridge University Press.

GREENWALD, A. G., CARNOT, C. G., BEACH, R., & YOUNG, B. (1987). Increasing voting behavior by asking people if they expect to vote. *Journal of Applied Psychology, 72,* 315–318.

GREENWALD, A. G., MCGHEE, D. E., & SCHWARTZ, J. L. K. (1998). Measuring individual differences in implicit cognition: The implicit association test. *Journal of Personality and Social Psychology, 74,* 1464–1480.

GREENWALD, A. G., NOSEK, B. A., & BANAJI, M. R. (2003). Understanding and using the implicit association test: I. An improved scoring algorithm. *Journal of Personality and Social Psychology, 85,* 197–216.

GRIFFIN, B. Q., COMBS, A. L., LAND, M. L., & COMBS, N. N. (1983). Attribution of success and failure in college performance. *Journal of Psychology, 114,* 259–266.

GRIFFITT, W. (1970). Environmental effects on interpersonal affective behavior. Ambient effective temperature and attraction. *Journal of Personality and Social Psychology, 15,* 240–244.

GRIFFITT, W. (1987). Females, males, and sexual responses. In K. Kelley (Ed.), *Females, males, and sexuality: Theories and research.* Albany: State University of New York Press.

GRIFFITT, W., & VEITCH, R. (1971). Hot and crowded: Influences of population density and temperature on interpersonal affective behavior. *Journal of Personality and Social Psychology, 17,* 92–98.

GRIFFITT, W., & VEITCH, R. (1974). Preacquaintance attitude similarity and attraction revisited: Ten days in a fallout shelter. *Sociometry, 37,* 163–173.

GROENENBOOM, A., WILKE, H. A. M., & WIT, A. P. (2001). Will we be working together again? The impact of future interdependence on group members' task motivation. *European Journal of Social Psychology, 31,* 369–378.

GROSS, A. E., & CROFTON, C. (1977). What is good is beautiful. *Sociometry, 40,* 85–90.

GROVE, J. R., HANRAHAN, S. J., & MCINMAN, A. (1991). Success/failure bias in attributions across involvement categories in sport. *Personality and Social Psychology Bulletin, 17,* 93–97.

GRUDER, C. L., COOK, T. D., HENNIGAN, K. M., FLAY, B., ALESSIS, C., & KALAMAJ, J. (1978). Empirical tests of the absolute sleeper effect predicted from the discounting cue hypothesis. *Journal of Personality and Social Psychology, 36,* 1061–1074.

GRUMAN, J. C., & SLOAN, R. P. (1983). Disease as justice: Perceptions of the victims of physical illness. *Basic and Applied Social Psychology, 4,* 39–46.

GRUNBERGER, R. (1971). *The 12-year-Reich: A social history of Nazi Germany 1933–1945.* New York: Holt, Rinehart & Winston.

GRUSH, J. E. (1980). Impact of candidate expenditures, regionality, and prior outcomes on the 1976 Democratic presidential primaries. *Journal of Personality and Social Psychology, 38,* 337–347.

GUDYKUNST, W. B. (1989). Culture and intergroup processes. In M. H. Bond (Ed.), *The cross-cultural challenge to social psychology.* Newbury Park, CA: Sage.

GUÉGUEN, N., & JACOB, C. (2001). Fund-raising on the Web: The effect of an electronic foot-in-the-door on donation. *CyberPsychology and Behavior, 4,* 705–709.

GUERIN, B. (1993). *Social facilitation.* Paris: Cambridge University Press.

GUERIN, B. (1994). What do people think about the risks of driving? Implications for traffic safety interventions. *Journal of Applied Social Psychology, 24,* 994–1021.

GUERIN, B. (1999). Social behaviors as determined by different arrangements of social consequences: Social loafing, social facilitation, deindividuation, and a modified social loafing. *The Psychological Record, 49,* 565–578.

GUERIN, B., & INNES, J. M. (1982). Social facilitation and social monitoring: A new look at Zajonc's mere presence hypothesis. *British Journal of Social Psychology, 21,* 7–18.

GUINESS, O. (1993). *The American hour: A time of reckoning and the once and future role of faith.* New York: Free Press.

GUNDERSEN, E. (2001, August 1). MTV is a many splintered thing. *USA Today*, p. 1D.

GUPTA, U., & SINGH, P. (1982). Exploratory study of love and liking and type of marriages. *Indian Journal of Applied Psychology, 19,* 92–97.

HACKMAN, J. R. (1986). The design of work teams. In J. Lorsch (Ed.), *Handbook of organizational behavior.* Englewood Cliffs, NJ: Prentice-Hall.

HADDOCK, G., & ZANNA, M. P. (1994). Preferring "housewives" to "feminists." *Psychology of Women Quarterly, 18,* 25–52.

HAEMMERLIE, F. M. (1987). Creating adaptive illusions in counseling and therapy using a self-perception theory perspective. Paper presented at the Midwestern Psychological Association, Chicago.

HAEMMERLIE, F. M., & MONTGOMERY, R. L. (1982). Self-perception theory and unobtrusively biased interactions: A treatment for heterosocial anxiety. *Journal of Counseling Psychology, 29,* 362–370.

HAEMMERLIE, F. M., & MONTGOMERY, R. L. (1984). Purposefully biased interventions: Reducing heterosocial anxiety through self-perception theory. *Journal of Personality and Social Psychology, 47,* 900–908.

HAEMMERLIE, F. M., & MONTGOMERY, R. L. (1986). Self-perception theory and the treatment of shyness. In W. H. Jones, J. M. Cheek, & S. R. Briggs (Eds.), *A sourcebook on shyness: Research and treatment.* New York: Plenum.

HAGERTY, M. R. (2000). Social comparisons of income in one's community: Evidence from national surveys of income and happiness. *Journal of Personality and Social Psychology, 78,* 764–771.

HALBERSTADT, J., & RHODES, G. (2000). The attractiveness of nonface averages: Implications for an evolutionary explanation of the attractiveness of average faces. *Psychological Science, 11,* 285–289.

HALL, J. A. (1984). *Nonverbal sex differences: Communication accuracy and expressive style.* Baltimore: Johns Hopkins University Press.

HALL, T. (1985, June 25). The unconverted: Smoking of cigarettes seems to be becoming a lower-class habit. *Wall Street Journal,* pp. 1, 25.

HAMBERGER, J., & HEWSTONE, M. (1997). Inter-ethnic contact as a predictor of blatant and subtle prejudice: Tests of a model in four West European nations. *British Journal of Social Psychology, 36,* 173–190.

HAMBLIN, R. L., BUCKHOLDT, D., BUSHELL, D., ELLIS, D., & FERITOR, D. (1969, January). Changing the game from get the teacher to learn. *Transaction,* pp. 20–25, 28–31.

HAMILTON, V. L., HOFFMAN, W. S., BROMAN, C. L., & RAUMA, D. (1993). Unemployment, distress, and coping: A panel study of autoworkers. *Journal of Personality and Social Psychology, 65,* 234–247.

HANEY, C., & ZIMBARDO, P. (1998). The past and future of U.S. prison policy: Twenty-five years after the Stanford Prison Experiment. *American Psychologist, 53,* 709–727.

HARDIN, G. (1968). The tragedy of the commons. *Science, 162,* 1243–1248.

HARDY, C., & LATANÉ, B. (1986). Social loafing on a cheering task. *Social Science, 71,* 165–172.

HARITOS-FATOUROS, M. (1988). The official torturer: A learning model for obedience to the authority of violence. *Journal of Applied Social Psychology, 18,* 1107–1120.

HARITOS-FATOUROS, M. (2002). *Psychological origins of institutionalized torture.* New York: Routledge.

HARKINS, S. G. (1981). Effects of task difficulty and task responsibility on social loafing. Presentation to the First International Conference on Social Processes in Small Groups, Kill Devil Hills, North Carolina.

HARKINS, S. G., & JACKSON, J. M. (1985). The role of evaluation in eliminating social loafing. *Personality and Social Psychology Bulletin, 11,* 457–465.

HARKINS, S. G., LATANÉ, B., & WILLIAMS, K. (1980). Social loafing: Allocating effort or taking it easy? *Journal of Experimental Social Psychology, 16,* 457–465.

HARKINS, S. G., & PETTY, R. E. (1981). Effects of source magnification of cognitive effort on attitudes: An information-processing view. *Journal of Personality and Social Psychology, 40,* 401–413.

HARKINS, S. G., & PETTY, R. E. (1982). Effects of task difficulty and task uniqueness on social loafing. *Journal of Personality and Social Psychology, 43,* 1214–1229.

HARKINS, S. G., & PETTY, R. E. (1987). Information utility and the multiple source effect. *Journal of Personality and Social Psychology, 52,* 260–268.

HARKINS, S. G., & SZYMANSKI, K. (1989). Social loafing and group evaluation. *Journal of Personality and Social Psychology, 56,* 934–941.

HARMON, A. (2003, June 29). Online dating sheds its stigma as Losers.com. *New York Times* (www.nytimes.com).

HARRIES, K. D., & STADLER, S. J. (1988). Heat and violence: New findings from Dallas field data, 1980–1981. *Journal of Applied Social Psychology, 18,* 129–138.

HARRIS, J. R. (1998). *The nurture assumption.* New York: Free Press.

HARRIS, M. J. (1994). Self-fulfilling prophecies in the clinical context: Review and implications for clinical practice. *Applied & Preventive Psychology, 3,* 145–158.

HARRIS, M. J., & ROSENTHAL, R. (1985). Mediation of interpersonal expectancy effects: 31 meta-analyses. *Psychological Bulletin, 97,* 363–386.

HARRIS, M. J., & ROSENTHAL, R. (1986). Four factors in the mediation of teacher expectancy effects. In R. S. Feldman (Ed.), *The social psychology of education.* New York: Cambridge University Press.

HARRISON, A. A. (1977). Mere exposure. In L. Berkowitz (Ed.), *Advances in experimental social psychology, (vol. 10).* New York: Academic Press, pp. 39–83.

HARVEY, J. H., TOWN, J. P., & YARKIN, K. L. (1981). How fundamental is the fundamental attribution error? *Journal of Personality and Social Psychology, 40,* 346–349.

HATFIELD, E. (1988). Passionate and compassionate love. In R. J. Sternberg & M. L. Barnes (Eds.), *The psychology of love.* New Haven, CT: Yale University Press.

HATFIELD, E., & RAPSON, R. L. (1987). Passionate love: New directions in research. In W. H. Jones & D. Perlman (Eds.), *Advances in personal relationships, vol. 1.* Greenwich, CT: JAI Press.

HATFIELD, E., & SPRECHER, S. (1986). *Mirror, mirror: The importance of looks in everyday life.* Albany: State University of New York Press.

HATFIELD, E., TRAUPMANN, J., SPRECHER, S., UTNE, M., & HAY, J. (1985). Equity and intimate relations: Recent research. In W. Ickes (Ed.), *Compatible and incompatible relationships.* New York: Springer-Verlag.

HATFIELD (WALSTER), E., ARONSON, V., ABRAHAMS, D., & ROTTMAN, L. (1966). Importance of physical attractiveness in dating behavior. *Journal of Personality and Social Psychology, 4,* 508–516.

HATFIELD (WALSTER), E., WALSTER, G. W., & BERSCHEID, E. (1978). *Equity: Theory and research.* Boston: Allyn & Bacon.

HAZAN, C., & SHAVER, P. R. (1994). Attachment as an organizational framework for research on close relationships. *Psychological Inquiry, 5,* 1–22.

HEADEY, B., & WEARING, A. (1987). The sense of relative superiority—central to well-being. *Social Indicators Research, 20,* 497–516.

HEAP, B., & KENT, J. (EDS.). (2000). *Towards sustainable consumption: A European perspective.* London: The Royal Society.

HEATHERTON, T. F., & VOHS, K. D. (2000). Personality processes and individual differences—interpersonal evaluations following threats to self: Role of self-esteem. *Journal of Personality and Social Psychology, 78,* 725–736.

HEBL, M. R., & HEATHERTON, T. F. (1998). The stigma of obesity in women: The difference is black and white. *Personality and Social Psychology Bulletin, 24,* 417–426.

HEBL, M. R., & MANNIX, L. M. (2003). The weight of obesity in evaluating others: A mere proximity effect. *Personality and Social Psychology Bulletin, 29,* 28–38.

HEESACKER, M. (1989). Counseling and the elaboration likelihood model of attitude change. In J. F. Cruz, R. A. Goncalves, & P. P. Machado (Eds.), *Psychology and education: Investigations and interventions.* (Proceedings of the International Conference on Interventions in Psychology and Education, Porto, Portugal, July 1987.) Porto, Portugal: Portugese Psychological Association.

HEILMAN, M. E. (1976). Oppositional behavior as a function of influence attempt intensity and retaliation threat. *Journal of Personality and Social Psychology, 33,* 574–578.

HEINE, S. J., LEHMAN, D. R., MARKUS, H. R., & KITAYAMA, S. (1999). Is there a universal need for positive self-regard? *Psychological Review, 106,* 766–794.

HELLMAN, P. (1980). *Avenue of the righteous of nations.* New York: Atheneum.

HENDERSON-KING, E. I., & NISBETT, R. E. (1996). Anti-black prejudice as a function of exposure to the negative behavior of a single black person. *Journal of Personality and Social Psychology, 71,* 654–664.

HENDRICK, C., & HENDRICK, S. (1993). *Romantic love.* Newbury Park, CA: Sage.

HENDRICK, C., & HENDRICK, S. (2003). Romantic love: Measuring Cupid's arrow. In S. J. Lopez & C. R. Snyder (Eds.), *Positive psychological assessment: A handbook of models and measures*. Washington, DC: American Psychological Association.

HENDRICK, S. S., & HENDRICK, C. (1995). Gender differences and similarities in sex and love. *Personal Relationships, 2,* 55–65.

HENDRICK, S. S., & HENDRICK, C. (1997). Love and satisfaction. In R. J. Sternberg & M. Hojjat (Eds.), *Satisfaction in close relationships*. New York: Guilford Press.

HENDRICK, S. S., HENDRICK, C., & ADLER, N. L. (1988). Romantic relationships: Love, satisfaction, and staying together. *Journal of Personality and Social Psychology, 54,* 980–988.

HENRY, W. A., III. (1994, June 27). Pride and prejudice. *Time,* pp. 54–59.

HENSLIN, M. (1967). Craps and magic. *American Journal of Sociology, 73,* 316–330.

HEPWORTH, J. T., & WEST, S. G. (1988). Lynchings and the economy: A time-series reanalysis of Hovland and Sears (1940). *Journal of Personality and Social Psychology, 55,* 239–247.

HERADSTVEIT, D. (1979). *The Arab-Israeli conflict: Psychological obstacles to peace, (vol. 28).* Oslo, Norway: Universitetsforlaget. Distributed by Columbia University Press. Reviewed by R. K. White (1980), *Contemporary Psychology, 25,* 11–12.

HEREK, G. (1993). Interpersonal contact and heterosexuals' attitudes toward gay men: Results from a national survey. *Journal of Sex Research, 30,* 239–244.

HEWSTONE, M. (2003). Intergroup contact: Panacea for prejudice? *The Psychologist, 16,* 352–355.

HEWSTONE, M., HANTZI, A., & JOHNSTON, L. (1991). Social categorisation and person memory: The pervasiveness of race as an organizing principle. *European Journal of Social Psychology, 21,* 517–528.

HIGBEE, K. L., MILLARD, R. J., & FOLKMAN, J. R. (1982). Social psychology research during the 1970s: Predominance of experimentation and college students. *Personality and Social Psychology Bulletin, 8,* 180–183.

HIGGINS, E. T., & BARGH, J. A. (1987). Social cognition and social perception. *Annual Review of Psychology, 38,* 369–425.

HIGGINS, E. T., & McCANN, C. D. (1984). Social encoding and subsequent attitudes, impressions and memory: "Context-driven" and motivational aspects of processing. *Journal of Personality and Social Psychology, 47,* 26–39.

HIGGINS, E. T., & RHOLES, W. S. (1978). Saying is believing: Effects of message modification on memory and liking for the person described. *Journal of Experimental Social Psychology, 14,* 363–378.

HILEMAN, B. (1999, August 9). Case grows for climate change. *Chemical and Engineering News,* pp. 16–23.

HILL, T., SMITH, N. D., & LEWICKI, P. (1989). The development of self-image bias: A real-world demonstration. *Personality and Social Psychology Bulletin, 15,* 205–211.

HINE, D. W., & GIFFORD, R. (1996). Attributions about self and others in commons dilemmas. *European Journal of Social Psychology, 26,* 429–445.

HINES, M., & GREEN, R. (1991). Human hormonal and neural correlates of sex-typed behaviors. *Review of Psychiatry, 10,* 536–555.

HINSZ, V. B., TINDALE, R. S., & VOLLRATH, D. A. (1997). The emerging conceptualization of groups as information processors. *Psychological Bulletin, 121,* 43–64.

HIRSCHMAN, R. S., & LEVENTHAL, H. (1989). Preventing smoking behavior in school children: An initial test of a cognitive-development program. *Journal of Applied Social Psychology, 19,* 559–583.

HIRT, E. R. (1990). Do I see only what I expect? Evidence for an expectancy-guided retrieval model. *Journal of Personality and Social Psychology, 58,* 937–951.

HIRT, E. R., ZILLMANN, D., ERICKSON, G. A., & KENNEDY, C. (1992). Costs and benefits of allegiance: Changes in fans' self-ascribed competencies after team victory versus defeat. *Journal of Personality and Social Psychology, 63,* 724–738.

HOFFMAN, C., & HURST, N. (1990). Gender stereotypes: Perception or rationalization? *Journal of Personality and Social Psychology, 58,* 197–208.

HOFFMAN, L. W. (1977). Changes in family roles, socialization, and sex differences. *American Psychologist, 32,* 644–657.

HOFFRAGE, U., HERTWIG, R., & GIGERENZER, G. (2000, May). Hindsight bias: A by-product of knowledge updating? *Journal of Experimental Psychology: Learning, Memory, and Cognition, 26,* 566–581.

HOFLING, C. K., BROTZMAN, E., DAIRYMPLE, S., GRAVES, N., & PIERCE, C. M. (1966). An experimental study in nurse-physician relationships. *Journal of Nervous and Mental Disease, 143,* 171–180.

HOGAN, R., CURPHY, G. J., & HOGAN, J. (1994). What we know about leadership: Effectiveness and personality. *American Psychologist, 49,* 493–504.

HOGG, M. A. (1992). *The social psychology of group cohesiveness: From attraction to social identity.* London: Harvester Wheatsheaf.

HOGG, M. A. (1996). Intragroup processes, group structure and social identity. In W. P. Robinson (Ed.), *Social groups and identities: Developing the legacy of Henri Tajfel.* Oxford: Butterworth Heinemann.

HOGG, M. A. (2003). Social identity. In M. R. Leary & J. P. Tangey (Eds.), *Handbook of self and identity.* New York: Guilford Press.

HOGG, M. A., HAINS, S. C., & MASON, I. (1998). Identification and leadership in small groups: Salience, frame of reference, and leader stereotypicality effects on leader evaluations. *Journal of Personality and Social Psychology, 75,* 1248–1263.

HOGG, M. A., TURNER, J. C., & DAVIDSON, B. (1990). Polarized norms and social frames of reference: A test of the self-categorization theory of group polarization. *Basic and Applied Social Psychology, 11,* 77–100.

HOLMBERG, D., & HOLMES, J. G. (1994). Reconstruction of relationship memories: A mental models approach. In N. Schwarz & S. Sudman (Eds.), *Autobiographical memory and the validity of retrospective reports.* New York: Springer-Verlag.

HOLMES, J. G., & REMPEL, J. K. (1989). Trust in close relationships. In C. Hendrick (Ed.), *Review of personality and social psychology, vol. 10.* Newbury Park, CA: Sage.

HOLTGRAVES, T. (1997). Styles of language use: Individual and cultural variability in conversational indirectness. *Journal of Personality and Social Psychology, 73,* 624–637.

HOORENS, V. (1993). Self-enhancement and superiority biases in social comparison. In W. Stroebe & M. Hewstone (Eds.), *European review of social psychology, vol. 4.* Chichester, England: Wiley.

HOORENS, V. (1995). Self-favoring biases, self-presentation and the self-other asymmetry in social comparison. *Journal of Personality, 63,* 793–819.

HOORENS, V., & NUTTIN, J. M. (1993). Overvaluation of own attributes: Mere ownership or subjective frequency? *Social Cognition, 11,* 177–200.

HOORENS, V., NUTTIN, J. M., HERMAN, I. E., & PAVAKANUN, U. (1990). Mastery pleasure versus mere ownership: A quasi-experimental cross-cultural and cross-alphabetical test of the name letter effect. *European Journal of Social Psychology, 20,* 181–205.

HOUSE, R. J., & SINGH, J. V. (1987). Organizational behavior: Some new directions for I/O psychology. *Annual Review of Psychology, 38,* 669–718.

HOUSTON, V., & BULL, R. (1994). Do people avoid sitting next to someone who is facially disfigured? *European Journal of Social Psychology, 24,* 279–284.

HOVLAND, C. I., LUMSDAINE, A. A., & SHEFFIELD, F. D. (1949). *Experiments on mass communication. Studies in social psychology in World War II, vol. 3.* Princeton, NJ: Princeton University Press.

HOVLAND, C. I., & SEARS, R. (1940). Minor studies of aggression: Correlation of lynchings with economic indices. *Journal of Psychology, 9,* 301–310.

HUBERMAN, B., & LUKOSE, R. (1997). Social dilemmas and internet congestion. *Science, 277,* 535–537.

HUDDY, L., & VIRTANEN, S. (1995). Subgroup differentiation and subgroup bias among Latinos as a function of familiarity and positive distinctiveness. *Journal of Personality and Social Psychology, 68,* 97–108.

HUESMANN, L. R., LAGERSPETZ, K., & ERON, L. D. (1984). Intervening variables in the TV violence-aggression relation: Evidence from two countries. *Developmental Psychology, 20,* 746–775.

HUESMANN, L. R., MOISE-TITUS, J., PODOLSKI, C-L., & ERON, L. D. (2003). Longitudinal relations between children's exposure to TV violence and their aggressive and violent behavior in young adulthood: 1977–1992. *Developmental Psychology, 39,* 201–222.

HUGENBERG, K., & BODENHAUSEN, G. V. (2003). Facing prejudice: Implicit prejudice and the perception of facial threat. *Psychological Science, 14,* 640–643.

HULL, J. G., & BOND, C. F., JR. (1986). Social and behavioral consequences of alcohol consumption and expectancy: A meta-analysis. *Psychological Bulletin, 99,* 347–360.

HULL, J. G., & YOUNG, R. D. (1983). The self-awareness-reducing effects of alcohol consumption: Evidence and implications. In J. Suls & A. G. Greenwald (Eds.), *Psychological perspectives on the self, vol. 2.* Hillsdale, NJ: Erlbaum.

HUNT, A. R. (2000, June 22). Major progress, inequities cross 3 generations. *Wall Street Journal,* pp. A9, A14.

HUNT, M. (1990). *The compassionate beast: What science is discovering about the humane side of human kind.* New York: William Morrow.

HUNT, M. (1993). *The story of psychology.* New York: Doubleday.

HUNT, P. J., & HILLERY, J. M. (1973). Social facilitation in a location setting: An examination of the effects over learning trials. *Journal of Experimental Social Psychology, 9,* 563–571.

HUNTER, J. A., STRINGER, M., & WATSON, R. P. (1991). Intergroup violence and intergroup attributions. *British Journal of Social Psychology, 30,* 261–266.

HUNTER, J. D. (2002, June 21–22). "To change the world." Paper presented to the Board of Directors of The Trinity Forum, Denver, Colorado.

HURTADO, S., DEY, E. L., & TREVINO, J. G. (1994). Exclusion or self-segregation? Interaction across racial/ethnic groups on college campuses. Paper presented at the American Educational Research Association annual meeting.

HUSTON, A. C., DONNERSTEIN, E., FAIRCHILD, H., FESHBACH, N. D., KATZ, P. A., & MURRAY, J. P. (1992). *Big world, small screen: The role of television in American society.* Lincoln: University of Nebraska Press.

HUSTON, T. L. (1973). Ambiguity of acceptance, social desirability, and dating choice. *Journal of Experimental Social Psychology, 9,* 32–42.

HUSTON, T. L., & CHOROST, A. F. (1994). Behavioral buffers on the effect of negativity on marital satisfaction: A longitudinal study. *Personal Relationships, 1,* 223–239.

HYMAN, H. H., & SHEATSLEY, P. B. (1956/1964). Attitudes toward desegregation. *Scientific American, 195*(6), 35–39, and *211*(1), 16–23.

ICKES, B. (1980). On disconfirming our perceptions of others. Paper presented at the American Psychological Association convention.

ICKES, W., LAYDEN, M. A., & BARNES, R. D. (1978). Objective self-awareness and individuation: An empirical link. *Journal of Personality, 46,* 146–161.

ICKES, W., SNYDER, M., & GARCIA, S. (1997). Personality influences on the choice of situations. In R. Hogan, J. Johnson, & S. Briggs (Eds.), *Handbook of personality psychology.* San Diego, CA: Academic Press.

IDSON, L. C., & MISCHEL, W. (2001). The personality of familiar and significant people: The lay perceiver as a social-cognitive theorist. *Journal of Personality and Social Psychology, 80,* 585–596.

ILO. (1997, December 11). Women's progress in workforce improving worldwide, but occupation segregation still rife. International Labor Association press release (www.ilo.org/public/english/bureau/inf/pr/1997/35.htm).

IMAI, Y. (1994). Effects of influencing attempts on the perceptions of powerholders and the powerless. *Journal of Social Behavior and Personality, 9,* 455–468.

INGHAM, A. G., LEVINGER, G., GRAVES, J., & PECKHAM, V. (1974). The Ringelmann effect: Studies of group size and group performance. *Journal of Experimental Social Psychology, 10,* 371–384.

INGLEHART, R. (1990). *Culture shift in advanced industrial society.* Princeton, NJ: Princeton University Press.

INGLEHART, R. (1997). *Modernization and postmodernization.* Princeton, NJ: Princeton University Press.

ISOZAKI, M. (1984). The effect of discussion on polarization of judgments. *Japanese Psychological Research, 26,* 187–193.

ISR Newsletter. (1975). Institute for Social Research, University of Michigan, *3*(4), 4–7.

ITO, T. A., MILLER, N., & POLLOCK, V. E. (1996). Alcohol and aggression: A meta-analysis on the moderating effects of inhibitory cues, triggering events, and self-focused attention. *Psychological Bulletin, 120,* 60–82.

ITO, T. A., & URLAND, G. R. (2003). Race and gender on the brain: Electrocortical measures of attention to the race and gender of multiply categorizable individuals. *Journal of Personality and Social Psychology, 85,* 616–626.

IYENGAR, S. S., & LEPPER, M. R. (2000). When choice is demotivating: Can one desire too much of a good thing? *Journal of Personality and Social Psychology, 79,* 995–1006.

IYER, P. (1993, Fall). The global village finally arrives. *Time*, pp. 86–87.

JACKMAN, M. R., & SENTER, M. S. (1981). Beliefs about race, gender, and social class different, therefore unequal: Beliefs about trait differences between groups of unequal status. In D. J. Treiman & R. V. Robinson (Eds.), *Research in stratification and mobility, vol. 2.* Greenwich, CT: JAI Press.

JACKS, J. Z., & CAMERON, K. A. (2003). Strategies for resisting persuasion. *Basic and Applied Social Psychology, 25,* 145–161.

JACKSON, J. M., & LATANÉ, B. (1981). All alone in front of all those people: Stage fright as a function of number and type of co-performers and audience. *Journal of Personality and Social Psychology, 40,* 73–85.

JACKSON, L. A. (1989). Relative deprivation and the gender wage gap. *Journal of Social Issues, 45*(4), 117–133.

JACKSON, L. A., HUNTER, J. E., & HODGE, C. N. (1995). Physical attractiveness and intellectual competence: A meta-analytic review. *Social Psychology Quarterly, 58,* 108–123.

JACOBY, S. (1986, December). When opposites attract. *Reader's Digest,* pp. 95–98.

JAFFE, Y., SHAPIR, N., & YINON, Y. (1981). Aggression and its escalation. *Journal of Cross-Cultural Psychology, 12,* 21–36.

JAMIESON, D. W., LYDON, J. E., STEWART, G., & ZANNA, M. P. (1987). Pygmalion revisited: New evidence for student expectancy effects in the classroom. *Journal of Educational Psychology, 79,* 461–466.

JANIS, I. L. (1971, November). Groupthink. *Psychology Today,* pp. 43–46.

JANIS, I. L. (1982). Counteracting the adverse effects of concurrence-seeking in policy-planning groups: Theory and research perspectives. In H. Brandstatter, J. H. Davis, & G. Stocker-Kreichgauer (Eds.), *Group decision making.* New York: Academic Press.

JANIS, I. L., KAYE, D., & KIRSCHNER, P. (1965). Facilitating effects of eating while reading on responsiveness to persuasive communications. *Journal of Personality and Social Psychology, 1,* 181–186.

JANIS, I. L., & MANN, L. (1977). *Decision-making: A psychological analysis of conflict, choice and commitment.* New York: Free Press.

JANKOWIAK, W. R., & FISCHER, E. F. (1992). A cross-cultural perspective on romantic love. *Ethnology, 31,* 149–155.

JEFFERY, R. (1964). The psychologist as an expert witness on the issue of insanity. *American Psychologist, 19,* 838–843.

JELLISON, J. M., & GREEN, J. (1981). A self-presentation approach to the fundamental attribution error: The norm of internality. *Journal of Personality and Social Psychology, 40,* 643–649.

JENNINGS, D. L., AMABILE, T. M., & ROSS, L. (1982). Informal covariation assessment: Data-based vs theory-based judgments. In D. Kahneman, P. Slovic, & A. Tversky (Eds.), *Judgment under uncertainty: Heuristics and biases.* New York: Cambridge University Press.

JOHNSON, B. T., & EAGLY, A. H. (1989). Effects of involvement on persuasion: A meta-analysis. *Psychological Bulletin, 106,* 290–314.

JOHNSON, B. T., & EAGLY, A. H. (1990). Involvement and persuasion: Types, traditions, and the evidence. *Psychological Bulletin, 107,* 375–384.

JOHNSON, D. J., & RUSBULT, C. E. (1989). Resisting temptation: Devaluation of alternative partners as a means of maintaining commitment in close relationships. *Journal of Personality and Social Psychology, 57,* 967–980.

JOHNSON, D. W., & JOHNSON, R. T. (2003). Field testing integrative negotiations. *Peace and Conflict, 9,* 39–68.

JOHNSON, J. D., JACKSON, L. A., & GATTO, L. (1995). Violent attitudes and deferred academic aspirations: Deleterious effects of exposure to rap music. *Basic and Applied Social Psychology, 16,* 27–41.

JOHNSON, J. G., COHEN, P., SMAILES, E. M., KASEN, S., & BROOK, J. S. (2002). Television viewing and aggressive behavior during adolescence and adulthood. *Science, 295,* 2468–2471.

JOHNSON, J. T., JEMMOTT, J. B., III., & PETTIGREW, T. F. (1984). Causal attribution and dispositional inference: Evidence of inconsistent judgments. *Journal of Experimental Social Psychology, 20,* 567–585.

JOHNSON, M. H., & MAGARO, P. A. (1987). Effects of mood and severity on memory processes in depression and mania. *Psychological Bulletin, 101,* 28–40.

JOHNSON, R. D., & DOWNING, L. L. (1979). Deindividuation and valence of cues: Effects of prosocial and antisocial behavior. *Journal of Personality and Social Psychology, 37,* 1532–1538.

JOHNSTON, L., O'MALLEY, P. M., & BACHMAN, J. G. (1996). *National survey results on drug use from the Monitoring the Future study, 1975–1995.* Rockville, MD: National Institute on Drug Abuse, U.S. Dept. of Health and Human Services, Public Health Service, National Institutes of Health, Washington, DC.

JOINER, T. E., JR. (1994). Contagious depression: Existence, specificity to depressed symptoms, and the role of reassurance seeking. *Journal of Personality and Social Psychology, 67,* 287–296.

JOINSON, A. N. (2001). Self-disclosure in computer-mediated communication: The role of self-awareness and visual anonymity. *European Journal of Social Psychology, 31,* 177–192.

JONES, E. E. (1976). How do people perceive the causes of behavior? *American Scientist, 64,* 300–305.

JONES, E. E., & HARRIS, V. A. (1967). The attribution of attitudes. *Journal of Experimental Social Psychology, 3,* 2–24.

JONES, E. E., & NISBETT, R. E. (1971). *The actor and the observer: Divergent perceptions of the cases of behavior.* Morristown, NJ: General Learning Press.

JONES, E. E., RHODEWALT, F., BERGLAS, S., & SKELTON, J. A. (1981). Effects of strategic self-presentation on subsequent self-esteem. *Journal of Personality and Social Psychology, 41,* 407–421.

JONES, J. M. (2003). TRIOS: A psychological theory of the African legacy in American culture. *Journal of Social Issues, 59,* 217–242.

JONES, J. M., & MOORE, D. W. (2003, June 17). Generational differences in support for a woman president. The Gallup Organization (www.gallup.com).

JONES, J. T., PELHAM, B. W., & MIRENBERG, M. C. (2002). Name letter preferences are not merely mere exposure: Implicit egotism as self-regulation. *Journal of Experimental Social Psychology, 38,* 170–177.

JONES, W. H., CARPENTER, B. N., & QUINTANA, D. (1985). Personality and interpersonal predictors of loneliness in two cultures. *Journal of Personality and Social Psychology, 48,* 1503–1511.

JONES, W. H., HOBBS, S. A., & HOCKENBURY, D. (1982). Loneliness and social skill deficits. *Journal of Personality and Social Psychology, 42,* 682–689.

JONES, W. H., SANSONE, C., & HELM, B. (1983). Loneliness and interpersonal judgments. *Personality and Social Psychology Bulletin, 9,* 437–441.

JOSEPHSON, W. L. (1987). Television violence and children's aggression: Testing the priming, social script, and disinhibition predictions. *Journal of Personality and Social Psychology, 53,* 882–890.

JOURARD, S. M. (1964). *The transparent self.* Princeton, NJ: Van Nostrand.

JOURDEN, F. J., & HEATH, C. (1996). The evaluation gap in performance perceptions: Illusory perceptions of groups and individuals. *Journal of Applied Psychology, 81,* 369–379.

JUDD, C. M., BLAIR, I. V., & CHAPLEAU, K. M. (2004). Automatic stereotypes vs. automatic prejudice: Sorting out the possibilities in the Payne (2001) weapon paradigm. *Journal of Experimental Social Psychology, 40,* 75–81.

JUDD, C. M., PARK, B., RYAN, C. S., BRAUER, M., & KRAUS, S. (1995). Stereotypes and ethnocentrism: Diverging interethnic perceptions of African American and White American youth. *Journal of Personality and Social Psychology, 69,* 460–481.

JUSSIM, L. (1986). Self-fulfilling prophecies: A theoretical and integrative review. *Psychological Review, 93,* 429–445.

JUSSIM, L. (1993). Accuracy in interpersonal expectations: A reflection-construction analysis of current and classic research. *Journal of Personality, 61,* 637–668.

JUSSIM, L., ECCLES, J., & MADON, S. (1996). Social perception, social stereotypes, and teacher expectations: Accuracy and the quest for the powerful self-fulfilling prophecy. *Advances in Experimental Social Psychology, 28,* 281.

KAGAN, J. (1989). Temperamental contributions to social behavior. *American Psychologist, 44,* 668–674.

KAHAN, T. L., & JOHNSON, M. K. (1992). Self effects in memory for person information. *Social Cognition, 10,* 30–50.

KAHN, M. W. (1951). The effect of severe defeat at various age levels on the aggressive behavior of mice. *Journal of Genetic Psychology, 79,* 117–130.

KAHNEMAN, D., & SNELL, J. (1992). Predicting a changing taste: Do people know what they will like? *Journal of Behavioral Decision Making, 5,* 187–200.

KAHNEMAN, D., & TVERSKY, A. (1979). Intuitive prediction: Biases and corrective procedures. *Management Science, 12,* 313–327.

KAHNEMAN, D., & TVERSKY, A. (1995). Conflict resolution: A cognitive perspective. In K. Arrow, R. Mnookin, L. Ross, A. Tversky, & R. Wilson (Eds.), *Barriers to the negotiated resolution of conflict.* New York: Norton.

KALICK, S. M. (1977). *Plastic surgery, physical appearance, and person perception.* Unpublished doctoral dissertation, Harvard University. Cited by E. Berscheid in An overview of the psychological effects of physical attractiveness and some comments upon the psychological effects of knowledge of the effects of physical attractiveness. In W. Lucker, K. Ribbens, & J. A. McNamera (Eds.), *Logical aspects of facial form (craniofacial growth series).* Ann Arbor: University of Michigan Press, 1981.

KAMEDA, T., & SUGIMORI, S. (1993). Psychological entrapment in group decision making: An assigned decision rule and a groupthink phenomenon. *Journal of Personality and Social Psychology, 65,* 282–292.

KAMMER, D. (1982). Differences in trait ascriptions to self and friend: Unconfounding intensity from variability. *Psychological Reports, 51,* 99–102.

KANAGAWA, C., CROSS, S. E., & MARKUS, H. R. (2001). "Who am I?" The cultural psychology of the conceptual self. *Personality and Social Psychology Bulletin, 27,* 90–103.

KANDEL, D. B. (1978). Similarity in real-life adolescent friendship pairs. *Journal of Personality and Social Psychology, 36,* 306–312.

KAPLAN, M. F. (1989). Task, situational, and personal determinants of influence processes in group decision making. In E. J. Lawler (Ed.), *Advances in group processes, vol. 6.* Greenwich, CT: JAI Press.

KAPLAN, M. F., WANSHULA, L. T., & ZANNA, M. P. (1993). Time pressure and information integration in social judgment: The effect of need for structure. In O. Svenson & J. Maule (Eds.), *Time pressure and stress in human judgment and decision making.* Cambridge: Cambridge University Press.

KARAU, S. J., & WILLIAMS, K. D. (1993). Social loafing: A meta-analytic review and theoretical integration. *Journal of Personality and Social Psychology, 65,* 681–706.

KARAU, S. J., & WILLIAMS, K. D. (1997). The effects of group cohesiveness on social loafing and compensation. *Group Dynamics: Theory, Research, and Practice, 1,* 156–168.

KARAVELLAS, D. (2000). Sustainable consumption and fisheries. In B. Heap & J. Kent (Eds.), *Towards sustainable consumption: A European perspective.* London: The Royal Society.

KARNEY, B. R., & BRADBURY, T. N. (1995). The longitudinal course of marital quality and stability: A review of theory, method, and research. *Psychological Bulletin, 118,* 3–34.

KASHIMA, E. S., & KASHIMA, Y. (1998). Culture and language: The case of cultural dimensions and personal pronoun use. *Journal of Cross-Cultural Psychology, 29,* 461–486.

KASHIMA, Y., & KASHIMA, E. S. (2003). Individualism, GNP, climate, and pronoun drop: Is individualism determined by affluence and climate, or does language use play a role? *Journal of Cross-Cultural Psychology, 34,* 125–134.

KASSER, T. (2000). Two versions of the American dream: Which goals and values make for a high quality of life? In E. Diener & D. Rahtz (Eds.), *Advances in quality of life: Theory and research.* Dordrecth, Netherlands: Kluwer.

KASSER, T. (2002). *The high price of materialism.* Cambridge, MA: MIT Press.

KASSIN, S. M., GOLDSTEIN, C. C., & SAVITSKY, K. (2003). Behavioral confirmation in the interrogation room: On the dangers of presuming guilt. *Law and Human Behavior, 27,* 187–203.

KATZ, A. M., & HILL, R. (1958). Residential propinquity and marital selection: A review of theory, method, and fact. *Marriage and Family Living, 20,* 237–335.

KATZ, J., BEACH, S. R. H., & JOINER, T. E., JR. (1999). Contagious depression in dating couples. *Journal of Social and Clinical Psychology, 18,* 1–13.

KAUFMAN, J., & ZIGLER, E. (1987). Do abused children become abusive parents? *American Journal of Orthopsychiatry, 57,* 186–192.

KAWAKAMI, K., DOVIDIO, J. F., MOLL, J., HERMSEN, S., & RUSSIN, A. (2000). Just say no (to stereotyping): Effects of training in the negation of stereotypic associations on stereotype activation. *Journal of Personality and Social Psychology, 78,* 871–888.

KEATING, J. P., & BROCK, T. C. (1974). Acceptance of persuasion and the inhibition of counterargumentation under various distraction tasks. *Journal of Experimental Social Psychology, 10,* 301–309.

KELLER, J., & DAUENHEIMER, D. (2003). Stereotype threat in the classroom: Dejection mediates the disrupting threat effect on women's math per-formance. *Personality and Social Psychology Bulletin, 29,* 371–381.

KELLERMAN, J., LEWIS, J., & LAIRD, J. D. (1989). Looking and loving: The effects of mutual gaze on feelings of romantic love. *Journal of Research in Personality, 23,* 145–161.

KELLEY, H. H., & STAHELSKI, A. J. (1970). The social interaction basis of cooperators' and competitors' beliefs about others. *Journal of Personality and Social Psychology, 16,* 66–91.

KELMAN, H. C. (1997). Group processes in the resolution of international conflicts: Experiences from the Israeli-Palestinian case. *American Psychologist, 52,* 212–220.

KELMAN, H. C. (1998). Building a sustainable peace: The limits of pragmatism in the Israeli-Palestinian negotiations. Address to the American Psychological Association convention.

KELTNER, D., & ROBINSON, R. J. (1996). Extremism, power, and the imagined basis of social conflict. *Current Directions in Psychological Science, 5,* 101–105.

KENDLER, K. S., NEALE, M., KESSLER, R., HEATH, A., & EAVES, L. (1993). A twin study of recent life events and difficulties. *Archives of General Psychiatry, 50,* 789–796.

KENNEDY, D. (2002). POTUS and the fish. *Science, 297,* 477.

KENNY, D. A. (1994). *Interpersonal perception: A social relations analysis.* Storrs, CT: Guilford Press.

KENRICK, D. T. (1987). Gender, genes, and the social environment: A biosocial interactionist perspective. In P. Shaver & C. Hendrick (Eds.), *Sex and gender: Review of personality and social psychology, vol. 7.* Beverly Hills, CA: Sage.

KENRICK, D. T., & GUTIERRES, S. E. (1980). Contrast effects and judgments of physical attractiveness: When beauty becomes a social problem. *Journal of Personality and Social Psychology, 38,* 131–140.

KENRICK, D. T., GUTIERRES, S. E., & GOLDBERG, L. L. (1989). Influence of popular erotica on judgments of strangers and mates. *Journal of Experimental Social Psychology, 25,* 159–167.

KENRICK, D. T., & MACFARLANE, S. W. (1986). Ambient temperature and horn-honking: A field study of the heat/aggression relationship. *Environment and Behavior, 18,* 179–191.

KENRICK, D. T., & TROST, M. R. (1987). A biosocial theory of heterosexual relationships. In K. Kelly (Ed.), *Females, males, and sexuality.* Albany: State University of New York Press.

KERNIS, M. H. (2003). High self-esteem: A differentiated perspective. In E. C. Chang & L. J. Sanna (Eds.), *Virtue, vice, and personality: The complexity of behavior.* Washington, DC: APA Books.

KERR, N. L. (1983). Motivation losses in small groups: A social dilemma analysis. *Journal of Personality and Social Psychology, 45,* 819–828.

KERR, N. L. (1989). Illusions of efficacy: The effects of group size on perceived efficacy in social dilemmas. *Journal of Experimental Social Psychology, 25,* 287–313.

KERR, N. L., & BRUUN, S. E. (1981). Ringelmann revisited: Alternative explanations for the social loafing effect. *Personality and Social Psychology Bulletin, 7,* 224–231.

KERR, N. L., & BRUUN, S. E. (1983). Dispensibility of member effort and group motivation losses: Free-rider effects. *Journal of Personality and Social Psychology, 44,* 78–94.

KERR, N. L., GARST, J., LEWANDOWSKI, D. A., & HARRIS, S. E. (1997). That still, small voice: Commitment to cooperate as an internalized versus a social norm. *Personality and Social Psychology Bulletin, 23,* 1300–1311.

KERR, N. L., HARMON, D. L., & GRAVES, J. K. (1982). Independence of multiple verdicts by jurors and juries. *Journal of Applied Social Psychology, 12,* 12–29.

KERR, N. L., & KAUFMAN-GILLILAND, C. M. (1994). Communication, commitment, and cooperation in social dilemmas. *Journal of Personality and Social Psychology, 66,* 513–529.

KERR, N. L., & KAUFMAN-GILLILAND, C. M. (1997). ". . . and besides, I probably couldn't have made a difference anyway": Justification of social dilemma defection via perceived self-inefficacy. *Journal of Experimental Social Psychology, 33,* 211–230.

KIDD, J. B., & MORGAN, J. R. (1969). A predictive information system for management. *Operational Research Quarterly, 20,* 149–170.

KIESLER, C. A. (1971). *The psychology of commitment: Experiments linking behavior to belief.* New York: Academic Press.

KIHLSTROM, J. F., & CANTOR, N. (1984). Mental representations of the self. In L. Berkowitz (Ed.), *Advances in experimental social psychology, vol. 17.* New York: Academic Press.

KIM, H., & MARKUS, H. R. (1999). Deviance of uniqueness, harmony or conformity? A cultural analysis. *Journal of Personality and Social Psychology, 77,* 785–800.

KIMMEL, A. J. (1998). In defense of deception. *American Psychologist, 53,* 803–805.

KINDER, D. R., & SEARS, D. O. (1985). Public opinion and political action. In G. Lindzey & E. Aronson (Eds.), *The handbook of social psychology,* 3rd ed. New York: Random House.

KINSLEY, M. (2003, April 21). The power of one. *Time,* p. 86.

KITAYAMA, S., & KARASAWA, M. (1997). Implicit self-esteem in Japan: Name letters and birthday numbers. *Personality and Social Psychology Bulletin, 23,* 736–742.

KITAYAMA, S., & MARKUS, H. R. (1995). Culture and self: Implications for internationalizing psychology. In N. R. Goldberger & J. B. Veroff (Eds.), *The culture and psychology reader.* New York: New York University Press.

KITAYAMA, S., & MARKUS, H. R. (2000). The pursuit of happiness and the realization of sympathy: Cultural patterns of self, social relations, and well-being. In E. Diener & E. M. Suh (Eds.), *Subjective well-being across cultures.* Cambridge, MA: MIT Press.

KITE, M. E. (2001). Changing times, changing gender roles: Who do we want women and men to be? In R. K. Unger (Ed.), *Handbook of the psychology of women and gender.* New York: Wiley.

KLAAS, E. T. (1978). Psychological effects of immoral actions: The experimental evidence. *Psychological Bulletin, 85,* 756–771.

KLECK, R. E., & STRENTA, A. (1980). Perceptions of the impact of negatively valued physical characteristics on social interaction. *Journal of Personality and Social Psychology, 39,* 861–873.

KLEIN, J. G. (1991). Negative effects in impression formation: A test in the political arena. *Personality and Social Psychology Bulletin, 17,* 412–418.

KLEIN, W. M., & KUNDA, Z. (1992). Motivated person perception: Constructing justifications for desired beliefs. *Journal of Experimental Social Psychology, 28,* 145–168.

KLEINKE, C. L. (1977). Compliance to requests made by gazing and touching experimenters in field settings. *Journal of Experimental Social Psychology, 13,* 218–223.

KLENTZ, B., BEAMAN, A. L., MAPELLI, S. D., & ULLRICH, J. R. (1987). Perceived physical attractiveness of supporters and nonsupporters of the women's movement: An attitude-similarity-mediated error (AS-ME). *Personality and Social Psychology Bulletin, 13,* 513–523.

KLOPFER, P. H. (1958). Influence of social interaction on learning rates in birds. *Science, 128,* 903.

KNIGHT, G. P., FABES, R. A., & HIGGINS, D. A. (1996). Concerns about drawing causal inferences from meta-analyses: An example in the study of gender differences in aggression. *Psychological Bulletin, 119,* 410–421.

KNIGHT, J. A., & VALLACHER, R. R. (1981). Interpersonal engagement in social perception: The consequences of getting into the action. *Journal of Personality and Social Psychology, 40,* 990–999.

KNOWLES, E. S. (1983). Social physics and the effects of others: Tests of the effects of audience size and distance on social judgment and behavior. *Journal of Personality and Social Psychology, 45,* 1263–1279.

KNUDSON, R. M., SOMMERS, A. A., & GOLDING, S. L. (1980). Interpersonal perception and mode of resolution in marital conflict. *Journal of Personality and Social Psychology, 38,* 751–763.

KOEHLER, D. J. (1991). Explanation, imagination, and confidence in judgment. *Psychological Bulletin, 110,* 499–519.

KOESTNER, R., & WHEELER, L. (1988). Self-presentation in personal advertisements: The influence of implicit notions of attraction and role expectations. *Journal of Social and Personal Relationships, 5,* 149–160.

KOESTNER, R. F. (1993). False consensus effects for the 1992 Canadian referendum. Paper presented at the American Psychological Association Convention.

KOMORITA, S. S., & BARTH, J. M. (1985). Components of reward in social dilemmas. *Journal of Personality and Social Psychology, 48,* 364–373.

KONRAD, A. M., RITCHIE, J. E., JR., LIEB, P., & CORRIGALL, E. (2000). Sex differences and similarities in job attribute preferences: A meta-analysis. *Psychological Bulletin, 126,* 593–641.

KOOLE, S. L., DIJKSTERHUIS, A., & VAN KNIPPENBERG, A. (2001). What's in a name? Implicit self-esteem and the automatic self. *Journal of Personality and Social Psychology, 80,* 669–685.

KOOMEN, W., & DIJKER, A. J. (1997). Ingroup and outgroup stereotypes and selective processing. *European Journal of Social Psychology, 27,* 589–601.

KOOP, C. E. (1987). Report of the surgeon general's workshop on pornography and public health. *American Psychologist, 42,* 944–945.

KOPPEL, M., ARGAMON, S., & SHIMONI, A. R. (2002). Automatically categorizing written texts by author gender. *Literary and Linguistic Computing, 17,* 401–412.

KORIAT, A., LICHTENSTEIN, S., & FISCHHOFF, B. (1980). Reasons for confidence. *Journal of Experimental Social Psychology: Human Learning and Memory, 6,* 107–118.

KORN, J. H., & NICKS, S. D. (1993). The rise and decline of deception in social psychology. Poster presented at the American Psychological Society convention.

KRACKOW, A., & BLASS, T. (1995). When nurses obey or defy inappropriate physician orders: Attributional differences. *Journal of Social Behavior and Personality, 10,* 585–594.

KRAUT, R. E., & POE, D. (1980). Behavioral roots of person perception: The deception judgments of customs inspectors and laymen. *Journal of Personality and Social Psychology, 39,* 784–798.

KRAVITZ, D. A., & MARTIN, B. (1986). Ringelmann rediscovered: The original article. *Journal of Personality and Social Psychology, 50,* 936–941.

KROGER, R. O., & WOOD, L. A. (1992). Are the rules of address universal? IV: Comparison of Chinese, Korean, Greek, and German usage. *Journal of Cross-Cultural Psychology, 23,* 148–162.

KROSNICK, J. A., & ALWIN, D. F. (1989). Aging and susceptibility to attitude change. *Journal of Personality and Social Psychology, 57,* 416–425.

KRUEGER, J. (1996). Personal beliefs and cultural stereotypes about racial characteristics. *Journal of Personality and Social Psychology, 71,* 536–548.

KRUEGER, J., & CLEMENT, R. W. (1994). The truly false consensus effect: An ineradicable and egocentric bias in social perception. *Journal of Personality and Social Psychology, 67,* 596–610.

KRUGER, J., & DUNNING, D. (1999). Unskilled and unaware of it: How difficulties in recognizing one's own incompetence lead to inflated self-assessments. *Journal of Personality and Social Psychology, 77,* 1121–1134.

KRUGER, J., EPLEY, N., & GILOVICH, T. (1999). Egocentrism over email. Paper presented to the American Psychological Society meeting.

KRUGER, J., & GILOVICH, T. (1999). "I cynicism" in everyday theories of responsibility assessment: On biased assumptions of bias. *Journal of Personality and Social Psychology, 76,* 743–753.

KRUGLANSKI, A. W., & WEBSTER, D. M. (1991). Group members' reactions to opinion deviates and conformists at varying degrees of proximity to decision deadline and of environmental noise. *Journal of Personality and Social Psychology, 61,* 212–225.

KRUGMAN, P. (2003, February 18). Behind the great divide. *New York Times* (www.nytimes.com).

KRULL, D. S., LOY, M. H-M., LIN, J., WANG, C-F., CHEN, S., & ZHAO, X. (1999). The fundamental attribution error: Correspondence bias in individualist and collectivist cultures. *Personality and Social Psychology Bulletin, 25,* 1208–1219.

KUBANY, E. S., BAUER, G. B., PANGILINAN, M. E., MUROKA, M. Y., & ENRIQUEZ, V. G. (1995). Impact of labeled anger and blame in intimate relationships. *Journal of Cross-Cultural Psychology, 26,* 65–83.

KUGIHARA, N. (1999). Gender and social loafing in Japan. *Journal of Social Psychology, 139*, 516–526.

KUIPER, N. A., & HIGGINS, E. T. (1985). Social cognition and depression: A general integrative perspective. *Social Cognition, 3*, 1–15.

KUIPER, N. A., & ROGERS, T. B. (1979). Encoding of personal information: Self-other differences. *Journal of Personality and Social Psychology, 37*, 499–514.

KULL, S. (2003, June 4). Quoted in Many Americans unaware WMD have not been found. Program on International Policy Attitudes (pipa.org/whatsnew/html/new_6_04_03.html).

KUNDA, Z. (1990). The case for motivated reasoning. *Psychological Bulletin, 108*, 480–498.

KWAN, V. S. Y., BOND, M. H., & SINGELIS, T. M. (1997). *Journal of Personality and Social Psychology, 73*, 1038–1051.

LAGERSPETZ, K. (1979). Modification of aggressiveness in mice. In S. Feshbach & A. Fraczek (Eds.), *Aggression and behavior change*. New York: Praeger.

LALONDE, R. N. (1992). The dynamics of group differentiation in the face of defeat. *Personality and Social Psychology Bulletin, 18*, 336–342.

LAMAL, P. A. (1979). College student common beliefs about psychology. *Teaching of Psychology, 6*, 155–158.

LANDERS, A. (1969, April 8). Syndicated newspaper column. Cited by L. Berkowitz in The case for bottling up rage. *Psychology Today*, September 1973, pp. 24–31.

LANER, M. R., & VENTRONE, N. A. (1998). Egalitarian daters/traditionalist dates. *Journal of Family Issues, 19*, 468–477.

LANER, M. R., & VENTRONE, N. A. (2000). Dating scripts revised. *Journal of Family Issues, 21*, 488–500.

LANGER, E. J. (1977). The psychology of chance. *Journal for the Theory of Social Behavior, 7*, 185–208.

LANGER, E. J., & IMBER, L. (1980). The role of mindlessness in the perception of deviance. *Journal of Personality and Social Psychology, 39*, 360–367.

LANGER, E. J., JANIS, I. L., & WOFER, J. A. (1975). Reduction of psychological stress in surgical patients. *Journal of Experimental Social Psychology, 11*, 155–165.

LANGER, E. J., & RODIN, J. (1976). The effects of choice and enhanced personal responsibility for the aged: A field experiment in an institutional setting. *Journal of Personality and Social Psychology, 334*, 191–198.

LANGLOIS, J., KALAKANIS, L., RUBENSTEIN, A., LARSON, A., HALLAM, M., & SMOOT, M. (1996). Maxims and myths of beauty: A meta-analytic and theoretical review. Paper presented to the American Psychological Society convention.

LANGLOIS, J. H., KALAKANIS, L., RUBENSTEIN, A. J., LARSON, A., HALLAM, M., & SMOOT, M. (2000). Maxims or myths of beauty? A meta-analytic and theoretical review. *Psychological Bulletin, 126*, 390–423.

LANGLOIS, J. H., & ROGGMAN, L. A. (1990). Attractive faces are only average. *Psychological Science, 1*, 115–121.

LANGLOIS, J. H., ROGGMAN, L. A., CASEY, R. J., RITTER, J. M., RIESER-DANNER, L. A., & JENKINS, V. Y. (1987). Infant preferences for attractive faces: Rudiments of a stereotype? *Developmental Psychology, 23*, 363–369.

LANGLOIS, J. H., ROGGMAN, L. A., & MUSSELMAN, L. (1994). What is average and what is not average about attractive faces? *Psychological Science, 5*, 214–220.

LANZETTA, J. T. (1955). Group behavior under stress. *Human Relations, 8*, 29–53.

LARSEN, R. J., & DIENER, E. (1987). Affect intensity as an individual difference characteristic: A review. *Journal of Research in Personality, 21*, 1–39.

LARSON, J. R., JR., FOSTER-FISHMAN, P. G., & KEYS, C. B. (1994). Discussion of shared and unshared information in decision-making groups. *Journal of Personality and Social Psychology, 67*, 446–461.

LARSSON, K. (1956). *Conditioning and sexual behavior in the male albino rat.* Stockholm: Almqvist & Wiksell.

LARWOOD, L. (1978). Swine flu: A field study of self-serving biases. *Journal of Applied Social Psychology, 18*, 283–289.

LARWOOD, L., & WHITTAKER, W. (1977). Managerial myopia: Self-serving biases in organizational planning. *Journal of Applied Psychology, 62*, 194–198.

LASSITER, G. D., & DUDLEY, K. A. (1991). The *a priori* value of basic research: The case of videotaped confessions. *Journal of Social Behavior and Personality, 6*, 7–16.

LASSITER, G. D., GEERS, A. L., HANDLEY, I. M., WEILAND, P. E., & MUNHALL, P. J. (2002). Videotaped interrogations and confessions: A simple change in camera perspective alters verdicts in simulated trials. *Journal of Applied Psychology, 87,* 867–874.

LASSITER, G. D., GEERS, A. L., MUNHALL, P. J., HANDLEY, I. M., & BEERS, M. J. (in press). Videotaped confessions: Is guilt in the eye of the camera? *Advances in Experimental Social Psychology.*

LASSITER, G. D., & MUNHALL, P. J. (2001). The genius effect: Evidence for a nonmotivational interpretation. *Journal of Experimental Social Psychology, 37,* 349–355.

LATANÉ, B., & DABBS, J. M., JR. (1975). Sex, group size and helping in three cities. *Sociometry, 38,* 180–194.

LATANÉ, B., & DARLEY, J. M. (1968). Group inhibition of bystander intervention in emergencies. *Journal of Personality and Social Psychology, 10,* 215–221.

LATANÉ, B., & DARLEY, J. M. (1970). *The unresponsive bystander: Why doesn't he help?* New York: Appleton-Century-Crofts.

LATANÉ, B., & NIDA, S. (1981). Ten years of research on group size and helping. *Psychological Bulletin, 89,* 308–324.

LATANÉ, B., WILLIAMS, K., & HARKINS. S. (1979). Many hands make light the work: The causes and consequences of social loafing. *Journal of Personality and Social Psychology, 37,* 822–832.

LAUMANN, E. O., GAGNON, J. H., MICHAEL, R. T., & MICHAELS, S. (1994). *The social organization of sexuality: Sexual practices in the United States.* Chicago: University of Chicago Press.

LAWLER, A. (2003a). Iraq's shattered universities. *Science, 300,* 1490–1491.

LAWLER, A. (2003b). Mayhem in Mesopotamia. *Science, 301,* 582–588.

LAWLER, A. (2003c). Ten millennia of culture pilfered amid Baghdad chaos. *Science, 300,* 402–403.

LAYDEN, M. A. (1982). Attributional therapy. In C. Antaki & C. Brewin (Eds.), *Attributions and psychological change: Applications of attributional theories to clinical and educational practice.* London: Academic Press.

LAZARSFELD, P. F. (1949). The American soldier—an expository review. *Public Opinion Quarterly, 13,* 377–404.

LEARY, M. R. (1998). The social and psychological importance of self-esteem. In R. M. Kowalski & M. R. Leary (Eds.), *The social psychology of emotional and behavioral problems.* Washington, DC: American Psychological Association.

LEARY, M. R. (1999). Making sense of self-esteem. *Current Directions in Psychology, 8,* 32–35.

LEARY, M. R., & KOWALSKI, R. M. (1995). *Social anxiety.* New York: Guilford Press.

LEDOUX, J. (1994, June). Emotion, memory and the brain. *Scientific American,* pp. 50–57.

LEDOUX, J. (1996). *The emotional brain: The mysterious underpinnings of emotional life.* New York: Simon & Schuster.

LEE, F., HALLAHAN, M., & HERZOG, T. (1996). Explaining real-life events: How culture and domain shape attributions. *Personality and Social Psychology Bulletin, 22,* 732–741.

LEE, J. A. (1988). Love-styles. In R. J. Sternberg & M. L. Barnes (Eds.), *The psychology of love.* New Haven, CT: Yale University Press.

LEFCOURT, H. M. (1982). *Locus of control: Current trends in theory and research.* Hillsdale, NJ: Erlbaum.

LEIPPE, M. R., & ELKIN, R. A. (1987). Dissonance reduction strategies and accountability to self and others: Ruminations and some initial research. Presentation to the Fifth International Conference on Affect, Motivation, and Cognition, Nags Head Conference Center.

LEMYRE, L., & SMITH, P. M. (1985). Intergroup discrimination and self-esteem in the minimal group paradigm. *Journal of Personality and Social Psychology, 49,* 660–670.

LEON, D. (1969). *The Kibbutz: A new way of life.* London: Pergamon Press. Cited by B. Latané, K. Williams, & S. Harkins (1979), Many hands make light the work: The causes and consequences of social loafing. *Journal of Personality and Social Psychology, 37,* 822–832.

LERNER, M. J. (1980). *The belief in a just world: A fundamental delusion.* New York: Plenum.

LERNER, M. J., & MILLER, D. T. (1978). Just world research and the attribution process: Looking back and ahead. *Psychological Bulletin, 85,* 1030–1051.

LERNER, M. J., & SIMMONS, C. H. (1966). Observer's reaction to the "innocent victim": Compassion or rejection? *Journal of Personality and Social Psychology, 4,* 203–210.

LERNER, M. J., SOMERS, D. G., REID, D., CHIRIBOGA, D., & TIERNEY, M. (1991). Adult children as caregivers: Egocentric biases in judgments of sibling contributions. *The Gerontologist, 31,* 746–755.

LEVENTHAL, H. (1970). Findings and theory in the study of fear communications. In L. Berkowitz (Ed.), *Advances in experimental social psychology, vol. 5.* New York: Academic Press.

LEVIN, D. T. (2000). Race as a visual feature: Using visual search and perceptual discrimination tasks to understand face categories and the cross-race recognition deficit. *Journal of Experimental Psychology: General, 129,* 559–574.

LEVINE, J. M. (1989). Reaction to opinion deviance in small groups. In P. Paulus (Ed.), *Psychology of group influence: New perspectives.* Hillsdale, NJ: Erlbaum.

LEVINE, J. M., & MORELAND, R. L. (1985). Innovation and socialization in small groups. In S. Moscovici, G. Mugny, & E. Van Avermaet (Eds.), *Perspectives on minority influence.* Cambridge: Cambridge University Press.

LEVINE, R. (2003). *The power of persuasion: How we're bought and sold.* New York: Wiley.

LEVINSON, H. (1950). *The science of chance: From probability to statistics.* New York: Rinehart.

LEVY, S. R., STROESSNER, S. J., & DWECK, C. S. (1998). Stereotype formation and endorsement: The role of implicit theories. *Journal of Personality and Social Psychology, 74,* 1421–1436.

LEVY-LEBOYER, C. (1988). Success and failure in applying psychology. *American Psychologist, 43,* 779–785.

LEWINSOHN, P. M., HOBERMAN, H., TERI, L., & HAUTZINER, M. (1985). An integrative theory of depression. In S. Reiss & R. Bootzin (Eds.), *Theoretical issues in behavior therapy.* New York: Academic Press.

LEWINSOHN, P. M., & ROSENBAUM, M. (1987). Recall of parental behavior by acute depressives, remitted depressives, and nondepressives. *Journal of Personality and Social Psychology, 52,* 611–619.

LEWIS, C. S. (1952). *Mere Christianity.* New York: Macmillan.

LEWIS, D. O. (1998). *Guilty by reason of insanity.* London: Arrow.

LEYENS, J-P., CAMINO, L., PARKE, R. D., & BERKOWITZ, L. (1975). Effects of movie violence on aggression in a field setting as a function of group dominance and cohesion. *Journal of Personality and Social Psychology, 32,* 346–360.

LI, N. P., BAILEY, J. M., KENRICK, D. T., & LINSENMEIER, J. A. W. (2002). The necessities and luxuries of mate preferences: Testing the tradeoffs. *Journal of Personality and Social Psychology, 82,* 947–955.

LICHTBLAU, E. (2003, March 18). U.S. seeks $289 billion in cigarette makers' profits. *New York Times* (www.nytimes.com).

LICHTENSTEIN, S., & FISCHHOFF, B. (1980). Training for calibration. *Organizational Behavior and Human Performance, 26,* 149–171.

LICKLITER, R., & HONEYCUTT, H. (2003). Developmental dynamics: Toward a biologically plausible evolutionary psychology. *Psychological Bulletin, 129,* 819–835.

LIEHR, P., MEHL, M. R., SUMMERS, L. C., & PENNEBAKER, J. W. (2004). Connecting with others in the midst of stressful upheaval on September 11, 2001. *Applied Nursing Research, 17,* 2–6.

LILIENFELD, S. O., WOOD, J. M., & GARB, H. N. (2000). The scientific status of projective techniques. *Psychological Science in the Public Interest, 1,* 27–66.

LINDSKOLD, S., & ARONOFF, J. R. (1980). Conciliatory strategies and relative power. *Journal of Experimental Social Psychology, 16,* 187–198.

LINDSKOLD, S., BENNETT, R., & WAYNER, M. (1976). Retaliation level as a foundation for subsequent conciliation. *Behavioral Science, 21,* 13–18.

LINDSKOLD, S., BETZ, B., & WALTERS, P. S. (1986). Transforming competitive or cooperative climate. *Journal of Conflict Resolution, 30,* 99–114.

LINDSKOLD, S., & COLLINS, M. G. (1978). Inducing cooperation by groups and individuals. *Journal of Conflict Resolution, 22,* 679–690.

LINDSKOLD, S., & FINCH, M. L. (1981). Styles of announcing conciliation. *Journal of Conflict Resolution, 25,* 145–155.

LINDSKOLD, S., & HAN, G. (1988). GRIT as a foundation for integrative bargaining. *Personality and Social Psychology Bulletin, 14,* 335–345.

LINDSKOLD, S., HAN, G., & BETZ, B. (1986a). The essential elements of communication in the GRIT strategy. Personality and Social Psychology Bulletin, 12, 179–186.

LINDSKOLD, S., HAN, G., & BETZ, B. (1986b). Repeated persuasion in interpersonal conflict. Journal of Personality and Social Psychology, 51, 1183–1188.

LINDSKOLD, S., WALTERS, P. S., KOUTSOURAIS, H., & SHAYO, R. (1981). Cooperators, competitors, and response to GRIT. Unpublished manuscript, Ohio University.

LINEHAM, M. M. (1997). Self-verification and drug abusers: Implications for treatment. Psychological Science, 8, 181–184.

LINVILLE, P. W., GISCHER, W. G., & SALOVEY, P. (1989). Perceived distributions of the characteristics of in-group and out-group members: Empirical evidence and a computer simulation. Journal of Personality and Social Psychology, 57, 165–188.

LIPSITZ, A., KALLMEYER, K., FERGUSON, M., & ABAS, A. (1989). Counting on blood donors: Increasing the impact of reminder calls. Journal of Applied Social Psychology, 19, 1057–1067.

LITTLE, A., & PERRETT, D. (2002). Putting beauty back in the eye of the beholder. The Psychologist, 15, 28–32.

LIVINGSTON, R. W. (2001). What you see is what you get: Systematic variability in perceptual-based social judgment. Personality and Social Psychology Bulletin, 27, 1086–1096.

LOCKE, E. A., & LATHAM, G. P. (1990). Work motivation and satisfaction: Light at the end of the tunnel. Psychological Science, 1, 240–246.

LOCKSLEY, A., ORTIZ, V., & HEPBURN, C. (1980). Social categorization and discriminatory behavior: Extinguishing the minimal intergroup discrimination effect. Journal of Personality and Social Psychology, 39, 773–783.

LOEWENSTEIN, G., & SCHKADE, D. (1999). Wouldn't it be nice? Predicting future feelings. In D. Kahneman, E. Diener, & N. Schwarz (Eds.), Understanding well-being: Scientific perspectives on enjoyment and suffering. New York: Russell Sage Foundation, pp. 85–105.

LOFLAND, J., & STARK, R. (1965). Becoming a worldsaver: A theory of conversion to a deviant perspective. American Sociological Review, 30, 862–864.

LOFTIN, C., MCDOWALL, D., WIERSEMA, B., & COTTEY, T. J. (1991). Effects of restrictive licensing of handguns on homicide and suicide in the District of Columbia. New England Journal of Medicine, 325, 1615–1620.

LOFTUS, E. F., & KLINGER, M. R. (1992). Is the unconscious smart or dumb? American Psychologist, 47, 761–765.

LOMBARDO, J. P., WEISS, R. F., & BUCHANAN, W. (1972). Reinforcing and attracting functions of yielding. Journal of Personality and Social Psychology, 21, 359–368.

LONNER, W. J. (1980). The search for psychological universals. In H. C. Triandis & W. W. Lambert (Eds.), Handbook of cross-cultural psychology, vol. 1. Boston: Allyn & Bacon.

LORD, C. G., ROSS, L., & LEPPER, M. (1979). Biased assimilation and attitude polarization: The effects of prior theories on subsequently considered evidence. Journal of Personality and Social Psychology, 37, 2098–2109.

LORENZ, K. (1976). On aggression. New York: Bantam Books.

LOVETT, F. (1997). Thinking about values (report of December 13, 1996, Wall Street Journal national survey). The Responsive Community, 7(2), 87.

LOWE, R. H., & WITTIG, M. A. (1989). Comparable worth: Individual, interpersonal, and structural considerations. Journal of Social Issues, 45, 223–246.

LOWENSTEIN, D. (2000 May 20). Interview. The World (www.cnn.com/TRANSCRIPTS/0005/20/stc.00.html).

LUEPTOW, L. B., GAROVICH, L., & LUEPTOW, M. B. (1995). The persistence of gender stereotypes in the face of changing sex roles: Evidence contrary to the sociocultural model. Ethology and Sociobiology, 16, 509–530.

LUNTZ, F. (2003, June 10). Quoted by T. Raum, "Bush insists banned weapons will be found." Associated Press (story.news.yahoo.com).

LYDON, J., & DUNKEL-SCHETTER, C. (1994). Seeing is committing: A longitudinal study of bolstering commitment in amniocenesis patients. Personality and Social Psychology Bulletin, 20, 218–227.

LYKKEN, D. T. (1997). The American crime factory. Psychological Inquiry, 8, 261–270.

LYKKEN, D. T. (1999). Happiness. New York: Golden Books.

References 429

Lynch, B. S., & Bonnie, R. J. (1994). Toward a youth-centered prevention policy. In B. S. Lynch & R. J. Bonnie (Eds.), *Growing up tobacco free: Preventing nicotine addiction in children and youths.* Washington, DC: National Academy Press.

Lynn, M., & Oldenquist, A. (1986). Egoistic and nonegoistic motives in social dilemmas. *American Psychologist, 41,* 529–534.

Lyons, L. (2003, September 23). Oh, boy: Americans still prefer sons. *Gallup Poll Tuesday Briefing* (www.gallup.com).

Lyubomirsky, S. (2001). Why are some people happier than others? The role of cognitive and motivational processes in well-being. *American Psychologist, 56,* 239–249.

Ma, V., & Schoeneman, T. J. (1997). Individualism versus collectivism: A comparison of Kenyan and American self-concepts. *Basic and Applied Social Psychology, 19,* 261–273.

Maass, A. (1998). Personal communication from Universita degli Studi di Padova.

Maass, A., & Clark, R. D., III. (1984). Hidden impact of minorities: Fifteen years of minority influence research. *Psychological Bulletin, 95,* 428–450.

Maass, A., & Clark, R. D., III. (1986). Conversion theory and simultaneous majority/minority influence: Can reactance offer an alternative explanation? *European Journal of Social Psychology, 16,* 305–309.

Maass, A., Volparo, C., & Mucchi-Faina, A. (1996). Social influence and the verifiability of the issue under discussion: Attitudinal versus objective items. *British Journal of Social Psychology, 35,* 15–26.

Maccoby, E. E. (2002). Gender and group process: A developmental perspective. *Current Directions in Psychological Science, 11,* 54–58.

MacDonald, G., Zanna, M. P., & Holmes, J. G. (2000). An experimental test of the role of alcohol in relationship conflict. *Journal of Experimental Social Psychology, 36,* 182–193.

MacDonald, T. K., & Ross, M. (1997). Assessing the accuracy of predictions about dating relationships: How and why do lovers' predictions differ from those made by observers? Unpublished manuscript, University of Lethbridge.

Mack, D., & Rainey, D. (1990). Female applicants' grooming and personnel selection. *Journal of Social Behavior and Personality, 5,* 399–407.

MacKay, J. L. (1980). Selfhood: Comment on Brewster Smith. *American Psychologist, 35,* 106–107.

MacLeod, C., & Campbell, L. (1992). Memory accessibility and probability judgments: An experimental evaluation of the availability heuristic. *Journal of Personality and Social Psychology, 63,* 890–902.

Macrae, C. N., & Bodenhausen, G. V. (2000). Social cognition: Thinking categorically about others. *Annual Review of Psychology, 51,* 93–120.

Macrae, C. N., Bodenhausen, G. V., Milne, A. B., & Jetten, J. (1994). Out of mind but back in sight: Stereotypes on the rebound. *Journal of Personality and Social Psychology, 67,* 808–817.

Macrae, C. N., & Johnston, L. (1998). Help, I need somebody: Automatic action and inaction. *Social Cognition, 16,* 400–417.

Maddux, J. E. (1993). The mythology of psychopathology: A social cognitive view of deviance, difference, and disorder. *The General Psychologist, 29*(2), 34–45.

Maddux, J. E., & Gosselin, J. T. (2003). Self-efficacy. In M. R. Leary, & J. P. Tangney (Eds.), *Handbook of self and identity.* New York: Guilford Press.

Maddux, J. E., & Rogers, R. W. (1983). Protection motivation and self-efficacy: A revised theory of fear appeals and attitude change. *Journal of Experimental Social Psychology, 19,* 469–479.

Madon, S., Jussim, L., & Eccles, J. (1997). In search of the powerful self-fulfilling prophecy. *Journal of Personality and Social Psychology, 72,* 791–809.

Major, B. (1989). Gender differences in comparisons and entitlement: Implications for comparable worth. *Journal of Social Issues, 45,* 99–116.

Major, B. (1993). Gender, entitlement, and the distribution of family labor. *Journal of Social Issues, 49,* 141–159.

Malamuth, N. M., & Check, J. V. P. (1981). The effects of media exposure on acceptance of violence against women: A field experiment. *Journal of Research in Personality, 15,* 436–446.

Malkiel, B. G. (1999). *A random walk down Wall Street,* rev. ed. New York: Norton.

MANIS, M., CORNELL, S. D., & MOORE, J. C. (1974). Transmission of attitude-relevant information through a communication chain. *Journal of Personality and Social Psychology, 30,* 81–94.

MANN, L. (1981). The baiting crowd in episodes of threatened suicide. *Journal of Personality and Social Psychology, 41,* 703–709.

MARCUS, D. K., & MILLER, R. S. (2003). Sex differences in judgments of physical attractiveness: A social relations analysis. *Personality and Social Psychology Bulletin, 29,* 325–335.

MARCUS, S. (1974). Review of *Obedience to authority.* New York Times Book Review, January 13, pp. 1–2.

MARCUS-NEWHALL, A., PEDERSEN, W. C., CARLSON, M., & MILLER, N. (2000). Displaced aggression is alive and well: A meta-analytic review. *Journal of Personality and Social Psychology, 78,* 670–689.

MARKEY, P. M., WELLS, S. M., & MARKEY, C. N. (2002). In S. P. Shohov (Ed.), *Advances in Psychology Research, 9,* 94–113. Huntington, NY: Nova Science.

MARKMAN, H. J., FLOYD, F. J., STANLEY, S. M., & STORAASLI, R. D. (1988). Prevention of marital distress: A longitudinal investigation. *Journal of Consulting and Clinical Psychology, 56,* 210–217.

MARKS, G., & MILLER, N. (1987). Ten years of research on the false-consensus effect: An empirical and theoretical review. *Psychological Bulletin, 102,* 72–90.

MARKUS, H., & KITAYAMA, S. (1991). Culture and the self: Implications for cognition, emotion, and motivation. *Psychological Review, 98,* 224–253.

MARKUS, H., & WURF, E. (1987). The dynamic self-concept: A social psychological perspective. *Annual Review of Psychology, 38,* 299–337.

MARSH, H. W., & YOUNG, A. S. (1997). Causal effects of academic self-concept on academic achievement: Structural equation models of longitudinal data. *Journal of Educational Psychology, 89,* 41–54.

MARSHALL, R. (1997). Variances in levels of individualism across two cultures and three social classes. *Journal of Cross-Cultural Psychology, 28,* 490–495.

MARSHALL, W. L. (1989). Pornography and sex offenders. In D. Zillmann & J. Bryant (Eds.), *Pornography: Research advances and policy considerations.* Hillsdale, NJ: Erlbaum.

MARTIN, R. (1996). Minority influence and argument generation. *British Journal of Social Psychology, 35,* 91–103.

MARUYAMA, G., RUBIN, R. A., & KINGBURY, G. (1981). Self-esteem and educational achievement: Independent constructs with a common cause? *Journal of Personality and Social Psychology, 40,* 962–975.

MARVELLE, K., & GREEN, S. (1980). Physical attractiveness and sex bias in hiring decisions for two types of jobs. *Journal of the National Association of Women Deans, Administrators, and Counselors, 44*(1), 3–6.

MARX, G. (1960). *Groucho and me.* New York: Dell.

MASUDA, T., & KITAYAMA, S. (2004). Perceiver-induced constraint and attitude attribution in Japan and the U.S.: A case for culture-dependence of corre-spondence bias. *Journal of Experimental Social Psychology, 40,* 409–416.

MAYER, J. D., & SALOVEY, P. (1987). Personality moderates the interaction of mood and cognition. In K. Fiedler & J. Forgas (Eds.), *Affect, cognition, and social behavior.* Toronto: Hogrefe.

MCALISTER, A., PERRY, C., KILLEN, J., SLINKARD, L. A., & MACCOBY, N. (1980). Pilot study of smoking, alcohol and drug abuse prevention. *American Journal of Public Health, 70,* 719–721.

MCCARREY, M., EDWARDS, H. P., & ROZARIO, W. (1982). Ego-relevant feedback, affect, and self-serving attributional bias. *Personality and Social Psychology Bulletin, 8,* 189–194.

MCCARTHY, J. F., & KELLY, B. R. (1978a). Aggressive behavior and its effect on performance over time in ice hockey athletes: An archival study. *International Journal of Sport Psychology, 9,* 90–96.

MCCARTHY, J. F., & KELLY, B. R. (1978b). Aggression, performance variables, and anger self-report in ice hockey players. *Journal of Psychology, 99,* 97–101.

MCCAULEY, C. (1989). The nature of social influence in groupthink: Compliance and internalization. *Journal of Personality and Social Psychology, 57,* 250–260.

MCCAULEY, C. R. (2002). Psychological issues in understanding terrorism and the response to terrorism. In C. E. Stout (Ed.), *The psychology of terrorism, vol. 3.* Westport, CT: Praeger/Greenwood.

McCauley, C. R., & Segal, M. E. (1987). Social psychology of terrorist groups. In C. Hendrick (Ed.), *Group processes and intergroup relations: Review of personality and social psychology, vol. 9.* Newbury Park, CA: Sage.

McConahay, J. B. (1981). Reducing racial prejudice in desegregated schools. In W. D. Hawley (Ed.), *Effective school desegregation.* Beverly Hills, CA: Sage.

McCullough, J. L., & Ostrom, T. M. (1974). Repetition of highly similar messages and attitude change. *Journal of Applied Psychology, 59,* 395–397.

McFarland, C., & Ross, M. (1985). The relation between current impressions and memories of self and dating partners. Unpublished manuscript, University of Waterloo.

McFarland, S. G., Ageyev, V. S., & Abalakina-Paap, M. A. (1992). Authoritarianism in the former Soviet Union. *Journal of Personality and Social Psychology, 63,* 1004–1010.

McFarland, S. G., Ageyev, V. S., & Djintcharadze, N. (1996). Russian authoritarianism two years after communism. *Personality and Social Psychology Bulletin, 22,* 210–217.

McGillicuddy, N. B., Welton, G. L., & Pruitt, D. G. (1987). Third-party intervention: A field experiment comparing three different models. *Journal of Personality and Social Psychology, 53,* 104–112.

McGinn, A. P. (1998, June 20). Hidden forces mask crisis in world fisheries. Worldwatch Institute (www.worldwatch.org).

McGuire, A. (2002, August 19). Charity calls for debate on adverts aimed at children. *The Herald* (Scotland), p. 4.

McGuire, W. J. (1964). Inducing resistance to persuasion: Some contemporary approaches. In L. Berkowitz (Ed.), *Advances in experimental social psychology, vol. 1.* New York: Academic Press.

McGuire, W. J., & McGuire, C. V. (1986). Differences in conceptualizing self versus conceptualizing other people as manifested in contrasting verb types used in natural speech. *Journal of Personality and Social Psychology, 51,* 1135–1143.

McGuire, W. J., McGuire, C. V., Child, P., & Fujioka, T. (1978). Salience of ethnicity in the spontaneous self-concept as a function of one's ethnic distinctiveness in the social environment. *Journal of Personality and Social Psychology, 36,* 511–520.

McGuire, W. J., McGuire, C. V., & Winton, W. (1979). Effects of household sex composition on the salience of one's gender in the spontaneous self-concept. *Journal of Experimental Social Psychology, 15,* 77–90.

McGuire, W. J., & Padawer-Singer, A. (1978). Trait salience in the spontaneous self-concept. *Journal of Personality and Social Psychology, 33,* 743–754.

McKelvie, S. J. (1995). Bias in the estimated frequency of names. *Perceptual and Motor Skills, 81,* 1331–1338.

McKelvie, S. J. (1997). The availability heuristic: Effects of fame and gender on the estimated frequency of male and female names. *Journal of Social Psychology, 137,* 63–78.

McKenna, F. P., & Myers, L. B. (1997). Illusory self-assessments—Can they be reduced? *British Journal of Psychology, 88,* 39–51.

McKenna, K. Y. A., & Bargh, J. A. (1998). Coming out in the age of the Internet: Identity demarginalization through virtual group participation. *Journal of Personality and Social Psychology, 75,* 681–694.

McKenna, K. Y. A., & Bargh, J. A. (2000). Plan 9 from cyberspace: The implications of the Internet for personality and social psychology. *Personality and Social Psychology Review, 4,* 57–75.

McKenna, K. Y. A., Green, A. S., & Gleason, M. E. J. (2002). What's the big attraction? Relationship formation on the Internet. *Journal of Social Issues, 58,* 9–31.

McNeill, B. W., & Stoltenberg, C. D. (1988). A test of the elaboration likelihood model for therapy. *Cognitive Therapy and Research, 12,* 69–79.

Mealey, L., Bridgstock, R., & Townsend, G. C. (1999). Symmetry and perceived facial attractiveness: A monozygotic co-twin comparison. *Journal of Personality and Social Psychology, 76,* 151–158.

Meehl, P. E. (1954). *Clinical vs. statistical prediction: A theoretical analysis and a review of evidence.* Minneapolis: University of Minnesota Press.

Meindl, J. R., & Lerner, M. J. (1984). Exacerbation of extreme responses to an out-group. *Journal of Personality and Social Psychology, 47,* 71–84.

Merari, A. (2002). Explaining suicidal terrorism: Theories versus empirical evidence. Invited address to the American Psychological Association.

MESSÉ, L. A., & SIVACEK, J. M. (1979). Predictions of others' responses in a mixed-motive game: Self-justification or false consensus? *Journal of Personality and Social Psychology, 37,* 602–607.

MESSICK, D. M., & SENTIS, K. P. (1979). Fairness and preference. *Journal of Experimental Social Psychology, 15,* 418–434.

METALSKY, G. I., JOINER, T. E., JR., HARDIN, T. S., & ABRAMSON, L. Y. (1993). Depressive reactions to failure in a naturalistic setting: A test of the hopelessness and self-esteem theories of depression. *Journal of Abnormal Psychology, 102,* 101–109.

MICHAELS, J. W., BLOMMEL, J. M., BROCATO, R. M., LINKOUS, R. A., & ROWE, J. S. (1982). Social facilitation and inhibition in a natural setting. *Replications in Social Psychology, 2,* 21–24.

MIKULA, G. (1984). Justice and fairness in interpersonal relations: Thoughts and suggestions. In H. Taijfel (Ed.), *The social dimension: European developments in social psychology, vol. 1.* Cambridge: Cambridge University Press.

MIKULINCER, M., FLORIAN, V., & HIRSCHBERGER, G. (2003). The existential function of close relationships: Introducing death into the science of love. *Personality and Social Psychology Review, 7,* 20–40.

MILGRAM, A. (2000). My personal view of Stanley Milgram. In T. Blass (Ed.), *Obedience to authority: Current perspectives on the Milgram paradigm.* Mahwah, NJ: Erlbaum.

MILGRAM, S. (1965). Some conditions of obedience and disobedience to authority. *Human Relations, 18,* 57–76.

MILGRAM, S. (1974). *Obedience to authority.* New York: Harper and Row.

MILGRAM, S., & SABINI, J. (1983). On maintaining social norms: A field experiment in the subway. In H. H. Blumberg, A. P. Hare, V. Kent, & M. Davies (Eds.), *Small groups and social interaction, vol. 1.* London: Wiley.

MILLAR, M. G., & TESSER, A. (1992). The role of beliefs and feelings in guiding behavior: The mismatch model. In L. Martin & A. Tesser (Eds.), *The construction of social judgment.* Hillsdale NJ: Erlbaum.

MILLER, A. G. (1986). *The obedience experiments: A case study of controversy in social science.* New York: Praeger.

MILLER, A. G. (2004). What can the Milgram obedience experiments tell us about the Holocaust? Generalizing from the social psychological laboratory. In A. G. Miller (Ed.), *The social psychology of good and evil.* New York: Guilford Press.

MILLER, A. G., ASHTON, W., & MISHAL, M. (1990). Beliefs concerning the features of constrained behavior: A basis for the fundamental attribution error. *Journal of Personality and Social Psychology, 59,* 635–650.

MILLER, A. G., GILLEN, G., SCHENKER, C., & RADLOVE, S. (1973). Perception of obedience to authority. *Proceedings of the 81st Annual Convention of the American Psychological Association, 8,* 127–128.

MILLER, D. T., DOWNS, J. S., & PRENTICE, D. A. (1998). Minimal conditions for the creation of a unit relationship: The social bond between birthdaymates. *European Journal of Social Psychology, 28,* 475.

MILLER, J. B. (1986). *Toward a new psychology of women,* 2nd ed. Boston: Beacon Press.

MILLER, J. G. (1984). Culture and the development of everyday social explanation. *Journal of Personality and Social Psychology, 46,* 961–978.

MILLER, K. I., & MONGE, P. R. (1986). Participation, satisfaction, and productivity: A meta-analytic review. *Academy of Management Journal, 29,* 727–753.

MILLER, L. C. (1990). Intimacy and liking: Mutual influence and the role of unique relationships. *Journal of Personality and Social Psychology, 59,* 50–60.

MILLER, L. C., BERG, J. H., & ARCHER, R. L. (1983). Openers: Individuals who elicit intimate self-disclosure. *Journal of Personality and Social Psychology, 44,* 1234–1244.

MILLER, L. C., BERG, J. H., & RUGS, D. (1989). Selectivity and sharing: Needs and norms in developing friendships. Unpublished manuscript, Scripps College.

MILLER, N., & MARKS, G. (1982). Assumed similarity between self and other: Effect of expectation of future interaction with that other. *Social Psychology Quarterly, 45,* 100–105.

MILLER, N., PEDERSEN, W. C., EARLEYWINE, M., & POLLOCK, V. E. (2003). A theoretical model of triggered displaced aggression. *Personality and Social Psychology Review, 7,* 75–97.

MILLER, N. E. (1941). The frustration-aggression hypothesis. *Psychological Review, 48,* 337–342.

MILLER, P. A., & EISENBERG, N. (1988). The relation of empathy to aggressive and externalizing/antisocial behavior. *Psychological Bulletin, 103,* 324–344.

MILLER, P. C., LEFCOURT, H. M., HOLMES, J. G., WARE, E. E., & SALEY, W. E. (1986). Marital locus of control and marital problem solving. *Journal of Personality and Social Psychology, 51,* 161–169.

MILLER, R. L., BRICKMAN, P., & BOLEN, D. (1975). Attribution versus persuasion as a means for modifying behavior. *Journal of Personality and Social Psychology, 31,* 430–441.

MILLER, R. S. (1997). Inattentive and contented: Relationship commitment and attention to alternatives. *Journal of Personality and Social Psychology, 73,* 758–766.

MILLER, R. S., & SIMPSON, J. A. (1990). Relationship satisfaction and attentiveness to alternatives. Paper presented at the American Psychological Association convention.

MILLETT, K. (1975, January). The shame is over. *Ms.,* pp. 26–29.

MINARD, R. D. (1952). Race relationships in the Pocohontas coal field. *Journal of Social Issues, 8*(1), 29–44.

MIRELS, H. L., & McPEEK, R. W. (1977). Self-advocacy and self-esteem. *Journal of Consulting and Clinical Psychology, 45,* 1132–1138.

MITA, T. H., DERMER, M., & KNIGHT, J. (1977). Reversed facial images and the mere-exposure hypothesis. *Journal of Personality and Social Psychology, 35,* 597–601.

MITCHELL, T. R., & THOMPSON, L. (1994). A theory of temporal adjustments of the evaluation of events: Rosy prospection and rosy retrospection. In C. Stubbart, J. Porac, & J. Meindl (Eds.), *Advances in managerial cognition and organizational information processing.* Greenwich, CT: JAI Press.

MITCHELL, T. R., THOMPSON, L., PETERSON, E., & CRONK, R. (1997). Temporal adjustments in the evaluation of events: The "rosy view." *Journal of Experimental Social Psychology, 33,* 421–448.

MONSON, T. C., & SNYDER, M. (1977). Actors, observers, and the attribution process: Toward a reconceptualization. *Journal of Experimental Social Psychology, 13,* 89–111.

MOODY, K. (1980). *Growing up on television: The TV effect.* New York: Times Books.

MOORE, D. L., & BARON, R. S. (1983). Social facilitation: A physiological analysis. In J. T. Cacioppo & R. Petty (Eds.), *Social psychophysiology.* New York: Guilford Press.

MOORE, D. W. (2003, March 11). Half of young people expect to strike it rich: But expectations fall rapidly with age. Gallup News Service (www.gallup.com/poll/releases/pr030311.asp).

MOR, N., & WINQUIST, J. (2002). Self-focused attention and negative affect: A meta-analysis. *Psychological Bulletin, 128,* 638–662.

MORIER, D., & SEROY, C. (1994). The effect of interpersonal expectancies on men's self-presentation of gender role attitudes to women. *Sex Roles, 31,* 493–504.

MOSCOVICI, S. (1985). Social influence and conformity. In G. Lindzey & E. Aronson (Eds.), *The handbook of social psychology,* 3rd ed. Hillsdale, NJ: Erlbaum.

MOSCOVICI, S., LAGE, S., & NAFFRECHOUX, M. (1969). Influence of a consistent minority on the responses of a majority in a color perception task. *Sociometry, 32,* 365–380.

MOSCOVICI, S., & ZAVALLONI, M. (1969). The group as a polarizer of attitudes. *Journal of Personality and Social Psychology, 12,* 124–135.

Motherhood Project. (2001, May 2). Watch out for children: A mothers' statement to advertisers. Institute for American Values (www.watchoutforchildren.org).

MOYER, K. E. (1976). *The psychobiology of aggression.* New York: Harper & Row.

MOYER, K. E. (1983). The physiology of motivation: Aggression as a model. In C. J. Scheier & A. M. Rogers (Eds.), *G. Stanley Hall Lecture Series, vol. 3.* Washington, DC: American Psychological Association.

MUCCHI-FAINA, A., MAASS, A., & VOLPATO, C. (1991). Social influence: The role of originality. *European Journal of Social Psychology, 21,* 183–197.

MUELLER, C. W., DONNERSTEIN, E., & HALLAM, J. (1983). Violent films and prosocial behavior. *Personality and Social Psychology Bulletin, 9,* 83–89.

MULLEN, B. (1986a). Atrocity as a function of lynch mob composition: A self-attention perspective. *Personality and Social Psychology Bulletin, 12,* 187–197.

MULLEN, B. (1986b). Stuttering, audience size, and the other-total ratio: A self-attention perspective. *Journal of Applied Social Psychology, 16,* 139–149.

MULLEN, B., & BAUMEISTER, R. F. (1987). Group effects on self-attention and performance: Social loafing, social facilitation, and social impairment. In C. Hendrick (Ed.), *Group processes and intergroup relations: Review of personality and social psychology, vol. 9.* Newbury Park, CA: Sage.

MULLEN, B., BROWN, R., & SMITH, C. (1992). Ingroup bias as a function of salience, relevance, and status: An integration. *European Journal of Social Psychology, 22,* 103–122.

MULLEN, B., BRYANT, B., & DRISKELL, J. E. (1997). Presence of others and arousal: An integration. *Group Dynamics: Theory, Research, and Practice, 1,* 52–64.

MULLEN, B., & COPPER, C. (1994). The relation between group cohesiveness and performance: An integration. *Psychological Bulletin, 115,* 210–227.

MULLEN, B., & GOETHALS, G. R. (1990). Social projection, actual consensus and valence. *British Journal of Social Psychology, 29,* 279–282.

MULLEN, B., & HU, L. (1989). Perceptions of ingroup and outgroup variability: A meta-analytic integration. *Basic and Applied Social Psychology, 10,* 233–252.

MULLEN, B., & RIORDAN, C. A. (1988). Self-serving attributions for performance in naturalistic settings: A meta-analytic review. *Journal of Applied Social Psychology, 18,* 3–22.

MULLER, S., & JOHNSON, B. T. (1990). Fear and persuasion: A linear relationship? Paper presented to the Eastern Psychological Association convention.

MULLIN, C. R., & LINZ, D. (1995). Desensitization and resensitization to violence against women: Effects of exposure to sexually violent films on judgments of domestic violence victims. *Journal of Personality and Social Psychology, 69,* 449–459.

MURPHY, C. (1990, June). New findings: Hold on to your hat. *The Atlantic,* pp. 22–23.

MURPHY, C. M., & O'FARRELL, T. J. (1996). Marital violence among alcoholics. *Current Directions in Psychological Science, 5,* 183–187.

MURRAY, S. L., GELLAVIA, G. M., ROSE, P., & GRIFFIN, D. W. (2003). Once hurt, twice hurtful: How perceived regard regulates daily marital interactions. *Journal of Personality and Social Psychology, 84,* 126–147.

MURRAY, S. L., HOLMES, J. G., GELLAVIA, G., GRIFFIN, D. W., & DOLDERMAN, D. (2002). Kindred spirits? The benefits of egocentrism in close relationships. *Journal of Personality and Social Psychology, 82,* 563–581.

MURRAY, S. L., HOLMES, J. G., MACDONALD, G., & ELLSWORTH, P. C. (1998). Through the looking glass darkly? When self-doubts turn into relationship insecurities. *Journal of Personality and Social Psychology, 75,* 1459–1480.

MURSTEIN, B. L. (1986). *Paths to marriage.* Newbury Park, CA: Sage.

MUSON, G. (1978, March). Teenage violence and the telly. *Psychology Today,* pp. 50–54.

MYERS, D. G. (2000). *The American paradox: Spiritual hunger in an age of plenty.* New Haven, CT: Yale University Press.

MYERS, D. G., & BISHOP, G. D. (1970). Discussion effects on racial attitudes. *Science, 169,* 778–789.

MYERS, J. N. (1997, December). Quoted by S. A. Boot, Where the weather reigns. *World Traveler,* pp. 86, 88, 91, 124.

MYERS, N. (2000). Sustainable consumption: The meta-problem. In B. Heap & J. Kent (Eds.), *Towards sustainable consumption: A European perspective.* London: The Royal Society.

NADLER, A., GOLDBERG, M., & JAFFE, Y. (1982). Effect of self-differentiation and anonymity in group on deindividuation. *Journal of Personality and Social Psychology, 42,* 1127–1136.

NAGAR, D., & PANDEY, J. (1987). Affect and performance on cognitive task as a function of crowding and noise. *Journal of Applied Social Psychology, 17,* 147–157.

NAIL, P. R., MACDONALD, G., & LEVY, D. A. (2000). Proposal of a four-dimensional model of social response. *Psychological Bulletin, 126,* 454–470.

NATIONAL CENTER FOR HEALTH STATISTICS. (1991). Family structure and children's health: United States, 1988, *Vital and Health Statistics, Series 10, No. 178,* CHHS Publication No. PHS 91–1506 by Deborah A. Dawson.

NATIONAL COUNCIL FOR RESEARCH ON WOMEN. (1994). Women and philanthropy fact sheet. *Issues Quarterly, 1*(2), 9.

NATIONAL RESEARCH COUNCIL. (2002). *Youth, pornography, and the Internet.* Washington, DC: National Academy Press.

NATIONAL SAFETY COUNCIL. (2001). Data from 1995 to 1999 summarized in personal correspondence from Kevin T. Fearn, NSC Research and Statistics Department.

NATIONAL TELEVISION VIOLENCE STUDY. (1997). Thousand Oaks, CA: Sage.

NEEDLES, D. J., & ABRAMSON, L. Y. (1990). Positive life events, attributional style, and hopefulness: Testing a model of recovery from depression. *Journal of Abnormal Psychology, 99,* 156–165.

NEIMEYER, G. J., MacNAIR, R., METZLER, A. E., & COURCHAINE, K. (1991). Changing personal beliefs: Effects of forewarning, argument quality, prior bias, and personal exploration. *Journal of Social and Clinical Psychology, 10,* 1–20.

NELSON, L. J., & MILLER, D. T. (1995). The distinctiveness effect in social categorization: You are what makes you unusual. *Psychological Science, 6,* 246.

NEMETH, C. (1979). The role of an active minority in intergroup relations. In W. G. Austin & S. Worchel (Eds.), *The social psychology of intergroup relations.* Monterey, CA: Brooks/Cole.

NEMETH, C., & WACHTLER, J. (1974). Creating the perceptions of consistency and confidence: A necessary condition for minority influence. *Sociometry, 37,* 529–540.

NEMETH, C. J. (1997). Managing innovation: When less is more. *California Management Review, 40,* 59–74.

NEMETH, C. J. (1999). Behind the scenes. In D. G. Myers, *Social psychology,* 6th ed. New York: McGraw-Hill.

NEMETH, C. J., BROWN, K., & ROGERS, J. (2001a). Devil's advocate versus authentic dissent: Stimulating quantity and quality. *European Journal of Social Psychology, 31,* 1–13.

NEMETH, C. J., CONNELL, J. B., ROGERS, J. D., & BROWN, K. S. (2001b). Improving decision making by means of dissent. *Journal of Applied Social Psychology, 31,* 48–58.

NEW YORK TIMES. (2002, May 26). Fighting to live as the towers died (www.nytimes.com).

NEWCOMB, T. M. (1961). *The acquaintance process.* New York: Holt, Rinehart and Winston.

NEWELL, B., & LAGNADO, D. (2003). Think-tanks, or think tanks. *The Psychologist, 16,* 176.

NEWMAN, A. (2001, February 4). Rotten teeth and dead babies. *New York Times Magazine* (www.nytimes.com).

NEWMAN, H. M., & LANGER, E. J. (1981). Post-divorce adaptation and the attribution of responsibility. *Sex Roles, 7,* 223–231.

NEWMAN, L. S. (1993). How individualists interpret behavior: Idiocentrism and spontaneous trait inference. *Social Cognition, 11,* 243–269.

NEWPORT, F., MOORE, D. W., JONES, J. M., & SAAD, L. (2003, March 21). Special release: American opinion on the war. *Gallup Poll Tuesday Briefing* (www.gallup.com/poll/tb/goverpubli/s0030325.asp).

NIAS, D. K. B. (1979). Marital choice: Matching or complementation? In M. Cook & G. Wilson (Eds.), *Love and attraction.* Oxford: Pergamon.

NICHOLS, J. (2003, February 9). Man overdoses online as chatters watch him die. *Grand Rapids Press,* p. A20.

NIE, N. H., & ERBRING, L. (2000, February 17). *Internet and society: A preliminary report.* Stanford, CA: Stanford Institute for the Quantitative Study of Society.

NIEMI, R. G., MUELLER, J., & SMITH, T. W. (1989). *Trends in public opinion: A compendium of survey data.* New York: Greenwood Press.

NISBETT, R. E. (1990). Evolutionary psychology, biology, and cultural evolution. *Motivation and Emotion, 14,* 255–263.

NISBETT, R. E., & SCHACHTER, S. (1966). Cognitive manipulation of pain. *Journal of Experimental Social Psychology, 2,* 227–236.

NIX, G., WATSON, C., PYSZCZYNSKI, T., & GREENBERG, J. (1995). Reducing depressive affect through external focus of attention. *Journal of Social and Clinical Psychology, 14,* 36–52.

NOLAN, S. A., FLYNN, C., & GARBER, J. (2003). Prospective relations between rejection and depression in young adolescents. *Journal of Personality and Social Psychology, 85,* 745–755.

NOLLER, P., & FITZPATRICK, M. A. (1990). Marital communication in the eighties. *Journal of Marriage and the Family, 52,* 832–843.

NORC. (1996). General social survey. National Opinion Research Center, University of Chicago (courtesy Tom W. Smith).

NOREM, J. K. (2000). Defensive pessimism, optimism, and pessimism. In E. C. Chang (Ed.), *Optimism and pessimism.* Washington, DC: APA Books.

NOREM, J. K., & CANTOR, N. (1986). Defensive pessimism: Harnessing anxiety as motivation. *Journal of Personality and Social Psychology, 51,* 1208–1217.

NOTARIUS, C., & MARKMAN, H. J. (1993). *We can work it out*. New York: Putnam.

NURMI, J-E., & SALMELA-ARO, K. (1997). Social strategies and loneliness: A prospective study. *Personality and Individual Differences, 23*, 205–215.

NURMI, J-E., TOIVONEN, S., SALMELAARO, K., & ERONEN, S. (1996). Optimistic, approach-oriented, and avoidance strategies in social situations: Three studies on loneliness and peer relationships. *European Journal of Personality, 10*, 201–219.

NUTTIN, J. M., JR. (1987). Affective consequences of mere ownership: The name letter effect in twelve European languages. *European Journal of Social Psychology, 17*, 318–402.

O'BRIEN, L. T., & CRANDALL, C. S. (2003). Stereotype threat and arousal: Effects on women's math performance. *Personality and Social Psychology Bulletin, 29*, 782–789.

ODDONE-PAOLUCCI, E., GENUIS, M., & VIOLATO, C. (2000). A meta-analysis of the published research on the effects of pornography. In C. Violata (Ed.), *The changing family and child development*. Aldershot, England: Ashgate Publishing.

O'DEA, T. F. (1968). Sects and cults. In D. L. Sills (Ed.), *International encyclopedia of the social sciences, vol. 14*. New York: Macmillan.

OHBUCHI, K., & KAMBARA, T. (1985). Attacker's intent and awareness of outcome, impression management, and retaliation. *Journal of Experimental Social Psychology, 21*, 321–330.

O'LEARY, K. D., CHRISTIAN, J. L., & MENDELL, N. R. (1994). A closer look at the link between marital discord and depressive symptomatology. *Journal of Social and Clinical Psychology, 13*, 33–41.

OLSON, J. M., ROESE, N. J., & ZANNA, M. P. (1996). Expectancies. In E. T. Higgins & A. W. Kruglanski (Eds.), *Social psychology: Handbook of basic principles*. New York: Guilford Press, pp. 211–238.

OLWEUS, D. (1979). Stability of aggressive reaction patterns in males: A review. *Psychological Bulletin, 86*, 852–875.

OLWEUS, D., MATTSSON, A., SCHALLING, D., & LOW, H. (1988). Circulating testosterone levels and aggression in adolescent males: A causal analysis. *Psychosomatic Medicine, 50*, 261–272.

ORBELL, J. M., VAN DE KRAGT, A. J. C., & DAWES, R. M. (1988). Explaining discussion-induced cooperation. *Journal of Personality and Social Psychology, 54*, 811–819.

ORENSTEIN, P. (2003, July 6). Where have all the Lisas gone? *New York Times* (www.nytimes.com).

ORIVE, R. (1984). Group similarity, public self-awareness, and opinion extremity: A social projection explanation of deindividuation effects. *Journal of Personality and Social Psychology, 47*, 727–737.

ORNSTEIN, R. (1991). *The evolution of consciousness: Of Darwin, Freud, and cranial fire: The origins of the way we think*. New York: Prentice-Hall.

OSBERG, T. M., & SHRAUGER, J. S. (1986). Self-prediction: Exploring the parameters of accuracy. *Journal of Personality and Social Psychology, 51*, 1044–1057.

OSBORNE, J. W. (1995). Academics, self-esteem, and race: A look at the underlying assumptions of the disidentification hypothesis. *Personality and Social Psychology Bulletin, 21*, 449–455.

OSGOOD, C. E. (1962). *An alternative to war or surrender*. Urbana: University of Illinois Press.

OSGOOD, C. E. (1980). GRIT: A strategy for survival in mankind's nuclear age? Paper presented at the Pugwash Conference on New Directions in Disarmament, Racine, Wis.

OSKAMP, S. (1991). Curbside recycling: Knowledge, attitudes, and behavior. Paper presented at the Society for Experimental Social Psychology meeting, Columbus, Ohio.

OSKAMP, S. (2000). A sustainable future for humanity? How can psychology help? *American Psychologist, 55*, 496–508.

OSTERHOUSE, R. A., & BROCK, T. C. (1970). Distraction increases yielding to propaganda by inhibiting counterarguing. *Journal of Personality and Social Psychology, 15*, 344–358.

OSTROM, T. M., & SEDIKIDES, C. (1992). Out-group homogeneity effects in natural and minimal groups. *Psychological Bulletin, 112*, 536–552.

OYSERMAN, D., COON, H. M., & KEMMELMEIER, M. (2002a). Rethinking individualism and collectivism: Evaluation of theoretical assumptions and meta-analyses. *Psychological Bulletin, 128*, 3–72.

OYSERMAN, D., KEMMELMEIER, M., & COON, H. M. (2002b). Cultural psychology, a new look: Reply to Bond (2002), Fiske (2002), Kitayama (2002), and Miller (2002). *Psychological Bulletin, 128*, 110–117.

OZER, E. M., & BANDURA, A. (1990). Mechanisms governing empowerment effects: A self-efficacy analysis. *Journal of Personality and Social Psychology, 58,* 472–486.

PADGETT, V. R. (1989). Predicting organizational violence: An application of 11 powerful principles of obedience. Paper presented at the American Psychological Association Convention.

PAK, A. W., DION, K. L., & DION, K. K. (1991). Social-psychological correlates of experienced discrimination: Test of the double jeopardy hypothesis. *International Journal of Intercultural Relations, 15,* 243–254.

PALLAK, S. R., MURRONI, E., & KOCH, J. (1983). Communicator attractiveness and expertise, emotional versus rational appeals, and persuasion: A heuristic versus systematic processing interpretation. *Social Cognition, 2,* 122–141.

PALMER, D. L. (1996). Determinants of Canadian attitudes toward immigration: More than just racism? *Canadian Journal of Behavioural Science, 28,* 180–192.

PALMER, E. L., & DORR, A. (Eds.). (1980). *Children and the faces of television: Teaching, violence, selling.* New York: Academic Press.

PANDEY, J., SINHA, Y., PRAKASH, A., & TRIPATHI, R. C. (1982). Right-left political ideologies and attribution of the causes of poverty. *European Journal of Social Psychology, 12,* 327–331.

PAPASTAMOU, S., & MUGNY, G. (1990). Synchronic consistency and psychologization in minority influence. *European Journal of Social Psychology, 20,* 85–98.

PAPE, R. A. (2003, September 22). Dying to kill us. *New York Times* (www.nytimes.com).

PARK, B., & ROTHBART, M. (1982). Perception of out-group homogeneity and levels of social categorization: Memory for the subordinate attributes of in group and out-group members. *Journal of Personality and Social Psychology, 42,* 1051–1068.

PARKE, R. D., BERKOWITZ, L., LEYENS, J. P., WEST, S. G., & SEBASTIAN, J. (1977). Some effects of violent and nonviolent movies on the behavior of juvenile delinquents. In L. Berkowitz (Ed.), *Advances in experimental social psychology, vol. 10.* New York: Academic Press.

PARKS, C. D., & RUMBLE, A. C. (2001). Elements of reciprocity and social value orientation. *Personality and Social Psychology Bulletin, 27,* 1301–1309.

PASCARELLA, E. T., & TERENZINI, P. T. (1991). *How college affects students: Findings and insights from twenty years of research.* San Francisco: Jossey-Bass.

PATTERSON, D. (1996). *When learned men murder.* Bloomington, IN: Phi Delta Kappan.

PATTERSON, G. R., CHAMBERLAIN, P., & REID, J. B. (1982). A comparative evaluation of parent training procedures. *Behavior Therapy, 13,* 638–650.

PATTERSON, G. R., LITTMAN, R. A., & BRICKER, W. (1967). Assertive behavior in children: A step toward a theory of aggression. *Monographs of the Society for Research in Child Development, 32,* (Serial No. 113), 5.

PATTERSON, T. E. (1980). The role of the mass media in presidential campaigns: The lessons of the 1976 election. *Items, 34,* 25–30. Social Science Research Council, 605 Third Avenue, New York, NY 10016.

PAYNE, B. K. (2001). Prejudice and perception: The role of automatic and controlled processes in misperceiving a weapon. *Journal of Personality and Social Psychology, 81,* 181–192.

PEDERSEN, W. C., GONZALES, C., & MILLER, N. (2000). The moderating effect of trivial triggering provocation on displaced aggression. *Journal of Personality and Social Psychology, 78,* 913–927.

PEGALIS, L. J., SHAFFER, D. R., BAZZINI, D. G., & GREENIER, K. (1994). On the ability to elicit self-disclosure: Are there gender-based and contextual limitations on the opener effect? *Personality and Social Psychology Bulletin, 20,* 412–420.

PELHAM, B. W., MIRENBERG, M. C., & JONES, J. T. (2002). Why Susie sells seashells by the seashore. Implicit egotism and major life decisions. *Journal of Personality and Social Psychology, 82,* 469–487.

PENNEBAKER, J. W., & LAY, T. C. (2002). Language use and personality during crises: Analyses of Mayor Rudolph Giuliani's press conferences. *Journal of Research in Personality, 36,* 271–282.

PENTON-VOAK, I. S., JONES, B. C., LITTLE, A. C., BAKER, S., TIDDEMAN, B., BURT, D. M., & PERRETT, D. I. (2001). Symmetry, sexual dimorphism in facial proportions and male facial attractiveness. *Proceedings of the Royal Society of London, 268,* 1–7.

PEOPLE. (2003, September 1). Nipped, tucked, talking, pp. 102–111.

PEPLAU, L. A., & GORDON, S. L. (1985). Women and men in love: Gender differences in close heterosexual relationships. In V. E. O'Leary, R. K. Unger, & B. S. Wallston (Eds.), *Women, gender, and social psychology.* Hillsdale, NJ: Erlbaum.

PEREIRA, J. (2003, January 10). Just how far does First Amendment protection go? *Wall Street Journal,* pp. B1, B3.

PERLOFF, L. S. (1987). Social comparison and illusions of invulnerability. In C. R. Snyder & C. R. Ford (Eds.), *Coping with negative life events: Clinical and social psychological perspectives.* New York: Plenum.

PERLS, F. S. (1969). *Ego, hunger and aggression: The beginning of Gestalt therapy.* New York: Random House. Cited by Berkowitz in "The case for bottling up rage," *Psychology Today,* July 1973, pp. 24–30.

PESSIN, J. (1933). The comparative effects of social and mechanical stimulation on memorizing. *American Journal of Psychology, 45,* 263–270.

PESSIN, J., & HUSBAND, R. W. (1933). Effects of social stimulation on human maze learning. *Journal of Abnormal and Social Psychology, 28,* 148–154.

PETERSON, B. E., DOTY, R. M., & WINTER, D. G. (1993). Authoritarianism and attitudes toward contemporary social issues. *Personality and Social Psychology Bulletin, 19,* 174–184.

PETERSON, C., SCHWARTZ, S. M., & SELIGMAN, M. E. P. (1981). Self-blame and depression symptoms. *Journal of Personality and Social Psychology, 41,* 253–259.

PETERSON, C., & STEEN, T. A. (2002). Optimistic explanatory style. In C. R. Snyder & S. J. Lopez (Eds.), *Handbook of positive psychology.* London: Oxford University Press.

PETERSON, R. S., & NEMETH, C. J. (1996). Focus versus flexibility: Majority and minority influence can both improve performance. *Personality and Social Psychology Bulletin, 22,* 14–23.

PETTIGREW, T. F. (1958). Personality and socio-cultural factors in intergroup attitudes: A cross-national comparison. *Journal of Conflict Resolution, 2,* 29–42.

PETTIGREW, T. F. (1969). Racially separate or together? *Journal of Social Issues, 2,* 43–69.

PETTIGREW, T. F. (1978). Three issues in ethnicity: Boundaries, deprivations, and perceptions. In J. M. Yinger & S. J. Cutler (Eds.), *Major social issues: A multidisciplinary view.* New York: Free Press.

PETTIGREW, T. F. (1986). The intergroup contact hypothesis reconsidered. In M. Hewstone & R. Brown (Eds.), *Contact and conflict in intergroup encounters.* Oxford: Basil Blackwell.

PETTIGREW, T. F. (1988). Advancing racial justice: Past lessons for future use. Paper for the University of Alabama Conference: "Opening Doors: An Appraisal of Race Relations in America."

PETTIGREW, T. F. (1997). Generalized intergroup contact effects on prejudice. *Personality and Social Psychology Bulletin, 23,* 173–185.

PETTIGREW, T. F. (1998). Intergroup contact theory. *Annual Review of Psychology, 49,* 65–85.

PETTIGREW, T. F., JACKSON, J. S., BRIKA, J. B., LEMAINE, G., MEERTENS, R. W., WAGNER, U., & ZICK, A. (1998). Outgroup prejudice in western Europe. *European Review of Social Psychology, 8,* 241–273.

PETTIGREW, T. F., & MEERTENS, R. W. (1995). Subtle and blatant prejudice in western Europe. *European Journal of Social Psychology, 25,* 57–76.

PETTIGREW, T. F., & TROPP, L. R. (2000). Does intergroup contact reduce prejudice: Recent meta-analytic findings. In S. Oskamp, (Ed.), *Reducing prejudice and discrimination.* Mahwah, NJ: Erlbaum, pp. 93–114.

PETTY, R. E., & CACIOPPO, J. T. (1977). Forewarning cognitive responding, and resistance to persuasion. *Journal of Personality and Social Psychology, 35,* 645–655.

PETTY, R. E., & CACIOPPO, J. T. (1979). Effects of forewarning of persuasive intent and involvement on cognitive response and persuasion. *Personality and Social Psychology Bulletin, 5,* 173–176.

PETTY, R. E., & CACIOPPO, J. T. (1986). *Communication and persuasion: Central and peripheral routes to attitude change.* New York: Springer-Verlag.

PETTY, R. E., CACIOPPO, J. T., & GOLDMAN, R. (1981). Personal involvement as a determinant of argument-based persuasion. *Journal of Personality and Social Psychology, 41,* 847–855.

PETTY, R. E., & KROSNICK, J. A. (Eds.). (1995). *Attitude strength: Antecedents and consequences.* Hillsdale, NJ: Erlbaum.

PETTY, R. E., SCHUMANN, D. W., RICHMAN, S. A., & STRATHMAN, A. J. (1993). Positive mood and persuasion: Different roles for affect under high and low elaboration conditions. *Journal of Personality and Social Psychology, 64,* 5–20.

PETTY, R. E., & WEGENER, D. T. (1999). The elaboration likelihood model: Current status and controversies. In S. Chaiken & Y. Trope (Eds.), *Dual-process theories in social psychology,* pp. 41–72. New York: Guilford press.

PETTY, R. E., WHEELER, S. C., & BIZER, G. Y. (2000). Attitude functions and persuasion: An elaboration likelihood approach to matched versus mismatched messages. In G. R. Maio & J. M. Olson (Eds.), *Why we evaluate: Functions of attitudes,* pp. 133–162. Mahwah, NJ: Erlbaum.

PEW. (2003). Views of a changing world 2003. The Pew Global Attitudes Project. Washington, DC: Pew Research Center for the People and the Press (people-press.org/reports/pdf/185.pdf).

PHILLIPS, D. L. (2003, September 20). Listening to the wrong Iraqi. *New York Times* (www.nytimes.com).

PINCUS, J. H. (2001). *Base instincts: What makes killers kill?* New York: Norton.

PINGITORE, R., DUGONI, B. L., TINDALE, R. S., & SPRING, B. (1994). Bias against overweight job applicants in a simulated employment interview. *Journal of Applied Psychology, 79,* 909–917.

PINKER, S. (1997). *How the mind works.* New York: Norton.

PINKER, S. (2002). *The blank slate.* New York: Viking Press.

PIPHER, M. (2002). *The middle of everywhere: The world's refugees come to our town.* New York: Harcourt.

PLAKS, J. E., & HIGGINS, E. T. (2000). Pragmatic use of stereotyping in teamwork: Social loafing and compensation as a function of inferred partner-situation fit. *Journal of Personality and Social Psychology, 79,* 962–974.

PLATZ, S. J., & HOSCH, H. M. (1988). Cross-racial/ethnic eyewitness identification: A field study. *Journal of Applied Social Psychology, 18,* 972–984.

PLAUT, V. C., MARKUS, H. R., & LACKMAN, M. E. (2002). Place matters: Consensual features and regional variation in American well-being and self. *Journal of Personality and Social Psychology, 83,* 160–184.

PLINER, P., HART, H., KOHL, J., & SAARI, D. (1974). Compliance without pressure: Some further data on the foot-in-the-door technique. *Journal of Experimental Social Psychology, 10,* 17–22.

POMERLEAU, O. F., & RODIN, J. (1986). Behavioral medicine and health psychology. In S. L. Garfield & A. E. Bergin (Eds.), *Handbook of psychotherapy and behavior change,* 3rd ed. New York: Wiley.

POPENOE, D. (2002). The top ten myths of divorce. Unpublished manuscript, National Marriage Project, Rutgers University.

PORTER, N., GEIS, F. L., & JENNINGS (WALSTEDT), J. (1983). Are women invisible as leaders? *Sex Roles, 9,* 1035–1049.

POSTMES, T., & SPEARS, R. (1998). Deindividuation and antinormative behavior: A meta-analysis. *Psychological Bulletin, 123,* 238–259.

POWELL, J. (1989). *Happiness is an inside job.* Valencia, CA: Tabor.

POZO, C., CARVER, C. S., WELLENS, A. R., & SCHEIER, M. F. (1991). Social anxiety and social perception: Construing others' reactions to the self. *Personality and Social Psychology Bulletin, 17,* 355–362.

PRAGER, I. G., & CUTLER, B. L. (1990). Attributing traits to oneself and to others: The role of acquaintance level. *Personality and Social Psychology Bulletin, 16,* 309–319.

PRATKANIS, A. R., GREENWALD, A. G., LEIPPE, M. R., & BAUMGARDNER, M. H. (1988). In search of reliable persuasion effects: III. The sleeper effect is dead. Long live the sleeper effect. *Journal of Personality and Social Psychology, 54,* 203–218.

PRATTO, F. (1996). Sexual politics: The gender gap in the bedroom, the cupboard, and the cabinet. In D. M. Buss & N. M. Malamuth (Eds.), *Sex, power, conflict: Evolutionary and feminist perspectives.* New York: Oxford University Press.

PRATTO, F., STALLWORTH, L. M., & SIDANIUS, J. (1997). The gender gap: Differences in political attitudes and social dominance orientation. *British Journal of Social Psychology, 36,* 49–68.

PRENTICE, D. A., & CARRANZA, E. (2002). What women and men should be, shouldn't be, are allowed to be, and don't have to be: The contents of prescriptive gender stereotypes. *Psychology of Women Quarterly, 26,* 269–281.

PRENTICE-DUNN, S., & ROGERS, R. W. (1980). Effects of deindividuating situational cues and aggressive models on subjective deindividuation and aggression. *Journal of Personality and Social Psychology, 39,* 104–113.

PRENTICE-DUNN, S., & ROGERS, R. W. (1989). Deindividuation and the self-regulation of behavior. In P. B. Paulus (Ed.), *Psychology of group influence,* 2nd ed. Hillsdale, NJ: Erlbaum.

PRESSON, P. K., & BENASSI, V. A. (1996). Illusion of control: A meta-analytic review. *Journal of Social Behavior and Personality, 11,* 493–510.

PRICE, G. H., DABBS, J. M., JR., CLOWER, B. J., & RESIN, R. P. (1974). At first glance—Or, is physical attractiveness more than skin deep? Paper presented at the Eastern Psychological Association convention. Cited by K. L. Dion & K. K. Dion (1979). Personality and behavioral correlates of romantic love. In M. Cook & G. Wilson (Eds.), *Love and attraction.* Oxford: Pergamon.

PRITCHARD, I. L. (1998). The effects of rap music: On aggressive attitudes toward women. Master's thesis, Humboldt State University.

PROHASKA, V. (1994). "I know I'll get an A": Confident overestimation of final course grades. *Teaching of Psychology, 21,* 141–143.

PRONIN, E., KRUGER, J., SAVITSKY, K., & ROSS, L. (2001). You don't know me, but I know you: The illusion of asymmetric insight. *Journal of Personality and Social Psychology, 81,* 639–656.

PRONIN, E., LIN, D. Y., & ROSS, L. (2002). The bias blind spot: Perceptions of bias in self versus others. *Personality and Social Psychology Bulletin, 28,* 369–381.

PRUITT, D. G. (1986). Achieving integrative agreements in negotiation. In R. K. White (Ed.), *Psychology and the prevention of nuclear war.* New York: New York University Press.

PRUITT, D. G. (1998). Social conflict. In D. Gilbert, S. T. Fiske, & G. Lindzey (Eds.), *Handbook of social psychology,* 4th ed. New York: McGraw-Hill.

PRUITT, D. G., & KIMMEL, M. J. (1977). Twenty years of experimental gaming: Critique, synthesis, and suggestions for the future. *Annual Review of Psychology, 28,* 363–392.

PRUITT, D. G., & LEWIS, S. A. (1975). Development of integrative solutions in bilateral negotiation. *Journal of Personality and Social Psychology, 31,* 621–633.

PRUITT, D. G., & LEWIS, S. A. (1977). The psychology of integrative bargaining. In D. Druckman (Ed.), *Negotiations: A social-psychological analysis.* New York: Halsted.

PRUITT, D. G., & RUBIN, J. Z. (1986). *Social conflict.* San Francisco: Random House.

PRYOR, J. B., & REEDER, G. D. (1993). *The social psychology of HIV infection.* Hillsdale, NJ: Erlbaum.

PUBLIC OPINION. (1984, August/September). Vanity fare, p. 22.

PURVIS, J. A., DABBS, J. M., JR., & HOPPER, C. H. (1984). The "opener": Skilled user of facial expression and speech pattern. *Personality and Social Psychology Bulletin, 10,* 61–66.

PUTNAM, R. (2000). *Bowling alone.* New York: Simon & Schuster.

PYSZCZYNSKI, T., HAMILTON, J. C., GREENBERG, J., & BECKER, S. E. (1991). Self-awareness and psychological dysfunction. In C. R. Snyder & D. O. Forsyth (Eds.), *Handbook of social and clinical psychology: The health perspective.* New York: Pergamon.

QUARTZ, S. R., & SEJNOWSKI, T. J. (2002). *Liars, lovers, and heroes: What the new brain science reveals about how we become who we are.* New York: William Morrow.

QUATTRONE, G. A. (1982). Behavioral consequences of attributional bias. *Social Cognition, 1,* 358–378.

QUATTRONE, G. A., & JONES, E. E. (1980). The perception of variability within in-groups and out-groups: Implications for the law of small numbers. *Journal of Personality and Social Psychology, 38,* 141–152.

RAINE, A., LENCZ, T., BIHRLE, S., LACASSE, L., & COLLETTI, P. (2000). Reduced prefrontal gray matter volume and reduced autonomic activity in antisocial personality disorder. *Archives of General Psychiatry, 57,* 119–127.

RAINE, A., STODDARD, J., BIHRLE, S., & BUCHSBAUM, M. (1998). Prefrontal glucose deficits in murderers lacking psychosocial deprivation. *Neuropsychiatry, Neuropsychology, & Behavioral Neurology, 11,* 1–7.

RAJECKI, D. W., BLEDSOE, S. B., & RASMUSSEN, J. L. (1991). Successful personal ads: Gender differences and similarities in offers, stipulations, and outcomes. *Basic and Applied Social Psychology, 12,* 457–469.

RANK, S. G., & JACOBSON, C. K. (1977). Hospital nurses' compliance with medication overdose orders: A failure to replicate. *Journal of Health and Social Behavior, 18,* 188–193.

RAPOPORT, A. (1960). *Fights, games, and debates.* Ann Arbor: University of Michigan Press.

REEDER, G. D., McCORMICK, C. B., & ESSELMAN, E. D. (1987). Self-referent processing and recall of prose. *Journal of Educational Psychology, 79,* 243–248.

REGAN, D. T., & CHENG, J. B. (1973). Distraction and attitude change: A resolution. *Journal of Experimental Social Psychology, 9,* 138–147.

REICHER, S., SPEARS, R., & POSTMES, T. (1995). A social identity model of deindividuation phenomena. In W. Storebe & M. Hewstone (Eds.), *European review of social psychology, vol. 6.* Chichester, England: Wiley.

REIFMAN, A. S., LARRICK, R. P., & FEIN, S. (1991). Temper and temperature on the diamond: The heat-aggression relationship in major league baseball. *Personality and Social Psychology Bulletin, 17,* 580–585.

REIS, H. T., NEZLEK, J., & WHEELER, L. (1980). Physical attractiveness in social interaction. *Journal of Personality and Social Psychology, 38,* 604–617.

REIS, H. T., & SHAVER, P. (1988). Intimacy as an interpersonal process. In S. Duck (Ed.), *Handbook of personal relationships: Theory, relationships and interventions.* Chichester, England: Wiley.

REIS, H. T., WHEELER, L., SPIEGEL, N., KERNIS, M. H., NEZLEK, J., & PERRI, M. (1982). Physical attractiveness in social interaction: II. Why does appearance affect social experience? *Journal of Personality and Social Psychology, 43,* 979–996.

REITZES, D. C. (1953). The role of organizational structures: Union versus neighborhood in a tension situation. *Journal of Social Issues, 9*(1), 37–44.

REMLEY, A. (1988, October). From obedience to independence. *Psychology Today,* pp. 56–59.

RENAUD, H., & ESTESS, F. (1961). Life history interviews with one hundred normal American males: "Pathogenecity" of childhood. *American Journal of Orthopsychiatry, 31,* 786–802.

RENNER, M. (1999). *Ending violent conflict.* Worldwatch Paper 146, Worldwatch Institute.

RESSLER, R. K., BURGESS, A. W., & DOUGLAS, J. E. (1988). *Sexual homicide patterns.* Boston: Lexington Books.

RHODES, G., SUMICH, A., & BYATT, G. (1999). Are average facial configurations attractive only because of their symmetry. *Psychological Science, 10,* 52–58.

RHODEWALT, F., & AGUSTSDOTTIR, S. (1986). Effects of self-presentation on the phenomenal self. *Journal of Personality and Social Psychology, 50,* 47–55.

RHOLES, W. S., NEWMAN, L. S., & RUBLE, D. N. (1990). Understanding self and other: Developmental and motivational aspects of perceiving persons in terms of invariant dispositions. In E. T. Higgins & R. M. Sorrentino (Eds.), *Handbook of motivation and cognition: Foundations of social behavior, vol. 2.* New York: Guilford Press.

RICE, B. (1985, September). Performance review: The job nobody likes. *Psychology Today,* pp. 30–36.

RICH, F. (2001, May 20). Naked capitalists: There's no business like porn business. *New York Times* (www.nytimes.com).

RICHARD, F. D., BOND, C. F., JR., & STOKES-ZOOTA, J. J. (2003). One hundred years of social psychology quantitatively described. *Review of General Psychology, 7,* 331–363.

RICHARDSON, L. F. (1960). Generalized foreign policy. *British Journal of Psychology Monographs Supplements, 23.* Cited by A. Rapoport in *Fights, games, and debates.* Ann Arbor: University of Michigan Press, 1960, p. 15.

RIORDAN, C. A. (1980). Effects of admission of influence on attributions and attraction. Paper presented at the American Psychological Association convention.

ROBBERSON, M. R., & ROGERS, R. W. (1988). Beyond fear appeals: Negative and positive persuasive appeals to health and self-esteem. *Journal of Applied Social Psychology, 18,* 277–287.

ROBERTSON, I. (1987). *Sociology.* New York: Worth.

ROBINS, R. W., & BEER, J. S. (2001). Positive illusions about the self: Short-term benefits and long-term costs. *Journal of Personality and Social Psychology, 80,* 340–352.

ROBINS, R. W., SPRANCA, M. D., & MENDELSOHN, G. A. (1996). The actor-observer effect revisited: Effects of individual differences and repeated social interactions on actor and observer attributions. *Journal of Personality and Social Psychology, 71,* 375–389.

ROBINSON, J. (2002, October 8). What percentage of the population is gay? *Gallup Tuesday Briefing* (www.gallup.com).

ROBINSON, M. D., & RYFF, C. D. (1999). The role of self-deception in perceptions of past, present, and future happiness. *Personality and Social Psychology Bulletin, 25,* 595–606.

ROBINSON, M. S., & ALLOY, L. B. (2003). Negative cognitive styles and stress-reactive rumination interact to predict depression: A prospective study. *Cognitive Therapy and Research, 27,* 275–291.

ROBINSON, R. J., KELTNER, D., WARD, A., & ROSS, L. (1995). Actual versus assumed differences in construal: "Naive realism" in intergroup perception and conflict. *Journal of Personality and Social Psychology, 68,* 404–417.

ROBINSON, T. N., WILDE, M. L., NAVRACRUZ, L. C., HAYDEL, F., & VARADY, A. (2001). Effects of reducing children's television and video game use on aggressive behavior. *Archives of Pediatric and Adolescent Medicine, 155,* 17–23.

ROCHAT, F. (1993). How did they resist authority? Protecting refugees in Le Chambon during World War II. Paper presented at the American Psychological Association convention.

ROCHAT, F., & MODIGLIANI, A. (1995). The ordinary quality of resistance: From Milgram's laboratory to the village of Le Chambon. *Journal of Social Issues, 51,* 195–210.

ROEHLING, M. V. (2000). Weight-based discrimination in employment: Psychological and legal aspects. *Personnel Psychology, 52,* 969–1016.

ROGERS, C. R. (1958). Reinhold Niebuhr's *The self and the dramas of history:* A criticism. *Pastoral Psychology, 9,* 15–17.

ROGERS, C. R. (1980). *A way of being.* Boston: Houghton Mifflin.

ROGERS, R. W., & MEWBORN, C. R. (1976). Fear appeals and attitude change: Effects of a threat's noxiousness, probability of occurrence, and the efficacy of coping responses. *Journal of Personality and Social Psychology, 34,* 54–61.

ROGERS, R. W., & PRENTICE-DUNN, S. (1981). Deindividuation and anger-mediated interracial aggression: Unmasking regressive racism. *Journal of Personality and Social Psychology, 41,* 63–73.

ROKEACH, M., & MEZEI, L. (1966). Race and shared beliefs as factors in social choice. *Science, 151,* 167–172.

RONEY, J. R. (2003). Effects of visual exposure to the opposite sex: Cognitive aspects mate attraction in human males. *Personality and Social Psychology Bulletin, 29,* 393–404.

ROOK, K. S. (1984). Promoting social bonding: Strategies for helping the lonely and socially isolated. *American Psychologist, 39,* 1389–1407.

ROSENHAN, D. L. (1973). On being sane in insane places. *Science, 179,* 250–258.

ROSENTHAL, R. (1985). From unconscious experimenter bias to teacher expectancy effects. In J. B. Dusek, V. C. Hall, & W. J. Meyer (Eds.), *Teacher expectancies.* Hillsdale, NJ: Erlbaum.

ROSENTHAL, R. (1991). Teacher expectancy effects: A brief update 25 years after the Pygmalion experiment. *Journal of Research in Education, 1,* 3–12.

ROSENTHAL, R. (2002). Covert communication in classrooms, clinics, courtrooms, and cubicles. *American Psychologist, 57,* 839–849.

ROSENTHAL, R. (2003). Covert communication in laboratories, classrooms, and the truly real world. *Current Directions in Psychological Science, 12,* 151–154.

ROSENZWEIG, M. R. (1972). Cognitive dissonance. *American Psychologist, 27,* 769.

ROSS, L. (1977). The intuitive psychologist and his shortcomings: Distortions in the attribution process. In L. Berkowitz (Ed.), *Advances in experimental social psychology, vol. 10.* New York: Academic Press.

ROSS, L. (1981). The "intuitive scientist" formulation and its developmental implications. In J. H. Havell & L. Ross (Eds.), *Social cognitive development: Frontiers and possible futures.* Cambridge, England: Cambridge University Press.

ROSS, L. (1988). Situationist perspectives on the obedience experiments. Review of A. G. Miller's *The obedience experiments. Contemporary Psychology, 33,* 101–104.

ROSS, L., AMABILE, T. M., & STEINMETZ, J. L. (1977). Social roles, social control, and biases in social-perception processes. *Journal of Personality and Social Psychology, 35,* 485–494.

ROSS, L., & WARD, A. (1995). Psychological barriers to dispute resolution. In M. P. Zanna (Ed.), *Advances in experimental social psychology, vol. 27.* San Diego, CA: Academic Press.

Ross, M., & Buehler, R. (1994). Creative remembering. In U. Neisser & R. Fivush (Eds.), *The remembering self*. New York: Cambridge University Press.

Ross, M., McFarland, C., & Fletcher, G. J. O. (1981). The effect of attitude on the recall of personal histories. *Journal of Personality and Social Psychology, 40*, 627–634.

Ross, M., & Newby-Clark, I. R. (1998). Construing the past and future. *Social Cognition, 16*, 133–150.

Ross, M., & Sicoly, F. (1979). Egocentric biases in availability and attribution. *Journal of Personality and Social Psychology, 37*, 322–336.

Ross, M., Thibaut, J., & Evenbeck, S. (1971). Some determinants of the intensity of social protest. *Journal of Experimental Social Psychology, 7*, 401–418.

Rossi, A. S., & Rossi, P. H. (1990). *Of human bonding: Parent-child relations across the life course*. Hawthorne, NY: Aldine de Gruyter.

Roszell, P., Kennedy, D., & Grabb, E. (1990). Physical attractiveness and income attainment among Canadians. *Journal of Psychology, 123*, 547–559.

Rotenberg, K. J. (1997). Loneliness and the perception of the exchange of disclosures. *Journal of Social and Clinical Psychology, 16*, 259–276.

Rothbart, M., & Birrell, P. (1977). Attitude and perception of faces. *Journal of Research Personality, 11*, 209–215.

Rothbart, M., Fulero, S., Jensen, C., Howard, J., & Birrell, P. (1978). From individual to group impressions: Availability heuristics in stereotype formation. *Journal of Experimental Social Psychology, 14*, 237–255.

Rothbart, M., & Taylor, M. (1992). Social categories and social reality. In G. R. Semin & K. Fielder (Eds.), *Language, interaction and social cognition*. London: Sage.

Rotter, J. (1973). Internal-external locus of control scale. In J. P. Robinson & R. P. Shaver (Eds.), *Measures of social psychological attitudes*. Ann Arbor, MI: Institute for Social Research.

Rotton, J., & Frey, J. (1985). Air pollution, weather, and violent crimes: Concomitant time-series analysis of archival data. *Journal of Personality and Social Psychology, 49*, 1207–1220.

Rouhana, N. N., & Bar-Tal, D. (1998). Psychological dynamics of intractable ethnonational conflicts: The Israeli-Palestinian case. *American Psychologist, 53*, 761–770.

Ruback, R. B., Carr, T. S., & Hoper, C. H. (1986). Perceived control in prison: Its relation to reported crowding, stress, and symptoms. *Journal of Applied Social Psychology, 16*, 375–386.

Rubin, J. Z. (1986). Can we negotiate with terrorists: Some answers from psychology. Paper presented at the American Psychological Association convention.

Rubin, L. B. (1985). *Just friends: The role of friendship in our lives*. New York: Harper & Row.

Rubin, Z. (1973). *Liking and loving: An invitation to social psychology*. New York: Holt, Rinehart and Winston.

Ruiter, R. A. C., Kok, G., Verplanken, B., & Brug, J. (2001). Evoked fear and effects of appeals on attitudes to performing breast self-examination: An information-processing perspective. *Health Education Research, 16*, 307–319.

Rule, B. G., Taylor, B. R., & Dobbs, A. R. (1987). Priming effects of heat on aggressive thoughts. *Social Cognition, 5*, 131–143.

Rusbult, C. E., Johnson, D. J., & Morrow, G. D. (1986). Impact of couple patterns of problem solving on distress and nondistress in dating relationships. *Journal of Personality and Social Psychology, 50*, 744–753.

Rusbult, C. E., Martz, J. M., & Agnew, C. R. (1998). The investment model scale: Measuring commitment level, satisfaction level, quality of alternatives, and investment size. *Personal Relationships, 5*, 357–391.

Rusbult, C. E., Morrow, G. D., & Johnson, D. J. (1987). Self-esteem and problem-solving behaviour in close relationships. *British Journal of Social Psychology, 26*, 293–303.

Russell, B. (1930/1980). *The conquest of happiness*. London: Unwin Paperbacks.

Russell, G. W. (1983). Psychological issues in sports aggression. In J. H. Goldstein (Ed.), *Sports violence*. New York: Springer-Verlag.

Ryan, R. (1999, February 2). Quoted by A. Kohn, In pursuit of affluence, at a high price. *New York Times* (via www.nytimes.com).

Saad, L. (2002, November 21). Most smokers wish they could quit. Gallup News Service (www.gallup.com/poll/releases/pr021121.asp).

SAAD, L. (2003, April 22). Giving global warming the cold shoulder. The Gallup Organization (www.gallup.com).

SABINI, J., & SILVER, M. (1982). *Moralities of everyday life.* New York: Oxford University Press.

SACCO, W. P., & DUNN, V. K. (1990). Effect of actor depression on observer attributions: Existence and impact of negative attributions toward the depressed. *Journal of Personality and Social Psychology, 59,* 517–524.

SACK, K., & ELDER, J. (2000, July 11). Poll finds optimistic outlook but enduring racial division. *New York Times* (www.nytimes.com).

SACKS, C. H., & BUGENTAL, D. P. (1987). Attributions as moderators of affective and behavioral responses to social failure. *Journal of Personality and Social Psychology, 53,* 939–947.

SAGARIN, B. J., RHOADS, K. V. L., & CIALDINI, R. B. (1998). Deceiver's distrust: Denigration as a consequence of undiscovered deception. *Personality and Social Psychology Bulletin, 24,* 1167–1176.

SALES, S. M. (1972). Economic threat as a determinant of conversion rates in authoritarian and nonauthoritarian churches. *Journal of Personality and Social Psychology, 23,* 420–428.

SALES, S. M. (1973). Threat as a factor in authoritarianism: An analysis of archival data. *Journal of Personality and Social Psychology, 28,* 44–57.

SANDE, G. N., GOETHALS, G. R., & RADLOFF, C. E. (1988). Perceiving one's own traits and others': The multifaceted self. *Journal of Personality and Social Psychology, 54,* 13–20.

SANDERS, G. S. (1981a). Driven by distraction: An integrative review of social facilitation and theory and research. *Journal of Experimental Social Psychology, 17,* 227–251.

SANDERS, G. S. (1981b). Toward a comprehensive account of social facilitation: Distraction/conflict does not mean theoretical conflict. *Journal of Experimental Social Psychology, 17,* 262–265.

SANDERS, G. S., BARON, R. S., & MOORE, D. L. (1978). Distraction and social comparison as mediators of social facilitation effects. *Journal of Experimental Social Psychology, 14,* 291–303.

SANDERSON, C. A., & CANTOR, N. (2001). The association of intimacy goals and marital satisfaction: A test of four mediational hypotheses. *Personality and Social Psychology Bulletin, 27,* 1567–1577.

SANISLOW, C. A., III., PERKINS, D. V., & BALOGH, D. W. (1989). Mood induction, interpersonal perceptions, and rejection in the roommates of depressed, nondepressed-disturbed, and normal college students. *Journal of Social and Clinical Psychology, 8,* 345–358.

SANITIOSO, R., KUNDA, Z., & FONG, G. T. (1990). Motivated recruitment of autobiographical memories. *Journal of Personality and Social Psychology, 59,* 229–241.

SAPADIN, L. A. (1988). Friendship and gender: Perspectives of professional men and women. *Journal of Social and Personal Relationships, 5,* 387–403.

SARTRE, J-P. (1946/1948). *Anti-Semite and Jew.* New York: Schocken Books.

SATO, K. (1987). Distribution of the cost of maintaining common resources. *Journal of Experimental Social Psychology, 23,* 19–31.

SATTERFIELD, A. T., & MUEHLENHARD, C. L. (1997). Shaken confidence: The effects of an authority figure's flirtatiousness on women's and men's self-rated creativity. *Psychology of Women Quarterly, 21,* 395–416.

SAVITSKY, K., EPLEY, N., & GILOVICH, T. (2001). Do others judge us as harshly as we think? Overestimating the impact of our failures, shortcomings, and mishaps. *Journal of Personality and Social Psychology, 81,* 44–56.

SAX, L. J., LINDHOLM, J. A., ASTIN, A. W., KORN, W. S., & MAHONEY, K. M. (2002). *The American freshman: National norms for Fall, 2002.* Los Angeles: Cooperative Institutional Research Program, UCLA.

SCHACHTER, S., & SINGER, J. E. (1962). Cognitive, social and physiological determinants of emotional state. *Psychological Review, 69,* 379–399.

SCHAFER, R. B., & KEITH, P. M. (1980). Equity and depression among married couples. *Social Psychology Quarterly, 43,* 430–435.

SCHAFFNER, P. E., WANDERSMAN, A., & STANG, D. (1981). Candidate name exposure and voting: Two field studies. *Basic and Applied Social Psychology, 2,* 195–203.

SCHEIN, E. H. (1956). The Chinese indoctrination program for prisoners of war: A study of attempted brainwashing. *Psychiatry, 19,* 149–172.

SCHIFFENBAUER, A., & SCHIAVO, R. S. (1976). Physical distance and attraction: An intensification effect. *Journal of Experimental Social Psychology, 12,* 274–282.

SCHIMEL, J., ARNDT, J., PYSZCZYNSKI, T., & GREENBERG, J. (2001). Being accepted for who we are: Evidence that social validation of the intrinsic self reduces general defensiveness. *Journal of Personality and Social Psychology, 80,* 35–52.

SCHIMEL, J., PYSZCZYNSKI, T., GREENBERG, J., O'MAHEN, H., & ARNDT, J. (2000). Running from the shadow: Psychological distancing from others to deny characteristics people fear in themselves. *Journal of Personality and Social Psychology, 78,* 446–462.

SCHKADE, D. A., & KAHNEMAN, D. (1998). Does living in California make people happy? A focusing illusion in judgments of life satisfaction. *Psychological Science, 9,* 340–346.

SCHKADE, D. A., & SUNSTEIN, C. R. (2003, June 11). Judging by where you sit. *New York Times* (www.nytimes.com).

SCHLENKER, B. R. (1976). Egocentric perceptions in cooperative groups: A conceptualization and research review. Final Report, Office of Naval Research Grant NR 170–797.

SCHLENKER, B. R., & LEARY, M. R. (1982). Social anxiety and self-presentation: A conceptualization and model. *Psychological Bulletin, 92,* 641–669.

SCHLENKER, B. R., & LEARY, M. R. (1985). Social anxiety and communication about the self. *Journal of Language and Social Psychology, 4,* 171–192.

SCHLENKER, B. R., & MILLER, R. S. (1977a). Egocentrism in groups: Self-serving biases or logical information processing? *Journal of Personality and Social Psychology, 35,* 755–764.

SCHLENKER, B. R., & MILLER, R. S. (1977b). Group cohesiveness as a determinant of egocentric perceptions in cooperative groups. *Human Relations, 30,* 1039–1055.

SCHLENKER, B. R., WEIGOLD, M. F., & HALLAM, J. R. (1990). Self-serving attributions in social context: Effects of self-esteem and social pressure. *Journal of Personality and Social Psychology, 58,* 855–863.

SCHLESINGER, A., JR. (1949). The statistical soldier. *Partisan Review, 16,* 852–856.

SCHLESINGER, A., JR. (1991, July 8). The cult of ethnicity, good and bad. *Time,* p. 21.

SCHLOSSER, E. (2003, March 10). Empire of the obscene. *New Yorker,* pp. 61–71.

SCHMADER, T., & JOHNS, M. (2003). Converging evidence that stereotype threat reduces working memory capacity. *Journal of Personality and Social Psychology, 85,* 440–451.

SCHMITT, D. P. (2003). Universal sex differences in the desire for sexual variety; tests from 52 nations, 6 continents, and 13 islands. *Journal of Personality and Social Psychology, 85,* 85–104.

SCHOENEMAN, T. J. (1994). Individualism. In V. S. Ramachandran (Ed.), *Encyclopedia of human behavior.* San Diego, CA: Academic Press.

SCHOENFELD, B. (1995, May 14). The loneliness of being white. *New York Times Magazine,* 34–37.

SCHOFIELD, J. (1982). *Black and white in school: Trust, tension, or tolerance?* New York: Praeger.

SCHOFIELD, J. W. (1986). Causes and consequences of the colorblind perspective. In J. F. Dovidio & S. L. Gaertner (Eds.), *Prejudice, discrimination, and racism.* Orlando, FL: Academic Press.

SCHOOLER, J. W. (2002). Verbalization produces a transfer inappropriate processing shift. *Applied Cognitive Psychology, 16,* 989–997.

SCHOR, J. B. (1998). *The overworked American.* New York: Basic Books.

SCHULZ, J. W., & PRUITT, D. G. (1978). The effects of mutual concern on joint welfare. *Journal of Experimental Social Psychology, 14,* 480–492.

SCHUMAN, H., & SCOTT, J. (1989). Generations and collective memories. *American Sociological Review, 54,* 359–381.

SCHWARTZ, B. (2000). Self-determination: The tyranny of freedom. *American Psychologist, 55,* 79–88.

SCHWARTZ, B. (2004). *The tyranny of choice.* New York: Ecco/HarperCollins.

SCHWARTZ, S. H., & GOTTLIEB, A. (1981). Participants' post-experimental reactions and the ethics of bystander research. *Journal of Experimental Social Psychology, 17,* 396–407.

SCHWARZ, N., BLESS, H., & BOHNER, G. (1991). Mood and persuasion: Affective states influence the processing of persuasive communications. In M. Zanna (Ed.), *Advances in experimental social psychology, vol. 24.* New York: Academic Press.

SCHWARZ, N., & CLORE, G. L. (1983). Mood, misattribution, and judgments of well-being: Informative and directive functions of affective states. *Journal of Personality and Social Psychology, 45*, 513–523.

SCHWEINLE, W. E., ICKES, W., & BERNSTEIN, I. H. (2002). Empathic inaccuracy in husband to wife aggression: The overattribution bias. *Personal Relationships, 9*, 141–159.

SCOTT, J. P., & MARSTON, M. V. (1953). Nonadaptive behavior resulting from a series of defeats in fighting mice. *Journal of Abnormal and Social Psychology, 48*, 417–428.

SEARS, D. O. (1979). Life stage effects upon attitude change, especially among the elderly. Manuscript prepared for Workshop on the Elderly of the Future, Committee on Aging, National Research Council, Annapolis, MD, May 3–5.

SEARS, D. O. (1986). College sophomores in the laboratory: Influences of a narrow data base on social psychology's view of human nature. *Journal of Personality and Social Psychology, 51*, 515–530.

SEDIKIDES, C. (1993). Assessment, enhancement, and verification determinants of the self-evaluation process. *Journal of Personality and Social Psychology, 65*, 317–338.

SEGAL, H. A. (1954). Initial psychiatric findings of recently repatriated prisoners of war. *American Journal of Psychiatry, 61*, 358–363.

SEGALL, M. H., DASEN, P. R., BERRY, J. W., & POORTINGA, Y. H. (1990). *Human behavior in global perspective: An introduction to cross-cultural psychology.* New York: Pergamon.

SEGERSTROM, S. C. (2001). Optimism and attentional bias for negative and positive stimuli. *Personality and Social Psychology Bulletin, 27*, 1334–1343.

SEIBT, B., & FORSTER, J. (2004). Stereotype threat and performance: How self-stereotypes influence processing by inducing regulatory foci. *Journal of Personality and Social Psychology, 87*, 38–56.

SELIGMAN, M. (1994). *What you can change and what you can't.* New York: Knopf.

SELIGMAN, M. E. P. (1975). *Helplessness: On depression, development and death.* San Francisco: W. H. Freeman.

SELIGMAN, M. E. P. (1991). *Learned optimism.* New York: Knopf.

SELIGMAN, M. E. P. (1992). Power and powerlessness: Comments on "Cognates of personal control." *Applied and Preventive Psychology, 1*, 119–120.

SELIGMAN, M. E. P. (1998). The prediction and prevention of depression. In D. K. Routh & R. J. DeRubeis (Eds.), *The science of clinical psychology: Accomplishments and future directions.* Washington, DC: American Psychological Association.

SELIGMAN, M. E. P. (2002). *Authentic happiness: Using the new positive psychology to realize your potential for lasting fulfillment.* New York: Free Press.

SEMIN, G. R., & DE POOT, C. J. (1997). Bringing partiality to light: Question wording and choice as indicators of bias. *Social Cognition, 15*, 91–106.

SENGUPTA, S. (2001, October 10). Sept. 11 attack narrows the racial divide. *New York Times* (www.nytimes.com).

SENGUPTA, S. (2003, May 27). Congo war toll soars as U.N. pleads for aid. *New York Times* (www.nytimes.com).

SENTYRZ, S. M., & BUSHMAN, B. J. (1998). Mirror, mirror, on the wall, who's the thinnest one of all? Effects of self-awareness on consumption of fatty, reduced-fat, and fat-free products. *Journal of Applied Psychology, 83*, 944–949.

SETA, C. E., & SETA, J. J. (1992). Increments and decrements in mean arterial pressure levels as a function of audience composition: An averaging and summation analysis. *Personality and Social Psychology Bulletin, 18*, 173–181.

SETA, J. J. (1982). The impact of comparison processes on coactors' task performance. *Journal of Personality and Social Psychology, 42*, 281–291.

SHACKELFORD, T. K., & LARSEN, R. J. tor of psychological, emotional, and physiological distress. *Journal of Personality and Social Psychology, 72*, 456–466.

SHAFFER, D. R., PEGALIS, L. J., & BAZZINI, D. G. (1996). When boy meets girls (revisited): Gender, gender-role orientation, and prospect of future interaction as determinants of self-disclosure among same- and opposite-sex acquaintances. *Personality and Social Psychology Bulletin, 22*, 495–506.

SHARMA, N. (1981). Some aspect of attitude and behaviour of mothers. *Indian Psychological Review, 20*, 35–42.

SHAVITT, S. (1990). The role of attitude objects in attitude functions. *Journal of Experimental Social Psychology, 26*, 124–148.

SHELDON, K. M., ELLIOT, A. J., YOUNGMEE, K., & KASSER, T. (2001). What is satisfying about satisfying events? Testing 10 candidate psychological needs. *Journal of Personality and Social Psychology, 80,* 325–339.

SHEPPERD, J. A. (2003). Interpreting comparative risk judgments: Are people personally optimistic or interpersonally pessimistic? Unpublished manuscript, University of Florida.

SHEPPERD, J. A., & WRIGHT, R. A. (1989). Individual contributions to a collective effort: An incentive analysis. *Personality and Social Psychology Bulletin, 15,* 141–149.

SHERIF, M. (1966). *In common predicament: Social psychology of intergroup conflict and cooperation.* Boston: Houghton Mifflin.

SHERMAN, D. K., NELSON, L. D., & ROSS, L. D. (2003). Naive realism and affirmative action: Adversaries are more similar than they think. *Basic and Applied Social Psychology, 25,* 275–289.

SHERMAN, J. W. (1996). Development and mental representation of stereotypes. *Journal of Personality and Social Psychology, 70,* 1126–1141.

SHERMAN, J. W., LEE, A. Y., BESSENOFF, G. R., & FROST, L. A. (1998). Stereotype efficiency reconsidered: Encoding flexibility under cognitive load. *Journal of Personality and Social Psychology, 75,* 589–606.

SHERMAN, S. J., CIALDINI, R. B., SCHWARTZMAN, D. F., & REYNOLDS, K. D. (1985). Imagining can heighten or lower the perceived likelihood of contracting a disease: The mediating effect of ease of imagery. *Personality and Social Psychology Bulletin, 11,* 118–127.

SHIH, M., PITTINSKY, T. L., & AMBADY, N. (1999). Stereotype susceptibility: Identity salience and shifts in quantitative performance. *Psychological Science, 10,* 80–83.

SHORT, J. F., JR. (ED.). (1969). *Gang delinquency and delinquent subcultures.* New York: Harper & Row.

SHOSTAK, M. (1981). *Nisa: The life and words of a !Kung woman.* Cambridge, MA: Harvard University Press.

SHOWERS, C., & RUBEN, C. (1987). Distinguishing pessimism from depression: Negative expectations and positive coping mechanisms. Paper presented at the American Psychological Association convention.

SHRAUGER, J. S. (1983). The accuracy of self-prediction: How good are we and why? Paper presented at the Midwestern Psychological Association convention.

SHRAUGER, J. S., RAM, D., GRENINGER, S. A., & MARIANO, E. (1996). Accuracy of self-predictions versus judgments by knowledgeable others. *Personality and Social Psychology Bulletin, 22,* 1229–1243.

SIDANIUS, J., & PRATTO, F. (1999). *Social dominance: An intergroup theory of social hierarchy and oppression.* New York: Cambridge University Press.

SIDANIUS, J., PRATTO, F., & BOBO, L. (1994). Social dominance orientation and the political psychology of gender: A case of invariance? *Journal of Personality and Social Psychology, 67,* 998–1011.

SIEFF, E. M., DAWES, R. M., & LOEWENSTEIN, G. F. (1999). Anticipated versus actual responses to HIV test results. *American Journal of Psychology, 112,* 297–311.

SIGALL, H. (1970). Effects of competence and consensual validation on a communicator's liking for the audience. *Journal of Personality and Social Psychology, 16,* 252–258.

SILKE, A. (2003). Deindividuation, anonymity, and violence: Findings from Northern Ireland. *Journal of Social Psychology, 143,* 493–499.

SILVER, M., & GELLER, D. (1978). On the irrelevance of evil: The organization and individual action. *Journal of Social Issues, 34,* 125–136.

SIMMONS, W. W. (2000, December). When it comes to having children, Americans still prefer boys. *The Gallup Poll Monthly,* pp. 63–64.

SIMONTON, D. K. (1994). *Greatness: Who makes history and why.* New York: Guilford Press.

SIMPSON, J. A. (1987). The dissolution of romantic relationships: Factors involved in relationship stability and emotional distress. *Journal of Personality and Social Psychology, 53,* 683–692.

SIMPSON, J. A., CAMPBELL, B., & BERSCHEID, E. (1986). The association between romantic love and marriage: Kephart (1967) twice revisited. *Personality and Social Psychology Bulletin, 12,* 363–372.

SIMPSON, J. A., GANGESTAD, S. W., & LERMA, M. (1990). Perception of physical attractiveness: Mechanisms involved in the maintenance of romantic relationships. *Journal of Personality and Social Psychology, 59,* 1192–1201.

SINGER, M. (1979). Cults and cult members. Address to the American Psychological Association convention.

SKAALVIK, E. M., & HAGTVET, K. A. (1990). Academic achievement and self-concept: An analysis of causal predominance in a developmental perpsective. *Journal of Personality and Social Psychology, 58,* 292–307.

SKITKA, L. J. (1999). Ideological and attributional boundaries on public compassion: Reactions to individuals and communities affected by a natural disaster. *Personality and Social Psychology Bulletin, 25,* 793–808.

SLAVIN, R. E. (1990, December/January). Research on cooperative learning: Consensus and controversy. *Educational Leadership,* pp. 52–54.

SLOVIC, P. (1972). From Shakespeare to Simon: Speculations—and some evidence—about man's ability to process information. *Oregon Research Institute Research Bulletin, 12*(2).

SLOVIC, P., & FISCHHOFF, B. (1977). On the psychology of experimental surprises. *Journal of Experimental Psychology: Human Perception and Performance, 3,* 455–551.

SMEDLEY, J. W., & BAYTON, J. A. (1978). Evaluative race-class stereotypes by race and perceived class of subjects. *Journal of Personality and Social Psychology, 3,* 530–535.

SMELSER, N. J., & MITCHELL, F. (EDS.). (2002). *Terrorism: Perspectives from the behavioral and social sciences.* Washington, DC: National Research Council, National Academies Press.

SMITH, A. (1976). *The wealth of nations.* Book 1. Chicago: University of Chicago Press. (Originally published 1776.)

SMITH, A. E., JUSSIM, L., & ECCLES, J. (1999). Do self-fulfilling prophecies accumulate, dissipate, or remain stable over time? *Journal of Personality and Social Psychology, 77,* 548–565.

SMITH, A. E., JUSSIM, L., ECCLES, J., VAN NOY, M., MADON, S., & PALUMBO, P. (1998). Self-fulfilling prophecies, perceptual biases, and accuracy at the individual and group levels. *Journal of Experimental Social Psychology, 34,* 530–561.

SMITH, D. E., GIER, J. A., & WILLIS, F. N. (1982). Interpersonal touch and compliance with a marketing request. *Basic and Applied Social Psychology, 3,* 35–38.

SMITH, H. (1976). *The Russians.* New York: Balantine Books. Cited by B. Latané, K. Williams, & S. Harkins in Many hands make light the work. *Journal of Personality and Social Psychology, 37,* 1979, pp. 822–832.

SMITH, H. J., & TYLER, T. R. (1997). Choosing the right pond: The impact of group membership on self-esteem and group-oriented behavior. *Journal of Experimental Social Psychology, 33,* 146–170.

SMITH, H. W. (1981). Territorial spacing on a beach revisited: A cross-national exploration. *Social Psychology Quarterly, 44,* 132–137.

SMITH, P. B., & TAYEB, M. (1989). Organizational structure and processes. In M. Bond (Ed.), *The cross-cultural challenge to social psychology.* Newbury Park, CA: Sage.

SMITH, T. W. (1998, December). American sexual behavior: Trends, socio-demographic differences, and risk behavior. National Opinion Research Center GSS Topical Report No. 25.

SMOREDA, Z., & LICOPPE, C. (2000). Gender-specific use of the domestic telephone. *Social Psychology Quarterly, 63,* 238–252.

SNODGRASS, M. A. (1987). The relationships of differential loneliness, intimacy, and characterological attributional style to duration of loneliness. *Journal of Social Behavior and Personality, 2,* 173–186.

SNYDER, C. R. (1978). The "illusion" of uniqueness. *Journal of Humanistic Psychology, 18,* 33–41.

SNYDER, C. R. (1980, March). The uniqueness mystique. *Psychology Today,* pp. 86–90.

SNYDER, C. R., & FROMKIN, H. L. (1980). *Uniqueness: The human pursuit of difference.* New York: Plenum.

SNYDER, C. R., & HIGGINS, R. L. (1988). Excuses: Their effective role in the negotiation of reality. *Psychological Bulletin, 104,* 23–35.

SNYDER, C. R., & SMITH, T. W. (1986). On being "shy like a fox": A self-handicapping analysis. In W. H. Jones, J. M. Cheek, S. R. Briggs (Eds.), *Shyness: Perspectives on research and treatment.* New York: Plenum.

SNYDER, M. (1981). Seek, and ye shall find: Testing hypotheses about other people. In E. T. Higgins, C. P. Herman, & M. P. Zanna (Eds.), *Social cognition: The Ontario symposium on personality and social psychology.* Hillsdale, NJ: Erlbaum.

SNYDER, M. (1983). The influence of individuals on situations: Implications for understanding the links between personality and social behavior. *Journal of Personality, 51,* 497–516.

SNYDER, M. (1984). When belief creates reality. In L. Berkowitz (Ed.), *Advances in experimental social psychology, vol. 18.* New York: Academic Press.

SNYDER, M., CAMPBELL, B., & PRESTON, E. (1982). Testing hypotheses about human nature: Assessing the accuracy of social stereotypes. *Social Cognition, 1,* 256–272.

SNYDER, M., & ICKES, W. (1985). Personality and social behavior. In G. Lindzey & E. Aronson (Eds.), *Handbook of social psychology,* 3rd ed. New York: Random House.

SNYDER, M., TANKE, E. D., & BERSCHEID, E. (1977). Social perception and interpersonal behavior: On the self-fulfilling nature of social stereotypes. *Journal of Personality and Social Psychology, 35,* 656–666.

SOKOLL, G. R., & MYNATT, C. R. (1984). Arousal and free throw shooting. Paper presented at the Midwestern Psychological Association convention, Chicago.

SOLBERG, E. C., DIENER, E., & ROBINSON, M. D. (2003). Why are materialists less satisfied? In T. Kasser & A. D. Kanner (Eds.), *Psychology and consumer culture: The struggle for a good life in a materialistic world.* Washington, DC: APA Books.

SOLOMON, S., OGILVIE, D. M., COHEN, F., GREENBERG, J., & PYSZCZYNSKI, T. (2005). American roulette: The effects of reminders of death on support for George W. Bush in the 2004 presidential election. *Analyses of Social Issues and Public Policy, 5,* 177–187.

SOMMER, R. (1969). *Personal space.* Englewood Cliffs, NJ: Prentice-Hall.

SPARRELL, J. A., & SHRAUGER, J. S. (1984). Self-confidence and optimism in self-prediction. Paper presented at the American Psychological Association convention.

SPECTOR, P. E. (1986). Perceived control by employees: A meta-analysis of studies concerning autonomy and participation at work. *Human Relations, 39,* 1005–1016.

SPEER, A. (1971). *Inside the Third Reich: Memoirs.* (P. Winston & C. Winston. trans.). New York: Avon Books.

SPENCER, S. J., STEELE, C. M., & QUINN, D. M. (1999). Stereotype threat and women's math performance. *Journal of Experimental Social Psychology, 3,* 4–28.

SPIEGEL, H. W. (1971). *The growth of economic thought.* Durham, NC: Duke University Press.

SPITZBERG, B. H., & HURT, H. T. (1987). The relationship of interpersonal competence and skills to reported loneliness across time. *Journal of Social Behavior and Personality, 2,* 157–172.

SPIVAK, J. (1979, June 6). *Wall Street Journal.*

SPIVEY, C. B., & PRENTICE-DUNN, S. (1990). Assessing the directionality of deindividuated behavior: Effects of deindividuation, modeling, and private self-consciousness on aggressive and prosocial responses. *Basic and Applied Social Psychology, 11,* 387–403.

SPRECHER, S. (1987). The effects of self-disclosure given and received on affection for an intimate partner and stability of the relationship. *Journal of Personality and Social Psychology, 4,* 115–127.

SPRECHER, S., ARON, A., HATFIELD, E., CORTESE, A., POTAPOVA, E., & LEVITSKAYA, A. (1994). Love: American style, Russian style, and Japanese style. *Personal Relationships, 1,* 349–369.

SPRECHER, S., SULLIVAN, Q., & HATFIELD, E. (1994). Mate selection preferences: Gender differences examined in a national sample. *Journal of Personality and Social Psychology, 66,* 1074–1080.

SPRECHER, S., & TORO-MORN, M. (2002). A study of men and women from different sides of earth to determine if men are from Mars and women are from Venus in their beliefs about love and romantic relationships. *Sex Roles, 46,* 131–147.

STANGOR, C., JONAS, K., STROEBE, W., & HEWSTONE, M. (1996). Influence of student exchange on national stereotypes, attitudes and perceived group variability. *European Journal of Social Psychology, 26,* 663–675.

STANGOR, C., LYNCH, L., DUAN, C., & GLASS, B. (1992). Categorization of individuals on the basis of multiple social features. *Journal of Personality and Social Psychology, 62,* 207–218.

STARK, R., & BAINBRIDGE, W. S. (1980). Networks of faith: Interpersonal bonds and recruitment of cults and sects. *American Journal of Sociology, 85,* 1376–1395.

STASSER, G. (1991). Pooling of unshared information during group discussion. In S. Worchel, W. Wood, & J. Simpson (Eds.), *Group process and productivity.* Beverly Hills, CA: Sage.

STATISTICS CANADA. (2001). www.statcan.ca

STAUB, E. (1989). *The roots of evil: The origins of genocide and other group violence.* Cambridge: Cambridge University Press.

STAUB, E. (1999). Behind the scenes. In D. G. Myers, *Social psychology,* 6th ed. New York: McGraw-Hill.

STAUB, E. (2003). *The psychology of good and evil: Why children, adults, and groups help and harm others.* New York: Cambridge University Press.

STAUB, E., & PEARLMAN, L. A. (2004). Advancing healing and reconciliation. *Journal of Genocide Studies, 24,* 297–334.

STEELE, C. M. (1997). A threat in the air: How stereotypes shape intellectual identity and performance. *American Psychologist, 52,* 613–629.

STEELE, C. M., & ARONSON, J. (1995). Stereotype threat and the intellectual test performance of African Americans. *Journal of Personality and Social Psychology, 69,* 797–811.

STEELE, C. M., & SOUTHWICK, L. (1985). Alcohol and social behavior I: The psychology of drunken excess. *Journal of Personality and Social Psychology, 48,* 18–34.

STEELE, C. M., SPENCER, S. J., & ARONSON, J. (2002). Contending with group image: The psychology of stereotype and social identity threat. In M. P. Zanna (Ed.), *Advances in experimental social psychology,* pp. 34, 379–440. San Diego, CA: Academic Press.

STEIN, A. H., & FRIEDRICH, L. K. (1972). Television content and young children's behavior. In J. P. Murray, E. A. Rubinstein, & G. A. Comstock (Eds.), *Television and social learning.* Washington, DC: Government Printing Office.

STEIN, D. D., HARDYCK, J. A., & SMITH, M. B. (1965). Race and belief: An open and shut case. *Journal of Personality and Social Psychology, 1,* 281–289.

STEPHAN, W. G. (1986). The effects of school desegregation: An evaluation 30 years after Brown. In R. Kidd, L. Saxe, & M. Saks (Eds.), *Advances in applied social psychology.* New York: Erlbaum.

STEPHAN, W. G. (1987). The contact hypothesis in intergroup relations. In C. Hendrick (Ed.), *Group processes and intergroup relations.* Newbury Park, CA: Sage.

STEPHAN, W. G. (1988). School desegregation: Short-term and long-term effects. Paper presented at the national conference "Opening doors: An appraisal of race relations in America," University of Alabama.

STEPHAN, W. G., BERSCHEID, E., & WALSTER, E. (1971). Sexual arousal and heterosexual perception. *Journal of Personality and Social Psychology, 20,* 93–101.

STERNBERG, R. J. (1988). Triangulating love. In R. J. Sternberg & M. L. Barnes (Eds.), *The psychology of love.* New Haven, CT: Yale University Press.

STERNBERG, R. J. (1998). *Cupid's arrow: The course of love through time.* New York: Cambridge University Press.

STERNBERG, R. J. (2003). A duplex theory of hate and its development and its application to terrorism, massacres, and genocide. *Review of General Psychology, 7,* 299–328.

STILLINGER, C., EPELBAUM, M., KELTNER, D., & ROSS, L. (1991). The "reactive devaluation" barrier to conflict resolution. Unpublished manuscript, Stanford University.

STOCKDALE, J. E. (1978). Crowding: Determinants and effects. In L. Berkowitz (Ed.), *Advances in experimental social psychology, vol. 11.* New York: Academic Press.

STONE, A. A., HEDGES, S. M., NEALE, J. M., & SATIN, M. S. (1985). Prospective and cross-sectional mood reports offer no evidence of a "blue Monday" phenomenon. *Journal of Personality and Social Psychology, 49,* 129–134.

STONE, J. (2000, November 6). Quoted by Sharon Begley, The stereotype trap. *Newsweek.*

STONE, J., LYNCH, C. I., SJOMELING, M., & DARLEY, J. M. (1999). Stereotype threat effects on Black and White athletic performance. *Journal of Personality and Social Psychology, 77,* 1213–1227.

STONER, J. A. F. (1961). A comparison of individual and group decisions involving risk. Unpublished master's thesis, Massachusetts Institute of Technology, 1961. Cited by D. G. Marquis in Individual responsibility and group decisions involving risk. *Industrial Management Review, 3,* 8–23.

STORMS, M. D. (1973). Videotape and the attribution process: Reversing actors' and observers' points of view. *Journal of Personality and Social Psychology, 27,* 165–175.

STORMS, M. D., & THOMAS, G. C. (1977). Reactions to physical closeness. *Journal of Personality and Social Psychology, 35,* 412–418.

STOUFFER, S. A., SUCHMAN, E. A., DEVINNEY, L. C., STAR, S. A., & WILLIAMS, R. M., JR. (1949). *The American soldier: Adjustment during army life, vol. 1.* Princeton, NJ: Princeton University Press.

STRACK, F., & DEUTSCH, R. (2004). Reflective and impulsive determinants of social behavior. *Personality and Social Psychology Review, 8,* 220–247.

STRACK, S., & COYNE, J. C. (1983). Social confirmation of dysphoria: Shared and private reactions to depression. *Journal of Personality and Social Psychology, 44,* 798–806.

STRAUS, M. A., & GELLES, R. J. (1980). *Behind closed doors: Violence in the American family.* New York: Anchor/Doubleday.

STRAUSBERG, M. A. (2003, September 24). U.S. Muslim data. Personal correspondence from The Gallup Poll Data Librarian.

STROEBE, W., INSKO, C. A., THOMPSON, V. D., & LAYTON, B. D. (1971). Effects of physical attractiveness, attitude similarity, and sex on various aspects of interpersonal attraction. *Journal of Personality and Social Psychology, 18,* 79–91.

STROESSNER, S. J., HAMILTON, D. L., & LEPORE, L. (1990). Intergroup categorization and intragroup differentiation: Ingroup-outgroup differences. Paper presented at the American Psychological Association convention.

STROESSNER, S. J., & MACKIE, D. M. (1993). Affect and perceived group variability: Implications for stereotyping and prejudice. In D. M. Mackie & D. L. Hamilton (Eds.), *Affect, cognition, and stereotyping: Interactive processes in group perception.* San Diego, CA: Academic Press.

STRONG, S. R. (1978). Social psychological approach to psychotherapy research. In S. L. Garfield & A. E. Bergin (Eds.), *Handbook of psychotherapy and behavior change,* 2nd ed. New York: Wiley.

STRONG, S. R., WELSH, J. A., CORCORAN, J. L., & HOYT, W. T. (1992). Social psychology and counseling psychology: The history, products, and promise of an interface. *Journal of Personality and Social Psychology, 39,* 139–157.

STURM, M., PEROVICH, D. K., & SERREZE, M. C. (2003, October). Meltdown in the North. *Scientific American,* pp. 60–67.

SULLIVAN, A. (1999, September 26). What's so bad about hate? *New York Times Magazine* (www.nytimes.com).

SULS, J., WAN, C. K., & SANDERS, G. S. (1988). False consensus and false uniqueness in estimating the prevalence of health-protective behaviors. *Journal of Applied Social Psychology, 18,* 66–79.

SUMMERS, G., & FELDMAN, N. S. (1984). Blaming the victim versus blaming the perpetrator: An attributional analysis of spouse abuse. *Journal of Social and Clinical Psychology, 2,* 339–347.

SUNSTEIN, C. R. (2001). *Republic.com.* Princeton, NJ: Princeton University Press.

SVENSON, O. (1981). Are we all less risky and more skillful than our fellow drivers? *Acta Psychologica, 47,* 143–148.

SWANN, W. B., JR. (1996). *Self-traps: The elusive quest for higher self-esteem.* New York: Freeman.

SWANN, W. B., JR. (1997). The trouble with change: Self-verification and allegiance to the self. *Psychological Science, 8,* 177–180.

SWANN, W. B., JR., & GILL, M. J. (1997). Confidence and accuracy in person perception: Do we know what we think we know about our relationship partners? *Journal of Personality and Social Psychology, 73,* 747–757.

SWANN, W. B., JR., & PREDMORE, S. C. (1985). Intimates as agents of social support: Sources of consolation or despair? *Journal of Personality and Social Psychology, 49,* 1609–1617.

SWANN, W. B., JR., WENZLAFF, R. M., KRULL, D. S., & PELHAM, B. W. (1991). Seeking truth, reaping despair: Depression, self-verification and selection of relationship partners. *Journal of Abnormal Psychology, 101,* 293–306.

SWEDISH INFORMATION SERVICE. (1980). *Social change in Sweden,* September, No. 19, p. 5. (Published by the Swedish Consulate General, 825 Third Avenue, New York, NY 10022.)

SWEENEY, J. (1973). An experimental investigation of the free rider problem. *Social Science Research, 2,* 277–292.

SWEENEY, P. D., ANDERSON, K., & BAILEY, S. (1986). Attributional style in depression: A meta-analytic review. *Journal of Personality and Social Psychology, 50,* 947–991.

SWETS, J. A., DAWES, R. M., & MONAHAN, J. (2000). Psychological science can improve diagnostic decisions. *Psychological Science in the Public Interest, 1,* 1–26.

SWIM, J. K. (1994). Perceived versus meta-analytic effect sizes: An assessment of the accuracy of gender stereotypes. *Journal of Personality and Social Psychology, 66,* 21–36.

SWIM, J. K., AIKIN, K. J., HALL, W. S., & HUNTER, B. A. (1995). Sexism and racism: Old-fashioned and modern prejudices. *Journal of Personality and Social Psychology, 68,* 199–214.

SWIM, J. K., & COHEN, L. L. (1997). Overt, covert, and subtle sexism. *Psychology of Women Quarterly, 21,* 103–118.

SWIM, J. K., COHEN, L. L., & HYERS, L. L. (1998). Experiencing everyday prejudice and discrimination. In J. K. Swim & C. Stangor (Eds.), *Prejudice: The target's perspective.* San Diego, CA: Academic Press.

SWIM, J. K., & HYERS, L. L. (1999). Excuse me—What did you just say?!: Women's public and private reactions to sexist remarks. *Journal of Experimental Social Psychology, 35,* 68–88.

SWIM, J. K., & STANGOR, C. (EDS.). (1998). Prejudice: The target's perspective. San Diego, CA: Academic Press.

SWINDLE, R., JR., HELLER, K., BESCOSOLIDO, B., & KIKUZAWA, S. (2000). Responses to nervous breakdowns in America over a 40-year period: Mental health policy implications. *American Psychologist, 55,* 740–749.

SYMONS, C. S., & JOHNSON, B. T. (1997). The self-reference effect in memory: A meta-analysis. *Psychological Bulletin, 121,* 371–394.

SYMONS, D. (1979). *The evolution of human sexuality.* New York: Oxford University Press.

TAFARODI, R. W., LO, C., YAMAGUCHI, S., LEE, W. W-S., & KATSURA, H. (2004). The inner self in three countries. *Journal of Cross-Cultural Psychology, 35,* 97–117.

TAJFEL, H. (1970, November). Experiments in intergroup discrimination. *Scientific American,* pp. 96–102.

TAJFEL, H. (1981). *Human groups and social categories: Studies in social psychology.* London: Cambridge University Press.

TAJFEL, H. (1982). Social psychology of intergroup relations. *Annual Review of Psychology, 33,* 1–39.

TAJFEL, H., & BILLIG, M. (1974). Familiarity and categorization in intergroup behavior. *Journal of Experimental Social Psychology, 10,* 159–170.

TAMRES, L. K., JANICKI, D., & HELGESON, V. S. (2002). Sex differences in coping behavior: A meta-analytic review and an examination of relative coping. *Personality and Social Psychology Review, 6,* 2–30.

TANNEN, D. (1990). *You just don't understand: Women and men in conversation.* New York: William Morrow.

TARMANN, A. (2002, May/June). Out of the closet and onto the Census long form. *Population Today, 30,* 1, 6.

TAYLOR, D. M., & DORIA, J. R. (1981). Self-serving and group-serving bias in attribution. *Journal of Social Psychology, 113,* 201–211.

TAYLOR, K. M., & SHEPPERD, J. A. (1998). Bracing for the worst: Severity, testing, and feedback timing as moderators of the optimistic bias. *Personality and Social Psychology Bulletin, 24,* 915–926.

TAYLOR, S. E. (1979). Remarks at symposium on social psychology and medicine, American Psychological Association convention.

TAYLOR, S. E. (1981). A categorization approach to stereotyping. In D. L. Hamilton (Ed.), *Cognitive processes in stereotyping and intergroup behavior.* Hillsdale, NJ: Erlbaum.

TAYLOR, S. E. (1989). *Positive illusions: Creative self-deception and the healthy mind.* New York: Basic Books.

TAYLOR, S. E. (2002). *The tending instinct: How nurturing is essential to who we are and how we live.* New York: Times Books, Henry Holt.

TAYLOR, S. E., CROCKER, J., FISKE, S. T., SPRINZEN, M., & WINKLER, J. D. (1979). The generalizability of salience effects. *Journal of Personality and Social Psychology, 37,* 357–368.

TAYLOR, S. E., & FISKE, S. T. (1978). Salience, attention, and attribution: Top of the head phenomena. In L. Berkowitz (Ed.), *Advances in experimental social psychology, vol. 11.* New York: Academic Press.

TAYLOR, S. E., FISKE, S. T., ETCOFF, N. L., & RUDERMAN, A. J. (1978). Categorical and contextual bases of person memory and stereotyping. *Journal of Personality and Social Psychology, 36,* 778–793.

TAYLOR, S. E., LERNER, J. S., SHERMAN, D. K., SAGE, R. M., & McDOWELL, N. K. (2003). Portrait of the self-enhancer: Well adjusted and well liked or maladjusted and friendless? *Journal of Personality and Social Psychology, 84,* 165–176.

TAYLOR, S. P., & CHERMACK, S. T. (1993). Alcohol, drugs and human physical aggression. *Journal of Studies on Alcohol,* Supplement No. 11, 78–88.

TEGER, A. I. (1980). *Too much invested to quit.* New York: Pergamon Press.

TEIGEN, K. H. (1986). Old truths or fresh insights? A study of students' evaluations of proverbs. *British Journal of Social Psychology, 25,* 43–50.

TELCH, M. J., KILLEN, J. D., McALISTER, A. L., PERRY, C. L., & MACCOBY, N. (1981). Long-term follow-up of a pilot project on smoking prevention with adolescents. Paper presented at the American Psychological Association convention.

TESSER, A. (1988). Toward a self-evaluation maintenance model of social behavior. In L. Berkowitz (Ed.), *Advances in experimental social psychology, vol. 21.* San Diego, CA: Academic Press.

TESSER, A., ROSEN, S., & CONLEE, M. C. (1972). News valence and available recipient as determinants of news transmission. *Sociometry, 35,* 619–628.

TESTA, M. (2002). The impact of men's alcohol consumption on perpetration of sexual aggression. *Clinical Psychology Review, 22,* 1239–1263.

TETLOCK, P. E. (1983). Accountability and complexity of thought. *Journal of Personality and Social Psychology, 45,* 74–83.

TETLOCK, P. E. (1985). Integrative complexity of American and Soviet foreign policy rhetoric: A time-series analysis. *Journal of Personality and Social Psychology, 49,* 1565–1585.

TETLOCK, P. E. (1998). Close-call counterfactuals and belief-system defenses: I was not almost wrong but I was almost right. *Journal of Personality and Social Psychology, 75,* 639–652.

TETLOCK, P. E. (1999). Theory-driven reasoning about plausible pasts and probable futures in world politics: Are we prisoners of our preconceptions? *American Journal of Political Science, 43,* 335–366.

TGM. (2000, May 30). Canadian teens forsaking television for the Internet (an Angus Reid poll reported by the Toronto Globe and Mail). *Grand Rapids Press.*

THOMAS, K. W., & PONDY, L. R. (1977). Toward an "intent" model of conflict management among principal parties. *Human Relations, 30,* 1089–1102.

THOMAS, L. (1978). Hubris in science? *Science, 200,* 1459–1462.

THOMPSON, L. (1990a). An examination of naive and experienced negotiators. *Journal of Personality and Social Psychology, 59,* 82–90.

THOMPSON, L. (1990b). The influence of experience on negotiation performance. *Journal of Experimental Social Psychology, 26,* 528–544.

THOMPSON, L. (1998). *The mind and heart of the negotiator.* Upper Saddle River, NJ: Prentice-Hall.

THOMPSON, L., & HREBEC, D. (1996). Lose-lose agreements in interdependent decision making. *Psychological Bulletin, 120,* 396–409.

THOMPSON, L., VALLEY, K. L., & KRAMER, R. M. (1995). The bittersweet feeling of success: An examination of social perception in negotiation. *Journal of Experimental Social Psychology, 31,* 467–492.

THOMPSON, L. L., & CROCKER, J. (1985). Prejudice following threat to the self-concept. Effects of performance expectations and attributions. Unpublished manuscript, Northwestern University.

THOMPSON, S. C., ARMSTRONG, W., & THOMAS, C. (1998). Illusions of control, underestimations, and accuracy: A control heuristic explanation. *Psychological Bulletin, 123,* 143–161.

THOMSON, R., & MURACHVER, T. (2001). Predicting gender from electronic discourse. *British Journal of Social Psychology, 40,* 193–208 (and personal correspondence from T. Murachver, May 23, 2002).

THORNTON, B., & MAURICE, J. (1997). Physique contrast effect: Adverse impact of idealized body images for women. *Sex Roles, 37,* 433–439.

TIDEMAN, S. (2003, undated). Announcement (of Operationalizing Gross National Happiness conference, February 18–20, 2004). Distributed via the Internet.

TIME. (1992, March 30). The not so merry wife of Windsor, pp. 38–39.

TIMKO, C., & MOOS, R. H. (1989). Choice, control, and adaptation among elderly residents of sheltered care settings. *Journal of Applied Social Psychology, 19,* 636–655.

TJADEN, P., & THOENNES, N. (2000). *Prevalence, incidence, and consequences of violence against women: Findings from the National Violence Against Women Survey* (National Institute of Justice Report No. NCJ-172837). Washington, DC: U.S. Department of Justice, National Institute of Justice.

TOMORROW, T. (2003, April 30). Passive tense verbs deployed before large audience; stories remain unclear (www240.pair.com/tomtom/pages/ ja/ja_fr.html).

TORMALA, Z. L., & PETTY, R. E. (2002). What doesn't kill me makes me stronger: The effects of resisting persuasion on attitude change. *Journal of Personality and Social Psychology, 83,* 1298–1313.

TRAVIS, L. E. (1925). The effect of a small audience upon eye-hand coordination. *Journal of Abnormal and Social Psychology, 20,* 142–146.

TREWIN, D. (2001). *Australian social trends 2001.* Canberra: Australian Bureau of Statistics.

TRIANDIS, H. C. (1981). Some dimensions of intercultural variation and their implications for interpersonal behavior. Paper presented at the American Psychological Association convention.

TRIANDIS, H. C. (1994). *Culture and social behavior.* New York: McGraw-Hill.

TRIANDIS, H. C. (2000). Culture and conflict. *International Journal of Psychology, 55,* 145–152.

TRIANDIS, H. C., BONTEMPO, R., VILLAREAL, M. J., ASAI, M., & LUCCA, N. (1988). Individualism and collectivism: Cross-cultural perspectives on self-ingroup relationships. *Journal of Personality and Social Psychology, 54,* 323–338.

TRIPLETT, N. (1898). The dynamogenic factors in pacemaking and competition. *American Journal of Psychology, 9,* 507–533.

TROLIER, T. K., & HAMILTON, D. L. (1986). Variables influencing judgments of correlational relations. *Journal of Personality and Social Psychology, 50,* 879–888.

TROPP, L. R., & PETTIGREW, T. F. (2004). Intergroup contact and the central role of affect in intergroup prejudice. In C. W. Leach & L. Tiedens (Eds.), *The social life of emotion.* Cambridge: Cambridge University Press.

TROST, M. R., MAASS, A., & KENRICK, D. T. (1992). Minority influence: Personal relevance biases cognitive processes and reverses private acceptance. *Journal of Experimental Social Psychology, 28,* 234–254.

TROUILLOUD, D. O., SARRAZIN, P. G., MARTINEK, T. J., & GUILLET, E. (2002). The influence of teacher expectations on student achievement in physical education classes: Pygmalion revisited. *European Journal of Social Psychology, 32,* 591–607.

TSANG, J-A. (2002). Moral rationalization and the integration of situational factors and psychological processes in immoral behavior. *Review of General Psychology, 6,* 25–50.

TURNER, C. W., HESSE, B. W., & PETERSON-LEWIS, S. (1986). Naturalistic studies of the long-term effects of television violence. *Journal of Social Issues, 42*(3), 51–74.

TURNER, J. C. (1981). The experimental social psychology of intergroup behaviour. In J. Turner & H. Giles (Eds.), *Intergroup behavior.* Oxford, England: Basil Blackwell.

TURNER, J. C. (1987). *Rediscovering the social group: A self-categorization theory.* New York: Basil Blackwell.

TURNER, J. C. (1991). *Social influence.* Milton Keynes, England: Open University Press.

TURNER, M. E., & PRATKANIS, A. R. (1994). Social identity maintenance prescriptions for preventing groupthink: Reducing identity protection and enhancing intellectual conflict. *International Journal of Conflict Management, 5,* 254–270.

TURNER, M. E., PRATKANIS, A. R., PROBASCO, P., & LEVE, C. (1992). Threat cohesion, and group effectiveness: Testing a social identity maintenance perspective on groupthink. *Journal of Personality and Social Psychology, 63,* 781–796.

TV GUIDE. (1977, January 26), pp. 5–10.

TVERSKY, A., & KAHNEMAN, D. (1973). Availability: A neuristic for judging frequency and probability. *Cognitive Psychology, 5,* 207–302.

TVERKSY, A., & KAHNEMAN, D. (1974). Judgment under uncertainty: Heuristics and biases. *Science, 185,* 1123–1131.

TWENGE, J. M., BAUMEISTER, R. F., TICE, D. M., & STUCKE, T. S. (2001). If you can't join them, beat them: Effects of social exclusion on aggressive behavior. *Journal of Personality and Social Psychology, 81,* 1058–1069.

TWENGE, J. M., CATANESE, K. R., & BAUMEISTER, R. F. (2002). Social exclusion causes self-defeating behavior. *Journal of Personality and Social Psychology, 83,* 606–615.

TWENGE, J. M., CATANESE, K. R., & BAUMEISTER, R. F. (2003). Social exclusion and the deconstructed state: Time perception, meaninglessness, lethargy, lack of emotion, and self-awareness. *Journal of Personality and Social Psychology, 85,* 409–423.

TZENG, M. (1992). The effects of socioeconomic heterogamy and changes on marital dissolution for first marriages. *Journal of Marriage and the Family, 54,* 609–619.

UMBERSON, D., & HUGHES, M. (1987). The impact of physical attractiveness on achievement and psychological well-being. *Social Psychology Quarterly, 50,* 227–236.

United Nations. (1991). *The world's women 1970–1990: Trends and statistics.* New York: United Nations.

UPI. (1970/1967). September 23, 1967. Cited by P. G. Zimbardo in The human choice: Individuation, reason, and order versus deindividuation, impulse, and chaos. In W. J. Arnold & D. Levine (Eds.), *Nebraska symposium on motivation,* 1969. Lincoln: University of Nebraska Press.

VALLIANT, G. E. (1997). Report on distress and longevity. Paper presented to the American Psychiatric Association convention.

VALLONE, R. P., GRIFFIN, D. W., LIN, S., & ROSS, L. (1990). Overconfident prediction of future actions and outcomes by self and others. *Journal of Personality and Social Psychology, 58,* 582–592.

VALLONE, R. P., ROSS, L., & LEPPER, M. R. (1985). The hostile media phenomenon: Biased perception and perceptions of media bias in coverage of the "Beirut Massacre." *Journal of Personality and Social Psychology, 49,* 577–585.

VAN BOVEN, L., & GILOVICH, T. (2003). To do or to have? That is the question. *Journal of Personality and Social Psychology, 85,* 1193–1202.

VAN KNIPPENBERG, D., & WILKE, H. (1992). Prototypicality of arguments and conformity to ingroup norms. *European Journal of Social Psychology, 22,* 141–155.

VAN LANGE, P. A. M. (1991). Being better but not smarter than others: The Muhammad Ali effect at work in interpersonal situations. *Personality and Social Psychology Bulletin, 17,* 689–693.

VAN LANGE, P. A. M., TARIS, T. W., & VONK, R. (1997). Dilemmas of academic practice: Perceptions of superiority among social psychologists. *European Journal of Social Psychology, 27,* 675–685.

VAN LANGE, P. A. M., & VISSER, K. (1999). Locomotion in social dilemmas: How people adapt to cooperative, tit-for-tat, and noncooperative partners. *Journal of Personality and Social Psychology, 77,* 762–773.

VAN VUGT, M., VAN LANGE, P. A. M., & MEERTENS, R. M. (1996). Commuting by car or public transportation? A social dilemma analysis of travel mode judgements. *European Journal of Social Psychology, 26,* 373–395.

VAN YPEREN, N. W., & BUUNK, B. P. (1990). A longitudinal study of equity and satisfaction in intimate relationships. *European Journal of Social Psychology, 20,* 287–309.

VANDELLO, J. A., & COHEN, D. (1999). Patterns of individualism and collectivism across the United States. *Journal of Personality and Social Psychology, 77,* 279–292.

VANDERSLICE, V. J., RICE, R. W., & JULIAN, J. W. (1987). The effects of participation in decision-making on worker satisfaction and productivity: An organizational simulation. *Journal of Applied Social Psychology, 17,* 158–170.

VAUX, A. (1988). Social and personal factors in loneliness. *Journal of Social and Clinical Psychology, 6,* 462–471.

VEYSEY, B. M., & MESSNER, S. F. (1999). Further testing of social disorganization theory: An elaboration of Sampson and Groves's "Community structure and crime." *Journal of Research in Crime and Delinquency, 36,* 156–174.

VIGNOLES, V. L., CHRYSSOCHOOU, X., & BREAKWELL, G. M. (2000). The distinctiveness principle: Identity, meaning, and the bounds of cultural relativity. *Personality and Social Psychology Review, 4,* 337–354.

VISSER, P. S., & KROSNICK, J. A. (1998). Development of attitude strength over the life cycle: Surge and decline. *Journal of Personality and Social Psychology, 75,* 1389–1410.

VITELLI, R. (1988). The crisis issue assessed: An empirical analysis. *Basic and Applied Social Psychology, 9,* 301–309.

VON HIPPEL, W., SILVER, L. A., & LYNCH, M. B. (2000). Stereotyping against your will: The role of inhibitory ability in stereotyping and prejudice among the elderly. *Personality and Social Psychology Bulletin, 26,* 523–532.

WAGSTAFF, G. F. (1983). Attitudes to poverty, the Protestant ethic, and political affiliation: A preliminary investigation. *Social Behavior and Personality, 11,* 45–47.

WALFISH, D. (2001). National count reveals major societal changes. *Science, 292,* 1823.

WALL, B. (2002, August 24–25). Profit matures along with baby boomers. *International Herald Tribune,* p. 13.

WALLACE, C. P. (2000, May 8). Germany's glass ceiling. *Time,* p. B8.

WALLACE, M. (1969, November 25). *New York Times.*

WALLER, J. (2002). *Becoming evil: How ordinary people commit genocide and mass killing.* New York: Oxford University Press.

WALSTER (HATFIELD), E. (1965). The effect of self-esteem on romantic liking. *Journal of Experimental Social Psychology, 1,* 184–197.

WALSTER (HATFIELD), E., ARONSON, V., ABRAHAMS, D., & ROTTMAN, L. (1966). Importance of physical attractiveness in dating behavior. *Journal of Personality and Social Psychology, 4,* 508–516.

WALSTER (HATFIELD), E., WALSTER, G. W., & BERSCHEID, E. (1978). *Equity: Theory and research.* Boston: Allyn & Bacon.

WARD, W. C., & JENKINS, H. M. (1965). The display of information and the judgment of contingency. *Canadian Journal of Psychology, 19,* 231–241.

WASON, P. C. (1960). On the failure to eliminate hypotheses in a conceptual task. *Quarterly Journal of Experimental Psychology, 12,* 129–140.

WATKINS, D., AKANDE, A., & FLEMING, J. (1998). Cultural dimensions, gender, and the nature of self-concept: A fourteen-country study? *International Journal of Psychology, 33,* 17–31.

WATKINS, D., CHENG, C., MPOFU, E., OLOWU, S., SINGH-SENGUPTA, S., & REGMI, M. (2003). Gender differences in self-construal: How generalizable are Western findings? *Journal of Social Psychology, 143,* 501–519.

WATSON, D. (1982, November). The actor and the observer: How are their perceptions of causality divergent? *Psychological Bulletin, 92,* 682–700.

WATSON, R. I., JR. (1973). Investigation into deindividuation using a cross-cultural survey technique. *Journal of Personality and Social Psychology, 25,* 342–345.

WEBSTER, D. M. (1993). Motivated augmentation and reduction of the overattribution bias. *Journal of Personality and Social Psychology, 65,* 261–271.

WEGNER, D. M., & ERBER, R. (1992). The hyperaccessibility of suppressed thoughts. *Journal of Personality and Social Psychology, 63,* 903–912.

WEHR, P. (1979). *Conflict regulation.* Boulder, CO: Westview Press.

WEINER, B. (1981). The emotional consequences of causal ascriptions. Unpublished manuscript, UCLA.

WEINSTEIN, N. D. (1980). Unrealistic optimism about future life events. *Journal of Personality and Social Psychology, 39,* 806–820.

WEINSTEIN, N. D. (1982). Unrealistic optimism about susceptibility to health problems. *Journal of Behavioral Medicine, 5,* 441–460.

WEISS, J., & BROWN, P. (1976). Self-insight error in the explanation of mood. Unpublished manuscript, Harvard University.

WENER, R., FRAZIER, W., & FARBSTEIN, J. (1987, June). Building better jails. *Psychology Today,* pp. 40–49.

WHEELER, L., & KIM, Y. (1997). What is beautiful is culturally good: The physical attractiveness stereotype has different content in collectivistic cultures. *Personality and Social Psychology Bulletin, 23,* 795–800.

WHITE, G. L. (1980). Physical attractiveness and courtship progress. *Journal of Personality and Social Psychology, 39,* 660–668.

WHITE, H. R., BRICK, J., & HANSELL, S. (1993). A longitudinal investigation of alcohol use and aggression in adolescence. *Journal of Studies on Alcohol,* Supplement No. 11, 62–77.

WHITE, J. A., & PLOUS, S. (1995). Self-enhancement and social responsibility: On caring more, but doing less, than others. *Journal of Applied Social Psychology, 25,* 1297–1318.

WHITE, J. W., & KOWALSKI, R. M. (1994). Deconstructing the myth of the nonaggressive woman. *Psychology of Women Quarterly, 18,* 487–508.

WHITE, M. (2000). *Historical atlas of the twentieth century* (users.erols.com/mwhite28/warstat8.htm).

WHITE, P. A., & YOUNGER, D. P. (1988). Differences in the ascription of transient internal states to self and other. *Journal of Experimental Social Psychology, 24,* 292–309.

WHITE, R. K. (1996). Why the Serbs fought: Motives and misperceptions. *Peace and Conflict: Journal of Peace Psychology, 2,* 109–128.

WHITE, R. K. (1998). American acts of force: Results and misperceptions. *Peace and Conflict, 4,* 93–128.

WHITMAN, D. (1996, December 16). I'm OK, you're not. *U.S. News and World Report,* p. 24.

WHITMAN, R. M., KRAMER, M., & BALDRIDGE, B. (1963). Which dream does the patient tell? *Archives of General Psychology, 8,* 277–282.

WHYTE, G. (1993). Escalating commitment in individual and group decision making: A prospect theory approach. *Organizational Behavior and Human Decision Processes, 54,* 430–455.

WICKER, A. W. (1971). An examination of the "other variables" explanation of attitude-behavior inconsistency. *Journal of Personality and Social Psychology, 19,* 18–30.

WIDOM, C. S. (1989). Does violence beget violence? A critical examination of the literature. *Psychological Bulletin, 106,* 3–28.

WIEGMAN, O. (1985). Two politicians in a realistic experiment: Attraction, discrepancy, intensity of delivery, and attitude change. *Journal of Applied Social Psychology, 15,* 673–686.

WIESEL, E. (1985, April 6). The brave Christians who saved Jews from the Nazis. *TV Guide,* pp. 4–6.

WIESELQUIST, J., RUSBULT, C. E., FOSTER, C. A., & AGNEW, C. R. (1999). Commitment, pro-relationship behavior, and trust in close relationships. *Journal of Personality and Social Psychology, 77,* 942–966.

WILDER, D. A. (1978). Perceiving persons as a group: Effect on attributions of causality and beliefs. *Social Psychology, 41,* 13–23.

WILDER, D. A. (1981). Perceiving persons as a group: Categorization and intergroup relations. In. D. L. Hamilton (Ed.), *Cognitive processes in stereotyping and intergroup behavior.* Hillsdale, NJ: Erlbaum.

WILDER, D. A. (1990). Some determinants of the persuasive power of in-groups and out-groups: Organization of information and attribution of independence. *Journal of Personality and Social Psychology, 59,* 1202–1213.

WILDER, D. A., & SHAPIRO, P. N. (1984). Role of out-group cues in determining social identity. *Journal of Personality and Social Psychology, 47,* 342–348.

WILDSCHUT, T., PINTER, B., VEVEA, J. L., INSKO, C. A., & SCHOPLER, J. (2003). Beyond the group mind: A quantitative review of the interindividual-intergroup discontinuity effect. *Psychological Bulletin, 129,* 698–722.

WILLIAMS, J. E., & BEST, D. L. (1990a). *Measuring sex stereotypes: A multination study.* Newbury Park, CA: Sage.

WILLIAMS, J. E., & BEST, D. L. (1990b). *Sex and psyche: Gender and self viewed cross-culturally.* Newbury Park, CA: Sage.

WILLIAMS, J. E., SATTERWHITE, R. C., & BEST, D. L. (1999). Pancultural gender stereotypes revisited: The Five Factor model. *Sex Roles, 40,* 513–525.

WILLIAMS, J. E., SATTERWHITE, R. C., & BEST, D. L. (2000). Five-factor gender stereotypes in 27 countries. Paper presented at the XV Congress of the International Association for Cross-Cultural Psychology, Pultusk, Poland.

WILLIAMS, K. D. (2002). *Ostracism: The power of silence.* New York: Guilford Press.

WILLIAMS, K. D., CHEUNG, C. K. T., & CHOI, W. (2000). Cyberostracism: Effects of being ignored over the Internet. *Journal of Personality and Social Psychology, 79,* 748–762.

WILLIAMS, K. D., HARKINS, S., & LATANÉ, B. (1981). Identifiability as a deterrent to social loafing: Two cheering experiments. *Journal of Personality and Social Psychology, 40,* 303–311.

WILLIAMS, K. D., JACKSON, J. M., & KARAU, S. J. (1992). Collective hedonism: A social loafing analysis of social dilemmas. In D. A. Schroeder (Ed.), *Social dilemmas: Social psychological perspectives.* New York: Praeger.

WILLIAMS, K. D., & KARAU, S. J. (1991). Social loafing and social compensation: The effects of expectations of coworker performance. *Journal of Personality and Social Psychology, 61,* 570–581.

WILLIAMS, K. D., NIDA, S. A., BACA, L. D., & LATANÉ, B. (1989). Social loafing and swimming: Effects of identifiability on individual and relay performance of intercollegiate swimmers. *Basic and Applied Social Psychology, 10,* 73–81.

WILLIAMS, T. M. (ED.). (1986). *The impact of television: A natural experiment in three communities.* Orlando, FL: Academic Press.

WILLIS, F. N., & HAMM, H. K. (1980). The use of interpersonal touch in securing compliance. *Journal of Nonverbal Behavior, 5,* 49–55.

WILLS, T. A. (1981). Downward comparison principles in social psychology. *Psychological Bulletin, 90,* 245–271.

WILSON, E. O. (1978). *On human nature.* Cambridge, MA: Harvard University Press.

WILSON, E. O. (2002, February). The bottleneck. *Scientific American, 286,* 83–91.

WILSON, G. (1994, March 25). Equal, but different. *The Times Higher Education Supplement, Times of London.*

WILSON, R. S., & MATHENY, A. P., JR. (1986). Behavior-genetics research in infant temperament: The Louisville twin study. In R. Plomin & J. Dunn (Eds.), *The study of temperament: Changes, continuities, and challenges.* Hillsdale, NJ: Erlbaum.

WILSON, T. D. (1985). Strangers to ourselves: The origins and accuracy of beliefs about one's own mental states. In J. H. Harvey & G. Weary (Eds.), *Attribution in contemporary psychology.* New York: Academic Press.

WILSON, T. D. (2002). *Strangers to ourselves: Discovering the adaptive unconscious.* Cambridge, MA: Harvard University Press.

WILSON, T. D., DUNN, D. S., KRAFT, D., & LISLE, D. J. (1989). Introspection, attitude change, and attitude-behavior consistency: The disruptive effects of explaining why we feel the way we do. In L. Berkowitz (Eds.), *Advances in experimental social psychology, vol. 22.* San Diego, CA: Academic Press.

WILSON, T. D., & GILBERT, D. T. (2003). Affective forecasting. *Advances in Experimental Social Psychology, 35,* 346–413.

WILSON, T. D., LASER, P. S., & STONE, J. I. (1982). Judging the predictors of one's mood: Accuracy and the use of shared theories. *Journal of Experimental Social Psychology, 18,* 537–556.

WILSON, T. D., LINDSEY, S., & SCHOOLER, T. Y. (2000). A model of dual attitudes. *Psychological Review, 107,* 101–126.

WINTER, F. W. (1973). A laboratory experiment of individual attitude response to advertising exposure. *Journal of Marketing Research, 10,* 130–140.

WISMAN, A., & KOOLE, S. L. (2003). Hiding in the crowd: Can mortality salience promote affiliation with others who oppose one's worldviews? *Journal of Personality and Social Psychology, 84,* 511–526.

WITTENBERG, M. T., & REIS, H. T. (1986). Loneliness, social skills, and social perception. *Personality and Social Psychology Bulletin, 12,* 121–130.

WITTENBRINK, B., JUDD, C. M., & PARK, B. (1997). Evidence for racial prejudice at the implicit level and its relationship with questionnaire measures. *Journal of Personality and Social Psychology, 72,* 262–274.

WIXON, D. R., & LAIRD, J. D. (1976). Awareness and attitude change in the forced-compliance paradigm: The importance of when. *Journal of Personality and Social Psychology, 34,* 376–384.

WOHL, M. J. A., & ENZLE, M. E. (2002). The deployment of personal luck: Sympathetic magic and illusory control in games of pure chance. *Personality and Social Psychology Bulletin, 28,* 1388–1397.

WOLF, S. (1987). Majority and minority influence: A social impact analysis. In M. P. Zanna, J. M. Olson, & C. P. Herman (Eds.), *Social influence: The Ontario symposium on personality and social psychology, vol. 5.* Hillsdale, NJ: Erlbaum.

WOLF, S., & LATANÉ, B. (1985). Conformity, innovation and the psycho-social law. In S. Moscovici, G. Mugny, & E. Van Avermaet (Eds.), *Perspectives on minority influence.* Cambridge: Cambridge University Press.

WOOD, J. V., HEIMPEL, S. A., & MICHELA, J. L. (2003). Savoring versus dampening: Self-esteem differences in regulating positive affect. *Journal of Personality and Social Psychology, 85,* 566–580.

WOOD, J. V., SALTZBERG, J. A., & GOLDSAMT, L. A. (1990a). Does affect induce self-focused attention? *Journal of Personality and Social Psychology, 58,* 899–908.

WOOD, J. V., SALTZBERG, J. A., NEALE, J. M., STONE, A. A., & RACHMIEL, T. B. (1990b). Self-focused attention, coping responses, and distressed mood in everyday life. *Journal of Personality and Social Psychology, 58,* 1027–1036.

WOOD, W., & QUINN, J. M. (2003). Forewarned and forewarmed? Two meta-analytic syntheses of forewarnings of influence appeals. *Psychological Bulletin, 129,* 119–138.

WOODZICKA, J. A., & LAFRANCE, M. (2001). Real versus imagined gender harassment. *Journal of Social Issues, 57*(1), 15–30.

WORCHEL, S., & BROWN, E. H. (1984). The role of plausibility in influencing environmental attributions. *Journal of Experimental Social Psychology, 20,* 86–96.

WORCHEL, S., ROTHGERBER, H., DAY, E. A., HART, D., & BUTEMEYER, J. (1998). Social identity and individual productivity within groups. *British Journal of Social Psychology, 37,* 389–413.

WORD, C. O., ZANNA, M. P., & COOPER, J. (1974). The nonverbal mediation of self-fulfilling prophecies in interracial interaction. *Journal of Experimental Social Psychology, 10,* 109–120.

WORRINGHAM, C. J., & MESSICK, D. M. (1983). Social facilitation of running: An unobtrusive study. *Journal of Social Psychology, 121,* 23–29.

WRIGHT, D. B., BOYD, C. E., & TREDOUX, C. G. (2001). A field study of own-race bias in South Africa and England. *Psychology, Public Policy, & Law, 7,* 119–133.

WRIGHT, P., & RIP, P. D. (1981). Retrospective reports on the causes of decisions. *Journal of Personality and Social Psychology, 40,* 601–614.

WRIGHT, R. (1998, February 2). Politics made me do it. *Time,* p. 34.

WRIGHT, R. (2003, June 29). Quoted by Thomas L. Friedman, "Is Google God?" *New York Times* (www.nytimes.com).

WRIGHT, S. C., ARON, A., MCLAUGHLIN-VOLPE, T., & ROPP, S. A. (1997). The extended contact effect: Knowledge of cross-group friendships and prejudice. *Journal of Personality and Social Psychology, 73,* 73–90.

WYLIE, R. C. (1979). *The self-concept Theory and research on selected topics, vol. 2.* Lincoln: University of Nebraska Press.

YBARRA, O. (1999). Misanthropic person memory when the need to self-enhance is absent. *Personality and Social Psychology Bulletin, 25,* 261–269.

YOUNG, W. R. (1977, February). There's a girl on the tracks! *Reader's Digest,* pp. 91–95.

YOVETICH, N. A., & RUSBULT, C. E. (1994). Accommodative behavior in close relationships: Exploring transformation of motivation. *Journal of Experimental Social Psychology, 30,* 138–164.

YUKL, G. (1974). Effects of the opponent's initial offer, concession magnitude, and concession frequency on bargaining behavior. *Journal of Personality and Social Psychology, 30,* 323–335.

YZERBYT, V., ROCHER, S., & SCHADRON, G. (1997). Stereotypes as explanations: A subjective essentialistic view of group perception. In R. Spears, P. J. Oakes, N. Ellemers, & S. A. Haslam (Eds.), *The social psychology of stereotyping and group life.* Oxford: Basil Blackwell.

YZERBYT, V. Y., & LEYENS, J-P. (1991). Requesting information to form an impression: The influence of valence and confirmatory status. *Journal of Experimental Social Psychology, 27,* 337–356.

ZAJONC, R. B. (1965). Social facilitation. *Science, 149,* 269–274.

ZAJONC, R. B. (1968). Attitudinal effects of mere exposure. *Journal of Personality and Social Psychology, 9,* Monograph Suppl. No. 2, part 2.

ZAJONC, R. B. (1970, February). Brainwash: Familiarity breeds comfort. *Psychology Today,* pp. 32–35, 60–62.

ZAJONC, R. B. (1998). Emotions. In D. Gilbert, S. T. Fiske, & G. Lindzey (Eds.), *Handbook of social psychology,* 4th ed. New York: McGraw-Hill.

ZAJONC, R. B. (2000). Massacres: Mass murders in the name of moral imperatives. Unpublished manuscript, Stanford University.

ZANNA, M. P., & PACK, S. J. (1975). On the self-fulfilling nature of apparent sex differences in behavior. *Journal of Experimental Social Psychology, 11,* 583–591.

ZEBROWITZ-MCARTHUR, L. (1988). Person perception in cross-cultural perspective. In M. H. Bond (Ed.), *The cross-cultural challenge to social psychology.* Newbury Park, CA: Sage.

ZILLMANN, D. (1989a). Aggression and sex: Independent and joint operations. In H. L. Wagner & A. S. R. Manstead (Eds.), *Handbook of psychophysiology: Emotion and social behavior.* Chichester, England: Wiley.

ZILLMANN, D. (1989b). Effects of prolonged consumption of pornography. In D. Zillmann & J. Bryant (Eds.), *Pornography: Research advances and policy considerations.* Hillsdale, NJ: Erlbaum.

ZILLMANN, D., & PAULUS, P. B. (1993). Spectators: Reactions to sports events and effects on athletic performance. In R. N. Singer, N. Murphey, & L. K. Tennant (Eds.), *Handbook of research on sport psychology.* New York: Macmillan.

ZILLMANN, D., & WEAVER, J. B., III. (1999). Effects of prolonged exposure to gratuitous media violence on provoked and unprovoked hostile behavior. *Journal of Applied Social Psychology, 29,* 145–165.

ZILLMER, E. A., HARROWER, M., RITZLER, B. A., & ARCHER, R. P. (1995). *The quest for the Nazi personality: A psychological investigation of Nazi war criminals.* Hillsdale, NJ: Erlbaum.

ZIMBARDO, P. G. (1970). The human choice: Individuation, reason, and order versus deindividuation, impulse, and chaos. In W. J. Arnold & D. Levine (Eds.), *Nebraska symposium on motivation, 1969.* Lincoln: University of Nebraska Press.

ZIMBARDO, P. G. (1971). *The psychological power and pathology of imprisonment.* A statement prepared for the U.S. House of Representatives Committee on the Judiciary, Subcommittee No. 3: Hearings on Prison Reform, San Francisco, CA, October 25.

ZIMBARDO, P. G. (1972). The Stanford prison experiment. A slide/tape presentation produced by Philip G. Zimbardo, Inc., P. O. Box 4395, Stanford, CA. 94305.

ZIMBARDO, P. G. (2002, April). Nurturing psychological synergies. *APA Monitor,* pp. 5, 38.

ZIMBARDO, P. G. (2004). A situationist perspective on the psychology of evil: Understanding how good people are transformed into perpetrators. In A. G. Miller (Ed.), *The social psychology of good and evil.* New York: Guilford Press.

ZIMBARDO, P. G., EBBESEN, E. B., & MASLACH, C. (1977). Influencing attitudes and changing behavior. Reading, MA: Addison-Wesley.

ZUCKER, G. S., & WEINER, B. (1993). Conservatism and perceptions of poverty: An attributional analysis. *Journal of Applied Social Psychology, 23,* 925–943.

ZUCKERMAN, E. W., & JOST, J. T. (2001). What makes you think you're so popular? Self-evaluation maintenance and the subjective side of the "friendship paradox." *Social Psychology Quarterly, 64,* 207–223.

Line-Art Credits

———————— ❖ ————————

Cartoon 1-1

Reprinted with permission by Jason Love at www.jasonlove.com

Figure 3-1

From H. Markus & S. Kitayama, "Culture and the Self: Implications for Cognition, Emotion, and Motivation," *Psychological Review*, 98, 1991, pp. 224–253. Copyright © 1991 by the American Psychological Association. Reprinted with permission.

Figure 5-1

From T.F. Heatherton & K. D. Vohs, "Interpersonal Evaluations Following Threats to Self: Role of Self-Esteem," *Journal of Personality and Social Psychology*, 78, pp. 725–736. Copyright © 2000 by the American Psychological Association. Reprinted with permission.

Figure 11-3

From Jody Dill & Craig Anderson, "Loneliness, Shyness, and Depression: The Etiology an dInterpersonal Relationships of Everyday Problems in Living," in *Recent Advances in Interpersonal Approaches to Depression*, edited by T. Joiner and J. C. Coyne. Copyright © 1998 by the American Psychological Association. Reprinted with permission.

Figure 13-1

Reprinted with permission of the Pew Research Center for the People and the Press.

Figure 13-2

From Eagly & Wood (eds.), "Explaining sex differences in social behavior:A Meta-Analytic Perspective" in *Personality and Social Psychology Bulletin*, No. 17, pp. 306–315. Copyright © 1991 by Sage Publications, Inc. Reprinted by permission of Sage Publications, Inc.

Figure 14-2

From *Obedience to Authority* by Stanley Milgram (NY: HarperCollins).

Figure 14-3

From the Milgram Obedience Experiment, from S. Milgram, "Some conditions of obedience ad disobedience to authority" in *Human Relations*, 18, 1, pp. 73. Copyright © 1965 Plenum Press, renewed 1993 by Alexandra Milgram.

Figure 26-1

From R. B. Zajonc, "Attitudinal effects of mere exposure" in *Journal of Personality and Social Psychology*, Monograph Suppl. No. 2, part 2. Copyright © 1968 by the American Psychological Association. Reprinted with permission.

Photo Credits

———— ❖ ————

Name Index

❖

Subject Index

❖

481